India Today

EDITORIAL ADVISER

Damodar R. SarDesai
Navin and Pratima Doshi Chair in Indian History (Emeritus)
and Professor Emeritus, History, University of California, Los Angeles

India Today

AN ENCYCLOPEDIA OF LIFE IN THE REPUBLIC

—— VOLUME TWO: L–Z ——

Arnold P. Kaminsky
and Roger D. Long, Editors

 ABC-CLIO

Santa Barbara, California • Denver, Colorado • Oxford, England

Copyright 2011 ABC-CLIO, LLC

Library of Congress Cataloging-in-Publication Data

India today : an encyclopedia of life in the Republic/Arnold P. Kaminsky and
Roger D. Long, editors.
     p. cm.
Includes bibliographical references and index.
ISBN 978-0-313-37462-3 (hard back : alk. paper) — ISBN 978-0-313-37463-0 (ebook)
1. India—Social life and customs—Encyclopedias. 2. India—History —1947—Encyclopedias.
I. Kaminsky, Arnold P. II. Long, Roger D.
DS428.2.I535 2011
954.0503—dc23

                    2011025913

ISBN: 978-0-313-37462-3
EISBN: 978-0-313-37463-0

15 14 13 12 11   1 2 3 4 5

This book is also available on the World Wide Web as an eBook.
Visit www.abc-clio.com for details.

ABC-CLIO
An Imprint of ABC-CLIO, LLC

ABC-CLIO, LLC
130 Cremona Drive, P.O. Box 1911
Santa Barbara, California 93116-1911

This book is printed on acid-free paper ∞
Manufactured in the United States of America

Contents

✦

Alphabetic List of Entries

✦

Topic Finder

✦

Below are the entries for *India Today* listed under broad topics. For more detailed access, consult the index at the back of volume 2.

Green Revolution
International Monetary Fund,
    Relations with
Monetary Policy
Money and Foreign Exchange Markets
National Rural Employment Guarantee Act
Nongovernmental Organizations
Outsourcing and Offshoring
Reserve Bank of India
Special Economic Zones
Stock Exchange Markets
Tourism
World Bank, Relations with
World Economic Forum
World Trade Organization, Relations with

EDUCATION

Aligarh Muslim University
Asiatic Society of Bengal
Asiatic Society of Mumbai
District Primary Education Program
Education, Development
Election Commission
Election of 2009
Gandhi Peace Foundation
Indian Institutes of Technology
Jamia Millia Islamia University
Orientalism
Postcolonial Studies
Ramakrishna Mission
Village Education Committees

GOVERNMENT, LAW, AND ADMINISTRATION

Archaeological Survey of India
Armed Forces
Cabinet
Constitution
Intelligence Services

Judiciary System
Mandal Commission
Panchayat System and Local Government
Parliament
President
Prime Minister
Right to Information
Secularism
Shah Bano Case

INDIVIDUALS

Advani, Lal Krishna
Bachchan, Harivansh Amitabh
Bedi, Kiran
Benegal, Shyam
Birla Family
Dalai Lama, 14th
Gandhi, Feroze Varun
Gandhi, Maneka
Gandhi, Mohandas Karamchand
Gandhi, Rahul
Gandhi, Sonia
Khan, Aamir
Khan, Ali Akbar
Khan, Vilayat
Roy, Arundhati
Shankar, Ravi
Singh, Khushwant
Singh, Manmohan
Subramaniam, Lakshminarayana
Surya, Vasantha
Thackeray, Balasaheb Keshav
Thapar, Romila
Yadav, Lalu Prasad
Yadav, Mulayam Singh

MEDIA AND TELECOMMUNICATION

All India Radio
Doordarshan

L

Lacadive Islands. *See* Lakshwadeep

✦ LADAKH

The region Ladakh comprises almost one-third of the state Jammu and Kashmir and is the highest region in India, with steep, narrow valleys between the Himalayan and Kara-koram mountains. The altitude ranges from 9,800 feet at Leh, the capital, to 11,300 feet at Zoji-la Pass, peaking to 23,000 feet at Nun-Kun. Ladakh is divided into two districts, Kargil and Leh, the inhabitants of the former being mostly Shia Muslims and of the latter mostly Vajrayana Buddhists. The district is one of the most sparsely populated parts of India, with a population of approximately 260,000 people. Ladakh is governed by the Autonomous Hill Development Council (AHDC) Act of 1995. Both Leh and Kargil districts are governed by councils who work with villages for social services such as health and education, land use, and taxation. Due to its location between Pakistan and China, Ladakh is a major military outpost for the Indian Army.

The Ladakhi language is based on the Tibetan language family but is different enough to constitute a separate language, although it is written in the Tibetan script. The word *Ladakh* means "land of high passes," and it is also called "moonland" because of its lack of rainfall, its meager vegetation, and its mountainous landscape. Ladakh is bordered by Pakistan-occupied Kashmir on the west, China on the north and east, and Lahul and Spiti of the Indian state of Himachal Pradesh on the southeast. The largest ethnic group is Buddhist, approximately

View of Leh, capital of India's most northern region, Ladakh, a center of Tibetan Buddhism. (Belayamedvedica/Dreamstime.com)

81 percent of the population, followed by 15 percent of the population, which is Muslim, and 4 percent Hindu. Because of Ladakh's high altitude, agriculture is possible for only a few months of the year, between May and September. The main crops are barley, wheat, and some vegetables such as cauliflower, potatoes, and peas. The livestock raised include yaks, cows, sheep, and goats. The water supply comes from the run-off of melting snow and glaciers that is are funneled into canals for drinking and for irrigation. Land is held by small farmers who bring their crops to small local markets or to the main market at Leh.

Ladakh is the repository of many historic Tibetan-style monasteries that are filled with murals, sculptures, metal images, and *tangkas* (painted scrolls) all relating to the life of the Buddha and attendant deities. Ladakh has about 5,000 lamas (monks) who live at these monasteries. Two of the oldest monasteries are Lamayuru and Alchi. Laramyuru, situated in an isolated mountain site about 75 miles west of Leh was started in the 11th century CE. Formerly holding 400 lamas, the site houses only about 50 now. It is famous for its 2-story-high 11-headed, 1,000-armed Lord of the Western Paradise. Alchi Monastery, founded in 1000 CE, is famous for its 1,000-year-old wall paintings in brilliant shades of red and blue. Located about 40 miles west of Leh, it is distinct in that it is not situated on a hill or mountain; instead, it was built on a level with the village. Thiksey, on the outskirts of Leh, is on a hill overlooking the city and the Indus River and was founded in 1430. It is renowned for its ancient collection of Buddhist texts and small bronze sculptures. Hemis, founded in 1630, is the biggest and wealthiest monastery and it is noted for its large yearly festival that is now becoming a tourist attraction.

Ladakh's history reflects four competing influences: Indian, Tibetan, Kashmiri, and British. During the Mauryan Dynasty (322–ca. 185 BCE), in the 3rd century BCE, an emissary from Emperor Ashoka (ca. 273–232) brought Buddhism to Ladakh. The region was later part of the Kushan Empire (ca. 48–220 CE) and linked the major commercial trade routes between China, Central Asia, and India. Contact with Tibet came during the 7th century during the reign of Songstan Gampo (ca. 605–649), founder of the Tibetan Empire. Tibetans migrated to Ladakh, intermarrying with the local Buddhist Mon and Dard populations. The kings of Ladakh, the Lha Chen Dynasty, descended from a branch of the Tibetan kings after 842 CE with the breakup of the Tibetan Empire, and greater Tibetanization occurred after this time.

In Kashmir, the first Muslim king, Rinchana, (1320–1323) was a Ladakhi Buddhist prince who converted to Islam. From that period, Islam spread especially in the western part of Ladakh. The Namghal Dynasty was established in 1533 by Choyang Namgyal, who was also a descendant of the former kings of Tibet, so that Ladakh had close ties to both Kashmir and Tibet. In 1685, the king of Ladakh, Deldan Namgyal (1642–1694), received aid from Kashmir, then part of the Mughal Empire, in order to defeat an invading Tibetan and Mongol army, and this led to greater Kashmiri influence. Kashmir became part of the Sikh Empire under Maharaja Ranjit Singh (1780–1839; maharaja 1801–1839), who appointed a Dogra, Gulab Singh (1792–1857), as the governor of Jammu. When Gulab Singh refused to support the Sikhs during the Anglo-Sikh War of 1846, he was rewarded by the British and became the maharaja of the combined state of Jammu, Kashmir, and Ladakh. After Indian Independence in 1947, Gulab Singh's great-grandson, Maharaja Hari Singh (1895–1961), the Hindu ruler of the combined region, signed articles of accession to become part of India, and this included Ladakh. This accession to India was disputed by newly created Pakistan, and tribesmen from the North-West Frontier province crossed the border and invaded Kashmir and Ladakh. Pakistan felt that the entire state should be part of Pakistan because over 90 percent of the state's population was Muslim. Ladakh pushed back the invaders but Kashmir was divided along a Line of Control. It has been the site of numerous border disputes and several wars and skirmishes, one of which, the Kargil War of 1999 between India and Pakistan in the western part of Ladakh, threatened the important Srinagar (Kashmir) to Leh highway. The Indian Army eventually pushed back Pakistan's troops to its previous position behind the Line of Control.

RUTH K. ROSENWASSER

See also Dalai Lama, 14th

Further Reading
Jina, Prem Singh. *Ladakh: The Land and the People.* New Delhi: Indus Publishing, 1996.
Official Site of Ladakh Autonomous Hill Development Council, Leh. Accessed April 26, 2011. http:// leh.nic.in.

Rizvi, Janet. *Ladakh: Crossroads of High Asia*. Delhi: Oxford University Press, 1996.

Rizvi, Janet. *Trans-Himalayan Caravans: Merchant Princes and Peasant Traders in Ladakh*. Delhi: Oxford University Press, 1999.

✦ LAKSHWADEEP

Lakshwadeep (a hundred thousand islands), also known as the Lacadive Islands, is at 11 square miles, the smallest and least populated Union Territory with just over 60,000 inhabitants. Located some 200 miles from the southwest coast of India there are nearly 40 islands and islets. The capital, situated on one of the four main islands, is Kavaratti. Over 80 percent of the population speaks Malayalam; others speak Jeseri and Mahl. The main industry revolves around coconuts and coconut-fiber products, although a growing number of tourists come from India to enjoy the spectacular beaches, water sports, and the marine life and clear water. The administrator governs the islands. Lakshwadeep sends one member to the lower house of Parliament, the Lok Sabha, in New Delhi.

ROGER D. LONG

See also Constitution; Territories

Further Reading

Nag, P., ed. *Lakshadweep: The Coral Paradise of India*. Kolkata: National Atlas and Thematic Mapping Organization, Government of India, 2005.

Planning Commission, Government of India. *Lakshadweep Development Report*. New Delhi: Academic Foundation, 2007.

Sirajuddin, S. M. *All India Anthropometric Survey: Lakshadweep Islands*. Kolkata: Anthropological Survey of India, 2006.

Union Territory of Lakshadweep. Accessed April 26, 2011. http://www.lakshadweep.nic.in.

Vijayakumar, V. *Traditional Futures: Law and Custom in India's Lakshadweep Islands*. New Delhi: Oxford University Press, 2006.

✦ LAND TENURE

The system of land tenure not only affects the prospects of agrarian transformation but also has implications for the well-being of rural households in general. The Indian land tenure system that has evolved over centuries is marked by a great deal of diversity and regional variation. The system of land tenure in India during the British period (1757–1947) underwent major changes. There were basically three different types of land tenure systems in colonial India: the *zamindari* system, the *mahalwari* system, and the *ryotwari* system. In the *zamindari* system it was the responsibility of the landlords, called *zamindar*, to collect land revenue from the peasants and to submit their share of the revenue to the government; in the *mahalwari* system it was the village headman who was to collect and deposit the revenue on behalf of the whole village; and under the *ryotwari* system the individual farmer was responsible for the payment of revenue directly to the government.

The *zamindari* system was created by the East India Company in 1793, when the "permanent settlement" was introduced by Lord Cornwallis. Under this system, *zamindars* were declared full proprietors of large areas of land and were entrusted with the task of collecting rent from the farmers. Thus a class of intermediaries was created between the state and the farmers. At the time of independence, this system was prevalent in West Bengal, Bihar, Orissa, Uttar Pradesh, Andhra Pradesh, and Madhya Pradesh. The *zamindari* system often led to exploitation of the peasantry in a variety of ways, including forced labor and compulsory "gifts."

Soon after independence, steps were taken to abolish the *zamindari* system. Although *zamindari* abolition was one of the relatively satisfactory measures undertaken under the land reforms program, the exemption given to land under "personal cultivation" was used as a pretext for retaining large chunks of land by the *zamindars*. The other components of India's land reform program included imposition of ceilings on land ownership and transfer of surplus land to the landless; tenancy reforms to provide security of tenure and regulate rent; and consolidation of land holdings. By and large, land reforms were only a partial success, except in a few states, such as West Bengal and Kerala. But in many parts of the country, owing to the political and social power of the landlords, poor land records, the informal nature of the tenancy contracts, and ineffective administrative agencies at the grassroots level, land reforms were poorly implemented.

Although tenancy has declined in India, it continues to be a feature of both advanced and backward agriculture. The phenomenon of "reverse tenancy" under which relatively large farmers lease land from small and marginal farmers is being found in areas of advanced agriculture such as the Punjab and Haryana. With the gradual move toward the liberalization of agricultural trade and marketing, corporate involvement in agriculture has been on the rise. On the one hand, there has been a demand for the relaxation and the withdrawal of the restriction on land-leasing, so that there is more flexibility in the land-lease market. On the other hand, serious reservations have been raised against such moves that tend to displace farmers from land, their main source of livelihood.

DEEPAK K. MISHRA

See also Economy; Food Security; Poverty and Wealth; Water Conflict

Further Reading
Chaudhuri, B. "Agrarian Relations: Eastern India." In *The Cambridge Economic History of India*, vol. 2, *c1757–1970*, edited by Dharma Kumar, 86–177. Cambridge: Cambridge University Press, 1983.
World Bank. *India: Re-energizing the Agricultural Sector to Sustain Growth and Reduce Poverty*. New Delhi: Oxford University Press, 2005.

✦ LANGUAGES AND SCRIPTS

India is an area of great linguistic diversity and is called a "nation of nations," with each "nation" possessing its own language and dialects. There are 22 official languages and 47 important languages, as well as tribal languages and dialects; altogether, according to one estimate, there are cumulative totals of 179 languages and 544 dialects. Within this variety there are four major language groups. These are Indo-Aryan, Dravidian, Austro-Asiatic, and Tibeto-Burman. Among these it is the Indo-Aryan language group that is spoken by the majority of Indians. In spite of this bewildering diversity, the entire region could be considered as a single linguistic area, since regardless of the languages' affiliations to any of the four major groups, they share a number of cultural, religious, and social features due to shared geographical proximity and historical past.

Most north Indian languages seem to have derived from a single language called Arya, which was introduced to India by groups of nomadic migrants who arrived through the Himalayan passes more than 3,000 years ago. Over time, the Aryan language successively spread over large parts of northern and central India, and it also evolved to become today's various north Indian languages. These modern languages are also in many ways different from the ancient spoken Arya and its immediate successor, Sanskrit. Sanskrit first evolved into Prakrit (natural speech). Further refinement of Prakrit as a literary language occurred around the 10th century, and it was soon after this we find the development of modern regional languages such as Bengali, Hindi, Punjabi, and Gujarati.

The Dravidian family of languages is mainly concentrated in southern India. In terms of numbers of speakers, Dravidian languages are the fourth or fifth largest of the world's language families. And in India every fifth person speaks a Dravidian language. The Dravidian language family has four subgroups: South Dravidian, consisting of Badaga, Irula, Kannada, Kodagu, Kota, Malayalam, Tamil, Toda, and Tulu; South-Central Dravidian, including Gondi, Konda, Kui, Kuvi, Manda, Pengo, and Telugu; Central Dravidian, containing Gadaba, Kolami, Naiki, and Parji; and North Dravidian, consisting of Brahui, Kurux, and Malto.

The vast majority of the Dravidian speakers are concentrated in southern and central India from the Vindhya Mountains (a cultural and linguistic divider) to Cape Comorin and are located mainly in the states of Tamil Nadu, Andhra Pradesh, Karnataka, and Kerala.

The Munda language family is currently spoken in eastern India. Munda and its related sister languages, such as Khasi of Assam, are branches of the Austro-Asiatic family of languages. This family includes various languages of Southeast Asia, such as Mon-Khmer of present-day Cambodia and Nicobarese in the Nicobar Islands. This linguistic evidence in the form of loan words found in Vedic and later in Indo-Aryan texts also suggest the possibility of an early Austro-Asiatic language that may well have been spoken in the Punjab and the Ganges-Yamuna Doab. But so far, no direct, concrete evidence for its widespread use in the distant prehistoric past has appeared.

The northern rim of South Asia bordering the foothills and the mountain chains of the high Himalayas is inhabited by Tibeto-Burman speakers. The early history of this area is unknown and the earliest widely accepted reference to the people of this area is the mountain people called Kirata, who are mentioned in Vedic texts. The language of Kathmandu Valley in Nepal was Nawari until the mid-18th century, when it was replaced by Nepali; Nawari belongs to the Tibeto-Burman language group, as do the present-day dominant languages in Ladakh and Bhutan, along with the dialect of the Sherpa people.

Apart from the four families mentioned, there are a few languages in India that show no identifiable relationship with any language inside or outside the Indian subcontinent. These include Burushaski, a language in Kashmir; Nahali, a language in central India; and Vedda, a language of the earliest hunter gatherers of Sri Lanka. These languages are spoken to a limited extent today but some of them may have been of great importance in prehistoric times.

Loan words in old Indo-Aryan and early Dravidian hints of the existence of pre-Aryan and pre-Dravidian languages. The modern locations of some of these languages were not necessarily their prehistoric homeland.

The earliest epigraphical record of a decidedly Indian script that could be deciphered is the rock and pillar edicts of the Mauryan emperor Ashoka (272–231 BCE). They were mostly written in two of the earliest Indian scripts—Brahmi and the other Kharosthi—but the language used in these inscriptions is the Magadhi-Prakrit dialect of Ashoka's capital Pataliputra in Magada (Bihar). Some 200 scripts, both ancient and modern, from the Indian subcontinent as well as Tibet and Southeast Asia claim their descent from Brahmi, a term used for writing in general (the art of Brahma).

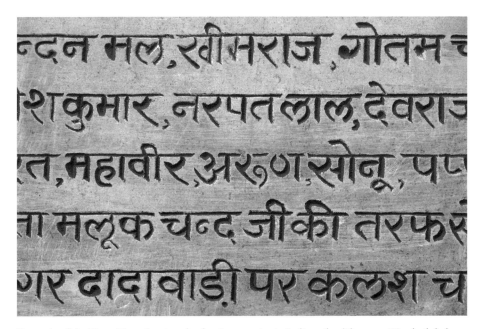

Example of the Deva-Nagari script, the dominant script in India today. There are 22 scheduled languages in India, with nearly 400 additional identifiable languages. (Honorata Kawecka)

By the beginning of the first millennium, Brahmi writing had already branched off into two distinct script families, the northern and the southern. Each of these families had a number of separate scripts and, although they had a common origin, their shape had visibly changed. The currently dominant script, Deva-Nagari (script for the city of gods), has 48 letters: 13 are vowels, and the remaining 35 are consonants. They can represent every sound in Sanskrit. Along with Sanskrit, other modern languages from northern India are also written in Deva-Nagari such as Hindi and Nepali, the official languages of India and Nepal, as well as the widely used language of western India, Marathi. Deva-Nagari, like other Brahmi-based scripts, is written from left to right. It became the parent of other Indic scripts such as Gurmukhi, which has been used by the Sikhs since the 1500s to write their sacred texts in the Punjabi language. Gurumukhi is closely connected with the emergence of Sikhism and was a modified form of an earlier Indic script called Landa that was used for writing Punjabi, Landa, and Sindhi. It was chosen for writing Punjabi by the early Sikh gurus. In modern Pakistan, keeping with its Islamic heritage, Punjabi is written in the Perso-Arabic script. Another important script that derived from Nagari was the proto-Bengali script. It led to the development of modern Bengali script (another widely used script in eastern India), along with scripts used for writing Santhali (an Austric tribal language), Assamese, and Manipuri, which is closely related to the Gujarati script used in western India. Other daughters of Gupta script are the Pali script, Tibetan, and Sarada, and it is one of the sources for the Tamil script, the oldest Dravidian language in southern India.

The Pali script, along with Grantha (of the late 5th-century Pallava Dynasty), was to be the parent script for many south and southeast Asian languages including old Thai, Burmese, Kavi (old Javanese), and Sinhalese. Sarada, another daughter of Pali (and which gave rise to the Takri script used for the Dogri language in Jammu), was used for writing the Kashmiri language (which could also be written in Deva-Nagari). But Kashmir, being predominately an Islamic region, adopted the Persio-Arabic script as its national script.

The south Indian scripts of the Dravidian-speaking people are a smaller family than the northern group. Here, the most important one that derived from the Brahmi script was Kadamba. This gave rise to old Kanarese, the parent script of both modern Kanarese and Kannada, both of which emerged around 1500 CE. Another important southern script was Grantha (which means "book" in Sanskrit), which originated 800 years ago. It became the parent of Malayalam script and was commonly used for writing the Sanskrit language in southern India. It also was to influence the development of Tamil script around 750 CE and the Tamil script called Tamil-eluthu, which derives from the northern group. All Indic scripts are adaptations to the language's sound system. In Pakistan, the official language, Urdu, though similar to Hindi in speech, uses the Persio-Arabic script. The Persio-Arabic script, unlike Deva-Nagari, is inadequate for expressing the complex grammar of the new Indo-Aryan speech, and this makes reading Urdu somewhat difficult. Since the early days of the first Islamic sultanates of the mid-11th century to the mid-19th century, the Persian language and the Persio-Arabic script remained the official literary medium in all north Indian–based kingdoms and empires, including the early British colonial state. After 1830, the English language, and the Latin script, became the dominant means of both the spoken and the written language.

Today, largely due to foreign travel and globalization, English has again become the lingua franca of the educated professional classes of India. The rise of the English language and the use of the Latin script also has to do with the failure of Hindi and its Deva-Nagari script to become the single pan-Indian elite language. The English spoken by most Indians, earlier derogatorily referred to as "chi-chi" and now sometimes called "Hinglish," has achieved the status of a language in itself with a growing and widely admired corpus of literature and its own Nobel Prize–winning authors.

RAMAN N. SEYLON

See also Hinglish; Media and Telecommunications; Newspapers, Indian-Language

Further Reading
Campbell, George L. *Handbook of Scripts and Alphabets.* New York: Routledge, 1997.
Cardona, George, and Dhanesh Jain. *The Indo-Aryan Languages.* London: Routledge, 2007.
Christin, Anne-Marie. *A History of Writing: From Hieroglyph to Multimedia.* Paris: Flammarion, 2002.
Kannaiyan, V. *Scripts: In and around India.* Chennai: Commissioner of Museums, Government Museum, 2000.
Masica, Colin P. *The Indo-Aryan Languages.* Cambridge: Cambridge University Press, 1991.
Southworth, Franklin C. *Linguistic Archaeology of South Asia.* London: Routledge, 2005.
Steever, Sanford B. *The Dravidian Languages.* London: Routledge, 1998.

✦ LITERATURE

The literature of India is composed in various languages, each of which has its own distinct tradition. However, owing to a pan-Indian Sanskrit tradition, Arabic-Persian influences, the colonial experience, a common set of mythologies, and above all, close interaction between these linguistic and literary traditions, significant resemblances are found among these regional cultures and traditions, which together form the canon of Indian literature.

The English word "literature" has derived from the Latin root *litera*, meaning "a letter," thus invoking a connection with something written. This connection, however, does not hold true in the context of India. The hymns of the *Rigveda* (ca. 1500 BCE), generally regarded as the earliest extant text of India, were composed orally. Hence, it is also known as a part of the *shruti*, or oral tradition. Much later, around the first century of the Common Era, Bharata composed the earliest extant dramaturgy of India, *Natyasastra.* Bharata used the word *kavya*, which literally meant "poetry," to denote any literary creation: written, oral, or visual. According to Bharata, there are two types of poetry: *kavya drisyakavya* (visual poetry) and *shravya kavya* (oral poetry). While drama forms a part of visual poetry, long narrative poems are part of oral poetry. Thus orality has been considered to be an indispensable part of Indian literature, and contemporary Indian literature also acknowledges the impact of oral traditions.

Aspects of literature composed in various regions of India vary due to cultural and linguistic differences and several sociopolitical reasons. This regional literature has developed in its own way through interaction with other Indian and non-Indian literature and cultures, forming its own unique literary history. Broadly speaking, Indian literature can be divided into three major periods: literature of the ancient period, covering from around 1500 BCE up to approximately 700 CE; literature of the medieval period, spanning from around 700 to around 1800 CE; and literature of the modern period, beginning roughly around 1800 and running to the present.

The 19th century marked a major turning point in the trajectory of Indian literature, as English education was formally introduced during this period by the British colonizers. The existing court languages of India—mainly Sanskrit and Persian—were gradually replaced by English, and the exposure to Western culture through English and interactions among various regional traditions have shaped modern Indian literature. The period is characterized by several movements, countermovements, schools, and styles, which are often overlapping at both the national as well as regional levels. A number of authors have contributed in more than one field of literature and sometimes in multiple languages as well. Modern Indian literature can be divided into two broad sections: prose on the one hand, and poetry and drama on the other.

Prose. Storytelling has been a part of the Indian tradition as far as it has been recorded. However, the novel as a genre only began to flourish in India from the late 19th century when early novelists were influenced by British novels. However, the rich Sanskrit and folk traditions of India have also greatly influenced Indian novels, resulting in a genre very much different from British novels.

Bankim Chandra Chatterjee (1838–1894) was a particularly famous early novelist of India who was influenced by English literature. He wrote novels in English as well as in Bengali. The short story also began to emerge as a very popular and powerful literary genre at the end of the 19th century thanks to a large number of magazines, journals, and periodicals that regularly published short stories. It was mainly Rabindranath Thakur (1861–1941), generally known as Rabindranath Tagore, who popularized this genre in India. As a result of their oeuvres and their influences, Chatterjee and Tagore were said to be the founders of modern Indian literature.

As a result of colonial politics, the sociopolitical situation of India changed rapidly during this period and this was reflected in the literature of the time. Social issues became a common theme in various forms of regional literature. The rise of a new class of people, the "babus," and a critique of the treatment of women became crucial themes. Chatterjee's *Vishavriksha* (*The Poison Tree*) of 1873 was a seminal text that depicted the dilemma of women in the newly emerging nuclear families.

From the 19th century a number of female authors came to the forefront. Rassundari Devi's (ca. 1809–?) *Amar Jiban* (*My Life*) of 1876 is the first autobiography by an Indian woman. Pandita Ramabai (1858–1922), Rokeya Sakhawat Hossain (1880–1932), Krupabai Satthianadhan (1862–1894), and Tarabai Shindhe (ca. 1850–1910) are some of the most important authors of the early modern period to criticize gender discrimination and caste hierarchy. Rokeya Hossain's short story "Sultana's Dream" is one of the earliest stories of science fiction in India; she describes a "ladyland" much more advanced in science and technology than the mundane patriarchal society of the time.

During the first half of the 20th century the Indian nationalist movement had a profound impact on Indian prose as well as verse, and the nationalist movement, in turn, was influenced by the literature of the day. There was, in short, a symbiotic relationship between the two. Bakim Chandra Chatterjee's Bengali novel *Anandamath* (*Abbey of Bliss*), published in 1882, was one of those novels that had a lingering impact on the Indian nationalist movement, as the song "Bande Mataram" ("Hail to Thee Mother") was first sung at the 1896 session of the Indian National Congress (founded in 1885) and became very popular. Many people were upset that it did not become the national anthem in 1950 and there are calls by the right-wing Bharatiya Janata Party (founded in 1980) that it should be adopted as the national anthem. In addition, Indian literature was also influenced by the international Marxist-Socialist movement. *Umrao Jan Ada*, an Urdu novel by Mirza Mohammad Hadi Ruswa (1857–1931), has been called the first realist novel of India. It was published in 1899 and narrated the life of a courtesan in Lucknow to the backdrop of the 1857 rebellion. In 1929 Bibhutibhushan Bandopadhyay (1894–1950) published his famous novel *Pather Panchali* (*Song of the Road*) in Bengali, drawing on a particular form of Bengali folk song called *panchali*. The novel is one of the numerous instances of the confluence of the written and the oral traditions in the Indian context. In 1936 Munshi Premchand (1880–1936) published *Godaan* (*The Gift of a Cow*) in Hindi, in a novel that depicted the miserable conditions of Indian peasants living under British rule. In the same year, the Progressive Writers' Association was set up in India, which marked the progressive trend in Indian literature. Sarat Chandra Chattopadhyay (1876–1938), a Bengali novelist and a contemporary of Premchand, was also famous for his depiction of rural Bengal.

Raja Rao, who lived between 1908 and 2006, wrote *Kanthapura*, which was one of the earliest English novels in India. Published in 1938, the novel deals with Gandhian philosophy, that is, the ideas of Mahatma Mohandas Karamchand Gandhi (1869–1948), and its impact on the Indian nationalist movement. Since then, a number of novels, short stories, and poems by Indian authors have been published in English. Nirad C. Chaudhuri (1897–1999), Mulk Raj Anand (1905–2004), and R. K. Narayan (1906–2001) are particularly famous for their English fiction and their essays.

The partition of India and Pakistan in 1947 followed by communal riots in various parts of India created a long-lasting impact on Indian literature, so much so that even after more than 60 years of independence, partition has remained an important theme in contemporary

R. K. Narayan in 1999. Narayan depicted life in India with grace and humor, offering witty, perceptive descriptions of Indian life. His novels and short stories, many of them highly autobiographical, have brought the characters of his imaginary town of Malgudi to an appreciative international audience. (THE HINDU/AFP/Getty Images)

Indian literature. The violence and trauma of the partition period intimately associated with the independence of the country has become a recurring motif in Indian novels, short stories, and poems. *Train to Pakistan* by Khushwant Singh (b. 1915) and *Midnight's Children* by Salman Rushdie (b. 1947) are two of the most famous novels dealing with this traumatic event. While Singh focuses on the violence immediately following independence, Rushdie traces the journey of these twin countries after independence.

Postindependence literature is remarkable also for its humanistic and progressive trends. Social problems, especially those of caste and gender hierarchy, come up as recurring themes. Vyankatesh Madgulkar (1927–2001) published the novella *Bangarvadi* in 1955 about a poor village. Shripad Narayan Pendse (1913–2007) published *Garambica Bapu* (*Wild Bapu of Garambi*) in 1952. Thakazhi Sivasankara Pillai (1912–1999) published *Chemmeen* (*Prawns*) in 1956. Shrilal Shukla (b. 1925) published *Raag Darbari* in 1968. Mahasweta Devi (b. 1926) published *Aranyer Adhikar* (*The Occupation of the Forest*) in 1977. U. R. Ananthamurthy (b. 1932) published *Samskara,* which can be translated as "culture" or "ritual" or "death rites," in 1966. Anita Desai (b. 1935) published *In Custody* in 1984. Amitav Ghosh (b. 1956) published *The Shadow Lines* in 1988. Upamanyu Chatterjee (b. 1959) published *English August: An Indian Story* in 1988. Arundhati Roy (b. 1961) published *The God of Small Things* in 1997, which won the Booker Prize the same year. These are among the most famous contemporary novels dealing with varying aspects of the sociopolitical struggles in India and of the plight of rural or urban India.

The rise of a number of promising women authors and the foregrounding of feminist issues are other distinct features of this period. The Urdu author Ismat Chughtai (1911–1991) is particularly famous for her short story "Lihaaf" ("The Quilt"), which was published in 1941. With its implicit reference to lesbianism, the story appeared as a severe critique of Indian society. Mahasweta Devi (b. 1926), a famous activist-author, penned numerous novels, short stories, and essays in Bengali highlighting the exploitations of the "lower" caste people. Nabaneeta Dev Sen (b. 1938), C. S. Laxmi (b. 1944) (who also writes under the pen name Ambai), Urmila Pawar (b. 1945), Vaidehi (b. 1945) (whose real name is Janaki Srinivasa Murthy), Mrinal Pande (b. 1946), and B. M. Zuhara (b. 1952) are some of the eminent women authors on the contemporary Indian literary scene. Many of them champion the cause of women in their work.

Dalit literature is one of the most prominent aspects of contemporary Indian writing. The word *dalit* means "oppressed." The term refers to groups of people from various parts of the country who have traditionally been regarded as "untouchables." A number of Dalit authors have created a major impact on the content as well as the form of Indian literature. Dalit authors such as Baby Kamble (b. 1929), Urmila Pawar (b. 1945), Bama Faustina (b. 1958), and others have introduced a new literary genre in the Indian canon, the *testimonio* (testimony). Although Kamble and Pawar write in Marathi, Bama's autobiography *Karukku* (1992) is regarded as the first Tamil Dalit text.

There is also a large group of authors of Indian origin who live outside India and who have achieved international acclaim. Among such authors are Bharati Mukherjee (b. 1940), Rohinton Mistry (b. 1952), Jhumpa Lahiri (b. 1967), and Kiran Desai (b. 1971).

Poetry and Drama. Like prose, early modern poetry and drama were also influenced by classical European and English poetry. Madhusudan Dutta (1824–1873) was a famous Bengali poet who introduced free verse poems in Bengali literature. Rabindranath Tagore was awarded the Nobel Prize for Literature in 1913 for a collection of 103 poems called *Gitanjali* (*Song Offerings*), which were published in the same year. In 1922 he published *Lipika*, a book that was considered by many to be the first work of prose poems in India.

The impact of the nationalist movement is evident in Tagore's patriotic poems and songs. In fact, his writings also influenced the trajectory of the Indian nationalist movement to a large extent. The Tamil poet Subramania Bharati (1882–1921) and the Bengali poets Dwijendralal Roy (1863–1913) and Kaji Najrul Islam (1899–1976) are also known for their patriotic poems and songs. Narmadashankar Dave (1833–1886) (popularly known as Narmad), Kerala Varma (1845–1914), Kumaran Asan (1873–1922), and Mohammad Iqbal (1877–1938) are among the most distinguished poets of this period who have successfully blended Western influences with ancient Indian traditions in their poems.

Romanticism began to flourish in Indian poetry from the early 20th century. Suryakant Tripathi (1896–1961) (also known as Nirala), Mahadevi Varma (1907–1987), Harivanshrai Bachchan (1907–2003), Balamani Amma (1909–2004), Sachidananda H. Vatsyaya (1911–1987) (also known by his pen name Agyeya), and the internationally renowned Faiz Ahmed Faiz (1911–1984) are some of the remarkable poets of this period who emphasized personal experience and lyricism in their works. The poems of this period are characterized by their stress on individuality, nature, emotion, childhood, and nostalgia. These poems, to a large extent, resemble English Romantic poetry.

However, attempts to develop a new poetry became evident from the 1930s on. From this period a number of poets began to move away from traditional meters and styles and to create a new and different kind of verse. Such attempts produced varying results among various regional traditions. In Bengali literature this period was known as *Kallol yug* ("era of the literary magazine *Kallol*"), when poets such as Buddhadev Basu (1908–1974), Jibonanando Das (1899–1954), and others strove to break free from the empty lyricism of popular Bengali poems. In Hindi literature this was the period of *pragativad* (progressivism) followed by *prayogvad* (experimentalism). While Bengali poets were influenced more by Western poets, such as T. S. Eliot (1888–1965), Baudelaire (1821–1867), and others, some poets writing in Hindi sought inspiration from Japanese haiku. In fact, Indians' exposure to non-Indian cultures through English played a major role behind such movements.

Gradually, the style and form of poetry changed. Everyday language has become a part of poetic diction, and prose poems have become popular. The rising sociopolitical conscious-ness, especially issues like gender, class, and caste discrimination, is well manifested in the poems of Subhas Mukhopadhyay (1919–2003), Shankha Ghosh (b. 1932), Raghuvir Sahay (1929–1990), Arun Kolkatkar (1932–2004), Dilip Chitre (b. 1938), Kamala Das (1934–2009), Namdeo Dhasal (b. 1949), and others. Dhasal is one of the most prominent Dalit poets of contemporary India and also an activist who has voiced his protest against the marginalization of Dalits in his poems and novels. *The Golden Gate*, a novel in verse by Vikram Seth (b. 1952), marks a breakthrough in the structure of Indian novels. In 2007, Dogri author Gian Singh Pagoch received the Sahitya Akademi (India's National Academy of Letters) Award for his epic *Mahatma Vidur*.

Toru Dutt (1856–1877) is one of the first Indian authors to write novels as well as poems in English. She is followed by a number of other poets, including Sarojini Naidu (1879–1949), Nissim Ezekiel (1924–2004), Jayanta Mahapatra (b. 1928), and Arvind Krishna Mehrotra (b. 1947). During the second half of the 20th century a number of bilingual poets appeared, such as A. K. Ramanujan (1929–1993), Kamala Das, Arun Kolatkar (1932–2004), and Dilip Chitre, who write in their mother tongue as well as in English.

The 20th-century sociopolitical scene marked the rise of a number of women poets. Swarnakumari Devi (1855–1932) was one of the earliest women writers of India who wrote poems and novels, and she also edited a magazine called *Bharati*. Amrita Pritam (1919–2005) was the first Indian woman who won the Sahitya Akademi Award (in 1956) for her poem *Sunehure*. Mahadevi Varma (1907–1987), Balamani Amma (1909–2004), Nabaneeta Dev Sen (b. 1938), Hira Bansode (b. 1939), Padma Sachdev (b. 1940), and Sujata Bhatt (b. 1956) are some of the other women who have had a significant impact on Indian poetry.

The forms of traditional Indian drama also began to change from the mid-19th century. Early modern playwrights, such as Madhusudan Dutta (1824–1873), Bharatendu Haris-hchandra (1850–1885), Girish Chandra Ghosh (1844–1912), D. L. Roy (1863–1913), and others, offered pictures of colonial India in their plays. Harishchandra, considered to be the father of modern Hindi literature, is particularly well known for his political satire *Andher Nagari* (*The Dark City*). While Dutta is famous for his farces criticizing the newly educated Bengali "babus," Roy and Ghosh are renowned for their historical and social plays. Roy's *Shahjahan* (1910) and *Chandragupta* (1911) and Ghosh's *Chitanya Lila* (1884), *Siraj-Ud-Daula* (1905), and other plays became extremely popular. The use of ancient myths and historical characters to satirize contemporary society is quite prominent in works by contemporary authors, poets, and playwrights alike. Ghosh also translated Shakespeare's *Macbeth* into Bengali. Tagore was remarkable in his attempt at blending ancient Indian dramatic traditions and folk traditions in modern plays, and they eventually shaped the course of modern Indian plays. His plays such as *Dakghor* (*Post Office*), *Raktakorobi* (*Red Oleanders*), and *Raja* (*The King*) are radically different from those of his predecessors. In fact, folk theaters like *yatra*, *nautanki*, and *yakshagana* have had a significant impact on modern Indian plays.

In 1942 a group of playwrights and actors formed the Indian People's Theatre Association (IPTA) in order to make people aware of the prevailing sociopolitical situation. In 1944 the IPTA produced *Nabanna*, a pathbreaking play written by Bijon Bhattacharya (1917–1978) with World War II and the Bengal Famine of 1943 as backdrops. The IPTA, however, stopped functioning after 1947, and various theater groups emerged in its place. Bahurupee was one of the most famous groups; it staged its own productions as well as plays written by other playwrights.

Besides group theater, there were also several individual playwrights who achieved great success. Bhisham Sahni (1915–2003), Habib Tanvir (1923–2009), Mohan Rakesh (1925–1972), Chandrashekhar Kambar (b. 1937), Mahesh Elkunchwar (b. 1939), and Ratan Thiyam (b. 1948) are among the notable playwrights of modern India. Badal Sirkar (b. 1925) wrote *Evam Indrajit*—a complex play dealing with the existential struggle and identity crisis of modern human beings—first staged in 1967, this play marked a major turning point in Indian drama. In 1975 Tanvir's *Charandas Chor* (*Charandas, the Thief*), a successful blend of folk tradition and modern theater, marked a radical change in the form of Indian plays. Utpal Dutt (1929–1993) penned *Tiner Taloar* (The Tin Sword), a play based on *Pygmallion* (1913) by George Bernard Shaw (1856–1950) and it also became very famous. A critique of the sociopolitical situation of India is apparent in contemporary plays. Vijay Tendulkar (1928–2008) produced *Shantata! Court Chalu Aahe* (Silence! The Court Is in Session) and *Ghashiram Kotwal* (*Ghashiram, the Constable*), and Girish Karnad (b. 1938) wrote *Tughlak* (1964). These are some of the most popular plays that satirize the prevailing sociopolitical situation. Karnad's *Hayavadana* is another important play that brings into focus the identity crisis of modern Indians. In fact, sociopolitical turmoil along with issues of gender and caste discrimination have become the concern of a number of contemporary playwrights and have been manifested in *Kaeji Rath* by Sajood Sailani (b. 1936), in *Curfew* by Lakshman Srimal (b. 1944), and in various other plays. Mahesh Dattani (b. 1958) penned *Seven Circles Round the Fire*, an outstanding play that depicts an affair between a hermaphrodite and an upper-class man. His *On a Muggy Night in Mumbai* is another pathbreaking play that deals with homosexual love.

NILANJANA BHATTACHARYA

See also Media and Telecommunications; Theater

Further Reading

Chattarejee, Suniti Kumar, ed. *The Cultural Heritage of India,* vol. 5. Kolkata: Ramakrishna Mission Institute of Culture, 2001.

Contemporary Indian Literature. 4th ed. New Delhi: Sahitya Akademi, 1997.

Das, Sisir Kumar. *A History of Indian Literature, 1800–1910: Western Impact, Indian Responses.* New Delhi: Sahitya Akademi, 1991.

Das, Sisir Kumar. *A History of Indian Literature, 1911–1956: Struggle for Freedom, Triumph and Tragedy.* New Delhi: Sahitya Akademi, 1995.

Datta, Amaresh, ed. *Encyclopedia of Indian Literature.* New Delhi: Sahitya Akademi, 1987.

Dharwadker, Vinay, and A. K. Ramanujan, eds. *The Oxford Anthology of Modern Indian Poetry.* New Delhi: Oxford University Press, 1994.

George, K. M., ed. *Modern Indian Literature: An Anthology,* vol. 1, *Survey and Poems.* New Delhi: Sahitya Akademi, 1994.

George, K. M., ed. *Modern Indian Literature: An Anthology,* vol. 2, *Fiction.* New Delhi: Sahitya Akademi, 1994.

Satchidanandan, K., ed. *Indian Poetry: Modernism and After, a Seminar.* New Delhi: Sahitya Akademi, 2001.

Talati-Parikh, Sitanshi. "Modern Indian Drama." In *Western Drama through the Ages: A Student Reference Guide,* vol. 1, edited by Kimball King, 161–176. Westport, CT: Greenwood, 2007.

Tharu, Susie, and K. Lalitha, eds. *Women Writing in India: 600 BC to the Present.* Delhi: Oxford University Press, 1991.

✦ LOOK EAST POLICY

India's Look East policy is a multifaceted approach geared toward developing and strengthening economic and strategic ties with the nations of Southeast Asia. Partly seen as India's larger regional strategy to boost its position as a regional power, the policy has received significant attention within and outside the country. Southeast Asia has witnessed remarkable economic growth in the recent past and India's relatively better economic performance in the postliberalization period has fueled hope for mutually beneficial trade relations among the growing economies of the region. On the part of India, this multifaceted strategy aims to establish strategic links with individual countries, evolve closer political and economic ties with the Association for Southeast Asian Nations (ASEAN), and to showcase India's potential as a partner in regional trade and investment relations. Observers feel that India's Look East policy, at least partly, is a response to the increasing economic, political, and strategic connections between China and ASEAN. Domestically it is also seen as part of a strategy to develop India's relatively backward northeastern region.

The Look East policy is seen in the context of increasing economic partnership between ASEAN and the People's Republic of China. China was accepted by ASEAN as a dialogue partner in 1996 and since then China has been actively involved in strengthening its economic partnership with these nations. In 2001, China unilaterally offered to open its market in some key sectors to the ASEAN countries and in 2002 a Framework Agreement on Comprehensive Economic Cooperation was signed. This strategy is also seen as an important step toward integrating the backward southwestern part of China with the ASEAN economies. India's engagement with the ASEAN countries has to be seen in the context of this regional configuration of economic cooperation in Asia.

As part of the strategy, India has actively attempted to strengthen its relations with ASEAN, and at least partly it has become successful in doing so. India became a sectoral dialogue partner with ASEAN in 1992, a full dialogue partner in 1995, a member of the Council for Security Cooperation in the Asia-Pacific, and a summit partner (on par with China, Japan, and Korea) in 2002. In 2002, the first India-ASEAN business summit was held in Delhi. In August 2009, India signed a free-trade agreement (FTA) for goods with ASEAN, which resulted in tariff liberalization in a large number of products traded between the 10-member ASEAN nations and India. Negotiations are going on to reach an agreement on trade in services and investment. This is considered to be a very significant development in the context of India's longstanding suspicion toward regional multilateralism.

Initial speculations suggest that India's plantations (tea, coffee, rubber, and spices), marine products, and textile and garment industries are going to face tough competition from the ASEAN countries on account of this FTA in goods. Certain segments of India's manufacturing industries, however, feel that the agreement will open up new opportunities.

The other important dimension of this policy is the greater "sensitivity towards a large number of smaller countries of Southeast Asia" and the discernable change in India's attitude toward Myanmar's military junta. There has been a reversal of the earlier policy of reservations toward the military government and India is among the few countries that have provided aid to the military regime in Myanmar. India is currently building a highway and railroad north of the new capital, Mandalaya.

Domestically, this policy of closer economic and political ties with its eastern neighbors is seen as a significant part of the new development policy for the economically backward states of northeastern India. These states, though rich in oil and mineral resources, have remained weakly integrated with the Indian economy and have been falling behind the national economic growth rate after the liberalization period. The northeastern region (NER) of India has 98 percent of its boundary with neighboring countries and is connected with the rest of India through a narrow corridor at Siliguri. The region has also witnessed secessionist and militant movements of diverse kinds for a long time. In response to the region's backwardness, the government of India has initiated a number of infrastructure and other projects in the past few years. India's Look East policy is expected to provide new growth impetus for this land-locked region. The North Eastern Region Vision 2020, a document produced by the Ministry of Development of North Eastern Region, states: "the immediate priority is to build the required infrastructure right up to the border areas, establishing connectivity and communication links to the cross-border points through which trade and economic exchanges with the countries neighboring the North Eastern Region are proposed to be promoted under the Look East Policy." However, as of now, critics feel that India's Look East policy is more centrally anchored with regional security policy rather than with a regionally rooted development strategy. The future success of the strategy depends on the extent to which India's involvement with the ASEAN countries, and other neighboring countries, is linked to the regional bottlenecks in terms of poor connectivity and weak market linkages in the northeastern region. In an address to the "Look East" Summit in Kolkata (2010), Arunachal Governor J. J. Singh outlined the imperatives of developing the region. The challenge, he noted, is not only to open up new vistas of economic cooperation but also to manage the borders effectively, "especially with regard to cross border migration, terrorism, drugs and arms supply and other forms of non-conventional security threats for ensuring the rights and traditions of local ethnic groups comprehensively in the context of global forces of change."

DEEPAK K. MISHRA

See also Foreign Policy; Myanmar, Relations with; Singapore, Relations with; Southeast Asia, Relations with; Vietnam, Relations with

Further Reading

Arunachalam, P. *India-ASEAN Free Trade Agreement: Challenges and Changes*. New Delhi: Serials Publications, 2011.

Department of Development of North Eastern Region and North Eastern Council. *North Eastern Region Vision, 2020*. New Delhi: Government of India, 2008.

Khanna, Sushil. "Look East, Look South: Backward Border Regions in India and China." www.burmalibrary.org/docs4/LookEast-LookSouth-08REVISED.pdf.

Pal, P., and M. Dasgupta. "The ASEAN-India Free Trade Agreement: An Assessment." *Economic and Political Weekly* 44 (38) (2009): 11–14.

✦ LUCKNOW

Lucknow, the capital of Uttar Pradesh, is situated on the bank of the river Gomti and has an estimated population of 5 million people. Lucknow is famous for its fine cuisine and gracious living, music, Urdu and Hindi literature, and fine architecture. Although Lucknow was able to maintain a semblance of communal harmony between the Hindus and Muslims during the traumatic days of the partition period, postindependence politics based on religious and caste issues has besmirched its rich and tolerant history. Voting trends in Uttar Pradesh, the largest state in India, are monitored very closely by all political parties, as it is the key to winning a majority at the center. In addition to its status as the political epicenter of India, the city has highly reputed academic, medical, and research institutions, as well as old established and respected high schools, and boasts its own high court, a medical college, two universities, a central drug research institute, and tutoring schools for students aspiring to do well in competitive exams. Lucknow's educational, commercial, and legal infrastructure has facilitated its growth in the information technology sector, in banking, in retail, and in construction. All major national companies are present in Lucknow. Lucknow is one of the few cities in northern India that has been selected for the Smart City project, which uses information technology for economic development.

The present city was built within the environs of the ruins of Lakshmanpur, a land, according to legend, gifted by Lord Rama, hero of the epic *Ramayana*, to his younger brother Lakshman. This city rose to prominence when the Nawabs of Awadh, the descendents of a Persian noble family of Nishapur, Khurasan, decided to shift their capital from Faizabad-Ayodhya to Lucknow in 1775. The Nawabs (an honorary title given to them by the Mughal emperors) of Awadh were encouraged by the English East India Company, founded in 1600, to reassert their separate identity as Shia Muslims in the last decades of the 18th century. Saadat Khan (ca. 1680–1839; nawab 1724–1739), whose former name was Muhammad Amin, was the founder of the dynasty. He never rose up in open revolt against the Mughal emperor but simply took advantage of the emperor's weak position and set himself up as an independent king. He ensured the family's prosperity when he designated his nephew, who was married to his only daughter, to be his successor.

Street market in the old section of Lucknow, the bustling capital of Uttar Pradesh. Lucknow was renowned as a cosmopolitan city with a strong cultural and artistic tradition supported by a refined aristocratic class in the 18th and 19th centuries. (Dinodia/StockphotoPro)

The Nawabs of Awadh contributed to making Lucknow a vibrant city both culturally and economically through their encouragement of artisanal production, music, architectural projects, and handicrafts. Most notably, the rulers of Awadh took the annual Shia commemoration of Imam Hussain's martyrdom (Imam Hussain was the Prophet Mohammad's grandson) at the Battle of Karbala in 680, also known as the Remembrance of Muharram, and made it highly ritualistic and elaborate. Although the Nawabs of Awadh built specific edifices like *Bara Imambara* (a house to remember Imam Husain) to observe Muharram, the first month of the Islamic calendar, they also publicly involved other religious communities as well. The handicrafts of Lucknow are highly renowned, especially the *Chikankari*, an intricate embroidery involving 38 types of stitches (*morri, katao,* and *bakhia*) produced on textiles. The artisans, mostly women, create designs of *Chikankari* on cotton, muslin, chiffon, and silk for sale locally and internationally. Lucknow eateries still thrive on 19th-century traditional Nawabi cuisine, where food is produced on a slow fire (*dum* style). Great attention is paid to the flavors, the ingredients, and the way the food is served.

FATIMA A. IMAM

See also Uttar Pradesh

Further Reading
Graff, Violette, ed. *Lucknow: Memories of a City.* New Delhi: Oxford University Press, 1997.
Llewellyn-Jones, Rosie, ed. *Lucknow: City of Illusion.* Munich: Prestal Verlag, 2006.
Llewellyn-Jones, Rosie. *The Lucknow Omnibus.* New York: Oxford University Press, 2001.
Llewellyn-Jones, Rosie, ed. *Lucknow, Then and Now.* Mumbai: Marg, 2003.
Official Website of Lucknow District. Accessed April 26, 2011. http://lucknow.nic.in/.

M

♦ MADHYA PRADESH

Madhya Pradesh is a state in the central part of India whose history goes back millennia. Evidence abounds that Madhya Pradesh has been populated since the Neolithic period. It was at this time that the earliest waves of humans arrived in the region and continued what appeared to be a seminomadic lifestyle. Gradually the various tribes began to settle, developing agriculture and building cities. Arts, science, and government flourished in the region centuries before the arrival of the Aryans and the Vedic religion, two forces that would later dominate India.

The first powerful kingdom of the area was known as the Avanti and held considerable sway over a vast swath of central India. Later during the Vedic Age (ca. 2000–650 BCE), Madhya Pradesh continued to prosper and benefited from the cultural enrichment and technological progress that characterized this era. This included organization of society along a class system (*varnas*), rules of marriage, and creation of an organized religion based on the Vedas, the Upanishads, and the Puranas.

Later Madhya Pradesh would become a part of the Mauryan Empire (323–185 BCE), India's first unified kingdom, and embraced Buddhism, the religion of its rulers. The state had the distinct honor of being chosen by the Mauryan emperor Ashoka the Great (304–232 BCE) as the location for the first Buddhist stupa in human history, the great Stupa of Sanchi. This historic monument still stands today and is a popular attraction for Buddhist pilgrims and tourists alike, attracting visitors from all over the world.

In the first millennium of the Common Era, Madhya Pradesh would see the rise and fall of a number of kingdoms. The region became a battlefield for many competing political forces both from within India proper and from the invasions of Turks, Huns, Mongols, and Muslim armies who sought to conquer and control the rich territory.

Throughout the Middle Ages, each successive wave of invasion and fighting ushered in a rebirth and development of new cultural and architectural characteristics for Madhya Pradesh's cities and a destruction of much of what came before. Among the few remaining structures from this period are the impressive temples of Khajuraho, built by the Hindu kings of the Chandela Dynasty (10th–13th century CE). These striking temples depicting human sexuality miraculously survived the onslaught of Muslim invasions and Islamic rule for more than 1,000 years. Like Sanchi, they too attract tourists who come from far and wide to see these remarkable temples and their incredible carvings.

Madhya Pradesh came under Mughal control in the 16th century and remained under Muslim rule until the 18th century, when control of the region was once again contested by an outside force. This time it was the British, whose imperial ambitions led them to colonize the coastlines of India first and then expand into the heartland. By 1861 the British were in complete control of Madhya Pradesh, and it became part of British India. After Indian independence from Britain in August 1947, modern Madhya Pradesh was created out of the former princely states and colonial holdings of British India.

At the time of its modern political organization in 1956, Madhya Pradesh was the largest of India's 29 states. However, its size was reduced in November 2000 when the new state of Chhattisgarh was carved out of southeastern Madhya Pradesh. Nonetheless, Madhya Pradesh is home to more than 60 million people and is nearly 200,000 square miles in size.

Given its geographical location at the center of India, Madhya Pradesh has always been a vitally important part of India's government and political well-being. As part of India's federal system, Madhya Pradesh contributes representatives to India's Parliament and has its own state-level government, consisting of a 230-seat Legislative Assembly. Although there are many political parties active in Madhya Pradesh, the state is dominated by two major parties, the Indian National Congress (INC), founded in 1885, and the Bharatiya Janata Party (BJP), founded in 1980. In 2010 the BJP held the reins of government after winning landslide elections in 2003 and 2008.

Madhya Pradesh ranks 7th in economic output among India's 29 states and ranks 10th in per capita gross domestic product. Since 1999, the state has had a steady growth rate of approximately 3.5 percent. The growth rate would have been more, but the separation of Chhattisgarh from Madhya Pradesh in 2000 cut an estimated 30 percent from the overall economic output. Much of the productivity of Madhya Pradesh is in the agricultural sector, particularly forest products, which are valuable for their variety and are used in ayurvedic (traditional medicine) practices throughout India and the world. Madhya Pradesh also produces sugar, soybeans, oil seeds, and a variety of grains for domestic consumption. Even with this agricultural output, however, Madhya Pradesh has a large number of poor and hungry people. Recent studies have equated the hunger in Madhya Pradesh with that in Ethiopia and Chad.

In industry, Madhya Pradesh once hosted Union Carbide, one of the oldest and most influential petrochemical corporations in the world. The joint U.S.-Indian venture was located in the city of Bhopal and became headline news in 1984 when on December 3 an estimated 42 tons of toxic methyl isocyanate gas were accidentally released into the atmosphere. In what would become the worst industrial disaster ever recorded, up to 10,000 people died within 72 hours of the gas leak, and 25,000 have died from diseases related to gas exposure since that time. As a result, few major international companies call Madhya Pradesh home, having only one S&P 500 (Standard & Poor index of the top 500 companies of large-cap American stocks) located within the state.

The population within Madhya Pradesh is diverse. India's tribal communities, some of whose earliest inhabitants lived outside of the *varna* system for much of India's history, continue to thrive and make up a large percentage of the state's overall population. These communities have kept many of their customs and traditions alive, in large part due to their relative isolation from the political turmoil that shaped India's landscape over the centuries. Along with tribal groups, a large segment of Madhya Pradesh is populated by followers of the Hindu faith, the ancestors of whom migrated to the area in successive waves over the centuries. Supplementing these two groups are small numbers of Jains, Sikhs, Christians, and Muslims.

In matters of customs and culture, most of the population follows Hindu traditions and ceremonies of marriage, birth, and death. Even the tribal groups have adopted much of the Hindu tradition as part of their local customs. Clothing varies among the groups as well, yet there are clear clothing choices that dominate the cultural scene in Madhya Pradesh. These include the *lungi* (*dhoti* or sarong worn around the waist), various forms of head coverings (*safa* or turban), the *kurta* (a loose shirt falling below the waist and worn by both men and women), the *salwar* (loose pajama-like trousers), and *saris* (a garment of unstitched cloth of four to nine yards worn by women). Clothes are often brightly colored and are chosen for their ability to protect the wearer from Madhya Pradesh's hot summers and moderately cool winters.

STEVEN B. SHIRLEY

See also Bharatiya Janata Party; Bhopal Gas Disaster

Further Reading

Brown, M. Bhopal "Gas Disaster Legacy Lives on 25 Years Later." *Telegraph*, August 6, 2009. http://www.telegraph.co.uk/news/worldnews/asia/india/5978266/Bhopal-gas-disasters-legacy-lives-on-25-years-later.html.

Lakshmana, C. M. *Demographic Change and Gender Inequality: A Comparative Study of Madhya Pradesh and Karnataka.* Bangalore: Institute for Social and Economic Change, 2007.

"Madhya Pradesh: The Heart of Incredible India." Accessed April 27, 2011. http://www.mp.gov.in. http://indiabudget.nic.in/es2006–07/chapt2007/tab97.pdf.

Sen, Probir. *Madhya Pradesh: Unhurried, Unspoilt, Undiscovered.* New Delhi: Wisdom Tree, 2010.

Sharma, Aruna. *The Heartland of Divinity: Fairs and Festivals of Madhya Pradesh.* New Delhi: Wisdom Tree, 2010.

Madras. *See* Tamil Nadu

✦ MAHARASHTRA

Maharashtra (meaning "great nation") is a state located on the west coast of India on the Arabian Sea. With a 2001 population of 96.9 million people, it is India's second most populous state. Maharashtra is the third-largest state in terms of land area, covering an area of approximately 191,000 square miles. Dubbed India's "economic powerhouse," it has the highest gross domestic product of any state in the country and makes the largest contribution to national industrial output. Maharashtra became a state on May 1, 1960—celebrated annually as Maharashtra Day—when the former state of Bombay was divided into the ethnolinguistic states of Maharashtra, where most of the people speak Marathi; and Gujarat, where most of the people speak Gujarati. The newly formed state of Maharashtra also included Marathi-speaking parts of Madhya Pradesh and the princely state of Hyderabad that had been reassigned to the state of Bombay in 1956. Maharashtra's political capital is Mumbai, and its official language is Marathi.

With the Arabian Sea to the west, Maharashtra borders the states of Gujarat and Madhya Pradesh on the north, Chhattisgarh and Andhra Pradesh on the east, and Goa and Karnataka on the south. Maharashtra is made up of 35 districts divided into 5 geographic regions: Konkan, Marathwada (or Aurangabad division), Khandesh (or Nashik division), Desh (or Pune division), and Vidarbha (made up of the Nagpur and Amravati divisions). The Sahyadri (or Western Ghat) mountain range runs north to south parallel to the coast. East of the Sahyadris is the Deccan Plateau. The state's three major rivers are the Godavri, Krishna, and Tapi. Although a majority of Maharashtra's population is rural, it is India's second most urban state, with 42 percent living in urban areas in 2001.

Once a part of Ashoka's Mauryan Empire (304–232 BCE), parts of modern-day Maharashtra came under the rule of the Satavahana Dynasty around 230 BCE. Based in Paithan in the Marathwada region, the Satavahana Dynasty was the first Maharashtra-based empire to emerge, ruling over parts of the region for roughly 400 years. The rock caves at Ajanta and Ellora are among the lasting cultural legacies of this empire and are rightly celebrated as some of the most remarkable edifices in the world. Around 400 CE the Satavahanas were succeeded by the Vakatakas and then the Chalukyas. Power struggles ensued among these empires as well as the Hoysala and Yadava kingdoms well into the 12th century. Between the 11th and 13th centuries, the Yadava Kingdom nurtured Maratha arts and culture from its capital in Devagiri (near present-day Aurangabad). It was during the Yadava Empire in 1290 that the saint and poet Dnyeneshwar (1275–1296) wrote the beloved Marathi poem *Dnyaneshwari*, which was a commentary on the sacred Hindu scripture, the *Bhagavad Gita*. During this period Sanskrit literature also flourished in the region. In the late 13th century the region sustained attacks from the sultans of Delhi, and the Yadava Kingdom fell in 1317.

Between the 14th and 17th centuries, the area was under the control of the Delhi Sultinate. In 1327 the Muslim emperor Muhammed bin Tughlaq (ca. 1300–1351) moved his capital from Delhi to Devagiri, changing the city's name to Daulatabad. For the next 400 years a succession of Muslim emperors ruled over the Deccan, including the Tughlaqs (1321–1398), the Bhamani Dynasty (1347–1482), and a series of smaller shahdoms. Throughout this period, Muslim rule was continually challenged by the region's Hindu Maratha chiefs. However, the Marathas did not pose a serious threat to Maharashtra's Mughal rulers, as civil wars prevented them from uniting against the more unified opposition. In the mid-17th century, however, the Maratha chief Shivaji Bhonsale, or Chhattrapati Shivaji Maharaj (1630–1680; r. 1674–1680), successfully united these forces and led a successful insurrection against Mughal rule in the region. Shivaji signed a truce with Bijapur's emperor Adil Shah in 1660, after which Shivaji's kingdom was firmly established and he built a civil administration in the region. Until his death in 1680, however, Shivaji's army engaged in bitter battles with Aurangzeb (1618–1707), the Mughal governor of the Deccan (1636–1644, 1652–1658) and Mughal emperor (1658–1707), as well as British and Portuguese forces. Maratha hold was further fortified in the early 18th century when Shivaji's grandson adopted the formal designation *peshwa* ("prime minister"). Maratha Peshwas ruled over the region, although not without considerable struggle, for roughly 200 years.

During this time the Europeans had arrived and were establishing a foothold in western India. While the Portuguese maintained a strong presence in the area, most British trading activities were concentrated in the northeastern city of Calcutta on the bank of the river Hooghly. Trade between England and western India meanwhile was conducted primarily from the Gujarati city of Surat. In the late 18th and early 19th centuries, the East India Company struggled with the Marathas for control of Maharashtra. After defeating the Marathas in the Third Anglo-Maratha War in 1818, the company established its regional dominance and created the Bombay Presidency, encompassing much of present-day Maharashtra and Gujarat. Meanwhile, the territories of Goa, Daman, and Diu were still under Portuguese control, and areas to the east were overseen by the nizam of Hyderabad. In the 1820s the company relocated its administrative and commercial activities from Surat to Bombay, and many Gujarati merchants and traders soon followed. After the Mutiny of 1857, the British Crown consolidated its India holdings, and the East India Company relinquished control of the Bombay Presidency. Until India gained independence in August 1947, the British colonial administration governed the Bombay Presidency from its regional headquarters in the fort area of southern Bombay.

After independence, the organization of India's provinces, states, and administrative regions was an irrational jumble, reflecting part colonial legacy and part political compromise. The idea had earlier been proposed to reorganize the states along linguistic lines, although India's new leadership, including Prime Minister Jawaharlal Nehru (1889–1964; prime minister

1947–1964), opposed the idea on the grounds that such a reorganization would weaken national unity. After a leader in the movement to create a Telugu-speaking state fasted to death in 1952, however, the prime minister acquiesced and created the Telugu-speaking state of Andhra Pradesh, paving the way for complete state reorganization. In 1956 the Indian States Reorganization Committee recommended the creation of 14 ethnolinguistic states. Under the States Reorganization Act of 1956, the Marathi-speaking regions of Vidarbha and Marathwada became part of Bombay state, but Bombay state remained a bilingual Marathi and Gujarati state. Opposing this decision, a group of Marathi activists formed the Samyukta Maharashtra Samiti in February 1956 to fight for the creation of a Marathi-speaking state. Bombay state's Gujarati population generally opposed the state's division, fearing the loss of the city of Bombay that had been built largely with Gujarati capital, although with Maratha labor.

For the next four years, Bombay politics were dominated by debates over state reorganization. Although the movement was initially dominated by members of the Indian National Congress (INC), founded in 1885 and also known as the Congress Party, Maharashtrian Socialists, Communists, and other leftist groups were brought into the movement to show broad support for a Marathi state. The movement meanwhile turned violent in early 1960 when Chief Minister Morarji Desai (1896–1995; chief minister of Bombay 1952–1960; prime minister 1977–1979) ordered the police to fire on a crowd of Samyukta Maharashtra protestors, killing 105 people. As a result, Desai was forced to step down from his post. The public outrage over this event helped fuel the movement for the creation of a Marathi-speaking state, and the state of Maharashtra was created on May 1, 1960, with the city of Bombay as its administrative and legislative capital.

Since its formation, Maharashtra generally speaking has been an INC stronghold. With the exception of the 1978 election in which the Janata Party took the largest share of seats in the Maharashtra Legislative Assembly, the INC (in its various incarnations and splinter parties) held on to power. Maharashtra politics have generally been dominated by members of rural Maratha castes who have held power in village councils and control over the state's agricultural cooperatives. Consequently, politics in the state have tended to be dominated by the INC and are predominantly rural and decidedly anti-Brahmin. This political landscape began to change in the late 1980s and early 1990s, however, culminating in 1995 with the INC defeat and the formation of a coalition government by the right-wing Bharatiya Janata Party (BJP), founded in 1980, and the Shiv Sena Party, founded in 1966.

While support for the Mumbai-based Shiv Sena Party had been growing steadily since its formation in 1966, the party made its first strong standing in statewide elections in 1990 when it ran in cooperation with the Hindu nationalist BJP. Although the party was still unable to take a majority of seats in 1990, a scandal in Maharashtra's INC, paired with the Shiv Sena's strategic use of violence, sealed the coalition's electoral success. The BJP and Shiv Sena won enough seats to put together a majority and form the government in 1995. In addition to several high-profile scandals, the ruling INC government had suffered waning public support after its seemingly inept response to the 1993 earthquake in Marathwada. The coalition's political capture was short-lived, however, and an INC-led coalition returned to power in 1999.

In Maharashtra's October 2009 elections a coalition of the INC and the Nationalist Congress Party (NCP) formed in May 1999 after three INC members were expelled from the party for rejecting the idea that a foreigner, the Italian-born Sonia Gandhi (b. 1946) and widow of former prime minister Rajiv Gandhi (1944–1991; prime minister 1984–1989), could lead the INC after the coalition won a decisive victory across the state. Of the 288 seats in the state's Legislative Assembly, 144 seats were secured by either INC or NCP candidates. The BJP and Shiv Sena meanwhile won 46 and 45 seats, respectively.

LIZA WEINSTEIN

See also Bharatiya Janata Party; Mumbai; Shiv Sena; Thackeray, Balasaheb Keshav

Further Reading

Government of Maharashtra. Accessed April 27, 2011. http://www.maharashtra.gov.in.

Kosambi, Meera. *Intersections: Socio-Cultural Trends in Maharashtra*. New Delhi: Orient Longman, 2000.

Kumar, Ravinder. *Western India in the Nineteenth Century: A Study in the Social History of Maharashtra*. New York: Routledge, 2004.

Talwalker, Clare. "Shivaji's Army and Other 'Natives' in Bombay." *Comparative Studies of South Asia, Africa, and the Middle East* 16(2) (1996): 114–122.

Vora, Rajendra. "Shift in Power from Rural to Urban Sector." *Economic and Political Weekly*, January 13–20, 1996.

✦ MALDIVES

Maldives is a small island nation located in the Indian Ocean, with Male as its capital. India and Sri Lanka, with which Maldives has close historical, cultural, and economic ties, are its neighbors. The total land area of Maldives is fewer than 186 square miles. The estimated population in 2009 was 396,334. The official language is Dhivehi.

Maldives is an Islamic nation whose people were converted to Sunni Islam in the mid-12th century. The nation was long ruled by a hereditary sultanate. Maldives became a British protectorate in 1887 and secured independence on July 26, 1965. After the abolition of the hereditary sultanate in 1968, Maldives, through a referendum, became a republic. The nation has a highly centralized presidential form of government. Under a major political reform agenda, political parties were unanimously given legal recognition by the People's Majlis in 2005. Maumoon Abdul Gayoom (b. 1937), the longest-ruling head of government in Asia, ruled the island state for 30 years (1978–2008). In November 1988 Sri Lankan Tamil mercenaries attempted to overthrow Gayoom in a coup, but it was immediately foiled with India's military assistance. In the first multiparty presidential elections held in October 2008, Gayoom was defeated by his political rival, Mohamed Nasheed (b. 1967), who was sworn in as president of Maldives on November 11, 2008. The Maldivian economy is primarily based on fisheries, although the natural beauty of Maldives has been attracting a large number of tourists, mainly from Europe and South Asia, who richly contribute to the state's revenue. Maldives has the highest per capita income in South Asia.

B. M. JAIN

See also South Asian Association for Regional Cooperation

Further Reading

Brown, John S., ed. *Columbia Chronologies of Asian History and Culture.* New York: Columbia University Press, 2000.

Metz, Helen Chapin, ed. *Maldives: A Country Study.* Washington, DC: Library of Congress, 1994.

Robinson, Francis. *The Cambridge Encyclopedia of India, Pakistan, Bangladesh, Sri Lanka, Nepal, Bhutan and the Maldives.* New York: Cambridge University Press, 1989.

✦ MANDAL COMMISSION

The Mandal Commission, named after Bindheshwari Prasad Mandal (1918–1982) from Bihar, who was a member of the lower house of Parliament, the Lok Sabha, was established in 1979 by the Indian government under Prime Minister Morarji Desai (1896–1995; prime minister 1977–1979) of the Janata Party to identify socially or educationally backward communities and to recommend reservations (or minimum quotas) for them in government service and in public universities. The first report of this commission was submitted in late 1980 and then was recirculated to pass a law during the National Front government led by Prime Minister Vishwanath Pratap Singh (1931–2008; prime minister 1989–1990) in 1990. The Mandal Commission identified almost 52 percent of the Indian population who did not have access to educational institutions and government employment. The commission recommended 27 percent job quotas for members of the lower castes, known as Other Backward Classes (OBC), in all central government offices including the judiciary, the police, banks, railways, and the private sector. The report suggested that state governments follow the same criteria. The commission also proposed that the same quota should be applied in OBC's admissions and promotions and that a separate central ministry should monitor the progress made in the implementation of the quota system.

When Singh announced on August 7, 1990, that his government would implement the changes specified by the Mandal Commission, widespread protests broke out across the country. Students belonging to the upper castes played a leading role in the protests, and many of them committed self-immolation in protest over the government's repressive response. The fragile coalition central government could not withstand the onslaught on the reservations policy and fell from power less than a year after being sworn in. The most important dimension of the Mandal Commission's report was its recommendation to start investigations into the conditions of OBCs among the Sikh, Buddhist, Christian, and Muslim communities. This issue of reservations for other backward classes, those who are not recognized in the Indian Constitution as protected citizens such as Scheduled Castes (untouchables), also known as Dalits, and Scheduled Tribes, also known as Adivasis, receded into the background during the communal fervor that ripped the country apart in the early 1990s and brought a coalition of right-wing Hindu parties, most notably the Bharatiya Janata Party, founded in 1980, to power. Since then the central and state governments have partially applied the Mandal Commission recommendations, but the southern Indian states have been more open and liberal in increasing job and educational quotas for the OBCs.

The issue of reservations in jobs and educational institutions came to the fore again with the formation of the National Commission for Minorities in 1992, which was charged with monitoring and evaluating the progress of the reservations policy. The commission identifies specific needs of socially backward classes that can be met through job quotas and reservations in schools, colleges, professional institutions, and universities. The recommendations and initiatives of the commission are routinely challenged by upper-caste Indian communities, leading to injunctions of judicial rulings. For instance, in 2008 the Supreme Court upheld the United Progressive Alliance (UPA) government's plan to provide a 27 percent quota to OBCs in central educational institutions excluding the "creamy layer" (the affluent sections of OBCs). The Court also validated the 93rd Amendment of the Constitution (2005), which gives power to the central government to increase the OBC quota in institutions of higher learning. OBC communities have since received greater opportunities through the recommendations submitted by the Mishra Commission (2007), which proposed 15 percent reservations for Dalits, Muslims, and Christians in educational institutions and jobs and their inclusion into the OBC category.

The UPA government, reelected in 2009 and led by Manmohan Singh (b. 1932; prime minister 2004–), reiterated its government's commitment to providing equal opportunity to every Indian citizen irrespective of caste, class, or religion in national economic activities, education, and employment.

FATIMA A. IMAM

See also Constitution

Further Reading
Engineer, Asghar Ali, ed. *Mandal Commission Controversy*. New Delhi: Ajanta Publications, 1991.
National Commission for Minorities. Accessed April 27, 2011. http://ncm.nic.in/.
Panandiker, V. A. Pai, ed. *The Politics of Backwardness: Reservation Policy in India*. New Delhi: Konark, 1997.

Manipur. *See* Northeastern States

Maoists. *See* Naxalite Movement

✦ MARWARIS

Commercial activity in India has historically been dominated by certain merchant banking communities such as the Marwaris, Khatris, and Khojas in the north Indian hinterland; Gujarati *banias*, Lohanas, Bhatias, Parsis, and Muslim traders in Western India; the Sindhis (especially from the *bhaiband* class) in the northwestern parts of undivided India; and the Chettiars and Komatis in southern India. One community that has been able to maintain its economic prowess in the subcontinent since at least the 15th century and from which prominent business figures continue to emerge even in the 21st century is that of the Marwaris.

The word "Marwari" is derived from Marwar, the erstwhile state of Jodhpur, but it is used to refer to anyone whose homeland is Rajasthan. Comprising a heterogeneous mix of caste groups within the *bania* (trader) caste, a number of *jatis* (subcastes), and persons of both Hindu and Jain persuasion, the term has been widely used to refer to immigrant traders from Rajasthan, especially in regions where they have settled. The immigrant traders themselves identified with the title from the late 19th century, as it helped them conceal their internal differences and present themselves as a unified community.

Rajasthani traders have a long history of migration for trade purposes. From at least the early 15th century, they are known to have traded all over the north Indian hinterland, especially in up-country markets, and often migrated in search of economic opportunities or to regions where they were offered special trading privileges by rulers. Their traditional interests included trading along caravan routes, money lending, acting as treasurers to ruling dynasties, and financing warring princes. From the 17th century Rajasthani traders moved to eastern India, especially Bengal. The coming of European traders and the establishment of British ascendancy over the subcontinent furthered this migration. Taking advantage of the rise of new commercial centers, the expansion of commercial agriculture, the new safety of travel established by the British, and the commercial opportunities of the Pax Brittanica, they arrived in large numbers in Bombay and Calcutta from the mid-19th century and later moved to Madras, various places in central India, and Assam.

The immigrant traders soon became indispensable in the new economic order as brokers, middlemen, and subcontractors, and by the last decades of the 19th century they gained control over the main segments of the bazaar economy. Given their long tradition of trading and their strong links with the hinterland of northern India, these traders were also involved in financing peasant cultivators and were able to ensure the seasonal flows of goods that the Europeans required. Widespread networks and complex financial arrangements interlocked

Marwaris together at several levels and generated credit flows, enabling these indigenous merchants to deliver goods at all levels of the economy. Financing of the massive movement of goods and crops occurred under their auspices, as did agricultural and craft production, which was dependent on them advancing loans to peasants and artisans. Through credit networks and the use of sophisticated financial instruments (*hundi*), the traders could control the indigenous money market and ensure the flow of goods and credit across the subcontinent. Thus, the Marwaris came to occupy a position of advantage within the colonial economy. Among the commodities in which they dealt were Manchester piece goods, of which they became the principal distributors; grain; oilseeds; raw cotton; jute; and other unprocessed goods. As brokers, the Marwaris became *banias* or guarantee brokers to important European houses and helped in bringing in new orders and in financing and guaranteeing bills. In addition to trading, the Marwaris developed considerable interests in speculative markets and engaged in futures trading in opium, spices, hessian (a coarse woven cloth), and jute.

Community networks played a critical role in helping Marwari newcomers settle. Typically they were housed in a *bassa* (community lodging) and worked as apprentices to well-settled traders before launching out on their own. This experience initiated the newcomers into the ways of city life, introduced them to the codes of mercantile morality that held the immigrants together, and inducted them into community networks. By the mid-19th century, the immigrant traders had also set up community institutions to regulate internal affairs, determine current rates of interest, settle disputes, and represent the community at diverse forums.

From this advantageous position, the Marwaris were able to expand into industry in the post–World War I era. The war presented enormous opportunities in both trading and speculation for bazaar traders, as European shipping was tied up with war needs. These profits, the dominance by Marwaris over hinterland trade, and their familiarity with different layers in the jute sector from procurement of raw materials to baling, speculation, and their control over jute shares enabled the Marwaris of eastern India to break into the European monopoly of the jute industry. Thus, in 1919 three Marwari firms—Birla Jute Manufacturing Company, Halwasia Jute Mills, and Hukumchand Jute Mills, Ltd.—entered the jute-production business. While the majority of the community remained traders and moneylenders, the larger business groups were able to enter into cotton and sugar in the 1920s, followed by cement, paper, coal, light engineering, iron and steel, and pharmaceuticals in the 1930s and 1940s. The interwar years thus witnessed their entry into technologically advanced areas and their emergence as industrialists in places far removed from Calcutta and Bombay. New groups emerged in almost every decade from the ranks of the Marwari bazaar traders, while their bazaar links and interests remained strong. The 1940s also saw older Marwari business groups enter areas, such as tea, from which European businesses were anxious to withdraw in the lead-up to independence and foray into new areas such as staple fiber, aluminum, fertilizers, and rayon pulp. By the 1950s the community was growing toward being the most prominent on the Indian industrial scene, second only to the Parsees.

A number of factors and historical circumstances were responsible for the widespread success of Marwari traders. Their corporate organization, their shared code of business ethics, their strong kin and locality networks, and a flexible nexus between family and firm gave them advantages in commercial pursuits. They also maintained a highly versatile trading and financial portfolio that enabled them to shift their priorities when faced with challenges and take advantage of new opportunities.

Apart from commercial prowess, the Marwari community also played an important part in public life. Marwari traders were especially close to the Hindu nationalist politician and educationist Madan Mohan Malaviya (1861–1946) and enthusiastically supported several causes of Hindu resurgence that Malaviya championed such as cow protection, vegetarianism, and the propagation of Sanskrit and Hindi. A deeply religious community, the Marwaris also grew close to Mahatma Mohandas Karamchand Gandhi (1969–1948) from the late 1920s. A *bania* himself, Gandhi appeared as one of their own, and they were especially attracted to his religious persona. Their association with him grew to be both political and religious. Alongside smaller traders, prominent members of the community such as Jamnalal Bajaj (1884–1942), Ghanshyamdas Birla (1894–1983), and Hanuman Prasad Poddar (1892–1971) took an active interest in national politics.

In postindependence India, the large Marwari business houses consolidated their economic power under the new industrial policy of Prime Minister Jawaharlal Nehru (1889–1964; prime minister 1947–1964). This policy, which appeared to restrict industrial growth, advantaged large groups that grew their share of capital, fixed assets, and capital stock. In 1964 the Monopolies Inquiry Committee found that 10 of the 37 largest industrial houses belonged to the Marwaris. In the last 60 years the community has continued to dominate the industrial sphere, although many new players have emerged, and even in the late 1980s four Marwari houses accounted for a third of the total assets of the top 10 business houses in India. Half of the nation's private industrial assets were controlled by the community as late as 1997.

Yet there are challenges that the community faces. The Marwaris are widely stereotyped as miserly, untrustworthy, greedy, and clannish and are treated as outsiders even in regions where they have resided for several generations. Strong anti-Marwari sentiments have erupted at times of economic distress, and Marwari traders have been blamed for hoarding, adulterating, and creating artificial scarcity of essential commodities since the famous Deccan Agriculturist Riots of 1875, when peasants in rural Maharashtra blamed Marwari moneylenders for their economic distress. There have been other instances, such as the Bengal famine of 1943, when the Marwaris were accused of hoarding and causing false shortages. In more recent years, anti-Marwari agitations have been witnessed in Orissa in the 1980s and in Assam in the 1960s and again in the 1990s. Negative perceptions also affect large Marwari business houses, which are perceived to be run on kin ties, to be family dominated, to be unprofessional, to favor community and caste members, and to value profits and pace of growth rather than quality.

The recent liberalization of the Indian economy (post-1991) and the increased competition that it has heralded have led to the decline of some Marwari groups, but many have remained in the limelight. Prominent Marwaris have also continued to emerge on the industrial scene, the latest being Lakshmi Mittal (b. 1950), whose acquisition of Arcelor S.A. in 2006 made him the largest steel maker in the world. Yet it remains to be seen how Marwari businesses will respond to the challenges and opportunities that liberalization is bringing to India and how the community will fare in 21st-century India.

MEDHA KUDAISYA

See also Economy; Kolkata; Rajasthan

Further Reading

Hardgrove, Anne. *Community and Public Culture. The Marwaris in Calcutta.* New Delhi: Oxford University Press, 2004.
Kudaisya, Medha. *The Life and Times of G. D. Birla.* New Delhi, Oxford University Press, 2003.
Kudaisya, Medha, and Ng Chin-Keong, eds. *Chinese and Indian Merchants: Historical Antecedents.* Leiden: Brill, 2009.
Timberg, Thomas. *The Marwaris: From Traders to Industrialists.* New Delhi: Vikas, 1978.
Tripathi, Dwijendra. *The Oxford History of Indian Business.* New Delhi: Oxford University Press, 2004.

Masjid-i-Jahanuma. *See* Jama Masjid Mosque

✦ MAURITIUS, RELATIONS WITH

India and Mauritius have a shared historical past spanning several centuries. Migration from India to Mauritius has taken place since the 15th century, with Indians primarily going to Mauritius as indentured laborers. Over time a sizable percentage of the indigenous population of Mauritius has undergone a process of assimilation and acculturation with India's diverse cultural heritage.

The visit of Indian nationalist leader Mohandas Karamchand Gandhi (1869–1948) in 1901 and his decision to send Manilal Doctor (1881–1956), a London-educated lawyer and politician, to Mauritius to garner support for India's struggle for freedom strongly influenced the people of Mauritius, who themselves were striving for independence. In 1968 when the island finally achieved independence, March 12—the starting date of Gandhi's historic Dandi Salt March in 1930—was selected as the date of independence and the national day of Mauritius.

Since the independence of Mauritius, India has taken a proactive part in promoting human resources and the economic development of the country. India has provided the necessary expertise for sectors of the economy targeted for rapid economic development such as in the Export Processing Zones and in tourism. India has assisted Mauritius with the implementation of the Four-Year Plan by sending technical experts and workers. In addition, India also provided heavy machinery and equipment that were used for infrastructural development in construction and surface transportation. The Four-Year Plan was followed by the 1978 Agreement on Economic, Technical and Scientific and Cultural Cooperation and the establishment of a Comprehensive Economic Cooperation Agreement between India and Mauritius. The diplomatic relationship between Mauritius and India is a warm one, and the bilateral relationship between the two countries is expected to grow significantly in the foreseeable future.

MOHAMMED BADRUL ALAM

See also Diaspora, Indian

Further Reading

Chandrasekhar, Sripati S. *From India to Mauritius: A Brief History of Immigration and the Indo-Mauritian Community.* LaJolla, CA: Population Review Books, 1988.
Eisenlohr, Patrick. *Little India: Diaspora, Time, and Ethnolinguistic Belonging in Hindu Mauritius.* Berkeley: University of California Press, 2006.
Prasad, Sunil. *India and Mauritius: Relationship of Two Centuries.* New Delhi: Chanakya Publications, 2000.

✦ MEDIA AND TELECOMMUNICATIONS

The media and telecommunications sectors in India today are thriving, exhibiting varying degrees of public-private partnership and providing a wider range of choice and content to larger numbers of people in both rural and urban areas than ever before. The major watershed event occurred in 1991 when the Indian economy was deregulated and opened up to foreign competition and investment. The result is that the telecommunications sector is the third-largest recipient of foreign direct investment (FDI). The 1990s and 2000s have been dominated by developments in television—especially through cable and satellite television—as well as the boom in the Internet, particularly since 1995 with the availability of commercial Internet. There has also been a major increase in the regional-language newspaper industry, and this is linked to increasing literacy, technological improvements, rising disposable incomes, the emergence of a rural middle class, the rapidly expanding urban middle class, a widening public-political sphere, and greater participation in public affairs at the local level.

Indian print journalism presents an unrivaled example of success with rising newspaper circulation, thus bucking the global trend toward falling advertising revenue. Since the 1980s the dominance of English-language newspapers in terms of circulation and readership numbers has been replaced by Indian-language newspapers, spearheaded by those in Hindi, although English national dailies and magazines still command a disproportionately higher

Busy newsroom at New Delhi Television (NDTV), one of India's private news channels, April 2003. (AP Photo/Gautam Singh)

degree of prestige and political influence. According to a March 2007 survey conducted by the Office of the Registrar of Newspapers for India (RNI), the total number of registered newspapers and periodicals in 2007 was 65,032, which included 7,131 dailies and 22,116 weeklies. These include publications in more than 124 languages and dialects, with Hindi having the largest number of registered newspapers and periodicals at 24,927, followed a distant second by those in English at 9,064. There have been dramatic improvements in the reach and penetration of the press as well. The National Readership survey of 2005 claimed a total readership of 200 million, which is almost 1 in 5 readers or about 20 percent of the Indian population, with almost 50 percent of those based in rural India. As reported by the RNI in 2008, the largest daily newspaper in the country by readership is the Hindi-language *Dainik Jagran*, at 55.7 million, and among the most widely read English dailies are, in descending order, the *Times of India*, the *Hindustan Times*, and the *Hindu*.

However, the success of the Indian press is firmly rooted in its imperial past. When India gained independence in 1947, the country had a bustling and thriving journalistic community and a press conducted in both English and vernacular languages. From the early 19th century when the first Indian printer and publisher set up business in Calcutta (Kolkata) in 1807, the Indian press grew into a prominent vehicle for the articulation of Indian nationalist anti-imperial sentiment and provided a rare forum for political participation under British rule after the British Crown takeover in 1858. The first telegraph line was opened between Calcutta and Diamond Harbour to the south of Calcutta in 1851, and from the late 1850s until independence the main news agency operating within India was the British-owned company Reuters, which was founded in 1851. Reuters in India monopolized foreign news services and through its affiliates also dominated domestic news. Following independence, the company lost its monopoly and soon ceased to operate completely in India. Today the main news agency is the nonprofit Press Trust of India (PTI), which came into operation in 1949 and now boasts more than 500 newspapers and all major television and radio channels and includes foreign media organizations, such as the BBC, on its books. Although smaller than the PTI, the other major news agency is the United News of India (UNI), which began functioning in 1961. There is also an Internet-based news and photo exchange arrangement among nonaligned countries, including India, called the Non-Aligned Movement News Network (NNN).

Radio broadcasting was introduced into India by the British between World War I and World War II, with All India Radio (AIR) broadcasting from 1936. At independence in 1947, however, India only had 6 radio stations and 18 transmitters covering 11 percent of the population and 2.5 percent of the land area of India. By the end of 2007, this number had increased to include 231 radio stations and 373 transmitters covering 99.14 percent of the population and 91 percent of India. While news can only be broadcast on the government-controlled AIR channels, nonnews sectors have been privatized and are open completely to FDI, with more than 100 private channels and cable networks in operation in 2009.

Television services began in India as part of the AIR network under government control, beginning in the capital of New Delhi in 1965, Bombay (Mumbai) in 1972, and Calcutta (Kolkata), and Madras (Chennai) in 1975. Delhi Doordarshan (DD), as the premier television organization, came into existence on September 15, 1976. Color television made its appearance in 1982, with the main impetus for its introduction provided by the Asian Games hosted by India in Delhi that year. In 1997 a new Broadcasting Corporation of India, the Prasar Bharati, came into existence subsuming DD and AIR, and five years later a 24-hour news channel was introduced on Indian television. Today there are more than 64 television centers in operation throughout the country functioning on a three-tier system with national, regional, and local broadcasting. From slow beginnings, the broadcast media has been opened to limited FDI, and today the consumer is spoiled by the choices available from cable and satellite broadcasters, with dozens of indigenous channels as well as a substantial number of foreign channels, including the BBC, Channel 5, MTV, Star, CNN, PBS, CBS, ITV, Sky, History, and National Geographic.

The first telephone services were introduced by the British only six years after the invention of the telephone in Calcutta during 1881–1882, with the first automatic exchanges being opened in Simla during 1913–1914. However, for a long time even after independence, the coverage and quality of telephone service remained very poor. In the last few decades major strides have been made to improve coverage and the range of options available to the consumer. In 2000 the Bharat Sanchar Nigam Ltd (BSNL), a new undertaking by the new public sector to cover all forms of telephone service, came into operation. There has also been a major impetus to increase the private sector share of telephone operations, which in March 2008 stood at 73.5 percent at a time when the network of telephone connections in the country was around 300.49 million. The rural areas, which have traditionally been poorly assisted by this service, have also seen heavy investment with the introduction in 2007 of broadband service, although optimal coverage will require a great deal more work in terms of infrastructure and services. By 2010 there were around 545 million mobile phone subscribers in India, placing the country second in the world for mobile phone use, behind only China and ahead of the United States.

CHANDRIKA KAUL

See also All India Radio; Doordarshan; *Hindu, The*; *Hindustan Times*; *Indian Express*; *India Today*; Newspapers, Indian-Language; Radio; Television; *Times of India, The*

Further Reading
Central Intelligence Agency. *The World Factbook: India, 2010.* https://www.cia.gov/library/publica tions/the-world-factbook/geos/in.html.
India 2009: A Reference Annual. New Delhi: Ministry of Information & Broadcasting, 2009.
Kaul, Chandrika. *Reporting the Raj: The British Press and India, c. 1880–1922.* Manchester, UK: Manchester University Press, 2003.
Ninan, Sevanti. *Headlines from the Heartland: Reinventing the Hindi Public Sphere.* New Delhi, Sage, 2007.

✦ MEDICAL TOURISM

India is a popular destination for international travelers seeking private health care. Medical tourism in fact is experiencing high annual growth rates, and government bodies in India, such as the Ministry of Tourism, have initiated a range of programs to encourage and market medical tourism, including marketing campaigns, improved airport and transportation services, and tax incentives.

The most popular treatments requested by tourists include alternative medicine treatment, bone marrow transplants, cosmetic surgery, dentistry, infertility treatments, joint replacements, oncology services, and specialized surgeries such as eye and heart surgery. Major cities that cater to medical tourists are Chennai, Mumbai, and New Delhi.

India offers several key advantages for medical tourists, including affordability, the immediate availability of treatment, high standards of care, medical expertise, the availability of the latest medical technology, easy communication with doctors and nurses in English, and India's popularity as a favorite tourist destination. Package deals for patients often include prearrangements, flights, transfers, hotel and hospital stays, postoperative care, and even a vacation. This contrasts with the high costs and long waiting times in countries such as Canada and the United States and in Europe, the lack of up-to-date technology in the Middle

East, and the nonavailability of treatment in some poorer countries in Africa and the other countries of the subcontinent.

Although health care delivery is largely unregulated in India, medical services for tourists report a growing compliance with international quality standards. A number of private Indian hospitals have been inspected by the Joint Commission International in the United States, the Trent International Accreditation Scheme in the United Kingdom, and other global accreditation organizations as well. India has also set up its own accreditation boards; one is the National Accreditation Board for Hospitals and Healthcare Providers, which is under the supervision of the Quality Council of India. These organizations inspect and accredit health care facilities and hospitals worldwide that use internationally recognized procedures and standards.

There are some problems associated with medical care in India. As Western countries have leading medical services and high quality standards, undergoing treatment overseas is sometimes viewed as inferior and risky. There is some variation in quality and accreditation in Indian hospitals, and many do not meet international standards. Postoperative complications can occur for patients who undertake vacation activities or travel back to their home country shortly after surgery, and these might be more difficult to solve after patients leave the hospital. Another problem is the resolution of complaints or any litigation that reaches the courts. In addition, the industry faces tough competition from health facilities in countries in the region such as Thailand, Malaysia, and Singapore. Some people also believe that there are ethical issues for India to resolve with regard to medical tourists: tourists occupy the time of doctors and nurses and take up bed space and facilities in an already overburdened health care system; tourists create further inequalities, as medical tourism facilities are far superior to those that cater to the average Indian; tourists create fears that higher salaries and career opportunities in private health care lure professionals from the public sector and the rural areas; tourists create uncertainty over the extent to which the large profits generated from private health care benefit public health and public health systems; and tourists raise the issue of the illegal purchase of organs and tissues for transplantation.

GARETH DAVEY

See also Ayurvedic Medicine; Diet and Health; Health Care; HIV/AIDS; Mental Health Care

Further Reading

Bookman, Milica Z., and Karla Bookman. *Medical Tourism in Developing Countries.* New York: Palgrave Macmillan, 2007.

Medicine, Ayurvedic. *See* Ayurvedic Medicine

✦ MEGHALAYA

Meghalaya, meaning the "Abode of Clouds," is a state, or federal unit, of the Indian Union located in the northeastern region of the country. Comprising plateaus and hills, this picturesque state boasts of having the wettest site on the planet. Shillong, often called the "Scotland of the East," is the capital. Meghalaya was a part of the larger state of Assam before it attained full statehood in 1972 in the North-Eastern Areas (Reorganisation) Act.

Meghalaya is bounded by Assam on the north and Bangladesh on the south and lies on a latitude range of 20°1′N and 26°5′N and a longitude range of 85°49′E and 92°53′E. The total geographical area of Meghalaya is about 14,000 square miles, and the state falls under 3 autonomous district councils—Khasi, Garo, and Jaintia—in accordance with the Sixth Schedule of the Indian Constitution. These 3 autonomous councils are further divided into 7 administrative districts, 2 subdivisions, 6 special administrative units, and 30 community development blocks. The headquarters of the 7 districts are as follows: East Khasi Hills District, headquartered in Shillong; Ri Bhoi District, headquartered in Nongpoh; West Khasi Hills District, headquartered in Nongstoin; East Garo Hills District, headquartered in William Nagar; West Garo Hills District, headquartered in Tura; South Garo Hills District, headquartered in Baghmara; and Jaintia Hills District, headquartered in Jowai.

Geologically very rich, the whole state of Meghalaya is a plateau with a wide variety of natural vegetation ranging from tropical mixed forests of the Garo Hills to deciduous pine forests in the Khasi-Jaintia Hills. Sal, pine, firs, bamboo, wild bananas, and grasslands are important varieties of flora in the plateau.

The Khasis of Meghalaya belong to the Mon-Khmer subfamily of the Austric stock of people. The nearest groups who speak similar languages are the Mundas of the Chottanagpur Plateau, the Mons of Lower Burma, and the Khmer of Cambodia and Thailand. These groups started settling down in their present habitat at different periods of time and commonly trace their original settlement to the meeting point of the Brahmaputra Valley before it was dominated by the Bodo-Kacheri plains people. The Garo peoples share ancestral ties with the greater Bodo-Kacheri peoples. However, the inhabitants of the frontier regions display significant cultural influences from the people of Bangladesh and Assam.

The Khasis have their own origin myth. They believe that many centuries ago a particular hill, U Lum Sohpet Bneng ("The Navel of Heaven"), originally connected heaven and earth. On the side of heaven there were seven huts where men lived. Due to man's sins, heaven was separated from earth, so man was left to himself. By this folktale, the Khasis claim to be of divine origin. Christianity is the dominant religion today, but it has several traits of animism and pagan worship instilled in it.

The total population of Meghalaya is nearly 2.5 million, with an average density of around 65 persons per square mile. Three principal groups of people reside here: The Garos live in the East and West Garo Hills, and the Khasis and Pnars dominate the Khasi and Jaintia

Khasi women at a market in the Indian state of Meghalaya, November 2010. The Khasis are a matrilineal society where property is inherited by the youngest daughter. In Khasi culture, the woman looks after the home, the father finds the means to support the family, and the maternal uncle settles all family matters. (Samrat/Dreamstime.com)

Hills. They primarily follow a matrilineal system. English is the official language of the state, but the principal spoken languages are Khasi, Pnar, and Garo.

Before the British incursion into the region in the 19th century, Meghalaya was comprised of independent Khasi, Garo, and Jaintia kingdoms. In 1835 the British incorporated Meghalaya into Assam, although the region enjoyed a semi-independent status for a short while by virtue of a treaty relationship with the British Crown. The topography and climate of Meghalaya made it a much-favored location for Europeans. Administrators and missionaries alike built headquarters or bases for their operations in Meghalaya. After the transfer of power in August 1947, the state, then known as United Khasi and Jaintia Hills, became part of the larger state of Assam, with Shillong as the capital.

With the reorganization of states in India under the 1971 North-Eastern Areas (Reorganisation) Act, Meghalaya attained full-fledged statehood on January 21, 1972, with a Legislative Assembly elected every five years. The Legislative Assembly has 60 members, and Meghalaya has 2 representatives in the Lok Sabha, the lower house of Parliament, one each from Shillong in Khasi Hills and Tura in Garo Hills. Meghalaya also has 1 representative in the Rajya Sabha, the upper house of Parliament. The ceremonial head of the state is the governor, who is appointed by the government of India. However, real executive powers are held by the chief minister, who is elected through a majority vote of the Legislative Assembly.

Meghalaya has a traditional governance system based on clan hierarchy. In the customary Khasi system of governing, each clan has its own council known as the Durbar Kur, which is presided over by the clan headman. The Durbar Kur manages the internal affairs of the clan and even today coexists with modern forms of governance. Every village also has a local assembly known as the Durbar Shnong ("Village Council"), which is presided over by the village headman. These councils play an important administrative role in rural areas in regard to aspects of community land, sanitation, education, health, and the resolution of disputes.

Matters relating to more than one village are dealt with by another council, the Raid Durbar, that is comprised of members of adjacent Khasi villages. The Raid Durbar is presided over by an elected headman known as *basan*, *lyngdoh*, or *sirdar*. Above the Raid Durbar there is a final political authority called the Syiemship. The Syiemship is the congregation of several raids and is headed by an elected chief known as the *syiem* ("king"). At various levels the Raid Durbar coexists, both formally and informally, with constitutional forms of government and is of immense importance in Khasi society. With some minor exceptions, the traditional governance systems of the Jaintias and the Garos are similar to that of the Khasis.

Meghalaya does not have large industries, but the smaller-scale industries comprise sericulture, flour mills, preservation, and engineering units concentrated either in the urban centers or located along the Shillong-Guwahati National Highway in an area called Byrnihat. Important medium-scale industries are confined to cement manufacture, plywood, chemical factories, and oil mills. Animal husbandry and dairy farming are important livelihood sources. Meghalaya has about 540,000 cattle, 29,000 buffaloes, 180,000 goats, 2.07 million pigs, and 1.419 million birds in the poultry business.

Meghalaya is rich in mineral resources, particularly in coal, limestone, and uranium. During 1983–1984 the Department of Atomic Energy discovered two high-quality uranium ore deposits of 9.22 million tons at Killung and Rangam. After initial explorations in 1987, the Uranium Corporation of India (UCIL), a government of India undertaking, extracted about 630 tons of uranium from a open cast mine, 6.2 square miles in size, near Domiasiat. However, strong local opposition forced the UCIL to wind up operations in the early 1990s. The UCIL is now proposing an open cast mining project worth 8,140 million rupees. The proposed mining and processing project—the Kylleng-Pyndengsohing Uranium Project in Mawthabah—will require 867 acres from 6 villages and will impact 72 other villages that fall within a 12-mile radius of the project area. There is strong opposition to the project from environmental organizations and local communities. They allege that public opinion was not incorporated into decision making on the project, which involves large-scale environmental degradation and the exposure of the local population to nuclear radiation.

Meghalaya, unlike most other states of India, follows a matrilineal system whereby lineage and inheritance are traced through the female line. In this system the youngest daughter inherits all the property and acts as the caretaker of her parents. However, the men, usually the mother's brother, have considerable influence in property-related decision making. But the matrilineal system also means that women sometimes take on a huge amount of responsibility both within the household and in the public sphere.

SUSHMITA KASHYAP

See also Northeastern States

Further Reading
Bhargava, Gopal K., and S. C. Bhatt. *Meghalaya*. Delhi: Kalpaz, 2006.
Bhattacharyya, N. N. *Meghalaya: Land, People and Economy*. New Delhi: Rajesh Publications, 2008.
Government of Megalaya: The Megalaya State Portal. Accessed April 27, 2011. http://www.meghalaya .nic.in.
Sharma, S. K. *Meghalaya*. New Delhi: Mittal, 2006.

✦ MENTAL HEALTH CARE

Mental health care in India is directed by the Ministry of Health and Family Welfare as part of the general health service. The National Mental Health Plan, set up in 1982, serves as the nation's mental health policy. The plan aims to ensure the availability and development of mental health services and training for mental health care practitioners. A number of health-related acts have been approved by the Lok Sabha, the lower house of the Parliament of India, including the Mental Health Act (1987) that regulates the treatment, care, and rights of the mentally ill and created a central government authority to regulate the provision of mental health services.

Patients are treated in primary health centers and general hospitals as inpatients or outpatients. Most mental hospitals are supervised by local, state, or central governments. There has also been a growth in private psychiatric services as well as in charitable trusts, voluntary groups, and other nongovernment organizations. Health professionals are trained in modern medicine and use the same illness classification systems, drugs, and behavioral methods as in the West. However, traditional medical practitioners constitute an important part of health care provision in India. The two medical systems practiced by these practitioners are ayurveda, "the science of life," that would be considered an alternative medical system as, among other things, it prescribes herbs, massage, and yoga; and Unani or Yunani (meaning "Greek Medicine"), which is based on the Greek concepts of the four humors: phlegm, blood, yellow bile, and black bile. Traditional medical systems are more popular in the rural areas, where such systems are readily available and comparatively inexpensive.

The family plays an important role in the care of the mentally ill in India, which is responsible for decisions about seeking help and the treatment process. However, family and community reactions to the mentally ill are often negative and can sometimes result in neglect, rejection, and stigma.

Although there has been a significant improvement in health care provision since independence, a pressing need exists for better mental health resources. Problems include the limited number of mental health facilities and professionals, the concentration of services in urban areas, minimal government funding, and the inability of patients to pay for treatment. The overwhelming majority of the people of India live in rural areas and do not have satisfactory health service facilities, services, or access to health care practitioners. There is also no central organization for mental health services and no nationwide data on the prevalence and incidence of mental illnesses. Consequently, the majority of mentally ill people in India go without adequate diagnosis, treatment, and aftercare. Another major issue is the rights of mentally ill people.

Despite these challenges, mental health services in India have improved a great deal in a short period of time. The government and other agencies are active in mental health promotion, and there have been improvements in the quality of care. Some of these improvements include an increase in government funding, the training of mental health personnel, innovations in the private sector, the integration of Indian and Western approaches, and an increase in nongovernmental organizations related to aftercare programs and human rights.

GARETH DAVEY

See also Ayurvedic Medicine; Diet and Health; Health Care; HIV/AIDS

Further Reading
Sebastia, Brigitte, ed. *Restoring Mental Health in India: Pluralistic Therapies and Concepts.* New Delhi: Oxford University Press, 2009.

✦ MIDDLE CLASS

The term "middle class" in relation to India is predominantly used with respect to the subcontinent's drastic shift from a planned economy to an open market economy in the early 1990s and with a gross domestic product of 6.5 percent. Abroad, attention is generally focused on the new market segments of millions of new customers with surplus money to spend on a plethora of consumer durables and automobiles as well as the growth of the service sectors, ranging from information technologies to business product outsourcing (e.g., call centers). India has capitalized on its large educated English-speaking population to become a major exporter of information technology services and software workers, who constitute key segments of the middle class. Moreover, the middle class has gained international attention due to the presence of some 26 million overseas Indians, many of whom have been referred to as "cultural ambassadors" by several Indian politicians. Overseas Indians contribute to India's growth by sending substantial remittances to family members and by investing in real estate or other growing industries in the country. The Indian middle class is also frequently compared to its Chinese equivalent in order to define similarities and differences in terms of economic, political, and social changes.

It is important to note that the middle class as a social category did not suddenly emerge in 1991 when India opened up its economy. The Indian middle class is as old as any Western country's middle class and is directly related to the spread of high capitalism, the development of bourgeois society, industrialization, the advent of the East India Company (1600–1858), and British colonial rule (1858–1947). Employment in the colonial administration and work in towns and trading centers were especially fertile ground for the development of middle-class culture and infrastructure. An important subgroup of the established Indian middle class was the *bhadralok*, members of the educated and cultivated status group of the so-called respectable people in Bengal. Sometimes you can find them depicted in indigenous popular culture and satirical magazines around 1900, such as when a pot-bellied man would be made fun of for his attempts to mimic the British colonial lifestyle. While such iconography must be understood as persiflage, it nevertheless underlines a well-established view that Indian modernity is copied from the West because Indians cannot develop their own modernity. Such a problematic Orientalist view of a singular Western modernity has been challenged by Indian and non-Indian scholars who have argued for alternative, multiple, or multicentered modernities.

Based on the large colonial administration, postindependence India continued to elaborate a middle class predominantly on the grounds of its huge government administration. The middle classes of the open market economy mark a shift from the administrative sector to the private service sector. Accompanied by reservation politics introduced in the late 1980s that facilitated access to higher education and to positions in the government administration for underprivileged castes and classes, the new middle classes are said to be less defined by birth, such as caste, than by merit and ambition. The idea of the American Dream has nurtured that of the Indian Dream and encouraged the emergence of a confident Indian who sees himself or herself at the same level as anyone from a Western country. This possibility has shaped the notion of world-class Indianness. However, despite the fact that by law caste must not be considered in terms of a person's individual career and other forms of discrimination, in practice caste membership continues to govern social concepts of the middle class, such as marriage (endogamy).

The definition of today's middle class in surveys varies greatly in terms of income, underlining the relevance of recognizing the existence of different middle classes according to income but also to aspiration. There is no single category that allows us to define the term "middle class" in India. One approach is to look at occupation patterns, education, and income. The new middle classes are a highly heterogeneous group and are made up of people in professional, administrative, managerial, clerical, and other white-collar occupations. Survey categories defining the middle classes are (in ascending order) "aspirers," "seekers," "strivers," and the "near rich." Images-KSA Technopak, Gurgaon, a global management consulting firm, in its survey of urban consumers titled "Consumer Outlook 2005," published in *India Retail Report 2005*, differentiated the new middle classes into 32 million "technologies babies" (8–19 years of age), 16 million "impatient aspirers" (20–25 years of age), 41 million "balance seekers" (25–50 years of age), and 9 million "arrived veterans" (51–60 years of age). According to a survey by the management consulting firm McKinsey's Global Institute, in 2007 the middle class encompassed 50 million people and is projected to grow tenfold in the next 20 years. Other statistics speak of more than 100 million and even 300 million middle-class people, based on today's predictions. India is thus one of the largest consumer markets worldwide, with an overwhelming dominance of consumption taking place in the urban regions (62 percent). In 2004 the National Council for Applied Economic Research (NCAER) published a report titled "The Great Indian Middle Class" and estimated that in 2010 almost 4 million households will belong to the "near rich" to "super rich" categories, with an annual income of 1 million to more than 10 million rupees (e.g., around $24,000 to $240,000). The McKinsey Global Institute has predicted that by 2025, more than 291 million Indians will move up the economic ladder and cross the poverty line. This seems to be a very optimistic prognosis and part of what Ruchira Ganguly-Scrase and Timothy J. Scrase have called the great myth of economic liberalization. Underlying India's image of globalization's "El Dorado" is the increasing withdrawal of the state's financial and social safety nets and the transformation of Indian society into a risk society, that is, a society increasingly challenged by human-made problems as a result of modernization. The aspiration to move up is paired with the fear of falling or being left behind. Thus, other concepts aspired to seem to be at risk and are simultaneously mythologized; that is, being seen as part of the community, both local and global, and fully participating in it are considered important. In this context education, and in particular English and higher education, become increasingly important for the middle class and the upwardly mobile.

The fear of falling by the aspiring and even the affluent middle classes in India who hang between high and low is a fear that many people share. The option to choose among a wide variety of material goods, lifestyle designs, and relationships is not only attractive but is also threatening and in fact highly risky, with responsibilities taken and borne by individuals. The constant pressure to perform suitable conspicuous acts of consumption and be up to date with the latest lifestyle trends is also a way of ensuring that you do not fall down and behind. In this context, the production and circulation of moral narratives of risk and rise are crucial in order to negotiate and legitimize what is socially acceptable and what is not. For members of the thriving middle class, often stigmatized as parvenus by the established elites, lifestyle experts and the media have become a safety net and an educational platform for getting the best and fastest access to crucial know-how. But access is restricted, and conditions and rules are constantly shifting due to a host of different forces.

In tandem with the glamor and fascination of this economic miracle came the critique that the fruits of economic growth were enjoyed by the affluent classes, ignoring the fact that more than 50 percent of households in India are in the "deprived" category. The NCAER report on the middle classes of 2004 defines the "deprived" (for 2001–2002) as annually earning below 90,000 rupees and consisting of about 135 million households. The inflation rate of 10.7 percent for consumer goods has shown how everyday life of the "simple" middle class and poor is affected. In 2005, 27.5 percent of the Indian population lived below the poverty line, with 25.7 percent in urban areas and 28.3 percent in rural areas. The per capita income per month defining the poverty line in Delhi was 613 rupees ($14). Reuters reports that 77 percent of Indians, about 836 million people, "live on less than half a dollar a day in one of the world's hottest economies," referring to the report of the state-run National Commission for Enterprises in the Unorganized Sector (NCEUS). The survey states that a majority of the people from the informal sector in fact live on less than 20 rupees (45 cents) per day.

Challenging purely quantitative approaches toward defining a social group such as the middle classes in India, the term "middle-classness" was introduced to highlight the importance of membership to a particular group and its relevance for developing "suitable" strategies to establish membership in the middle class. The desire to belong to the middle class is not necessarily restricted to a person's income. Instead, the practices and status symbols linked to the term

A young middle class family visiting the Jama Masjid mosque in Delhi, February 2008. The middle classes have become a very important group in India's booming consumer market. (Paul Prescott/Dreamstime.com)

"middle class" are constantly being negotiated by those who might already belong and those who do not belong to this group but aspire to do so. Middle-classness must be visualized and performed in order to be recognized and experienced. Conspicuous consumption—the conscious display of affluence—is part and parcel of a person's right to belong to the middle class or the elite. In this light many new spaces and practices have emerged, mainly in urban sites, as stages for these practices and new social groups related to the opening of the market economy. These range from large shopping malls to golf courses to gated communities and special economic zones. An increasingly visible middle class youth culture occupies spaces such as cafes, bars, nightclubs, and restaurants. Along with this a new infrastructure of experts has emerged, such as wedding planners; interior designers; beauty, wellness, and fitness consultants; spiritual lifestyle masters; and therapists. The mass media, ranging from magazines to television programs and blogs, celebrate, criticize, and shape their dominant consumers, the middle class. India's gigantic film industry, in particular Bombay cinema (Bollywood), spins off narratives of confident cosmopolitan and yet patriotic middle-classness and elite lifestyles.

New professional groups and new leisure sites and practices are the most obvious markers of India Shining—a political slogan referring to the overall feeling of economic optimism after plentiful rains in 2003 and the success of the *Indian IT boom*. The slogan was popularized by the then-ruling *Bharatiya Janata Party* (BJP) for the 2004 *Indian general elections*. Several of the sites, spaces, and events at which this Indian Dream becomes visible and almost tangible have resulted from the process of economic liberalization started in 1991. Global capitalism, especially in the new millennium, has produced a large and heterogeneous middle class that is distinctly different from the old middle class. The dramatic speed at which India opened up to the world market and enjoyed rapid economic growth has also contributed to the production of new lifestyles that allow members of the new middle classes to both adapt to this change in terms of mobility and flexibility and learn to perform and display the newly gained wealth and confidence. One of the most obvious testing grounds and stages of new lifestyles are the city, the media, and religious practices (e.g., pilgrimage and marriage). They are the arenas where new identities are contested, where desires, pleasures, and anxieties are given a face, a narrative, and direction, by a host of lifestyle experts, the media, and social events.

The new enthusiasm about belonging to the world class has various origins. Until the early 1990s, India seemed to be on the receiving end of modernity, positioned at the margins of the developed world and predominantly defined as a backward country. This image was propagated by both the Indian political and economic elites and Western countries and can be traced back to the expansionist and Eurocentric politics of imperialism and colonialism. The imperial metropolis was conceived as being center stage, while the colonies were placed at its periphery. Flows of knowledge, power, and goods were perceived as monodirectional, moving from a center to its margins. Only if the margins became like the center, the argument went, could these nations become modern. This asymmetrical relationship in the perception of Indians and non-Indians, however, has changed since the beginning of the millennium:

India, along with China, is about to join the league of First World countries and alliances, and the state as well as nongovernmental organizations and individual players herald the view that an age of Indian confidence and strength has begun.

In the age of open market economies, class has become the key focus and platform of cultural production and consumption—particularly the affluent segment of the new middle classes, or the new rich—underlining the fact that these groups share a consensus about their new roles, social positions, and lifestyles. They have a common capacity for dis-cretionary spending and new forms of consumption and public display, which are derived largely from international middle-class fashion. However, this heterogeneous, dynamic, and predominantly metropolitan segment of Indian society has yet to come to terms with the idea of its own identity in the national and global economy and the public culture.

The Indian middle class must actually be coined in the plural: "middle classes." The middle class in India is highly heterogeneous and dynamic, a complexity that depends on a variety of factors that determine a person's and a group's context including region, religion, caste, and education. All of this makes it difficult to talk of "the" middle class in India. While the Indian middle class's growth is predictable, its manifold facets and practices keep changing in unexpected directions.

CHRISTIANE BROSIUS

See also Economy

Further Reading

Brosius, Christiane. *India's Middle Class: New Forms of Urban Leisure, Consumption and Prosperity.* New Delhi: Routledge, 2010.

Delanty, Gerard, ed. *Europe and Asia: Beyond East and West.* London: Routledge, 2006.

Fernandes, Leela. *India's New Middle Class: Democratic Politics in an Era of Economic Reform.* Minneapolis: University of Minnesota Press, 2006.

Ganguly-Scrase, Ruchira, and Timothy J. Scrase. *Globalisation and the Middle Classes in India: The Social and Cultural Impact of Neoliberal Reforms.* London: Routledge, 2009.

Jaffrelot, Christophe, and Peter van der Veer, eds. *Patterns of Middle Class Consumption in India and China.* New Delhi: Sage, 2008.

Liechty, Mark. *Suitably Modern: Making Middle-Class Culture in a New Consumer Society.* Princeton, NJ: Princeton University Press, 2003.

Pinches, Michael. "Cultural Relations, Class and the New Rich of Asia." In *Culture and Privilege in Capitalist Asia,* edited by Michael Pinches, 1–55. London: Routledge, 1999.

Säävälä, Minna. "Entangled in the Imagination: New Middle Class Apprehensions in an Indian Theme Park." *Ethnos* 71(3) (2006): 390–414.

Säävälä, Minna. *Middle-class Moralities: Everyday Struggle over Belonging and Prestige in India.* New Delhi: Orient Blackswan, 2010.

Varma, Pavan. *The Great Indian Middle Class.* New Delhi: Penguin, 1998.

✦ MIDDLE EAST, RELATIONS WITH

India has historically had close relations with the countries of the Middle East. Travelers, traders, and rulers from Persia and Arabia have enhanced the cultural richness of the Indian subcontinent. After independence from the British in August 1947, India continued to have good relations with the Middle East, particularly with Egypt and Iran. In the Arab-Israeli conflict, India pursued a pro-Arab policy. This was both in order to counteract Pakistani influence in the region and to secure access to Middle East petroleum resources. India concentrated on developing a close relationship with Egypt on the strength of the ties between Prime Minister Jawaharlal Nehru (1889–1964; prime minister 1947–1964) with Egyptian president Gamel Abdul Nasser (1918–1970; president 1954–1970).

In the late 1960s and in the 1970s, India successfully improved bilateral relations by developing mutually beneficial economic exchanges with a number of Islamic countries, particularly Iran, Iraq, Saudi Arabia, and the other Persian Gulf states that had formed the Gulf Cooperation Council (GCC) in 1981. The strength of India's economic ties also enabled the country to build strong relationships with Iran and Iraq. Indian–Middle Eastern relations were further strengthened by New Delhi's anti-Israeli stance in the Arab-Israeli wars of 1967 and 1973 and by Indian support for the fourfold oil price rise in 1973 by the Organization of Petroleum Exporting Countries (OPEC).

The Islamic Revolution in Iran and the Soviet invasion of Afghanistan, both of which occurred in 1979, changed the balance of power in the Middle East and complicated India's relations with these countries. The significance of Egypt as a leader of the Arab world also declined during this period, and Saudi Arabia and the other oil-rich Gulf monarchies now gained prominence in Middle Eastern political affairs. In the 1980s, India performed a delicate diplomatic balancing act. New Delhi took a position of neutrality in the Iran-Iraq War (1980–1988), maintained warm ties with Baghdad, and built workable political and economic relations with the new Islamic government in Tehran. India's support for the Palestinian cause continued during this period. India also continued its diplomatic relations with Lebanon in spite of the ensuing civil war there. During the escalation of violence in Beirut the Indian embassy was temporarily closed, but apart from this brief closure, India maintained its diplomatic representation in Beirut throughout the civil war.

The 1990s also saw a change in India's policy. The Indian government stepped back from its staunch anti-Israeli stance and support for the Palestinian cause. In 1992 India recognized the State of Israel and established diplomatic relations. This was also in line with India's attempts to get closer to the United States, which was the only remaining superpower after the dissolution of the Soviet Union in 1991. India's new opening to Israel brought important technical, intelligence, and military benefits and more influence in Washington. Following in this direction, New Delhi voted for the United Nations (UN) resolution authorizing the use of force to expel Iraqi troops from Kuwait and rejected Iraq's linkage of the Kuwaiti and Palestinian problems.

India continues to have good relations with the Middle East in the post-9/11 environment. In 2003 India preserved its neutrality over the U.S.-led invasion of Iraq to topple the government led by President Saddam Hussein (1937–2006; president 1979–2003). There was talk of contributing Indian troops to the military action, but due to anti-U.S. protests within India, the decision to send troops was cancelled. India normalized its ties with the new democratically elected government of Iraq in 2005, seeking to restart trade and cooperation. Indian businesses applied for contracts for reconstruction projects to the Iraqi government, and simultaneously activities of Iraqi businesses in India have also been growing rapidly. Iraq is also one of the major suppliers of crude oil to India. In a significant departure from its previous position, in 2005 due to its pro-U.S. foreign policy, India voted against Iran in the UN on the question of Iran's nuclear program. This was in contradiction to the older pro-Iranian Indian stance and significantly harmed Indo-Iranian relations.

India is very reliant upon Middle Eastern oil and gas and must maintain cordial relations with most of the major suppliers, including Iran, the United Arab Emirates, Qatar, and Saudi Arabia as well as Iraq. Similarly, India is also a major consumer for these states. The GCC as a collective entity has tremendous significance for India. India's historical ties with GCC states, coupled with increasing imports of oil and gas, growing trade and investment opportunities, and the presence of 3.5 million Indian workers in the region, are of vital interest to India. India's economic linkages with the GCC increased steadily during 1970s, 1980s and 1990s, especially due to growth in oil imports. India has also provided soldiers to the United Nations Interim Force in Lebanon (UNIFIL) since 1998 and has about 850 soldiers currently deployed in the eastern sector of the 13-mile buffer zone north of the Israeli border. The Indian government continues to build on its close economic, cultural, and political ties with the Middle East by adapting to the changing realities of the international environment.

A pattern of interdependence is emerging between India and the GCC due to their strategic positions and central roles in the current energy security discourse. Development-induced growth in India during the 1990s resulted in higher energy consumption, increasing oil demand, and a growing reliance on oil. The process of deregulation of the petroleum industry in India was completed in 2002 with a significant lifting of curbs by the Indian government on foreign direct investment in the petroleum sector. On the supply side there has been a declining Western market share of Gulf oil and declining oil revenues for the Gulf states. However, due to vast reserves and low cost production capabilities, this will stabilize, and they will regain their position as a key oil supplier. Even though India has taken significant measures to diversify the sources of oil and gas, the current trends of consumption clearly indicate that the dependence on the Gulf is likely to remain.

From a strategic point of view, India and the GCC share the desire for political stability and security in the region. Their common political and security concerns translate into efforts for peace, security, and stability in the Gulf region and South Asia and create further opportunities for GCC-India cooperation in the future. The areas for cooperation are also widening beyond investments, trade and commerce, and sharing and development of human resources to include security.

STUTI BHATNAGAR

See also Foreign Policy; Gulf States, Indian Labor in

Further Reading
Janardhan, N. "Gulf Security and India." *Gulf Asia Bulletin*, no. 1 (January 2007): 28–31.
Jorfi, Abdul Amir. "Iran and India: Age Old Friendship." *India Quarterly* 50(4) (October–December 1994): 65–92.
Mudiam, Prithvi Ram. *India and the Middle East.* London: British Academic Press, 1994.
Pradhan, Samir Ranjan. *India, GCC and the Global Energy Regime: Exploring Interdependence and Outlook for Collaboration.* New Delhi: Academic Foundation, 2008.
Singh, Madhur. "India and Iran: Getting Friendly?" *Time*, April 24, 2008. http://www.time.com/time /world/article/0,8599,1734777,00.html.

✦ MISSILE PROGRAM

Among all the developing countries that have weapon of mass destruction (WMD) capabilities, India alone has achieved a unique degree of success. Outside the group of the five legally accepted nuclear weapon states under the Nuclear Non-Proliferation Treaty, India possesses the most sophisticated ballistic and cruise missile programs in the world. They have developed to the extent that New Delhi can now design, build, and test any type of missile and deploy short- and medium-range nuclear-tipped ballistic and cruise missiles in an operational mode against Pakistan and China. India views its nuclear and missile programs as the key to maintaining strategic stability in the Asia-Pacific region, safeguarding against potential nuclear threats from Pakistan and China, and attaining Great Power status.

Indians are not completely new to the world of rocketry and missilery. The use of such technology by India dates back to the 18th century during the reign of Hyder Ali (1722–1782; r. 1761–1782) of Mysore (Karnataka) and his son Tipu Sultan (1750–1799; r. 1782–1799), the "Tiger of Mysore." Fighting the British East India Company, Tipu Sultan's army used a variety of rockets in a supporting role in the battles at Sirangapatam in the 1790s. This was the world's first use of rockets for fighting modern wars. The rockets were reverse-engineered by British rocket metallurgy pioneer William Congreve (1772–1828) and later became known as Congreve Rockets.

Efforts to design and build missiles span nearly four decades. India embarked on a number of plans to develop missiles in the early 1970s that would strengthen the country's defenses. Prominent among them was Project Indigo, which led to an Indo-Swiss joint agreement to design and manufacture an intermediate-range missile; Project Valiant, which involved the development of a long-range ballistic missile; and Project Devil, which was aimed at reverse-engineering the Soviet SA-2 surface-to-air missile (SAM). While Project Indigo never came to fruition, Project Valiant and Project Devil were developed but with limited success. They were ended in 1974 and 1980, respectively.

A comprehensive missile-development program known as the Integrated Guided Missile Development Program (IGMDP) was begun in 1983 under the leadership of the aeronautical engineer and later president of India (2002–2007) Dr. Abdul Kalam (b. 1931). He had previously been the project director of the Satellite Launch Vehicle-3 program at the Indian Space Research Organization. The IGMDP was undertaken by the Defense Research and Development Organization (DRDO) in partnership with other Indian government laboratories and research centers. With an initial budget of $133 million, the program envisaged simultaneously taking up the design and development of five missiles that would provide the nation with a comprehensive missile-based defense umbrella within 10 years. The five missiles included the short-range Trishul (Trident) SAM, the Akash (Sky) SAM, the smokeless high-energy Nag (Snake) antitank guided missile, the Prithvi (Earth) surface-to-surface missile, and the Agni (Fire) intermediate-range missile. Of these, only Prithvi and Agni are ballistic missiles with the capability of delivering nuclear warheads.

Indian Air Force (IAF) personnel march past a short-range Prithvi ballistic missile at the IAF Day Parade in New Delhi. India successfully test-fired two nuclear-capable Prithvi-II surface-to-surface missiles at Chandipur, Orissa, October 2009. (AP Photo/Mustafa Quraishi)

Prithvi, which was first test-fired in 1988, has three versions. Prithvi-I, or the army version, has a range of 93 miles and a payload capacity of 2,204 pounds. The Indian Army has raised two missile groups, the 333rd and 334th, both based in Secunderabad (Andhra Pradesh), to handle all logistical and operational details related to Prithvi-I. Prithvi-II, the air force version, has a range of 155 miles with a warhead weight of 1,100–1,543 pounds. The Indian Air Force has raised two missile squadrons based in Hyderabad (Andhra Pradesh). Prithvi-III, also called Dhanush (Bow), has two variants of 155- and 217-mile ranges and a warhead weight of 1,100 pounds.

This missile, which in 2010 was under development, is a surface- and ship-launched ballistic missile whose purpose is to provide the Indian Navy with the third leg of the triad (land, air, and sea) delivery system for nuclear systems.

The intermediate-range Agni has four versions: Agni-I, Agni-II, Agni-III, and Agni-IV. Agni-I, which was first test-fired in 2002, has a 434-mile range and a 2,204-pound payload capacity and would probably replace short-range and liquid-fueled Prithvis for nuclear-targeting missions against Pakistan. Agni-II, which was flight-tested in 1999, has a 2,204 pound payload and a range of 1,200 miles, which it can cover in 11 minutes. The Indian Army has raised two missile groups, the 444th and the 555th, to induct and manage Agni-I and Agni-II variants. Agni-III is a two-stage solid fuel missile that can carry a 1.5 ton nuclear warhead 1,800-plus miles. With this missile, India has achieved credibility in its nuclear deterrent posture vis-à-vis China, something that India has been striving to achieve for a long time. The Agni-IV, with a range 3,100 miles, is now under development.

The Shaurya (Valor) is another short-range SAM developed by the DRDO outside the IGMDP for use by the Indian Army. Capable of hypersonic speeds, the Shaurya has a range of 372 miles and a payload capacity of a one-ton conventional or nuclear warhead. The missile was first tested in November 2008.

Realizing the importance of cruise missiles for their edge in accuracy and precision over ballistic missiles, India has introduced the BrahMos, supersonic cruise missile, the product of an Indian-Russian joint venture, into its armed forces. The missile is named after two great rivers, the Brahmaputra in India and the Moskva in Russia. BrahMos has a range of 173–186 miles and payload of 440–661 pound. The missile can be launched from submarines, ships, aircraft, or silos. It is believed that the technologies acquired and developed under the program will most likely help India develop nuclear-capable long-range cruise missiles in the medium and long term.

In July 2007 Indian defense scientists announced the proposed development of a subsonic cruise missile called Nirbhay (Fearless) with a range of 621 miles that can be deployed on multiple platforms. With its terrain-hugging capability, the missile would be able to avoid being detected by ground radar.

In February 2008 India carried out a successful test of the K-15 (Sagarika or Oceanic) submarine-launched ballistic missile, which can deliver a 1,102-pound nuclear payload to distances of between 466 and 621 miles. The Sagarika program is believed to be driven by India's long-term goals of achieving a secure sea-based second-strike nuclear capability.

In January 2008 the government announced the formal end of the IGMDP program since most of the missiles developed under the program had been introduced into service. According to Dr. S. Pralhada, director of the DRDO, new missile and weapons systems will be developed in new five-year programs and will include both private industry as well as foreign partners in order to lower costs.

Despite its emergence as a world-class missile power, India is not a member of the 34-member Missile Technology Control Regime (MTCR), which was established in 1987 to restrict the proliferation of WMD-capable ballistic missiles, cruise missiles, and unmanned aerial vehicles and their associated technology to nonmissile states. India rejects the MTCR on the grounds that it is a victim of such technology-denial regimes that are insensitive to India's national security needs and, the Indian government believes, interfere with the peaceful uses of space technology. Although India is not a member of the MTCR, the Indian government has been informally observing MTCR guidelines and has refrained from selling its missiles or missile-related technologies to other states. While stringent export controls by technology-denial regimes have slowed down many Indian projects (especially the development of an independent space launch capability and the building of a missile deterrent capability against China) and increased its costs, these have also made the Indian missile program largely an indigenous one with almost all of the equipment developed by Indian scientists.

Unlike the 1970s and 1980s when political symbolism and scientific expertise steered India's missile program, it is now guided by a clear strategic vision and a determination to bring about time-bound technological outcomes. Clearly the missile program has not only become central to India's minimal nuclear-deterrent posture, but more significantly it has emerged as the symbol of an independent, self-reliant, vibrant, and strategically autonomous Indian state.

UPENDRA CHOUDHURY

See also Space Program

Further Reading
Choudhury, Upendra. "Too Close for Comfort." *Bulletin of Atomic Scientists* 59(2) (2003): 22–25.
Nuclear Threat Initiative. "Missile Overview." http://www.nti.org/e_research/profiles/India/Missile /index.html.
Sachdeva A. K. *Space Age Gladiators: Surface to Surface Missiles and Air Strategy; An Indian Point of View.* New Delhi: Knowledge World, 2000.

✦ MIZORAM

Mizoram is the 23rd state of the Indian Union and is located in the northeastern region of India. The state boasts the highest literacy rate in the country. Mizoram literally means "Land of the Highlanders" in Mizo, a language of the Kuki-Chin branch of the Tibeto-Burman group of languages. Mizoram was called the Lushai Hills District by the British; after the transfer of power in August 1947, it was renamed Mizo Hills District in 1954. The present name was given in 1972 when it was made a Union Territory. On February 20, 1987, Mizoram became a part of the Indian federal structure when it was made into a state, with Aizawl as its capital. While Mizoram is home to a number of ethnic groups, the Mizo people hold the majority position in terms of population, education, and jobs. Mizoram is infamous for its periodic famine that occurs during the bamboo flowering season and has also been in the news for the migration of some Mizos to Israel.

Mizoram is at located at a latitude of 21°58′ and 24°35′N and a longitude 92°15′ and 93°29′E. It occupies an important strategic position, having a long international border of almost 450 miles, and is flanked by Bangladesh on the west and Myanmar on the east and south. On the Indian side, Mizoram shares borders with Manipur, Assam, and Tripura to the north and has the most diverse topography in northeastern India with a varied range of flora and fauna. As many as 21 major hill ranges of different heights run through the length and breadth of the state, with the highest peak, Phawngpui ("Blue Mountain"), towering almost 6,800 feet above sea level. Phawngpui is famous for its orchids and rhododendrons.

There are various wildlife sanctuaries and national parks in Mizoram, including the Ngengpui Wildlife Sanctuary, the Khawnglung Wildlife Sanctuary, Phawngpui National Park, the Thorangtlang Wildlife Sanctuary, and the Lengteng Wildlife Sanctuary. The summers are pleasant, and winters are cool. During winter the temperature varies from approximately 51 to 69 degrees, and in summer temperatures are between 68 and 84 degrees. The entire area is under the regular influence of monsoons, with heavy rains from May to September. The average rainfall is 100 inches per annum.

The origin of the Mizos is shrouded in mystery. In Mizo oral tradition, they were said to have emerged from the netherworld through an opening in a huge rock. The generally accepted theory is that the Mizos and other subtribes were part of a great Mongoloid wave of migration from China, with people first settling in Myanmar and later moving to Mizoram. It is possible that the Mizos came from Shinlung or Chhinlungsan located on the banks of the river Yalung in China. In Myanmar they first settled in Shan State and then moved on to the Kabaw Valley, then Khampat, and later in the middle of the 16th century to the Chin Hills. Mizo folk songs talk about kinship ties with the Burmese. Other theories suggest that the Mizos lived in Shan State for about 300 years before they moved across the river Tiau to India in the middle of the 16th century. Legends narrate that the early Mizos were cave dwellers.

Even today, no dependable inscriptions on the prehistoric and protohistoric periods of the Lushai people are available. Therefore, oral traditions, folklore, and accounts by foreign travelers are very valuable chronicles. We do know, however, that the modern era began in 1890 with annexation by the British.

According to the 2001 census, the population of Mizoram was 888,573. Most of these people are in tribes linked linguistically or ethnically. These ethnic groups are collectively known as the Lushais or are otherwise called Mizos, both of which are umbrella terms. The Mizos are divided into many subtribes, the largest of which is the Lushais, comprising almost two-thirds of the state's population. Other Mizo tribes include the Hmar, Mara, Paite, Lai, Ralte, and Lakher. Kuki and Chin peoples are also related to the Mizos. Notable among them are the Bru and Riang tribes from Tripura and the Chakma of Arakanese origin. There are also ethnic groups from other parts of India as a result of migration through government jobs and trade, but their numbers are minimal. The sex ratio at 938 females to 1,000 males is slightly higher than the national average of 933 females to 1,000 males.

In addition to the Mizos, the Lakhers are an important tribe living in the hills of the India-Myanmar border. In appearance some of them are typically Naga and some are typically Kuki, while others appear to belong to neither of these groups. Superficially the Lakhers appear to definitely be a Kuki tribe, but their language and material culture associate them with the Lushais and Chins. Their terms of relationship are more Kuki than Naga, and their weapons, including their ceremonial *daas*, are Kuki. The Lakhers are matrilineal. These matrilineal traditions suggest at first sight Mon-Khmer associations, but except perhaps for the locality in which the Lakhers are found, they might equally well be Bodo. In short, the Lakhers may be classed insofar as their material culture and language are concerned with the Kuki tribes who had migrated in prehistoric times down the valley of the Chindwin to their present habitat.

In 2001 the state became the second most-literate Indian state, with an overall literacy of 88.49 percent. Today, with a 97 percent literacy rate, Mizoram has replaced Kerala as India's most literate state. The Mizos had no literature of their own until 1894, when the Roman script was introduced by Christian missionaries.

Mizoram was previously animistic, but Christianity spread rapidly with the arrival of Christian missionaries. Now the majority population is Christian, and most are members of the Presbyterian Church. The other three major churches are Mizoram Baptist, Roman Catholic, and the Salvation Army. There is also a Jewish sect, called the Bnei Menashe, that considers itself one of the lost tribes of Israel. Several hundred Chins, Kukis, and Mizos have formally converted to Orthodox Judaism but see themselves not as converts but instead as ethnically Jewish. The Jewish population of the Bnei Menashe currently is estimated to be 9,000. The landscape is dotted with many churches and temples.

Mizoram is a part of the federal system of the Indian Union and has a Legislative Assembly of 40 members. The chief minister, appointed by the central government, is the chief political officer. Political awakening among the Mizos started during the British administration with the creation of the first political party, the Mizo Common People's Union, on April 9, 1946. It was later renamed the Mizo Union. During the transfer of power, the Mizo Union demanded the inclusion of all the Mizo-inhabited areas adjacent to Lushai Hills. However, a new party called United Mizo Freedom (UMFO) demanded that Lushai Hills should join Burma and not India. As a result, a certain amount of autonomy was granted by the government and enshrined in the Indian Constitution. When the Lushai Hills Autonomous District Council came into being in 1952, chieftainships among the Mizos were legally abolished. The arrangements for autonomy, however, were vague and did not meet the aspirations of the Mizos, and they soon started to demand a separate hill state.

The Young Mizo Association (YMA) is the oldest and largest social organization in Mizoram. It is an association in which every Mizo adult is entitled to be a member by paying a prescribed membership fee. Since its inception in 1935, the YMA has been an important voice in the region. Although the organization has become politicized, the essential aims of the YMA are the development of Mizoram and honoring Christian values.

In 1959 Mizoram was devastated by a great famine known as the Mautam Famine. The famine was caused by excessive flowering of a certain bamboo called *mautam*, which attracts rodents that feed on the bamboo flowers and proliferate in great numbers. Once the bamboo flowers are all devoured, the rats ravage paddy and other crops, sometimes destroying huge tracts overnight. The 1959 occurrence led to plague and famine, and people kept themselves alive by eating roots and leaves gathered in the jungle. Others moved to faraway places, while a considerable number of people died of starvation. One result of the famine was that in September 1960 the Mizo National Famine Front (MNFF) started under the leadership of Pu Laldenga (d. 1990), a bank clerk in Aizawl, and the party gained a great deal of support because of its famine relief work.

The MNFF dropped the word "Famine" and a new political organization, the Mizo National Front (MNF), was born on October 22, 1961, under Laldenga's leadership. The aim of the party was to push for the sovereign independence of Mizoram through armed rebellion. As a result the MNF was outlawed in 1967, but disturbances in the region continued. Laldenga met with prime minister Rajiv Gandhi (1944–1991; prime minister 1984–1989), and the MNF was disbanded following the Mizoram Accord of June 30, 1986, whereby the MNF renounced violence. The MNF laid down arms, and Laldenga was appointed the first chief minister of the new full-fledged State of Mizoram. He held the chief ministership from 1986 until 1988.

Mizo society is clan-based and follows customary law. Under this system, village elders and appointed chiefs discuss all matters concerning local governance and adjudicate disputes. Customary law is patriarchal and holds more sway than the Indian legal system. Before a money economy was introduced, most of the punishment was in terms of fines paid in kind, such as giving a *mithun* (bison), a pig, or a fowl.

Mizos also have a *zawlbuk* (bachelor's house) system in which young men become socialized. The dormitory is usually situated at the heart of the village. After work the men gather in the *zawlbuk* and engage in storytelling, wrestling, and crafts work or socialize. Most important meetings are also held in the hall of the dormitory. Boys stay with their parents until puberty and after that attain full membership in the *zawlbuk*. This system is no longer strictly followed, although in most Lushai and Pawi villages the institution still exists. The Lakher tribe, however, being matrilineal, do not have the *zawlbuk* system.

Four factors can account for the near abolition of the system. The village chiefs had sole authority over the *zawlbuk*, and prior to 1947 during the British colonial period the powers of the chief shrank considerably. In postcolonial India chieftanship was legally abolished, thus undermining the legitimacy of the *zawlbuk* system. Also, the adoption of Christian values slowly changed indigenous practices and customs. The extinction of the *zawlbuk* system was almost inevitable when formal educational institutions were introduced among the Mizos.

Mizo society is largely patrilineal in nature. The eldest son inherits the father's property, as women do not have inheritance rights under customary law. In the absence of sons, the property goes to the nearest male kin. If a man dies leaving behind a widow and minor children, the widow takes care of the property until the children come of age. In case the widow remarries anyone except the brother of the deceased, the property and care of the children become the responsibility of the brother or uncle of the deceased.

When somebody dies, the villagers are informed by various means including a gunshot fired from the house of the deceased. Mizos believe in the afterlife and ancestor worship. During the funeral ceremony for a deceased person, friends and relatives gather in the house and celebrate with the beating of drums and by feasting with locally prepared rice beer and meat. In case of an unnatural death, no such feasting is done.

Mizo marriages are generally preceded by long courtships during which the suitor, with the parents' permission, can sleep in the girl's house. The girl's family does not give any dowry. Instead the bridegroom's family has to offer a bride-price that is negotiated among the elders of the two families over rice beer. On the wedding day both sides slaughter a certain number of pigs and exchange gifts such as axes, cotton thread, or traditional jewelry before the bride enters the groom's house. A person can divorce at will, but certain customary procedures must be followed. The main issues concern the refund or payment of the unpaid bride-price, depending on who has filed for divorce. However, with the conversion of most tribes to Christianity, many of these customs are not strictly followed. Older people still follow customary traditions, but young people tend to be more relaxed about them.

Mizos are a fun-loving people and like to celebrate with dances, feasts, and songs. The most popular Mizo dance is the bamboo dance, which is also seen in many Southeast Asian countries such as the Philippines. Other popular dances are the Khal Lam, Sawlakin, and Tlanglam. The traditional musical instruments are drums and flutes. The women are natural weavers, and almost every woman can weave intricate and colorful patterns. The *puan*, a striped loin cloth worn by both men and women, is the traditional garment of the Mizos. These garments are of varied shades and designs and are usually produced on looms.

SUSHMITA KASHYAP

See also Northeastern States

Further Reading

Lalhriatpuii. *Economic Participation of Women in Mizoram*. New Delhi: Concept Publishing, 2010.

Nunthara, C. *Local Self Government in Mizoram*. New Delhi: Institute of Social Sciences, 2007.

Official Website of Mizoram. Accessed April 27, 2011. http://www.mizoram.nic.in.

Patnaik, Jagadish K. *Mizoram, Dimension and Perspectives: Society, Economy, and Polity*. New Delhi: Concept Publishing, 2008.

Zoengpari. *Psychosocial Life of Mizos.* Delhi: Abhijit Publications, 2006.

Modern Art. *See* Art, Modern

✦ MONETARY POLICY

The evolution of monetary policy can be traced back to the developmental objectives of creating an institutional framework for industrial growth, the creation of rural credit for agricultural development and expansion, and the establishment of balanced regional growth as laid down in the various Five-Year Plans. The First Five-Year Plan, originally presented to the Lok Sabha, the lower house of the Indian Parliament, by Prime Minister Jawaharlal Nehru (1889–1964; prime minister 1947–1964) on December 8, 1951, stated that central banking in a planned economy could not be confined to the regulation of the overall supply of credit or the regulation of the flow of bank credit. Central banking would instead have to take a direct and active role, first in creating or helping to create the machinery needed for financing developmental activities and second in ensuring that finance flows in the directions intended.

The two major objectives of monetary policy in India are to maintain price stability and to ensure the adequate availability of credit to sustain overall growth. The emphasis on these objectives has varied depending on the circumstances of the day. Price stability as the predominant objective of monetary policy emerged as high public investments and consequent high fiscal deficits led to inflationary pressures in the early stages of planned development.

In the 1960s, bank credit—aggregate as well as sectoral—was the intermediate target of monetary policy. The targeting of credit was meshed with the aim of central banking to push development projects. This targeting of credit was the instrument through which the Reserve Bank of India (RBI) influenced monetary policy and was the means by which the RBI could achieve the ultimate objectives of monetary policy. However, even while targeting credit, the RBI also took monetary aggregates into account. In this context, a number of studies found that the demand for money in India was relatively stable. Consequently, the RBI, on the recommendations of the Chakravarty Committee, which was set up to examine the workings of monetary policy and reported in 1985, accepted a monetary targeting framework to target broad money (M3) in line with the expected rate of growth of the gross domestic product and an acceptable level of inflation. M3 means the different types of money available including notes and coins, traveler's checks of nonbank issuers, demand deposits, savings deposits, and various deposits of cash and money market accounts. Accordingly, the RBI sets an indicative broad money expansion target in its Annual Policy Statement, which is announced every year in April. A multiple indicator approach, besides a broad money target, was also adopted by the RBI in April 1998. These indicators include movement in interest rates, trade, capital flows, the exchange rate, and the availability of credit to other sectors of the economy. The multiple indicator approach serves as a comprehensive guide for monetary policymaking, given that the uncertain environment in which monetary authorities operate makes a single model or a limited set of indicators an insufficient guide for the conduct of monetary policy.

With monetary policy reforms, a shift took place from simply relying on traditional instruments of monetary policy, that is, open market operations and changes in the bank rate for short-term interest rates as an important instrument of monetary policy. The RBI is now able to influence short-term interest rates by adjusting the liquidity in the system through the Liquidity Adjustment Facility.

The RBI also reactivated the bank rate in April 1997 as a reference rate, which served as the signaling device for monetary policy. The interest rates on different types of accommodation from the RBI are also linked to the bank rate. Any change in the bank rate also affects the prime lending rates of commercial banks. The use of the cash reserve ratio as an instrument of monetary control has been reduced. The cash reserve ratio was lowered from the peak rate of 15 percent in 1981 to 5 percent in 2004, rising again to 9 percent on August 30, 2008.

The changes in how monetary policy operates have also had an impact on the RBI's balance sheet in terms of size and composition and sources of income and expenditure. In this context the RBI has more clearly articulated the process of how it formulates monetary policy, how it has been more consultative, and how it has reformed the way it formulates monetary policy.

The conduct of monetary policy is governed by a number of factors. The objective of price stability comes to the fore in the wake of high and volatile prices for food, fuel, and metals. On the other hand, the global economic crisis that began in late 2008 required stability in the financial sector and increasing demand in the market. Another challenge in the formulation of monetary policy is to maintain linkages between different segments of the financial market, including money, government securities, and the foreign exchange market.

The Annual Policy Statement for 2009–2010 highlighted several immediate challenges faced by the Indian economy that needed to be addressed through monetary policy. These were supporting the drivers of aggregate demand to enable the economy to return to its high growth rate, restoring credit flow to all the productive sectors of the economy, unwinding fiscal stimulus over time in an orderly manner in order to return to a path of credible fiscal consolidation, financial stability in the face of a severe global economic crisis, withdrawal of the large liquidity in an orderly manner to avoid possible risks of upward inflationary pressures and asset price bubbles, and addressing the key challenge of ensuring an interest rate environment that supports revival of investment demand.

RASHMI UMESH ARORA

See also Asian Development Bank; Central Banking, Development Aspects; Economy; Financial Institutions, Development; International Monetary Fund, Relations with; Reserve

Bank of India; Stock Exchange Markets; World Bank, Relations with; World Economic Forum; World Trade Organization, Relations with

Further Reading
Reserve Bank of India. *The Report of the Committee to Review the Working of the Monetary System (Chairman: Sukhamov Chakravarty).* Mumbai: Reserve Bank of India, 1985.
Reserve Bank of India. *Report on Currency and Finance, 2004–05.* Mumbai: Reserve Bank of India, 2006.
Venugopal Reddy, Y. *Monetary and Financial Sector Reforms in India: A Central Banker's Perspective.* New Delhi: UBS Publishers, 2000.

✦ MONEY AND FOREIGN EXCHANGE MARKETS

The money market is the part of the monetary system engaged in the lending and borrowing of short-term funds. The Indian money market witnessed exponential growth after the globalization initiative in 1991 and is integral for financial institutions that employ short-term instruments for meeting financial requirements of various sectors such as agriculture, finance, and manufacturing. The Reserve Bank of India (RBI), established on April 1, 1935, has played a major role in regulating and controlling the money market, which has exhibited outstanding performance over the past 20 years.

Money market instruments take care of borrowers' short-term needs and render liquidity to lenders. For India's monetary policy, call/notice money and repo transactions are most critical. Call/notice money consists of overnight money and money at short notice (i.e., up to 14 days). The Indian financial sector in the 1970s and 1980s was governed by a heavily regulated system of nationalized banking, directed credit, and automatic monetization of government deficits. Rate ceilings were frequent in those days of volatile call money rates, and the market remained narrow and undeveloped. Extensive attempts were made to increase the number of money market participants following recommendations made by the Chakravarty Committee in 1985 and the Vaghul Committee in 1987. Currently India has two major types of entities participating in the call/notice market: (1) market makers that lend and borrow and (2) lenders only. Banks (commercial and cooperative) and primary dealers act as market makers. Their total number is 112, and they are allowed to lend as well as to borrow. All-India financial institutions, mutual funds, and insurance companies are permitted to operate as lenders only, and there are 53 of them. The average daily turnover in this market is about $120 billion. The various types of money market instruments are treasury bills, repurchase agreements, commercial papers, certificates of deposit, and banker's acceptance.

The RBI intervenes when necessary in order to eliminate disparities in the market. Whenever there is a liquidity crunch, the RBI opts to either reduce the cash reserve ratio (CRR) or infuse more money into the financial system. In a recent initiative to overcome the liquidity crunch in the money market, the RBI infused more than $750 billion along with reductions in the CRR.

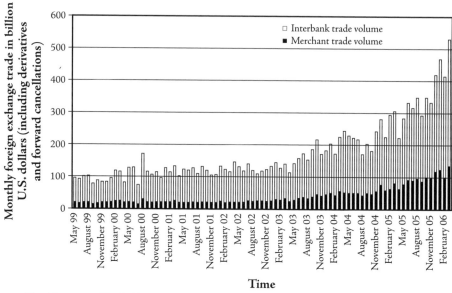

Note: Not corrected for double counting
Source: RBI Building

Figure 3   Foreign exchange trading activity

The foreign exchange market in India took off in 1978 when the government began to allow banks to trade foreign exchange with one another. Today more than 70 percent of the trading in foreign exchange continues to take place in the interbank market. The market consists of more than 90 authorized dealers, mostly banks, that conduct currency trades among themselves, emerging with neutral positions at the end of the trading day.

Trading is regulated by the Foreign Exchange Dealers Association of India (FEDAI), a self-regulatory association of dealers incorporated under Section 25 of the Companies Act of 1956. The FEDAI's major activities include framing rules that govern the conduct of interbank foreign exchange business among banks vis-à-vis the public and acting as a liaison with the RBI for reforms and development of the foreign exchange market. Since 2001, clearing and settlement functions in the foreign exchange market are largely carried out by the Clearing Corporation of India Limited (CCIL). The CCIL handles transactions of approximately $3.5 billion per day, accounting for about 80 percent of the total transactions.

The process of liberalization has significantly boosted the foreign exchange market in the country by allowing both banks and corporations greater flexibility in holding and trading foreign currencies. The Sodhani Committee, set up in 1994, recommended greater freedom to participating banks, allowing them to fix their own trading limits, set interest rates on foreign currency (FCNR) deposits, and use derivative products. The foreign exchange market has more than tripled in the last few years, recording a compounded annual growth rate exceeding 25 percent. This includes swaps, forwards, and forward cancellations. Figure 3 shows the growth of foreign exchange trading in India between 1999 and 2006. The interbank foreign exchange trading volume has continued to account for the dominant share (more than 77 percent) of total trading during this period.

PARAMITA GUPTA

See also Asian Development Bank; Central Banking, Development Aspects; Economy; Financial Institutions, Development; International Monetary Fund, Relations with; Monetary Policy; Reserve Bank of India; Stock Exchange Markets; World Bank, Relations with; World Economic Forum; World Trade Organization, Relations with

Further Reading
Chakrabarti, Rajesh. "Foreign Exchange Markets in India." Working Paper Series, Indian School of Business, 2005.
FEDAI: Foreign Exchange Dealers' Association of India. Accessed April 27, 2011. http://www .fedai.org.in.
"Reserve Bank of India Bulletin." Reserve Bank of India: India's Central Bank. Accessed April 27, 2011. http://www.bulletin.rbi.org.in.

✦ MUMBAI

The city of Mumbai, located on India's west coast and formerly known as Bombay, is India's largest city and the political capital of the State of Maharashtra. Dubbed *urbs prima in Indus* (India's foremost city), Mumbai is regarded as the country's financial, commercial, and entertainment capital. Home to India's largest (and Asia's oldest) stock exchange and the Indian headquarters of many domestic and multinational corporations as well as Bollywood, the massive Hindi-language film and television industry, Mumbai contributes more than any other city to India's gross domestic product and income tax coffers. Yet despite its economic might, Mumbai is also marked by severe socioeconomic and health disparities, with a majority of its population living in slums and squatter settlements and lacking access to adequate sanitation facilities and potable water.

The city of Mumbai was originally a string of seven small islands separating the Arabian Sea from a protected harbor. During the 18th and 19th centuries the seven islands merged into one continuous island through both naturally rising water levels and engineered landfills. Until the arrival of Europeans in the 16th century, the area was reportedly referred to as Mumbai by its earliest inhabitants, members of the Marathi-speaking Koli fishing community. The name was given for Mumbadevi, a goddess important to the Kolis. During Portuguese (1534–1661) and then British (1661–1947) possession, the area was called Bombay, a version of the Portuguese phrase for "good bay." This etymology has been disputed by some historians, however, and other explanations for the city's name can be found. Under

British rule, Bombay was both a city and the capital of a vast presidency comprising Gujarat, western Maharashtra, and parts of Karnataka and Sindh in Pakistan. Aden was also governed from Bombay. As a result of the Government of India Act of 1935, Sindh became a separate province of British India, and Bombay became much smaller and a province. The city of Bombay, however, continued to be the financial, educational, entertainment, and political hub of western India. In November 1995 the city's name was officially changed to Mumbai when a coalition headed by the conservative Shiv Sena Party, founded in 1966, came to power at the state level. The renaming signaled a reassertion of the city's Marathi origins and a rejection of its European and non-Maharashtrian past. However, many residents continue to call the city Bombay as well as use its Hindi and Gujarati pronunciations, Bombai and Mambai.

According to Census of India, 11.9 million people were living in Greater Mumbai in 2001. Comprising an area of nearly 300 square miles, Greater Mumbai is one of the world's most densely populated cities, with a density of approximately 54,000 persons per square mile. In 2007 the United Nations (UN) estimated the population of the Mumbai urban agglomeration at 18.98 million people. According to these numbers, Mumbai is the fourth-largest urban agglomeration in the world. With an annual average growth rate estimated at 2.32 percent, Mumbai is predicted to become the world's second-largest city by 2020.

In 2001 the gender ratio in Greater Mumbai was 811 females per 1000 males. This compares to a nationwide ratio of 933 females per 1,000 males. Although Mumbai's gender ratio has gradually improved over the past century, it is still significantly lower than the national average. The percentage of Mumbai's population living in slums in 2001 was estimated at 52.5 percent, or 6.25 million people. This is regarded as a conservative estimate, as some estimates have placed the city's slum population as high as 8 million people, or 60 percent of the city's overall population.

Mumbai has long been regarded as India's most cosmopolitan city, with all of the country's major religious, linguistic, and ethnic communities represented. In 2001, 67.4 percent of Mumbai's population was Hindu, with 18.6 percent Muslim, 5.2 percent Buddhist, and the remaining 9 percent comprised of the city's visible minority Christian, Sikh, Parsi, and Jewish communities. Roughly half of Mumbai's population is Maharashtrian. The remaining half is made up of Gujaratis, Sindhis, Parsis, southern Indians, and northern Indians from Bihar, Uttar Pradesh, and the Punjab. About 5 percent of the population is comprised of members of the Scheduled (formerly Untouchable) Castes, with the largest numbers representing the Bhambi, Mahar, and Mang castes. Less than 1 percent is made up of members of Scheduled Tribes.

For as long as recorded history, the islands of Mumbai were inhabited by members of the Son Koli caste. In the mid-14th century the islands came under Muslim rule when a military outpost was established on one of the islands. For the next 150 years a series of Muslim and Hindu rulers, based largely in Gujarat, struggled for control of the region. Yet the area was not viewed as commercially or militarily important when the Portuguese landed on the sparsely populated islands in the early 16th century and established administrative control in October 1535.

Cityscape of Mumbai, Maharashtra, one of the world's biggest and most dynamic cities, and home of the world's largest film industry, Bollywood. (iStockphoto)

During their 136-year rule the Portuguese gave the islands and bay the name Bombay, but they remained uninterested in developing the area as a commercial or military outpost. In fact, it was their missionaries who left the most indelible mark on the city by converting a large segment of the population to Catholicism. Decendents of these early converts, referred to as East Indian Christians, remain visible in Mumbai today and still carry Portuguese surnames. In 1661 the islands of Bombay were included in the dowry of Catherine de Braganza (1638–1705), the sister of Portugal's king, upon her marriage to King Charles II (1630–1685; r. 1665–1685) of England the following year. In 1668 the British Crown leased the seven islands—then called Bombay, Colaba, Old Woman's Island, Mahim, Mazagaon, Parel, and Worli—to the English East India Company (founded on December 31, 1600) at the rate of 10 pounds per year. The East India Company retained administrative control of Bombay until 1858, when the British government consolidated its holdings of British India and established a new colonial administration in the city of Bombay.

The city's roots as a commercial center date to the early 1800s, when local entrepreneurs began shipping Bihari and Malwa opium from Bombay to China. These activities posed a direct challenge to the East India Company's opium monopoly based in Calcutta and helped establish Bombay as a center for native investment and entrepreneurship. By the 1820s, Bombay's native business community included members of such diverse groups as Gujaratis, Parsis, Marwaris, *banias*, Iranian Jews, Dawoodi Bohras, and Konkani Muslims. This diversity and cosmopolitan character are often cited, even today, as Mumbai's most significant commercial advantage.

In the mid-1800s, capital from the opium trade was invested in several industrial enterprises, most notably in textile manufacturing. In 1854 a Parsi merchant, Cowasjee Nanabhoy Davar (1815–1873), built India's first mechanized cotton textile mill in Bombay, the Bombay Spinning and Weaving Company. By the end of the 1850s, dozens of other cotton textile mills had been established in the city. Activity in the mills increased sharply in the 1860s, when the American Civil War (1861–1865) cut off North American exports of cotton to England. Lancaster and Manchester, the center of the cotton industry in England, turned to Bombay and the city's new textile mills to provide them with the required short staple cotton and processed cotton textiles. By the end of the 19th century, there were 83 textile mills in the city employing approximately 10 percent of the population.

Bombay further bolstered its position as India's commercial capital throughout the 20th century as textile profits were invested in capital intensive industries, including light engineering, pharmaceuticals, petrochemicals, and fertilizers. The city remained important as a shipping port and emerged as the center of India's oil industry. Hindi-language cinema grew more popular in the period immediately following independence, and a thriving film and television industry developed in the city. Referred to both informally and increasingly formally as Bollywood, Bombay's film industry grew steadily during the late 20th century to become one of the world's largest, measured by profit and productivity.

The textile industry fell into decline in the 1960s and 1970s due to aging facilities and increased competition from China and Southeast Asia. An infamous 18-month strike and mass layoffs in the early 1980s further weakened the industry. By the early 1990s, Mumbai's industrial workforce was one-fifth the size it had been in the late 1970s. Workers were gradually replaced by power looms, and those who remained employed were shifted from the formal sector to the unorganized, largely informal sector.

The city's economy underwent dramatic restructuring in the 1980s and 1990s. Manufacturing employment fell significantly, driven by steep losses in the textile sector. Meanwhile, the largest employment gains were in the communications sector as well as in the finance, insurance, and real estate industries. Foreign investment helped fuel Mumbai's economy in the period following India's economic liberalization in 1991, and international financial groups began trading on Bombay's Stock Exchange. Despite challenges from high-growth technology centers in southern India, Mumbai remains an engine of the Indian economy. In addition to the Bombay Stock Exchange and the Reserve Bank of India, Mumbai remains home to an active shipping port, the Indian headquarters of most private financial institutions, and a booming real estate industry.

Despite the presence of these powerful institutions, a significant proportion of Mumbai's economy remains in the unorganized or informal sector. With large segments of retail, domestic service, and small-scale manufacturing operating outside of the formal sector, most of the city's workers lack access to adequate wages and benefits and safe working conditions.

Mumbai has also played a major role in India's political history, playing host to the first session of the Indian National Congress (INC), also known as the Congress Party, in December 1885 and other significant events in India's struggle for independence. After independence, Mumbai remained an INC stronghold, and the city's political elite have long had strong ties to New Delhi.

In the late 1950s the city sat at the center of the Samyukta Maharashtra movement, founded in 1956 by Keshavrao Jedhe (1886–1959) in the struggle over the creation of linguistic states. As plans were being drafted to divide Bombay state into Marathi- and Gujarati-speaking states, debates raged over where the city of Bombay would go. Marathi members of the Samyukta Maharashtra movement argued that Bombay was an integral part of the state of Maharashtra, while the city's Gujarati business communities claimed the city as their own. Meanwhile, a third group argued that Bombay did not belong to a single linguistic group and proposed the designation of Bombay as a Union Territory like the national capital, New Delhi. On May 1, 1960, the Samyukta Maharashtra movement was successful, and Mumbai was designated the capital of Maharashtra.

Despite strong INC support throughout the 1960s, Mumbai has also been home to regional political movements that have directly challenged the party's dominance. The Shiv Sena, a right-wing political party formed in Mumbai in 1966 by Balasaheb Thackeray (b. 1926), emerged as a formidable political movement in the 1970s and 1980s by mobilizing ethnic pride and anti-Muslim sentiments among the city's middle and working classes. The violent underpinnings of the Shiv Sena's message and tactics fell into sharp relief in the early 1990s when the city erupted in religious riots and the party's leadership fanned the flames of conflict. The two largest political parties in Mumbai remain the INC and the Shiv Sena, although the Bharatiya Janata Party (founded in 1980), the Republican Party of India that came out of the Scheduled Castes Federation founded by the Scheduled Caste leader Dr. Bhimrao Ramji Ambedkar (1891–1956) in 1942, the Nationalist Congress Party (founded in 1999), and the Maharashtra Navnirman Sena (founded in 2006 as an offshoot of the Shiv Sena by Raj Thackeray [b. 1968]) also have a political presence in the city.

LIZA WEINSTEIN

See also Bharatiya Janata Party; Maharashtra; Thackeray, Balasaheb Keshav; Shiv Sena

Further Reading
Dwivedit, Sharada, and Rahul Mehrotra. *Bombay: The Cities Within.* Bombay: Eminence Designs, 2001.
Mehta, Suketu. *Maximum City: Bombay Lost and Found.* New York: Knopf, 2004.
Pacione, Michael. "City Profile: Mumbai." *Cities* 23(3) (2006): 229–238.
Patel, Sujata, and Alice Thorner, eds. *Bombay: Metaphor for Modern India.* New York: Oxford University Press, 1995.
Patel, Sujata, and Alice Thorner, eds. *Bombay: Mosaic of Modern Culture.* Bombay: Oxford University Press, 1995.
Patel, Sujata, and Jim Masselos, eds. *Bombay and Mumbai: The City in Transition.* New York: Oxford University Press, 2003.

✦ MUSIC, DEVOTIONAL

Bhajans (the devotional music of Bhakti sects), Qawwails (Sufi devotional music), and Shab Kirtan (the devotional music of the Sikhs) are central to three major religious traditions of South Asia. Devotional music in India is not only found in devotional settings but is also a potentially lucrative music market in South Asia. Devotional music is predominantly vocal, often sung in groups, and is almost always accompanied by drums, idiophones, or handclapping.

For the most part, devotional music represents one of the major folk traditions of the subcontinent. As such, it is sung by nonprofessionals in religious gatherings. Starting with the availability of cheap cassettes, the mass marketing of devotional music has drawn highly skilled and talented professional musicians and musical groups into the commercial genre. The oldest form of devotional music is the chanting and singing of the Hindu holy books the Vedas, especially the *Samaveda*, which is typically sung by a group of devotees. Both Qawwali and Bhajan forms date as far back as the 1300s. Qawwalis emerged in the Sufi traditions of South Asian Sufism, some with roots in Central Asia. Bhajans, or their ancestors, have been part of Bhakti movements and sects since about the same period. Shabad Kirtan grew out of the emphasis on musical worship by the founders of Sikhism in the 16th century. All three forms are informed but not ruled by the classical Hindustani and Karnatik raga systems.

Nothing can be more deeply rooted in the Hindu Bhakti tradition than Bhajans. Bhajans are songs of love for God or of self-surrender. Virtually all Bhakti sects have their own sets of Bhajans and ways of singing them. References found in Bhajans to attributes or anecdotes of gods or goddesses typically mime human relationships. While Sanskrit is prominent, Bhajans are found in virtually any of South Asia's vernacular languages. Famous medieval composers of Bhajans are Tulsidas (1532–1623), Mirabai (ca. 1498–ca. 1547), any of various composers known as Surdas, and many others. Their Bhajans have become part of the tradition of classical music to be regularly included in vocal concerts as light but solo vocal performances. Professional Bhajan singers are able to become quite popular singing the same repertoire. Bhajans are also found in medieval syncretic devotional sects such as those of Kabir (1440–1518) and Guru Nanak (1469–1539), where they form the basis for the Sikhs' Shabad Kirtan. Another form of the Bhajan is the Hindu Kirtan wherein songs usually directed toward the Hindu gods Krishna, Ram, or Vishnu are accompanied by drumming and group dancing approaching the ecstatic.

Qawwali is a form of Sufi devotional music particularly popular in South Asian areas with a historically strong Muslim presence such as in the Punjab in both Pakistan and India, in the Gangetic Valley, and to a lesser degree in Bangladesh and Kashmir, which have their own strong folk traditions. Originally performed mainly at Sufi shrines or gatherings, Qawwali has gained mainstream popularity thanks to the rise of the mass media in South Asia.

Qawwali originated with the Sufi saints of Central Asia, as is the case for South Asian Sufism. Amir Khusrau Dehlavi (1253–1325), who wrote in both Persian and medieval Hindi, is strongly associated with the origins of Qawwali in South Asia, and Qawwali singing is especially important to Chishti Sufis. However, the performance of Qawwali is South Asian and is characterized by one or two strong leaders accompanied by a male chorus singing in unison and by vigorous drumming. Themes are largely invocations and praise directed to Allah, the prophet Muhammad, Imam Ali, or Sufi saints and are often interspersed with poetry sung in Urdu, Punjabi, and, infrequently, Multani, Persian, or older forms of Hindi, and even Bengali in Bangladesh.

J. ANDREW GREIG

See also Hinduism; Islam; Khan, Ali Akbar; Khan, Vilayat; Religion; Shankar, Ravi; Sikhism

Further Reading

Hyder, Syed Akbar, and Carla Petievich. "Qawwali Songs of Praise." In *Islam in South Asia in Practice*, edited by Barbara Daly Metcalf, 93–100. Princeton, NJ: Princeton University Press, 2009.

Jacoviello, S. "Nusrat Fateh Ali Khan: The Strange Destiny of a Singing Mystic." *Semiotica* (183) 2011: 319–341.

Qureshi, Regula. *Sufi Music of India and Pakistan: Sound, Context and Meaning in Qawwali*. Cambridge: Cambridge University Press, 1986.

✦ MUSLIMS

India is home to one of the largest Muslim communities in the world. Muslims comprise 13.4 percent of India's 1.1 billion population and are the largest minority community in the nation. With a history of more than a millennium on the subcontinent, Muslims in India have coexisted in one of the most diverse and pluralistic societies in the world. They are the majority community in Kashmir and Lakshadweep. In addition, they live in large numbers in Uttar Pradesh, West Bengal, and Bihar. Despite being a minority, members of the Muslim community have made major contributions in different walks of life and often excel in several of them. However, Muslims continue to struggle with poverty, low literacy rates, and the lack of access to educational institutions, especially in higher education, and they are underrepresented in government offices at all levels.

The present community of Muslims in India is the result of a long historical process. The first Muslims in India were the Arab traders who appeared on the western coast as early as the 7th century, and many of them intermarried with local women and started families. In the northern parts of the Indian subcontinent, Muslim settlement started with the arrival of Turks, Afghanis, Persians, and Central Asians in the 10th and 11th centuries, although the first invasion of India by land occurred by the Arab commander Muhammad bin Qasim (ca. 695–715) in 711 CE. Members of these groups ruled India intermittently from the period of the Delhi Sultanate (1206–1526) through the Mughal Empire (1526–1858). They also spread out to other parts of the subcontinent including southern India, where several independent political states and social entities emerged. Over time the number of Muslims in India increased as their communities prospered and as members of the local population converted to Islam. The reasons for conversion included political aspiration, social uplift as people sought to escape the caste system if they were untouchables or from the lower castes, and being attracted to the egalitarianism promised by Islam that does not recognize caste or class. Sufis also played an important role in the spread of Islam since they were very accommodating of cultural practices and customs found in indigenous traditions. In addition, Indians recognized Sufism because it had an affinity with the Hindu tradition of devotion known as Bhakti. The Muslims in India today thus come from different ethnicities, sects, caste backgrounds, linguistic groups, and an interesting mixture of variations on all these factors.

According to the census of 2001, the number of Muslims in India is 138 million. At 13.4 percent of the Indian population, they are next only to the Hindus, who constitute 80.5 percent of the population. The sex ratio among Muslims is 936 females per 1,000 males, which is just above the national average of 933 females to 1,000 males. Their literacy rate is 59.1 percent, compared to the national average of 64.8 percent. Similarly, the literacy rate among Muslim women is 50.1 percent, certainly below that of their male counterparts as well as the overall female literacy rate in India, which is 53.7 percent. Other data also affirm Muslims as trailing in the national figures on the education and economic development index, among other categories. The total fertility rate (TFR), however—that is, the average number of children a woman would bear during her lifetime—is .7 percent higher among Muslim women than the national figure. But this rate varies among Muslims in different socioeconomic levels. As is reflected in statistics found worldwide, educated and financially stable families have lower fertility rates than the poor and the uneducated. The fertility rate also fluctuates from region to region. For instance, the fertility rate among Muslims is lower in southern states than in the states in northern and central India.

Contrary to popular belief, the worldwide Muslim community is not monolithic, and neither is the Muslim community in India. Although Sunnis make up the majority of India's Muslims, Shias have been politically and economically influential. The existence of divisions and factions within each of the two sects further defies the notion of one single and strictly coherent community. Although Islam does not recognize or acknowledge the validity of a class or caste system, Muslims in India identify themselves as *ashrafs*, or those with Arab or foreign ancestry; *ajlafs*, or middle-caste Hindu converts; and *arzals*, or converts from the untouchable castes. Another grouping is also that of the upper-caste Hindu converts. This stratification is further reflected in social categories such as Scheduled Castes, Scheduled Tribes, and Other Backward Classes. Historically, a good number of low-caste Hindus converted to Islam but remained impoverished and browbeaten, with most of them continuing their traditional occupations and their low occupational status. Similarly, Muslim converts carried their regional culture and often their traditions into their new religion. Muslim society in India is therefore distinguished by social, sectarian, economic, and regional variations.

Muslim interactions with other communities in India are generally cordial in everyday life but are not free on occasion from conflicts and violent clashes. Muslims have contributed to the rich culture of India in food, dress, architecture, music, art, and languages, and it is noteworthy that the Indian culture we know today is a result of the coming together of multiple cultures. However, the prevalence of a common culture has not prevented conflicts from taking place. Communal riots between Hindus and Muslims occurred on numerous occasions before and after India attained independence in 1947. Although different riots need to be understood in their own local and situational contexts, the organized movement Hindutva (Hinduness, or Hindu nationalism) and its counterpart Muslim extremist ideologies have provided a combustible fuel to such incidents. A notorious series of bloody riots took place in Gujarat in 2002 in which more than 2,000 Muslims lost their lives, and a number of Hindus were also murdered in retaliation. Earlier, Hindu-Muslim riots broke out across India in December 1992 following the demolition of Babri Mosque at Ayodhya in Uttar Pradesh by Hindu activists who claimed that the site was the birthplace of the Hindu god Lord Rama. Such incidents take place every few years and lead to ghettoization in many areas, as Muslims feel safer living within the confines of their own community. But the limited nature and duration of such vicious incidents owes a great deal to the secular foundations of India and its enduring commitment to secularism.

As a community, Muslims have played a key role in the politics of the nation. Many Muslims fought for India's independence and also laid down their lives in the cause of freedom.

Thousands of devout Muslims congregate at the Jama Masjid Mosque in Old Delhi for prayers on the first day of the Eid celebration marking the end of Ramadan. (AP/Wide World Photos)

At the time of the Partition of British India into the sovereign states of India and Pakistan, a number of Muslims chose to live in India, both defying the call for a separate Islamic homeland for Muslims (Pakistan) and choosing to remain in an India led by a secular-minded Hindu prime minister, Jawaharlal Nehru (1889–1964; prime minister 1947–1964). The result is that Muslims continued to make a major contribution to national political life in postcolonial India. Muslims have served in parliamentary, ministerial, gubernatorial, cabinet, and other high positions within federal, state, and local governments. Even the highest office in the nation, the presidency of India, has been held by Muslims on three different occasions: Zakir Hussain (1897–1969; president 1967–1969), Fakhruddin Ali Ahmad (1905–1977; president 1974–1977), and A. P. J. Abdul Kalam (b. 1931; president 2002–2007). Muslims have also served as vice president, including the vice president serving in 2009, Mohammad Hamid Ansari (b. 1934; vice president 2007–). Despite significant Muslim representation at the top, there have been demands from some Muslim organizations to enhance their political representation in Parliament and in political parties by calling for quotas based on proportional representation.

Education is another field where Muslims have the dual distinction of being both ahead in some areas but generally behind their Hindu confreres. Muslims are among the most highly educated people in India but as a community are ranked among the most marginalized when it comes to overall higher education levels and rate of literacy. In postcolonial India the leadership and vision of renowned Muslim scholars Maulana Abul Kalam Azad (1888–1958) and Saiyid Nurul Hasan (1921–1993) in the field of education is unparalleled. The Muslim community has also produced innumerable professors, engineers, medical professionals, corporate executives, teachers, scientists, technologists, artists, and actors, among a long list of professions where Muslims have made major contributions. Under constitutional provisions, schools and institutions of higher learning are operated by Muslims. Such institutions of national eminence include Aligarh Muslim University in Uttar Pradesh and Jamia Millia Islamia in Delhi. They have produced some of the greatest Muslim intellectuals and leaders in the nation. A majority of Muslims, however, go to madrasas or Islamic seminaries. Darul Ulum, founded in 1866 and located in Deoband, Uttar Pradesh, and Nadwatul Ulama, founded in 1894 and located in Lucknow, are among the most renowned madrasas in India. In general, madrasas operate with a very low budget and are always short of funds. In addition, they are located in substandard educational facilities. Nonetheless it is largely to their credit that the larger Muslim community is found to be literate and educated, since the madrasas offer education and accommodation either free of cost or for a token amount. The downside of this picture is the low overall literacy rate of Muslims.

Muslim representation in both the private and public sectors is also way below the average proportion for their population. Although jobs in the private sector have occupied the center stage of employment in India since the country's deregulation of the economy in 1991, government jobs are still sought after for the financial security and status they bring. Muslims hold only 4 percent of government jobs, and the percentage of Muslims holding jobs in the private sector is also very low. This percentage gets even lower when it comes to the higher echelons of the civil service. Under the current reservation system for deprived socioreligious groups in India, some Muslim communities qualify for government positions, and this has helped enhance Muslim representation. The demand for increasing the number of reservations for Muslims in government positions has been raised, as has the demand for increased numbers of Muslims in the army, the police, and other agencies. Studying the social, economic, and educational status of Muslims in India, the Sachar Committee, chaired by Justice Rajindar Sachar, chief justice of the high court at Delhi, presented its 403-page report in 2006 and recommended an incentive-based diversity index and a program of affirmative action in the private sector.

The contribution of Muslims can be noted in different fields. In literature, their contribution is more than acknowledged. Muslim writers from India have composed some of the most noted writings in Arabic and Persian, but their contribution to the literature of several Indian languages is also highly noteworthy. Beginning with poets such as Mirza Ghalib (1797–1869) and prose writers such as Muhammad Husain Azad (1830–1910), the body of Urdu literature has mostly been shaped and contributed by Muslim litterateurs. Some of the notable modern writers include Kaifi Azmi (1919–2002), Qurratulain Hyder (1926–2007), Ismat Chughtai (1911–1991), Rahi Masoom Raza (1927–1992), and Bashir Badr (b. 1945). Muslim writers have equally enriched the literature of the Assamese, Bengali, Bhojpuri, English, Gujarati, Hindi, Kannada, Kashmiri, Malyalam, Marathi, Punjabi, Tamil, and Telugu languages. Nazrul Islam (1899–1976) in Bengali, Waris Shah (1722–1798) in Punjabi, Abdur Rahman (b. 1937) in Tamil, K. T. Muhammad (1927–2008) in Malayalam, Habba Khatoon (16th century) in Kashmiri, and Malik Muhammad Jaisi (1477–1542), who wrote in the Avadhi dialect of Hindi, are only a few examples.

Muslims have made a significant contribution in the field of Indian art and cinema. Muslim actors, actresses, directors, producers, screenwriters, lyricists, composers, singers, and technicians have carved a niche for themselves in Bombay cinema ever since the beginnings of the industry. Actor Dilip Kumar (aka Yusuf Khan; b. 1922), singer Mohammad Rafi (1924–1980), actress Madhubala (aka Mumtaz Begam Jehan Dehlavi; 1933–1969), screenwriter Jan Nisar Akhtar (1914–1976), and director Kamal Amrohi (1918–1993) have been the doyens of Indian cinema. Even today, actors such as Aamir Khan (b. 1965), Shahrukh Khan (b. 1965), and Salman Khan (b. 1965) are some of the most popular and successful stars in the industry. Similarly, M. F. Husain (b. 1915) currently is the most recognized Indian painter and has been called the "Picasso of India," while Ebrahim Alkazi (b. 1925) and Habib Tanvir (1923–2009) established themselves as the leading theater personalities of India. In the field of Indian classical music, Muslims such as the vocalist Bade Ghulam Ali Khan (1902–1968), the *shehnai* player Bismillah Khan (1916–2006), the *tabla* players Alla Rakha (1919–2000) and Zakir Hussain (b. 1951), and the *sarod* player Amjad Ali Khan (b. 1946) have dominated its Hindustani school.

Muslims in India today also face challenges as they live a life of promise. Poverty, low literacy, and lack of access to quality educational facilities and good teachers are major issues facing the community. Another serious challenge that Muslims face is the rise of religious fundamentalism. Historically part of a pluralistic culture, India's Muslims have not been free from violence, but recent incidents of terrorism have threatened their liberal and secular credentials. The promise of life in India comprises the economic growth that India has enjoyed since the 1990s and benefits all communities, including Muslims. This economic expansion of India has improved their economic well-being. With further growth and expansion of the Indian economy, the status of Muslims is expected to improve, and so will the statistics that show their relative backwardness. Similarly, widespread and greater access to educational opportunities will further improve their social, economic, and political life.

M. RAISUR RAHMAN

See also Ayodhya; Communalism; Jama Masjid Mosque; Nizari Ismailis; Religion

Further Reading

Ahmad, Imtiaz, ed. *Caste and Social Stratification among Muslims in India.* New Delhi: Manohar, 1978.

Hasan, Mushirul. *Legacy of a Divided Nation: India's Muslims since Independence.* Boulder, CO: Westview, 1997.

Metcalf, Barbara Daly. *Islamic Contestations: Reflections on Muslims in India and Pakistan.* New York: Oxford University Press, 2004.

Mujeeb, M. *The Indian Muslims.* London: Allen and Unwin, 1967.

Sikand, Yoginder. *Muslims in India since 1947: Islamic Perspectives on Inter-faith Relations.* New York: RoutledgeCurzon, 2004.

Social, Economic and Educational Status of the Muslim Community of India: A Report. New Delhi: Government of India, November 2006.

✦ MYANMAR, RELATIONS WITH

The relationship between the Republic of India and the Union of Myanmar (prior to 1989 known as Burma) is predicated on historical ties, including the shared cultural and religious heritage of these neighbors. The Indian origin of many Burmese words is indicative of the almost constant traffic between these two cultures. Their shared tradition of Buddhism, wide-ranging commercial and political links, and the enduring legacies of British colonialism ensure that the two countries have a great deal in common. Indian support for the independence of Burma in 1948 continues to provide a measure of mutual goodwill and admiration.

The shared history of British colonial rule becomes even more potent when considered alongside large-scale Indian migration to colonial Burma. Many of these migrants were employed in the military, the bureaucracy, and the administration. Before World War II (1939–1945), Indians were the dominant group in some of Burma's major centers, including the city of Rangoon, and their influential role led to anti-Indian attacks. After independence, further political hardships in Burma motivated many to leave the country. While most of the descendants of these migrants returned to India or moved to other parts of the world, some have remained in Burma, where they constitute a small but commercially successful segment of the urban population. The descendants of these Indians still constitute about 2 percent of the population.

At the governmental level, there have been repeated episodes of tension punctuated by mutual accusations of harboring armed rebels. Such accusations have largely centered on rebel groups with bases along the Indo-Burmese frontier and include the United Liberation Front of Asom in India and the Kachin Independence Army in Myanmar. Both rebel groups are accused of seeking a safe haven in the neighboring country and of using their international links to consolidate their operational successes with improved training and logistics. Their reputed links to the regional narcotics trade have often been used to justify attacks on them.

Since 1988 the State Law and Order Restoration Council/State Peace and Development Council has governed Myanmar, and ties between the two countries have improved. This improvement has emerged during a period when the Myanmar military established its control of the Indo-Myanmar frontier through its cease-fire agreement with the Kachin Independence Army.

The two governments have increased cooperation along their 909-mile frontier, and there are now formal trading points between the two countries. At the same time, India is attempting to fence the entire length of the border to stop illegal crossings. Seeking economic solutions to political conflict in northeastern India means that ambition for even greater links and the upgrading of an often decrepit infrastructure are priorities for both countries. The World War II–era Stilwell Road between northeastern India and southwestern China that snakes its way across the mountains of northern Myanmar may one day become a key component of infrastructure linking Asia's two most populous countries. Such a conduit of economic and cultural resources would see Myanmar playing an even greater role in the future security and prosperity of northeastern India.

Recent efforts to increase trade and diplomatic ties have led to a partial thawing in official relations. From India's perspective the rationale for friendlier relations is that Indian foreign policy analysts identify China's strategic designs on the Indian Ocean as a potential threat. Chinese access to the Indian Ocean is best facilitated through Myanmar, and the dangers that this suggests have come to preoccupy some Indian strategic planners.

Disrupting opportunities for even closer ties was the lingering issue of the treatment of Myanmar prodemocracy leader Aung San Suu Kyi (b. 1945) and her incarceration under house arrest, although she was released from captivity in November 2010. Some Indian commentators considered their country's failure to more fully advocate on her behalf a betrayal of Indian democratic principles. Others are far more circumspect and remain focused on the threat that a stronger Chinese influence in Myanmar presents. They equivocate on Myanmar's democracy and are prepared to overlook the government's human rights abuses if that will help secure India's strategic future. Nonetheless, there has been public concern about arms sales to the Myanmar government, particularly in the period immediately after the 2007 crackdown on protests by Buddhist priests. There are indications that the Indian government is continuing to consider its options with respect to further engagement with Myanmar.

High-level official visits have become more frequent between the two countries, and these formal links have been consolidated by participation in multilateral forums including the Bay of Bengal Initiative for Multi-Sectoral Technical and Economic Cooperation (BIMSTEC) and the Mekong-Ganga Cooperation. Both organizations include South Asian and Southeast Asian members and are based on the logic of history, geography, and economics. It is ultimately those ties that will lead to further links between India and Myanmar. Both countries hope to capitalize on what remain largely underdeveloped efforts to cooperate and collaborate on issues of shared concern.

NICHOLAS FARRELLY

See also China, Relations with; Look East Policy; Southeast Asia, Relations with

Further Reading

Bhattacharya, Swapna. *India-Myanmar Relations, 1886–1948.* Calcutta: K. P. Bagchi, 2007.

Egreteau, Renaud. "India's Ambitions in Burma: More Frustration Than Success?" *Asian Survey* 48(6) (2008): 936–957.

Haacke, Jürgen. *Myanmar's Foreign Policy: Domestic Influences and International Implications.* New York: Routledge, 2006.Figure 3   **Foreign exchange trading activity**

N

✦ NAGALAND

Nagaland is situated in the extreme northeastern corner of India and is considered by many to be one of the most interesting of India's 29 states. It is bordered by Arunachal Pradesh to the north, Assam to the west, and Manipur to the south. Nagaland, so named for its tribal inhabitants, the Naga people, is roughly 10,000 square miles in size and has a climate that is dominated by the five-month-long monsoon season beginning in May and ending in September of each year.

The abundance of rain and the tropical latitude ensure that Nagaland is rich in flora and fauna. Bamboo, oak, magnolia, and pine trees are abundant. Nagaland's wildlife is also diverse, including large mammals, such as elephants, wild buffaloes, and bears. Nagaland is also home to a rich variety of small primates, including pigtailed macaques, the slow loris, and hoolock gibbons. One may also find big cats in Nagaland, including the leopard and tiger, though in recent decades both have become endangered species.

Nagaland, though populated for thousands of years, was only organized as a political state in the Republic of India on December 1, 1963, 16 years after Indian independence in 1947. The majority of the Naga people embraced the union with India on specified terms, which included a high level of autonomy from the central government in New Delhi to run their own economic and political affairs. Today, Nagaland is governed by a legislative assembly of 60 representatives elected by popular vote. It is dominated by four political parties, with the Nagaland People's Front currently in power. Stability of the state remains a priority, with Nagaland having suffered low-level nationalist insurgencies since its union with India.

Nagas shout slogans and march in a rally demanding integration of all Naga-inhabited areas in Senapati, about 50 miles south of Kohima, capital of the northeastern Indian state of Nagaland, May 13, 2006. (AP Photo/K. Sharatchandra)

Economically, Nagaland's standard of living ranks in the middle of India's 29 states. Agriculture remains the most important economic activity, with up to 90 percent of the population engaged in some aspect of the sector. Harvests of rice, millet, sugarcane, and forest products account for much of the agricultural output, but new attention is being paid to silk production as a way to boost the standard of living for the state's residents. Due to the political violence that erupted in the 1970s and the 1980s, the tourist sector was hurt as potential visitors avoided the area in large numbers. The insurgency between ethnonationalists seeking complete independence from India and government forces ended with a cease-fire brokered in the mid-1990s. Since that time Nagaland has promoted itself as both a safe and tourist-friendly destination.

Tourism is an increasingly important aspect of Nagaland's economy. It helps that, although the state is geographically isolated compared to much of India, Nagaland is easily reached by automobile, train, or jet aircraft. To capitalize on this fact, Nagaland's state government and many private companies have been pushing for more visitors, even opening websites dedicated to Nagaland tourism. These sites feature videos and other materials highlighting the state's colorful tribes, festivals, and unique culture. In many ways, Nagaland is showcasing itself as a place for ecotourism and anthropological tourism, a destination where one can learn about tribal diversity and enjoy some of India's best-preserved tropical forests at the same time.

The vast majority of Nagaland's population identify themselves with one of the region's 14 major tribes and speak languages of the Tibeto-Burman language family. These languages provide important clues to the origins of the people. For example, linguists have traced common cultural and ethnic links shared by the Nagas to groups living in Bhutan, Nepal, Assam, and Burma, as well as to smaller tribes found in northern Thailand and southwestern China. Research has further shown that the indigenous languages of the Naga tribes had no written script; instead, the area borrowed first from Sanskrit and later from the Latin alphabet introduced by Christian missionaries.

It is estimated today that up to 90 percent of the Naga people claim Christianity as their main religion. Surprisingly, Nagaland resisted absorbing both the Hindu and Buddhist beliefs of India, with only traces of their influence found in the region. Instead, the tribes came to embrace Christianity in the 19th and 20th centuries; the Christianity that developed, however, was a blend of Christian and indigenous beliefs. Like many of the world's premodern populations, the people of Nagaland had earlier religious beliefs and practices based upon animism, the worship of nature; these often included such practices as headhunting.

Although the practice of headhunting has long been abandoned, many Nagas hold firm to animist beliefs, recognizing and worshiping spirits in nature, such as divinities that live in the forests, rocks, and rivers of the region. Another aspect of animism still found in Nagaland is the shaman or medicine man. Shamans were common fixtures in villages of the past and can still be found today, overseeing various village rites and festivals celebrated throughout the year.

The national costume and clothing of Nagaland is also different from most of the rest of India. The Nagas eschew the more common dress, including the ever-present *salwar* or *lungi* and even the *sari*. Instead, one will find Nagas attired in handloomed sarongs and shawls, brightly colored and decorated according to tribal customs.

STEVEN B. SHIRLEY

See also Northeastern States

Further Reading
Danda, A. K., et al., eds. *North-East India: Ethno-Cultural Perspectives and Process*. Calcutta: Indian Anthropological Society, 1998.
Hokishe, S. *Emergence of Nagaland: Socio-economic and Political Transformation and the Future*. New Delhi: Vikas, 1986.
Horam, M. *Naga Insurgency: The Last Thirty Years*. New Delhi: Cosmo, 1988.
"Know India . . . Now." Accessed April 28, 2011. http://www.nagalandonline.in.
Singh, K. Suresh, N. K. Das, and C. L. Imechen, eds. *People of India: Nagaland*. Calcutta: Seagull Books, 1994.

✦ NATIONAL ALLIANCE OF PEOPLE'S MOVEMENTS

The National Alliance of People's Movements (NAPM), which originated in 1992, is a nationwide coalition of a diverse range of individuals, groups, and movements that works toward the fulfillment of a democratic, autonomous, and egalitarian state. While rapidly growing urban India and the consumer market benefit industrial and business elites and the swelling ranks of the middle class, the majority of people continue to live in rural areas and comprise a diverse population of marginal farmers, Adivasis (tribals), and marginalized castes. The NAPM wages a struggle against the hegemonic and exploitative policies associated with the "New Economic Policy" of privatization, liberalization, and partnership in global capitalism. The policy, it argues, irretrievably damages the environment and demeans the sacrifice of the toiling masses; in addition, it alienates, uproots, and displaces the people living on the margins in both urban and rural areas.

The NAPM advocates fundamental change and a people-oriented sustainable development model. It opposes the uncontrolled powers of global and domestic capital, and the policies and conditions imposed by the International Monetary Fund (IMF), the World Bank, and the World Trade Organization (WTO), which have all diminished the role of the state in the vital areas of health and education, as well as in the economy as a whole. The NAPM supports legal protection for the people's right of access to forests, common land, and water, and aims to revitalize the rural economy, including measures to improve the lives of forest dwellers, rural artisans, and those engaged in rural industries. It opposes the current industrial policy, which, it believes, abandons social responsibility and devalues human labor. It supports legislation regarding the minimum wage, safety regulation, health care, working hours, and environmental protection.

The NAPM also focuses on microwatershed development and river basins as a unit of planning and opposes big dams and the development of other infrastructure projects, such as the creation of special economic zones. These encroach upon the resources and livelihood of marginal farmers and Adivasis. The creation of nuclear and mining projects and the exploitation of minerals and natural wealth also cause enormous damage to the lives of the downtrodden and to the environment. The organization opposes communalism and values the protection of plural cultures; condemns organized violence, both private and state; advocates gender equity; and demands extensive electoral reform. It has championed the Right to Information, the National Rural Employment Guarantee Scheme, the Right to Food, and the rights of hawkers and slum dwellers. The NAPM has opposed both extremist and state violence in the Adivasi areas and the abuse of state machinery through such legislation as the Armed Forces Special Powers Act.

YOGESH SNEHI

See also Asian Development Bank; Central Banking, Development Aspects; Economy; Financial Institutions, Development; International Monetary Fund, Relations with; Monetary Policy; National Rural Employment Guarantee Act; Reserve Bank of India; Stock Exchange Markets; World Bank, Relations with; World Economic Forum; World Trade Organization, Relations with

Further Reading

Drèze, Jean, Meera Samson, and Satyajit Singh, eds. *The Dam and the Nation: Displacement and Resettlement in the Narmada Valley.* New Delhi: Oxford University Press, 1997.

Friends of the River Narmada. Accessed April 28, 2011. http://narmada.org.

National Alliance of People's Movements. Accessed April 28, 2011. http://www.napm-india.org.

✦ NATIONAL RURAL EMPLOYMENT GUARANTEE ACT

The National Rural Employment Guarantee Act (NREGA) of 2005, also known as the Mahatma Gandhi National Rural Employment Guarantee Act 2005, is a law that guarantees at least 100 days of work a year at statutory minimum wages to every household whose adult members volunteer to do unskilled manual work. Whenever adult members register themselves, in writing or orally, with the local Gram Panchayat, they are issued a Job Card, which is valid for at least five years, and as a matter of right are entitled to work within 15 days of the application. (A Gram Panchayat is a local government at the village or small-town level; it can be set up with a minimum population of 300.)

Initially, the NREGA was established in 200 districts of India on February 2, 2006, and then extended to an additional 130 districts in 2007–2008. (On April 1, 2007, 113 districts were established, and 17 districts in Uttar Pradesh were established on May 15, 2007.) The remaining districts were established on April 1, 2008, which extended the NREGA to the entire country.

A guarantee of employment is important social security legislation. For the more than 60 percent of the rural population that is dependent on agriculture, the NREGA provides a minimum subsistence entitlement and is especially effective during an economic slowdown or recession.

The NREGA ensures twin benefits for rural development. While it guarantees work, it also helps in building and strengthening the rural infrastructure through the construction of roads, the repairing of water channels for water conservation and flood control, the recovering of waste land, and afforestation. It also provides a viable alternative against hunger. Significantly, if a registered member is not provided employment within the stipulated time, he or she is entitled to an unemployment allowance.

Rural development has been an intrinsic part of various government schemes, but most of them failed in achieving their objectives primarily because of bureaucratic hassles and a policy that never made people aware of such schemes. The NREGA goes beyond the limited purview of these schemes. It is an act of the Parliament and provides legal entitlements to laborers for work at minimum wages fixed by the central and state government. This also strengthens the bargaining power of unorganized workers.

Along with providing the guarantee of a job, the NREGA has also restructured power relationships in rural India. More women and people from the margins of caste and class, Dalits (formerly called untouchables), small and marginal farmers, and the landless have benefited from the economic and social entitlements of the act. The Right to Information Act also provides an additional tool for ensuring accountability and transparency in the functioning of the NREGA.

There are, however, some major shortcomings that affect the implementation of the NREGA. Among the major challenges are the inordinate delays in the payment of wages, poor worksite facilities like crèches, and corruption through the siphoning of large funds by the faking of old assets. These have been reported in states such as Uttar Pradesh and

Madhya Pradesh. The augmentation of schemes for rural development also remains a major challenge, owing to a shift in the work cycle of laborers during the harvest season.

Some of these challenges have been addressed through the opening of individual or joint bank accounts for laborers and enabling payment through proposed ATM-like machines, the use of information technology (IT) for monitoring completed work, and the institution of social audits of NREGA funds.

YOGESH SNEHI

See also Central Banking, Development Aspects; Economy; Financial Institutions, Development

Further Reading

Dey, Nikhil, Jean Drèze, and Reetika Khera. *Employment Guarantee Act: A Primer.* New Delhi: National Book Trust, 2006.

Gopal, K. S. "NREGA Social Audits: Myths and Reality." *Economic and Political Weekly* 44(3) (2009): 70–74.

"Mahatma Gandhi National Rural Employment Guarantee Act 2005." Ministry of Rural Development, Government of India. Accessed April 28, 2011. http://nrega.nic.in.

Narayan, Sudha. "Employment Guarantee, Women's Work and Child Care." *Economic and Political Weekly* 43(9) (2008): 10–13.

National Volunteers Organization. *See* Rashtriya Swayamsevak Sangh

✦ NAXALITE MOVEMENT

The Naxalite, or Naxalbari, movement was centered on the struggle for land and labor rights for the tribal people of the Naxalbari region in West Bengal and was led by radicals from the Communist Party of India (Marxist), or CPI(M), against the local landlords and the Darjeeling tea estate owners. This rebellion (or insurgency) lasted barely 52 days, from the last week of May to mid-July 1967. This peasant rebellion took its name from the Naxalbari region, where 60-odd villages cover an area of about 300 square miles in the Darjeeling district. This area is the slender neck of eastern India, squeezed in between former East Pakistan (Bangladesh) below and the foothills of the Himalayas, China, Bhutan, and Nepal above. It was also an area ideal for many insurrection movements, as it provided mountain hideouts, natural forest cover, and possible foreign sanctuaries.

The people of this part of West Bengal are tribal, mainly Santals, with a population of 1,200,000 by the 1961 census. They were employed by the landlords, or *jotedars*, under the *adhiar* land tenure system on a contractual basis. Under the *adhiar* system, the landlord provided capital in the form of seeds, plows, and bullocks needed for crop cultivation. In exchange, the landlord got a share of the harvested crops. Labor relations in the region were highly exploitative, and disputes over the shares of the produce and eviction of the peasant laborers were common occurrences. There was also unrest in the famous Darjeeling tea estates, where tribal peasants had been cultivating rice on surplus estate lands. They feared eminent eviction by the estate owners.

The general election of 1967 was a major event in Indian political history. The fourth general election for independent India, it saw a number of major electoral defeats for the ruling Congress Party in statewide elections. It was a humiliating setback for the Congress Party, which had fought for India's independence and delivered India from British rule just 20 years earlier. In Bengal, the election also brought an end to the 20-year continuous rule by the Congress Party. A political coalition called United Front government came to power under Ajoy Mukherjee with an alliance of 14 parties, including the pro-Russian Communist Party of India (CPI) and the pro-Chinese CPI(M), which were bitter rivals.

Maverick Communist activists had been working in this state since the mid-1950s, organizing the tribal peoples for protests on a wide range of issues. The most important of these was to stop the arbitrary eviction of the tribal workers from the lands they had previously cleared and cultivated. The tribal people, for their part, depended on Communist activists to help them deal with the exploitative relations with wealthy *jotedars*, who were often absentee landlords, and moneylenders, who kept the cultivators in near serflike status. The leading Communist activists were Kanu Sanyal, an upper-caste Brahmin with a charismatic personality from a nearby town. Kanu Sanyal was a dedicated Communist Party worker who had learned the tribal language and lived among the peasants, organizing meetings, leading protests, and handling court cases on their behalf. His close associate was Jangul Santal, a Santal tribal activist who was also an active member of the CPI(M). Their chief was a radical Communist ideologue named Charu Mazumdar, a small, well-read, 59-year-old upper caste Marxist visionary with a heart condition. Mazumdar was dedicated to the ideas of China's chairman Mao-Tse-Tung. He wanted to set up a Marxist revolutionary base to stage peasant uprisings all across the Indian countryside and eventually win political power, imitating Mao's own example in the Chinese countryside. Mazumdar played a major role in building up cells in this area, but unlike Kanu Sanyal, he was not a charismatic person and preferred to act behind the scenes.

The CPI being part of the winning United Front coalition government led to rumors and fearmongering. The CPI had convinced the landlords that their small and medium-sized lands would be confiscated by the new government and turned over to its tribal cultivators. In response, and as a precautionary proactive measure, there was a spate of evictions of tribal sharecroppers. There were also attacks, carried out by thugs hired by landlords, on sharecroppers who had previously challenged and won their right to remain on the lands they had cultivated. The trigger for the Naxalite rebellion was one such attack on a tribal man who had been awarded land by the court under the existing tenancy legislation. This time, the tribal people chose to retaliate by attacking the landlords and seizing their lands with the support of the local Communist activists from CPI(M).

On May 25, 1967, the tribal activists drove the local landlords away from their lands and hoisted red flags in their fields. The local police and the administration were also forced to flee the area of conflict, and this area was declared a "liberated zone." Tribal militia, armed with their traditional bows and arrows and occasional firearms, began to mobilize and to defend the area against any future police actions. Committees were formed in every village, setting up a parallel administration and taking over courts and schools. Raids were undertaken on the homes of rich landlords to confiscate their rice stocks and cancel or burn all tenant-related documents or deeds alleged to have been used to oppress and cheat the peasants.

Roving armed bands began to collect taxes and administer vigilante justice. Death sentences were passed on the more oppressive landlords. The state minister, on June 12, 1967, declared that a "reign of terror" had descended on Darjeeling district, and the CPI(M) sent a top-level delegation to defuse the crisis. However, the local Communist chapter would not yield. The CPI(M) Politburo, by the end of June, came up against its own activists during the Naxalbari rebellion. It expelled Charu Mazumdar, Kanu Sanyal, Jangul Santal, and their follow rebels from the party ranks for advocating what is called an "adventurous line of action." All this happened under the glare of national and international publicity. The peasant rebels from Naxalbari won the sympathy and admiration of the radical leftist students at the Calcutta Presidency College, who organized public meetings and demonstrations and set up a support group called "Naxalbari Peasants Struggle Aid." This support group was later, in 1969, to become the nucleus of the separate Marxist Party, the Communist Party of India (Marxist-Leninist), or CPI(ML).

As rebel activities continued unabated, Radio Peking (Beijing) broadcast the Chinese government's own support and sympathy for the Naxalbari rebels on June 28 by describing the Naxalbari incident as the "front paw of a revolutionary armed struggle by the Indian people under the guidance of Chairmen Mao-Tse-Tung." It called the United Front government the tool of the reactionaries engaged in deceiving the people of West Bengal. This was the first evidence that China was also paying close attention to events unfolding in West Bengal and its disenchantment with its Indian political disciple, the CPI(M). This public denouncement by Radio Peking was something of a shock for the CPI(M) hierarchy, which had considered itself a loyal adherent of the Pro-Chinese Communist Party. At the same time, the message had a tremendous impact on the morale of the Naxalbari-based party rebels, who saw it as a vindication of their independent action. The government of India interpreted the Chinese radio broadcast as blatant interference in its internal affairs and an act of Chinese subversion to undermine its own authority and legitimacy in this volatile area. The state and the local police forces were ordered to locate and arrest the agitators and crush the rebellion.

The rebellion lasted only 52 days, and its end came on July 12, 1967, when a major police action was launched to round up the rebels and to arrest its leaders. The casualty rate was surprisingly low, as only one person died during the final police action. The total casualties for the entire rebellion were 18 tribal women and children, who were killed while allegedly being used as human shields (according to the police version) in an earlier shootout. In the final push, the rebels offered no resistance, and the key leaders Kanu Sanyal, Charu Mazumdar, and Jangul Santal were all arrested and jailed. They were later released in March 1969, when another Marxist-led coalition state government come to power.

This movement came at a critical period of Indian history, five years after its humiliating military defeat in a brief but bruising border skirmish with the Chinese. At this time, the government of India was very sensitive to any public statements from Beijing that could be interpreted as interference in India's domestic and international affairs. It was in no mood to allow any form of Chinese patronage to any group within its territory. It also came at a time when China itself faced internal power struggles within the Communist Party in the form of the so-called "cultural revolution" and was eager to support other radical Communist-led insurgencies in its neighborhood. It also occurred at a period of Indian economic stagnation, with a declining per capita income, and the nation on the verge of a large-scale famine in Bihar. There were also food shortages in other provinces, with millions of India's citizens kept alive by emergency food aid from the United States.

Finally, there were the college-educated students whose future looked bleak at a time of massive unemployment, and they had a lot of free time and were ready to engage in radical political activities. It was also the late 1960s and the high point of leftist student protests and riots, which was part of the global youth cultural scene. In West Bengal, the better-organized radical Marxist parties with a lot of prestige attracted the more socially conscious students. They also offered ready solutions to the present predicaments through mass revolution, the overthrow of an exploitive system, and the establishment of a just order based on Chairman Mao's Chinese Communist model. The slogan of the day among the Calcutta Presidency College student activists was "Mao-Tse-Tung Zindabad," or "Long live Chairman Mao-Tse-Tung."

The only major casualty of the Naxalbari rebellion seems to have been the provincial coalition government under Ajoy Mukherjee, which was dismissed by the central government of India in November 1967. In spite of its brief life span, and the relatively small loss of life, the Naxalbari peasant revolt had a far-reaching impact as a model for politically motivated tribal-peasant rebellions throughout India. Even today, such radical Naxalbari-style insurgencies, now called "Maoist" by the popular press, are considered the biggest internal threat to the security of India. Since 2009 the government of India has labeled all Maoist groups as terrorists and issued greater power to its police, the Central Reserve Police Force (CRPF) paramilitary force, and the armed forces to deal with them accordingly.

RAMAN N. SEYLON

See also Land Tenure; Northeastern States; West Bengal

Further Reading

Abbas, Khwaja Ahmad. *The Naxalites*. Delhi: Lok Pubications, 1979.

Banerjee, Sumanta. *India's Simmering Revolution: The Naxalite Uprising*. London: Zed Books, 1984.

Banerjee, Sumanta. *In the Wake of Naxalbari: A History of the Naxalite Movement in India*. Calcutta: Subarnarekha Calcutta, 1980.

Dasgupta, Biplab. *The Naxalite Movement*. Bombay: Allied Publishers, 1974.

Duyker, Edward. *Tribal Guerrillas: The Santals of West Bengal and the Naxalite Movement*. New York: Oxford University Press, 1987.

Ghosh, Sankar. *The Naxalite Movement: A Maoist Experiment*. Calcutta: Firma K. L. Mukhopadhyay, 1974.

Jawaid, Sohail. *The Naxalite Movement in India: Origin and Failure of the Maoist Revolutionary Strategy in West Bengal, 1967–1971*. New Delhi: Associated Publishing House, 1979.

Johari, Jogdish Chandra. *Naxalite Politics of India*. Delhi: Research Publications, 1972.

Mukherjee, Arun Prosad. *Maoist "Spring Tthunder": The Naxalite Movement, 1967–1972*. Kolkata: K. P. Bagchi, 2007.

Ray, Rabindra. *The Naxalites and Their Ideology*. New York: Oxford University Press, 1988.

Sen, Asit. *An Approach to Naxalbari*. Calcutta: Institute of Scientific Thoughts, 1980.

Singh, Prakash. *The Naxalite Movement in India*. New Delhi: Rupa, 2007.

✦ NEW DELHI

New Delhi (also known as Delhi) is one of the nine districts of Delhi in the National Capital Territory of Delhi, the capital of the Republic of India, and the capital of the government of the National Capital Territory of Delhi. Located on the banks of the Yamuna River, in northwestern India on the Indo-Gangetic Plain, it has a population of more than 18 million people, spread out over more than 160 square miles, and is expanding rapidly, with about 250,000 people migrating to the city every year. Its population density of more than 75,000 people per square mile makes it one of the largest cities in the world. Numerous languages are spoken in Delhi, although the predominant languages are Hindi, Punjabi, Urdu, and English. Along with Mumbai and Kolkata it is one of the three greatest cities of India and is renowned for its social and intellectual dynamism. The business, political, and media center for India, Delhi rivals the great conurbations of the world, and more than 20 million people pass through its Indira Gandhi International Airport every year.

The city has a humid subtropical climate, with an average high of 102 degrees Fahrenheit in May and an average low of 45 degrees in January. Most of its average 28 inches of rainfall comes during the monsoon rains of July and August, when city streets are often flooded, people wade up to their knees in water, and traffic comes to a standstill. At other times people bake in the dry summer heat, made worse by a blanket of dust and pollution hovering over the city, which is caused by the acutely congested traffic and factories and workshops, and worsened by the numerous dung fires that people light to cook their meals, especially in the evenings. Airplanes are sometimes grounded in winter for hours when the smoke mixes with fog, reducing visibility. New Delhi is thus one of the most populous, most crowded, most polluted, and fastest-growing cities in the world.

King George V (1865–1936; king of the United Kingdom and emperor of India, 1910–1936), announced on December 12, 1911, that the capital of British India would be moved from Calcutta to Delhi in a new city to be built adjacent to the old city. New Delhi was designed by British architects Edwin Lutyens (1869–1944) and Herbert Baker (1862–1946) and inaugurated on February 13, 1931. Delhi, however, because of its strategic location, had been the center of habitation for millennia. It is located on the site of an early capital mentioned in the *Mahabharata*, of circa 1000 BCE; was Islamicized around the 12th century; and was made the great city of the Mughals after Babur (1483–1531; Mughal emperor 1526–1531) captured the city in 1526. It has been the capital of at least half a dozen dynasties or empires.

Delhi is, therefore, a city containing numerous sights both ancient and modern. Nothing remains of its ancient Aryan past, but the most significant of Delhi's top tourist sites are the Qutub Minar, a minaret almost 238 feet high built by Muslim ruler Qutub-ud-din Aibak, the first sultan of Delhi (1206–1210) between 1193 and 1368; the tomb of the first Mughal emperor, Humayun (1508–1556; Mughal emperor 1530–1540, 1555–1556); the Red Fort (*Lal Qila*), completed by Mughal emperor Shah Jahan (1592–1666; Mughal emperor 1628–1658) in 1648; and Jama Masjid Mosque, the largest mosque in India,

Aerial view of Connaught Place, a thriving and bustling business and commercial center as well as an entertainment district filled with restaurants, bars, and shops; it is considered to be the center of New Delhi. (Sipra Das/The India Today Group/Getty Images)

completed in 1656. Its pre-Muslim history is represented by the 22-foot-high iron pillar of Chandragupta II, emperor (ca. 380–415) during the Gupta Empire (319–547). Sites from the British period include Rashtrapati Bhavan, the official residence of the president; Parliament House, containing both the upper (Rajya Sabha) and the lower (Lok Sabha) houses of Parliament; the Secretariat Building, housing government ministries; and India Gate, commemorating the lives of servicemen from World War I. Numerous temples are also found in Delhi, from the modernist Bahai Lotus Temple to the Hindu Akshardham Temple and Lakshminarayan Temple to the Sikh Gurdwara Bangla Sahib; numerous churches and cathedrals are found there as well.

Delhi is one of the great educational centers of the world, with a large number of world-class universities, including Delhi University, Jamia Millia Islamia, and Jawaharlal Nehru University. It houses the remarkable National Museum and the Nehru Memorial Museum, which is not only a museum on the life of Jawaharlal Nehru (1889–1964; prime minister 1947–1964), the second member of the Nehru dynasty, which has given India three prime ministers so far, but is also a vast treasure trove for scholars working on India's modern history.

New Delhi is a vibrant city that pulsates with energy from early morning to late at night. Its innumerable cafes and tea shops are the center of life for many Indians, especially the young, students, and the unemployed and the underemployed, who all gather in Connaught Place. The city contains some of the finest hotels and restaurants in the world and houses bazaars selling almost every imaginable product. It is a book lover's paradise. Buses, rickshaws, and taxis zoom around the city, helping to create the frenetic pace and atmosphere that characterizes the city. It is modernizing at a fast pace, almost as quickly as the new rapidly expanding metro, both underground and aboveground, speeds people to their destinations around the city and into the far suburbs. New Delhi is not just a remarkable city but also an incredible experience.

ROGER D. LONG

See also Jama Masjid Mosque

Further Reading

Favero, Paolo. *India Dreams: Cultural Identity among Young Middle Class Men in New Delhi.* Stockholm: Department of Social Anthropology, Stockholm University, 2005.

Irving, Robert. *Indian Summer: Lutyens, Baker and Imperial Delhi.* New Haven, CT: Yale University Press, 1981.

Jain, A. K. *Delhi under Hammer: The Crisis of Sealing and Demolition.* New Delhi: Rupa, 2010.

Jalil, Rakhshanda. *Invisible City: The Hidden Monuments of Delhi.* New Delhi: Niyogi Books, 2008.

Jolly, U. S. *Challenges for a Mega City: Delhi, a Planned City with Unplanned Growth.* New Delhi: Concept Publishing, 2010.

Khanna, Rahul. *The Modern Architecture of New Delhi, 1928–2007.* New Delhi: Random House India, 2008.

Legg, Stephen. *Spaces of Colonialism: Delhi's Urban Governmentalities.* Maiden, MA: Blackwell, 2007.

National Capital Territory of Delhi. Accessed April 28, 2011. http://delhi.gov.in.

New Delhi Municipal Council. Accessed April 28, 2011. http://ndmc.gov.in.

Sengupta, Ranjana. *Delhi Metropolitan: The Making of an Unlikely City*. New Delhi: Penguin, 2007.

Singh, B. P., ed. *The Millennium Book on New Delhi*. New Delhi: Oxford University Press, 2001.

Sundaram, Ravi. *Pirate Modernity: Delhi's Media Urbanism*. London: Routledge, 2010.

✦ NEWSPAPERS, INDIAN-LANGUAGE

India's newspaper market is highly complex and diverse. In 2008 newspapers were published in English and 22 other principal languages written in 14 different scripts. There has been a tremendous growth of Indian-language newspapers since independence in 1947, and especially since the late 1970s. Spearheaded by Hindi-language newspapers, this growth is largely driven by the increase in the level of literacy, improvements in consumer purchasing power, growing political awareness, the spread of computer technology and offset presses, and the use of marketing strategies by newspapers to reach out to the readers. It was in 1979 that Hindi dailies for the first time overtook English dailies in terms of circulation (3 million to 2.97 million, according to the Registrar of Newspapers India), and this gap kept widening during the 1980s and 1990s. According to the circulation figures for 2007, Hindi dailies lead with 8.48 million copies, while English dailies trail a distant second with 3.15 million copies.

Another way of understanding the growth of Indian-language newspapers is through the readership figures. In India, the culture of sharing a newspaper is prevalent, particularly among the readers of Indian-language newspapers. This is evident when looking at the difference between circulation and readership figures. The National Readership Survey for 2006 reported that vernacular newspapers have grown from 191 million readers to 203.6 million (of these, 81.6 million were readers of Hindi newspapers), while English newspapers have stagnated at around 21 million readers.

It must be noted that the dramatic rise of Hindi newspapers has taken place in the context of the growing ascendancy of electronic media. Many analysts believe that the advent of privately operated cable and satellite television channels will spell the death knell of newspapers. However, newspapers have adapted to technological innovations and repositioned themselves to continue as a vital medium of communication. By localizing their content and issuing regional-, district-, and local-level editions, Hindi newspapers have been able to create new constituencies of readership and, in the process, retain their share of advertising revenue in the face of growing competition from the electronic media. Through focusing on local news and stories of local interest, Hindi newspapers have brought news closer to the readers.

From the independence of India in August 1947 until the mid-1980s, politicians and bureaucrats hardly bothered with or even took notice of the news published in Hindi newspapers. English-language newspapers were considered the national newspapers, even though they had a low circulation. Now, politicians and bureaucrats cannot afford to ignore news published in Hindi and other regional-language newspapers.

Dainik Jagran was established by a revolutionary Indian freedom fighter, Puran Chandra Gupta (b. 1940). The first edition of the newspaper was brought out from Jhansi, Uttar Pradesh, in 1942, but in 1947 it was issued at Kanpur, also in Uttar Pradesh. Since its inception, *Dainik Jagran* has expanded steadily. According to the National Readership survey of 2006, it is the most widely read daily newspaper of India, with 21.24 million readers. It is the first Indian newspaper to have crossed the readership mark of 20 million copies a day.

Since its establishment in 1942 until 1989, *Dainik Jagran* was mostly only available in Uttar Pradesh. The only edition outside the state during this period was an edition published from Bhopal, Madhya Pradesh, which was launched in 1956. However, being based in Uttar Pradesh itself was a major advantage, as that state has the distinction of being the "Hindi heartland" and occupies an important place in the pan-Indian political landscape. After the Bhopal edition came out, the next expansion took place nearly two decades later, with the launch of an edition from Gorakhpur, Uttar Pradesh, in 1975. This was followed by the launch of local editions coming out from different cities in the state, including Lucknow (1979), the capital city of Uttar Pradesh. By the end of the 1980s *Dainik Jagran* was able to establish for itself a dominant presence in Uttar Pradesh. Thereafter, it started expanding outside the state.

Dainik Jagran launched its edition from New Delhi, the capital of India, in 1990, and launched its Jalandhar, Punjab, edition in 1999. *Dainik Jagran* now has a media presence across 12 states: Bihar, Chhattisgarh, Delhi (a Union Territory), Haryana, Himachal Pradesh, Jammu and Kashmir, Jharkhand, Madhya Pradesh, Punjab, Rajasthan, Uttar Pradesh, and Uttaranchal. Currently, *Dainik Jagran* publishes 37 editions and prints more than 200 subeditions, with each subedition carefully customized for the readership of its geographic area.

Much of the success of *Dainik Jagran* can be attributed to its ability to localize the content of each edition and to use the colloquial language of the area. As a result, the difference in the presentation style of a particular item of news in two different editions is easily noticeable. This is one of the important features of Hindi newspapers that cannot be found in the case of English newspapers. In the political arena, *Dainik Jagran* has also been notorious for supporting a right-wing Hindutva (Hinduness) ideology. During the Babri Masjid controversy in the late 1980s and early 1990s, which eventually led to the destruction of the mosque on December 6, 1992, *Dainik Jagran* reported the events in a highly sensational manner and stoked the passions of Hindu extremists. As a result, in its December 1991 Ayodhya Judgment, the Press Council of India criticized the Hindi Press in general, and *Dainik Jagran* in particular, for "offending the canons of journalistic ethics."

The chief editor of the newspaper, Narendra Mohan (1934–2002), was elected to the Rajya Sabha, the upper house of the Indian Parliament, and represented the extremist right-wing Bharatiya Janata Party (BJP), founded in 1980. Similarly, during the Kargil war between India and Pakistan in 1998, Prime Minister Atal Bihari Vajpayee (b. 1924), leader of the BJP, gave an exclusive interview to *Dainik Jagran*, which was printed widely in the English press, once again indicating the central role of the newspaper.

Giving its support to a right-wing political ideology greatly helped *Dainik Jagran* to expand, as a wave of support for Hindutva swept the northern Indian heartland. Thus, *Dainik Jagran* rode the rising wave of Hindutva sentiment in the late 1980s and early 1990s through its sensationalist and populist reporting style. However, it would be an oversimplification to attribute the entire success of *Dainik Jagran* merely to its support of Hindutva ideology. As noted above, the newspaper has 37 editions and more than 200 subeditions, which shows its strong appeal to a local audience. It also employs marketing strategies to create a new constituency of readers. The result is that *Dainik Jagran* became an important newspaper catering to a large number of Hindi-speakers in disparate parts of India.

Dainik Bhaskar was first published in 1958 by industrialist Dwarka Prasad Agarwal (b. 1933) as a family business from Bhopal, the capital of the state of Madhya Pradesh. For nearly 40 years the distributorship of the daily newspaper was confined to Madhya Pradesh, but in 1995 it expanded outside the state. In 2009 it is the second most-widely read newspaper in India after *Dainik Jagran,* with an estimated 20.95 million readers. It is the leading newspaper in the states of Madhya Pradesh, Rajasthan, Chandigarh (a Union Territory), and Haryana.

In 1992 *Dainik Bhaskar* became the leading newspaper in Madhya Pradesh. In the wake of the communal riots that broke out in Bhopal following the demolition of the Babri Masjid on December 6, 1992, *Dainik Bhaskar* appealed for communal harmony. Unlike a number of other Hindi newspapers, *Dainik Bhaskar* adopted a liberal and secular approach during the controversy and as a result was able to establish a following among the Muslim population, which is nearly 40 percent of the total population of Bhopal.

In an attempt to expand its base outside of Madhya Pradesh, *Dainik Bhaskar* embarked on an aggressive research and marketing campaign in the mid-1990s. Thus, in October 1995 newspaper executives identified Rajasthan as a potential market, a decision that was viewed as a high-risk venture since one company, Bennett, Coleman and Company, had just shut down the Jaipur edition of *Navbharat Times,* a Hindi newspaper. Moreover, *Rajasthan Patrika* was dominating the newspaper market in Rajasthan, and other Hindi newspapers such as *Rashthradoot* and *Nav Jyoti* had a strong presence in the state. Yet in spite of this market situation, the Agarwal family decided to launch its Rajasthan edition from Jaipur on December 19, 1996. Over the next 14 months a massive survey was conducted in 175,000 households in Jaipur, almost 50 percent of the total population, and 100 percent of the total readership. The survey aimed to understand people's preferences, their reading habits, and their expectations for a newspaper.

These multipronged marketing strategies helped *Dainik Bhaskar* make an entry into the newspaper market in Rajasthan and to surpass *Rajasthan Patrika* as the leading newspaper in the state, a position it had held since 1956. The success fascinated the Bhaskar Group, as it was their first venture outside the state of Madhya Pradesh. This was the first time in the history of the Hindi print media that a publisher employed marketing strategies to develop a new market and sell newspapers like any other consumer good. The success in Jaipur prompted the group to expand to other regions, and *Dainik Bhaskar* now prints 32 separate editions and more than 200 subeditions spread across nine states.

Dainik Bhaskar is also the first Hindi newspaper to start a newspaper for women. In order to provide exclusive coverage of issues of special interest to women, *Women Bhaskar* was launched in December 2007 from Indore, Madhya Pradesh. It is the first daily newspaper designed exclusively for women, and it is distributed along with the main edition of *Dainik Bhaskar*. Its success in Indore prompted the Bhaskar group to start a women's newspaper in Bhopal and in other cities across India.

Another important step in the process of publishing for the local market was the beginning of *Upcountry City Bhaskar,* a four-page weekly pullout that covers lifestyle and other local happenings in the countryside. The publication is targeted at a young readership, including women. As of 2010 this concept had not been tried by any other Hindi newspaper, as "upcountry" is usually considered less desirable for consumer-oriented lifestyles.

Like *Dainik Jagran,* its close competitor, *Dainik Bhaskar* focuses on local news and items of local interest. Of the 20 pages carried in each of its 32 separate editions, only 4 to 5 pages are common to all. Each edition is customized according to its locale and infused with colloquial language and local idioms. While explaining the sources of their publishing model, Girish Agarwal, managing director of the Bhaskar group, remarked to *Business India*, "We have borrowed aggressiveness from the Times group, networking from *Eenadu,* and content from the *Hindu.*" However, the two publishing models that *Dainik Bhaskar* follows are *USA Today* and the *Times of India.*

It is evident that the Bhaskar group is open to learning from and adopting different approaches used by successful newspapers in different countries. Such an approach of investing time, energy, and money in learning the secrets of successful newspapers and adopting their strategies has helped *Dainik Bhaskar* become a great success story in the Indian media market.

Punjab Kesari, a daily newspaper, was started at Jalandhar in 1965, with an initial print order of 1,500 copies. By 1977 the circulation had risen to nearly 72,000 copies per day. During the Emergency of 1975–1977, when the government of Indira Gandhi (1917–1984; prime minister 1966–1977, 1980–1984) imposed heavy censorship over the press, *Punjab Kesari* started encompassing its front page in a color magazine. *Punjab Kesari* thus has the distinction of being the first newspaper in India to use color on its front page. In 1983 *Punjab Kesari* launched an edition from Delhi, and by 1986 it had become the largest-selling Hindi daily in India.

Lala Jagat Narain (1889–1981), the founder of *Punjab Kesari,* was gunned down in September 1981 during the Khalistan insurgency that shook the Punjab during the 1980s. The reason for his murder was the perceived insult that he and his newspaper perpetuated on the sentiments of Sikhs by speaking out against a separate Khalistan. Insurgents also targeted *Punjab Kesari*'s agents and hawkers, and 53 of them were murdered. The newspaper established a "martyr's fund" and raised 42 million rupees from readers as compensation to be paid to the bereaved families. The large amount of money raised was a demonstration of the strong support commanded for the newspaper by its readers.

Punjab Kesari remained a dominant Hindi daily in the 1980s and in the first half of the 1990s. Instead of employing a marketing survey, *Punjab Kesari* utilized its connection with agents and hawkers to understand the preferences and demands of its readers. The result was that it kept changing the type of news it covered and the editorial content of the paper. It was the first Hindi daily newspaper, for example, to focus on offering a strong dose of local news.

However, critics and rivals among the Hindi dailies regard *Punjab Kesari* as the symbol of a declining standard of journalism. *Punjab Kesari* buys stories from the *National Enquirer*—a notorious tabloid widely sold in supermarkets and other outlets in the United States. Though this helped in assuring its initial success, it could not sustain its growth for long. As a result, it has now lost its dominant position in the Hindi newspaper market. The growth story of *Punjab Kesari* also illustrates India's highly competitive newspaper market and the need for a newspaper to adapt to the changing tastes of its readers in order to survive and flourish.

Anandabazar Patrika is an influential Bengali daily published from Kolkata. It was started in 1922 as an evening daily. For many years it has remained the largest-circulated single-edition regional-language daily of India. It has a daily circulation of more than 1 million copies. The readership figure of the newspaper stands at 7.29 million, according to the National Readership Survey of 2006. Despite being the largest-circulated daily, it did not receive significant advertisement until the 1980s. This was because of the perception prevalent among advertisers and advertising agencies that only readers of English newspapers have purchasing power. However, *Anandabazar Patrika* was able to convince the advertisers about the potential purchasing power of regional-language newspaper readers. Today, the rate of advertisement in the paper is highest among all regional-language newspapers.

Like other successful regional-language newspapers, *Anandabazar Patrika* uses simple and colloquial language. However, unlike other regional-language newspapers, which began to publish multiple editions to increase their readership, *Anandabazar Patrika* confined itself to Kolkata and Mumbai. Instead of launching its editions from small towns and rural areas, which would have made it a mass newspaper, *Anandabazar Patrika* is still based in metropolitan cities and mostly read by the highest strata of the society. This strategy of the paper is partly driven by the hope of attracting the biggest advertisers and charging the highest advertising rates.

Dina Thanthi, or *Daily Thanthi*, was founded in 1942 from Madurai, a provincial town in southern Tamil Nadu. It is the most-read Tamil newspaper of India, with 10.38 million readers, according to the National Readership Survey of 2006. The founder of the daily, S. P. Adithanar, was a lawyer trained in Britain. While in Britain, he was inspired by the English tabloid, the *Daily Mirror*, for its ability to reach a mass audience. It was his desire to publish a newspaper in the Tamil language that could reach ordinary people. It is believed that *Daily Thanthi* pioneered the technique of publishing from a number of centers. In the 1940s, Adithanar started editions from Madras, Salem, and Tiruchchirappalli. However, the Salem edition soon failed, while the Tiruchchirappalli edition was paused and restarted in 1954. The publisher used the public bus services to distribute the newspaper throughout the southern Tamil region.

In the past, readers in the far-flung areas away from the publication centers got their newspaper at least a day late. But Adithanar could provide a fresh newspaper to readers every morning in Tamil towns, which proprietors elsewhere in India could not do until 40 years later. It also used photographs extensively at a time when other newspapers found it difficult to do so because of limited technology and resources. *Daily Thanthi's* most notable feature is its emphasis on local news, particularly crimes. The use of colloquial language that resonates with the local society is another important reason for its success.

Daily Thanthi today has 14 editions. It also publishes editions from the neighboring states of Karnataka and Pondicherry to cater to the needs of the Tamil-speaking population in these states.

Eenadu was started in 1974 from Visakhapatnam. It is now the largest-read Telugu daily of India. According to the National Readership Survey of 2006, it has a readership base of 13.8 million, which made it the number three daily of India. *Eenadu* is owned by Ramoji Rao (b. 1936), who is a businessman and media baron. Ramoji Rao and his newspaper played an important role in the creation and success of the Telugu Desam Party, a regional political party in the state of Andhra Pradesh, which challenged the dominance of the Congress Party, a national political party.

Eenadu is believed to have pioneered the strategy of localization that has led to the tremendous growth of Indian-language newspapers since the 1980s. By 1989 *Eenadu* started publishing district editions for small towns in rural Andhra Pradesh. It began to publish an 8-page color tabloid with content tailored for the particular district where it was distributed, which went along with the 12 pages printed on the broadsheet. In order to get local news, *Eenadu* built a network of correspondents in the countryside. If their news was published, they received small sums of money. Telephones were used to send news of immediate importance to the head office. Otherwise, news was sent through the bus services. By localizing the paper, *Eenadu* was able to generate local bases of advertising, which became a major source of revenue. These methods of local news gathering and the creation of local advertising were subsequently followed by other regional-language and Hindi newspapers.

Today *Eenadu* uses such modern technology as the Internet to get news from remote areas. It has continuously invested huge capital to modernize the technology and the processes of news gathering. The success of *Eenadu* also shows the changing nature of Telugu journalism and the importance of associating and highlighting the local society.

Malayala Manorama was started as a four-page weekly newspaper in 1890 from Kottayam, a small town in the princely state of Travancore. It became a daily in 1928. It was also the first joint-stock publishing company of India, founded by Kandathil Varghese Mappillai (1857–1904) in 1888. *Malayala Manorama* was closed in September 1938 when the Travancore government became outraged at political opposition expressed in its columns and banned the newspaper. The editor of the paper, K. C. Mammen Mappillai (1873–1953), Kandathil Varghese Mappillai's nephew who had become editor upon the death of his uncle in 1904, by which time the newspaper was issued biweekly, was jailed and his property was confiscated. The newspaper was closed down after it printed reports of police and military atrocities. Mappillai's jailing showed the influence of the press and its power to mobilize the masses. The newspaper did not resume publication for nine years but finally did so on November 29, 1947, and it soon flourished.

The second edition of the paper was issued in Kozhikode in 1966, and since the early 1970s *Malayala Manorama* has become the leading newspaper in Kerala. Today it is the largest-read Malayalam daily, with 8.4 million readers, and is published from eight centers in Kerala. In 2002 it launched Manorama Online.

TABEREZ AHMED NEYAZI

See also Hindu, The; Hindustan Times; Indian Express; India Today; Media and Telecommunications; *Times of India, The*

Further Reading

Jeffrey, Robin. "Bengali: 'Professional, Somewhat Conservative' and Calcuttan." *Economic and Political Weekly*, 32(1997): 141–144.

Jeffrey, Robin. "Hindi: Taking to the *Punjab Kesari* Line." *Economic and Political Weekly* 32 (1997): 77–83.

Jeffrey, Robin. "Indian-Language Newspapers and Why They Grow." *Economic and Political Weekly* 28 (1993): 2004–2011.

Jeffrey, Robin. *India's Newspaper Revolution: Capitalism, Politics and the Indian-Language Press, 1977–99.* New Delhi: Oxford University Press, 2000.

Jeffrey, Robin. "Telugu: Ingredients of Growth and Failure." *Economic and Political Weekly* 32 (1997): 192–195.

Manorama Online. Accessed April 28, 2011. http://www.manoramaonline.com.

Neyazi, Taberez Ahmed. "Media Convergence and Hindi Newspapers: Changing Institutional and Discursive Dimensions, 1977–2007." PhD dissertation, National University of Singapore, 2009.

Sinha, Piyush Kumar, and Kunjesh Pariher. "Dainik Bhaskar—Jaipur." *Asian Case Research Journal* 6 (2002): 167–204.

Stahlberg, Per. *Lucknow Daily: How a Hindi Newspaper Constructs Society.* Stockholm: Stockholm Studies in Social Anthropology, 2002.

✦ NIZARI ISMAILIS

The Nizari Ismailis (generally known as the Ismailis) are a minority Shia Muslim community that resides in 25 different countries around the world, including India. The Ismailis are an ethnically, culturally, and linguistically diverse community united by their allegiance to their imam (spiritual leader) Prince Karim Aga Khan IV (b. 1936; Aga Khan 1957–), who is their 49th hereditary imam and a direct descendant of the Prophet Muhammad through Ali (598–661; caliph 656–661), who was the first imam and the Prophet's cousin and son-in-law, and through Ali's wife, Fatima (ca. 605–632), the daughter of the Prophet.

Ismaili Muslims hold Indian national flags and Ismaili religious flags as they wait to welcome their spiritual leader, Aga Khan IV in Hyderabad, Andhra Pradesh, May 2008. (AP Photo/ Mahesh Kumar)

Although they are officially known as the Shia Imami Ismaili Muslims, in India they are often referred to as Khojas or Aga Khanis. The term *khoja* is derived from the Persian *khwaja*, meaning "lord, master, or honorable person." Prior to their conversion the Nizari Ismailis of the Indian subcontinent were members of the Hindu Lohana caste and were addressed by the Hindu title of *thakur* (master). The term *khoja*, therefore, was a replacement for *thakur*. The Indian Ismailis are not concentrated in one part of India; rather, they reside in various states throughout India. The majority of Indian Ismailis are of Gujarati ancestry and migrated to other Indian states in the late 19th century due to deteriorating conditions in Gujarat.

Islam consists of two principal sects, the Shia and the Sunni, which both bear witness that there is only one God and that Muhammad is the final Messenger of God. A schism in the Islamic community occurred upon the death of the Prophet. The community was in need of a leader, but as Muhammad was the seal of the prophets, another prophet could not succeed him. A group of prominent Muslims took the matter into their own hands and chose Abu Bakr (ca. 573–634; caliph 632–634), a close companion of the Prophet and one of the earliest converts to Islam, to be the successor of the Messenger of God. The institution of the caliphate in Islam was thus established. In the meantime, a small group of Muslims (later known as the Shia) held that shortly before his death the Prophet had designated his cousin and son-in-law, Ali, as his successor and the imam.

The caliph, in Sunni understanding, was primarily a political leader who commanded armies, protected Islam, and governed following the Quran and the examples of the Prophet. He was not a religious leader and did not have supreme authority to interpret revelation. The doctrine of Imama in the Shia tradition states that the institution of Imamate is bestowed on the descendants of Ali and Fatima, the Prophet's daughter, through *nass*, or divine designation. The role of the imam is to guide his followers in temporal and spiritual matters, to preserve the message of the Quran, and to ensure it is interpreted according to the changing times.

The death of the fifth imam, Jafar al-Sadiq (702–765), resulted in the first major split among the Shia. A small minority, the Ismailis, accepted his elder son, Ismail (ca. 721–755), as his successor. The majority, the Ithna'ashariyya (Twelvers), accepted his younger son, Musa al-Kazim (745–799), as the next imam. The Ithna'ashariyya are the largest Shia group and are so called because of their conviction that their 12th imam went into concealment in the ninth century and that his reappearance is still being awaited. While the majority of sources relate that Ismail died before his father, the Ismailis denied this notion and claimed that the announcement of Ismail's death was a strategy to protect Ismail from the Abbasids, the third dynasty in Islam, which ruled 749–1258. Soon after the recognition of Musa al-Kazim as imam by the majority, the Ismaili imams went into hiding to avoid Abbasid persecution and initiated the *dawr al-satr*, or period of concealment. During this period the Ismaili *dawa* (missionary) movement flourished in Iraq, Persia, eastern Arabia, and Sindh. In 883 the *dawa* movement was initiated in the Indian subcontinent.

The *dawr al-satr* ended with the establishment of the Fatimid caliphate in North Africa in 909, and in 973 the caliphate's headquarters moved to Cairo. During the Fatimid caliphate (909–1171) there was a further split among the Ismailis after the death of the 18th imam, al-Mustansir I, in 1094. This resulted in the formation of those that accepted his elder son, Nizar (1045–1097, imam 1095–1097), as the succeeding imam, known as the Nizari Ismailis, and those who accepted his younger son, Mustali (imam 1094–1101), known as the Mustalian Ismailis. The Fatimid caliphate continued under the leadership of the Mustali Ismaili imams. In India the Mustalian Ismailis, popularly known as Bohras, are primarily found in Gujarat and Mumbai. The term *bohra* is derived from the Gujarati *vohorvu*, meaning "to trade." It is held, therefore, that either the Bohras were originally a trading community or that they were converted to Mustalian Ismailism from the Hindu Vohra caste. The Mustalian Ismailis believe that their final imam is in occultation, and they are waiting for his emergence. For the second time in their history, in about 1095, the Nizari Ismaili imams were forced to conceal their identity, this time in Persia for nearly 70 years. It was not until 1162 that the 23rd imam, Hasan II (imam 1162–1166), openly manifested himself as the imam and resumed his position as head of state and community. Hasan II and his successors ruled at the fortress of Alamut in the Persian Alburz Mountains until the Mongols invaded in 1256. In the late Alamut period the Nizari Ismaili leadership made extensive efforts to introduce the *dawa* activities into the Indian subcontinent.

For at least two centuries after the fall of Alamut, the Nizari imams lived covertly in predominantly Sunni Persia and were inaccessible to their followers. The Nizari Ismailis who survived the Mongol invasion escaped to Nizari Ismaili communities in Afghanistan, Central Asia, and Sindh, where they were guided by local *dais* (missionaries), *pirs* (preacher-saints), or *shaykhs*, who claimed access to the Nizari imams in Persia. In order to escape persecution, the Nizari Ismailis adopted the practice of *taqiyya*, or dissimulation and secrecy, often disguising themselves as Sufis (Muslim mystics), Twelver Shias, Sunnis, or Hindus, as it befitted the environment around them.

After the fall of Alamut, Sufi teachings, terminology, and ideas permeated into Persian Nizari Ismailism. At the same time, the Sufis began to use Nizari Ismaili doctrines. Due to this fusion, the Persian Nizari Ismailis began to adopt external Sufi ways of life. The Nizari Ismaili imams, still living covertly, presented themselves to outsiders as Sufi masters or *pirs*, and their followers adopted the title of *murids*, or disciples. The imams also adopted Sufi names. This practice was initiated by the 32nd imam, Mustansir Billah II (1029–1094; imam 1036–1094), who took on the name of Shah Qalandar. The Persian Nizari Ismailis concealed themselves under the guise of Sufism, and although they did not formally affiliate with any one Sufi *tariqa*, or order, by this time they appeared as any other Sufi *tariqa*.

During the 13th century mysticism flourished from Anatolia and Egypt to Delhi, and Persian literature thrived in India as much as in Persia. At the same time, the fervor of Sufism reached the Indian subcontinent, which saw the expansion of various Sufi schools. Alongside the rise of Sufism, the Indian subcontinent was in the midst of another transformation, the rise of the Bhakti tradition, particularly in northern India. Tradition asserts that the Ismaili imams sent *pirs* from Persia to the Indian subcontinent in the first half of the 13th century to initiate the *dawa*.

The *pirs* composed *ginans* (devotional songs) in local languages, including Gujarati, Kacchi, Sindhi, Siraiki (or Multani), Punjabi, Hindi, and Urdu, with terminology borrowed from Sanskrit, Arabic, and Persian. In addition to using vernacular languages, the *pirs* also appropriated widespread doctrines. Similar to medieval Indian devotional poetry, the *ginans* were transmitted orally. The earliest-known manuscript, dated to the 16th century, indicates that it may have been around this time that the *ginans* were first translated from an oral into a written tradition. Today the *ginans* are an integral part of the congregational worship of the Ismailis of South Asian ancestry in India, as well as in other parts of the world.

According to Ismaili tradition, the earliest *pir* to be sent to India by the imams was Satgur Nur. He is said to have lived sometime between the late 11th and early 12th centuries and was mainly active in Patan, Gujarat. He is well known for having converted the king of Gujarat, Siddharaja Jayasinha, along with all the residents of Patan, which was renamed Pirna Patan (the *pir*'s city). Satgur Nur's tomb is located in Nawsari, near Surat. The second major *pir* in India was Shams, who was primarily active in Uch and Multan. His dates are variously given as the early 12th century to the 14th century. Shams portrayed himself to be a Hindu *yogi* or wandering *dervish* in order to blend into his environment. Shams's mausoleum can be found in Multan. The next major *pir*, Sadr al-Din, was the great-grandson of Shams, and the largest number of *ginans* are attributed to him. He lived during the latter part of the 14th and early 15th century. Although his headquarters was in Uch, his work reached Sindh, the Punjab, Kutch, and Kathiawad. Sadr al-Din bestowed the title of Khoja on the Ismailis in India. He is also credited with the establishment of the first *jamaatkhana* (place of worship) in Kotdi, Sindh. Today, there are approximately 337 *jamaatkhanas* in India. In addition, Sadr al-Din is said to be the creator of the Khojki script, which was used exclusively by the Ismailis until the late 1960s to record religious literature, perhaps in order to deter hostility from those who were adverse to Ismaili practices and doctrine; it is no longer a living script. The death of Sadr al-Din took place anywhere between the late 14th and early 15th century. His shrine is located near Uch. Sadr al-Din was succeeded by his son Hasan al-Kabir al-Din, who maintained Uch as his center. Born in Uch in the 15th century, he was the first *pir* to be born in India. Hasan al-Kabir al-Din died in the latter part of the 15th century. His tomb lies outside Uch and is known locally as Hasan Darya.

The 46th Ismaili imam, Hasan Ali Shah (1804–1881), who received the honorific title of Aga Khan ("lord"), was the first of the Nizari Ismaili imams to migrate from Persia to the Indian subcontinent in 1842. In time he set up residences in Mumbai, Pune, and Bangalore. His son and successor, Aqa Ali Shah (1830–1885), Aga Khan II, in his brief Imamate of four years (1881–1885) and in his capacity as president of the Muhammadan National Association, promoted a system of quality education and social welfare for the benefit of all Indian Muslims. He was also appointed to the Bombay Legislative Council. Aga Khan II's son, Sultan Muhammad Shah al-Husayni (1877–1957), Aga Khan III, succeeded him in 1885 and continued to put reforms into place for the betterment of the Nizari Ismailis. He frequently traveled to Europe, where he befriended British royalty and other government officials. He was also an active participant in Indian politics and was part of the movement that eventually led to independence from British colonial rule. He was also entirely committed to the modernization of the Ismaili community and ensured that high-quality schools and hospitals were established for the benefit of all, regardless of ethnicity, gender, or religion. Aga Khan III was succeeded by his grandson, Prince Karim Aga Khan IV (b. 1936; Aga Khan 1957–), who is the present imam of the Ismailis. In an effort to continue the modernization policies, and to ensure improving socioeconomic and educational conditions, as well as access to primary health care, he founded the Aga Khan Foundation in 1967. As the foundation's work expanded into the three main areas of economic development, social development, and culture, the Aga Khan Development Network (AKDN) was established. AKDN is a system of numerous development agencies that operate mainly in Asia and Africa. In July 2007 Aga Khan IV celebrated his Golden Jubilee, marking 50 years of being the imam of the Ismaili community.

SHARMINA MAWANI AND ANJOOM MUKADAM

See also Islam; Religion

Further Reading

Asani, Ali S. *Ecstasy and Enlightenment: The Ismaili Devotional Literature of South Asia.* London: I. B. Tauris, 2002.

Bearman, P., et al., eds. *Encyclopaedia of Islam.* 2nd ed. Leiden: Brill, 2009.

Daftary, Farhad. *The Ismailis: Their History and Doctrine.* Cambridge: Cambridge University Press, 2007.

Daftary, Farhad. *A Short History of the Ismailis: Traditions of a Muslim Community,* Edinburgh, UK: Edinburgh University Press, 1998.

Esmail, Aziz. *A Scent of Sandalwood: Indo-Ismaili Religious Lyrics (Ginans),* vol. 1. Surrey: Curzon, 2002.

Nanji, Azim. "Ismailism." In *Islamic Spirituality: Foundation,* edited by Seyyed Hossein Nasr, 179–198. London: Routledge and Kegan Paul, 1987.

Nanji, Azim. *The Nizari Ismaili Tradition in the Indo-Pakistan Subcontinent.* New York: Caravan Books, 1978.

Shackle, Christopher, and Zawahir Moir. *Ismaili Hymns from South Asia: An Introduction to the Ginans.* London: School of Oriental and African Studies, University of London, 1992.

✦ NONGOVERNMENTAL ORGANIZATIONS

The nongovernmental organizations (NGOs) sector in India represents a vibrant civil society. While the evolution of this sector has been a slow process, it now plays an important role in development and public policy making. The inability of the state to meet the needs of the people has led either to the cooption of voluntary groups, which have been delegated power to perform certain functions, or to the rise of groups that have assumed an advocacy or activist role to change public policy. This grassroots connection and social networking with the community in the social services sector has made NGOs an important yet subordinate ally in the public policy process, and they have been slowly acknowledged as an important agency of social polity.

The World Bank and other agencies estimate that about 2 million NGOs are working in India, and 34,000 of them are classified on the basis of geography and activity: 53 percent are rural based, 47 percent are urban based, 49.6 percent are unregistered, 80 percent are corporate and people financed, 1.3 percent are government financed, and 7 percent are funded by global capital. Most NGOs are small operations; volunteers or a few part-time employees run about three-fourths of them. Since these organizations lack money to support themselves, the government allocates funds. Many funds also come from foreign groups and foundations. This money is regulated by the Foreign Contribution Regulation Act (FCRA) of 1976 under the Ministry of Home Affairs. NGOs must be registered as trusts or societies, or as private, limited, nonprofit companies under Section 25 of the Indian Companies Act, 1956. Section 2(15) of the Income Tax Act gives them tax exemption.

The rise of the NGO sector began with the establishment of the traditional voluntary service sector before independence in the form of Hindu charitable organizations and Christian missionaries. The former service-oriented organizations worked for the welfare of Hindu communities, and the latter provided educational opportunities and health care to the marginalized poor and tribes, who were also encouraged to convert to Christianity. These voluntary organizations performed a great role in the social and political transformation of the country. In postindependence India, many Gandhians established voluntary agencies to work closely with governmental programs on social and economical issues. The Gandhian values of *khadi* (homespun cloth) and propagation of *swadeshi* (self-rule) were facilitated by these organizations. They not only helped people fight for freedom but also spread the message of Mahatma Mohandas Karamchand Gandhi (1869–1948) among the rural poor in order to usher in a new era of self-sufficiency and self-reliance in the villages. These agencies worked with the communities in village and rural-development programs, cooperative agencies, and small handicraft industries. In addition, they organized cooperatives for market products and worked for adult education and the eradication of illiteracy.

By the 1960s it became clear that government programs could not solve the problems of the poor. To tackle major issues of social justice, inequality, caste, and class, NGO groups emerged and started to support and advocate the cause of the underprivileged. This evolved into NGOs going into the rural areas. As a result, NGOs became a familiar sight in the countryside.

In the beginning, funds were scarce as no institutional money was available, and the NGOs relied upon volunteerism. Soon the role of NGOs and their importance in rural development was recognized, and the central government felt the need to financially support these organizations in both urban and rural areas. This did not happen, however, until the 1980s. It was under the Sixth Five-Year Plan (1980–1985) that the government identified new areas in which NGOs could be involved, and they included renewable energy, environmental protection and sustainable development, family welfare, health and nutrition, education, water management, social welfare programs and tribal development, and disaster management. This was just the beginning. In the following Five-Year Plans, the government engaged the NGOs more actively, and these groups were expected to show how village and indigenous resources could be used and how human resources, rural skills, and local knowledge could be used in development.

Because of their interaction with local people, NGOs can be very effective in bringing change, and a network of NGOs has been created. These organizations also work as a go-between, negotiating between the state and the people. By the early 1980s the term NGO became popular, encouraging a new NGO era. Although NGOs were traditionally voluntary, their professional dimension was a later development. Many NGO groups have taken an alternative "social action" approach by politicizing the issue of poverty, directly challenging many of the social programs established by the government. NGOs in the areas of the environment, health, education, peace, human rights, consumer rights, and women's rights have shown how effective they can be in ushering in social and political change.

NGOs can be divided into the following three sectors: (i) operational NGOs, whose primary purpose is the design and implementation of development-related projects; (ii) advocacy

NGOs, whose primary purpose is to defend or promote a specific cause and who seek to influence policies and practices; and (iii) NGOs that engage in both operational and advocacy activities.

Operational NGOs are those that work in the area of development and empowerment projects, such as providing water and sanitation, building taps or pumps in rural villages, and training workers for skills that make them self-reliant and raise them out of poverty. Examples range from the Self Employed Women's Association (SEWA) to Sulabh International. SEWA has worked in the area of women's empowerment and has helped women become self-reliant. Sulabh International spearheaded a movement to build latrines in rural and urban communities where open fecal matter created health and sanitation problems.

Since the 1980s, many NGO groups across the country have moved in the direction of functioning as operational NGOs with the help of donor agencies, government funds, and microcredit organizations that have politicized the issue of poverty. Another critical area where operational NGOs have worked is in the prevention of HIV/AIDS and disaster management. India suffers from floods and droughts every year, and many NGOs are pressed into service during their aftermath. The NGO sector, in fact, has always been in the forefront of providing recovery, relief, and rehabilitation after natural calamities and disasters. One example was the NGOs' enormous response in the aftermath of the 2004 Indian Ocean tsunami. These actions of the NGO sector have compelled the government to seek assistance from NGO groups in developing, coordinating, and implementing new health and disaster management policies.

Another area where operational NGOs have assumed importance is in conservation and maintaining good water quality and biodiversity. Under the pressures of rapid industrialization, a rapid increase in population, and anthropogenic activities, biodiversity, human life, and ecological resolve are threatened. Both surface and groundwater resources are deteriorating and polluted with chemicals and other hazardous agents. Supplying clean drinking water, in fact, is one of the greatest challenges in the world today. There are grave threats to biodiversity, and animal species are dying and becoming extinct each day. The Center for Science and Environment, Eco Friends, Tarun Bharat Sangh, and World Wild Life Fund for Nature are NGOs that operate in these areas. They are trying to bring about awareness and induce people to take up measures for the protection of nature and the environment. Saving turtles, crocodiles, tigers, deer, lions, salmon, tree ferns, and many other species of plants and animals form their agenda.

Advocacy and activist NGOs are those that lobby for a cause and defend certain rights of the people that are being violated by government policies. They do not function in project management and development but mainly work toward raising awareness of an issue through protests, public rallies, and the media. Many of the recent NGO protests have been related to large dam and development projects where the government has left many people displaced without an adequate rehabilitation policy. There have also been movements for the protection of land and forests, like the Bhoodan Movement and Chipko Andolan. More recently, with the rise of neoliberalism and globalization, large corporations have moved in to control the water supply. Several organizations, like the Plachimada in Kerala, the Research Foundation for Science Technology and Ecology, and the Paani Morcha in Delhi, have taken up the cause against the backdoor privatization of water. One of the most successful social movements was the Narmada Bachao Andolan (NBA) movement, which fought for the rights of tribal people displaced by the large Sardar Sarovar Dam being built across the Narmada River near Navagam, Gujerat. Strong interventions by the NBA and other NGOs have forced the government to take up these issues more seriously and draft a rehabilitation policy. The NGO interventions in these issues has remained very strong, and, in some cases, they have forced a change in government policy and planning.

NGOs have also done pioneering work in the area of women's rights. In a largely traditional society like India's, women have been subject to discrimination, torture, dowry deaths, and multiple forms and contexts of domination. The women's movement began in the 1970s and has since made great strides in the protection of women's rights, with special reference to discrimination at work and at home and to unequal wages and domestic labor. The most important success of this movement was a 33 percent reservation for women in the Panchayats—the local-level bodies for village administration. This demand was further taken to Parliament, and in March 2010 the Rajya Sabha passed a bill for a 33 percent reservation for women in Parliament and in state legislatures. It still, however, awaits passage in the lower house, the Lok Sabha.

NGOs have their own strengths and weaknesses. Some of the major strengths have been their direct networking with local people. Given their work in the hinterland, they possess a much better sense of the issues on the ground than do the politicians hundreds of miles away; their strong field-based experiences can be incorporated into government policies. They are participatory in their approach and engage with the community and the state, forming a link between the two. The government's enactment of the right to information has opened new opportunities for NGOs in government planning and operations. The NGO Parivartan used this right of information to expose the World Bank's intervention in the tendering process for a water-distribution plant.

Most NGOs lack the visibility and importance that should be accorded to organizations of this nature. They are not central to the policy-making process and are generally successful mainly in small-scale interventions. In spite of their contributions, NGOs are limited in their financial and institutional capacity. In some cases an NGO may have between 2 and 5 employees; estimates are that about 5 percent have between 6 and 10 employees, and only about 8.5 percent (1 in every 12) NGOs employ more than 10 people. While funds are a constant source of concern, the accountability of these funds is also a serious issue. Some NGO workers have started regarding their advocacy as a livelihood rather than a social commitment. In many cases, the search for funds induces them to work for funding agencies. Many NGOs are searching for financial stability lest they perish in the absence of funds. In spite of their low levels of sustainability, there is an upsurge in the number of NGOs, and the sector has assumed a strong base. Their role as agents of social change has become exceedingly important. The NGO culture has changed from volunteerism into professionalism, but it still represents a vibrant civil society and citizens' democracy in action.

VANDANA ASTHANA

See also Asian Development Bank; Central Banking, Development Aspects; Economy; Environment; Feminism; Financial Institutions, Development; World Bank, Relations with

Further Reading

Kilby, P. *NGOs in India: The Challenges of Empowerment and Accountability*. London: Routledge, 2010.

Sooryamoorthy, R., and K. D. Gangrade. *NGOs in India: A Cross-Sectional Study*. Westport, CT: Greenwood, 2001.

Sundar, P. *Foreign Aid for Indian NGOs: Problems and Solutions*. London: Routledge, 2010.

✦ NONRESIDENT INDIANS AND PERSONS OF INDIAN ORIGIN

Nonresident Indian (NRI), or *Pravasi Bharatiya*, is the term used for an individual who was born in India and has Indian citizenship but who lives abroad. The term can be used for an Indian citizen who has taken up employment or is studying overseas but who aims to return to India. Every year, on January 7–9, the government recognizes the contributions made by NRIs at an event known as *Pravasi Bharatiya Divas* (Nonresident Indian Day). The dates are significant, as January 9, 1915, is the date that Mahatma Mohandas Karamchand Gandhi (1869–1948) returned to India from South Africa. The event was established in 2003. It is sponsored by the Ministry of Overseas Indian Affairs (MOIA) and the Federation of Indian Chambers of Commerce and Industry (FICCI), and NRIs who have made a significant contribution in their field or profession are recognized. Since 2006 there has been a branch of the *Pravasi Bharatiya Divas* in Europe.

The term NRI is often replaced by Person of Indian Origin (PIO) as people become citizens in their newly adopted countries. There are several other terms in addition to PIO, including expatriate Indian, overseas Indian, member of the Indian diaspora, and *pardesi*. In order to obtain PIO status one must apply for a PIO card, show evidence of a link to India, and pay a fee. The term PIO is an official status given by the government to those foreign nationals (with the exception of those living in Bangladesh and Pakistan) who have held an Indian passport, can trace their ancestry to India up to their great-grandparents, or are the spouse of a citizen of India or PIO. The benefits of having a PIO card include visa-free entry into India during the period of validity of the PIO card, exemption from registering with the authorities if the stay in India is less than six months, and the right to acquire, hold, transfer, and dispose of immovable properties in India, except for agricultural or plantation property. PIO cardholders are not, however, allowed to vote in Indian elections.

SHARMINA MAWANI AND ANJOOM MUKADAM

See also Diaspora, Indian; Diaspora in the United Kingdom; Diaspora in the United States

Further Reading
Balaram, P. "The Rise of the Non-Resident Indian." *Current Science* 85(10) (2003): 1398.

✦ NORTHEASTERN STATES

Spread over an area of 158,500 square miles, the northeastern states (NES) of India, commonly referred to as northeastern India, comprise the seven states of Arunachal Pradesh, Assam, Manipur, Meghalaya, Mizoram, Nagaland, and Tripura. Tenuously linked with the Indian mainland by a narrow stretch of land 13 miles in width, the region remained, as a result of British colonial policy, relatively isolated, physically and culturally, until 1950, a trend that allowed an internal homogeneity of sorts to develop.

The region is a combination of lowlands on the one hand, and of plateaus, hills, and mountains on the other, in a 3:7 ratio. Elevation varies from 96 to 426 feet in the former, and from 2,622 to 9,840 feet in most parts of the latter. Topography varies sharply along the northern reaches of Arunachal Pradesh, where elevation ranges from 13,000 to 26,082 feet. In the remaining parts of the region, topographic variation, and also elevation, is much lower. In the Meghalaya-Karbi plateau, the elevation ranges from 3,937 to 5,577 feet in general, barring the Shillong peak that reaches 6,433 feet; similar differences in relative relief along the eastern hills are far lower than the northern parts of Arunachal.

The climate is a blend of cold, humid monsoon in areas above the 6,500-foot contour line; wet subtropical in southern stretches of Arunachal, western Nagaland, Mizoram, and Manipur; and humid mesothermal monsoonal in the valley and plateau areas. Rainfall, copious throughout the region, is torrential in stretches like the Cherrapunji-Mawsynram-Pnursula belt of southern Meghalaya bordering Bangladesh; and in Cherrapunji more than 354 inches annually is a routine occurrence. In the rest of the region, average annual precipitation ranges from 39 inches to more than 157 inches, with about 60 percent being concentrated during the monsoon season of June to October.

Against such a backdrop, luxuriant tropical vegetation ranging from alpine, subtropical pine, and montane to tropical wet evergreen, semi-evergreen, and moist deciduous thrives, making the territory a global biodiversity hotspot. Forests are central to the region in terms of its economy and timber trade, tourism, and wildlife resorts, and shifting cultivation in the hill areas is closely interwoven with the region's forest wealth. The NES accounts for more than a quarter of India's area under forest, while covering only 7.7 percent of the country's total geographical area.

For the region as a whole, the forest cover stood at 54 percent of the total area in 1993 and increased to 66 percent in 2005, although doubts have been expressed over official data. Official reports state that forest cover varies between 80.9 percent (of the total geographical area) in Arunachal Pradesh, to 35 percent in Assam, with the other states placed between 76 percent in Manipur to 88.6 percent in Mizoram.

However, only 6.8 percent of forests in the region belong to the very dense category, and many protected areas are largely bereft of forest cover. Forest areas under state control are of three types: National Parks (NP), Wildlife Sanctuaries (WLS), and Reserved Forests (RF), in order of declining levels of protective enforcement and increasing levels of encroachment, settlement, and illegal logging. During 1993, 33.7 percent of the forest area was under RF, 14 percent was under NPs and WLSs, and the lion's share of 59.7 percent was under the "unclassified" category, the latter being almost entirely under community control in the hill areas, where autonomous councils administer the forest areas. In such community-owned areas, tribal communities decide matters such as the area to be brought under cultivation or the quantity of bamboo to be extracted for sale at paper mills; in some instances communities revere certain forests as sacred groves (SGs) that are often quite well preserved. Among the numerous community-protected SGs, the Mawphlang grove north of Shillong has been particularly well preserved for several generations.

Several Protected Areas (PAs), such as NPs, WLSs, and RFs, dot the landscape. With the opening up of the region with the coming of the British in the early 19th century and the years following the Treaty of Yandaboo in 1826, the forest wealth declined gradually and consistently. PAs today remain the last bastion for many of the region's rich flora and fauna species. The NPs in particular attract many domestic and international tourists, with the Kaziranga and Manas NPs being well-known tourist destinations. The former is a World Heritage Site and is rated as a conservation success story. It boasts of several species, such as the great one-horned rhinoceros, Indian tiger, wild Asiatic water buffalo, and swamp deer.

The population composition of the NES is marked by a bewildering ethnic diversity unparalleled elsewhere in India and perhaps by few corners of the world. Although at first glance seven states based on linguistic differences seem to portray a fair degree of ethnic homogeneity, the truth is that within individual states marked ethnic diversities flourish. Thus, in Nagaland more than 20 major tribes each speak different dialects, whereas in excess of 200 tribes exist in Arunachal Pradesh. In certain pockets of Assam bordering the other states, tribes such as the Hmars, the Kukis, the Paites, the Zemi Nagas, and the Dimasas exist side by side. The inaccessibility of the area, prompted by a difficult terrain, hindered communication, and spatial interaction and intermingling in the recent past have allowed diverse cultural groups to flourish.

However such ethnic diversities have not always meant peaceful coexistence, and interethnic rivals fighting over few economic resources have often been the region's bane, with the result that ethnic conflict has claimed many lives. Conflict-induced displacement in different corners of the NES at different points of time has been a frequent occurrence. In Assam's

Kokrajhar District, it is estimated that in excess of 250,000 persons were displaced as Internally Displaced Persons (IDPs) following conflicts between the Boros and the Santhals from 1996 to 1998. While the Boros are a plains tribe that inhabits large areas of Assam on the north bank of the Brahmaputra River, the Santhals were imported from the Chota Nagpur Plateau areas (present-day Jharkhand) during the 19th century to work the tea plantations of Assam.

In recent decades conflicts have not infrequently occurred between indigenous tribes, the Assamese, and cross-border international immigrants. The porous international border has allowed large numbers of undocumented illegal migrants to enter the NES, and Assam in particular. The Supreme Court in a 2005 judgment termed the waves of illegal migration flows as demographic aggression. However, since there are a slew of contentious issues at stake, very little has been achieved to resolve the issue.

The NES has a population density of 93 persons per square mile, less than half the 194 persons per square mile density in India as a whole. There are, however, sharp contrasts in density within the seven states. Assam and Tripura have densities above 186 persons per square mile, compared to 8 and 24 persons per square mile in Arunachal Pradesh and Mizoram respectively. The states of Manipur, Meghalaya, and Nagaland possess a density of around 60. The population densities of the NES reflect the nature of the terrain and the availability of valley land.

In terms of size, the states in descending order are Arunachal Pradesh (52,035 square miles), Assam (48,739 square miles), Meghalaya (13,936 square miles), Manipur (13,873 square miles), Mizoram (13,720 square miles), Nagaland (10,301 square miles), and Tripura (6,515 square miles). In terms of population size, the states in descending order are Assam, Tripura, Meghalaya, Manipur, Nagaland, Arunachal Pradesh, and Mizoram.

Although it has a low-density tract in comparison to the Indian average, the NES does not lag behind the country's aggregate in terms of the rate of population growth. On the contrary, the NES recorded a decadal population growth rate of 21.86 percent to that of 21.54 percent recorded by India as a whole. All the states, barring Assam and Tripura, grew faster than the average Indian growth rate during 1991–2001. Nagaland, with a growth rate of 64.46 percent, recorded the highest growth rate among all the states during the past decade.

In spite of this rapid growth during 1991–2001, northeastern India remains more rural than any other part of India. The proportion of urban population at 18.08 percent is considerably lower then the 27.82 percent norm in 2001. Interestingly, the relatively larger demographic states of Assam and Tripura had lower urban populations of 12.9 and 17 percent respectively than did their demographically smaller neighboring states.

In terms of sex ratio (the number of females per 1,000 males), the NES with 937 females was very similar to the national average of 933 females. Within the NES, Manipur, Meghalaya, and Tripura had relatively better sex ratios, with 978, 972, and 948 respectively. Among these, Meghalaya follows a matrilineal system, and the status of women in society is very high. This is often remarked upon when female literacy rates are considered.

Agriculture is the economic mainstay of the NES. Generally, subsistence agriculture prevails, although there are marked differences between lowland and highland areas. In the lowland areas wet rice (paddy) cultivation is the norm, and most areas are dependent on the monsoon rains rather than on irrigation. Productivity is not high, although yield levels have improved in recent years. The spread of modern agricultural techniques has been slow, with the mechanization of farms being the exception rather than the rule. However, changes such as cultivation of more than a single paddy crop, the use of high-yielding varieties of seeds, and the use of fertilizers have crept in. Agricultural operations, however, are often disrupted by several waves of floods that burst the banks of the large rivers, the Brahmaputra and the Barak. Although floods damage crops, and crop losses mount to millions of rupees annually, the silt carried and deposited by the annual floodwaters serves to enhance the soil fertility of the alluvial plains. The Brahmaputra flows through the midline of the length of the valley, and its floodwaters extend as broad swaths on its north and south banks. Although much of the valley land is annually replenished by silt, bank erosion caused by the river is an adverse spin off concomitant to flooding.

Agricultural operations in the lowlands thrive year after year with minimal technological input. The floodwaters, coupled with abundant rainfall, ensure that in spite of limited irrigation, satisfactory crop yields are maintained. The main crops, in addition to rice, are jute, tea, rubber, cotton, oilseeds, sugarcane, and potatoes. Fruits include oranges, bananas, grapes, pineapples, passion fruit, areca nuts, coconuts, guavas, mangos, jackfruit, and citrus fruits. In certain localities a wide array of medicinal plants and rare orchids are found.

In the highland areas, shifting cultivation (locally known as *jhum*) is practiced. A diverse range of crops are cultivated in the *jhum* areas. Sometimes 30–40 different crops are cultivated in the same *jhum* plot. Apart from serving to meet the subsistence requirements of the families dependent on *jhum*, growing a multiple mix of crops helps protect these farmers and their families from crop failure and crop-specific pest attacks. As with shifting cultivation in the uplands of Southeast Asia, *jhum* involves a shifting of plots rather than a rotation of crops. This is known as the *jhum* cycle and varies between 2 and 5 years across different areas in the region. In general, there has been a sharp reduction in the *jhum* cycle, and this has rendered the *jhum* system less sustainable, since a longer cycle and longer fallow periods allow for natural regeneration of soil fertility. Compared to the 10- to 20-year cycles in the past, current short cycles, on account of growing population and increased demands on land, have led to a reduction in the viability of the practice and an increase in its deleterious environmental effects. It has been alleged that *jhum* increases loss and aggravates flooding in downstream areas.

Jhum is not merely a method of cultivation in the upland areas of northeastern India. *Jhumming* has several rituals and traditions attached to it. Many of these traditions have been passed down the generations. Symbolic rituals include the sacrifice of chickens to aid in plot selection and in the prediction of the quality of the harvest, and the offering of prayers to appease spirits and ward off evil. Harvest operations, which are carried out using human power, are often a community affair marked by much gaiety and camaraderie. Partaking of rice beer and community feasting often mark such occasions and are a part and parcel of the *jhum* economy. While the use of draft animals, either a pair of cows or buffaloes, to plow the land is the norm in lowland agriculture, in contrast, minimal tools and a primitive dibbling stick and seeds sown using the broadcast method are standard practice. However, there are exceptions, and in certain areas, Nagaland in particular, an intricate system of terraced hillslopes is used to cultivate paddies in the absence of level land. Elsewhere in the Aratani plateau, near Ziro in Arunachal Pradesh, a unique indigenous system of irrigation developed over several generations transfers water from one rice field to another.

Beyond subsistence agriculture is the tea plantation economy in Assam. Initiated by the British, the Assam tea plantations continue to be a profitable venture. One of the effects has been the mushrooming of small tea growers in Assam as well as in the other nearby states. Small growers make use of the factories in larger tea gardens to process their tea leaves, since economies of scale inhibit them from making investments in factories and the machinery involved. To handle the tea output the Gauhati Tea Auction Center (GTAC) was set up in 1970 at Guwahati. Currently the GTAC is the largest auction center in the world in terms of the amount of crush, tear, and curl tea (black tea) handled. The method of processing black tea is also known as cut, twist, and curl.

The NES exhibit lower levels of development compared to the rest of India. The NES's contribution to the country's total industrial output is less than 2 percent. In terms of agriculture, only nominal amounts of surplus are generated, and the bulk of production remains confined to meeting subsistence requirements. To counter this, planning attempts have sought to boost less-developed areas like northeastern India. Special considerations have been given to the region in three ways: through the transfer of resources under planning assistance, through transfer of revenue resources, and by way of financial-institution investments in central public-sector undertakings (CPSU).

Under various Five-Year Plans, through the allocation of funds, a balanced regional development was attempted. From the Fourth Plan (1974–1978) onward, concerted efforts to boost the less-developed NES were made. For the developed states, 30 percent of plan assistance was provided in the form of grants and 70 percent in the form of loans, whereas for the NES the breakdown was 90 percent as grants and 10 percent as loans. Preferential treatment has been given in allocating funds to certain states in the NES, termed Special Category States (SCS), and these states were given better allocation of funds vis-à-vis the average. However, considering the low base level of development, such preferential treatment did not translate to improved levels of development and the amelioration of regional disparities. The Shukla Committee Report observed that in the infrastructure sector alone a staggering investment to the tune of 180 billion rupees (1 U.S. dollar = 50 rupees) was needed to bring the NES to par with the rest of India.

Apart from resource transfer under the Five-Year Plans, the transfer of revenue resources by the Finance Commissions (FCs) also sought to lessen inequalities between states. However, in this respect as well, the avowed policy was not always followed while disbursing funds. The first few FCs, from the first FC (1957–1962) until the ninth FC (1990–1995), did not fund the

NES favorably. The tenth FC (1995–2000) was distinctly favorable toward the NES in terms of the sharing of income tax revenues. In this context, the more money a state receives relative to its population numbers, the more the federal contribution is considered progressive. In terms of the sharing of union excise duties, the FC devolutions were progressive for the NES. From the eighth FC onward, economic backwardness became an important factor in allocating funds to states, and the NES, as a poor region by national standards, benefited accordingly.

A third dimension to funding development has been the role of financial institutions, the direction of flow of foreign direct investments (FDIs), and the distribution of assets of CPSUs. In this respect as well the NES did not benefit in a substantial manner, and tangible results did not accrue. Generally, low levels of infrastructure development have been a constricting factor.

Thus, in spite of efforts to reduce regional disparities and boost levels of development, the NES have lagged behind the development ladder. This has meant limited employment opportunities for the growing population, and stunted development has indirectly led to insurgency, militancy, and extortionist tendencies. There have been several demands for the creation of new states and even demands for secession from the Indian Union. While peace has ultimately prevailed in states like Mizoram and Nagaland, small (and not so small) pockets of dissent remain in Manipur, Nagaland, and Assam. In Manipur, in particular, there are numerous small groups of dissidents that have frequently tested state and union government resolve. The Armed Forces Special Powers Act (AFSPA) is a much contested act. It has been in operation in Manipur for the past eight years, and it gives the armed forces draconian powers; several instances of human rights violations have been alleged.

The NES has potential wealth from water stemming from the mighty rivers that crisscross it, particularly in Arunachal Pradesh and to a lesser extent in the other NES states. It is estimated that 40 percent of the country's total hydro potential lies with the NES. However, of this less than 2 percent has thus far been harnessed. It remains the case that the NES is India's powerhouse of tomorrow. In terms of existing power sources, oil and natural gas are one of its assets, and the region boasts of refineries at Digboi, Bongaigaon, Gauhati, and Numaligarh, of which the former is more than a century old. The NES has an estimated 500 billion cubic feet of natural gas reserves, and they are largely in Assam, Tripura, and Nagaland. They are capable of generating 3,000 megawatts for 30 years.

Other areas in which the NES has excellent resources are in coal, uranium, ethnic handicrafts, horticulture, fruit processing, agro-based industries, and ecotourism. In all, the land holds a great deal of potential, and its wealth is slowly unfolding as India increasingly pays attention to this far-flung region.

ANUP SAIKIA

See also Arunachal Pradesh; Assam; Economy; Meghalaya; Mizoram; Nagaland; National Rural Employment Guarantee Act

Further Reading

Basic Statistics of the North Eastern Region, 2006. Shillong: North Eastern Secretariat, 2008.

Forest Survey of India. *State of Forest Report, 2003.* Dehra Dun: Ministry of Environment and Forests, 2005.

Forest Survey of India. *State of Forest Report, 2005.* Dehra Dun: Ministry of Environment and Forests, 2008.

India: A Reference Manual 2008. New Delhi: Publications Division, Government of India, 2009.

Saikia, Anup. "NDVI Variability in North East India." *Scottish Geographical Journal* 125 (2009): 195–212.

Singh, V. P., et al., ed. *The Brahmaputra Basin Water Resources.* Dortrecht: Kluwer Academic, 2004.

Taher, M., and P. Ahmed. *Geography of North East India.* Guwahati: El Dorado Publications, 2000.

World Bank. *Development and Growth in Northeast India: The Natural Resources, Water, and Environment Nexus.* Washington, DC. World Bank, 2007.

Offshoring *See* Outsourcing and Offshoring

♦ ORIENTALISM

Orientalism is the name given to a particular kind of approach to the Orient (including India, where the argument has been particularly well received and has many adherents) and to things Oriental as put forward by Edward Said (1935–2003) in his book *Orientalism* (1978). Said argued that the domination of the Orient by the West had been sustained by a literature developed especially since the 18th century that represented the Orient in a particular way. This literature, he wrote, represented the East repeatedly as an exotic, subhuman "Other." Over the course of two centuries of reiteration and self-reference, this created a body of work that came to be accepted as one of systematic knowledge about the Orient.

Said believed that this literature was not an innocent misrepresentation of the Orient but intead was a cultural apparatus that operated "as representations usually do, for a purpose, according to a tendency, in a specific historical, intellectual, and even economic setting." Through analyses of literature on the Orient, he argued that this knowledge was produced in situations of unequal power and was mostly a prejudice serving political ends. Said enumerated four currents in 18th-century thought—expansion, historical confrontation, sympathy, and classification—upon which the intellectual and institutional structures of Orientalism were based. As evidenced in travelogues, novels, scholarly texts, and letters, he believed that the West constructed a discourse about the Orient that explained the East's differences in terms that were in accordance with Western standards and therefore judgmental. This made it possible to comprehend and consequently reject practices that were essentially different as belonging to an earlier rung of civilization that the West had already climbed. If one believed in this framing of the Orient, it was then acceptable and even desirable that the lands of the East should be subjugated and ruled by the so-called superior West.

SIPRA MUKHERJEE

See also Asiatic Society of Bengal; Asiatic Society of Mumbai; Postcolonial Studies

Further Reading
Said, Edward. *Culture and Imperialism.* London: Chatto and Windus, 1993.
Said, Edward. *Orientalism.* New York: Pantheon, 1978.

✦ ORISSA

Among states in the Indian Union, Orissa—Odhisha after March, 2011—ranks 12th in population and 10th in area. It is a maritime state with a coastline of 249 miles along the Bay of Bengal. Orissa covers an area of 60,199 square miles and has a population of 367 million. The state is surrounded by West Bengal, Bihar, and Jharkhand on the north; Andhra Pradesh on the south; the Bay of Bengal on the east; and Madhya Pradesh and Chhattisgarh on the west. Orissa, as a separate state from Bengal, received its exclusive identity as a province of the Oriya-speaking people in 1936 when India was still under British rule. Present-day Orissa consists of 30 districts, 58 subdivisions, 171 *tehsils,* and 314 development blocks.

Orissa has the distinct record of having had an independent dynasty of rulers from the 7th century until the 14th century, after which the province was ruled by the Mughals (1526–1858), the Marathas (1720–1819), and the British (1858–1947). The state is divided into four natural regions: the hilly areas on the north and northwest, the Eastern Ghats, the central and western plateaus, and the coastal plains. The hilly regions on the north and northwest and the central and plateau areas constitute the mineral belt of the state. These areas are regarded as parts of the Vindhya ranges of the Gondwana variety and cover major portions of the districts of Mayurbhanja, Keonjhar, Sundargarh, Bargarh, Angul, Sambalpur, Kalahandi, and Bolangir. The hilly terrain of the coastal regions are not continuous ranges but instead are a series of steep rugged ridges separated by precipitous valleys. About three-quarters of the area of Orissa has extensive mountainous regions.

The inhabitants of Orissa are mostly Oriyas, and their mother tongue is Oriya. The state is predominantly a traditional Hindu society, and the political, social, and economic bases of power are provided by the caste Hindus with Lord Jagannath, a form of the Hindu god Vishnu, as the symbol of Oriyan identity.

The dominant castes in contemporary Oriyan society are the Brahmins, Karans, and Khandayats. According to F. C. Bailey, an eminent historian, the Karans of Orissa in general and those of the city of Cuttack, one of the oldest cities in Orissa and its cultural and commercial capital, in particular are clever political operators and occupy almost all of the important political and administrative positions in the state. It is possible to argue that the legitimation of Karan power was derived from the Karans' status of being successors of the famous Gajapati kings of the Suryavamsa Dynasty who ruled over Kalinga (Orissa) and parts of Andhra Prasesh and West Bengal from 1435 until 1541.

Orissa also has a sizable tribal population, which is approximately 22 percent of the total population of the state. The tribes have their own languages depending on whether they are from the Bhuiyan, Savar, Gond, or Kondh tribes. The tribal economy is a subsistence economy and is based mainly on hunting, gathering, and fishing or a combination of hunting and gathering with shifting cultivation. The lifestyle among the tribes is not an easy one, and their problems are compounded due to land alienation, the perennial issue of indebtedness, antiquated agricultural practices, seasonal migration patterns, and the fact that the tribal members are largely uneducated. However, tribal peoples in some areas also benefit from their association with the Durga Puja, an important Hindu festival. The small village of Rameswapur in Orissa claims to hold the oldest Durga Puja on record. In spite of their marginal status and their migratory patterns, the tribes have fully taken part in the electoral process of the state. Sometimes they have been manipulated by different political parties,

Fishermen remove fish from their nets on a sandy beach in Orissa. India has many spectacular beaches and a huge fishing industry. (Jeremy Richards/Dreamstime.com)

while at other times they have been represented by their political mouthpiece, the Jharkhand Party, which has pockets of influence and has even decided the political fortunes of parties in power. The demands by a vociferous section of the tribal leaders for increased autonomy have added new political dimensions to regional rivalry in the state. These developments sit well with the demands for rural representation and a voice in the politics in state institutions and simultaneously in the mass political mobilization marked by an increasingly effective tribal organization.

Orissa has had a history of successfully managing the integration of princely states into its fold. Politically, Orissa originally consisted of only six districts but has included 26 Gadjats or Indian native states as well. Due to the efforts of Sardar Vallabhbhai Patel (1875–1950), home minister, deputy prime minister, minister of information and broadcasting, and, most importantly with regard to the princely states, minister of the states from 1947 until his death; and Dr. Harekrushna Mahatab (1899–1987), chief minister of Orissa during 1946–1950 and 1956–1961, the princely states finally agreed to sign the Instruments of Accession on December, 14, 1947, whereby they became part of India rather than semi-independent states and merged into Orissa's administrative structure on January, 1, 1948. On January 26, 1950, the day when India became a republic, the territorial map of Orissa was redrawn to include 13 districts. The government of J. B. Patnaik (b. 1927), which was in power for most of the 1980s and 1990s (Patnaik was chief minister during 1980–1989 and 1995–1999), had also taken some steps to create additional centers of administrative zones to benefit the people residing in the western and southern parts of Orissa. His son, Naveen Patnaik (b. 1946), the founder of the Biju Janata Dal party, was sworn in as the chief minister of Orissa after the elections of 2000 and won reelection in both 2004 and 2009. His victory is largely due to his image as an incorruptible politician and because he has attracted various companies to invest in Orissa's mineral belt.

In spite of development in industrialization, urbanization, communications, and education, Orissa still lags behind most of the other states of the Indian Union. There have been vociferous demands for the federal government to allocate more funds to the state as a special case, as a majority of Orissa's population lives below the poverty line. As Orissa moves toward modernization, conflicts arise with those propounding more traditional values. This clash of the traditional with the modern reflects the dynamism of Orissa's body politic. In March 2011, the 113th Amendment to the Indian Constitution changed the name to Odisha.

MOHAMMED BADRUL ALAM

Further Reading
Bailey, F. G. *Politics and Social Change: Orissa in 1959.* Berkeley: University of California Press, 1963.
Dash, S. C. *Orissa: State of Our Union.* Bhubaneswar: Government of Orissa, Public Relations Department, 1968.

Dutt, Tara. *Tribal Development in India*. New Delhi: Gyan, 2001.

Kulke, Hermann. *State Formation and Legitimation in India*. New Delhi: Manohar, 2001.

Nanda, S. *Coalitional Politics in Orissa*. Delhi: Sterling Publishers, 1979.

✦ OUTSOURCING AND OFFSHORING

Outsourcing involves contracting part of a business's activities to another domestic or international firm, while offshoring involves shifting a business activity to another country while keeping it within the same company. In both cases the primary intentions are the same: to save on costs, to complement other objectives such as increasing market share, and ultimately to increase profits through the ability to offer lower prices to consumers. Dealing with the business process and the supply chain complexity is the other key aim of outsourcing. In industry jargon, outsourcing (and offshoring) consists of business process outsourcing (BPO) and covers information technology (IT) software development and the IT services element, while another form of BPO—covering human resources (HR), finance, insurance, health, and after-sales call-center customer service—is referred to as information technology enabled services (ITES).

While outsourcing is currently famous through IT and other services, both of which India is known for as the most renowned destination, outsourcing began in earnest in the 1980s in the United States (in manufacturing) as the tool for realizing lean businesses, concentrating on a single or small set of products, as an alternative to the old conglomerate business model. The lean concept evolved further to use outsourcing to remove core processes from businesses to be subcontracted. Companies could then pick and choose among subcontractors to get ever-lower costs. While this reduced traditional costs and risk, it gave rise to a new set of costs and risks.

Outsourcing in India consists of IT (i.e., software and programming); traditional IT outsourcing, such as the remote management of whole systems and the beginnings of research and development; business back-office and front-office tasks and services (e.g., business administration and call centers); and manufacturing (e.g., clothing). Of these, IT and business back-office and front-office tasks and services are, at present, the most significant for India, all of which grew exponentially after 1995 compared to manufacturing, which has grown very slowly. As sectoral percentages of national income (gross domestic product [GDP]) for 1999–2000, all manufacturing constitutes 14.7 percent, with 11 percent of total employment, with finance, insurance, and real estate services and business services (including IT) being 13 and 1.2 percent, respectively. In 2005 the estimated contribution of IT offshoring and outsourcing to the Indian GDP for 2007–2008 was 7 percent, with an estimated workforce of approximately 1.5 million for that period and 2.23 million in 2009 (total employment in IT and BPO-ITES was said to be 4 million in 2008). The United States represents 60 percent of Indian IT and BPO-ITES activity. Total

Hewlett-Packard employees work at the company's business process outsourcing call center in Bangalore, Karnataka, August 2007. India's high-tech outsourcing industry is one of the largest in the world. (AP Photo/Aijaz Rahi)

services exports (which includes IT) increased in value from $5 billion to $60 billion from 1990 to 2006. Over the same period textile exports (which include clothing) increased from about $2 billion to about $8 billion. Foreign direct investment (FDI) has also been similarly muted. The IT and BPO-ITES industries are concentrated in the city of Bangalore in Karnataka but are also located in Hyderabad, Andhra Pradesh, and the more familiar cities of Mumbai (Bombay), Delhi, and Kolkotta (Calcutta). As of 2009, 7 Indian IT and BPO-ITES companies are in the top 15 global firms: HCL (India), Oracle, Xerox, Infosys (India), Accenture, IBM Global, Ciber (India), Cap Gemini, Genpact (India), Hewlett Packard-EDS, CSC, Cognizant (India), Intelligroup, Igate (India), and Patni (India).

The well-known success of Indian IT and business back-office and front-office tasks and services outsourcing resulted from low costs and low wages paid to workers and from the high quality of an elite segment of university graduates, specifically from the seven Indian institutes of technology and the six Indian institutes of management. This also resulted from English as India's second language; a history of sending highly skilled labor to the United States, resulting in cross-cultural and business knowledge familiarity; minimal reliance on India's physical infrastructure; the post-1991 Indian liberalization of the economy; and a strategic labor supply shortage in the United States of identically skilled IT labor. The acute IT shortage of engineers in the late 1990s that resulted from the Y2K software year "00" digit problem gave the final push that established Indian IT outsourcing internationally, which has resulted in the terms "Bangalored" or "Bangalore it."

By 2009, constraints on the further expansion of the sector had become a concern, as indicated by articles such as "The Coming Death of Indian Outsourcing." The Indian cost advantage of one to six (which at present is one to three) is in part a result of increasing salaries and a limited labor supply. Salary growth is around 15 percent per year, and if this growth continues, the cost ratio will be one-to-one by 2015. Only a fraction of India's large number of university graduates are suited to international work, hence the labor supply problem, and large numbers continue to emigrate.

Manufacturing's poor performance, particularly in the labor-intensive subsectors involved in outsourcing apparel (clothing), is in considerable measure due to the legacy of industrial restrictions referred to as the licence Raj as well as ongoing excessive labor regulations (to fire workers in companies with more than 100 workers, the state government's permission must be obtained). The industrial licensing and restrictions system operates as follows. Certain products—socks, for example—as of 2005 are permitted for manufacture only by small firms. India's clothing industry is therefore contrasted with those in China, Bangladesh, and Sri Lanka, where companies often employ thousands of workers under a single roof, while such companies in India remain small, frequently consisting of shops with fewer than 50 tailors. While clothing is a leading Indian outsourced export, the small export size, when compared to Bangladesh's much smaller workforce, indicates the effect of India's policy-induced economic constraints. The result is low productivity, low quality, and excessive pressure to reduce costs given a company's need to remain small. This leads to byzantine supply chains through subcontracting of subcontracting in order to meet deadlines that initial subcontractors cannot meet. The end result is the regular use of heavily exploited adult labor and incentives to use child labor in unregistered companies. A minimum estimate places child labor numbers at around 10 million. Western outsourcing firms find it very difficult to monitor this atomistic subcontractor supply chain structure, leading to consumer boycott risks due to repeated exposure of exploitative working conditions by journalists. Improved prospects for clothing sector outsourcing rests with the Indian government, dramatically speeding up the de-reserving of restricted goods that only began in 1997. As of 2005 some 600 goods were still restricted to production by small businesses. By January 2007 this was down to 239.

RISTO HÄRMÄ

See also Economy; Globalization; Indian Institutes of Technology; Special Economic Zones

Further Reading
Farrell, Diana, ed. *Offshoring: Understanding the Emerging Global Labor Market*. Boston: Harvard Business School Press, 2006.
Hale, Angela, and Jane Wills, eds. *Threads of Labour: Garment Industry Supply Chains from the Workers' Perspective*. Malden, MA: Blackwell, 2005.

Mitra, Sramana. "The Coming Death of Indian Outsourcing." *Forbes*, February 29, 2008. http://www .forbes.com/2008/02/29/mitra-india-outsourcing-tech-enter-cx_sm_0229outsource.html.

National Association of Software and Service Companies. Accessed April 28, 2011. http://www.nass com.in.

Panagariya, Arvind. *India: The Emerging Giant*. New York: Oxford University Press, 2008.

"The Tiger in Front: A Survey of India and China." *Economist*, March 5, 2005, 10.

"A World of Work: A Survey of Outsourcing." *Economist*, November 13, 2004, 4.

P

✦ PAKISTAN, RELATIONS WITH

India-Pakistan relations suffer from one of the longest ongoing conflicts in the world. The two nations have been involved in financial, military, and diplomatic disputes since India became independent and Pakistan was created in August 1947. The two countries have fought three major wars (1947–1948, 1965, and 1971) and one small-scale conflict (1999) and have frequently exchanged cross-border shots and barrages along the Line of Control (LOC) in Kashmir. Violent clashes have led to a whole host of differences, and mistrust between the two rivals has grown. For one reason or another, the gulf separating the two states continues to grow.

Understanding the events of the recent past helps us to understand the contemporary relations between India and Pakistan and possible future impacts as well. Throughout the 1990s, both countries were engaged in a series of dialogues to resolve outstanding disputes, in particular the long-lasting conflict over Kashmir. However, the talks ended in stalemate in 1998 when India demonstrated its nuclear capability and became a nuclear power. Soon after that in May 1998, due to enormous political pressure in Pakistan, the Pakistan Muslim League administration of Prime Minister Nawaz Sharif (b. 1949; prime minister 1990–1993, 1997–1999) conducted five consecutive nuclear tests in Baluchistan Province. As a result of this nuclear arms race, according to one estimate India had 60–70 nuclear warheads, and Pakistan possesses roughly 60 nuclear warheads. Concerns were thus heightened between May and July 1999 when India and Pakistan engaged in another small-scale conflict in Kashmir, the Kargil Conflict. Realizing the danger and the horrendous consequences of a nuclear exchange between the two countries, New Delhi and Islamabad exchanged details of their nuclear facilities in January 2009 as per the Agreement on the Prohibition of Attacks against Nuclear Installations and Facilities, which both countries signed in Islamabad.

The conflict has affected the potential for bilateral trade between India and Pakistan as well as trade conducted under the auspices of the South Asian Association for Regional Cooperation (SAARC), founded in 1985, of which both India and Pakistan are members. The South Asia Free Trade Area (SAFTA) created by SAARC is designed to enhance intraregional trade on the subcontinent. In 2007 bilateral trade was only $1.7 billion, which is much below the target of $10 billion set by SAARC. The volume of illegal trade between India and Pakistan is estimated to be $1.5 billion. Bilateral trade is only likely to reach its full potential once Pakistan gives India most favored nation (MFN) status, but this has not happened, and the MFN issue continues to be a major bone of contention between New Delhi and Islamabad.

The peace process has been an intermittent one, and in the recent past the only worthwhile development was in the form of the Indo-Pak Composite Dialogue. The dialogue was initiated in 2004 to explore solutions to a wide range of issues, such as the Kashmir dispute, the Sir Creek issue, the Wullar Barrage Project/Tulbul Navigation Project, terrorism and drug trafficking, economic and commercial cooperation, and promotion of friendly exchanges in various other fields. The process of the dialogue also suffered from a yearlong pause in 2007; it was restarted in May 2008 with a ministerial-level review of the fourth round of the dialogue. Even with tension in bilateral relations over the issue of a terrorist attack on the Indian embassy in Kabul on July 7, 2008, both countries moved on with the fifth round of the dialogue the same month. However, the dialogue made little progress because the controversial issue of cross-border terrorism was at the center stage of negotiations and could not be resolved.

The Indo-Pak Composite Dialogue has often been criticized for not producing results. However, a number of confidence-building measures have been agreed:

- In October 2005 an agreement was reached whereby both countries would inform the other with at least three days' notice before testing ballistic missiles within 25 miles of the international boundary and the LOC.
- The Memorandum of Understanding of June 2004 required measures to reduce the risk of accidental unauthorized use of nuclear weapons, and a nuclear hotline was set up to connect the foreign secretaries of both countries.
- To avoid the arrest of innocent fishermen who have strayed into each country's territorial waters, there is a hotline being created for better communications between the naval agencies of both countries.
- An important feature of the Composite Dialogue is the expansion of transportation linkages between India and Pakistan. The New Delhi–Lahore bus services was established in 1999, but by 2010 there were four other available bus routes: Srinagar-Muzaffarabad, Pooch-Rawalakot, Amritsar-Nankana Sahib, and Amritsar-Lahore.

The bus service between New Delhi and Lahore now runs three times a week, indicating the number of passengers desiring to travel between the two cities. In addition, there are two available train links: the Samjhota Express (between Amritsar and Lahore) and the Thar Express (between Munabao and Khokhrapar). There are now 12 flights connecting New Delhi and Mumbai in India with Lahore and Karachi in Pakistan. In 2008, both countries reached an agreement to expand the air routes and connect Chennai with Islamabad.

Nonetheless, the menace of terrorism has greatly constrained the peace process, and on several occasions the countries were on the verge of war due to cross-border terrorism. For example, relations were at their lowest level after an attack on the Indian Parliament on December 13, 2001, by the Muslim terrorist groups Lashkar-e-Taiba (Army of the Good), founded in 1990, and Jaish-e-Mohammed (Army of Mohammed or Army of the Prophet), founded in 2000, and a series of bomb blasts in Mumbai in July 2006 and later in November 2008. Both countries have understood the need to cooperate in fighting terrorists on both sides of the border, and for that purpose they are discussing the viability of a Joint Anti-Terrorism Mechanism (JATM) between India and Pakistan. In addition, the member states of SAARC, including India and Pakistan, have launched the SAARC Terrorist Offences Monitoring Desk (STOMD) in Colombo, Sri Lanka, as a result of the SAARC Regional Convention on Suppression of Terrorism, which was signed in Katmandu, Nepal, in 1987. There are also talks going on at SAARC to launch a regional police organization similar to the International Criminal Police Organization (Interpol), first established in 1923.

ZAHID SHAHAB AHMED

See also Foreign Policy; South Asian Association for Regional Cooperation

Further Reading

Ashraf, Fahmida. *India Pakistan Relations—Post Mumbai Attacks: Chronology of Indian Statements.* Islamabad: Institute of Regional Studies, 2009.

International Crisis Group. *Kashmir: The View from Islamabad.* Brussels: International Crisis Group, 2003.

Masood, Talat. "Pakistan's Kashmir Policy." *China and Eurasia Forum Quarterly* 4(4) (2006): 45–49.

Misra, Ashutosh. "Indo-Pakistan Talks 2004: Nuclear Confidence Building Measures (NCBMs) and Kashmir." *Strategic Analysis* 28(2) (2004): 347–351.

Mudiam, Prithvi Ram. "The India-Pakistan Dispute over Jammu and Kashmir and the United States." *Global Change, Peace & Security* 15(3) (2003): 263–276.

Patil, Sameer Suryakant. *Indo-Pak Composite Dialogue: An Update.* New Delhi: Institute of Peace and Conflict Studies, 2008.

Sridharan, E. "International Relations Theory and India-Pakistan Conflict." *India Review* 4(2) (2005): 103–124.

St. John, Anthony Wanis. "Third Party Mediation over Kashmir: A Modest Proposal." *International Peacekeeping* 4(4) (1997): 1–30.

Stockholm International Peace Research Institute. *SIPRI Yearbook 2008: Armaments, Disarmaments, and International Security.* Stockholm: Stockholm International Peace Research Institute, 2008.

✦ *PANCHAYAT* SYSTEM AND LOCAL GOVERNMENT

Implementing and designing poverty alleviation policies with the people's participation forms a key feature of the *panchayat* system of decentralized governance in India. Article 40 of the Indian Constitution directs the government to establish *panchayats* ("councils of five") to serve as institutions of local self-government, of which the elected village council (*gram panchayat*) is the basic unit. A *gram panchayat* includes between 1 and 5 revenue villages and a minimum of 20 wards (*chaupals*), and once elected *panchayat* members have a tenure of 5 years. A key element is the Gram Sabhas (the assembly), which is the formal vehicle for people's participation and where the annual report of activities is presented. The Gram Sabhas is open to everyone aged 18 and above. Districts in India are subdivided into *taluqs* or *tehsils*—areas that contain around 200–600 villages—where economic development and social welfare government departments have offices. Within the local governance infrastructure, a block is a large subunit of a district, and in some states blocks are of equal size with *taluqs* or *tehsils*. The district council (*zilla parishad*) is at the top level of the local governance system, and its jurisdiction includes all village and block councils within a district; membership includes the block council chairs.

In 1989 Prime Minister Rajiv Gandhi (1944–1991; prime minister 1984–1989) tried to enhance the role of *panchayats* in local government and economic development by introducing the Jawahar Employment Plan (*Jawahar Rozgar Yojana*), which provided funding directly to village councils to create jobs for the unemployed through public works projects. His government proposed the Sixty-Fourth Amendment Bill to make it mandatory for all states to establish a three-tiered (village, block, and district) system of *panchayats* in which representatives would be directly elected for five-year terms. *Panchayats* were to be given expanded authority and funding for local development efforts. Despite the popular appeal of transferring power to *panchayats*, the Sixty-Fourth Amendment Bill was rejected by Parliament, and in 1992 it was the 73rd and 74th amendments to the Indian Constitution that led to the constitutional status of *panchayats* as the third level of governance. Above this basic framework, most states in India have added other features to their *panchayat* legislation and have developed state-specific methods of local governance. These programs are undertaken not only by state governments but also by nongovernmental organizations, women's groups, self-help groups, and other political and grassroots activist organizations. Although the 73rd Amendment states that one-third of *panchayat* seats should be reserved for women, with a similar number for people from Scheduled Castes and Scheduled Tribes (depressed classes or untouchable or underprivileged classes), actual representation of these groups at the *panchayat* level and participation of women and poor households in Gram Sabha meetings is minimal, as social norms continue to dominate. Kerala is the only state in India with a fully functional and structured local government network, where measures for local governance accountability are recognized as a vital factor in effective public sector performance.

SHEEBA HÄRMÄ

See also Cabinet; Constitution; Parliament; President; Prime Minister

Further Reading
Adhikary, M. M., S. K. Acharya, and S. K. Musiar Ali. *Empowerment and Entitlement of Women in the Panchayat System.* Udaipur: Agrotech Publishing, 2009.
Bhandari, Ramesh. *Role and Status of Women in New Panchayati Raj System: Decentralisation and Rural Development.* New Delhi: Alfa Publication, 2009.
Mathur, Sangeeta. *Panchayati Raj System in South Asia.* Jaipur: Ritu Publications, 2010.

✦ PARLIAMENT

The progressive democratization of politics in Britain took the form of an increasing assertion of control by an elected Parliament over the executive. The chief means by which Parliament usurped the monarch's power of rule over subjects was responsible government. In the same tradition, both the prime minister and the cabinet are subject to control by the Indian Parliament in the regional and central legislatures created by the British during the period of British government control of India (1858–1947). This system has endured in its essential form since India became independent in 1947.

The powers of the Indian Parliament can be divided into legislative, financial, procedural, governmental, constitution-amending, and constitutive powers. Parliament enacts the law of the land, at least in theory. In reality, the legislative agenda is controlled by the government and is rubber-stamped by Parliament with the help of tightly maintained party discipline. If it chooses to act with the government, as is almost always the case, Parliament is all-powerful; if it chooses to act independently of the government, Parliament creates political instability and unpredictability in the affairs of the state. By choosing to act against the executive, Parliament indicates that the government has lost its confidence, and this brings the business of government to a standstill until fresh elections can be held.

The financial powers of Parliament are those empowering it to raise and spend money, including discussion and approval of the annual budget, which is usually introduced in mid-February. Only Parliament has the authority to levy taxes and spend money from the resulting consolidated fund. The procedural powers are those that permit Parliament to make rules for the conduct of its own business. Parliament formally controls the reins of government in that the cabinet is required to have the confidence of the Lok Sabha (the House of the People

Sansad Bhavan, Indian Parliament, New Delhi. Containing the Lower House, the Lok Sabha, the Upper House or Council of States, the Rajya Sabha, and a library, the circular parliament building opened in 1927; it is now a potent symbol of the world's largest democracy. (Shutterstock)

or the lower house of Parliament) and is collectively responsible to Parliament. Parliament is the main body for amending the Indian Constitution. Under its constitutive powers, Parliament can legislate to create or admit new states into the union of India, create a high court for a Union Territory and extend the jurisdiction of a high court to or restrict it from a Union Territory, and create or abolish the upper house for a state with the consent of its lower house.

The Parliament of India is bicameral. Its members are elected on the basis of universal adult suffrage. In the 15th general election in 2009, the number of eligible voters was a staggering 714 million, of whom some 420 million voted. The distribution of seats among the states is roughly in proportion to their population size. Of the 543 elective seats in the 15th Lok Sabha (2009–2014), 413 members of Parliament were in the general category, 81 were from Scheduled Castes (formerly known as untouchables), and 49 were from Scheduled Tribes. Any citizen of India who is at least 25 years old may seek election to the Lok Sabha from a constituency in which he or she has resided for a minimum period of 180 days. In a reserved constituency, only members of the Scheduled Castes and the Scheduled Tribes may run for office, but all adults within the constituency may vote. The two nominated seats are filled by the president with representatives of the Anglo-Indian community.

The system of voting is the single-member constituency, first past the post system. Each constituency is represented by only one member of Parliament in the Lok Sabha. Of those contesting from any constituency, the candidate with the highest number of votes is declared elected even if the total is well short of a majority. A proportional representation system would be more representative in a mathematically defined version of democracy. However, under Indian conditions (size, diversity, and complexity) this would almost certainly produce chaos.

The conduct of elections is entrusted by the Constitution to an election commission. The chief election commissioner is an independent official appointed by the president under conditions of service resembling those of senior judges. The tasks of the election commission include designing voting forms suitable for Indian conditions, determining the best dates for holding elections, and deciding whether the elections should be held simultaneously on consecutive days or at staggered intervals. The 15th general election was organized in five phases of voting spread over four weeks during April–May 2009.

By and large, the members of Parliament are chosen fairly. While individual seats may have been determined by musclemen or bribes, no general election in India has produced an overall result that was not a fair reflection of voter preferences. With growing consciousness of regional identity, a number of parties have risen to power in states and have formed coalition governments in New Delhi. The last time that a party was elected with an absolute majority in its own right in the Lok Sabha was in 1984.

Required to convene at least twice a year, the Lok Sabha normally meets annually in three sessions. The term of the Lok Sabha is for five years, although in an emergency this may be extended one year at a time but indefinitely. While Parliament may be dissolved and fresh elections held because a government has lost the confidence of the members of the Lok Sabha, the more common occurrence is for a prime minister to time a call for fresh elections with the goal of maximizing personal or party political gains.

The process of legislation involves three stages corresponding to the familiar three readings of bills in the British Parliament: the introduction and consideration of a bill followed by its enactment into law. The first reading consists of the bill being introduced along with an explanation of its aims and purposes. After the second reading a bill may be referred to a select committee, circulated for public response, or taken up for immediate consideration. The most substantial consideration of bills takes place in committee.

Ordinary bills can be introduced in either house, the Lok Sabha or the Rajya Sabha (the Council of States or the upper house of Parliament), and must be passed by both houses before they can be sent to the president. Ordinary bills become law once they have been signed by the president. Money bills can be introduced only in the Lok Sabha ("no taxation without representation"). While they may be taken up for discussion in the Rajya Sabha, the upper house cannot refuse assent to money bills, nor can it frustrate the passage of a money bill by the simple expedient of procrastination. The bill is deemed to have passed if not returned by the Rajya Sabha within 14 days.

The Lok Sabha is fundamentally akin to legislative assemblies in other parliamentary democracies, but the actual daily activity of India's Parliament can be quite different, reflecting its own unique sociopolitical environment.

The Rajya Sabha has 250 members, of whom 238 represent the states and Union Territories; the remaining 12 are nominated by the president acting on the advice of cabinet. Nominated members are chosen on the basis of their special knowledge or skills in the arts and sciences, in order to rectify a serious underrepresentation in Parliament of any particular group, or in an exercise of political patronage to reward party workers or major financial supporters. The distribution of Rajya Sabha seats among states is roughly in proportion to their population strengths, albeit with some effort at equalization.

Rajya Sabha members are elected for six-year terms, with a biennial turnover of one-third of the house. Unlike the Lok Sabha, the upper house is not subject to dissolution. The quorum of the Rajya Sabha is set at one-tenth (i.e., 25 members) of the total membership, with decisions being made by a majority of members actually present and voting. The presiding officer of the Rajya Sabha is the vice president of India.

The opposition in a parliamentary democracy is expected to play the role of an alternative government, complete with a shadow prime minister and cabinet-in-waiting. Because of the large number of political parties in India, the status of the leader of the opposition can be conferred only on the leader of a party that has at least 50 seats in the Lok Sabha. The main purpose of the opposition is to critique government actions and policies. By its existence and voice in Parliament, the opposition expresses the diversity of opinions in a country as large and varied as India. Party discipline ensures that the opposition loses when the votes on any motion are tallied. But statements in Parliament are heard in the country at large and are often listened to within the ranks of the ruling party. This is particularly relevant in a country such as India where the major parties are not sharply distinguished by ideological cleavages. Opposition arguments can resonate within the ruling party and can shape public policy by this indirect means. In turn, this has made the opposition parties in India more influential than would be suggested just by their numbers. In other words, although the debate in Parliament is ostensibly between the government and the opposition, in fact it can serve to structure the internal debate within the ruling party. This has been a distinctive feature of Indian politics.

RAMESH THAKUR

See also Cabinet; Constitution; *Panchayat* System and Local Government; Parliament; Prime Minister

Further Reading
Agrawal, Arun. "The Indian Parliament." In *Public Institutions in India: Performance and Design*, edited by Devesh Kapur and Pratap Bhanu Mehta, 77–104. Delhi: Oxford University Press, 2005.
India Parliament Guide. Washington, DC: USA International Business Publications, 2009.
Kashyap, Subhash C. *The Ten Lok Sabhas: From the First to the Tenth (1952–1991)*. Delhi: Shipra, 1992.
Morris-Jones, W. H. *Parliament in India*. Westport, CT: Greenwood, 1957.
Our Parliament: An Introduction to the Parliament of India. Delhi: National Book Trust, 2004.

✦ PARSIS

Parsis are the Indian followers of the Zoroastrian religion who had migrated to the western part of India during the eighth century CE. Today they are a well-settled minority community of approximately 70,000 members who preserve their religious and cultural identity. The Indian Parsis form the majority of and maintain close affiliations with the rest of the Zoroastrian community worldwide. Zoroastrianism, the oldest of the world's monotheistic religions, has influenced Judaism, Christianity, and Islam with its teachings of belief in a single cosmic deity, the struggle between good and evil, and the final day of judgment. Zoroastrianism originated in Iran after the settlement of the Aryans in the region. This led to the development of the traditions of both the Aryans and the indigenous Iranians. The traditional accounts of the Parsis relate that for more than 100 years before the defeat of Sassanian kings at the hands of Arabs in the seventh century, and before landing at the coastal town of Sanjan, Gujarat, Zoroastrians had wandered over various parts of India. The Hindu king Jadi Rana gave them refuge on the condition that the Zoroastrians would peacefully assimilate to the customs, dress, and language of the area. However, Parsis have maintained a strict observance of their faith by discouraging proselytizing. Nonetheless, as a community the Parsis are on the verge of extinction due to falling birthrates and the exclusion of children born to non-Parsi parents. By 2020 the population is expected to fall to 25,000.

Members of the Parsi community interact at a fire temple on the Parsi New Year Navroz in Ahmadabad, Gujarat, August 2009. Parsis, also known as Zoroastrians, are followers of the Persian prophet Zarathustra and first migrated to western India in the eighth century. (AP Photo/AjitSolanki)

The sacred fire, the central icon of the Zoroastrian faith, is regarded as a glowing image of the energy and reverential worth of God, known to the Parsis as Ahura Mazda. Most sacred fires are lit only for the duration of the religious worship. There are, however, many fire temples (*agiaries* or *atesh kadeh*) where the fire is kept burning at all times. Other objects, such as flowers and food, are displayed as symbols of divine creation. Mumbai has 41 fire temples, 4 Parsi cathedrals (*atesh bahrams*), and the Tower of Silence, where the funerary rituals are performed for the community. Since Parsis revere nature and do not want to defile the earth, the sky, or the water, they follow the system known as sky burials. The dead are placed inside a four-walled structure with an open top that exposes the corpses to the natural elements, including the vultures and the carrion crows that devour them.

The other important religious practice of the Parsis is the *navjote*, or initiation ceremony, during which boys and girls between the ages of seven and nine wear a *sudrah* (cotton shirt) and a *kusti* (a cord of 72 threads) around the waist. Like the initiation ceremonies, Parsi marriages are joyous occasions and are celebrated with the consumption of lots of food and drink. The nuptial benediction is offered in Zend, or Middle Persian of southwestern Iran during the Sassanian period, and in the Indian classical language Sanskrit. Parsis are encouraged to lead family lives, and celibacy is proscribed. Hereditary priests perform rites and ceremonies for the community, while the Parsi Panchayat (community government) regulates issues concerning the family and property. In spite of the Parsis having an exclusive cultural identity—the most noticeable acculturative practice is the adoption of the Gujarati language in preference to Persian—the Parsis have successfully immersed themselves into the social and political world of India, particularly in the city of Mumbai, and have played an important role in the legal system and most especially in business, where many Parsis have become exceedingly successful and wealthy. This transformation has been a remarkable one, as the Parsis were first of all a rural-based community but gradually rose to prominence in urban areas through their business acumen and the community's stress on educational achievement. This rise to prominence occurred especially during the colonial period, when they embraced the educational opportunities, including at the higher educational level, offered by the British, most notably at Elphinstone College, Mumbai, which was founded in 1857. The first Indian to be elected to the British House of Commons, in 1892, was a Parsi, Dadabhai Naoroji (1825–1917), who in 1850 was also the first Indian to be appointed a professor at Elphinstone College, his alma mater. The business houses of Tatas, Wadias, and Godrej, among other renowned Parsis corporations, carry forward the business tradition of the Parsis in contemporary India.

FATIMA A. IMAM

See also Mumbai; Religion

Further Reading
Palsetia, Jesse S. *The Parsis of India: Preservation of Identity in Bombay City.* Delhi: Manohar, 2008.

Parsis, Iranis, Zarathushtis—All under One Roof. Accessed April 28, 2011. http://zoroastrians.net/.

Taraprevala, Sooni. *Parsis, the Zoroastrians of India: A Photographic Journey, 1980–2000.* Mumbai: Good Books, 2000.

✦ PATNA

Patna, the capital of the state of Bihar, is located on the southern bank of the river Ganges. The city has a long history and derives its name from the word *patan* ("port"). Patna was an important center for inland river trade throughout the course of history. The city was known as Patliputra, Palibothra (as the Greeks called it), Kusumpur, Pushpapura, and Azimabad at different times in history. It was the seat of government for a long period as different empires and dynasties such as Magadha (5th century BCE), Nanda (5th–4th centuries BCE), Maurya (321–185 BCE), Sunga (185–73 BCE), Gupta (320–550 CE), and Pala (750–1174) made it their capital. In the British colonial period (1858–1947), Patna was an important center for the opium and indigo trades for European merchants.

Patna is the largest city of Bihar, has a total area of nearly 68 square miles, and is under the authority of the Patna Municipal Corporation. The city has been divided into 72 municipal wards with a total population of 1.366 million (2001 census). The Patna Municipal Corporation was established on August 15, 1952, in accordance with the Patna Municipal Corporation Act of 1951. The corporation consists of electoral representatives (known as ward councilors) from its 72 wards. These councilors further elect a mayor and an Empowered Standing Committee. Seventy-two wards are joined together in four circles, each administered by an executive officer appointed by the state government. The administration of the corporation is under the direct control of the municipal commissioner.

The city acts as the most significant business as well as the administrative hub of the entire region and receives a floating population of around 200,000 every day. With little industry, the city primarily functions as the service center for administration, health facilities, and education. The few industries include steel casting, cotton mills, warehousing, electronics, and leather and shoes. Altogether, around 250 small-scale industries are listed in and around the city. Around 250,000 people living below the poverty live in the area.

The development of the city has so far been haphazard. A master plan, however, known as the Jawarharlal Nehru National Urban Renewal Mission City Development Plan (2006–2012), was prepared by the Patna Regional Development Authority (a body of the state government of Bihar) to carry out a planned and evenly distributed development of the city. The plan intends to cover the urbanized portion of the Patna Regional Development Authority region of some 145 square miles by including areas of the Patna Municipal Corporation along with its satellite towns Danapur Nagarpalika, Phulwari Sharif Nagarpalika, Danapur Cantonment Area, and Khagaul Nagarpalika.

The plan aims to cover all the major aspects of urban life including water supply, drainage, and sanitation as well as the housing needs of an expanding city. The plan takes into account the seven famous monuments of the city—Agam Kuan, Durakhi Devi Temple, Choiti Patandevei, Begu Hajjam's Mosque, Kamaldah Jain Temple, Gol Ghar, and Har Mandir Takht—at a cost of just over 1 billion rupees.

SADAN JHA

See also Bihar

Further Reading
Ahmad, Qeyamuddin. *Patna through the Ages: Glimpses of History, Society & Economy*. New Delhi: Commonwealth Publishers, 1988.
Mukherjee, Sraman. "New Province, Old Capital: Making Patna." *Indian Economic and Social History Review* 46(2) (2009): 241–280.
Patna Municipal Corporation. Accessed April 28, 2011. http://www.patnanagarnigam.org.
Sachchidananda, and B. B. Mandal. *Crisis of Governance: The Case of Bihar*. New Delhi: Serials Publications, 2009.
Singh, Vivek Kumar, and Sudhir Kumar Jha. *Patna: A Monumental History*. Patna: Department of Art, Culture and Youth, 2008.

✦ PHILOSOPHY

Philosophy in modern India tends to take one of three often overlapping forms: engagement with issues internal to Western philosophy; a reconsideration of traditional Indian thought, especially that of Hinduism, Buddhism, and Jainism, in global contexts through the adaptation of Western philosophical terminology and frameworks; and a reconsideration of Western philosophical concepts in light of traditional Indian thought. This complexity stems from the fact that a separate sphere of philosophy, self-consciously distinguished from religion, is foreign to traditional Indian thought.

The question of whether Indian thought can be considered philosophical was first raised by the German philosopher G. W. F. Hegel (1770–1831). For Hegel, Indian thought cannot be considered philosophical since it remains entangled with religious speculation. Unlike Western philosophy, Indian thought is incapable of pure theory or knowledge for its own sake and is enslaved to religious practice. For Hegel, the concern with the supposed abstract oneness of meditative states discourages the critical self-reflection and independent thought characteristic of Western philosophy and secular modernity. Hegel's disavowal of Indian thought as philosophy accords with his assumption of the uniquely European nature of philosophy and overall vindication of the Enlightenment project. Arthur Schopenhauer (1788–1860), by contrast, considers Indian thought as properly philosophical. Focusing on early Buddhism and the *Upanishads*, Schopenhauer finds in Indian thought support for his critique of the Enlightenment's claims to detached objectivity and knowledge as pure theory.

These same concerns shape the inquiry of Indians themselves who take up the issue from the mid-19th century under British colonial rule. The question of what philosophy is, whether it is found outside the West and whether there is an Indian form of it, become inseparable from larger reconsiderations of India's intellectual heritage and the engagement of Indian traditions with modernity as part of the development of a distinctly Indian cultural identity. Consequently, Indian philosophy comes to be considered mostly in terms of religions of Indian origin, namely Hinduism, Buddhism and Jainism. A concern becomes whether any indigenous concept corresponds to the Western term "philosophy." The most notable candidates found are the Sanskrit *anvīkiki* ("methodological investigation") and *darśana* ("seeing"). Other Sanskrit equivalents invoked are *tattvajñāna* and *tattvavidyā* ("knowledge of reality"). However, while terms for "philosophy" are sought in Sanskrit, philosophizing itself mostly occurs in English. The term "philosophy," in its earliest appropriation in modern India, is thus associated with and made to ensure continuity between a primordial traditional past and a de-localized present anticipating a global future.

Traditionally, *darśana* does not denote philosophy separable from religious practice but rather denotes the view of a particular school, such as in the six schools (*ad-darśana*) of Hinduism. But in the latter half of the 19th century *darśana* became the main equivalent to the term "philosophy," propagated most influentially by the neo-Vedāntin reformer Swāmī Vivekānanda (1863–1902). The understanding of *darśana* as "philosophy" is invoked as an Indian equivalent on a world stage to refer to a universal phenomenon, placing India on equal terms with the West. Yet the visual connotations of *darśana* as "seeing" also come to enable the promotion of a distinctly Indian form of philosophizing. Vivekānanda equates philosophy in India with "clear *seeing*." His neo-Vedāntin successor Sarvepalli Radhakrishnan (1888–1975) refers to it as a "*vision* of truth." The experiential nature of Indian thought is emphasized and is contrasted favorably against Western thought. Thus, the dichotomy employed by Hegel between pure theory/knowledge for its own sake (as found in the West) and speculation subordinated to religious practice and spiritual experience (as found in India) is internalized in formative Indian appropriations of *darśana* as "philosophy." However, the values of the dichotomy are reversed: Western philosophy's concern for knowledge for its own sake and the eschewing of subjectivity are seen as leaving Western philosophy spiritually bereft, as it lacks a lived experiential component. Radhakrishnan's *Indian Philosophy* (1923) exemplifies this, as does Basant Kumar Mallik's (1879–1958) *The Individual and the Group* (1939) and *The Real and the Negative* (1940). This tendency is illustrated by the choice of the poet Rabindranath Tagore (1861–1941) as the first president of the Indian Philosophical Congress in 1925. The contributions to the first survey of philosophy in modern India, *Contemporary Indian Philosophy* (1936), coedited by Radhakrishnan, also consistently emphasize the distinctly spiritual and experiential nature of Indian philosophizing.

Professional philosophy first occurred at Calcutta University under Bajendranath Seal (1864–1938), the first, in 1899, to refer to comparative philosophy. His colleague Krishna Chandra Bhattacharya (1875–1949) began philosophy proper in India, overcoming the rational-spiritual/theory-practice dichotomy. Bhattacharya's analysis moved beyond mere reconsideration of Indian thought in Western terms, constituting philosophical development in its own right. Responding to the positivist reduction of philosophy to the methods of the natural sciences and the promotion of empirical psychology in the work of Gottlob Frege (1848–1925), Bhattacharya in *The Subject as Freedom* (1930) reworked Immanuel Kant's (1724–1804) transcendental model to develop what Bhattacharya terms "transcendental psychology" as a means of restoring the primacy of intentionality. Bhattacharya seeks to reinstate the place of subjectivity without falling back onto the metaphysical existence of the soul, instead positing the knowing subject as the very knowability of the object. He thus anticipates the phenomenology of Edmund Husserl (1859–1938) (whose *Ideas* Bhattacharya encountered in English in 1931). Bhattacharya builds on this to develop an account of subjectivity's alienation from the known object as a mode of freedom as the lived ground to which the will responds. In his posthumous *Studies in Philosophy* (1956), Bhattacharya applies the *rasa* ("taste" or "essence") theory from classical Indian aesthetics to the problem of the sacred in postmetaphysical modernity. Bhattacharya continues the discussion of the nature of philosophy itself, as does his son Kali Das Bhattacharya (1911–1984) in his *Alternative Standpoints in Philosophy* (1953). Kali Das Bhattacharya is also notable for his *Philosophy, Logic and Language* (1965) and *The Indian Concept of Man* (1982).

Indian phenomenology as foreshadowed by Krishna Chandra Bhattacharya is furthered by Jarava Lal Mehta (1912–1988) and Jitendra Nath Mohanty (b. 1928). Mehta's *The Philosophy of Martin Heidegger* (1967) highlights the significance of thought of Martin Heidegger (1889–1976) as a culmination of both the phenomenological and hermeneutic traditions of Western philosophy. Mehta's positioning outside of the West, unencumbered by post-Enlightenment Western philosophy's historical unease with religion, allows him to be one of the earliest to identify the religious implications of Heidegger's analysis of language and being for a postmetaphysical reenvisaging of negative theology. This enables an often overlooked continuity to be drawn from Heidegger's earlier focus on radical ontology to his later aesthetic turn. Mehta's *Transcendental Phenomenology* (1989) represents the culmination of his analysis of Heidegger, the phenomenological tradition and its influences on the Deconstructionist movement. Mohanty traces a similar trajectory; however, he takes Husserl's treatment of intentionality as his starting point in *The Concept of Intentionality* (1971), *Edmund Husserl's Theory of Meaning* (1976), and *Phenomenology* (1997). Both Mehta and Mohanty utilize the insights of phenomenology, especially its emphasis on the historical and cultural embeddedness of subjectivity, to self-critically reflect upon their own position as Indian thinkers working within Western philosophy. They thus develop sophisticated methodologies for undertaking philosophical dialogue across cultures. Mehta, in his *India and the West* (1985) and posthumous *Philosophy and Religion* (1990), utilizes Heidegger's insights into the ontological (i.e., "being") itself as a hermeneutic encounter to revisit the place of self-reflection as tradition-bound philosophizing in India. Ironically, Heidegger's concern with the uniquely European origins of philosophy, especially his reconsideration of Plato's conception of *theoria* and the transformative nature of self-knowledge, allows Mehta to reconsider classical Indian thought itself unencumbered by the religion-philosophy/theory-practice dichotomy. Similarly, Mohanty in his *Reason and Tradition in Indian Thought* (1992), *The Self and Its Other* (2000), and *Explorations in Philosophy* (2001) reappraises the assumptions of theory and practice, authority and knowledge, as a basis for rethinking the place of philosophizing in traditional India and modernity.

Representing different extremes of modern Indian philosophy are Bimal Krishna Matilal (1935–1991), Daya Krishna (1924–2007), and Gayatri Chakravorty Spivak (b. 1942). Matilal brings his training in both the Sanskritic tradition of logic (*tarka*) and mathematical logic under W. V. O. Quine (1908–2000) to bear on reconsiderations of Hindu, Buddhist, and Jain logic in light of modern analytical developments. In *Epistemology, Logic and Grammar in Indian Philosophical Analysis* (1971), *Language, Logic and Reality* (1985), and *Perception* (1986), Matilal pioneers a comparative framework within which to approach analytic philosophy, utilizing this to later engage in issues of ethics and personhood. Krishna, one of the most independent and original of modern Indian thinkers, questions the very assumption of the religious orientation of much classical Indian thought, instead emphasizing its purely theoretical nature in his *Indian Philosophy: A Counter Perspective* (1991). This allows Krishna to trace continuities between traditional and modern philosophizing. Spivak comes to prominence following her translation of Jacques Derrida's (1930–2004) *Of Grammatology* (1976). Spivak combines philosophical, literary, and sociopolitical analysis, critiquing the Enlightenment ideal of the autonomy of reason detached from political and ideological concerns. In "Can the Subaltern Speak?" (1988) and *A Critique of Postcolonial Reason* (1999), she argues that the claim of detached objectivity legitimizes colonial interests by masking the agenda of the colonizer and marginalizing the subjectivity of the colonized. Spivak criticizes Matilal's attempt to promote Indian thought in terms of the analytic tradition as contributing to this marginalization due to its internalization of Enlightenment paradigms of rationality. Krishna, in turn, is scathing toward the sort of postmodern critique espoused by Spivak.

With the notable exception of Spivak, most modern Indian thinkers have utilized Western philosophy to reconsider traditional Indian thought. Those working within the analytic tradition, such as Matilal and Krishna, have tended to emphasize the commonalities between traditional Indian thought and Western philosophy, while differences have tended to be highlighted by thinkers such as Mehta and Mohanty who work within continental traditions, such as phenomenology, that have tended to be more open to considering philosophy as occurring within the greater totality of unique lifeworlds. Beyond its independent developments, the significance of modern Indian philosophy lies in the ways that the hermeneutic encounter between Indian traditions and modernity have been utilized not only to reconsider the nature of philosophy itself but also to pioneer methodologies for undertaking philosophy in global, comparative, cross-cultural, and postcolonial settings.

ANDREW MCGARRITY

See also Religion

Further Reading

Halbfass, Wilhelm. *India and Europe: An Essay in Understanding.* Albany, NY: SUNY Press, 1988.

Jackson, William. "Steps towards the Whole Horizon: J. L. Mehta's Contributions to Hermeneutics and Phenomenology." *Asian Philosophy* 2(1) (1992): 21–38.

King, Richard. *Indian Philosophy: An Introduction to Hindu and Buddhist Thought.* Edinburgh, UK: Edinburgh University Press, 1999.

Lal, Basant Kumar. *Contemporary Indian Philosophy.* Patna: Motilal Banarsidass, 1973.

Raghuramaraju, A. *Debates in Indian Philosophy: Classical, Colonial and Contemporary.* New Delhi: Oxford University Press, 2006.

Schreiner, Peter. "The Indianness of Modern Indian Philosophy as a Historical and Philosophical Problem." *Philosophy East and West* 28 (1978): 21–37.

Pondicherry. *See* Puducherry

✦ POPULATION

Every sixth person in the world is an Indian. India's population, as per the 2001 population census, was 1.028 billion, consisting of 531.3 million males and 495.7 million females. The population in 2010 was estimated to be 1.173 billion according to the 2010 CIA *World Factbook,* while the provisional figure from the 2011 census is 1.21 billion. India accounts for 2.4 percent of the world's land area but supports 17.5 percent of the world population. It is one of the most densely populated countries in the world. India's population growth trajectory has been keenly studied for both academic reasons and policy purposes. Although there has been a marginal decline in the growth rate of the population from 2.14 percent during 1981–1991 to 1.93 percent during 1991–2001 and an estimated 1.376 percent in 2010, the growth rate continues to be high in comparison to many countries in Europe and North America. India is the second most-populous country in the world, behind only to China.

India's population density has increased steadily from 77 persons per .6 square mile to 324 persons per square kilometer in 2001. The difference in population density in different areas of the country is substantial, ranging from 9,340 in Delhi and 903 in West Bengal, the most thickly populated state among the major states, to 13 in Arunachal Pradesh. The high rate of population growth has its advantages as well as its disadvantages for social and economic development. On the one hand, a large population base ensures the supply of a large and growing labor force and also provides a large market for goods and services. On the other hand, in an agrarian country with a low rate of savings and low capital formation, a large population acts as a drag on resources, and the generation of capital for investment poses serious problems.

Historically, India has been a country with a relatively large population. This is primarily because of its soil, climate, and natural resources and its early development of agriculture that could support such large populations. The first census was conducted in 1872, but it was only from 1881 that the census was conducted every 10 years. Data from 1901 onward are considered to be more reliable than the earlier censuses. The pattern of population growth saw high fluctuations. Periods of high growth were followed by decreases, especially during 1871–1881, 1891–1901, and 1911–1921. This was largely due to huge famines in the 1870s and 1890s and the influenza epidemic of 1918 in which, according to one estimate, more than 15 million persons died. Nonetheless, India's population reached approximately 251 million in 1921. After that the population increased rapidly. The year 1921, also known as the year of the Great Divide, marks the difference in the patterns of growth. The rapid population growth during 1921–1951 occurred because of the decline in mortality rates and a large population whereby families were little affected by family planning programs and needed family members, especially sons, to supplement family income and to care for elders in old age. The decade 1951–1961 saw an explosive population growth whereby 78 million persons were added to the population. During 1961–1971 about 109 million persons were added, while the next decade, 1971–1981, saw an addition of 135 million persons. Furthermore, during 1981–1991 there was a net addition of 160 million persons, and the last decade of the century, 1991–2001, saw an increase of 184 million persons.

While high mortality rates caused by infectious and parasitic diseases, epidemics, and famines controlled population growth in the past, the rapid decline in mortality rates since 1921 and especially after 1947 led to a high growth rate that reached almost 2 percent during 1951–1961. In the subsequent decades the growth rate hovered around 2.2 percent per annum. The relative stability of the birthrate remained a major concern. It was only during 1991–2001 that the fall in the birthrate was faster than the death rate and that population growth was less than 2 percent. The significant point regarding the experience of the decade was that India had entered a phase of demographic transition characterized by declining fertility in some states. The increase in population has primarily occurred due to a significant reduction in the death rate. Demographic projections suggest that India will overtake China and become the most populous country of the world by the middle of this century.

Between Indian independence in 1947 and 1970, there was a significant decline in India's mortality rate. This decline was caused by a combination of factors, including reduction in the impact of several major communicable diseases and the prevention of famines. The mortality rate continued to decline steadily from 1970. Both the crude death rate (CDR) and the infant mortality rates (IMR) almost halved. While the CDR declined from 16 to less than 8 per 1,000, the IMR declined from 134 infant deaths to about 57 infant deaths per 1,000 live births in 2006. However, a rural-urban disparity continues to be a cause of concern. Life expectancy at birth in India has gone up from 32 years for 1950–1951 to 63 for 1999–2000.

India's total fertility rate (TFR), which measures the number of births per woman, has declined from around 6 in 1961 to just above 3 in 2010. Fertility has declined across the country but at different rates in rural and urban areas. There are marked contrasts in the fertility levels across the country. While Kerala and Tamil Nadu in southern India have already achieved replacement-level fertility rates, Uttar Pradesh and Bihar continue to have fertility rates considerably higher. In general, fertility rates are appreciably lower in the southern states. An analysis of the determinants of fertility reduction in India suggests that it has been achieved overwhelmingly through the increased use of modern contraceptive methods (mainly female sterilization). In particular, Kerala's remarkable achievement has often been linked to its better performance in social sector development. It is often pointed out that while Kerala and Tamil Nadu have been successful in radically reducing their fertility rates, many northern states such as Uttar Pradesh, Bihar, Madhya Pradesh, and Rajasthan all have very high fertility rates. These latter four states also have much lower levels of educational achievement, especially in female education, and general health care. It is these four states that are going to contribute an estimated 55 percent of total population growth in the quarter century between 2001 and 2026. The lower fertility levels and earlier fertility declines in the southern states has been attributed to the region's weaker patriarchal kinship structures and more equitable gender relations. These regional contrasts point out important aspects of the social and economic contexts that determine the extent and pace of fertility reduction in India. Although there appears to be a trend toward a broad convergence in levels of fertility between states, the interstate variations in fertility will likely continue for some time.

The urban population has increased from just 10.8 percent in 1901 to 27.8 percent in 2001. However, the growth of the urban population has declined since 1981. The slowing down of urban growth is largely due to a decline in the rate of the natural increase and a limited increase in the population of new towns. The process of urbanization in India is based on the larger cities. The share of Class I cities—that is, the number of metropolitan cities having a population of 1 million or more—increased from 12 in 1981 to 35 in 2001.

According to the 2001 census, 29.9 percent of the population were migrants. As per National Sample Survey (NSS) estimates, the percentage of migrants increased from 24.7 percent in 1993 to 26.6 percent for 1999–2000. Of the total migrants in 2001, 55 percent were rural-to-rural migrants, whereas 16 percent were migrants from rural to urban areas. While males migrate mostly for economic reasons (such as employment, business, and education), much of female migration in India is associational in nature; females mostly migrate when they get married. The majority of migrants in India migrate just short distances. This mobility usually goes from backward to relatively economically advanced states and cities. Recently, however, it has been observed that although regional imbalances have increased, the population has become relatively immobile. This is due to the growth of regional identity and regional pride and to city development plans that are hostile to the poor and to migrants.

India has a young age structure, with nearly 35 percent of the population below 15 years of age. Since 1971, however, and largely because of a decline in birthrates, there has been a significant decline in the proportion of children below the age of 15. At the same time, the proportion of the population aged 60 and above has increased steadily. In 2001 the share of the elderly population was 7.45 percent. The dependency ratio, defined as the ratio of nonworkers to workers, is high, which is why the contribution of children under 15 years of age is high.

Sex ratio, defined as the number of females per 1,000 males, is an important indicator of gender equality. The sex ratio in India has always been unfavorable to females, although there are regional variations. India's sex ratio declined from 972 in 1901 to 926 in 1991. In 2001 there was a marginal improvement as the sex ratio moved up to 933. Still, this is one of the lowest ratios in the world. Moreover, there are stark regional differences in the sex ratio; by and large, the southern states have a better record than the northern and northwestern states. Kerala has a sex ratio of 1058, which is comparatively high by global standards. There is a great deal of evidence to indicate that there has been a relative neglect in the health and well-being of women, particularly of infants and children, that has resulted in a lower survival rate for females in comparison to males. The relative disadvantage of females is also reflected in the low and declining child sex ratio (CSR). The CSR in India has come down from 945 in 1991 to 927 in 2001. The regional contrasts are again very significant, with the northwestern states of Punjab, Haryana, Gujarat, Madhya Pradesh, and Himachal Pradesh having a lower CSR than many southern states.

The work participation rate refers to the proportion of total workers to the total population expressed as a percentage. In general, the total work participation rate in India shows a rising trend since 1971. The trend is more pronounced in rural areas than in urban areas, where it has remained almost constant at 30 percent. In the case of females there has been an increase in the rate in both rural and urban areas. In the case of males, a slight decline in the rate is noticed for 1981–1991.

A majority of Indians are still dependent on agriculture for their livelihood, although there has been a decline in the share of agricultural workers from nearly 74 percent for 1972–1973 to nearly 57 percent for 2004–2005. Employment has undergone some significant changes in recent decades. Since the liberalization of the Indian economy in the 1990s the economy has performed well, but growth in employment has slowed down considerably. The 1990s have been described as a period of jobless growth, although there has been some recovery on the employment front since 1999–2000.

The literacy rate of the population in the age group seven years and above has risen to 65.4 percent in 2001 from 52.2 percent in 1991 and 43.6 percent in 1981. Despite a series of interventions by the government and nongovernmental organizations (NGOs), nearly one-third of Indians are still illiterate. In the rural areas literacy was 59 percent in 2001, while among rural females it was only 47 percent. The disadvantaged social groups also have relatively lower literacy rates. Illiteracy is disproportionately concentrated in seven states: Orissa, Madhya Pradesh, Andhra Pradesh, Uttar Pradesh, Arunachal Pradesh, Rajasthan, and Bihar. These states account for more than half of the illiterate people in the country. Programs such as Sarva Siksha Abhiyan—midday meal schemes—have been launched to achieve universal elementary education in India. Notwithstanding its phenomenal growth, higher education is still not accessible to the majority of people.

India's large population has been seen as a burden and as a Malthusian constraint on economic growth. Recently, however, emphasis has been placed on the benefits of such a large and young population in a globalizing and aging world. In 2004 the working population (15–64 years old) was 672 million, that is, nearly 62 percent of the total population. Even with the anticipated decline in fertility, it is estimated that India will have a substantially large population of young people. It is expected that by the year 2020 the average age of an Indian will be 29, compared to 37 for China and the United States, 45 for Western Europe, and 48 for Japan. This is expected to benefit the economy in many ways. First of all, a higher working-age population will mean the availability of a larger number of producers or workers, and a decline in the nation's saving rate is likely to increase the savings rate of the economy. Critics, however, point out that the large pool of young people could be productively employed only when India's significant deficits in education and health care are resolved. In the absence of policies enhancing the human capital base of the economy, the benefits of such demographic advantages will be seriously limited.

Population policies are policy measures designed to bring about desirable changes in the growth, composition, and quality of the population. Although the term "population policy" is often narrowly defined to mean family planning programs, or programs concerning

A teacher working with USAID conducts a family planning meeting for women in the densely populated and impoverished area of Sangam Vihar, New Delhi, August 1999. (AP Photo/John McConnico)

the reduction in the growth rate of the population, population policies in the wider sense encompass a gamut of issues concerning the number and the characteristics of the population.

There has always been a debate regarding the desirability of family planning programs. For the first decade and a half after India's independence in 1947, family planning programs were adopted on a modest scale, but the emphasis on family planning increased after the publication of the 1961 census data, which showed a growth rate that was greater than anticipated. The full-fledged Department of Family Planning was created in 1966, and an approach was adopted under which male and female family planning workers were recruited to provide alternative methods of contraception. During 1966–1969 the family planning program was made target-oriented, and more funds were provided. Achievement, however, fell far short of expectations.

The New National Population Policy of 1976 marked a departure from the earlier policies. Earlier policies were based on the understanding that while the government should continue to pursue family planning policies, population growth would be effectively controlled by the process of economic development and improvements in literacy. But the policy of 1976 clearly declared that to wait for education and economic development to bring about a decline in the fertility rate was not a practical solution, as the increase in population made economic development slow and more difficult to achieve. As a result, it was felt that a direct assault on population growth had to be made. The policy was a more proactive one, and some direct measures such as increasing the legal minimum age of marriage to 21 for males and 18 for girls were adopted. During the Emergency (1975–1977), however, compulsory sterilization and coercive family planning discredited the family planning program.

In the period after the Emergency there was again a revision in government policy toward family welfare. While targets were routinely revised and fresh goals were agreed upon, the use of coercive methods was not envisaged in the subsequent policy pronouncements. Relatively modest targets were fixed, and the structure of incentives for adoption and disincentives for nonadoption were devised.

National Population Policy 2000 (NPP 2000) has put emphasis on voluntary and informed choice, the consent of citizens while availing themselves of reproductive health care services, and the continuation of the target-free approach in administering family planning services. The policy signifies a shift from the earlier demographically driven target-oriented population policies to recognizing the centrality of human development, gender equity, and adolescent reproductive health and rights, among other factors. NPP 2000 aims at achieving net replacement levels (the TFR) by 2010 and is based on a broader set of interventions and recognizes the need to simultaneously address issues of child survival, maternal health, and contraception while increasing outreach and coverage of a comprehensive package of reproductive and child health services. In terms of agencies, there has been a more inclusive approach toward involving civil society groups, NGOs, and the corporate sector along with government agencies.

DEEPAK K. MISHRA

See also Economy

Further Reading

Central Intelligence Agency. *The World Factbook: India, 2010.* https://www.cia.gov/library/publications/the-world-factbook/geos/in.html.

Chandrashekhar, C. P., Jayati Ghosh, and A. Roychowdhury. "The 'Demographic Dividend' and Young India's Economic Future." *Economic and Political Weekly* 41(49) (2006): 5055–5064.

Council for Social Development. *India: Social Development Report.* New Delhi: Oxford University Press, 2006.

Dreze, J., and A. Sen. *India: Development and Participation.* New Delhi: Oxford University Press, 2002.

Dyson, T., and M. Moore. "On Kinship Structure, Female Autonomy and Demographic Behaviour in India." *Population and Development Review* 9(1) (1983): 35–75.

Dyson, T., R. Cassen, and L. Visaria, eds. *Twenty-First Century India: Population, Economy, Human Development and the Environment.* New Delhi: Oxford University Press, 2002.

Premi, M. K. *Population of India in the New Millennium: Census 2001.* New Delhi: National Book Trust, 2006.

✦ POSTCOLONIAL STUDIES

Postcolonial studies is an interdisciplinary field of academic specialization. Practitioners include literary and art critics as well as cultural historians and political scientists who focus on the analysis of issues related to the identity and expressions of populations who were the victims of modern European colonization. Some of the most influential representatives of postcolonial studies are from India.

Overseas European colonies were consolidated over several centuries until, by the time of World War I, the Europeans had settled in or were dominating more than three quarters of the globe. Following World War II, however, the bankruptcy of Britain and other nations with empires and the opposition to imperial rule organized by national liberation movements, which had been gathering momentum since the beginning of the 20th century, led to the fairly rapid disintegration of the European colonial empires and to the establishment of a myriad of politically autonomous nation-states. India gained its independence from the British at the stroke of midnight on August 14, 1947, ushering in a period of identity search and redefinition affecting a whole generation of intellectuals. Indian writer Salman Rushdie (b. 1947) encapsulated this phenomenon in his award-winning novel *Midnight's Children* (1981), which is still considered a particularly representative example of postcolonial literature. Through the narrative technique of magical realism, Rushdie presents the protagonist's life story as an allegory of Indian history before and especially after independence. The role of memory, through which people filter their experience of reality and establish their own idiosyncratic truth, is greatly emphasized in the novel, pointing to one of the basic themes of postcolonial studies: national identity is built on a scaffolding of collective memories, which reflect the way people are socially perceived and represented. The colonial encounter catalyzes a superiority/inferiority distinction between the colonizer and the colonized that becomes inexorably embedded in self-perception. Having been defined as qualitatively "other" by the colonial powers, those who were colonized cannot simply erase that identity by gaining political independence, particularly when the West maintains its indirect dominance on postcolonial societies (often ironically self-identified as "the Rest") through economic power and the prestige of its institutions.

The predicament of the continuing intellectual hegemony of the West is exactly what practitioners of postcolonial studies wish to address. Not surprisingly, this issue has especially attracted the attention of scholars who, while often born and raised in what are now postcolonial societies, have ended up living and working in Western academic settings. Thus, as argued by the Pakistani-Welsh theorist Sara Suleri (b. 1951), postcolonial theorists remain entangled in the colonial encounter since they choose to address, albeit critically, a mainly Western audience.

The issue of audience is a crucial one not only in postcolonial studies but also in the broader field of postcolonial literature in general, correlating as it does with the fact that the languages used by most postcolonial writers are the ones imposed by the colonizers. Being educated in postcolonial settings usually means acquiring these languages—English in particular—as a sort of lingua franca that provides the means for surmounting regional and ethnic particularism and for addressing a global audience. Consequently, postcolonial literature seems to be the result of a process adumbrated in the title of a foundational work of analysis: *The Empire Writes Back* (1989). But this "writing back" from the global periphery to its center reproduces just the client-patron relationship that should have ended with decolonization. One of the most influential postcolonial theorists, the Indian-born U.S.-based academic Gayatri Chakravorty Spivak (b. 1942), has characterized this process as one of "epistemic violence": the imposition of Western ways of knowing causing postcolonial subjects to be forever "caught in translation," that is, unable to express themselves without reference to alien categories.

The pervasive intellectual dominance of the West on "the Rest"—absorbed through linguistic and educational channels and molding the social identity of the postcolonial subjects—becomes particularly problematic when it is seen as being behind the very process of emancipation through which colonized societies successfully fought for and acquired political autonomy. The Indian political scientist Partha Chatterjee (b. 1947) highlights quite forcefully how the model of the nation-state adopted at independence by postcolonial societies such as India was clearly derived from the Western ideology of modernity and liberal democracy. This ideology, however, was linked to definitions of subjectivity and community that differ very profoundly from those catalyzed by Indian history. As a result, not only is the adoption of the institutional mechanisms of the democratic capitalistic state bound to clash with indigenous social structures, but even the Marxist critique of those mechanisms cannot be usefully adopted. The postcolonial experience highlights the local specificity of Western ideologies that were assumed to have universal application. Thus, one of the objectives of postcolonial studies is to provincialize Europe, as Indian historian Dipesh Chakrabarty indicates in the title of his influential work *Provincializing Europe* (2000).

In the view of perhaps the most influential representative of postcolonial studies, the Palestinian American literary critic Edward Said (1935–2003), it is the universalist assumptions of Western civilization that inevitably led to representing cultural differences in terms of superiority/inferiority, in the process justifying the West's imperial ambitions. In the analysis presented in his book *Orientalism* (1978), Said argues that even the most scholarly Western treatments of the languages, history, and cultural expressions of the Orient—Asia, North Africa, and the Middle East—were implicitly biased by the colonial encounter. As a result, the whole history of the Orient was rewritten from a Western point of view and then was used as the framework for remaking the colonial subjects in the image of their Western colonizers.

By highlighting the affiliation of knowledge with power, Said proposed discourse analysis as a useful tool for understanding the pervasive influence of ideology on all forms of expression, including scholarly research. This became the basis of much of the theoretical and methodological approach of postcolonial studies, leading on the one hand to a certain technical impenetrability of its texts and on the other hand to an overlap with related forms of cultural analysis, such as in India those emerging from the Centre for the Study of Developing Societies (CSDS), the Centre of Contemporary Studies (CCS), and the Subaltern Studies Collective. The main difference between the type of cultural studies produced in India and those produced by scholars of Indian origin operating in the West, however, has to do with the themes they address. While issues of nationhood, communal conflict, and globalization attract the attention of indigenously based scholars, issues of identity, individual rights, and cultural hybridity are addressed most often in the work of émigré scholars, or diasporic intellectuals as they are often called.

One of the most influential representatives of the latter group is the Indian-born, British-educated, and U.S.-based academic Homi K. Bhabha (b. 1949), who is also notorious for the opacity of his prose. Combining postmodern discourse analysis with Lacanian psychoanalysis, Bhabha argues that the only constructive strategy for addressing both the basic incommensurability of different cultures and the continuing hegemony of the West is hybridity. According to Bhabha, cultural assumptions are deconstructed by having the observed become the observer and by confusing categorizations of authenticity and "otherness" through mimicry, a set of ironically deceptive practices frustrating homogenizing efforts.

Two arguments put forth by the strongest critics of the textual turn in postcolonial studies are that the hybridity strategy may well be a successful approach for the personal adjustment of diasporic intellectuals themselves and that the celebration of social fragmentation and individual expression of multiple types of cultural diversity may fit particularly well in the context of globalized consumer capitalism. Among these critics, the Indo-Pakistani literary theorist Aijaz Ahmad (b. 1947), a fellow of the CCS, has possibly produced the most cogent critique of the heavy cost exacted by shifting the analysis of the postcolonial condition from the political-economic realm to the literary-cultural realm. As he concludes in his aptly titled work *In Theory* (1992), a reevaluation of the material conditions of postcolonial life, in the context of a historical reassessment of the revolutionary struggles leading to political independence, may uniquely reinvigorate the transformational potential of postcolonial studies, translating theory into practice. Or, as indicated by Sumit Sarkar (b. 1939), another Indian scholar calling for the need to reconfigure the political relevance rather than merely the academic relevance of postcolonial studies, what is needed is implementation of the Gramscian motto "Pessimism of the intellect, optimism of the will" by shifting from discourse to circumstance.

E. L. CERRONI-LONG

See also Asiatic Society of Bengal; Asiatic Society of Mumbai; Orientalism

Further Reading
Ahmad, A. *In Theory.* London: Verso, 1992.
Ashcroft, B., G. Griffiths, and H. Tiffin, eds. *The Empire Writes Back.* London: Routledge, 1989.
Bahri, D. "Introduction to Postcolonial Studies." Accessed April 28, 2011. http://english.emory.edu
    /Bahri/Intro.html.
Bhabha, Homi. K. *The Location of Culture.* London: Routledge, 1994.
Castle, G., ed. *Postcolonial Discourses.* Oxford, UK: Blackwell, 2001.
Chakrabarty, Dipesh. *Provincializing Europe: Postcolonial Thought and Historical Difference.* Princeton,
    NJ: Princeton University Press, 2000.
Chatterjee, P. *The Nation and Its Fragments: Colonial and Postcolonial Histories.* Princeton, NJ: Princeton
    University Press, 1993.
Rushdie, S. *Midnight's Children.* London: Jonathan Cape, 1981.
Said, Edward. *Orientalism.* New York: Pantheon, 1978.
Sarkar, Sumit. *Beyond Nationalist Frames: Postmodernism, Hindu Fundamentalism, History.* Blooming-
    ton: Indiana University Press, 2002.
Spivak, Gyatry Chakravorty. *A Critique of Post-Colonial Reason: Toward a History of the Vanishing Pres-
    ent.* Cambridge, MA: Harvard University Press, 1999.
Suleri, S. *The Rhetoric of English India.* Chicago: University of Chicago Press, 1992.
Young, R. *Postcolonialism: An Historical Introduction.* Oxford, UK: Blackwell, 2001.

✦ POVERTY AND WEALTH

Official data on poverty and wealth in India show a significant decline in poverty and an increase in wealth since 1980 compared to the preceding period. Using official Indian government estimates, the total population below the poverty line declined between 1983 and 1993–1994 by 8.5 percent, going from 44.5 to 36 percent, and between 1993–1994 and 2004–2005 by 8.2 percent, going from 36 to 27.8 percent. For the most recent data year, 2004–2005, using 2005 United Nations (UN) population data, this translated into 314.3 million out of a total population of 1.13 billion. This is down from 344.8 million in 1985, using UN 1985 population data and Indian 1983 poverty data. By comparison, the Indian middle class is frequently quoted as being 300 million people; in between this and the official poverty measure there are another 400 million people. However, given the high levels of malnutrition among children and women, it is at best uncertain that official Indian poverty data are a reliable measure of actual living standards or reductions in deprivation. The World Bank's most recent estimates of poverty for India, published in 2009, using the $1.25 a day poverty line—popularly referred to as the dollar-a-day measure of extreme poverty defined as inability to meet basic needs—puts the percentage of people in poverty at 41.6. The World Bank's 2009 $2 dollar-a-day poverty line measure of moderate poverty, where basic needs may just be met, records 75.6 percent living in poverty. The World Bank used an improved survey technique in 2008, so data published in the World Bank's report before this date are not strictly comparable with those from 2008 because the new technique more accurately shows what people consume, resulting in evidence that previous estimates underestimated the percentage in poverty.

Poverty lines such as these, whether the Indian government's or the World Bank's, classify individuals as poor using a monetary measure of food items with a margin for basic nonfood items. This measure leaves out significant proportions of the actual resources required for effective maintenance of health and education when compared with the idea of basic needs. Health and education are core indicators of human well-being, both of which can be low (inadequate) even if incomes are relatively high (above the poverty line), as existing research shows. What is required is a real, rather than monetary, measure of wealth in order to accurately measure poverty and deprivation. The term "real" here refers to the actual endowment of education that individuals hold and, alternatively, the skills or jobs that they perform, not the value of their salaries. Other indicators of the real level and distribution of wealth are the distributions of employment between sectors of the economy and health of the population.

Stark contrasts between the haves and have nots in India are omnipresent: between the few who can afford to buy expensive consumer products and the overwhelming majority of the population, which has to work very hard and long hours to eke out a living, like this rickshaw driver, October 2009. (Alain Lacroix/Dreamstime.com)

This is an important point in the Indian context given that the percentage of children suffering from malnutrition is greater than the percentage of officially measured total poor (children plus adults). The World Bank report *India's Undernourished Children* showed that child malnutrition is significantly worse in India than in sub-Saharan Africa; the number of children underweight at birth in sub-Saharan Africa is half India's number. In 2009, Forbes India reported a figure cited by Save the Children that 6 percent of gross domestic product (GDP) is lost through child mortality. Two million Indian children die before their fifth birthday, 25 percent of the world total of 8 million reported by the United Nations Children's Fund (UNICEF) in 2009. In 2008 UNICEF cited recent World Health Organization (WHO) data showing that more than 30 percent of Indian children under age 5 are stunted, with wasting measured as acute malnutrition affecting more than 15 percent of children under 5. Fifty percent of children under age 5 are underweight. Forty-six percent of children under age 3 have a body weight that is below the healthy range (i.e., are malnourished), representing almost 33 percent of malnourished children in all developing countries. To put this into perspective, 42 percent of the total Indian population is below age 18. Based on these measures, WHO places India well within the sub-Saharan human development level. Medicins sans Frontieres (Doctors without Borders [MSF]) remarked that this represented a major humanitarian emergency in a booming economy. Clearly deprivation is still more widespread when measured by other indicators of human well-being, such as the number of women suffering from malnutrition measured as anemia. In 2008 the MSF reported that 83 percent of Indian women are anemic. As a real indicator, education—the primary education-level skills imparted by government schools—was recently measured by a national survey by the Indian nongovernmental organization Pratham. The results showed that literacy and mathematics skills were significantly deficient. This was in the context of the last 10 years of significant investment in the government primary school sector under the Sarva Shiksha Abhiyan (SSA), the Education for All initiative.

Wealth is also conventionally valued in monetary terms by company share price and revenue and through other asset prices or the total value of national output. On these measures, wealth has clearly increased dramatically for India, with national output measured as real GDP per worker having doubled between the early 1980s and 2000. Yet wealth on these measures does not as yet adequately take into account depreciation of capital stock outside the typical business measurement context. Missing from depreciation measures are such things as human capital and natural resources, given what economists have long described as the inherent market failure to encompass the complete costs of production and consumption. For example, the World Bank, WHO, and Harvard University have developed the disability-adjusted life year (DALY), a measure of life years lost to premature death and years lived in ill health. From this is calculated the disease burden on countries, which shows the health gap with the healthiest countries. Human capital is affected by malnutrition, disease, and injuries, of which India suffers in excess, well above developed country standards. If wealth requires investment, the following is indicative: Forbes India reported in 2009 that

Indian government spending on health amounts to .9 percent of GDP, in contrast to, for example, Sierra Leone's 7.8 percent. In addition, parts of the capital stock such as agricultural land and transport infrastructure must be taken into consideration in wealth assessments. Recent research has shown that India's natural resources, such as water and agricultural land, have been significantly affected by overuse, causing depletion, particularly in the case of water, and contamination of both water and land caused by overuse of fertilizer and by external sources of pollution. While India's transport system is comprehensive, unlike many countries with similar levels of human development, particularly the railroad network, its rolling stock and freight handling systems are in need of complete redesign, not simply upgrading. Intermodal traffic is limited. India's rolling stock is of equivalent design and capacity to that of the United States in the 1950s. In addition, electricity supply is insufficient, with regular power outages. All of these physical infrastructure elements taken together have been widely quoted as being likely to prevent India's high GDP growth rate from continuing.

Wealthier countries with less income inequality and low absolute poverty tend to have significantly lower employment in agriculture and significant higher employment in manufacturing and services. Indian agricultural employment, which can be defined, as the Indian census does, as "farm worker" (farmers plus their workers), amounted to 67.1 percent of the total Indian workforce in 1991. By the census of 2001, this rate had fallen to 58.5 percent, although the absolute numbers had increased from 210 to 233 during that period. This must be distinguished from the total rural workforce, which includes nonfarm activity. The total rural workforce fell very little, from 79.1 percent in 1990–1991 to 77.2 by 1999–2000. This gives an indication of the geographic distribution of poverty and wealth, given that in 2004–2005 the unorganized sector of agricultural laborers had average years of schooling of 2.4 and 1.0 for males and females, respectively. Recent evidence has shown that since the reforms of 1991, high-value and skilled economic activity has been located in advanced regions and major urban areas. These economic activities, not mass manufacturing and construction employment, have accounted for India's high growth rate. Overall, the evolution of sectoral employment is shown in table 7. China in comparison saw change in employment by sector from 1986 to 2007 as follows: agriculture shrank from 61 to 41 percent; industry, which includes manufacturing, grew from 22 to 27 percent; and services grew from 17 to 32 percent of total employment.

Measured in conventional terms as real GDP, agriculture as a percentage of GDP changed from 46 percent in 1970–1971 to 32 percent in 1990–1991 and to 21 percent in

Table 7   Sectoral Distribution of Employment of the Indian Economy

	1972–1973	1977–1978	1983	1987–1988	1993–1994	1999–2000
Agriculture	74.0	72.3	68.4	65.5	60.4	56.7
Industry	11.4	12.3	13.7	15.5	15.8	17.6
Services	14.6	15.4	17.5	18.4	23.8	25.7

SOURCE: National Sample Survey Organisation, Government of India, 2001.

2004–2005. Industry increased from 22 percent of GDP in 1970–1971 to 27 percent in 1990–1991, where it has remained since. Manufacturing, with its potential to create mass employment in better-paid jobs, increased from 13 percent in 1970–1971 to 17 percent in 1990–1991, where it too has remained. Services, however, have increased from 32 percent of GDP in 1970–1971 to 41 percent in 1990–1991 and to 52 percent in 2004–2005 and has been responsible for all of the reduction in agriculture as a share of GDP. However, the type of services that have expanded have been overwhelmingly in low and unskilled work (in the informal sector). Notably, business services, which includes the much-publicized informa-tion technology (IT) and business process outsourcing (BPO) subsectors, constitute only 1.2 percent of the total Indian labor force and 13 percent of GDP (1999–2000). In 2005 the estimated contribution of IT offshoring and outsourcing to GDP was 7 percent, with an estimated workforce of approximately 1.5 million, for 2007–2008 and was 2.23 million for 2009 (total employment in IT and BPO-ITES was said to be 4 million in 2008). India had the highest average growth rate in the export of services during the 1990s, of which IT and BPO were the key components, at 17.5 percent, followed by China at 15.8 percent, while the Organization for Economic Cooperation and Development (OECD) countries with the highest rates for the same period were Canada and the United States at 7.3 and 6.1 percent, respectively. The United States represents 60 percent of Indian IT and BPO-ITES activ-ity. The better-paid formal sector, which includes services, industry, and manufacturing, con-sisted of 7.5 million workers (out of a total of 313 million workers) in 1991 and 8.7 million workers in 1998 and fell to 8.4 million workers in 2003. In comparison, in 2002 India had 6.2 million formal sector manufacturing jobs, while at about the same time China had 160 million such jobs. In contrast, India's industrial investment during the current high GDP growth phase since 1980 has been in capital intensive as well as in highly skilled areas. Some famous results have been Tata's Nano, the world's smallest gasoline car launched in 2008; the world's biggest steel company, Lakshmi Mittal's ArcelorMittal, measured by quantity of steel produced in 2008; and a best-selling electric car, the G-Wiz, made by the REVA Electric Car Company in Bangalore, Karnataka. Other successes include solar panels. The United Nations Industrial Development Organization (UNIDO) compiles data on value added in manufacturing measured on an index starting from the value 100. The World Bank's World Development Indicators 2007 report reprinted the index, which showed that for East Asia and the Pacific, the index reached nearly 450, an increase of nearly 450 percent from 1990 to 2005. On the same index, South Asia, of which India is the largest country, increased by only 250 percent over the same period. Even the construction sector shares of employment and GDP are not significant at 4.4 and 5.9 percent, respectively, for 1999–2000. Overall, as meas-ured by the World Bank, India was the 12th largest economy in the world in 2007, when its total monetary output value is measured as gross national income; China was the 4th largest.

In starker terms, Forbes India in 2008 determined that India now ranks 8th in the world for the number of billionaires, measured in U.S. dollars, and is ranked 2nd in the world for a country's combined billionaires' monetary wealth, behind the United States. The UN's 2009 human development index ranks India 134th of 182 countries measured, while India ranked 128th of 177 countries measured in 2007. The *Indian Economic Review* noted that for the top 5 percent of the population the comparison is with Europe, the United States, Japan, and Australia, while for the bottom 40 percent it is with sub-Saharan Africa.

RISTO HÄRMÄ

See also Agriculture; Economy; Outsourcing and Offshoring

Further Reading

Basu, Kaushik, ed. *The Oxford Companion to Economics in India.* New Delhi: Oxford University Press, 2007.

Chakravorty, Sanjay, and Somik V. Lall. *Made in India: The Economic Geography and Political Economy of Industrialization.* New Delhi: Oxford University Press, 2007.

Das, Gurcharan. *India Unbound: From Independence to the Global Information Age.* Rev. and updated ed. New York: Penguin, 2002.

Drèze, Jean, and Amartya Sen. *India: Development and Participation.* New Delhi: Oxford University Press, 2002.

Government of India, National Commission for Enterprises in the Unorganised Sector. *Report on Conditions of Work and Promotion of Livelihoods in the Unorganised Sector.* New Delhi: Academic Foundation, 2008.

Hiscock, Geoff. *India's Global Wealth Club: The Stunning Rise of Its Billionaires and the Secrets of Their Success.* Singapore: Wiley, 2008.

Medecins sans Frontieres. "Winners and Losers in India." March 31, 2008. http://doctorswithoutborders .org/news/article.cfm?id=2581&cat=field-news.

Nayak, Purushottam. *Human Development in North-East India.* New Delhi: Oxford University Press, 2009.

Panagariya, Arvind. *India: The Emerging Giant.* New York: Oxford University Press, 2008.

Plan India. *Because I Am a Girl: The State of the Girl Child in India, 2009.* New Delhi: Plan India, 2009.

World Bank. *India's Undernourished Children: A Call for Reform and Action.* Washington, DC: World Bank, 2006.

World Bank. *Poverty in India: The Challenge of Uttar Pradesh.* New Delhi: World Bank, 2002.

✦ PRESIDENT

In a parliamentary democracy, the offices of heads of state and the government are separate but not equal. In hereditary monarchies, the head of state is the king or queen; in republics, the head of state is an elected or appointed president. Formally, the president of India stands at the apex of the country's political system. The executive power of government is vested in the president, who is both the formal head of state and the symbol of the nation. He or she is not answerable to any court for actions taken in the course of performing official duties but is subject to impeachment by Parliament for violating the Indian Constitution. In reality, the office of president confers status bereft of power. The president has authority and dignity but no power to rule. Instead, he or she performs an essentially ceremonial role. The actual functions of government are carried out by the president only with the aid and advice of the prime minister and the cabinet.

The president is elected to office for five-year terms and may be reelected. Any Indian citizen who is at least 35 years old and is qualified for election to the Lok Sabha (the lower house of Parliament) is eligible to seek the presidency. The president is not elected by the people. Instead, in order to avoid creating a parallel center of authority in a parliamentary system of government, he or she is chosen by an electoral college consisting of the two houses of Parliament at the center and the state legislative assemblies. The method of election helps to keep in check presidential ambitions: chosen by legislators, presidents may not challenge those who have been directly elected by the people. The twin principles of uniformity among states and parity between the center and the states are meant to ensure the election of a truly national candidate. The lack of popular participation eliminates the tumult normally associated with elections in India but does serve to underline the dignity of the office.

The vice president is elected for a five-year term by the two houses of Parliament in a joint session. Responsibilities include presiding over the sessions of the Rajya Sabha (the upper house of Parliament), deputizing for the president as necessary, and succeeding the president if the office should fall vacant for any reason until new elections can be held. There is no expectation that the vice president would normally become the next president.

The choice of president and vice president requires political judgment and balance, especially over a period of time. The offices must be rotated between the major regions and components of the Indian population (especially Hindu and Muslim but also other minority groups such as the Sikhs). On July 25, 2007, Pratibha Devisingh Patil (b. 1934) was sworn in as the first woman president of India. The professional background of India's presidents has mostly been political. Patil is no exception, having served in the Maharashtra State Legislative Assembly during 1961–1985 and in the Rajya Sabha during 1985–1990 before being elected to the Lok Sabha in 1991.

The powers of India's president are normally just ornamental, comprising appointive, dismissive, legislative, and symbolic functions. The president appoints the prime minister and also, on the advice of the prime minister, the cabinet; the justices of the Supreme Court and state high courts; the attorney general and the comptroller and auditor general of India; members of special commissions and other high public officials; and the governors of states. The choice of prime minister is not a discretionary prerogative to be exercised by the president but instead is usually dictated by the party commanding a majority in the Lok Sabha. In most cases the power to appoint is matched by the power to dismiss. The prime minister formally holds office at the pleasure of the president; in reality, the prime minister retains office as long as he or she can demonstrate support of the majority in the Lok Sabha.

The president calls Parliament into session, nominates 12 members of the Rajya Sabha, has the right to address both houses of Parliament, and has the power to dissolve the lower house. A bill that has been passed by Parliament must be presented to the president for formal assent in order for it to become law. The president may withhold assent and return a bill—unless it is a money bill—for clarification, reconsideration, or possible amendment by Parliament. However, such a presidential veto can be overridden if both houses of Parliament simply pass the bill again. Some types of bills, such as those seeking to alter state boundaries, can be introduced in Parliament only on the president's recommendation.

Another legislative power given to the president is in the form of ordinances. When Parliament is not in session but immediate action is deemed necessary, the president is empowered by the Constitution to issue ordinances on the advice of the government. Although ordinances have the same force and effect as an act of Parliament, they must be laid before Parliament for formal enactment within six weeks of Parliament reconvening.

Thus, the president of India neither reigns nor rules over the country but instead represents and symbolizes the nation. The president is the commander in chief of the armed services, receives ambassadors from other countries, represents India on state visits abroad, presides on great state occasions, and has the power to grant pardons. However, in almost all cases presidential powers are exercised only on the advice of the prime minister and the cabinet.

Sometimes the election of the president can itself become the arena for a power struggle between rival political factions. When president Dr. Zakir Hussain (1897–1969) died in office in 1969, Vice President V. V. Giri (1894–1980) took over as acting president until the election of a new president, which was required to be held within six months. The official Congress Party candidate was N. Sanjiva Reddy (1913–1996), a politician from within the party. Prime Minister Indira Gandhi (1917–1964; prime minister 1966–1977, 1980–1984), however, who was locked in a struggle for power within the ruling party, let it be known that her preferred candidate was Giri. His election marked her triumph in Parliament over the Congress Party stalwarts who dominated the party organization.

Table 8 Presidents of India, 1950–2012

Name	In Office
Rajendra Prasad	1950–1962
Sarvepalli Radhakrishnan	1962–1967
Zakir Hussain	1967–1969
Varahagiri Venkata Giri	1969–1974
Fakhruddin Ali Ahmed	1974–1977
Neelam Sanjiva Reddy	1977–1982
Giani Zail Singh	1982–1987
R. Venkataraman	1987–1992
Shankar Dayal Sharma	1992–1997
Kocheril Raman Narayanan	1997–2002
Abdul J. Kalam	2002–2007
Pratibha Devisingh Patil	2007–2012

The discretionary latitude available to a president depends less on the office or the incumbent and more on the state of party politics in Parliament or in the cabinet. If a prime minister commands the loyalty of his or her cabinet and the confidence of Parliament and if the government in power is stable, there is little scope for independent presidential initiatives, although they can murmur dissent to unpopular bills and, by withholding assent temporarily, hope that public opinion sways the government to change course. If the government is a coalition of different parties based in different ideologies, interests, states, or regions, then the president can play a mediating and influential role in relations between the states and the central government.

RAMESH THAKUR

See also Cabinet; Constitution; *Panchayat* System and Local Government; Parliament; Prime Minister

Further Reading

Dubey, Scharada. *First among Equals: Presidents of India, 1950 to Present.* New Delhi: Westland, 2009.

Jal, Janak Raj. *Presidents of India, 1950–2000.* New Delhi: Regency Publications, 2003.

Manor, James. "The Presidency." In *Public Institutions in India: Performance and Design,* edited by Devesh Kapur and Pratap Bhanu Mehta, 105–127. New Delhi: Oxford University Press, 2005.

Noorani, A. G. *Constitutional Questions in India: The President, Parliament, and the States.* New Delhi: Oxford University Press, 2002.

Noorani, A. G. *The Presidential System: The Indian Debate.* New Delhi: Sage, 1989.

Singh, K. V. *Presidents of India: Dr. Rajendra Prasad to Smt. Pratibha Patil.* Delhi: Vista International Publishing House, 2007.

✦ PRIME MINISTER

The prime minister of India, like the counterpart in Westminster who provides the model for parliamentary systems of government, is the linchpin of the Indian system of government. In Britain the convention is firmly established that the prime minister must be a member of the lower house of Parliament. By contrast, Manmohan Singh, prime minister since 2004, is a member of India's upper house of Parliament.

The Indian Constitution defines the duties of the prime minister of India but not the powers of the office. Constitutional lawyers and political scientists have sought to identify the sources, agencies, and instruments of the prime minister's power and authority. Eight sources of prime ministerial power can be listed: headship of the Council of Ministers, party leadership, control of parliamentary activities, control of intelligence agencies, control of the bureaucracy, emergency powers, control of foreign policy, and personal charisma.

The prime minister is given almost total freedom in the appointment of members of Parliament to ministerial posts. In making the selections, the party leader nevertheless must ensure adequate representation first to regional and sectarian interests in the country, second to the various factions within the ruling party, and third to the balance of parliamentary seats held by coalition allies. Sometimes public opinion can force certain changes. After the terrorist attacks in Mumbai on November 26, 2008, for example, the home minister had to be dropped from the cabinet. As India has had to learn to live with coalition governments in New Delhi for the last two decades, prime ministers have had to manage fractious allies with large egos. Still, in general a prime minister can exercise considerable influence on parliamentary colleagues and therefore on the destiny of the country through the prerogative of constituting, reconstituting, and reshuffling the ministry and chairing the cabinet meetings.

The prime minister is the head of government by virtue of being the leader of the majority party in Parliament. A party is elected to office on the basis of a policy platform spelled out in an election manifesto. The party leader is exceptionally well placed to influence and shape the translation of the party manifesto into government policy. The extreme example of prime ministerial control of parliamentary activities was probably the period of emergency rule by Indira Gandhi during 1975–1977, when Parliament was in effect converted into a personal rubber stamp. All constitutional fetters were removed from the de facto exercise of power by the prime minister, and opposition benches were to be found chiefly in the country's jails. That one aberration aside, performance in parliamentary debates is itself a crucial test of a political leader's skills.

The peculiarities of Indian politics give unusually large scope for prime ministerial control of political life through domination of party processes. Thus, Prime Minister Rajiv Gandhi was the final arbiter of the choice of Congress Party candidates for elections from all constituencies through the length and breadth of the country, and the party organization became an instrument for the prime minister of India to control and dominate state politics as well. Unusually in the period since 2004, the party president, Sonia Gandhi, although a member of Parliament, has not held any cabinet post but has been the most powerful court of last appeal for deciding on both party and government policy. During the 2009 election campaign, the opposition parties proclaimed dismissively that while Singh presides, Sonia Gandhi decides.

Heads of government can also be partial to abusing their control of intelligence services for personal and party political purposes: the practice of sexing up intelligence has an old lineage. Intelligence agencies traditionally come under prime ministerial oversight, not the least because heads of government would mistrust potential rivals in charge of such key operations. The size and complexity of India, combined with a colonial past, saw the emergence of several intelligence agencies. Some of the more important contemporary ones are the Intelligence Bureau, including the Research and Analysis Wing (RAW); the Central Bureau of Investigation (CBI); the Criminal Investigation Department (Special Branch); and the Directorate of

Revenue Intelligence. Several prime ministers have been alleged to have used the intelligence agencies to keep abreast of moves and countermoves by potential challengers and to harass political opponents.

In addition to using intelligence agencies for maintaining a watching brief over opponents and potential rivals, the prime minister can exercise political control through the regular channels of bureaucracy (including the police). This is especially so in India, where the centralization of the elite administrative and police services facilitates vertical control of their activities. The scope for career and postcareer rewards (such as plum ambassadorships and state governorships) for officials was greatly expanded by consolidating centralization of political authority and of the economy. A bureaucratic command economy was created with government officials in charge of, for example, banks that had been nationalized. The opportunities for rewarding loyal officials through patronage appointments were thereby greatly multiplied.

The greatest opportunity for a prime minister of India to exercise total power within the Constitution comes during the declaration of a national emergency. It is not an exaggeration to say that the 1975–1977 experience was a period of prime ministerial dictatorship by Indira Gandhi.

The period of emergency rule was an aberration even by Indian standards. Increasingly in the modern world, heads of governments of all countries have begun to play the most visible role in determining their countries' foreign policies. India is no exception to the rule. The controversial India-U.S. civil nuclear cooperation deal, for example, bore the personal stamp of Manmohan Singh.

An international role in turn enhances the domestic status and stature of the prime minister. All major international conferences, such as the annual Commonwealth heads of governments and the G20 summit meetings in 2008 and 2009, are attended by the prime minister

Table 9   Prime Ministers of India, 1947–2010

Name	Party	In Office
Jawaharlal Nehru	Congress	1947–1964
Lal Bahadur Shastri	Congress	1964–1966
Indira Gandhi	Congress	1966–1977
Morarji Desai	Janata	1977–1979
Charan Singh	Janata	1979–1980
Indira Gandhi	Congress	1980–1984
Rajiv Gandhi	Congress	1984–1989
Vishwanath Pratap Singh	National Front	1989–1990
Chandra Shekhar	Samajvadi Janata	1990–1991
P. V. Narasimha Rao	Congress	1991–1996
H. D. Deve Gowda	United Front	1996–1997
Inder Kumar Gujral	United Front	1997–1998
Atal Bihari Vajpayee	Bharatiya Janata	1998–2004
Manmohan Singh	Congress	2004–

personally. Visits abroad to other countries and to such forums as the United Nations (UN) are treated as major political events where the prime minister is on show.

The final source of prime ministerial authority is the individual attributes and charisma of the person occupying the office. Singh is not the most charismatic leader but is exceptionally well credentialed, with an Oxbridge doctorate in economics.

RAMESH THAKUR

See also Cabinet; Constitution; *Panchayat* System and Local Government; Parliament; President

Further Reading
Dubey, Scharada. *Movers and Shakers: Prime Ministers of India, 1947 to 2009.* New Delhi: Westland, 2009.
Gaur, Mahendra, ed. *Indian Affairs: Prime Minister of India.* New Delhi: Kalpaz, 2005.
Kapur, Harish. *Foreign Policies of Prime Ministers of India.* New Delhi: Lancer Publishers, 2009.
Kochanek, Stanley A., and Robert L. Hardgrave. *India: Government and Politics in a Developing Nation.* 7th ed. Boston: Thomson-Wadsworth, 2008.
Manor, James ed. *Nehru to the Nineties: The Changing Office of Prime Minister in India.* London: Hurst, 1994.
Sharma, S. K. *Prime Ministers of India: Nehru to Manmohan Singh (1947–2007).* New Delhi: Anmol, 2007.

✦ PUDUCHERRY

Puducherry, prior to 2006 known as Pondicherry, is a legacy of French colonies and trading posts and consists of four territories: Puducherry (175 square miles), on the coast 100 miles south of Chennai; Karaikal (99 square miles), 100 miles farther south; Yanam (18 square miles), strung along the Godavari delta in Andhra Pradesh; and Mahe (a mere 5.5 square miles) on the western coast and surrounded by Kerala. The total population of the territory is just over 1 million. Puducherry is a major tourist site, known especially for its four beaches, and hosts the renowned Sri Aurobindo Ashram. The lieutenant governor administers the territory, which sends one member to New Delhi to the the Lok Sabha (the lower house of Parliament) and one member to the Rajya Sabha (the upper house of Parliament).

ROGER D. LONG

See also Territories

Further Reading
Chandni Bi, S. *Urban Centres of Pondicherry.* New Delhi: Icon Publications, 2006.
Official Website of the Government of Puducherry. Accessed April 28, 2011. http://www.pon.nic.in.

Planning Commission, Government of India. *Puducherry Development Report*. New Delhi: Academic Foundation, 2010.

Rai, Animesh. *The Legacy of French Rule in India, 1674–1954: An Investigation of a Process of Creolisation*. Pondicherry: French Institute of Pondicherry, 2008.

Raja, P., and Rita Nath Keshari. *Glimpses of Pondicherry*. Pondicherry: Busy Bee Books, 2005.

◆ PUNJAB

The Punjab (Panjab), or the land of the "five rivers," is a region straddling the border between Pakistan and India. The five rivers are the Jhelum, the Chenab, the Ravi, the Sutlej, and the Beas. The Punjab has a long history and rich cultural heritage, and the main religions practiced are Hinduism, Islam, and Sikhism. Prior to the independence of India in August 1947, the province played a significant role in the freedom struggle. Hindus, Muslims, and Sikhs lived together relatively harmoniously in the spirit of Punjabiyat, a common regional identity that cut across religious and linguistic lines. However, British divide et impera policies and other developments in identity politics soon began to change the situation, and each community began to assert itself politically in a new way.

Sikhs and Sikh politics have dominated the province. In 1872 Gursikhs, known as the Singh Sahibs, founded the Singh Sabha Movement in reaction to what it believed were wayward practices and beliefs within the Panth ("path" or "way"). The movement sought to reform Sikh practices through the publication of books, pamphlets, and newspapers and even by founding schools. The Singh Sabha was one of the foremost movements toward the assertion of Sikh identity. The Singh Sabha was viewed with suspicion by Hindus and Muslims, who created similar revivalist or fundamentalist movements.

Following in the footsteps of the Singh Sabha Movement, the Shiromani Akali Dal, a leading Sikh political party founded in December 1920, supported the Gurdwara Reform Movement, or the Akali Leher as it is sometimes called, to remove the *gurdwaras* (Sikh temples) from the arbitrary control of *mahants* (priests) and to bring them under popular control. The establishment of the Central Sikh League in 1919 paved the way for the Gurdwara Reform Movement. The Punjab government acceded to their demands and passed the Gurdwara Act on July 6, 1925, which transferred control of all historic Sikh *gurdwaras* from priests to a representative body of the Sikhs. The Gurdwara Reform Movement and the Gurdwara Act had profound consequences for Sikh consciousness and political action. The Shiromani Gurdwara Prabandhak Committee (SGPC) managed the *gurdwaras*, and the Akali Dal became the political arm of the Sikhs.

India's independence from British rule in August 1947 came at a huge price: the partition of the subcontinent and the Punjab and the creation of a new state for the Muslims, Pakistan. The Punjab, with its diverse population and history of coexistence, was the hardest hit, and the mass migration and murderous communal violence that preceded and followed the partition period deeply impacted the territorial and demographic structure of the state.

The migration of the Muslims left the Sikhs concentrated in a more compact geographical area and at the same time created a minority of Hindus. According to the census of 2001, the state of Punjab had a population of just over 24 million, 92 percent of whom claim Punjabi, a western Hindi dialect, as their mother tongue. More than 60 percent of the population is Sikh, with most of the remaining people being Hindu. The Punjab is one of the most highly urbanized states in India, with just over a third of the population living in towns or cities. Chandigarh is the capital. Ludhiana, with about 1.5 million people, is the largest city, with the next-largest city being the Sikh holy city of Amritsar, with about 1 million people. The province is divided into 17 districts.

One of the major issues that soon emerged after independence was the language dispute over Punjabi. The dispute spurred the Akali Dal's first major protest movement in independent India. In the censuses in the 1950s and 1960s, the Hindus of the Punjab recorded their mother tongue as Hindi instead of Punjabi, and this became a political struggle as Hindus took up the cause of Hindi and Sikhs advocated the use of Punjabi. In response, the Sikh community in the Punjab, under the leadership of the Shiromani Akali Dal, demanded a Punjabi-speaking state in which Punjabi would be the official language. The support given to both sides from Hindi and Punjabi newspapers and various religious organizations exacerbated tensions. As a result, Hindus and Sikhs became increasingly antagonistic toward each other, and the Sikhs began to be viewed as a separate community, or a minority, rather than as a people belonging to a particular province. The Punjab also witnessed an agricultural and development boom due to the success of the Green Revolution and the introduction of newly improved hybrid varieties of seeds. The new wealth in the state made both sides more assertive.

The issue was seemingly resolved in 1966 when the Punjab Reorganization Act was passed and the State of Haryana was carved out of the eastern province of Punjab to create a Hindi-speaking state; the western province retained a mostly Punjabi-speaking majority. The creation of Haryana, however, did not resolve the language issue, as a sizable Hindi-speaking population still existed within the boundaries of the Punjab, and conflict soon restarted on the status of the two languages. In a compromise measure, the Punjab Language Act of December 1967 made Punjabi the official language of the state and Hindi as the medium of communication with the Indian government owing the status of Hindi as the national language of the country. Tensions between the Sikh and Hindu populations continued, however, as both asserted their own religiously based identities.

In October 1973 the Akali Dal formulated the Anandpur Sahib Resolution. The resolution demonstrated the shift among Akalis as the party attempted to appeal to Sikh nationalists. The core political demand of the resolution was to preserve and keep alive the concept of a distinct and independent identity for the Panth and to create an environment in which the national sentiments and the aspirations of the Sikh Panth would find full expression. During this phase, proponents of an independent Sikh state—Khalistan—first given wide publicity by Jagjit Singh Chauhan (1929–2007) in 1971, came to the fore, and

A Sikh activist wears a t-shirt depicting Sikh leader Sant Jarnail Singh Bhindranwale after prayers at Sri Akal Takht at the Golden Temple, Amritsar, June 6, 2010. "Ghallughara Diwas" is the anniversary of the deadly 1984 Indian Army "Operation BLUESTAR" attack on the Golden Temple complex to arrest Bhindranwale and his militant followers who had initiated a movement for a separate Sikh state. (Narinder Nanu/AFP/Getty Images)

the Republic of Khalistan was actually proclaimed by Chauhan in 1980. Khalistan had its own flag and its own currency, the Khalistan dollar.

This began one of the most troubled and violent phases in the state's history. Faced with declining provincial authority under the centralizing federal government of Prime Minister Indira Gandhi (1917–1984; prime minister 1966–1977, 1980–1984), the Akalis mobilized the Sikh peasantry in a major campaign for Punjab's autonomy. The Khalistan movement, led in India by Jarnail Singh Bhindranwale (1947–1984) while Chauhan remained in exile in London, was also at its peak and most murderous stage, as the Hindu population in the state began to be targeted and incidents of violence began to increase with devastating effect. In this highly volatile environment, in June 1984 the government launched Operation BLUE-STAR on the Golden Temple in Amritsar. The operation was designed to capture Bhindranwale and his armed followers who had fortified the temple and to remove all the weapons that the separatists had stored in the sacred building.

Militarily successful, Operation BLUESTAR was a political disaster because the Indian Army's assault, which met very stiff resistance, badly damaged the holy shrine. This was considered the worst form of desecration of a beloved symbol of Sikhism and alienated the Sikh community both at home and abroad. The damage to the holy shrine led to the growth of extremism. On October 31, 1984, Prime Minister Indira Gandhi was assassinated by two of her Sikh bodyguards, Satwant Singh (1962–1989) and Beant Singh (d. 1984). Hindus retaliated by murdering Sikhs while the authorities merely looked on. Two years later the chief of Indian Army staff, A. S. Vaidya (1926–1986), who supervised the attack on the Golden Temple, was also assassinated. Gandhi's and Vaidya's assassins have all been declared martyrs by various Sikh groups. Beant Singh's widow and his father were elected by Sikhs to the Lokh Sabha, the lower house of Parliament. The 1980s and 1990s were filled with violence and vigorous state action when, it has been claimed, more than 10,000 Sikhs were killed. Postmilitancy politics in Punjab continue to be tense, although the secessionist movement has all but ended. Culturally and economically the Punjab continues to be a vibrant region that contributes significantly to the economy.

STUTI BHATNAGAR

See also Amritsar; Chandigarh; Sikhism

Further Reading
Banga, Indu, ed. *Five Punjabi Centuries: Polity, Economy, Society and Culture, c.1500–1990; Essays for J. S. Grewal.* New Delhi, Manohar, 1997.
Deol, Harnik. *Religion and Nationalism in India: The Case of the Punjab.* London: Routledge, 2000.
Government of the Punjab, India. Accessed April 28, 2011. http://punjabgovt.nic.in/.
Judge, Paramjit S. "Religion, Caste and Communalism in Punjab." *Sociological Bulletin* 51(2) (2002): 175–194.
O'Connell, Joseph T., ed. *Sikh History and Religion in the Twentieth Century.* Toronto: University of Toronto Press, 1988.
Singh, Khushwant. *A History of the Sikhs*, vol. 2, *1839–1988.* New Delhi: Oxford University Press, 1991.
Talbot, Ian. *Punjab and the Raj, 1849–1947.* Riverdale, MD: Riverdale Company, 1988.

Punjab Kesari. See Newspapers, Indian-Language

R

✦ RADIO

Since its beginnings in the 1920s, India radio has achieved its much-desired expansion. The Prasar Bharati Broadcasting Corporation (PBBC) is the public service broadcaster of India's television network (Doordashan) and the radio network AIR (All Indian Radio). Today 99 percent of India's 1 billion people have access to PBBC broadcasts. But the PBBC has been criticized for dull programming, unimaginatively conceived by bureaucrats and presented in a stiff and stilted manner, which has not endeared it to the listening public. Furthermore, the government is unwilling to give up control of the airwaves, whether it is by allowing the private sector to broadcast news, allowing foreign investment in radio broadcasting, or handing over the power and control of the medium to small rural communities to run their own community radio programming. Moreover, despite the information revolution and the onslaught of transnational media companies via satellite television, the government has still not formulated a coherent communications policy.

One of the future developments could be satellite radio. However, despite its wide reach, particularly when compared with FM radio, satellite radio lacks the ability to provide localized content, which FM radio can deliver. The high cost of receiving sets for satellite radio is also a major concern in India and is likely to play an important role in the popularity of satellite radio with the masses. Cable radio (provided by cable operators) and Internet radio are gaining in popularity. Today there are growing numbers of online radio stations.

In the 1950s, Ceylon (now Sri Lanka) was starting up its own commercial shortwave radio broadcasts to India. Film songs expelled from the Indian airwaves found a berth on

Radio Ceylon, and soon Hindi film music on that channel became prime-time listening for Indians. The highlight of the week was the hit parade, called *Bianca Geetmala*. It was broadcast on Wednesdays and was sponsored by the multinational Ciba company to promote its brand of toothpaste. Ameen Sayani, the younger brother of Hamid Sayani, another well-known broadcaster, hosted English-language programs for Radio Ceylon and seduced his listeners with his mellifluous voice, humor, and charm. The program ended with the dramatic announcement, amid a fanfare of trumpets, of the new top single of the hit parade. "In many northern and central Indian cities," write Eric Barnouw and S. Krishnawamy, "that moment found clusters of people huddled around tea shops and other places with radios." Many remember those moments fondly. Sathya Saran, editor of the women's magazine *Femina*, even kept diaries of the weekly winning songs: "I remember as a schoolgirl sitting glued to the radio with a large diary on my lap, writing down the name of songs, and their listings on the countdown show, as if it were completely necessary to my well being."

A survey of listener preferences revealed that out of 10 households with licensed radio sets, 9 were tuned to Radio Ceylon and the 10th set was broken. B. V. Keskar, realizing that he could not beat the popularity of Radio Ceylon with his personal preferences, agreed to allow film music back on AIR. Vividh Bharati, a new service that offered almost nonstop film music broadcasts via two powerful short-wave transmitters from Bombay and Madras, was created in 1957. In 1967 the service turned commercial and began accepting advertisements and sponsorship. Today there are 36 Vividh Bharati and other commercial stations on AIR. (Also in 1967, television, hitherto under the auspices of AIR, was deemed an important enough medium to be placed under separate management.)

In the succeeding years, as the cost of transistor radios began to fall, ownership increased exponentially. Transistor radios were also offered as free gifts to men who volunteered for a vasectomy (in keeping with the government's drive to promote family planning) during the 1970s. As the number of transmitters increased, so did the number of listeners. During the infamous years of the Emergency (1975–1977) declared by Prime Minister Indira Gandhi, the government blatantly used the radio to promote its agenda. There was a clampdown on all dissenting voices, and V. C. Shukla, the minister for information and broadcasting, instructed station directors that AIR was not "a forum run by the government to debate on the conflicting ideologies but to make people 'understand' government policies." AIR was soon dubbed "All Indi(r)a Radio" by the listening public.

Following the defeat of Prime Minister Gandhi and the removal of the Indian National Congress (INC) government after more than three decades of continuous power, proposals granting autonomy to the broadcast media were circulated. However, all of them were shelved when Gandhi returned triumphant after the 1980 election. Against a background of growing violence in the Punjab, Kashmir, and the northeastern regions in the 1980s, she planned to deploy radio for the purpose of national integration and communal harmony. Any hopes for autonomy of the broadcasting services were firmly quashed. In 1984 radio licenses were abolished, and from that point forward the funding for radio came from the public purse.

Since then the issue of autonomy has been raised several times but invariably shelved, either because of a change in government or due to a lack of bureaucratic will. In 1997 the Prasar Bharati, a government-funded body, was set up to oversee the broadcast media and ensure the autonomy of their services. Nevertheless, successive governments have continued to meddle in the composition of its board, half of whose members are appointed by the government. Today AIR remains a centralized bureaucracy disseminating via its expanded network of 210 broadcasting centers what it believes the listening public ought to hear rather than showing any real interest in what they might actually wish to hear. But with the growing competition from television, particularly cable and satellite television, the government has been under tremendous pressure to liberalize the airwaves. If private television channels—even foreign private channels—have been allowed to broadcast to the Indian public, some have argued, why have no Indian private radio channels been granted the same privileges?

In a case brought before it in 1995, the Supreme Court of India delivered a historic judgment by ruling that the airwaves did not constitute the government's exclusive private property. The Court deemed that the airwaves belonged to the people, and although the airwaves could be used for the promotion of the government's political agenda, they also had to be used for promoting the public good. The Court ordered the government to privatize at least a part of the airwaves. With great reluctance, the government agreed to the sale of some FM frequencies to private entrepreneurs in 2000, but several caveats accompanied the government's agreement to privatize the airwaves. Most importantly, no private FM channels would be allowed to disseminate news, and no foreign direct investment would be allowed in radio broadcasting. A total of 107 frequencies were placed on the market for use in 40 cities. Despite the considerable fanfare accompanying this event, only 22 private FM radio stations currently operate in 14 cities. Of these, Sun TV owns 4 stations that provide programs in the southern regional languages.

One of the main reasons for the small number of FM channels has been the high cost of the licenses. This was not imposed by the government but stemmed directly from the folly of the private entrepreneurs. Buoyed by the dot-com boom, they entered into a bidding frenzy. When the bubble burst, they discovered that they had entered into a contractual agreement with the government for an annual increase of 15 percent, regardless of earnings. Since advertising revenues in radio are small compared with those in television and print media, some private FM channels such as Win FM quietly folded. Those that survive are mostly affiliated with media companies.

To recoup the costs of investment and license fees, many of the private FM channels have gravitated toward the most lucrative popular Hindi film and pop music sector. Because they target the same young, urban, and educated middle classes to procure advertising revenue, most channels have ended up providing almost identical fare, delivered in the same breezy Hinglish (Hindi-English) patter. That these privatized FM channels are indistinguishable was made apparent by DRS, a marketing company survey in which listeners to the top three private FM channels—Mirchi, Red, and City Radio—were unable to distinguish among them. According to Anish Trivedi, formerly of Radio Mid-Day, "Unfortunately the radio industry in India doesn't have a choice any more. The fee structure forces it to attract as large an audience as it can get. While there is nothing wrong with this, I feel it limits the scope of the station, in terms of its programming. . . . My problem is having to assume that all listeners are idiots."

The tight control exercised by the state on the production and dissemination of content, on the one hand, and the homogenized fare that is palmed off as entertainment by the privatized channels, on the other, has resulted in a hegemony in which the state and the market have control over broadcasting. In such a situation, the listening public, both urban and rural, has no say whatsoever in the matter.

News and music are generally the main fare offered on Indian radio channels. The myriad channels of AIR are divided into five main sections that focus on rural areas (primary channels), cities (FM), the commercial service (nationwide), the nighttime channel (nationwide), and external broadcasts.

The main commercial section of AIR is centered on the 36 Vividh Bharati and other commercial stations on AIR. Vividh Bharati, which began in 1957, almost exclusively offers popular film music to the entire nation. The programming mix that is broadcast on primary channels in the regional languages includes news; film and nonfilm music; talks; discussions; interviews; programs on health, nutrition, hygiene, farming, and agriculture; special programs for women and children; sports programs; radio plays; and serials.

A mix of news and music—in Hindi, English, and regional languages—is the main fare of the 9 FM channels that serve the nine major cities (Delhi, Mumbai, Kolkata, Chennai, Bangalore, Panaji, Lucknow, Cuttack, and Jallandhar). They also feature chat shows, help lines, interactive phone-in programs, traffic news, and weather. The 4 FM II channels in Mumbai, Delhi, Kolkata, and Chennai are largely news-based. Plans for FM radio include 40 FM channels that are to be accorded to the education sector in conjunction with the Indira Gandhi National Open University for Gyan Vani (education) channels.

A nationwide nighttime program featuring news, music, and sports is broadcast in Hindi, English, and Urdu. The target audience is mostly the Indian male night-shift workers. AIR also features external broadcasts aimed at the neighboring countries and the Indian diaspora in the developed world. The broadcasts are produced in 27 languages (17 foreign and 10 Indian). The content of the programs is largely news, current affairs, reviews of the Indian press, music, and other subjects of cultural interest.

The most important function of AIR is the dissemination of news. AIR provides a total of 364 news bulletins daily. Around half of these emanate from Delhi and are in Hindi. These are then relayed across the country and are translated into regional languages and dialects. In addition, 45 regional news units located around the country produce 187 regional news bulletins. In total, news is disseminated in 64 regional languages and dialects.

Critics complain about the dull presentation of the news and that the language used on AIR is chaste and ornate. The style is stultified and rigid instead of friendly, and as Sayani Saran points out, its broadcasters make "a pronouncement" of everything. Furthermore, its news coverage is always deferential to the government and avoids all sensitive or controversial issues. Since political power rests in New Delhi and most news bulletins are composed in the capital before being translated into the regional languages and dialects, the news presentation also tends to be very Delhi-centric. (A similar pattern of control is visible in radio drama. In AIR's drama contests, regional plays must all be first translated into Hindi and then retranslated into the different regional languages for dissemination.) Consequently, the common perception is that news bulletins pay scant attention to local needs and that local news is lower in priority than is national news on local radio stations.

The government waged a similar crusade against foreign news media on television. Unable to stop the news broadcasts of transnational media companies such as BBC and CNN, the government decided to impose its will on foreign companies seeking to disseminate news in Hindi. The government thus pursued Rupert Murdoch's STAR TV news channel with remarkable vigor. Having seen profitability in India rise, STAR News, the news channel of STAR TV, had decided to switch to news services in Hindi. In order to adhere to the government's new guidelines on uplinking, STAR News sought Indian investors for the required 74 percent equity among Indian investors. This led to accusations from rival companies that STAR TV had allowed a plethora of Indian individuals to have a stake in the company but with no real control and that Murdoch would be the dominant influence behind the scenes, as was allegedly the case in the company's FM Radio City operations. Each night until the dispute was resolved, STAR News, produced in India, had to obtain the Indian government's permission to broadcast for the next seven days via its regional base in Hong Kong. The ritual continued until STAR News found Ananda Bazar Patrika, a Kolkata-based publisher, to acquire the 74 percent stake, and the company won a 10-year license to broadcast its news programs directly from its base in Mumbai.

ASHA KASBEKAR RICHARDS

See also All India Radio; Media and Telecommunications

Further Reading

All India Radio. Accessed April 28, 2011. http://www.allindiaradio.org/.

Baruah, U. L. *This Is All India Radio*. New Delhi: Publications Division, Ministry of Information and Broadcasting, 1983.

Chatterjee, P. C. *Broadcasting in India*. New Delhi: Sage, 1991.

"Lifeline for FM Radio." *Hindu*, August 17, 2004.

Luthra, H. R. *Indian Broadcasting*. New Delhi: Publications Division, Ministry of Information and Broadcasting, 1986.

Ministry of Information and Broadcasting. *Akash Bharati: Report of the Working Group on Autonomy for Akashvani and Doordarshan*. New Delhi: Publications Division, 1978.

Ministry of Information and Broadcasting. *Mass Media 2002*. New Delhi: Publications Division, 2002.

Ministry of Information and Broadcasting. *Prasar Bharati Review Committee Report*. New Delhi: Publications Division, 2000.

Ministry of Information and Broadcasting. *Report of the Expert Committee on the Marketing of Commercial Time of AIR and DD (Siddhartha Senate Committee)*. New Delhi: Publications Division, 1996.

Page, David, and William Crawley. *Satellites over South Asia*. New Delhi: Sage, 2001.

Prabhu, Anupa. "All We Need Is Radio Ga-ga." *Economic Times*, July 14, 2003.

"Radio Casualty." *Business India*, May 26–June 8, 2003.

Roy, Devlin. "Why No News Is Bad News." *Economic Times*, July 16, 2003.

Saran, Sathya. "Ruling the Airwaves." *Femina*, January 1, 2004.

Singhal, Arvind, and Everett M. Rogers. *India's Communication Revolution*. New Delhi: Sage, 2001.

Thomas, T. K., ed. *Autonomy for the Electronic Media: A National Debate on the Prasar Baharati Bill*. Delhi: Konark, 1990.

✦ RAILROADS

The greatest development in the mid-19th century under British rule, one that would have far-reaching consequences of welding India as a nation, took place in the realm of communications. First and foremost among these developments was the building of railways all across India, and it was this development that played a large role in the making of modern India in terms of economic and social development (including the perceptions of the people) and the forging of different geographical and linguistic areas into one unit. Along with the railways, there was the expansion and modernization of road transport such as the Grand Trunk Highway and the introduction of the telegraph (the Victorian Internet). Without these three communication systems, India could not have escaped its premodern economic pattern that was present until the early 19th century, with no access to an expanding internal and international market and no chance of stimulating the early industrial boom or expanding its agricultural products and cash crops, such as jute and cotton.

Indian railways have one of the grandest pieces of architecture of the late Victorian era. The best known among them was the Victoria Terminus, also known as the Chhatrapati Shivaji Terminus (CST), built between 1878–1887 and opened during the diamond jubilee of Queen Victoria. The terminus, designed by the famous architect F. W. Stevens and built in the Gothic-Saracenic style, features ornamental arches, ornate stained glass windows, and an imposing central dome. Other stations in the Gothic-Saracenic style that are also palatial in appearance include the Southern Railway Headquarters in Chennai (Madras), the Western Railway Headquarters at Churchgate in Mumbai (Bombay), the Central Station at Egmore in Chennai (Madras), and the Bengal-Nagpur Railway Headquarters at Kolkata (Calcutta), all of which are the finest examples of British Raj's public buildings. They could also be seen as architectural expressions of the colonial presence that exuded confidence and a sense of purpose. This was how the colonial administration wanted the Indian public to perceive its presence and role: as being one with a progressive mission and with all the trappings of power and grandeur. The railways were built for an empire that was meant to endure for a very long time. However, this imposing facade began to buckle in the early decades of the

Mumbai's Chhatrapati Shivaji Terminus (formerly Victoria Terminus), was opened in 1887 and is the city's main railroad station. With its Victorian neo-Gothic architecture, it is one of the most photographed buildings in all of India. Known as the "CST," the station teems with tens of thousands of commuters pouring through its doorways during the morning and evening rush hours. It has been designated by UNESCO as an outstanding World Heritage site. (Shutterstock)

20th century. Paradoxically, the very institutions and services that were meant to prop up the longevity of the British Raj also undermined its legitimacy. Here the railways played no small role in creating an India-wide nationalist movement.

After independence, India inherited a significant portion of the colonial railway network. New railway links had to be added to address the vital loss of key links due to partition. The priorities had also changed. The British-India government had favored the railways at the expense of large road networks, while the government of independent India focused on building the road networks at the expense of expanding or modernizing its railway system. This led to a greater volume of goods transported by roads.

The first priority after independence was to fill all the gaps in the colonial railway network, which was not designed to meet the requirements of a modern industrial society. The second priority was the standardization of the distance between tracks, or gauges (the unigauge project), and was not undertaken until the late 1990s. In 1853 the broad gauge of 5 feet 6 inches was adapted for India because it was steadier and could have dual civilian and military use. The broad gauge was used to link all the major cities. However, due to greater consideration of the economy, a new gauge of 3 feet ⅜ inch (meter gauge) was adapted for secondary and feeder links because it was cheaper mile per mile and could also be laid at a much faster rate. A smaller, narrower gauge was adapted for hill stations and many of the princely states. By the time of independence, India had a mixed bag of 9,942 miles of broad gauge, 9,321 miles of meter gauge, and 1,864 miles of narrow gauge of various sizes. After independence, due to a shift in priorities and the lack of funds needed for conversion, a three-gauge system was in use until 1995, when the decision was made that a single unigauge system should be adapted for all existing railway lines. At the current rate of progress, it would take another two decades for full conversion to a single broad gauge. By the year 2000, the broad gauge, which included further additions since independence, had 44,383 miles of track and hauled 90 percent of the nation's freight and 85 percent of its passenger transport.

Electrification of suburban routes was considered as far back as 1914, but no active steps were taken until 1922, when the first experimental train between Bombay and Kurla covered a distance of 9.5 miles; it was opened to the public three years later. Electricity was seen as the most efficient energy and was ideal for hauling heavy traffic. Electrification also had other advantages, such as reducing noise and air pollution and causing fewer disturbances to wildlife. So far less than a third of the railway system has been electrified, and the goal of electrification of the entire system is proceeding at a steady pace. The Mumbai suburban electric trains currently operate for 20 hours daily. At peak hours there is one train every two minutes, and trains often carry three times the permitted load.

Another means of tackling urban traffic problems is the building of underground railways, especially in large cities such as Calcutta, with its congested narrow roads and gridlock traffic jams. A decision was made as early as 1972 to create Calcutta Metro for speedier passenger service, and after many delays the service finally opened in 1995 with state-of-the-art technology. India-specific problems, such as heavy monsoon flooding, had to be addressed before India could have its own world-class underground metro system. Similar plans are being drawn up for New Delhi.

One of the priorities of the postindependence Indian government was total self-reliance, and for this purpose a state-of-the-art locomotive manufacturing unit was built at the Chittaranjan Locomotive Works and came into production in 1950. Chittaranjan Locomotive Works produced steam locomotives until 1972 and since then exclusively manufactures electric and diesel trains. A number of other manufacturing centers, both private and public, were constructed to build engine coaches and electrical parts for what still is Asia's largest rail network. Today the railways remains India's largest employer, as it was in the days of the British Raj. Currently, ambitious plans are being made to introduce monorails in major urban centers and to connect India's major cities by superfast trains.

RAMAN N. SEYLON

See also Economy; Indian Airlines

Further Reading

Bhandari, R. R. *Indian Railways: Glorious 150 Years.* New Delhi: Government of India, Ministry of Information and Broadcasting, Publication Division, 2005.

Ministry of Railways (Railway Board). *Annual Report and Accounts, 2004–05.* New Delhi: Government of India, Ministry of Railways, 2006.

Sahni, J. N. *Indian Railways One Hundred One Years: 1853 to 1953.* New Delhi: Government of India, Ministry of Railways, 1953.

Satow, Michael, and Ray Desmond. *Railways of the Raj.* New York: New York University Press, 1980.

Vaidyanathan, K. R. *150 Glorious Years of Indian Railways.* Mumbai: English Edition Publishers and Distributors, 2003.

✦ RAJASTHAN

India's largest state, noted for its enduring cultural traditions. Rajasthan is located in the northwestern part of India, bordered on the west by Pakistan and elsewhere by five neighboring Indian states, and is bisected by the rugged Aravalli Range, which stretches from the southwest to the northeastern corner of the state. West of this range the land is relatively flat, dry, and infertile, much of it dominated by the Thar Desert. In the eastern parts of the state the land is hilly and more fertile. Average rainfall also varies. The western deserts accumulate about 4 inches annually, while southeastern Rajasthan averages 26 inches, most of which falls during the summer monsoon season.

Rajasthan has been popularly linked to the Rajputs, a warrior caste that ruled much of the region beginning around the 7th century CE. With the advent of the Mughal Empire in the 16th century, many of the Rajput kingdoms aligned themselves with the Mughal court and were greatly influenced by the Mughals both economically and culturally. This led to an era of tremendous wealth and patronage of the arts, resulting in distinctive Rajput styles of art and architecture. Indeed, one popular term for the region as a whole, and the name by which it was known under British rule, was Rajputana ("the land of the Rajputs"). At the time of Indian independence in 1947, the region still included 19 princely states as well as areas that had been under direct British rule. Most of these joined in 1949 to form the state of Rajasthan ("the place of kings"), a term dating from the late 18th century and popularized by the writings of the British chronicler James Tod (1782–1835). With the incorporation of Ajmer and several smaller territories in 1956, Rajasthan assumed its present shape, with Jaipur as the capital. The state is divided into 33 districts and has a single-chamber Legislative Assembly with 200 seats.

Rajasthan encompasses an area of 132,140 square miles. The population according to the 2001 census was 56.5 million. The urban population, comprising 23.4 percent of the total, resides in 222 cities and towns, while 76.6 percent of the population lives in more than 41,000 villages. Almost 90 percent of the population identifies itself as Hindu, while 8.5 percent are Muslim. There are, in addition, small but influential communities of Jains and Sikhs. Approximately 12 percent of the population is from tribal communities, predominantly Bhils and Meenas. The most commonly spoken languages are Hindi, which has long been the official state language, and various dialects of Rajasthani, which was recently recognized as an official state language but has yet to be recognized as an official language at the national level. Rajasthani was generally considered to be a dialect of Hindi, although that perception has been changing in recent years, and many linguists recognize it today as a distinct language or cluster of related regional dialects.

With the martial heritage of the Rajputs, the colorful appearance of village and tribal peoples, living folk traditions, and magnificent ancient Jain temples at places such as Mount Abu and Osian, Rajasthan is known as one of the most culturally traditional states in India and is thereby one of the country's most popular tourist destinations. Since the elimination of privy purses for princes in 1971, many local erstwhile rulers have converted their forts into tourist attractions and their palaces into heritage hotels. In recent decades, Rajputs have played a prominent role in all sectors of the burgeoning tourist industry. The state government, private foundations, and private enterprises have placed a high priority on preserving, encouraging, and showcasing the traditional performing arts, music, and dance of Rajasthan. These are often on display at forts, museums, festivals, and tourist-oriented specially equipped, maintained, and idealized "villages."

Similarly, there have been efforts to encourage the production of the handicrafts for which Rajasthan is noted, such as miniature paintings, pottery, camel leather shoes, embroidery, and jewelry. Although jewelry is produced throughout the state, Jaipur is today an important global center

Jaipur city, Rajasthan. View from Ishwar Lat minaret near Tripolia gate. "The Pink City," founded in 1727, was India's first planned city. With its palaces, especially the Hawa Mahal, or "Palace of the Winds," Jaipur is one of India's most popular tourist destinations. (Alexander Zotov/Dreamstime.com)

for the production and trade of jewelry, gems, and semiprecious stones. Rajasthan is perhaps best known for the colorfulness of its woolen and cotton textiles, especially block-print and tie-dye cotton fabrics. Cotton prints from towns such as Sanganer and Bagru in the Jaipur District are well known, yet each region of Rajasthan produces its own distinctive patterns and styles.

Other major industries include cement production and the quarrying of marble and sandstone. The latter are not particularly new, as many palaces were constructed of local sandstone, and the marble used in the construction of the Taj Mahal came from the quarry at Makrana. Agricultural production focuses on grains such as wheat and millet, oil seeds, cotton, and sugarcane. Rajasthan is India's largest producer of opium for the pharmaceutical industry.

Rajasthan is known for its historic forts, palaces, and temples, yet it is also home to a number of colorful festivals that have become internationally known, especially the Pushkar Festival, the Marwar Festival in Jodhpur, the Camel Festival in Bikaner, and the Desert Festival in Jaisalmer. Some of these were originally annual fairs for trading livestock but have developed into major showcases for traditional arts, crafts, music, and dance.

Finally, Rajasthan features many distinctive religious shrines and related pilgrimages and fairs. Some important pilgrimages celebrate deified heroes such as Ramdevra, Tejaji, and Gogaji or premodern saints such as Dadu, Jambhoji, and Karni Mata. Thousands of pilgrims are attracted to major Jain shrines at Shri Mahavirji, Nakoda, and Rishabdeo. The most popular Muslim shrine in India is the *dargah* (tomb-shrine) of Khwaja Moinuddin Chishti at Ajmer, where the annual pilgrimage (*urs*) attracts hundreds of thousands of devotees.

JAMES M. HASTINGS

See also Jaipur

Further Reading

Bharucha, Rustom. *Rajasthan: An Oral History; Conversations with Komal Kothari*. New Delhi: Penguin, 2003.
Official Web Portal of the Government of Rajasthan. Accessed April 28, 2011. http://www.rajasthan .gov.in/.
Schomer, Karine, ed. *The Idea of Rajasthan: Explorations in Regional Identity*. Columbia, MO: South Asia Books, 2001.
Tod, James. *Annals and Antiquities of Rajasthan, or, the Central and Western Rajpoot States of India*. 1884; reprint, New Delhi: Munshiram Manoharlal, 2001.

✦ RAMAKRISHNA MISSION

The Ramakrishna Mission, or Vedanta Movement, is a worldwide Hindu spiritual and philanthropic movement named after the Indian saint Ramakrishna Paramahamsa (1836–1886), who preached a simple message of love and tolerance. The Ramakrishna

Mission is headquartered on 40 acres of land just outside of Kolkata at Belur on the west bank of the river Hooghly. Begun by a few Hindu monks, the mission was created in 1897 by Paramahamsa's disciples, foremost among whom was Swami Vivekananda (1863–1902), born Narendranath Dutta in Kolkata, who became a renowned figure in religious circles after he spoke about Hinduism at the Parliament of the World's Religions in Chicago in 1893. The Ramakrishna Mission and the Ramakrishna Math (monastery) form the core of the movement. The math serves as the center for the monastic activities of the order, providing space for the pursuit of spiritual discipline, and also serves as a center for secular activities. The latter include such philanthropic work as education, medicine, and helping people in distress. Together the organizations concretize the motto of the Ramakrishna movement: *Atmano mokshartham jagad hitaya cha* ("For one's own salvation and for the welfare of the world"). It was Vivekananda, with his emphasis on social work, who transformed the Hindu discourse on asceticism, devotion, and worship into the ethos of service to the nation. The Ramakrishna Mission preaches respect for all religions, advocates service to humanity as the highest form of worship, and has successfully blended together the monastic ideal of renunciation with that of altruistic service to society. Today the mission is one of the most successful of all religious orders, with 171 branches and thousands of disciples spread throughout the world.

SIPRA MUKHERJEE

See also Hinduism; Kolkata; Religion

Further Reading

Advaita Ashrama. *The Story of Ramakrishna Mission: Swami Vivekananda's Vision and Fulfilment.* Kolkata: Advaita Ashrama, 2006.

Beckerlegge, Gwilym. *The Ramakrishna Mission: The Making of a Modern Hindu Movement.* New York: Oxford University Press, 2000.

Ramakrishna Mission and Ramakrishna Monastery. Accessed April 28, 2011. http://www.belurmath.org.

✦ RASHTRIYA SWAYAMSEVAK SANGH

Boasting 4.5 million members in 2009, the Rashtriya Swayamsevak Sangh (RSS), or National Volunteers Organization, is a right-wing Hindu nationalist group that emerged in 1925 from the landscape of Hindu-Muslim riots, low-caste protest movements, and the national movement for independence. Keshava Baliram Hedgewar (1889–1940) of Maharashtra founded the group with five or six others at Nagpur and served as the first leader of the RSS, which became the core of the Sangh Parivar, or family of organizations dedicated to a nationalist project in postindependence India. Through its doctrine of "the whole world is one family," the RSS claims to renew Indian values and culture. This includes rejecting the caste system and working toward an egalitarian society, a position that RSS has backed by its large numbers of Dalit (untouchable) members. However, the party has maintained a hard-line stance on immigration, particularly the immigration of Bengali and Pakistani Muslims.

Contrary to the National Congress Party, founded in 1885 as the Indian National Congress, which advocated a nonviolent inclusive Indian nation whose focus was uniting against the British, the RSS favored the idea of a unified Hindu nation and was not opposed to militancy or the use of violence. According to its mission statement, the RSS believes that the word "Hindu" is an inclusive category that embodies certain life values, principles, and a holistic perception of the world. However, by propagating a Hindu majoritarian viewpoint, the party's rhetoric has strong anti-Muslim overtones.

The basis of RSS ideology originated from a pamphlet issued in 1923 titled *Hindutva—Who Is a Hindu?* that was written by V. D. Savarkar (1883–1966). K. B. Hedgewar drew out Savarkar's assertion that the term "Hindu" was a racial designation and further expanded the concept of ethnic nationality as developed by Madhav Sadashiv Golwalkar (1906–1973) in his *We, Our Nationhood Defined* (1939). In this treatise Golwalkar criticized India as falling behind socially and rejected the concept of territorial nationalism that the Congress Party supported, that is, a universalistic belief that all peoples and cultures inside India's borders were part of the Indian nation. Instead, he proposed a European model and used Nazi Germany as an example of why homogeneity was an unlikely possibility in a nation with varying ethnic groups. This also drew upon Savarkar's proposition that a common race and a shared civilization and culture make a nation, not mere geographic boundaries.

The RSS has had a contentious history and was banned by the Indian government in 1948, 1975, and 1992 for its involvement in the January 1948 assassination of Mahatma Gandhi (1869–1948), the Emergency in India declared by Prime Minister Indira Gandhi (1917–1984; prime minister 1966–1977, 1980–1984) between 1975 and 1977, and the Babri Mosque incident of 1992 when Hindus demolished a mosque believed to be the site of a Hindu temple. In all three instances the organization legally petitioned to have the ban lifted, won the legal battle, and had the organization reinstated.

While there is a branch of the RSS for women, the Rashtra Sevika Samiti, the main organization is for men only and places a strong emphasis on militant masculinity. One of the reasons that the RSS is accused of indoctrinating young men to be potentially violent and reactionary is the emphasis on physical exercise and strength, which are propagated through the *shakhas*, or local branches. The military-like structure of these schools begins with physical fitness routines that include yoga, games, and strength training. The singing of a *prarthana*, or hymn, to the motherland is also performed daily, and the schools also impart lessons emphasizing the RSS's doctrines. The ritual environment of the *shakhas*, infused with anti-Muslim messages and an ultranationalist stance, define the organization as a martial right-wing organization in the Indian political landscape.

Despite a controversial record, the RSS has a policy of *seva*, or public service, that followers study at camps similar to *shakhas*. The RSS has been notably active in relief efforts during times of natural disasters, earthquakes, cyclones, and regional floods. In 2001 the RSS was reported to have provided more than 30,000 volunteers to aid in searching for victims and removing rubble after the earthquake that devastated parts of Gujarat. The RSS is also credited with speaking out against anti-Sikh violence in the wake of Indira Gandhi's assassination in 1984. Nonetheless, many scholars and journalists remain critical of RSS tactics in the political arena, which are often labeled as extremist or militant.

JULI GITTINGER

See also Sangh Parivar; Vishwa Hindu Parishad

Further Reading
Golwalkar, M. S. *Bunch of Thoughts*. Bangalore: Vikrama Prakashan, 1966.
Golwalkar, M. S. *We, or Our Nationhood Defined*. Nagpur: Bharat Publications, 1939.
Jaffrelot, Christophe. *The Hindu Nationalist Movement in India*. New York: Columbia University Press, 1998.
RSS: Rashtriya Swayamsevak Sangh. Accessed April 28, 2011. http://www.rssonnet.org/.
van der Veer, Peter. *Imperial Encounters: Religion and Modernity in India and Britain*. Princeton, NJ: Princeton University Press, 2001.

✦ REGIONALISM AND REGIONAL SECURITY IN SOUTHERN ASIA

The new regionalism theory has been compared with old regionalism, which emerged in the early 20th century. The new regionalism theory is defined as a more comprehensive and multidimensional process that covers trade and economic integration, the environment, social policy, and security and democracy. In the new regionalism theory there is no mention of any direct way to deal with the issue of conflict resolution, although there is a mention of security as a common issue. Nevertheless, one missing aspect from the South Asian Association for Region Cooperation (SAARC) mechanism is proposed in the new regionalism theory: the growth of civil society striving for regional solutions to local and national problems. The significance of civil society is that not only economic networks but also sociocultural networks develop more quickly than formal political cooperation at the regional level. Therefore, unlike the top-down approach adopted by most of the regional cooperation systems based on the traditional paradigm, the new regionalism theory is mainly initiated through a bottom-up process, especially by the civil society actors. The process headed by nonstate actors is often referred to as regionalization.

The SAARC Charter (1985) declares that the member states of SAARC are "desirous of peace, stability, amity and progress in the region through strict adherence to the principles of the United Nations Charter and Non-Alignment, particularly respect for the principles of sovereign equality, territorial integrity, national independence, nonuse of force and noninterference in the internal affairs of other States and peaceful settlement of all disputes." The charter was signed in Dhaka, Bangladesh, by the heads of states of Bangladesh, Bhutan, India, Maldives, Nepal, Pakistan, and Sri Lanka.

Since its establishment, SAARC has initiated some important programs for regional economic integration and social cohesion, with the intent to establish equitable development at the regional level. With the overall aim of economic integration, the SAARC Chambers of Commerce and Industry was set up in 1992 to promote regional cooperation in the areas of trade and economic relations. However, a notable move toward furthering economic interdependence was the setting up of the South Asian Preferential Free Trade Agreement (SAPTA) in 1995. Historically South Asia has been a free-trade zone, as until 1947 the three major member states of SAARC—Bangladesh, India, and Pakistan—had been part of British India, which was a common market with an integrated monetary and communication system.

Ratified and entered into force in mid-2006, the South Asia Free Trade Area (SAFTA) builds on the provisions given in SAPTA, therefore extending its scope to include trade facilitation elements and preferred trade liberalization processes from a positive to a negative list approach. One of the key elements of SAFTA is the compensation given for revenue losses for smaller regional economies (Nepal, Bhutan, Bangladesh, and Maldives) in the event of tariff reductions. SAFTA required the developing countries in South Asia—that is, India, Pakistan, and Sri Lanka—to bring their duties down to 20 percent in the first phase of the two-year period ending in 2007. In the final five-year phase ending in 2012, the 20 percent duty will be reduced to zero in a series of annual cuts. However, the least developing country group in South Asia—consisting of Nepal, Bhutan, Bangladesh, and Maldives—gets an additional three years to reach zero duty: they have until 2015. Economic integration in South Asia is the prime objective of SAFTA via eliminating all sorts of barriers in trade, promoting free and fair movement of products, promoting fair competition and a free trade environment in regard to existing economic conditions, and establishing an institutional framework to promote and expand regional cooperation.

Apart from its goal of economic integration, a significant focus of SAARC is social cohesion among member countries so as to promote a vibrant South Asian identity. Some of the initiatives taken toward this end include:

1. SAARC Regional Convention on Suppression of Terrorism (1987).
2. SAARC Convention on Prevention and Combating Trafficking in Women and Children for Prostitution (2002).
3. SAARC Social Charter (2004).
4. Association of SAARC Speakers and Parliamentarians (1992).
5. SAARCLAW, an association for persons from the legal communities of the SAARC countries (1992).
6. SAARC Scheme for Promotion of Organized Tourism. The scheme was initiated with the overall objective of people-to-people contact in the region and more specifically as a step to facilitate the development of intraregional tourism.

7. SAARC Chairs, Fellowships and Scholarships Scheme. This initiative intends to provide cross-fertilization of ideas through greater interaction among students, scholars, and academics.

8. SAARC Youth Volunteers Program (SYVOP). The main objective of the SYVOP is to harness the idealism of youths for regional cooperation programs by enabling them to work in other countries in the field of agriculture and forestry.

Furthering SAARC objectives, the 14th SAARC Summit held in New Delhi in April 2007 took some significant steps. Member states agreed to increase the SAARC Development Fund, establish the South Asian University, create a SAARC Food Bank, and set up the SAARC Arbitration Council. At the same time, Afghanistan was formally invited to become a member.

The total of informal trade in the South Asian region is about $1.5 billion, which is 72 percent of formal trade for which estimates are available. Interestingly, of the $525 million of India's informal trade with Pakistan, almost half is traded officially first to Dubai and then to Pakistan via Iran and Afghanistan. The reason for this lies in the strained political relations between India and Pakistan. South Asian states seem unprepared for full-scale economic integration due to their fear of being swamped vis-à-vis the Indian economy because of its hegemonic behavior or losing their sovereignty to some extent.

Over the past two decades, SAARC has provided a forum for informal bilateral discussions especially when there has been an absence of formal interaction between the heads of states. For example, the 1991 SAARC Summit was an opportunity for the meeting between the Nepalese prime minister and the Bhutanese king to discuss the issue of refugees, and the May 1997 SAARC Summit enabled the Indian and Pakistani prime ministers to meet and discuss important bilateral issues. Indian and Pakistani officials also met on the sidelines of SAARC summits in Colombo and Katmandu to continue their debates on contemporary bilateral issues. This all was done outside the SAARC agenda.

However, SAARC is not always used as well as it could be. Three of the biggest economies within SAARC—India, Pakistan, and Sri Lanka—account for 89 percent of the gross domestic product (GDP) and 87 percent of the population of the region, yet each nation tackles problems on an individual basis rather than collectively because of political tensions among them. As a result, economic interdependence in the region is very low. Intraregional trade in SAARC is only 3–4 percent. Economic integration is usually seen as a first step toward the ideal of regionalism in any region, and SAARC has come under criticism for its failure to boost economic integration more than has been achieved.

The hope that SAARC would provide incremental benefits to South Asia had not been realized. Peaceful relations and the effective implementation of the SAARC Charter (1985) have been hindered by interstate conflicts between member states. For example, India and Pakistan have been battling through SAARC due to different priorities. As for India, conflict resolution comes after economic cooperation; with the case of Pakistan it is otherwise. The

Indian spectators applaud soldiers of the Indian Border Security Force during the ceremonial opening of the Indo-Pakistan border, October 25, 2009. (Dreamstime.com)

temptation to put either one—conflict resolution and normalization of bilateral issues— ahead of other issues has resulted in the lack of movement on both fronts.

When talking of interstate conflicts in South Asia, India is seen as the state at the center of the disputes. This has strengthened Pakistan's friendship with other smaller states, giving hope that a common stand could help to dilute Indian hegemony through SAARC. However, India and Pakistan are stuck over the Kashmir dispute.

For all the disappointments surrounding SAARC, it is evident that SAARC over the past two decades has been involved in the unprecedented rise in the interaction and networking among various institutions, agencies, and civil society organizations in South Asia. This unofficial cooperation has centered around various issues, especially the promotion of human rights, conflict resolution, health, business, and the performing arts. It has also been stated that through unofficial contacts SAARC was going to be the driving force behind the official SAARC process and that this constituted some sort of new regionalism. One drawback to the effectiveness of the organization is that SAARC has no provision for civil society groups to participate in SAARC summits.

Civil society organizations have been continuously making efforts to improve relations and to develop agendas for upcoming meetings. It was estimated that in 1998–1999 alone there were over 38 Track II channels working in South Asia. This shows the influence of civil society actors. It is often said that regionalization initiated by civil society in South Asia is creating regional peace constituencies.

There have been social movements from civil society organizations forging people-to-people forums in South Asia. This has also enabled civil society voices to be heard at the regional level. One such initiative is called South Asia Partnership International (SAP-I), with its member organizations in Bangladesh, Canada, India, Nepal, Pakistan, and Sri Lanka. For more than 20 years SAP-I has been promoting regionalism through civil society initiatives. Since 2001 this network has been organizing the People's Summit, which is designed to promote the people's agenda, as SAARC does not have the mechanism to enable civil society groups to interact with them. In addition, there are numerous think tanks in the region studying regionalism vis-à-vis SAARC and formulating recommendations to enhance its activities. For example, the South Asian Centre for Policy Studies (SACEPS) is based in Nepal; the Regional Centre for Strategic Studies (RCSS) based in Colombo, Sri Lanka; and the Islamabad Policy Research Institute (IPRI) is based in Islamabad, Pakistan. SACEPS has been active in debating the role of SAARC and in introducing measures to enhance regionalism. What needs to be done, however, is for civil society groups to have a formal relationship with SAARC.

Greater contact among the SAARC countries has the potential to develop into a launching pad for free trade, larger intraregional investments, and economic integration. Indian prime minister Atal Bihari Vajpayee (b. 1924; prime minister 1996, 1998–2004) even said that open borders and a single currency for South Asia were not unrealistic if the states of the region improved relations and eradicated mutual suspicion. SAARC has taken a gradual approach toward achieving this objective. The problem today is not regional cooperation but rather how to handle intraregional conflicts and to maintain good and just peaceful relations. This is done through conflict resolution or management mechanisms in most regional cooperation structures. With this in mind, a call was made by Pakistan in 2005, articulated by Foreign Minister Khurshid Mahmud Kasuri (b. 1941; foreign minister 2002–2007) and President Pervez Musharraf (b. 1943; president 2001–2008) to set up a conflict resolution mechanism within SAARC.

In the past, SAARC has adapted to changing needs and circumstances at the regional level and has expanded its mandate beyond the original spirit of its charter. SAARC has formulated special conventions on problems such as terrorism, drugs, and human trafficking and in this regard set up the SAARC Terrorism Offences Monitoring Desk (STOMD) and the SAARC Drug Offences Monitoring Desk (SDOMD), both based in Sri Lanka. SAARC has also provided opportunities for the leaders of India and Pakistan to continue discussions even at times of high tension.

South Asian nations are aware of the need to pursue the goal of regionalism under the umbrella of SAARC in order to overcome widespread poverty, promote conflict resolution, benefit from extended regional cooperation and economies of scale, and become more competitive and achieve higher growth rates.

ZAHID SHAHAB AHMED

See also Afghanistan, Relations with; Pakistan, Relations with; South Asian Association for Regional Cooperation; Sri Lanka, Relations with

Further Reading

Bailes, A. J. K. "Regionalism and Security in South Asia." In *Regionalism in South Asian Diplomacy*, 1–11. Stockholm: Stockholm International Peace Research Institute, 2007.

Gujral, S. I. K. "Shri I. K. Gujral's Inaugural Address at the Conference on SAARC 2015." In *SAARC 2015: Expanding Horizons and Forging Cooperation in a Resurgent Asia*, edited by K. K. Bhargava and M. P. Lama, 17–24. New Delhi: Friedrich-Ebert-Stiftung, 2007.

Hossain, M., and R. Duncan. *The Political Economy of Regionalism in South Asia*. Canberra: National Centre for Development Studies, Australian National University, 1998.

Kumar, R. *South Asian Union: Problems, Possibilities and Prospects*. New Delhi: Manas Publications, 2005.

Niklas, S. *Regional Cooperation and Conflict Management: Lessons from the Pacific Rim*. Uppsala: Uppsala University, 2002.

Pahariya, N. C. *SAFTA: An Instrument for Peace and Prosperity*. New Delhi: CUTS International, 2006.

Rahman, A. *SAARC: Not Yet a Community*. Honolulu: Asia Pacific Centre for Security Studies, 2006.

✦ RELIGION

In India there is no precise equivalent term for the word "religion" and it meanings, although it is certainly possible that a Westerner would identify and recognize as religious certain behavior and practices in India. Religion in India just might be conceived differently, or it might be designated by a completely different term. Actually, both of these points are true within the Indian cultural context. Traditionally, religion (if the term is applied recognizing its cross-cultural limitations) is intertwined with Indian culture, and it is thus difficult to really separate religion from Indian culture.

The closest approximation of the term "religion" in India is the notion of *dharma*, a very elusive term itself to precisely define. The term "dharma" originates from the Sanskrit root *dhar* ("to hold or uphold," "to maintain," "to support," "to be firm," or "to be durable"). In classical Indian texts, dharma can be viewed from two perspectives: physical and individual moral worlds. Both perspectives refer to a revealed and eternal dharma. The term "dharma" when applied to the universe signifies the cosmic laws that govern and maintain it, which are laws guarded by the gods. In addition to the physical realm, dharma also includes the moral world of humans. Within a moral context, dharma represents a set of personal and social obligations and duties that are dependent on a person's station in life and his or her social standing. These obligations associated with personal and moral dharma basically govern how a person should act. In this sense dharma embodies social custom. In short, dharma includes cosmic laws, social custom, legal requirements, and religious rules. The exact opposite of dharma is adharma (nondharma), which disrupts the cosmic harmony, disturbs the social fabric of society, and fragments an individual.

Beyond its meaning as the right way to behave and to maintain harmony in the cosmos, dharma can arguably be best grasped as a total way of life. And this way of life possesses legal, social, and religious rules that need to be followed by an individual. These rules include, for instance, dietary rules about what foods are allowed or forbidden, rules about with whom an individual can eat a meal, and hygienic rules related to proper bathing, brushing teeth, and grooming. As the social regulations of Indian life, dharma includes the social system and instructions about how the different groups are expected to interact with each other and outsiders, the judicial system and its violations and punishments, and rites of passage from before birth to death. These various rites (birth, initiation, marriage, and death being the most important) shape, refine, and perfect an individual into an adult member of society. This is both an outer and an inner process that is necessarily visible and invisible.

The source of dharma suggests most vehemently and lucidly its association with what the West refers to as religion. There are four sources of dharma, of which the most significant is the divinely revealed Vedas, which for ancient Hindus implies that all dharmas are grounded in revelation. This suggests that dharmas have a transcendent character and thus cannot be easily altered. Tradition is the second source of dharma and rests on the memory of the community. Memory is inferior and subordinate to revelation because it is not directly heard as with revelation, although that which is remembered is based on revelation. Good custom and human conscience are the final two sources of dharma. Good custom, or the way that righteous people live, is equated with a religious life and the acquiring of insight. These sources of dharma establish the traditional goals of life: artha (the attainment of economic well-being), kāma (desire, pleasure, or love), dharma (ritual, religion, ethics, social rules, civil and criminal laws), and moksha (liberation, release, redemption). All of these are considered legitimate goals to pursue. Two of these four goals of life are religiously oriented, which emphasizes the heavily religious connotations of dharma and makes it a close equivalent of what is ordinarily regarded as religion in the West.

If the term "dharma" represents the closest equivalent to religion in India, the characteristics of Hinduism set it apart from the major monotheistic faiths: Judaism, Christianity, Islam, Buddhism, and Jainism. Hinduism is polytheistic with strands of monotheism running through it by way of the various sectarian traditions. There is no single identifiable founder of Hinduism, as is the case with Buddhism, Christianity, and Islam. Hinduism does not possess a single unified religious organization such as a church. No single text or body of texts (although numerous texts are considered sacred), no single doctrine, and no one symbol are considered authoritative for all Hindus. Hinduism lacks a binding religious authority because there is no founder, no universal organization, and no authoritative scripture (although there are several contenders). Instead of a single sacred center, Hinduism embraces many of them to which people make pilgrimages. There are also many religious leaders, many texts, and many doctrines and symbols. It is difficult to get a cogent grasp of this multitude of religious phenomena. To make matters more confusing, there is no sharp distinction between divine and human beings in Hinduism, which makes it possible to pass from one status to the other. A couple of ways to differentiate between a deity and a human is to gaze at their eyes and feet. If a being does not blink or does not touch the ground with its feet, it is highly probable that the being is divine. In addition to a multitude of gods and goddesses, Hinduism is constituted by many sectarian movements usually centered on a single divine figure, many schools of thought, a multitude of temples and other sacred locations, and different beliefs and practices. In summary, these various features of Hinduism make it difficult to claim that it represents an orthodoxy, but as the dharma of the Indian people, Hinduism can be grasped as an orthopraxis, or the correct way to act within a religious belief system. Therefore, a Hindu possesses considerable freedom of belief, but an individual is more circumscribed with respect to correct behavior.

CARL OLSON

See also Hinduism

Further Reading

Glucklich, Ariel. *Religious Jurisprudence in the Dharmaśāstra.* New York: Macmillan, 1988.

Glucklich, Ariel. *The Sense of Adharma.* New York: Oxford University Press, 1994.

Olivelle, Patrick. *The Āśrama System: The History and Hermeneutics of a Religious Institution.* New York: Oxford University Press, 1993.

Olson, Carl. *The Many Colors of Hinduism: A Thematic-Historical Introduction.* New Brunswick, NJ: Rutgers University Press, 2007.

✦ RELIGIOUS POLLUTION

Within the context of the Hindu religious tradition, pollution is an important concept. Pollution is equated with dirt, which is matter out of place according to the insightful work of the anthropologist Mary Douglas (1921–2007) in her seminal work *Purity and Danger: An Analysis of Concepts of Pollution and Taboo* (1966). To become polluted means to be defiled, sullied, or dirty, which involves being in a wrong condition with respect to others, social norms, and cultural mores. It is possible to become polluted by improper personal actions, coming into contact with a defiled person, or having contact with an unclean substance, such as some form of bodily waste product (blood, spittle, semen, mucus, hair, nails, feces, or urine). As Douglas makes clear, dirt is misplaced matter that offends against order, which is symbolized by purity. Dirt is never a unique isolated event because it always presupposes an ordered symbolic social system and a systematic ordering and classification of matter, whose boundaries are culturally determined. Moreover, pollution is a type of danger that can result in disorder and can be committed intentionally or inadvertently. It is always incumbent upon the polluted person to remove this incorrect and dangerous condition by means of purification, such by using water or ingesting products of a cow.

Within Hindu religious tradition, there are three major forms of pollution: menstruation, death, and birth. During their menstrual period, women are isolated and live an ascetic lifestyle for five days. Pollution caused by death transmits defilement by genealogical linkage, and the closer the deceased is to survivors, the greater is the pollution for them.

The final major form of pollution is birth, which is culturally called happy pollution because the arrival of a newborn is a joyous event. Obviously, birth pollution is transmitted through kinship lines, although it typically involves a smaller group of kinsfolk than death pollution. The mother, for instance, is considered polluted for three months after giving birth, while her husband is polluted for a period of 11 days.

In addition to these major types of pollution, there are lesser types such as bodily emissions, contact with leather, sexual relations, shaving, cutting of hair, and paring of nails. Saliva generated by eating is another source of pollution. Within the context of classical Hinduism, the polluting nature of saliva due to eating involves restrictions on the transfer of food between different social groups. These food restrictions are related to the types of food. As a general rule, there are no restrictions on raw food, whereas cooked food involves numerous restrictions. Imperfect food (*kaccā*) is, for instance, boiled rice or possibly wheat flour cakes cooked without fat. This type of food is considered imperfect because it is cooked with water, which makes it vulnerable to impurity. Perfect food (*pakkā*) gains its status because it uses cow products in the cooking process that sanctify the food cooked with it.

A more unusual type of defilement is respect pollution, which is an intentional type of pollution. Intentional pollution is performed to demonstrate deference and respect to someone of higher status such as a guru or other type of holy person, which enables a person to express her or his inferior status. Since the human body is hierarchically ordered in Hinduism, with the head being the highest part and the feet being the lowest part, when a person touches the feet of

A Hindu devotee prostrates himself before a *mahant*, a religious leader, on the banks of the sacred river Ganges in Allahabad, Uttar Pradesh, July 2004. (AP photo/Rajesh Kumar Singh)

a superior person, the person doing the touching accepts the pollution of the exalted individual. This is also true of washing the feet of a holy person or embracing the feet of one's parents.

Within the context of Indian villages, ideas about pollution are directly related to the hierarchy of supernatural beings because the high gods, who are usually identified with Sanskrit deities such as Vishnu and Shiva, maintain the highest state of purity, whereas local village spirits are innately impure and malevolent. If the Sanskrit deities are polluted, they could become angry and inflict punishment against the offending person. The local supernatural figures are not consistently protected from impurity and often accept blood and flesh sacrifices, whereas these types of sacrificial offerings are considered polluting for the higher gods, who only accept vegetarian offerings. If village deities are maintained in a field of purity, they are useful to people because they can grant the requests of petitioners, whereas impurity can elicit their malevolent aspects.

Based on internal evidence from Indian classical texts and observations of village life, it can be affirmed that pollution flows, directly or through a conductor, from one being, substance, or fluid to another person. In contrast to pollution, purity cannot flow from person to person, although it can be lost by contact with a defiled person, substance, or fluid. Purity is thus an impermanent and relative condition that can be easily lost but never transferred. Purity exists, for instance, like an island within an ocean of pollution, which suggests that purity is artificially created and maintained. The maintenance of purity and the control of pollution represent a never-ending process.

CARL OLSON

See also Hinduism; Religion

Further Reading
Babb, Lawrence A. *The Divine Hierarchy: Popular Hinduism in Central India*. New York: Columbia University Press, 1975.
Douglas, Mary. *Purity and Danger: An Analysis of Concepts of Pollution and Taboo*. 1966; reprint, New York: Praeger, 2002.
Dube, S. C. *Indian Village*. London: Routledge and Kegan Paul, 1955.
Harper, Edward B. "Ritual Pollution as an Integrator of Caste and Religion." In *Religion in South Asia*, edited by Edward B. Harper, 151–196. Seattle: University of Washington Press, 1964.
Srinavas, M. N. *Religion and Society among the Coorgs of South India*. 1952; reprint, Calcutta: Asia Publishing House, 1965.

✦ RESERVE BANK OF INDIA

The Reserve Bank of India (RBI) dates back to 1773, when efforts were first initiated to establish a central bank in the country. This involved establishing a general bank in Bengal and Bihar. The efforts were not successful, however, as the bank failed soon after.

Later in 1914 the Chamberlain Commission recommended the amalgamation of three presidency banks into one central bank to be called the Imperial Bank of India, and the Imperial Bank Act was passed in 1920. The Imperial Bank, however, performed commercial banking functions as well as central banking functions. These functions included acting as the banker to the government and as a bankers' bank, while the functions of issue of currency notes and management of foreign exchange were the responsibility of central government.

On the recommendations of Royal Commission on Indian Currency and Finance, the decision was made to establish a central bank that performs exclusively central banking functions and does not perform commercial banking functions. The bill was initially introduced in the Legislative Assembly in January 1927 but was subsequently dropped due to differences in views regarding ownership, constitution, and composition of its Board of Directors. Meanwhile, two major reports influenced the decision on establishing the bank. These were the "Report of the Indian Central Banking Enquiry Committee" in 1931 and the "White Paper on Indian Constitutional Reforms" in 1933, which strongly recommended the establishment of the RBI. The bill was introduced again in 1933 and finally passed in 1934, and the Reserve Bank of India Act came into force on January 1, 1935. The Reserve Bank of India Act of 1934 provides the statutory basis of the functioning of the RBI, which commenced operations on April 1, 1935. The RBI was formed as the shareholders' institution in 1935. This, however, subsequently changed when the RBI was nationalized on January 1, 1949, according to the terms of the Reserve Bank of India (Transfer to Public Ownership) Act of 1948.

As in other organizations, the RBI is governed by a Central Board of Directors whose main function is general supervision and direction of RBI affairs. Board members are appointed by the government of India for the period of four years. The board is comprised of official and nonofficial directors. Besides the Central Board of Directors, there are also local boards for four regions (east, west, north and south). Each local board is comprised of five members. As in the case of the Central Board of Directors, members of the local boards are also appointed by the central government for a period of four years. The major functions of local boards are "to advise the Central Board on local matters and to represent territorial and economic interests of local cooperative and indigenous banks" and also "to perform such other functions as delegated by the Central Board from time to time."

The evolution of RBI during 1935–2008 can be examined for three periods: 1935–1950, a prenationalization phase termed a foundation phase when the RBI operated as a private bank; 1951–1990, or the developmental phase; and 1991 onward, or postliberalization phase.

According to the RBI, the objective of its establishment was to "regulate the issue of bank notes and keep the reserves with a view to securing monetary stability in India and generally to operate the currency and credit system of the country to its advantage." The major functions as laid down in the statute were issuing currency, acting as the banker to the government, and acting as a banker to other banks. These functions were earlier being carried out by the Controller of Currency and the Imperial Bank of India. During World War II and the postwar years, the major functions related to provision of war finance, repatriation of sterling debt, and exchange control operations. The major event during this phase was separation of Burma (Myanmar) from the Indian Union in 1937. The RBI, however, continued to act as the central bank for Burma until the Japanese occupation of Burma until April 1947. The RBI ceased to function as the central bank for Pakistan as of July 1, 1948. The developmental and other promotional roles had still not gained importance during the foundation phase.

The second phase (1951–1990) was the developmental phase, when emphasis was on institution building, financial sector development, and providing access to finance to various groups of people, regions, occupations, and sectors through rapid expansion of the bank branching network and credit. The RBI was also instrumental in institutional development and helped set up institutions such as the Deposit Insurance and Credit Guarantee Corporation of India, the Unit Trust of India, the Industrial Development Bank of India, the National Bank of Agriculture and Rural Development, and the Discount and Finance House of India to build the financial infrastructure of the country.

The economic reforms were launched in India in 1991, and with this the RBI's focus has shifted back to core central banking functions such as monetary policy, bank supervision and regulation, overseeing the payments system, and developing the financial markets. The other aspects that gained attention during this period are transparency, communications, and dissemination of information. The RBI's other thrust areas are financial inclusion and strengthening of credit delivery mechanisms for agriculture and small- and micro-sized enterprises, especially in the rural areas. The RBI is now an active participant in several important international institutions that seek to promote effective regulatory structures and financial and systemic stability. The RBI is a member of the Committee on Global Financial System, Markets Committee, and International Liaison Group under the aegis of the Basel Committee on Banking Supervision (BCBS) and is also gradually becoming an active member of the Financial Stability Forum and the BCBS. The RBI is also a shareholder in the Bank for International Settlements (BIS).

RASHMI UMESH ARORA

See also Central Banking, Development Aspects; Financial Institutions, Development; Monetary Policy

Further Reading
Reserve Bank of India. *Functional Evolution of Central Banking: Report on Currency and Finance, 2004–2005*. Mumbai: Reserve Bank of India, 2006.
Reserve Bank of India. *Report on Currency and Finance, 2004–2005*. Mumbai: Reserve Bank of India, 2006.
Subbarao, D. *Reserve Bank of India: Reflections on its Evolution*. Mumbai: Reserve Bank of India, 2009.

◆ RIGHT TO INFORMATION

A new chapter was added to the constitutional and people's history of India with the enactment of the Right to Information (RTI) Act on June 15, 2005. This freedom of information act provides for accountability and transparency in decision making and public spending in various sectors of the Indian government. The necessity for this piece of legislation was inspired by the need to enlarge the democratic space in Indian polity.

Before the enactment of the RTI in India, Tamil Nadu, Goa, and Madhya Pradesh had enacted their own RTI Act in 1997, followed by Rajasthan in 2000 and Delhi in 2001. The enactment of this legislation owes its inspiration to the collective consciousness of various grassroots organizations as they represent the aspirations of Indian people and their demand to develop a new political culture. Prominent among these organizations is Mazdoor Kisan Shakti Sangathan (MKSS) in Rajasthan that started the campaign for a minimum wage in rural India and exposed rampant corruption in schemes meant for rural development.

The RTI Act has given the people access to information that was earlier inaccessible and was supposedly confidential. This legislation enables any applicant to question and seek information about public issues such as the repair of roads, the absence of teachers in government schools, insufficient medicines in hospitals, the policy and procedures followed in making decisions, the functioning of the public distribution system, and the utilization of funds for various schemes of rural and urban development. To make the role of public authorities meaningful, the act lays emphasis on *suo moto* disclosures (disclosures made on the initiative of the government official, that is, voluntarily by the government official) on the schemes initiated by any department that spends public money.

The RTI Act instructs every government, a state government entity such as a utility company, and other departments or those that fall into the public domain to appoint a public information officer (PIO) who will be responsible for providing information sought by the public at large subject to the payment of a nominal fee specified in the Fee Rules. Significantly, this act stipulates a time frame of 30 days within which every PIO must provide the information sought by an applicant. The time frame cannot exceed 40 days in any single case. If a PIO fails to provide such information within this period, it is her or his obligation to give the applicant the reasons. The PIO can also be fined in case of willful nondisclosure, and applicants have been given the right to appeal the appellate authority against PIOs. The Central Information Commission (CIC) of the central government and the State Information Commission (SIC) in the respective states regulate the working of the RTI Act in their respective jurisdictions.

The pace of implementation of the RTI Act, however, continues to be abysmal. Apart from website portals, nothing significant has been done to publicize the act. The state governments plan to digitalize information and create a paper-free office for the CIC, something that may indeed be beneficial in the long run but excludes millions of people who are incapable of using information technology. Bureaucratic reluctance to make their decisions and work public is the single largest threat to the effective working of the RTI Act. In fact, the civil service bureaucracy at all levels has been trying to block public access to certain file notes that identify individuals, groups of individuals, organizations, appointments, and matters relating to inquiries and departmental proceedings. This raises questions about what the effect of the act would be after file notes are exempted. Any information that might have the potential of creating trouble for corrupt bureaucrats may be classified as file noting and be exempt from public disclosure. Furthermore, if the officials concerned are not named, on whom will the responsibility for actions and decisions be laid?

Although Prime Minister Manmohan Singh (b. 1932; prime minister 2004–) has categorically said that file notings relating to development plans, schemes, programs, and projects should be in the ambit of the RTI Act, there is immense pressure on the government and the CIC to exempt these from the act. The chief information commissioner has been imposing penalties and pressuring government departments to disclose file notings. This has not been viewed positively by officials who cherish their autonomy and their authority free from inspection; they even dislike public knowledge of their work. This dichotomy between the fundamental rights of every citizen to have access to information and the subsequent pressures from the very government that enacted the RTI Act to deny access can have serious implications for the working of the act in the coming years.

Ever since the inception of the RTI Act, it has been civil rights groups that have been focusing on the act's implementation. The most significant initiative in this direction is the organization of *jan sunwais* (public hearings). Parivartan, an RTI group based in Delhi has been, for instance, filing applications to seek information on issues of urban governance and the development of neglected slums and minor localities in the city. This group has been exposing rampant corruption through the diversion of funds meant for public welfare programs; the counterfeiting of papers dealing with work done, which in many cases remains nonexistent; and the checking of public utilities, especially access to water, public toilets, roads, and schools. Parivartan then organizes people to collectively question public servants or politicians through *jan sunwais*. These initiatives lead to the raising of public awareness and to the mobilization of people on issues of common interest and also foster social and communal solidarity.

While RTI groups credit the central government for the enactment of the RTI Act, they continue to pressure the government for effective implementation of the act. One of the most important demands of these groups is to inculcate the spirit of the RTI Act in the appointment of PIOs. This underlines the necessity to include, as the act states, "persons of eminence in public life with wide knowledge and experience in law, science and technology, social service, management, journalism, mass media or administration and governance." The end result, however, is that central and state commissions are completely bureaucratized and have been reduced to another tool for providing postretirement benefits for civil servants. The government has attempted structural adjustments in the wake of public pressure, but its attitude has largely been to avoid the enlargement of public debate on the RTI Act.

YOGESH SNEHI

See also Constitution

Further Reading

Commonwealth Human Rights Initiative (CHRI). *Compliance with the Right to Information Act: A Survey.* New Delhi: CHRI, 2009.

Mazdoor Kisan Shakti Sangathan. Accessed April 28, 2011. http://www.mkssindia.org.

Mentschel, Stefan. *Right to Information: An Appropriate Tool against Corruption?* New Delhi: Mosaic Books, 2005.

Pande, Suchi, and Shekhar Singh. *Right to Information Act 2005: A Primer.* New Delhi: National Book Trust, 2007.

Right to Information: A Citizen Gateway Information Service Portal. Accessed April 28, 2011. http://www.righttoinformation.gov.in.

Right to Information Act, 2005. New Delhi: Government of India Press, 2005.

✦ ROY, ARUNDHATI

Indian writer, social activist, and in 1998 one of *People* magazine's "50 Most Beautiful People in the World," Arundhati Roy was born in Shillong in 1961 and is the first Indian writer to win the British literary award known as the Booker Prize, which was awarded to her in 1997 for her first novel, *The God of Small Things.* In 1989 she wrote the screenplay for *In Which Annie Gives It Those Ones,* which was based on her experience as an architecture student, but she came to the public's attention in 1994 with her critique, titled "The Great Indian Rape

Arundhati Roy holds a copy of her novel *The God of Small Things* shortly after being awarded the prestigious Booker Prize, October 14, 1997. (AP Photo/Stefan Rousseau)

Trick," of Shekar Kapur's film *Bandit Queen*, based on the life of the outlaw Phoolan Devi (1963–2001). Roy, after winning the Booker Prize, has written and spoken on political issues and against globalization, India's nuclear activities, religious fundamentalism, and the U.S.-led wars in Afghanistan and Iraq. In 1998 she criticized India's nuclear weapons testing program at Pokran, Rajasthan, in "The End of Imagination," published in a collection of essays titled *The Cost of Living* in 1999. The same year she wrote "The Greater Common Good," arguing against the Narmada Dam project of some 30 large dams on the Narmada River. Her related protests with social activist Medha Patkar (b. 1954) led to Roy being briefly imprisoned. In 2002 the Lannan Foundation (founded in 1960) in Los Angeles awarded her the Prize for Cultural Freedom along with $350,000 in prize money, which she distributed among 50 people's movements, publications, educational institutions, and theater groups in India. In April 2003 South End Press released *War Talk*, which includes "Come September," a critique on the effects of the U.S.-led War on Terror, intervention in Chile, the Palestinian-Israeli conflict, and the war in Iraq. In 2005 she took an active role in the World Tribunal on Iraq. The Sydney Peace Prize, awarded by the Sydney Peace Foundation in Sydney, Australia, was awarded to Roy in 2004 for her social campaign and advocacy of nonviolence. In 2006, however, in protest of the massacre of protestors by Indian police and of the Indo-U.S. stand on economic policies, she declined to accept the Sahitya Akademi Award (national award from India's Academy of Letters) for her collection of essays titled *The Algebra of Infinite Justice*. In July 2009 Roy published a major work titled *Field Notes on Democracy: Listening to Grasshoppers*, a probing collection of essays on India's democracy and government.

SHEEBA HÄRMÄ

See also Environment; Human Rights; Globalization; Water Resources

Further Reading
Barsamian, David, and Naomi Klein. *The Chequebook and the Cruise Missile: Conversations with Arundhati Roy*. London: Harper Perennial, 2004.
Roy, Arundhati. *The Algebra of Infinite Justice*. London: Flamingo, 2002.
Roy, Arundhati. *Field Notes on Democracy: Listening to Grasshoppers*. Chicago: Haymarket Books, 2009.
Roy, Arundhati. *The God of Small Things*. New York: Random House, 1997.
Roy, Arundhati, "The Great Indian Rape Trick." http://www.sawnet.org/books/writing/roy_bq1.html.
Roy, Arundhati. *War Talk*. Cambridge, MA: South End, 2001.

✦ RUSSIA, RELATIONS WITH

Czar Peter the Great (1682–1725) was the first Russian czar to pay serious attention to India. Hostile powers in Central Asia, however, thwarted his attempts to create an overland trade route to India through Central Asia. Not until the beginning of the 19th century did

Russia again direct efforts toward India. The Russian relationship with Great Britain largely determined Russian relations with India until Indian independence in 1947. During the reign of Czar Paul I (r. 1796–1801), the Russian Empire allied with France in an attempt to threaten British territory in India. Paul abandoned Russia's earlier alliance with Great Britain when the two nations united in opposition to the French Revolution and in 1801 dispatched a group of Cossacks to conquer India. Paul died before the mission was completed, and the attack was cancelled. Nevertheless, strained relations with Great Britain continued through the 19th century as the Russian Empire expanded its territorial possessions in Central Asia. Great Britain and Russia vied for control of Central Asia in a struggle known as the Great Game. The struggle involved economic and political competition between the Russian and the British empires throughout Central Asia, including British possessions in the future nations of India and Pakistan.

The Bolshevik Revolution of 1917, in which revolutionary Russian leaders encouraged colonies to rise up against European colonizers, heightened tensions between the revolutionary Soviet government and Great Britain. But until the end of World War II, the Soviet Union lacked the political will and the resources to make good on its revolutionary rhetoric.

India's independence from Britain in August 1947 coincided with the beginning of the Cold War involving political, economic, and diplomatic competition on a global scale between the capitalist United States and the Socialist Soviet Union. Both powers attempted to expand their influence in newly decolonized European possessions. The United States and the Soviet Union offered two different approaches to modernization, one based on free enterprise and the other on state control of the economy. India's first prime minister, Jawaharlal Nehru (1889–1964; prime minister 1947–1964), attempted to maintain a position of nonalignment between the two powers. A number of factors, however, pushed Nehru into a closer relationship with the Soviet Union. By the 1950s, especially following the Chinese Revolution in 1949, Indian leaders identified much more with the Soviet model of state control and economic planning than with the American capitalist system. Nehru was impressed by the modernization of the Soviet economy without dependence on European and American capital. He borrowed the concept of state-directed industry from the Soviet Union: the idea of a comprehensive economic plan for all sectors of the economy. Nehru also believed that science and technology could lift India from its status as a former colony into a fully developed nation able to defend its interests on the world stage, much as the Bolshevik Revolution seemed to have transformed Russia.

Increasing support of India's rival Pakistan by the United States in the mid-1950s pushed Nehru closer to the Soviet Union. He traveled to the Soviet Union in June 1955, and the Soviet leader Nikita Khrushchev (1894–1971; premier 1958–1964) visited India later the same year. "Shout for us across the Himalayas whenever you need us," Khrushchev remarked in a gesture of friendship. India and the Soviet Union also shared a growing distrust of Communist China, leading to growing collaboration between the Soviet and Indian militaries in the 1960s and 1970s.

From the early 1960s the Soviets actively promoted their system and culture in India. The policy was part of a broader Soviet attempt to promote revolution in newly independent developing countries. Yuri Gagarin (1934–1968), after his famous flight as the world's first cosmonaut on April 12, 1961, visited India to help solidify the relationship and the collaboration in various fields between the two countries. He met Nehru as well as dozens of members of the cultural, scientific, and technical elite. Later, in April 1984, the Soviet Union launched the first Indian, Indian Air Force squadron leader Rakesh Sharma (b. 1949), into space aboard the Soviet spacecraft *Soyuz*.

The August 1971 Indo-Soviet Treaty of Peace, signed by Prime Minister Indira Gandhi (1917–1984; prime minister 1966–1977, 1980–1984) and Soviet leader Leonid Brezhnev (1906–1982; secretary-general 1964–1982), expanded political, economic, and cultural contacts between the two countries. Following India's wars with Pakistan in 1965 and 1971, the Soviets increased the delivery of weapons and advisers to India. By the 1970s, the Soviet Union became a primary supplier of weaponry and training for the Indian military, just as Pakistan depended heavily on U.S. weaponry and training.

The Soviets also expanded their participation in the Indian nuclear industry, especially after India exploded its first nuclear device on May 18, 1974, at Pokhran in Rajasthan. In response to the test, the United States withdrew its earlier support for India's civilian nuclear industry, and Moscow stepped in to fill the vacuum created by the exit of American nuclear industry advisers. By the early 1980s, Moscow committed Russia to helping India build civilian nuclear reactors, a collaborative effort that continued through the 1990s and the first decade of the 21st century.

Contacts between the two nations, however, were not limited to military, scientific, and technical exchanges. During the 1960s, thousands of middle-class Indians went to the Soviet Union to study. The Soviet Union reciprocated by sending thousands of technical advisers and engineers to India. Various aspects of Indian culture such as music and food enjoyed great popularity in Soviet society during the 1960s and 1970s. Thousands of Indians educated in Russia returned to teach Russian language and culture in Indian universities, some of which, such as the Jawaharlal Nehru University in New Delhi, developed renowned centers for the study of Russian history and politics.

The collapse of the Soviet Union in 1991 accelerated a growing liberalization of the Indian economy and a move away from a state-controlled model of economic development. The implosion of the Russian economy in the 1990s reduced Indian dependence on Soviet science and technology as well as Soviet weaponry, whose effectiveness had also been called into question by the disastrous Soviet-Afghan War (1979–1989). In the 1990s and the first part of the 21st century, ambitious young Indians chose the business and graduate schools of the United States rather than the study of engineering or physics in educational centers in Russia.

In the 21st century, relations between Russia and India have been based more on pragmatic economic interests rather than ideological programs. India and Russia share a common fear of Muslim-oriented terrorist groups and have a joint working group on combating international terrorism. When Russia began redeveloping its military and energy sectors in the 21st century, it aggressively marketed weaponry and nuclear power to India. Russia is, in fact, the chief supplier of arms to India. In 2004 India purchased the Russian aircraft carrier *Admiral Gorshkov* and renamed it *INS Vikramaditya*. The carrier was free, but India agreed to pay more than $2 billion for it to be refitted in Russia and to be equipped with Russian armaments. Delays pushed up the cost, and India agreed to pay an additional $1.2 billion with the expectation that the carrier would be commissioned in the Indian Navy in 2012.

India also purchased the BrahMos, a supersonic cruise missile that can be launched from land, air, or sea and even from submarines. It may cost India some $13 billion. In addition, India signed a joint venture deal with Russia to produce the Sukhoi PAK FA jet fighter and purchase 200 of the aircraft when they are produced. The first prototype flew in 2010. The second jointly developed aircraft to be part of the Indian military forces is the Sukhoi Su-30MKI, a multirole combat aircraft. India plans to have 280 in service by 2015 at an estimated cost of more than $10 billion. To transport its troops and equipment, India is in a third joint venture with Russia to produce the UAC/HAL II-214 military transport aircraft. Both countries will invest $300 million to make the aircraft, which is expected to be in service by 2016. Six other weapons systems from submarines to bombers will be bought or leased by India from Russia, making the Indo-Russian relationship an exceedingly important military one with enormous financial implications.

A July 2008 Indo-U.S. nuclear agreement seemed to give the United States an advantage in reentering the potentially lucrative Indian civilian nuclear industry but also opened the door to more Russian participation in India's nuclear sector. Retooling its space industry, Russia has also expanded efforts to service India's military and economic ambitions in space.

India's bilateral trade with Russia is modest. During 2006–2007 bilateral trade was only about $3 billion, with India's exports to Russia accounting for a third of the total. Nonetheless, the two countries set up a number of commissions and groups to further their economic relationship, such as the six Joint Working Groups under the auspices of the India-Russia Inter-Governmental Commission on Trade, Economic, Scientific, Technological and Cultural Cooperation to study how the two countries could develop their partnership in such areas as trade, finance, energy, mining, science and technology, information technology, culture, and tourism. Energy would be one lucrative area for cooperation. The commission held its 16th session in New Delhi in November 2010. The goal was to increase bilateral trade to $20 billion by 2015, a figure difficult to meet due to the continuing recession that began in 2008 but a goal indicative of the close relationship between the two countries and the optimism shared by both nations that their close historical and contemporary ties would continue unabated. It was to maintain the good relationship that Russian President Dmitry Medvedev visited India in December 2010.

ANDREW L. JENKS

See also Armed Forces; Foreign Policy

Further Reading

Conley, Jerome. *Indo-Russian Military and Nuclear Cooperation: Lessons and Options for U.S. Policy in South Asia*. Lanham, MD: Lexington Books, 2001.

Ganguly, Sreemati. *Indo-Russian Relations: The Making of a Relationship, 1992–2002*. Delhi: Shipra Publications, 2009.

Kundu, Nivedita Das, ed. *India-Russia Strategic Partnership: Challanges and Prospects*. New Delhi: Academic Foundation in association with Indian Council on World Affairs, 2010.

Mahapatra, Debidatta Aurodinda. *India-Russia Partnership: Kashmir, Chechnya, and Issues of Convergence*. New Delhi: New Century, 2006.

S

✦ SANGH PARIVAR

The Sangh Parivar, literally "family of organizations," refers to the group of Hindu nationalist organizations in India. While the Sangh Parivar includes approximately 20 different political groups, the triumvirate BJP-VHP-RSS contains by far the largest and strongest organizations of the group. The BJP is the Bharatiya Janata Party, the VHP is the Vishwa Hindu Parishad, and the RSS is the Rashtriya Swayamsevak Sangh.

The collection of political parties emerged in 1925 at the early stages of the movement for independence amid the backdrop of Hindu-Muslim riots. Keshav Baliram Hedgewar (1889–1940) founded the Rashtriya Swayamsevak Sangh (RSS) and served as its first leader. It became the core organization of the Sangh Parivar and was dedicated to a right-wing Hindu nationalist project. The Sangh Parivar, as it was officially termed, eventually came to include at least 12 major nationalist parties, including the VHP and the BJP. The group of organizations encompassed a wide range of interests, with the overarching goals of Hindu unity and national pride.

Founded in 1965 as an issue-oriented organization rather than a political one, the VHP worked for low-caste and tribal people's rights, and also promoted the ban on cow slaughter. The group emerged from a religious retreat led by Swami Chinmayananda (1916–1993) in 1962 and provided the RSS with legitimacy and connections to large religious groups, as well as manpower drawn from the *sadhus* (holy men) and workers connected with the VHP. Though some people speculated that the RSS was behind the religious organization to begin with, the VHP for years remained comparatively apolitical.

The Sangh Parivar was thrust into the political forefront in the 1980s, with the BJP as its most effective political party. Capitalizing on the need to rally around a strong Hindu party, and around an issue that could galvanize Hindus, the Sangh Parivar seized on the issue of the Babri Masjid in Ayodhya, Uttar Pradesh. Proposing to replace the Mughal mosque with a temple commemorating the Hindu god Rama's birthplace appealed to the residual resentment toward Muslims, not only for their role in Partition but for a whole host of transgressions against the Hindus historically. The destruction of temples and forcible conversions to Islam during the Mughal era (1525–1858) seemed to justify Hindu hatred, and with the BJP and VHP fanning the flames with virulent anti-Muslim speeches, more than 100,000 Hindu nationalist "volunteers" tore down the mosque in a matter of hours on December 6, 1992. Subsequent communal riots that broke out across India forced the Sangh Parivar to retreat on the building of the temple. However, even today, the proposition of building a Rama temple in Ayodhya is still part of the party platform.

The late 1990s marked an expansion of the Sangh Parivar into advocating a number of social movements, educational institutions, and the development of civil society. Though it encompasses a wide range of parties, ranging from the extreme militancy of the Bajrang Dal, the militant youth wing of the VHP, and the RSS and the BJP, the Sangh Parivar continues to represent more than 40 million Indians who are committed to making India what they consider to be the ideal Hindu nation.

JULI GITTINGER

See also Ayodhya; Bharatiya Janata Party; Rashtriya Swayamsevak Sangh; Vishwa Hindu Parishad

Further Reading
Jaffrelot, Christophe. *The Hindu Nationalist Movement in India.* New York: Columbia University Press, 1993.
Jaffrelot, Christophe, ed. *The Sangh Parivar: A Reader.* Delhi: Oxford University Press, 2005.
Jayawardena, Kumari, and Malathi De Alwis, eds. *Embodied Violence: Communalising Women's Sexuality in South Asia.* London: Zed Books, 1996.
Juergensmeyer, Mark. *The New Cold War? Religious Nationalism Confronts the Secular State.* Berkeley: University of California Press, 1993.
van der Veer, Peter. *Imperial Encounters: Religion and Modernity in India and Britain.* Princeton, NJ: Princeton University Press, 2001.
van der Veer, Peter. *Religious Nationalism: Hindus and Muslims in India.* Berkeley: University of California Press, 1994.

✦ SATHYA SAI BABA MOVEMENT

The Sathya Sai Baba movement is approximately 65 years old and has a single identifiable charismatic leader: Shri (honorific) Sathya Sai Baba (1926–2011), known to his devotees as *Bhagawan* (god), *Swami* (lord), or *Baba* (father). The Sathya Sai Baba movement is classified as a new religious movement by some scholars, as it transcends traditional religious boundaries; as a neo-Hindu revitalization or renewal movement by others; and as a globally successful sectarian Indic movement that draws from religious strains of the subcontinent.

Sathya Sai Baba's personal prefix, *Sathya* (truth), refers both to his given name of Sathyanarayana as well as to the quality his devotees belies him to have embodied. His birth in a rural, dominant-caste peasant family on November 23, 1926, in the remote village of Puttaparthi in Anantapur District in the Rayalseema (boundaries of kings) region of the south Indian state of Andhra Pradesh was, according to apostolic texts, accompanied by divine signs heralding the birth of a great soul. Detailed stories of his compassion, intelligence, musical skill, magical materializations of food and sweets, and healing abilities were all seen as signs of his omnipotence, omniscience, and omnipresence. After suffering a series of seizures at the age of 13, Sathya Sai Baba claimed that he was a reincarnation of Shirdi Sai Baba, a Muslim saint/seer (*faqir*) who died in 1918, which has led to some confusion among devotees of both sects. Later more reincarnations were attributed to him, including the great gods of Hinduism, Rama and Krishna; Siva and his consort, Shakti; Jesus Christ; and a future avatar called Prema Sai. So Sathya Sai Baba was thought by some to be a charismatic guru (teacher) and by others to be a reincarnated Muslim seer, a saint, or a *purna avatar* (full incarnation) of god, whose philosophy spanned various religious and sectarian traditions.

In his discourses, which number in the tens of thousands, Sathya Sai Baba divided his life into four 16-year phases: during the first phase he engaged in mischief and playful pranks (*balalilas*); during the second he performed miracles (*mahimas*); for the third he dedicated himself to general teaching (*upadesh*), while still performing miracles; and in the last segment (which would have begun around 1984) he dedicated his life to teaching select devotees his spiritual discipline (*sadhana*).

Sathya Sai Baba lived in the remote village of Puttaparthi in Anantapur District of southwestern rural Andhra Pradesh, one of the driest regions of India, about 110 miles from the city of Bangalore, on his 100-acre ashram, Prasanthi Nilayam. After his death on April 24, 2011, he was interred three days later under the podium where he met his disciples and preached.

Devotees had to travel to the ashram to have *darshan* (sacred viewing) of and be close to him. A primary aspect of Sathya Sai Baba's teachings was the spiritual benefit of *darshan* for his students. During *darshan* Sai Baba might interact with people, accept letters, materialize and distribute *vibhuti* (sacred ash), or call groups or individuals for interviews. *Darshan* was the center of all life in the ashram and took place twice a day, beginning with the singing of *bhajans* (sacred hymns), some composed by Sathya Sai Baba himself.

The Sathya Sai Baba movement—which, according to self-reporting, has between 6,000 and 8,000 centers and 50 million devotees all over the globe—is rapidly growing in the West and in East Asia. In 2001 sources within the movement provided a figure of 3,050 centers in approximately 167 countries all over the world. A likely figure of devotional strength suggested by the newsmagazine *India Today* is 20 million in 137 countries.

The Sathya Sai Baba movement is known to be the largest faith-based foreign-exchange earner for India, earning approximately 881.8 million rupees (approximately $5 million) or the year 2002–2003, and its net worth for the same year was approximately $6 billion. The Sai Baba international following is not confined to the Indian, primarily Hindu, diaspora, though those members form a significant part of the devotional base, but has expanded to include the middle classes of many different countries, religions, and cultures. Religious studies scholar Richard Weiss aptly called him "a prophet of the jet-set more than he is a guru of peasants." The devotees—professional, technocratic, "Westernized," or what sociologist Smriti Srinivas called an "urban following"—are characterized by their mobility, their affluence, and their focus on creating a healthy union between body, spirit, and mind.

The logo of the Sathya Sai organization (the Sarva Dharma image) consists of a five-petaled lotus flower displaying on its petals the symbols from five "world" religions (Hinduism, Christianity, Islam, Zoroastrianism, and Buddhism), and at its center is the lamp of knowledge. The symbol of the ecumenism of the Sai faith is found on all official communiqués of the Sathya Sai Baba movement and in iconic form in every Sai center in the world. In 1995 another emblem, also with five petals was added; on them are written the Sai faith's five central values: truth, nonviolence, love, peace, and right conduct, and the two symbols are used interchangeably. Doctrinally, the Sai faith is ecumenical, drawing ideas from all major world religions.

Guru Sathya Sai Baba greets followers after the inauguration of the Sathya Sai Baba International Centre, established to promote the appreciation of "world heritage," March 1999. Sathya Sai Baba, who claims millions of followers around the world, rarely travels and visited Delhi after a 17-year absence. There are an estimated 1,200 Sathya Sai Baba centers in 130 countries. (Tekee Tanwar/AFP/Getty Images)

Sathya Sai Baba's followers have created an international institutional edifice, which is managed by the Shri Sathya Sai Central Trust (SSCT) and is active through various branches of the International Sai Organization (ISO), also known as the International Sathya Sai Baba Organization. Organizationally the devotees are divided into three wings by the transnational Sathya Sai Seva Organization (SSSO)—the service wing, the education wing, and the devotion wing—based on their interest and aptitude, and they are assigned to various zones based on their country of origin. Each zone may consist of various nations—for example, zone one consists of the United States and Canada—and regions with local chapters. There are nine zones encompassing all the 137 countries where the movement has a presence.

The ISO is involved in service to humanity—distributing aid to the poor (especially those in war-torn or natural disaster zones, such as communities hit by the tsunami in 2004); providing potable water to communities in need; establishing educational institutions; and supporting medical facilities, homeless shelters, food banks, clothing drives, festival dinners, hospital visits, free clinics, and other participatory social services. The Sathya Sai Baba charitable work is understood by most to be the least controversial and most laudable aspect of the worldwide mission. Devotees spend considerable time doing *seva* (charitable work) as part of their mission to heal the world of contemporary problems. Internationally, Sathya Sai Baba devotees gather daily or weekly on Sundays (and/or Thursdays) for group devotional singing (*bhajans*), prayer, spiritual meditation, service to the community (*seva*), and participation in "Education in Human Values" (SSEHV), also known as Sai Sunday School.

The ISO straddles many new media; it issues translations of Sathya Sai Baba's many discourses both in cassette form and in books and journals; it creates and distributes a subscription newsletter called *Santhana Sarathi* (translated as "the way of the Charioteer," an analogy to the divine charioteer Krishna of the Hindu epic the *Mahabharata*); it runs a television broadcast station, Sai Cast, and a radio station, *Radio Sai*; it maintains several Internet sites, including *Heart 2 Heart* and virtual journals; and issues material keepsakes such as photographs and medallions, which are prized by devotees.

Sathya Sai Baba attracted his fair share of controversy and critics, both for his materializations and for cases of healing. The death of four youths in the Sai ashram in 1993 brought in its wake allegations of "sexual healing," popularly understood to be sexual misconduct with minor boys, against the Sai organization and Sathya Sai Baba himself. Sathya Sai Baba's magical materializations, which were filmed and aired in a BBC documentary *The Secret Swami* in 2004, have been seen by critics as nothing more than skillful prestidigitation, which angered devotees worldwide. A central theme of the BBC documentary was former devotee Alaya Rahm's sexual-abuse allegations against Sathya Sai Baba. Another documentary, *Seduced by Sai Baba*, produced by Denmark's national television and radio broadcast company, Denmark Radio, carried interviews containing allegations of abuse. Allegations of corruption, fiscal mismanagement, conspiracy, abuse, and even murder were leveled at Sathya Sai Baba and emphasized by a significant, though small, global anti-Sai movement, comprised primarily of disaffected "former devotees," as they call themselves. Indian and non-Indian news journals, including *India Today*, *The Week*, and *The Telegraph*, published critical pieces about Sathya Sai Baba, but despite his critics' claims of malfeasance, Sai Baba was never accused (much less convicted) of wrongdoing in an Indian court of law.

TULASI SRINIVAS

See also Hinduism; Religion

Further Reading

Babb, Lawrence A. *Redemptive Encounters: Three Modern Styles in the Hindu Tradition.* Prospect Heights, IL: Waveland, 2000.

Brown, Mick. "Divine Downfall". *Daily Telegraph,* October 28, 2000.

International Sai Organization. Accessed April 28, 2011. http://www.sathasai.org/.

Kent, Alexandra. *Divinity and Diversity: A Hindu Revitalization Movement in Malaysia.* Copenhagen: Nordic Institute of Asian Studies, 2005.

Palmer, Norris W. "Baba's World." In *Gurus in America,* edited by Thomas A. Forsthoefel and Cynthia Ann Humes, 99. Albany, NY: SUNY Press, 2005.

Srinivas, Smriti. *In the Presence of Sai Baba: Body, City, and Memory in a Global Religious Movement.* Boston: Brill, 2008.

Srinivas, Tulasi. *Winged Faith: Rethinking Globalization and Religious Pluralism through the Sathya Sai Movement.* New York: Columbia University Press, 2010.

Urban, Hugh B. "Avatar for Our Age: Sathya Sai Baba and the Cultural Contradictions of Late Capitalism." *Religion* (Elsevier) 33(1) (2003): 73–93.

Weiss, Richard. "The Global Guru: Sai Baba and the Miracle of the Modern." *New Zealand Journal of Asian Studies* 7(2) (December 2005): 5–19.

✦ SCHEDULED TRIBES

The term Scheduled Tribe refers to specific indigenous peoples of India who inhabit Scheduled Areas. Subject to legislation by Parliament, under Article 342 of the Constitution of India, the president has the power to declare any territory a Scheduled Area.

India is a country with a very large concentration of tribal people. Essentially, tribes are forest-based people whose lives are conditioned by the natural environment. They live off the land and are therefore concentrated in remote villages, forests, and hilly regions of the country. The essential characteristics of the tribal communities are primitive traits, geographical isolation, a distinct culture, an underprivileged condition, and isolation from the mainstream community. These are the criteria for determining whether an area is a Scheduled Area.

The Fifth Schedule of the constitution deals with the administration and control of Scheduled Areas and Scheduled Tribes in states other than Assam and Meghalaya. Some of the essential features of this administration are directives to the states by the union, submission of reports to the president by governors of states with Scheduled Areas, regulations by the governor with the approval of the president to prohibit or restrict the transfer of land by/or among members of the Scheduled Tribes, and regulation of the allotment of land and moneylending. The goal of these provisions is to protect tribals and prevent their exploitation by other social groups. The tribal areas in Assam, Meghalaya, Tripura, and Mizoram are appended to the Sixth Schedule in the constitution. These tribal areas are administered by autonomous district councils and regional councils with legislative and judicial functions.

The Ministry of Tribal Affairs, a branch of the government of India, looks after the affairs of the tribal communities. An offshoot of the branch of the Ministry of Social Justice and Empowerment, this new ministry was constituted in October 1999 to administer the policies, planning, and coordination for the development of Scheduled Tribes. The constitution also provides safeguards in the form of reserved positions for Scheduled Tribes in government services. The aim is to increase their representation in the services and to improve their social and financial position.

The tribal situation in the country is not homogeneous. In states such as Mizoram, more than 90 percent of the total population fall under the tribal category. In other states, such as Kerala, tribal members comprise less than 2 percent of the total population. The stages of development in different tribal groups also vary, from shifting cultivation and food gathering, to primitive forms of agriculture.

Tribals generally live in rural areas and constitute the labor class in the country. According to the Planning Commission estimate on poverty for the fiscal year 1993–1994, more than 90 percent of tribals live below the poverty line. The destruction and depletion of forests and their resources due to socioeconomic pressures continues to pose a serious threat to tribal alienation from their land and their livelihood.

A detailed review of tribal problems during the Fifth Five-Year Plan (1974–1979) provided a framework for the socioeconomic development of Scheduled Tribes and the prevention of their exploitation by other groups in society. A tribal subplan (TSP) strategy was devised. Amendments to the Fifth Schedule empowered the president to increase the size and number of Scheduled Areas in any state. In pursuance of this policy, the president has from time to time issued orders reassigning Scheduled Areas in some states. Accordingly, in Bihar, Gujarat, Himachal Pradesh, Maharashtra, Madhya Pradesh, Orissa, and Rajasthan, TSP areas have been made conterminous with Scheduled Areas. Under TSP, 194 Integrated Tribal Development Projects (ITDPs) were undertaken in areas where the Scheduled Tribe population was more than 50 percent of the total population. Further developments under TSP include the adoption of the Modified Area Development Approach (MADA) to cover smaller areas of tribal concentration (areas with a minimum 10,000 people of which 50 percent are Scheduled Tribes) during the Sixth Five-Year Plan; and identification of tribal clusters (areas with approximately 5,000 people of which 50 percent are Scheduled Tribes) during the Seventh Five-Year Plan. In the TSP states so far, 259 MADAs and 82 clusters have been identified. Spread over 17 states and 1 Union Territory, about 75 tribes have been identified as Primitive Tribal Groups (PTGs). They are characterized by inaccessible habitats, low rates of population growth, little or no literacy, and little movement beyond the hunter-gatherer stage.

The ministry of tribal affairs has implemented various programs for the welfare and development of the Scheduled Tribes. Among others, the programs include grants in aid; the construction of schools and hostels for tribal youth; establishment of village grain banks; guidance to tribal students in building careers and in finding employment; and financial aid to promote research and training for tribal development.

SECULARISM

Approximately 15 percent of the geographical area of the country is covered by prominent tribal areas. Article 342 of the constitution identified 533 tribes in the different states and Union Territories, with the state of Orissa having 62 tribal groups, the largest number in any state. Some of the major tribes are Boro in Assam, Bhil in Maharashtra, Gujjar in Himachal Pradesh, Bhil in Gujarat, Buxa in Uttar Pradesh, Bhil in Rajasthan, Banjara in Bihar, Garo in Meghalaya, Chakma in Tripura, Birhor in Orissa, Kammara in Tamil Nadu, Birhor in West Bengal, Lusai in Mizoram, Dafla in Arunachal Pradesh, Dhodi in Goa, Naga in Nagaland, Lepcha in Sikkim, Garra in Jammu and Kashmir, Jarawa in Andaman and the Nicobar Islands, and Dhodi in Daman and Diu. Some tribes can be found in more than one area of the country. Census data indicate an increase in the population of Scheduled Tribes since 1951. In 2001 the Scheduled Tribe population stood at 84.3 million, which was 8.19 percent of the total population of the country.

YOSAY WANGDI

See also Northeastern States

Further Reading

Basu, Durga Das. *Introduction to the Constitution of India.* 10th ed. New Delhi: South Asia Books, 1984.

Government of India. *Brochure on Reservation for Scheduled Castes and Scheduled Tribes in Services.* 8th ed. New Delhi: Ministry of Personnel, Public Grievances and Pensions, Department of Personnel and Training, 1993.

Government of India Ministry of Tribal Affairs. Accessed April 28, 2011. http://www.tribal.nic.in/.

Scripts. *See* Languages and Scripts

✦ SECULARISM

Secularism is a Western concept that originated with the Latin term *saeculum* (world, century, age) and implies that the outside world is different from the religious world with respect to beliefs and modes of behavior. Secularism reduces and replaces religion with other convictions. Some cultural observers have anticipated and predicted that secularism will replace religion in the not-too-distant future and that religion will wither away, die, and completely disappear. The fulfillment of this prognostication has not occurred, although religious adherence has declined in locations such as Europe. Religion, in fact, has proven to be more resilient than expected and to offer something valuable to ordinary people looking for guidance and meaning in life, something that they cannot find in secularism. The struggle between religion and secularism is being played out in India, which witnessed the rise of right-wing conservative and religiously affiliated Hindu political parties in recent decades under the Sangh Parivar, only to have a resurgence of the Congress Party, founded in 1885, win recent elections with its message, in part, of the advantages of secularism.

Secularism operates both privately and publicly by altering how people understand themselves and construct a worldview, and it also affects how they behave in public. Secularism is a complex process that includes the following: rationalization, industrialization, social differentiation, individualism, societalization, diversity, relativism, pluralism, modernization, technology, and egalitarianism. These various aspects of secularism do not affect cultures in the same way or to the same extent, and how the culture responds to any of these aspects is also unpredictable. It is important to acknowledge that the extent of the changes ushered in by secularism depends on the local context. There is no universal form of secularism that affects all societies in the same way.

The various elements of secularism operate to undermine religion. Rationalization, for instance, disrupts a person's faith by calling it into question. Industrialization creates a wedge between family life and economic life outside the home. Industrialization also demands specialization of economic roles that can result in the fragmentation of home life. Social differentiation grows in concert with the development of industrialization and specialization, as socioeconomic classes become more divided. Dividing workers into blue collar and white collar is symptomatic of differentiating workers. As socioeconomic developments call for a higher educational level to meet the challenges offered by new types of jobs, the educated adopt more independent modes of thinking that make them less willing to blindly accept religious beliefs and follow religious leaders. Individualism is also a factor that undermines blind adherence to religious messages by creating more autonomy for the person and stressing the importance of the individual over the community. Individualism also tends to make religion into something private. By finding oneself in a pluralistic context, the presumed uniqueness of one's religion is undermined, making one's allegiance to a religion voluntary and encouraging a person to choose among competing religions.

Societalization refers to the organization of life by the nation-state, which replaces the customary role of religion. In the case of India, the traditional caste system and its accompanying social privileges are not recognized by the constitution. This is a good example of the nation-state becoming a force that legitimates the social world instead of religion. Moreover, the diversity of religious cultures suggests relativism, which calls for tolerance to ensure social harmony. Throughout its history, relativism has not been a major problem in India, which has demonstrated considerable tolerance with regard to belief, although the culture has been less tolerant with regard to behavior. A modern exception to this trend is the tension between Hindu groups and Muslims.

The disruption of communal bonds, traditional employment patterns, and social status are caused by modernization and technology. Their promise of a better life is so appealing that they reduce the need for a person to turn to religion for answers to the problems of life. In such a scenario, there is no need to depend on religion because contingency is reduced and certainty heightened by relying on modern technology. The plethora of religious teachers (gurus) in India is indicative that this has not occurred on a large scale in India.

Although secularism became significant in modern times in the West, the term secularism was not used in India until the late 1940s, when elements of it were introduced into the Indian constitution. In contemporary India, there are five identifiable groups debating the pros and cons of secularism in India. The liberal position insists that religion and politics belong in different realms. In fact, the secularism of Prime Minister Jawaharlal Nehru (1889–1964; prime minister 1947–1964) was based on a conviction that religion represents an erroneous worldview that will yield to a more rational understanding of the world as scientific thought and economic growth advance. Liberals indicate that the rise of conservative, right-wing political parties, such as the Vishwa Hindu Parisad (VHP), founded in 1964, and Bharatiya Janata Party (BJP), founded in 1980, are symptomatic of responses to a cultural crisis created by secularism. The Indian sociologists T. N. Madan (b. 1933) and Ashis Nandy (b. 1937) argue for a different perspective on the topic because secularism was never indigenous to India, and it is therefore inappropriate to apply the notion to India. A third position is represented by nationalists who argue that the recognition of minorities represents a pseudosecularism. In contrast to the nationalists, Rajeev Bhargawa wants to incorporate values shared by many religions into the public life of India, a sort of secular religion embraced by all. Finally, by means of her genealogical approach, Shabnum Tejani finds that Indian secularism represents a formulation of nationalism that involves synthesizing liberal discourses with individual definitions of the democratic majority as broadly Hindu. The establishment of secularism in India occurred during the course of constituent assembly debates, which emerged around the issue of political safeguards for minorities between 1946 and 1950. Thus, secularism was invoked as an agreement against reservations for religious minorities. Moreover, it was widely accepted that for India to become a secular state there was a need to ensure freedom of religion. The advent of independence had a significant impact on the debate about secularism, serving as an embodiment of the values of unity and tolerance that marked a break with past political history.

CARL OLSON

See also Ayodhya; Bharatiya Janata Party; Rashtriya Swayamsevak Sangh; Sangh Parivar; Vishwa Hindu Parishad

Further Reading
Madan, T. N. "Secularism in Its Place." *Journal of Asian Studies* 46(4) (1987): 747–759.
Needham, A. Dingwaney, and R. Sunder Rajan, eds. *The Crisis of Secularism in India.* Durham NC: Duke University Press, 2007.
Tejani, Shabnum. *Indian Secularism: A Social and Intellectual History, 1890–1950.* Bloomington: Indiana University Press, 2008.

✦ SECURITY, INTERNAL

Internal security refers to the maintenance of security within the entire country. India has been facing major challenges to its internal security as traditional security threats, such as the danger of conventional and nuclear war, have been overshadowed by the dangers of domestic armed insurgencies and terrorist activities. India's internal security situation cannot be understood without taking into account its physical parameters. It is the seventh-largest country in the world; it has land boundaries of nearly 10,000 miles; it contains more than 600 island territories, has a coastline of more than 4,500 miles, and includes an Exclusive Economic Zone of more than 1,500,000 square miles. Finally, it has land frontiers and maritime boundaries with Pakistan, Bangladesh, China, Nepal, Bhutan, and Myanmar.

With a complex physical and sociocultural milieu, India's internal security concerns have been greatly influenced by the forces operating from both within and outside the country. Internal factors include its history, geography, colonial legacy, burgeoning population, sharp social and economic disparities, and complex sociocultural and ethnoreligious traditions that interplay freely in a secular democracy. Similarly, the continuing tensions between India and Pakistan over Kashmir, the geopolitics of the South Asian region (such as the Soviet Union's intervention in Afghanistan in 1979 and the subsequent political turmoil in Afghanistan and Pakistan), the strategic objectives of the neighboring countries, and the increasing influence of radical Islamic ideas are some of the major external factors that have contributed to internal instability.

India faces multiple internal security threats. Militancy in Kashmir, left-wing extremism, and insurgency in the northeastern states are some of the gravest threats. According to the New Delhi–based South Asia Terrorism Portal, at least 231 of the country's 608 districts are currently affected, at differing intensities, by various insurgent and terrorist movements. In addition, wide areas of the country appear to have "fallen off the map" of good governance and are acutely susceptible to violent political mobilization, lawlessness, and organized criminal activity. In 2008 alone, more than 1,000 civilians were killed in terrorist attacks, Naxalite violence, and militant activities in the northeastern states and in Jammu and Kashmir.

Militancy in the form of kidnapping and murders began to manifest itself in Kashmir in 1989. Since then, the character of militancy in the state has undergone a radical transformation. Initially it was waged by local Kashmiri militants with official Pakistani political, diplomatic, and military support, as Islamabad considered Kashmir the "unfinished agenda of partition." Toward the mid-1990s, however, militancy in the state was hijacked by Pakistan since the idea of merging Kashmir with that country did not find much favor among the local Kashmiri militants. After the tit-for-tat nuclear tests of 1998, Pakistan's confidence that it could raise the threshold of conflict without the risk of military retaliation increased with the direct involvement of its army to change the status quo in Kashmir. The result was the Kargil incident of 1999. While the Kargil debacle caused political turmoil in Pakistan and resulted in a military takeover, India experienced a substantial rise in violence and killings in Jammu and Kashmir and other parts of the country by Pakistan-based terrorist organizations. These

An Indian soldier takes cover as the luxurious Taj Mahal Hotel in Mumbai burns during the gun battle between the Indian military and Muslim terrorists inside the hotel, November 29, 2008. (AP Photo/David Guttenfelder)

included the 2000 attack on the Red Fort, the 2001 attack on the Indian Parliament, the 2006 Mumbai subway attack, and the 2008 Mumbai assault. Of these, the Parliament attack of 2002 and the Mumbai attack of 2008 triggered an intense military confrontation between the two nuclear rivals, as India accused Pakistan of complicity in these attacks.

Although political violence is under control in Kashmir, Pakistan-based terrorist groups, such as Jaish-e-Mohammad (the Army of Mohammad) and Lashkar-e-Taiba (the Army of the Pure), have spread their terror activities to the hinterland. The Mumbai attack in 2008 clearly established that these terror groups are resorting to spectacular acts of mass murder in urban centers, with the goal of intimidating and terrorizing the public. In addition, these groups are increasingly targeting national assets, and they have established links with other fundamentalist and terrorist organizations in different parts of the country.

Left-wing extremism, also known as Naxalism or Maoism, originated in India in 1968 and constitutes what Prime Minister Manmohan Singh (b. 1932; prime minister 2004–) has described as the "single biggest internal security challenge" confronting the country. While the number of Maoist-affected states in the country is currently pegged at 14, the movement has demonstrated the intent and the potential to spread across the length and breadth of the country. The People's War Group (PWG), the Maoist Communist Center (MCC), Party Unity, and the Communist Party of India (Marxist) are some of the most dreaded Naxalite groups.

Greatly influenced by Bengali revolutionary Charu Mazumdar (1918–1972) and his theory of "class struggle" and "class violence," the Naxalites operate in forest and tribal areas because they offer ideal conditions to carry out guerrilla warfare. They indulge in such terrorist acts as attempts to annihilate the so-called "class enemy," mass killings, attacks on public installations, and the conduct of summary trials. Their method of operation revolves around stealth, speed, and surprise, and so they target unprepared and sleepy police stations in order to seize arms and ammunition.

Though their "ideology" and "methodology" are imported, the basic causes of Naxalism are indigenous. There is a widespread perception that "land reforms" and efforts at the redressing of genuine grievances of the tribal population have only been superficial and that the "exploiters" continue to "exploit" the poor and the landless agriculturists. Since the issues raised by the Naxalites are people-centric and have a certain legitimacy in the eyes of the common people, the group as been very difficult to control.

The northeastern region consists of seven states with 10 percent of India's land mass. Linked to India by a narrow 43-mile stretch between Bangladesh and Bhutan; sharing an uninterrupted border of nearly 2,300 miles with China, Burma, Bangladesh, and Bhutan; and composed of ethnic groups that also reside in the neighboring countries, the whole area has been in a state of turmoil since the early years of independence. Ethnic heterogeneity, linguistic diversity, a change in the demographic profile of the region due to illegal migration from Bangladesh, historical and geopolitical development, and the lack of economic growth and infrastructure development are some of the major factors that have contributed to insurgency in the Northeast. Moreover, for geopolitical reasons, the neighboring countries bordering these states also encourage secessionist activities by way of providing arms, ammunition, and shelter to the insurgents.

Prominent terrorist and insurgent groups active in the northeastern region include the United Liberation Front of Assam, National Democratic Front of Bodoland, National Socialist Council of Nagaland, National Liberation Front of Tripura, All Tripura Tiger Force, and People's Liberation Army. In addition, these groups are divided into numerous factions, with different demands and principles. They claim to be the "watchdog of the people" and carry out numerous violent acts.

To manage its internal security, the Ministry of Home Affairs, the equivalent of the U.S. Department of Homeland Security, is the ministry responsible for the overall internal security of the country. It acts through a number of police, military, and intelligence organizations. These include special security forces to guard airports and other high-profile targets, and 12 paramilitary forces, such as the Central Reserve Police Force, the Assam Rifles, the Border Security Force, the Indo-Tibetan Border Police, the Special Frontier Force, the Sashastra Seema Bal, the Central Industrial Security Force, and the National Security Guard. The army usually participates in internal security duties as a last resort. Several intelligence agencies monitor terrorist activities. The Intelligence Bureau (IB), a division of the Ministry of Home Affairs, collects intelligence inside India, and the Research and Analysis Wing (RAW) is the external intelligence agency. A joint intelligence committee analyzes intelligence data from IB and RAW, as well as from a handful of military intelligence agencies, which usually provide tactical information gathered while carrying out counterterrorist activities.

India has responded to the problem of internal security through both political and military means. It has tried to reach a political solution by giving greater constitutional autonomy and undertaking developmental activities. The military option has been used to wear the rebels down and bring them to the negotiating table. While this approach has been successful in some cases, like the Punjab (1983–1991) and Mizoram (1966–1986), it has not succeeded in many other situations. There are two major reasons: the first is structural and the second is political. The "Union and State Lists" enshrined in the Indian constitution and the issue of a state's sphere of jurisdiction under its federal structure inhibit coordination among the various arms of the central and state governments. In fact, there is insufficient cooperation between the center and the states, and among states themselves. At the political level, the main obstacle is a lack of consensus among the major political parties on vital issues of national concern. After the Mumbai terrorist attack in 2008, the central government announced a number of measures to strengthen internal security, including the establishment of a National Investigative Agency and a tough antiterrorism law.

UPENDRA CHOUDHURY

See also Intelligence Services; Jammu and Kashmir; Naxalite Movement; Northeastern States

Further Reading

Choudhury, Upendra. "Internal Security under Seize: Need for Constitutional Correctives." In *Reviewing the Constitution*, edited by B. L. Fadia, 138–171. Udaipur: Himanshu Publishers, 2001.

Shrikant, Paranjpe, ed. *India's Internal Security: Issues and Perspectives.* New Delhi: Kalinga Publications, 2009.

South Asia Terrorism Portal. Accessed April 28, 2011. http://satp.org.

Vohra, N. N. "National Governance and Internal Security." Paper available at the Institute for Defence Studies and Analyses, New Delhi. www.idsa.in/NNVora170108.htm.

Security, Regional. *See* Regionalism and Regional Security in Southern Asia

Self Employed Women's Association (SEWA). *See* Women's Reform Movements

✦ SHAH BANO CASE

Contemporary debates between political parties in India largely revolve around the definition of secularism as it exists in the Indian landscape. Deemed a watershed event, the Shah Bano case brought the debate of religious law versus civil law into sharp relief, making secularism a central issue in elections in the 1990s and in the new millennium.

Shah Bano was a 62-year-old Muslim woman and mother of five who was divorced by her husband. Unable to support herself, she appealed through the court system in 1978 for a modest financial settlement from her ex-husband, even though under Muslim Personal Law she was not entitled at that time to any support from him. Seven years later her case was considered by the Supreme Court, which ruled that because Indian women had been able to seek financial recourse through the civil courts since the Hindu Succession Act of 1956, being Muslim did not preclude her from being a citizen of the state and therefore deriving all the benefits of citizenship. Therefore, she was also entitled to this recourse. This was seen by the Muslim community as impinging upon Muslim Personal Law, which, among other things, deals with legal matters concerning marriage, divorce, and inheritance.

Then, in 1986, the Congress Party–dominated Parliament passed the Muslim Women (Protection of Rights on Divorce) Act, whose most controversial provision was that it gave a Muslim woman the right to maintenance for the period of *iddat* (three lunar cycles) after the divorce, in addition to the repayment of *mahr* (dower or brideprice). This was controversial on many levels. From the liberal camp, it was seen as unjust to Muslim women that they were denied the extended maintenance other women in India received. Others felt it was unfair to Hindu men, who were forced to pay alimony for longer than three months. Above all, it was seen as an instance of the government invading religious domains, particularly by the Sangh Parivar, a right-wing group of Hindu organizations founded in 1965. Sangh Parivar argued that the Muslim Women Act went against the secular nature of the state, and thus encouraged further division of the Hindu and Muslim communities.

During the course of this event, the Congress Party of Prime Minister Rajiv Gandhi (1944–1991; prime minister 1984–1989) was criticized from all sides of the political spectrum by eventually allowing Muslim Personal Law to prevail and reversing the initial court decision, which had become one of the greatest points of contention among the right-wing Hindu community. The Shah Bano case became reconstituted as a cause that had a devastating effect on communal relations. Even today the Sangh Parivar considers the case emblematic of the dire effects of "pseudosecularism." The accusation that certain parties are complicit in nonsecular practices, thus living by a double-standard, was an indictment directed at the Congress Party for its evident lack of evenhandedness with all communities involved in the Shah Bano case.

JULI GITTINGER

See also Islam; Muslims

Further Reading
Hawley, John Stratton, ed. *Fundamentalism and Gender*. New York: Oxford University Press, 1994.
Lawrence, Bruce B., and Aisha Karim, eds. *On Violence: A Reader*. Durham, NC: Duke University Press, 2007.

Ludden, David, ed. *Contesting the Nation: Religion, Community, and the Politics of Democracy in India.* Philadelphia: University of Pennsylvania Press, 1996.

Pathak, Zakia, and Rajeswari Sunder Rajan. "Shahbano." *Signs* 14(3) (Spring 1989): 558–582.

Rajan, Rajeswari Sunder. *The Scandal of the State: Women, Law, and Citizenship in Postcolonial India.* Durham, NC: Duke University Press, 2003.

✦ SHANKAR, RAVI

Ravi Shankar (b. 1920) is the world's best-known Indian musician. Shankar, sometimes known simply as Ravi, has performed Hindustani music, north India's classical music, all over the world on the sitar, a long-necked, multistringed lute. He greatly expanded the visibility of the sitar and Hindustani music by collaborations with prominent Western musicians, such as the violinist Yehudi Menuhin (1916–1999), Beatles member George Harrison (1943–2001), and the American composer Philip Glass (b. 1937). His influence has also been acknowledged by many other musicians. For instance, jazz saxophonist John Coltrane (1926–1967) was a fan of

World renowned sitarist Ravi Shankar is seen playing his sitar in an iconic 1967 photograph. (AP Photo)

Shankar's. In addition to his many decades of performing in the most prestigious concert halls and venues of the world, Shankar has an extensive discography of about 120 recordings, 2 of which have won Grammy awards. Shankar also cowrote the Oscar-nominated score for the film *Gandhi* (1982), and he composed the highly acclaimed music for the three films of the Apu Trilogy (1955–1959) directed by Satyajit Ray (1921–1992). He has written two autobiographies in English.

Shankar has long been an innovator within the traditional repertoire of north Indian classical music. He changed the sound of the sitar and introduced flashier playing techniques that sometimes drew criticism from more conservative musicians. His creative approach, however, opened the music up to more experimental fusions, as demonstrated on his 1987 album *Tana Mana*. During the 1960s, largely due to his association with the Beatles and his performances at the Monterey Pop Festival (1967) and the

Concert for Bangladesh (1971), his sound, in the minds of many people, became synonymous with psychedelia. While enjoying the large crowds and the adulation, Shankar insisted that the arduous technical and spiritual discipline needed to perform his music excluded the use of drugs.

Born into a family of Bengali Brahmin intellectuals in Varanasi, Uttar Pradesh, Shankar won his artistic spurs in Paris during the 1930s in the dance troupe of his elder brother, Uday (1900–1977). Allauddin Khan (1862–1972), a sarod player and multi-instrumentalist composer who became one of the most renowned Indian music teachers of the 20th century, and the father of renowned sarod player Ali Akbar Khan (1922–2009), joined Uday's troupe for a year, during which time Shankar became his disciple. In 1938 Shankar gave up his career as a dancer and began a period of intense study of the sitar and Hindustani music with Allauddin Khan, and later married his daughter, Annapurna Devi (b. 1927). By the 1950s, Shankar was an established artist in India performing regularly in concerts and on the radio. In 1956 he toured the United States and made his seminal recording: *Three Ragas*. His international career soon took off, and he eventually became regarded as an elder statesman of world music.

Shankar has received many honors, including the Music Council UNESCO award (1975), the Magsaysay Award from Manila (1992), the French Legion of Honor (2000), and an honorary knighthood from Queen Elizabeth II (2001). The government of India has recognized his contributions to Indian culture by bestowing its most prestigious awards: the Padma Vibhushan (1981) and the Bharat Ratna (1999). In 1986 he was nominated to the Rajya Sabha, India's upper legislative chamber. Shankar lives in California and New Delhi with his wife Sukanya (b. 1954) and their daughter, the sitarist Anoushka Shankar (b. 1981). He is also the father of the singer Norah Jones (b. 1979).

J. ANDREW GREIG

See also Khan, Ali Akbar; Khan, Vilayat; Music, Devotional

Further Reading
Shankar, Ravi. *My Music, My Life*. New York: Simon and Schuster, 1968.
Shankar, Ravi. *Raga Mala: The Autobiography of Ravi Shankar*. New York: Welcome Rain, 1999.

◆ SHIV SENA

The Shiv Sena (Shivaji's Army) political party is a right-wing regional political party based in the state of Maharashtra. It was formed in Bombay (Mumbai) in 1966 by journalist and cartoonist Balasaheb "Bal" Thackeray (b. 1923). Named for the 17th-century Maratha warrior Shivaji Bhosle, or Chhatrapati Shivaji Maharaj (1630–1680), Shiv Sena was created as a single-issue movement to challenge the perceived dominance of south Indians in Mumbai's professional occupations. Since the late 1960s, however, its platform has expanded, but the party has retained a focus on Marathi ethnic chauvinism and Hindu nationalism. In 2010 Shiv Sena held a majority of the seats in the Mumbai Municipal Corporation, the city government of Mumbai and some of its suburbs. It held power at the state level as part of a coalition government between 1995 and 1999. At the national level it is part of the center-right coalition, the National Democratic Alliance (NDA), which was founded in 1998 and formed the government of India between 1998 and 2004 led by Prime Minister Atal Bihari Vajpayee (b. 1924).

Bal Thackeray founded the party during an acute recession in the late 1960s, building support by whipping up anti–south Indian (primarily anti-Tamil) sentiments and drawing upon images of strength associated with Maharashtra's warrior history. The party initially spread its message of Maratha pride on the editorial pages of Thackeray's weekly political journal *Marmik* and, later, in the party-sponsored daily newspaper *Saamna*. It also built support through neighborhood-level committees, or *shakas*—a structure borrowed from the Rashtriya Swayamsevak Sangh (RSS). Despite the party's use of local *shakas*, Shiv Sena has maintained a highly centralized structure, tightly controlled by Thackeray himself.

The party's popularity has ebbed and flowed over its 40-year history. Its support first surged in the early 1970s when it captured a majority of the seats in the Mumbai Municipal Corporation. By the close of the 1970s, however, it was losing support in Mumbai, and despite its efforts to become a statewide party, it held no seats in the Maharashtra Assembly. In the 1980s the party benefited from two political shifts. First, a lengthy strike in Mumbai's textile mills, followed by widespread mill closings, challenged the power of Mumbai's labor unions. The Shiv Sena seized this opportunity to build support among the disgruntled Maratha working class. Secondly, the Shiv Sena adopted the increasingly popular discourse of Hindu nationalism, or Hindutva ("Hinduness"), a word coined in 1923 by Hindu nationalist Vinayak Damodar Savarkar (1883–1966). By reframing its message in terms of Hindutva, Shiv Sena could build support in areas outside of Mumbai, where southern Indians were not perceived as a threat. By the end of the 1980s, Shiv Sena had emerged as a formidable political force in Maharashtra. In the 1990 Maharashtra Assembly elections, the party won 18 percent of the seats. In the next election, in 1995, Shiv Sena took a quarter of the seats and formed a coalition government with the right-wing Hindu nationalist party Bharatiya Janata Party (BJP), which had been founded in 1980.

In office for just five years, the government built a lasting legacy by officially changing Bombay's name to Mumbai (and overseeing numerous other name changes throughout the state) and facilitating significant investments in housing and infrastructure in Mumbai. Although the coalition lost power in the 1999 elections, Shiv Sena has remained a formidable opposition party. A leadership struggle in the party beginning in the mid-2000s, however, has threatened the party's stability. Soon after Bal Thackeray selected his son, Udhav Thackeray (b. 1960), as his successor in 2003, his nephew and political disciple, Raj Shrikant Thackeray (b. 1968), formed a new political party, the Maharashtra Navnirman Sena (Maharashtra Reformation Army) and took many of the party's supporters with him. With the movement's base divided, Shiv Sena appeared weaker than it had in many years.

LIZA WEINSTEIN

See also Maharashtra; Mumbai

Further Reading
Banerjee, Sikata. *Warriors in Politics: Hindu Nationalism, Violence, and the Shiv Sena in India.* Boulder, CO: Westview, 2000.
Hansen, Thomas Blom. *The Saffron Wave: Democracy and Hindu Nationalism in Modern India.* Princeton, NJ: Princeton University Press, 1999.
Hansen, Thomas Blom. *Wages of Violence: Naming and Identity in Postcolonial Bombay.* Princeton, NJ: Princeton University Press, 2001.
Jaffrolet, Christophe. *The Hindu Nationalist Movement in India.* New York: Columbia University Press, 1996.
Katzenstein, Mary Fainsod. *Ethnicity and Equality: The Shiv Sena Party and Preferential Policies in Bombay.* Ithaca, NY: Cornell University Press, 1979.
Mehta, Suketu. *Maximum City: Bombay Lost and Found.* New York, Knopf, 2004.
Patel, Sujata, and Alice Thorner. *Bombay: Metaphor for Modern India.* New Delhi: Oxford University Press, 1995.

✦ SIKHISM

Sikhism is the youngest of the world's monotheistic religions. It originated in the Punjab (the region of the five rivers) in northwestern India in the 15th century. Founded by Guru Nanak (1469–1539), Sikhism today has more than 25 million adherents worldwide. About 90 percent of the world's Sikhs live in India and are largely concentrated in the Punjab.

The adherents of Sikhism are called Sikhs. The word *Sikh* is derived from the Pali *sikkha* and the Sanskrit *sisya*, which both mean "disciple." Sikhs believe in one God, the same God for all people of all religions. They adhere to the teachings of ten gurus (teachers), which started with Guru Nanak, born in 1469, and ended with the 10th and last guru, Gobind Singh (1675–1708). The gurus espoused peace, social harmony, and equality of all peoples regardless of caste, with the 10th guru introducing a more militant philosophy in the face of persecution during the Mughal rule of India in the 16th century.

Since his sons were assassinated, Guru Gobind Singh, the 10th and last guru, proclaimed that the line of personal gurus ended with him. Thereafter, the supreme loyalty of the Sikhs was transferred from the personal guru to the holy book, the *Guru Granth Sahib*, and the *Khālsa*, the core group of committed followers from the larger Sikh community that Gobind Singh initiated in 1699.

The Sikh place of worship is called a *gurdwara* (temple), which literally means the "gateway to the guru." People of all faiths are welcome to the *gurdwara*. Sikhism emphasizes *panth* (community) and community service. So every *gurdwara* has a *langar* (a common kitchen), where Sikhs are expected to contribute in preparing a vegetarian meal to be shared by

Sikh pilgrims at the Full Moon Festival, Amritsar, Punjab, May 2010. (Atilla Jandi/Dreamstime.com)

everyone in the spirit of community and equality. While Sikhs do not mandate pilgrimage to holy sites because they believe that God is everywhere, Harmandir Sahib (Golden Temple) in Amritsar in the Punjab is considered as Sikhism's central and most sacred shrine. The *Adi Granth* (the original holy book) is housed at the Golden Temple.

Guru Nanak, the first guru, was born and raised a Hindu. At that time, Punjabis were either Muslims or Hindus. Hinduism and Islam grew side by side for more than 900 years before Sikhism emerged in the Punjab in the 15th century. Sikhism is often viewed as an offshoot of Hinduism, strongly influenced by the Hindu Sants, a meditative and devotional group in the Hindu *bhakti* (devotion) movement. It was also influenced by Islam, particularly by Sufi mysticism. It shuns the idolatry and polytheism of Hinduism and rejects the Hindu caste system and the authority of the Brahmins. Instead, it advocates equality for all men, regardless of caste, race, or gender. Like Islam, Sikhism focuses on one God, who is the truth and omniscient, omnipresent reality. God is formless and reveals himself through creation. It is one's duty to meditate on this creation. Through meditation, a person could be one with the creator. Through meditation and devotion, a person could attain *mokshsa*, the state of unity with the divine that ends the cycle of reincarnation or transmigration.

While Sikhism in its early history advocated tolerance of Hindus and Muslims, Sikhism evolved into a militant religion. It began to identify God with power. Due to continuing persecution during the reign of the Muslim Mughals, who invaded India from Afghanistan in the 16th century, Sikhs realized that they were called to be both soldiers and saints. Starting in

1526, northern India was ruled by the Mughal Dynasty. While there were friendly relations between the Mughals and the Sikhs at the beginning, the Mughals became suspicious of Sikhism due to its growing number of followers, and Sikhs suffered persecution at the hands of Mughal emperors. Emperor Jahangir executed Guru Arjan Dev (5th guru) for presumably corrupting Islamic teachings. For refusing to convert to Islam, Tegh Bahadur (9th guru) was beheaded during the reign of Emperor Aurangzeb. During the era of Hargobind (6th guru) and after Arjan's death, Sikhism slowly acquired militancy, and Amritsar was fortified. But it was during the time of Gobind Singh that Sikhism shifted from Guru Nanak's focus on inner peace and meditation to martial discipline and the arming of followers to defend the faith.

Gobind Singh changed the face of Sikhism when he created the *Khālsa* (community of the pure) from the broader Sikh *panth*. He introduced the rite of *pahul* (initiation by the sword) during the inauguration of this new brotherhood of soldier-saints. He introduced the "Five Ks," which identify many Sikhs to this day: a Sikh was not to cut his *kesh* (the hair of his head or beard), he was to wear a *kangha* (comb), a *kara* (steel bracelet), and *kachh* (short pants); and, he was to carry a *kirpān* (a double-edged sword). Henceforth, Gobind Singh was known as *Singh* (lion). He required male Sikhs to likewise assume the surname "Singh." Women could also be members of the Khālsa. They were given a single-edged sword and vested with the title *Kaur* (princess). The evolution of Sikhism from a meditative to militant religion has been the subject of theological and scholarly interest then and now.

When the Mughal Empire declined, a Sikh kingdom under the rule of Maharaja Ranjit Singh (1799–1839) arose and flourished in the Punjab, with Lahore as the capital and borders reaching as far as China and the Kyber Pass in present-day Afghanistan. With the death of Ranjit Singh, the Sikh kingdom of the Punjab fell into disarray. Then, after the defeat of the Sikhs in the Anglo-Sikh Wars of 1846 and 1848, the Punjab was annexed by Britain in 1849.

When Britain granted independence to India in 1947, and with the partition of the Indian subcontinent into India and Pakistan, what was then known as British Punjab was likewise partitioned. East Punjab became part of India, with West Punjab allocated to Pakistan. More than 2 million Sikhs were forced to emigrate to the East Punjab, leaving their ancestral homes and sacred sites behind in West Punjab. Both the Sikhs and Hindus became embroiled in the bloody war against the Muslims in Pakistan, which resulted in over a million deaths.

When the Hindus and Muslims acquired their own homelands at the end of British rule, Sikhs clamored for a separate Sikh state to be called Khalistan. While the Sikh demand for a separate nation was denied, the Indian central government gave them autonomy within the state of the Punjab. As a religion, Sikhism is difficult to dissociate from politics. In fact, the Akali Dal (Akali Religious Party), formed in 1920 and active to this day despite incessant factionalism, argues that religion and politics are integrated and inseparable in Sikhism. The Akalis claim to represent both the religious and political interests of the Sikhs.

Tragic milestones in the contemporary history of Sikhism occurred in 1984, when Indian prime minister Indira Gandhi ordered the Indian Army to storm the Golden Temple at Amritsar in June. Known as Operation BLUESTAR, this military assault was intended to force a Sikh extremist group holed up in the temple complex to surrender. This group was headed by Jarnail Singh Bhindranwale, a religious instructor and politician, who fought for Sikh rights and variably espoused Sikh autonomy or secession, as the case may be, using both terrorism and parliamentary means. Operation BLUESTAR killed not only Bhindranwale and his followers but also innocent faithful visiting the shrine. Sikhs condemned this desecration of their holy temple and the loss of many lives. A few months later, in October 1984, Gandhi was assassinated by her Sikh bodyguards in retaliation for the Amritsar assault. The assassination was followed by the Anti-Sikh Riots of 1984, which generated more Sikh casualties and outrage against the central government of India.

While the Sikhs lived for centuries as a religious majority in the land of the Punjab, they have always been a religious minority in the Indian subcontinent, a land dominated by Hinduism and Islam. Today, while Sikhs comprise only 2 percent of India's total population, they manage to preserve their own distinct identity and culture. Many *gurdwaras* have programs for children to learn Punjabi and the Gurmukhi script for writing the Punjabi language. However, there has been a growing resistance among Sikh youth to following old customs and traditions, particularly the wearing of turbans. In 2004 the election of Manmohan Singh as India's 14th and current prime minister was a welcome development in the Sikh community since he is the first Sikh to hold this office.

Sikhs who emigrated to other countries also live as religious minorities in their new homelands. In the 20th century, Sikh communities began to grow in North America and Europe. Today, the largest Sikh community outside of India can be found in Great Britain. Modest Sikh populations can also be found in Canada and in the United States. Per the U.S. Census Report in 2006, there are presently 500,000 Sikhs in the United States, most of whom live in California, Washington, New York, and New Mexico. After the 9/11 Al Qaeda attack on the World Trade Center in New York in 2001, there was a surge of hate crimes toward Sikhs in the United States, since many confused the turban-wearing Indian Sikhs with Muslims. Smaller Sikh communities can also be found in East Africa, Singapore, Malaysia, Iran, Fiji, Australia, and Hong Kong, among others.

All Sikhs celebrate the birthdays of Guru Nanak and Guru Gobind Singh and the anniversary of the martyrdom of Guru Arjan. They also commemorate the anniversary of the *Khālsa* every year during the Vaisakhi, a Punjabi harvest festival held at the beginning of the solar year.

GLORIA G. GONZALES

See also Amritsar; Punjab

Further Reading
Kapur, Rajiv A. *Sikh Separatism: The Politics of Faith.* London: Allen and Unwin, 1986.
McLeod, W. H. *The Sikhs: History, Religion, and Society.* New York: Columbia University Press, 1989.

Sikhism. Accessed April 28, 2011. http://sikhs.org.
Singh, Khushwant. *A History of the Sikhs*, vols. 1 and 2. Princeton, NJ: Princeton University Press, 1963.

Sikkim. *See* Himalaya

◆ SINGAPORE, RELATIONS WITH

Of all the 10 countries in the Association of Southeast Asian Nations (ASEAN), founded in 1967, with which India has developed a relationship since the beginning of its Look East policy in 1993, Singapore stands at the top. Singapore was one of the first to actively respond in the early 1990s to India's new policies to liberalize and globalize its economy. And in the post–Cold War and post–Soviet Union (1991) atmosphere, it became far easier for Singapore to endorse India's standing as a rising regional power. The strategic and military ties between the two countries were strengthened when Singapore threw its weight in ASEAN to support India's membership of the United Nations (UN) Security Council, although that has not, in 2010, yet been accomplished. In 2003 a bilateral agreement provided for expansion of cooperation between the two nations in joint military training and the development of weapons and systems technology. Cooperation was most notable in the maritime field, with the navies of the two states holding joint exercises in the MILAN (the Hindi term *milan* means "meeting" and is a biennial gathering of regional navies hosted by the Indian Navy) and SIMBEX (Singapore India Maritime Bilateral Exercise) programs near India's Andaman and Nicobar Islands. New agreements were also signed to promote the exchange of intelligence in fighting terrorism.

The economic statistics of bilateral trade and investment show very impressive growth, with the promise of strong growth in the future as well. Thus, there has been a dramatic growth in bilateral trade and a substantial investment on Singapore's part in India's infrastructure. As of 2006, the tiny island republic was India's eighth-largest source of investment at US$3 billion, an amount expected to rise to $5 billion in 2010 and from there to double in 2015. Singapore-India cumulative foreign direct investment for the period April 2000 to July 2009 was US$8.57 billion. Singapore has notably invested in upgrading India's ports and airports and in developing information technology (IT) parks and special economic zones. Additionally, there has been close collaboration in aerospace and space programs, and in aviation, energy, and biotechnology.

Among the special acts of collaboration is the creation of the Ascendas Information Technology Park in Bangalore in 2005. The Government Investment Corporation (GIC) of Singapore registered itself in India as a financial institutional investor and committed itself heavily in housing finance development corporations. In 2006 Singapore was India's ninth largest trading partner, accounting for 3.8 percent of India's total trade. Trade jumped from US$2.2 billion in 2001 to a little short of $10 billion five years later. In the five years from 2004 to 2009, India's imports from Singapore increased by 26.88 percent, while its exports doubled at 100.8 percent. More than 50 percent of Singapore's exports to India are re-exports.

The tourist traffic has also grown at an impressive rate. India is Singapore's fourth most popular tourist destination. Indian authorities reported the issue of more than 650,000 visas to visitors from Singapore in 2006. And conversely, Singapore (along with Penang and Pattaya) vie as the most popular family holiday destinations for middle- and higher-level executives and businessmen in India's major cities.

Economic relations have kept pace with the growing political and strategic relationship. India's Confederation of Indian Industry (CII) and the Singapore Business Federation have collaborated to promote a better economic relationship, resulting in the governments of the two countries signing the Comprehensive Economic Cooperation Agreement (CECA) in 2005. CECA eliminated trade and tariff barriers, made possible better access to banks and financial institutions, and provided for increased bilateral cooperation in education, science and technology, intellectual property rights, and commercial aviation. Singapore relaxed its conditions for visas to Indian professionals, especially in IT, medicine, engineering, and finance, enabling workers in these fields to migrate to the island nation and work there. In 2010 Singapore issued a license to India's Industrial Credit and Investment Corporation of India (ICICI) Bank as a full-fledged bank with authority to open multiple branches. That made ICICI the second Indian bank (after the State Bank of India) to hold that status in Singapore.

DAMODAR R. SARDESAI

See also Southeast Asia, Relations with

Further Reading
Kumar Nagesh, Sen Rahul, and Asher Mukul, eds. *India-ASEAN Economic Relations: Meeting the Challenges of Globalization*. Singapore: Institute of Southeast Asian Studies, 2006.

✦ SINGH, KHUSHWANT

A prominent Indian journalist and novelist, Khushwant Singh was born on February 2, 1915, in Hadali, Punjab, which now lies in Pakistan. He is a significant postcolonial writer in the English language and is known for his clear-cut secularism, wit, and deep passion for poetry. He was educated at Government College, Lahore; St. Stephen's College, Delhi; and King's College, London, before reading for the bar at the Inner Temple, also in London.

After qualifying in law, Singh returned to India and set up a legal practice in Lahore. However, he struggled in his practice for several years before the partition of India in August 1947.

635
SINGH, KHUSHWANT

Partition forced him to abandon his practice, and with his family he moved and settled in New Delhi. Shortly afterward, he was offered a job in the diplomatic service in the Ministry of External Affairs (MEA), which took him first to London and later to Canada. He also served in Paris with the United Nations (UN) Educational, Scientific and Cultural Organization. However, he found life in the bureaucracy to his disliking and left the MEA. In 1951 he joined All India Radio as a journalist.

Since then he has written for almost all the major national and international newspapers in India and abroad, published many books, and made numerous TV and radio appearances at home and abroad. He was the founder-editor of *Yojana* (1951–1953), editor of the *Illustrated Weekly of India* (1979–1980), chief editor of *New Delhi* (1979–1980), and editor of the *Hindustan Times* (1980–1983). His Saturday column "With Malice Towards One and All" in the *Hindustan Times* is by far one of the most popular columns of the day. As a writer and a journalist, he is known for his candor and brutally honest style of writing, which despite often landing him in controversy has not deterred or changed his style of expression.

Singh's many books—the U.S. Library of Congress lists 99 works by and about him—enjoy a worldwide readership. His *A History of the Sikhs* is a classic two-volume book on Sikh history and is used as a reference work by many scholars. His novel *Train to Pakistan* was made into a film and won him international acclaim and the Grove Press Award in 1954. Other well-known novels include *Delhi* and *The Company of Women*. He has also written the biography *Maharaja Ranjit Singh* and the historical work *Fall of Sikh Kingdom*. Singh's translation of *Japji*—the hymns of Guru Nanak (the founder of the Sikh faith)—and commentary on the *Bhagavadgita*, titled *From Mind to Supermind*, are a testament to his secular mindset. Another book, *Declaring Love in Four Languages*, written jointly with Sharda Kaushki, presents a selection of the finest poems in English, Hindi, Urdu, and Punjabi. He has also translated renowned Punjabi poet Amrita Pritam's poem *Pinjar* (Skeleton) into English.

Singh was a member of the Rajya Sabha (upper house of the Indian Parliament) from 1980 to 1986. Among other honors, he was awarded the Padma Bhushan in 1974 by the president of India. He returned the decoration in 1984, however, in protest against the Union Government's siege of the Golden Temple in Amritsar, popularly known as Operation Bluestar. Undeterred, the Indian government awarded Singh an even more prestigious honor, the Padma Vibhushan, in the year 2007. In 1999 he was honored with "Order of Khalsa" (*Nishaan-e-Khalsa*), the highest decoration bestowed by the Sikh community.

STUTI BHATNAGAR

See also Amritsar; Literature; Sikhism

Further Reading
Dhawan, R. K. *Three Contemporary Novelists: Khushwant Singh, Chaman Nahal, Salman Rushdie.* New Delhi: Classical Publishing, 1985.

Shahane, Vasant Anant. *Khushwant Singh*. New York: Twayne, 1972.

Singh, Khushwant. *Truth, Love and a Little Malice: An Autobiography*. New York: Viking, 2002.

Singh, Rohini, ed. *A Man Called Khushwant Singh*. New Delhi: UBS Publishers, 1996.

✦ SINGH, MANMOHAN

Manmohan Singh (b. 1932) became prime minister of India in 2004. He is the first Sikh to hold that office. Equally important, he is seen as the architect of India's economic reforms in the 1990s, which liberalized the Indian economy and opened it to foreign investment, thereby making it a partner in the global economy. He has been awarded national and international awards, including the Padma Vidbushan (1987) and the Euro Money and Asia Money Award for Finance Minister of the Year (1993).

Singh was brought up in Amritsar, Punjab, after his family moved from the place of his ancestors, Gah (Pakistan), in 1947. That year India was divided into the sovereign states of India and Pakistan. After completing his undergraduate degree from the University of the Punjab, Chandigarh, in 1952, and then his master's degree in 1954, he went to St. John's College, at the University of Cambridge. There he earned a degree in 1957 and ended as a Wrenbury Scholar, before transferring to Nuffield College, at the University of Oxford, where he received his PhD in 1962. His doctoral thesis, a critique of Indian trade policies, was entitled "India's Export Performance, 1951–1960, Export Prospects and Policy Implications."

Manmohan Singh is the prime minister of India and the country's first Sikh prime minister. (Shutterstock)

Upon his return to India, Singh taught at his alma mater, the University of the Punjab, between 1957 and 1965. Between 1966 and 1969 he worked at the United Nations (UN) Conference on Trade and Development, and in the following decade he worked at the Ministry of Foreign Trade and then for the cabinet minister for foreign trade. He also taught at the University of Delhi. In 1971 to 1972 he became the economic adviser to the Ministry of Foreign Trade, moving up to be the chief economic adviser to the Ministry of Finance (1972–1976). Between November 1976 and April 1980 he served as secretary of the Ministry of Finance, serving on such commissions as the Atomic Energy Commission and the Space Commission. In April 1980 he became the secretary of the Planning Commission, and he held that position until September 1982, when he was appointed governor of the Reserve Bank of India. He served as governor for three years before moving on, in 1985, for a two-year stint as deputy chairman of the Planning Commission of India. Between August 1987 and November 1990 he served as secretary-general and commissioner of the South Committee in Geneva, Switzerland. During these decades he acquired a wealth of knowledge by serving on a number of other councils, commissions, and associations.

During the 1990s Singh was ushered into the political limelight when he was chosen to be India's finance minister, and he was elected to the upper house of Parliament, the Rajya Sabha. He won election in October 1991 from Assam on the Congress Party ticket. In the Rajya Sabha he became the Leader of the Opposition and was reelected in 1995, 2001, and 2007. He served as the adviser to the prime minister on economic affairs between December 1990 and March 1991, before being appointed minister of finance, a position he held from June 1991 to May 1996. He then took on the portfolio of the minister of external affairs, holding it between November 2005 and October 2006. He returned for a short term as minister of finance between November 2008 and January 2009. As the finance minister, Singh gave a compelling speech about how India would recover from the near-collapse of its economy. Using the words of the renowned French intellectual and writer Victor Hugo (1802–1885), he stated that no power on earth could stop an idea whose time has come.

After the Congress Party–led United Progressive Alliance (UPA) won the general elections of 2004 Singh was, in a surprise move, chosen as the prime minister. First sworn in on May 22, 2004, he is only the second prime minister in India's history to be reelected after a full five-year term; the other was India's first prime minister Jawaharlal Nehru (1889–1964; prime minister 1947–1964). Singh distinguished himself as prime minister through his economic reforms, which changed the path that the Indian economy had been following for more than four decades. He introduced an ambitious economic recovery program, which led Indian commercial and IT sectors to achieve record growth and expansion. He simplified the Indian tax system and removed government regulations and bureaucratic controls to create a business and investment climate favorable to Indian businesses and entrepreneurs, as well as to global multinational corporations. At the same time, he is a strong advocate of the mixed economic model, in which the public sector remains a strong presence in dealing with infrastructure and agriculture.

Singh is the only Indian prime minister who has not won a general election from a seat in the lower house of Parliament, the Lok Sabha. Although he is intellectual, thoughtful, unassuming, and gentle-looking, albeit with a strong voice, his critics consider him to be a weak and indecisive leader, but he enjoys strong support from India's educated and middle classes, and he has emerged as a consensus builder among often assertive, unruly, and divergent allies in the UPA. Presiding over such a coalition, Singh continued his economic reforms to encourage growth in the industrial as well as the agrarian sectors. He has worked consistently to make the Indian government's bureaucracy more accountable for its actions. In a gesture toward engendering communal harmony between Hindus and Sikhs, Singh offered a public apology in Parliament on August 12, 2005, for the Indian government's role in the anti-Sikh riots of 1984, which was well received by the Sikh community. These riots had broken out after the assassination of Prime Minister Indira Gandhi (1917–1984; prime minister 1966–1977, 1980–1984) by her Sikh bodyguards.

Singh has adopted a pragmatic and friendly approach toward India's neighbors. When alleged Pakistani citizens attacked the financial capital, Mumbai, on November 26, 2008, however, relations with Pakistan became strained once again, but India has been praised for its restraint. Singh's government has also worked to ease tensions between India and China; one sign of normalization in relations was the opening in 2006 of the Nathula pass, which goes from the state of Sikkim to Tibet, after 40 years. Although, his government has reversed policies in dealing with India's former ally Iran. Amid loud criticism from the Opposition, Singh signaled the end of cooperation over Iran's nuclear program.

After his economic reforms, the most noteworthy accomplishment of Singh's government has been the highly contentious U.S.-India nuclear deal, signed in New Delhi by Singh and U.S. president George W. Bush (b. 1946; president 2001–2009) on March 2, 2006. The U.S.-India nuclear agreement allows India access to U.S. nuclear facilities and nuclear technology. As part of the deal, the United States agreed to help India develop civilian nuclear technology, and India is permitted to take part in international nuclear research activities. As a result of the violent opposition to the deal, Singh's government faced a no-confidence motion in Parliament on July 22, 2008, and only survived through abstentions and political deals with regional parties to win by 19 votes (275 votes to 256). In doing so, however, Singh lost the support of leftist parties from his coalition.

Nonetheless, the Indian people gave a decisive verdict in favor of the Congress-led coalition parties in March 2009 by reelecting Singh in the general elections. He commenced his second term in May 2009 with a team of his own choice, which was assembled to tackle the internal security threats, the recession that began in December 2007, and continuing problems with infrastructure. The first initiative of the new UPA government was to implement the lessons learned from the 2008 Mumbai terrorist attacks regarding lack of preparedness by security forces. Antiterror hubs have been set up in New Delhi, Mumbai, Kolkata, Chennai, and Bangalore and are manned by specially trained army commandos. The second initiative has been to upgrade and enhance the efficiency of the government: an ambitious project toward the goal of e-governance is the Unique Identification project (UID), which will provide a unique ID for each resident of the country. In addition, a high-level panel of experts has been appointed, with members such as Nobel Laureate Amartya Sen (b. 1933) and business tycoon L. N. Mittal (b. 1950), to advise the government on how to enhance private-public partnerships to stimulate economic growth. Singh's concern to improve the nation's communications and transportation system was demonstrated when he announced that his government would invest heavily in building hundreds of miles of freeways. In his Independence Day speech on August 15, 2009, Singh reiterated his government's seven priorities of agriculture, water, education, health care, employment, urban renewal, and infrastructure to continue the trajectory of growth and development of the previous five years. Internationally, Singh's expertise on economic planning and recovery was demonstrated in the G-20 Summit in September 2009, when his policy prescriptions were included in the group's communiqué. Indian diplomatic circles were highly appreciative and enthusiastic about his invitation from U.S. president Barack Obama (b. 1961; president 2009–) to be the first state guest in the White House during the Thanksgiving Day holidays on November 24, 2009.

FATIMA A. IMAM

See also Economy; Prime Minister

Further Reading

Singh, Manmohan. *India's Export Trends and the Prospects for Self-Sustained Growth.* Oxford, UK: Clarendon, 1964.

Singh, Manmohan. "Prime Minister of India Dr. Manmohan Singh." Accessed April 28, 2011. http://manmohansingh.org.

Singh, Manmohan. *Prime Minister Manmohan Singh: Selected Speeches.* 2 vols. New Delhi: Publication Division, Ministry of Information and Broadcasting, Government of India, 2005–2006.

✦ *SLUMDOG MILLIONAIRE* (MOVIE)

The movie *Slumdog Millionaire*, directed by British filmmaker and producer Danny Boyle (b. 1956) with Loveleen Tandan, an Indian film director and casting director, was an international success in 2008. The film won eight Oscars, including Best Film and Best Director. Indian attitudes toward the film, however, were ambivalent, ranging from outright rejection by the cultural chauvinists to acceptance among film fans. There were celebrations in Mumbai when the Oscar announcements were made on February 22, 2008. Related to this ambivalence is an ongoing debate about how the film should be classified—whether it is an Indian film, or a film about India made by a sympathetic foreigner, or a film inspired by the success of contemporary Bollywood. In any case, there is no doubt that Boyle warmed to his subject as production progressed, and the result is a film that captures many of the dilemmas of India's rapidly modernizing society: the corruption, communalism, and brutality on the part of the police, and the changing attitudes of the young toward social conventions that have glued India together for centuries.

The film is based on the 2005 novel *Q&A* by Vikas Swarup, the Indian diplomat and novelist. It was his first novel and has since been renamed *Slumdog Millionaire* to cash in on the film's success. It was transformed into a script by Simon Beaufoy (b. 1966), the British screenwriter. Funding for the production was obtained from a variety of sources, including Celador Films and Film4 Production (United Kingdom) and Warner International Pictures (United States). The film was shot in England and on location in India. It was well received on release, but its later box office and critical successes were achieved in incremental stages. In the year after winning the Oscar, the film grossed $377 million. Reviews of the film in the West emphasized its debt to Bollywood, while in India there was some disquiet over the title. *Slumdog*, it is alleged, is not a word commonly used in the *bustees* (slums) of Mumbai, and its use was viewed as derogatory. However, it is now reported that the word has been incorporated into *Hinglish*, the lingua franca of contemporary urban India.

The narrative trajectory of the film is complex. It tells the life story of Jamal Malik, a young Muslim who is a *chai wallah* (tea bearer) at a call center in Mumbai. His success on the game show *Kaun Banega Crorepati* (KBC; Who Wants to Be a Millionaire?), originally presented on Indian television by renowned Indian film actors Amitabh Bachchan (b. 1942) in 2000 and 2001 and then Shah Rukh Khan (b. 1965) for one year after a four-year hiatus, is greeted with suspicion, and he is arrested and beaten by the police. Jamal tells his story to an essentially sympathetic police inspector, revealing that each answer he provides on the show relates to an episode in his life, such as getting Amitabh Bachchan's autograph as a child and the death of his mother in the communal riots of 1993. (These episodes are shown in flashback in the film.) After their mother's death Jamal and his brother, Salim, are recruited into a begging gang, from which they escape to become, by accident, tourist guides at the Taj Mahal in Agra. On their return to Mumbai, Salim throws in his lot with a local gangster, while Jamal embarks on a search for Latika, a young girl whom the brothers had befriended in their begging days. Jamal finds that Latika has grown into a beauty but is the mistress of a local gangster. Jamal convinces the inspector that he is genuine, and he is released to complete his quest on KBC. It then becomes apparent that Jamal has undertaken this task in order to win Latika away from the gangster. She escapes with the assistance of Salim and Jamal, whom she meets on a railroad station platform, and they are reunited. The film concludes with a Bollywood song-and-dance routine as the credits role.

Slumdog Millionaire was hugely successful with audiences in the West but was controversial in India, where concerns remained about its overreliance on English to cater to the global audience, its representations of Hindus (who kill the boy's mother), the fate of the young actors who were plucked from the slums to portray the characters in their youth, and its perceived lack of cultural authenticity.

BRIAN SHOESMITH

See also Bachchan, Harivansh Amitabh; Bollywood; Film Industry

Further Reading

Swarup, Vikas. *Q&A: A Novel*. New York: Scribner, 2005.

✦ SOAP OPERAS

The genre of soap opera has its origins in the daytime serials that were broadcast on radio and sponsored by giant soap manufacturers, such as Proctor and Gamble, in the United States during the 1930s. Because the stories were targeted toward women doing their household work during the day, the soap opera characteristically features women-centric stories and chiefly (though not only) addresses a female audience.

In India, soap operas are a relatively new phenomenon, and most people refer to them as "serials." They are produced in a variety of Indian languages, including Hindi, Bengali, Marathi, and Tamil. The most popular and well-known serials are in Hindi. Indian prime-time soaps came into their own with the efflorescence of private television channels in the 1990s, such as the Star network, Zee TV, and Sony.

Soaps in India share common features with global soaps in their generic conventions; however, there are differences as well. Key features of Indian soaps can be outlined as follows:

1. Open-ended narratives told in serial/episodic form that resist narrative closure;
2. Multiple characters, plots, and subplots;
3. Use of time at a dual level—one that parallels actual time and implies that soap characters' lives go on whether we watch or not; and two, one in which the narrative takes a generational leap to introduce new characters and new story lines;
4. Emphasis on dialog and attempt at resolution;
5. Mixing of melodrama, myth, realism, and forms of entertainment;
6. The use of hook, recap, and precap;
7. Male characters whose actions move the narrative forward;
8. Women as the central protagonists;
9. The family home as the main setting for the show.

Of the points above, genre mixing and the use of hook, recap, and precap are distinctively India's. With regard to genre, Indian soaps draw on a variety of sources, both from India and the West, but retain a distinctively Indian flavor. Soaps in India represent a continuation of the culture's pre-cinematic dramatic forms and stories, transformed by the capitalist economy of scale and the power of the mass media. Where they differ from their Western counterparts is in the dramatic traditions from which they emerge. For most Indians, dramatic conventions are drawn from the two great epics, the *Ramayana* and *Mahabharata*, as well as from other folk legends, folk stories, and regional performances from the different states of India. The *Ramayana* and *Mahabharata* are stories of large joint families, their relationships and intrigues, and their family values and traditions. Indian soaps have also been influenced by the expensive and stylish production values of such U.S. prime-time soaps as *Dynasty*, *Dallas*, or *Grey's Anatomy*, as well as daytime dramas such as *The Bold and the Beautiful*, *General Hospital*, and *All My Children*. In addition, Indian soaps show the influence of successful mainstream Bollywood films.

Scene still from the Indian soap opera *Mahabharata*, 1989. Soap operas are immensely popular. (Hemant Pithwa/The India Today Group/Getty Images)

Another Indian soap convention is the use of hook, recap, and precap. The beginning of every episode starts with a recap of the previous day's events, bringing the viewer up to date, and then a voice-over invites the audience to *"aaiye, ab dekhtey hain aagey"* ("come, let us watch further"). This is the hook or enticement. Indian soaps use another ploy that is peculiarly Indian in order to lure their viewers to watch the next episode. This is what is termed a "precap." The term "precap" is a uniquely Indian term, literally the opposite of "recap." The precap is a preview of the next day's episode.

Precap is similar to the incorrect, though extremely handy, "prepone," the opposite of "postpone." Instead of using the term "bring forward," many people simply say "prepone" to contrast with "postpone." It is common parlance in India and has come to connote what is referred to as "Indian-English." Terms such as this are perfectly understood and accepted in India.

Indian soap opera production and consumption differ in many ways from that of the West. First, production houses in India are mostly family-run businesses. Examples include Ekta Kapoor's Balaji Telefilms, which gave India its first prime-time soaps, including *Kyunki Saas Bhi Kabhi Bahu Thi* (Because the Mother-in-Law Was Also Once a Daughter-in-Law, which aired on Star Plus) and *Kahaani Ghar Ghar Kii* (The Story of Every Home, which aired on Star Plus). Sunjoy Waddhwa's production house Sphere Origins first challenged Balaji Telefilms' supremacy with *Saat Phere . . . Saloni Ka Safar* (Seven Rounds of the Sacred Fire [during Marriage] . . . Saloni's Journey, which aired on Zee TV) and *Balika Vadhu* (Child

Bride, which aired on Colors). A third example is Rajan Shahi's production house, with soaps such as *Sapna Babul Ka . . . Bidaai* (The Dream of Every Father . . . His Daughter's Departure from her Natal Home to Her In-Laws' Home, aired on Star Plus) and *Yeh Rishta Kya Kehlata Hai* (What Is This Relationship Called, which aired on Star Plus).

A second distinction is the belief that Indians have in astrology, numerology, and *vaastu* (similar to feng shui), when it comes to success in their professional and personal lives. For instance, the soaps produced by Balaji Telefilms are often referred to as the "K soaps" because all their titles start with the letter K. It is said that Ekta Kapoor was advised by her astrologers to use this letter of the alphabet for success. Similarly, producer Sunjoy Waddhwa and his wife, Comall, spell their names in this unusual way (rather than the more usual "Sanjay" and "Komal") because they have been advised to do so by astrologers. Third is a belief in the strength of prayers and the visibility of statues and deities in all the offices of production houses. All the offices have statues of Hindu deities with offerings of fresh flowers and burning incense sticks. Fourth are the incredibly long working hours that production houses and studios keep, working through days and nights, weekends, and even national holidays.

Fifth is the manner in which television soaps are aired in India. Overseas, particularly in the United States, there are season breaks for prime-time soap operas. In India, there are no season breaks. People watch the same soaps Monday through Friday throughout the year. Soap characters, in turn, become like *dal-chawal* (lentils and rice, often a staple diet in India). Sixth is a constant allusion to family. Employees of production houses, as well as the soap stars themselves, refer to being all members of the same family. When a beloved character on a soap opera dies, many people cannot bear to stay on the set to watch that particular episode of shooting. Star TV has instituted the Star Parivaar (family) Awards for the best soap operas.

Until the 1990s, when India opened its doors to economic liberalization, the country had only one state-run television channel, Doordarshan. The most popular soaps on Doordarshan were *Hum Log* (We People, 1984) and *Buniyaad* (Foundation, 1986). These two were modeled along the lines of what are termed Sabido's method of education-entertainment. Simply put, the Sabido method produces radio and television dramas that impart social messages and values.

Hum Log and *Buniyaad* were important soaps in Indian television history because they were launched on the eve of economic reform in India; for the first time Indians had a shared sense of participating in the lives of the characters they saw on screen. Audiences created an imagined community of shared concerns, and issues stemming from the lives of the characters depicted in the soaps became questions that were debated both in the public and private spheres. The shows also made stars like Alok Nath household names. Nath played the role of Haveliram in *Buniyaad*, and after that he played the benevolent patriarch in many Bollywood films and other soaps. He is currently the loving and understanding father on the top-rated soap *Sapna Babul Ka . . . Bidaai*. Similarly, actress Kiran Juneja, who played the role of Veerawali in *Buniyaad*, married award-winning Bollywood director Ramesh Sippy and has acted in several Bollywood films and soaps.

In 2000 soap opera production and viewing changed dramatically with the launch of India's first prime-time soap, *Kyunki Saas Bhi Kabhi Bahu Thi*. The success of *Kyunki*, with its story of the Virani family, was followed by *Kahaani Ghar Ghar Kii*, the story of the Aggarwal family.

With *Kyunki* and *Kahaani*, Ekta Kapoor set a new trend of soap narratives based on urban, rich, joint families. Kapoor also raised the bar for production values; introduced catchy title songs and an opening montage; brought in aspirational lifestyles that also espoused *parivaar aur parampara* (family and tradition); used expensive and stylized sets; and created an upmarket look, reminiscent of popular Bollywood films of the 1990s. The costumes and jewelry featured on the shows set fashion trends, and people also copied the decor of the homes depicted in the soaps. Nothing like this had been seen before on Indian television.

The central women characters—Tulsi in *Kyunki* and Parvati in *Kahaani*—became the ideal wives and *bahus* (daughters-in-law); they also became household names, not only in India but also overseas in the United States, the United Kingdom, Europe, Australia, the Middle East, and the Far East. Smriti Irani, who played the role of Tulsi, and Sakshi Tanwar, who essayed the role of Parvati, are better known by their screen names. Such was their popularity that matrimonial advertisements in Indian newspapers marketed products by urging prospective brides to be like Tulsi and Parvati. The men also had their share of the fan following. When Tulsi's husband, Mihir Virani, "died," such was the public uproar to bring him back that the computers at Star TV and Balaji Telefilms crashed owing to the spate of emails from fans. So, Mihir Virani "returned from the dead," but with a new face—this time, the role was played by Ronit Bose Roy, a very popular actor of the small screen, who has been termed the "Amitabh Bachchan of television" in India. Ronit Bose Roy also played the role of the suave and handsome Mr. Rishabh Bajaj on Balaji Telefilm's *Kasautii Zindagii Kay* (The Trials of Life, aired on Star Plus), and he currently plays the rich landlord, Dharamraj Mahiyavanshi, in yet another Balaji Telefilms production *Bandini* (Imprisoned, aired on NDTV Imagine).

Kyunki and *Kahaani* also gave rise to the ubiquitous use of the term *saas-bahu*. In actuality, these were not merely *saas-bahu* sagas, but such was the success of *Kyunki*, which uses both words in its title, that the term stuck, and Bollywood films as well as reality shows and talent shows now use *saas-bahu* in their titles.

Kyunki and *Kahaani*, with their joint family sagas, went off the air after an eight-year run. Smriti Irani started her own production house, Ugraya Entertainment, and produces other shows, none of which have come close to *Kyunki*'s success. Irani's association with *Kyunki* led to the Bharatiya Janata Party (BJP), one of the political parties in India, to offer her a ticket in their elections. After *Kahaani* wound up, Tanwar has not acted in any other soap. She has, however, appeared in a recent Bollywood film *Coffee House* (2009, directed by Gurbir Singh Grewal), which did not do very well at the box office, and she is awaiting release of her second film, *Saloon*. Tanwar also works as the creative head for a friend's television production on Doordarshan.

The first two soaps to challenge the supremacy of *Kyunki* and *Kahaani* were issue based—they were stories that dealt with the problems that dark-skinned girls face in India, where a premium is put on fair skin, particularly in the marriage market. *Saat Phere* made a heroine of the brave Saloni; and *Bidaai* recounts the story of two cousins, the fair-skinned and beautiful Sadhana, who loves her dark-skinned cousin Ragini. Sadhana, played by Sara Khan, a former beauty-contest winner, and Ragini played by Parul Chauhan, are currently very popular actresses. *Bidaai*'s success has led to their participation in other shows, including dance talent shows and reality shows. Such is their popularity that they frequently go overseas to London and the United States. Their trips are financed by members of the Indian diaspora, who invite them to participate in such festive events as Diwali (the festival of lights).

Currently, the soaps with the highest ratings are those dealing with social concerns and issues in India. Soap narratives have moved away from the big city of Mumbai to smaller towns and villages. This demand for a different, new kind of content and setting is being driven by the inescapable fact of viewership increasing in the smaller towns of India. The producers of soaps, and advertising sponsors in turn, have to account for this increasing audience base.

The television channel Colors (a Viacom company), in particular, has made a name for itself with such soaps. They led with *Balika Vadhu* (Child Bride), which deals with the issue of child marriages, followed by *Uttaran* (Hand-Me-Down), which tells the story of a poor girl whose mother works in the house of a rich girl. *Na Aana Is Des Laado* (Don't Come to This Country, Darling Daughter) deals with female feticide, and most recently *Bairi Piya* (Vengeful Lover) is set against the backdrop of the very real stories of poor farmers' suicides in India. Avika Gor, who plays the child bride Anandi in *Balika Vadhu*, has won accolades for her acting, and the older women who are authority figures—such as Dadisa, the grandmother in *Balika Vadhu*, essayed by award-winning theater actress Surekha Sikri, and Ammaji in *Na Aana Is Des Laado*, played by actress Meghna Malik—are winning kudos for their acting prowess.

The cultural product that is prime-time soaps in India—particularly from the year 2000 onward—has borrowed from several sources and brought its own conventions and traditions of performance to bear on the form, giving it a distinctly Indian identity. The story of prime-time soaps in India, which are the flagship programs of television channels, is a fascinating one. It is as compelling as the narratives in the soaps that continue to bring audiences back day after day, and keep them engaged for years on end. This genre has retained its top position in viewership ratings. Prime-time soaps have made the small screen a big medium in reaching out to people.

The centrality of women in soap stories has been maintained from the 1980s until now, and production values remain high. Currently, a decade into the 21st century, however, we are seeing a move away from telefiction toward telereality. Whether this trend will continue, as the K soaps earlier did, remains to be seen in this fast-moving and dynamic field.

We need to remember that the story of prime-time soap operas in India has only just begun. But in the few short years of its existence, it has already opened up a large space in which they are discussed and debated, critiqued and celebrated. Soap stories rebuff easy answers, require ongoing reexamination and reinterpretation, and demand constant heightened interaction from both producers and audiences.

SHOMA MUNSHI

See also Television

Further Reading

Bajpai, Shailaja. "Reality Check." *Indian Express*, October 13, 2009. http://www.indianexpress.com/news/reality-check/528446/.

Desai, Santosh. "Reflections on a Box: That Epic Moment When We Spotted Ourselves on TV." *Outlook India*, October 19, 2009. http://www.outlookindia.com/article.aspx?262211.

Geraghty, Christine. "The Study of Soap Opera." In *A Companion to Television*, edited by Janet Wasko, 308–323. Malden, MA: Blackwell, 2005.

Munshi, Shoma. *Prime Time Soap Operas on Indian Television*. London: Routledge, 2010.

✦ SOMANATHA TEMPLE

The southern Gujarat coast, where the Temple of Somanatha is located, is an ancient auspicious place for Hindu pilgrimage due to its location at the confluence of three rivers, including the mythical Sarasvati. The story relating to Somanatha is mentioned in the sacred *puranas* and in the Hindu epic the *Mahabharata*. In earlier times, this area was called *Prabhas* or *Prabhasa-Pattna* (*Prabhasa* means "brilliance"), but there was no mention of the famous Shiva temple in any of the early accounts. Most modern historians believe that the large stone temple was constructed sometime during the 10th century by the Chaulukya (also known as Solankis) kings, who were the overlords for this stretch of the Gujarati coast. The early temple was a modest wooden structure featuring pillars reinforced with lead. It may have been renovated and fortified by the Chaulukya ruler named Mularaja (940–995 CE) in the 10th century. Apart from being a major center of pilgrimage and worship, it was also a storehouse of wealth, holding solid gold icons, jewelry, and coins that came as pilgrim donations or from temple investments in the overland and Indian ocean trades.

The Gujarati coast is also the location of a major port, known as Somanatha-Veraval, which was one of the three major ports in Gujarat and mainly involved with the horse trade. The Brahmins of Somanatha Temple, just like Brahmin communities in other parts of northern India, were very active participants in this lucrative trade, for which medieval India had an insatiable appetite. The care and breeding of horses had always been a problem in India due to lack of suitable fodder and difficult climatic conditions; therefore, imported high-spirited military horses had a short duration in active service. This caused a constant demand for new replacements, and all good-quality war horses had to be imported from Arabia, Persia, or

Central Asia at a very high cost. It was estimated that 10,000 horses were shipped annually to this coast of India, and that each horse fetched 220 gold dinars. Apart from cavalry, horses were also needed for temple rituals and as status symbols for the rich.

The Somanatha-Veraval port is linked with two major ancient trade routes: One was the Indian Ocean sea trade, which stretched from the South China Sea to the East African and Arabian coasts. The other was its overland caravan counterpart. The Arabian and Persian horses were imported through the oceanic route, while the Central Asian horses from Tajikistan and Korasan, passing through the caravansaries at Ghazni, Afghanistan, with its prosperous expatriate Indian merchant settlements, reached western India through the overland route. The temple earnings from this profitable horse trade were reinvested for further purchases, making Somanatha one of the wealthiest temples in India.

The other sources of income for Somanatha Temple, just like other major Hindu temples, were donations and taxes paid by the pilgrims. Such large amounts of wealth coming into this temple town naturally attracted predatory attacks from local *rajahs* and foreign raiders. Earlier, rival Hindu *rajahs* raided pilgrims and looted their donations, and the coastal shipping was targeted by sea pirates, who also had links with local rulers. It is within this context that we should view the most famous raid on Somanatha Temple by Mahmud of Ghazni, the Muslim Turkish ruler of Ghazni, Afghanistan. It was much more than a raid, according to the nationalist historian K. M. Munshi; for Hindus across India, it was an "unforgettable national disaster." This conventional view has been contested in the recent writings of the historian Romila Thapar, who offers us, in the best "Rashomon" fashion, multiple and often conflicting interpretations of the raid, including the various causes, the real objectives, and its mixed legacy. The summaries of three of these contending versions are given below, beginning with the conventional one.

The Arab medieval historian, Zakari'ya Al Kazwini, better known as Al Kazwini, in his work *Asaru-I Bilad wa Akhbaru-l Ibad*, or "The Monuments of Countries and Memoirs of Men" (composed around 1270 CE), offers us the colorful conventional account of Mahmud's raid on Somanatha. According to Al Kazwini's version, there in the middle of the wondrous temple of Somanatha was a levitating figure of Shiva linga (the representation of the Hindu god Shiva), which stayed afloat by a clever use of the magnetic lodestone, and it naturally amazed all those who witnessed it, whether they were Hindus or Muslims. When Mahmud decided to wage war against the Hindus, he made a great effort to capture and destroy this temple in the hope that the Hindus would become Muslims. Mahmud arrived there in the middle of 1026, and the Indians made a desperate resistance to protect their temple; some 50,000 of the defenders were slain. Mahmud looked upon the floating Shiva linga with wonder and gave orders to loot the temple. Mahmud then destroyed the Shiva linga with his own hands. The value of the gold found within the temple is said to have exceeded 20,000 gold dinars (6.5 tons of gold). For this deed, Mahmud was honored by the caliph of Islam, in Baghdad.

There are a number of Muslim versions of this conventional account, but curiously there is no Hindu version to corroborate the wondrous floating Shiva linga. However, there is one obscure Hindu reference about Mahmud's raid on Somanatha in the Hindu calendar (Shaka) year 1025–1025 CE, but that reference was also found in a Muslim source. This may well be an indication that the story of the raid was embellished with fictive narratives to make it seem highly symbolic—the triumph of Islam over the unbelievers.

The second version, and an equally plausible one, is the one that associates the image of the Shiva linga at Somanatha with the image of the pre-Islamic Arabian goddess Manat.

According to this version by Farrukhi Sistani (10th–11th centuries CE), the court poet of Mahmud of Ghazni, who claimed to have accompanied Mahmud during his Indian raids, the Somanatha in earlier times used to attract pre-Islamic "pagan" Arab pilgrims. They equated the term Somanatha to Su-Manat (the place of Manat), a major pre-Islamic goddess of the shrine at Kabah in the holy city of Mecca. During this early period she was identified as one of the three daughters of Allah (along with Al-Lat and Al Uzza). Later, these Arabian goddesses were abolished by the Prophet Muhammad. The image of the goddess Manat also was represented by a big block of black stone similar to the image of the Shiva linga. Hence, this Muslim Turkish attack on the Somanatha Temple and the destruction of the linga were not only seen as breaking the Hindu "unbeliever's" temple idol but also as destroying the image of a "false" Arabian goddess, whose obliteration was ordered by the prophet himself. It is in this context that the destruction of the famous Shiva linga could be seen as a doubly pious iconoclastic deed. It was for this that Mahmud was honored by the caliph of Islam and thereby gained political legitimacy.

Here it should also be noted that Mahmud's own fanaticism was not exclusively reserved for the non-Muslim Hindus, as he also waged war against Sultan Daud, the Muslim ruler of Multan in the Punjab, who was an Ismaili Shiite. It was stated in the chronicles of Farrukhi Sistani that some 50,000 Shiite heretics also perished along with 50,000 Hindu unbelievers.

The third version is a modern interpretation that gives an economic twist to this famous iconoclastic raid. According to this version, the raid was not only meant to acquire booty, but also to cripple the Arab monopolistic hold on the lucrative horse trade from the port of Somanatha-Veraval in Gujarat. The destruction of the port city would greatly benefit the rival influential horse merchants based in the town of Ghazni, as the slack in oceanic horse imports would be quickly taken up by the overland supply route passing through Ghazni. There is some evidence to support this version, as Mahmud's raid was zealously resisted not only by the Hindus but also by the local resident Arabs. One Sanskrit inscription tells of Vohara (Bohra) Farid, the son of Vohara Mahmud, who joined in the defense of Somanatha for the local ruler Brahmadeva. He was killed during the raid, and the inscription was commissioned as a memorial to him.

Until quite recently, most historians saw Mahmud's raid on Somanatha Temple as the beginning of the 1,000-year-old Hindu-Muslim divide, which was to shape all future relations between Hinduism and Islam. Thapar, however, maintains that this view is a relatively recent interpretation, or rather the interpolation by colonial historians, based on questionable sources. The earliest authoritative voice to favor this view was that of Alexander

Dow (1735–1779), the East India Company official and author of the three-volume *History of Hindustan*, which is about the 17th-century Indian Muslim historian Muhammad Quasion Firishta (1560–1620). Firishta's work was a highly embellished version of earlier sources, written more in the spirit of the Arabian Nights tales than as a sober objective historical chronicle. This imagined past became highly politicized and gained national prominence during the first Anglo-Afghan War (1839–1842), which was a punitive expedition to avenge an earlier humiliating defeat, when almost all of the British Indian Army was ambushed and massacred by local Afghan tribal groups as they made their way back to India. As a fitting vengeance for the massacre, the governor-general Lord Ellenborough ordered the uprooting of the supposed gates of Somanatha, which according to tradition fitted the tomb of Mahmud of Ghazni. This was to make amends for 800 years of "Hindu trauma," and serve as a lasting symbol of the British reconquest of Afghanistan. This act raised a storm of protest within the British Parliament at Westminster. Ellenborough was accused of appeasing the Hindus at the expense of Muslim sentiments and pandering to the monstrous "Linga-ism." On closer examination, this Afghan war trophy proved to be a disappointment, as its workmanship was Egyptian and entirely Islamic in style, not of Hindu craftsmanship. It was said to have been later stored away in an Agra fort, only to be eaten by white ants.

The legacy of the raid on Somanatha Temple was brought to the Indian public's attention during the early 20th century, not by local folk memory or medieval ballads, but in the pages of historical fiction writer Bankin Chandra Chatterji's novel *Jaya Somanatha*. It was published in 1927, when the Indian nationalist movement was in full swing. This fictive work and its emotive historical counterparts were to influence a whole generation of Hindu nationalists, including an amateur historian and a politician from Gujarat named K. M. Munchi, who later became the minister for food and civil services in the first postindependence cabinet under Prime Minister Jawaharlal Nehru. Munchi, the author of *Somanatha: The Shrine Eternal*, led a powerful Hindu nationalist lobby to restore the temple of Somanatha as one of the first tasks of the newly elected government of independent India. Munchi ignored the opposition from India's professional archaeologists and historians, who accused him of "vandalizing" a known archaeological site for political gain. For Munchi and his Hindu nationalist lobby, the act of removing the old temple ruins and replacing them with a modern structure was to eliminate the very symbols of Hindu's inability to challenge centuries of Islamic iconoclasm and to free Hindus from an inherent "occupation mentality." It was also meant to legitimize the power and the politics of the emerging Hindu nationalism inside postindependence India's political arena. A new stone temple was built in 1951, using the finest architectural style from Gujarat. But this spending of public money to settle a medieval religious grievance, in what is a secular multicultural India, did not have overwhelming support from the governing Congress Party hierarchy, including from Nehru. Nehru was against the Indian government's sponsorship of building a sectarian Hindu shrine and was appalled at the extravagant cost of its consecration ritual at a time when India had more pressing needs, including the ever-present threat of food shortage and famine. It is debatable if this rebuilding of the Shiva temple at the coast of southern Gujarat in 1951, or the destruction of the Babri Masjid at Ayodhya in 1989 by Hindu nationalists, has, in any way, restored the self-confidence or self-worth of the majority of Indians. Such retributory actions, based on unreliable and contentious historical accounts, only led to further alienation among the minority Indian Muslims and sullied the reputation of a supposedly secular and multicultural India.

RAMAN N. SEYLON

See also Ayodhya; Hinduism

Further Reading

Dowson, John, and H. M. Elliot. *The History of India as Told by Its Own Historians*, vol 10. Delhi: Low Price Publications, 1996.

Kulke, Hermann, and Dietmar Rothermund. *History of India*. New York: Routledge, 1998.

More, V. N. *Somanatha Temple*. Calcutta: Aryavarta Samskrti Samsad, 1948.

Munshi, K. M. *Jaya Somanath*. Bombay: Bharatiya Vidya Bhavan, 1976.

Thapar, Romila. *A History of India*, vol. 1. Harmondsworth, Middlesex, UK: Penguin, 1990.

Thapar, Romila. *Somanatha: The Many voices of History*. New York: Penguin, 2004.

✦ SOUTH ASIAN ASSOCIATION FOR REGIONAL COOPERATION

The South Asian Association for Regional Cooperation (SAARC) was created on December 8, 1985, after a series of extensive dialogues and brainstorming sessions between the representatives of the following seven SAARC member states: Bangladesh, Bhutan, India, the Maldives, Nepal, Pakistan, and Sri Lanka. The SAARC Secretariat was established in Kathmandu, Nepal. At the 14th SAARC Summit, held in New Delhi in April 2007, Afghanistan was admitted as the eighth SAARC member state. The Secretariat is headed by the secretary-general, who is appointed from the SAARC member states in alphabetical order for a period of three years. Dr. Sheel Kant Sharma of India became the ninth secretary-general of the SAARC on March 1, 2008, for a term of three years. Dr. Sharma is the second secretary-general from India; previously Kant Koshore Bhargava served in the same post from October 1989 to December 1991. The secretary-general is assisted by eight directors from member states. The director from India, Mr. Vinay Mohan Kwatra, serves as a director to the office of the secretary-general of SAARC.

There is a great interest in the SAARC from the outside, mainly due to the fact that the region is an emerging economy and also a huge market—more than a billion people—for foreign investment. In 2010 China, Japan, the Republic of Korea, the United States, Iran, Mauritius, Australia, Myanmar, and the European Union attained the status of SAARC observers.

The SAARC aims at economic cooperation and social development in the region. But under the overarching theme of cooperation in socioeconomic development, the SAARC promoted multilateral cooperation in such areas of mutual concern as agriculture and rural development, energy security, the environment, human resource development, people-to-people contact, poverty alleviation, science and technology, tourism development, and the expansion of transport linkages in South Asia. To reach out to the people of South Asia, the SAARC has established the following SAARC regional centers: SAARC Agricultural Information Center, Dhaka; SAARC Meteorological Research Center, Dhaka; SAARC Tuberculosis Center, Kathmandu; SAARC Documentation Center, New Delhi; SAARC Human Resources Development Center, Islamabad; SAARC Coastal Zone Management Center, Maldives; SAARC Information Center, Kathmandu; SAARC Energy Center, Islamabad; SAARC Disaster Management Center, New Delhi; SAARC Cultural Center, Matara (Sri Lanka); and SAARC Forestry Center in Thimphu (Bhutan).

Annual SAARC summits are considered as the highest authority; the 15th SAARC Summit was held in Colombo, Sri Lanka, in 2009, and the 16th SAARC Summit was held in Bhutan in April 2010. SAARC summits are supposed to happen annually, but in 25 years there were only 15 summits due to bilateral tensions and economic difficulties of the member states.

The intraregional trade in SAARC was nominal; therefore, the heads of the states signed the SAARC Preferential Trading Agreement (SAPTA) on December 7, 1995. As a commitment

Indian prime minister Manmohan Singh, center, and Bhutanese prime minister Lyonpo Khandu Wangchuk, right, congratulate Afghan president Hamid Karzai on his country's induction into the South Asian Association for Regional Cooperation (SAARC) during the inaugural session of the 14th SAARC Summit in New Delhi, April 2007. (AP Photo/Manish Swarup)

to SAPTA, the SAARC identified 226 items for trade on tariff concessions. India agreed to extend tariff concessions of up to 50 percent on more than 100 items. However, SAPTA wasn't enough to expand the intra-SAARC trade; therefore, at the 9th SAARC Summit in Male (May 1997), the South Asian leaders made a transition from SAPTA to SAFTA (South Asia Free Trade Area). India wholeheartedly accepted this development because it was linked to New Delhi's proposal on the SAARC Economic Community. SAFTA was signed on January 6, 2004, at the 12th SAARC held in Islamabad, and the agreement was actualized on January 1, 2006. To achieve the ideal of a South Asian Economic Union, the SAARC tries to facilitate intraregional trade; for instance, SAARCFINANCE connects the governors of central banks in South Asia. In addition, the SAARC has managed to reach the following crucial agreements: SAARC Limited Multilateral Agreement on Avoidance of Double Taxation and Mutual Administrative Assistance in Tax Matters (2005); SAARC Agreement on Mutual Administrative Assistance in Customs Matters (2005); Agreement for Establishment of SAARC Arbitration Council (2005); and the Agreement on the Establishment of South Asian Standards Organization (SARSO) in 2008. The SAARC's economic agenda under the umbrella of SAFTA continues to cruise at a moderate pace, due not only to political differences between India and Pakistan but also to diverse standards vis-à-vis free trade in the region.

The 21st-century SAARC is looking outward for greater cooperation with individual states, regional blocs, and international development agencies. The SAARC is open to learning lessons from other regional organizations and therefore has forged cooperation with the Association of Southeast Asian Nations (ASEAN) and the European Commission. The SAARC has memoranda of understanding to promote collaboration with the United Nations Conference on Trade and Development (UNCTAD), United Nations Children's Fund (UNICEF), United Nations Development Program (UNDP), United Nations Economic and Social Commission for Asia and Pacific (UNESCAP), United Nations Office on Drugs and Crime (UNODC), Canadian International Development Agency (CIDA), Deutche Geselschaft fur Technische Zusammenarbeit (GTZ), United Nations Industrial Development Organization (UNIDO), and International Standards Organization (ISO), just to name a few.

Besides working relationships with governmental, intergovernmental, and development agencies, the SAARC has forged collaborations with the private sector through SAARC Chamber of Commerce and Industry (SCCI), SAARC-LAW, South Asian Federation of Accountants (SAFA), South Asia Foundation (SAF), and Foundation of SAARC Writers and Literature (FOSWAL).

Decades after its establishment, the SAARC has moved out of the framework-consensus building stage into the implementation phase. Leaders at the SAARC felt the timely need of implementing projects to benefit the people of South Asia because mere agreements are of no use to prove the value of the organization. In this regard, the initiatives of the SAARC Food Bank and South Asian University in New Delhi, and the SAARC Development Fund

(SDF), which will have its secretariat in Thimphu, are worth mentioning. The SDF has been launched with an initial fund of $300 million, out of which $100 million are donated by India. The SDF has three windows (social, economic, and infrastructure) and has already implemented projects in India and Pakistan through collaborations with local nongovernmental organizations (NGOs), namely the Self-Employed Women's Association (SEWA) in India and the SUNGI Foundation of Pakistan.

ZAHID SHAHAB AHMED

See also Bangladesh, Relations with; Foreign Policy; Maldives; Pakistan, Relations with; Sri Lanka, Relations with

Further Reading
Chaturvedi, S. K., S. K. Sharma, and Madhurendra Kumar. *SAARC: Economic Cooperation*, vol. 4, *Encyclopaedia of SAARC*. New Delhi: Pragun, 2006.
Chaturvedi, S. K., S. K. Sharma, and Madhurendra Kumar. *SAARC: Past and Present*, vol. 1, *Encyclopaedia of SAARC*. New Delhi: Pragun, 2006.
Sharma, Rashmi. *India and SAARC*. New Delhi: Regal Publications, 2007.
Sharma, Rashmi. *SAARC*. New Delhi: Regal Publications, 2007.

✦ SOUTHEAST ASIA, RELATIONS WITH

Until the end of the Cold War in 1991, India's relationship with the countries of Southeast Asia, despite their geographic proximity, was only of marginal importance. Particular countries or events in the region concerned India mostly if they had international significance, disturbed global peace, or were part of a general problem, such as colonialism and the struggle to overthrow it. A new concern was evident around the end of colonial rule in India, which occurred in August 1947. Prime Minister Jawaharlal Nehru (1889–1964; prime minister 1947–1964) first called for an Asian Relations Conference to be held in March–April 1947 in New Delhi. He later called for conferences to be held on Indonesia in 1949; on India's efforts to hammer out the Geneva Agreements on Indochina in 1954; and on Indian readiness to accept the chairmanship of the three-member International Control Commissions (International Commission for Supervision and Control in Vietnam) for Vietnam, Cambodia, and Laos in 1954. India also believed in the new Asian and African awakening, as demonstrated by its leadership of the Bandung Conference in Indonesia in 1955.

India's policy toward Southeast Asia after the rise of Communist China in 1949 was based on keeping friendly relations with China. This was evident in India's treaties with China in 1954, and subsequently with several individual states, including some in Southeast Asia. The treaties were based on the five principles of peaceful coexistence, or Panch Sheel. India strongly opposed the U.S.-led policies of containment toward Communism and its policies of building alliances against the Communist bloc in the Cold War era. The United States offered the states of the region membership in the Southeast Treaty Organization (SEATO), whose expressly stated goal was to stem the tide of Communism south of the 17th Parallel. The organization, born in Manila, the Philippines, in August 1954 could enlist only two Southeast Asian states—Thailand and the Philippines—but not Burma, Indonesia, Cambodia, or Laos, which proclaimed their neutrality. Under the leadership of the trio of Nehru, Gamel Abdul Nasser (1918–1970) of Egypt, and Josip Broz Tito (1892–1980) of Yugoslavia, the Non-Aligned Movement (NAM) created a third bloc, obviating the need for a majority of Southeast Asian nations to join the U.S.-led military alliances against the Soviet-Chinese bloc. Divided Vietnam did not officially join either "bloc," but North Vietnam's Hanoi shared India's fears that pro-West alliances would signal the return of colonialism to the region.

As India-China relations soured following India's grant of asylum to the Dalai Lama, Tenzin Gyatso (b. 1935), and his nearly 35,000 followers fleeing Tibet in 1959, and the subsequent Chinese attack against India in the short but consequential India-China War in 1962, China reverted to its historical claim that Southeast Asia was in its sphere of influence. The Soviet diplomatic and military equipment given to India in the Sino-Indian conflict reflected the growing Sino-Soviet rift, which also showed the differing Soviet and Chinese positions in the ensuing Vietnam conflict against the United States. The promulgation of the Lin Biao (1907–1971) doctrine (1965) supporting "wars of liberation" provided the backdrop for Chinese support of the Vietnam conflict against the U.S.-backed Saigon regime in South Vietnam. North Vietnam's preference for the distant Soviet Union rather than for China, its traditional and geographically close neighbor, antagonized the latter, bringing a convergence of interests between India and Vietnam. This became even more pronounced in the Cambodia situation, where both Vietnam and India supported the Heng Samrin (b. 1934) regime (1979–1993), which was opposed by Beijing (and Washington). The new alignment of powers continued as China attacked Vietnam in February 1979, with China's paramount leader, Deng Hsiao Ping (1904–1997), publicly stating that China would teach Vietnam a "lesson" as it had done to India in 1962. It was no wonder that such "convergence" of interests between India and Vietnam against China would bring about a "strategic partnership" between New Delhi and Hanoi. In the late 1980s India played an important role in the international efforts in Paris to bring peace to a much-troubled Cambodia. India offered the benefit of its valuable experience in international peacekeeping, as it sent 1,700 civilian, military, and police personnel to Cambodia, to help both the United Nations (UN) Advanced Missions and the UN Transitional Authority in that country.

India remained aloof from the Association of Southeast Asian Nations (ASEAN), from the time of its creation in 1967, when there were only six pro-Western members, until the end of the Cold War in 1991. In the intervening period, for the most part, India regarded ASEAN as an instrument of U.S. policies in the region. India's economically restrictive "Socialist" policies had also inhibited the creation of good economic relations with the fast-growing economies of most of the ASEAN members, notably Malaysia, Singapore,

Indonesia, and Thailand. In 1975, in the aftermath of the Vietnam War and the much reduced U.S. presence in the region, India took a much more active interest in the area for its own sake and not just in the interests of global peace. The states of the region were concerned about the growing role Beijing would assume to fill the superpower vacuum created by the U.S. withdrawal, and there was growing interest among several ASEAN members for India to have a greater role in the region as a counterbalance to China. ASEAN was keen to assert its own independent standing and not just serve as a "lackey" of the United States. It also projected itself as an inclusive organization for the whole region, as it proceeded to admit both nonaligned as well as Communist states. Even Vietnam, Laos, and Cambodia, originally the reason for ASEAN's existence, were admitted; so was Myanmar, which had long remained neutral between the Communist and anti-Communist camps in Southeast Asia. Also, ASEAN had widened its economic relations to include the markets of China and Vietnam. For the first time, India took steps toward improving its relations with ASEAN, which, as noted, it had previously scorned for its dependence on the West, particularly the United States. In January 1992 ASEAN approved India as a "sector dialog partner" in the fields of trade, information technology, labor development, and tourism. Three years later, in 1995, India was made a "full dialog partner" of ASEAN. The following year, India advanced to become a full member of the ASEAN Regional Forum (ARF). More significantly, in 2002, India and ASEAN began holding annual India-ASEAN Summit Meetings.

Almost simultaneously with the promulgation of India's economic liberalization policies came the 1991 pronouncement of Prime Minister P. V. Narasimha Rao (1921–2004; prime minister 1991–1996) that India would develop a Look East policy. This had crucial strategic and economic consequences. From that time India determinedly plowed a path of integration, particularly economic, with the rising Southeast Asian economic powerhouse. Significantly, Rao first talked about the new policy while visiting Singapore, which would become the prime state for the dramatic improvement in bilateral trade and would make substantial financial investments in India.

India's Look East policy was applied to each of the countries of Southeast Asia, and the results were dramatic in the field of trade. In 1993–1994 the India-ASEAN trade was a mere US$2.5 billion, the balance of trade being largely in favor of the ASEAN nations. In the new millennium, the increases in bilateral trade were such as to make Indo-ASEAN trade the fourth largest for India after the European Union, the United States, and China. In the decade since 2000, the Indo-ASEAN trade's compounded annual growth rate (CAGR) was 27 percent, the total trade volume in fiscal 2009 being US$48 billion and expected to grow at an even higher CAGR in the new decade. Such a growth rate was helped tremendously by the signing in October 2009 in Thailand of the India-ASEAN Free Trade Agreement (FTA). Signed by the economic ministers of 11 countries, it covers a population of 1.7 billion people whose gross domestic product (GDP) then totaled US$2.3 trillion. The FTA, which took six years to negotiate, opened up possibilities for the economic integration of the South and Southeast Asian region. It will lift import tariffs on more than 80 percent of the region's products between 2013 and 2016. The customs duty on "sensitive goods," such as black tea and coffee, pepper, and rubber, will be reduced by 5 percent and eliminated by 2019, giving adequate time for borrowers in both regions to adjust. However, the FTA lists 489 items in agriculture, textiles, and chemicals that are exempted from tariff reduction.

India and ASEAN in 2010 negotiated an Agreement on Trade in Services and Investments. In the words of the co-chairperson of the ASEAN-India Trade Negotiating Committee, ASEAN would thereafter "seek a fast-track approach" with India for a "single" follow-up accord on liberalizing the two-way flow of services and investments. Accordingly, four meetings were scheduled in the first half of 2010 on a "request-offer basis" for negotiations, with the targeted date of August 2010 for the "final deal," which occurred in late October 2010. India has requested specific deals on employment in the ASEAN countries for English-speaking personnel in teaching, medicine and nursing, accounting, architecture, information technology, tourism, finance management, and banking.

DAMODAR R. SARDESAI

See also Foreign Policy; Singapore, Relations with; Vietnam, Relations with

Further Reading
Ayoob, Mohammed. *India and Southeast Asia: Indian Perceptions and Policies.* 1990; reprint, London: Routledge, 2000.
Kumar Nagesh, Sen Rahul, and Asher Mukul, eds. *India-Asean Economic Relations: Meeting the Challenges of Globalization.* Singapore: Institute of Southeast Asian Studies, 2006.
SarDesai, D. R. *Indian Foreign Policy in Cambodia, Laos and Vietnam, 1947–64.* Berkeley: University of California Press, 1968.

✦ SPACE PROGRAM

The Indian Space Program began with the establishment of the Indian National Committee for Space Research in August 1962 under the chairmanship of Dr. Vikram Sarabhai (1919–1971) "to look after all aspects of space research in India." Thereafter, the Space Commission and the Department of Space were established in June 1972, marking the formal beginning of the Indian space program. Since then India has grown into one of the "Big Three" Asian space powers, along with China and Japan.

The Space Commission is the nodal agency for coordinating research and development activities in space science and technology. The executive wing of the commission is the Department of Space, which operates through the Indian Space Research Organization (ISRO) that was set up in 1969 and is one of the leading space research organizations in the world. The corporate headquarters of ISRO is located in Bangalore, Karnataka, but activities related to satellites, launch vehicles, and applications are carried out at numerous centers throughout the country. The Vikram Sarabhai Space Center (VSSC) at Trivandrum, Kerala, the largest ISRO center, is responsible for launch vehicles. The principal rocket and satellite testing and launching station is Satish Dhawan Space Center at Sriharikota Island in Andhra Pradesh. The ISRO Satellite Center in Bangalore has the primary responsibility for the design, development, assembly, and testing of satellites. The Space Application Center at Ahmedabad, Gujarat, is responsible for the development of sensors and payloads. The National Remote Sensing Agency at Secunderabad, north of the city of Hyderabad, Andhra Pradesh, utilizes modern remote sensing techniques for planning and management of the country's natural resources and provides operational support for various users. Other institutes working in this area include the Physical Research Laboratory (PRL) at Ahmedabad, which conducts basic research in space sciences. The Master Control Facility at Hassan in Karnataka is a tracking station for launching satellites.

India began its space program with the aim of attaining self-reliance in satellites for various uses and in the launch vehicles that would put them in specified orbits. Research in these two streams began in the early 1970s. India launched its first experimental geostationary communication satellite, the Ariane Passenger Payload Experiment (APPLE), in 1981 through the French Space Organization. This indigenously built satellite helped scientists to gain experience in the design, development, and operation of the geostationary satellites to provide telecommunication and weather monitoring services. The success of the APPLE project led to the establishment of the Indian National Satellite System (INSAT) in 1983. INSAT consists of 21 satellites, of which 11 are in service, and it is the largest domestic communication system in the Asia-Pacific region.

Unlike the communication satellites, work on the remote sensing satellites began a little earlier. While *Aryabhata*, the first Indian remote sensing satellite, was launched in 1975, *Bhaskar-1* and *Bhaskar-2*, the other remote sensing satellites, were launched in 1979 and 1981 respectively. Designed and built in India, these satellites were launched by the Soviet Union from Baikanor, Kazakhstan, and led to the establishment of the Indian Remote Sensing Satellites (IRS) system in March 1988. With 10 satellites in operation, it is the largest constellation of remote sensing satellites for civilian use in operation today in the world.

Besides satellites, India has achieved remarkable success in the field of launch vehicles technology. In the 1960s and the 1970s, the country successfully developed a sounding rockets program, and by the 1980s research had yielded the Satellite Launch Vehicle-3 project, which was intended to carry an 88-pound payload to a height of nearly 320 miles. Its first experimental flight in 1979 and it third test in 1981, however, ended in failure. The fourth test in 1983 marked the completion of the project and also the experimental phase of the space program.

The second launch vehicle was the Augmented Satellite Launch Vehicle (ASLV), capable of putting 330-pound class payloads into a 250-mile low-earth orbit. Two successful launches of this vehicle were conducted in 1992 and 1994, when SROSS (Stretched Rohini Satellite

The Polar Satellite Launch Vehicle (PSLV-C6) sits on a launch pad at the Satish Dhawan Space Center of the Indian Space Research Organization at Sriharikota, Andhra Pradesh, May 2005. India's heaviest remote sensing satellite to date, CARTO-SAT-1, was launched by the PSLV-C6 later that month. (AP Photo/M. Lakshman)

Series, meant for atmospheric research and other scientific investigations) were placed in the intended orbits. India further applied its energies, resulting in the creation in 1994 of the Polar Satellite Launch Vehicle (PSLV), which launched IRS satellites weighing 2,204–2,645 pounds into 500–560 polar sun-synchronous orbit. Up to September 2009, 15 of 16 total PSLV launches had been successful. However, India's most significant achievement in the launch vehicle area is the Geosynchronous Satellite Launch Vehicle (GSLV) technology that enabled it to launch its INSAT-II–type satellites (4,409–5,511 pounds) into geostationary orbit. There have been five launches of the GSLV; the last was on September 2, 2007, and successfully put the INSAT-4CR satellite in geostationary orbit, placing India among the five top space-faring nations of the world. Currently, the country is developing its top-end advance launch vehicle called GSLV Mark-III, which is conceived and designed to make India fully self-reliant in launching the INSAT-4 class, heavier communication satellites of 9,920–11,023 pounds with an indigenously developed cryogenic upper stage. The first test is expected in 2011.

India's first mission beyond earth's orbit is Chandrayaan-1, a lunar spacecraft that successfully entered the lunar orbit on November 8, 2008. Although the Chandrayaan's mission was abruptly cut short on August 29, 2009, against its design life of two years, it, along with NASA's Lunar Reconnaissance Orbiter, played a major role in discovering water molecules in the moon's soil and rocks. India plans to follow up Chandrayaan-1 with Chandrayaan-2 and unmanned missions to Mars and a near-earth spacecraft in the near future.

Space has become the mainstay of the national infrastructure, providing critical services to the country's overall development. For instance, the INSAT system is extensively utilized for telecommunications, meteorological observations, radio and television broadcasting, satellite-aided search and rescue operations, and navigation and mobile satellite communication purposes. Similarly, remote-sensing satellites have already become the mainstay of the natural resource management system. Moreover, technology developed under the space program has been used in the nation's Integrated Guided Missile Development Program so as to meet the security needs of the country. India's first satellite launch vehicle, the SLV-3, for instance, played a major role in the development of the Agni series of missiles. The PSLV and GLSV combined together also offer India an intercontinental ballistic missile capability and make the country self-reliant in launching heavy IRS- and INSAT-type military satellites.

India's progress in space technology has attracted worldwide attention and demand, with leasing agreements for marketing IRS data and for the supply of space hardware and services. For example, under an agreement with the U.S. company EOSAT, data from India's IRS satellites are received and distributed worldwide. Several other contracts for the supply of space hardware and services to international customers have also been undertaken by ISRO in the recent past, with a huge earning of 10 billion rupees in 2008–2009 alone. India also believes in cooperating in space with agencies all over the world. A high-level United Nations (UN) team selected India for setting up a UN Center for Space Science and Technology Education. It was created at Dehradun, Uttaranchal, in 1995.

UPENDRA CHOUDHURY

See also Missile Program

Further Reading

Choudhury, Upendra. "India as a Space Power: How the Defense Versus Development Debate Became Outdated." *Indian Journal of Politics* 40(2–3) (April–September 2006): 115–128.

Indian Space Research Organization: Space Technology in the Service of Human Kind. Accessed April 28, 2011. http://www.isro.org.

Sankar U. *The Economics of India's Space Program: An Exploratory Analysis.* New Delhi: Oxford University Press, 2008.

✦ SPECIAL ECONOMIC ZONES

Special economic zones (SEZ) are especially demarcated territories within a nation-state that are established primarily to encourage the formation of capital through the production of goods and services. The practice of setting up such specialized zones can be traced back to 1965, when Asia's first export processing zone (EPZ) was set up at Kandla, in the state of Gujarat. Seven more EPZs came into existence by the late 1990s. Under the new scheme, however, all the existing EPZs were converted into SEZs. In April 2000 the government of India announced its first SEZ policy to supposedly overcome the limitations of bureaucratic controls, infrastructure, and fiscal regime, and to stimulate economic growth through foreign investment in the country. Later, in 2005, the government enacted the Special Economic Zones Act, which was supplemented by the SEZ Rules, which came into effect on February 10, 2006.

The SEZ Act was enacted with the primary objective of the "generation of additional economic activity, promotion of exports of goods and services, promotion of investment from domestic and foreign sources, creation of employment opportunities and the development of infrastructure facilities." This act envisaged a single-window SEZ approval mechanism through a 19-member interministerial board of approval, which would process all proposals for establishing such zones. To attract large-scale investment in this sector, the government offered impressive incentives and facilities that included major tax exemptions from export income and profits, central and state sales tax, service tax, customs and excise duties, and duty-free imports. It envisioned that the economic activity generated from SEZs would give multiplier thrust to the economy and surpass the regulatory compromises and fiscal losses, which were estimated by the Finance Ministry to be 1,600 billion rupees by 2010.

By the end of June 2009, the government of India gave approval to 1,201 government SEZs and 600 state/private SEZs set up before 2006, and notified 500 zones under the SEZ Act, totaling a whopping 2,301 zones within four years of enactment of the SEZ Act. Besides this, the government claims that a total area of 768 square miles required for the proposed SEZs would not be more than .066 percent of the total land area and not more than .122 percent of the total agricultural land in India. The policy of land acquisitions has, however, come under severe criticism from all segments of civil society and has opened up a Pandora's box of limitations associated with the SEZ Act. The establishment of an SEZ requires substantial procurement of land by promoters, and the state had been using the colonial Land Acquisition Act, 1894, to enforce acquisitions of fertile land from marginalized communities. Significantly, the Act of 1894 is applicable only for acquiring land for "public purposes," but in the context of SEZs it has been used for providing benefit to private players. Often, primarily agricultural or forest land was allegedly acquired through coercion and state violence. In addition, allegations that the landowners were compensated with payment below the market price and left to fend for themselves, without any source of income and employment, became louder.

In the wake of violent protests by farmers, landless workers, fish workers, and artisans across India—from Barnala (Punjab), Jhajjar (Haryana), Kakinada (Andhra Pradesh), Nandagudi and Mangalore (Karnataka), Singur and Nandigram (West Bengal), Jagatsinghpur (Orissa), Raigad (Maharashtra), and Goa—the government suspended all land acquisitions for new SEZs in February 2007 until a new rehabilitation policy for the displaced is announced. Subsequently, the government introduced the Land Acquisition (Amendment) Bill, 2007, and the Rehabilitation and Resettlement Bill, 2007, and announced the National Rehabilitation and Resettlement Policy, 2007, to address the grave problems resulting from land acquisitions for establishing SEZs. Due to a ban on compulsory acquisitions, small and mid-sized SEZ developers started buying land directly from owners. But the developers of large SEZs faced difficulties in acquiring contiguous land. Later, in August 2009, the government issued guidelines to allow states to acquire land for SEZs if the land owners have withdrawn or not filed objections against acquisition.

The issue of the viability of SEZs has generated intense debates in the social and political spheres. The primary reasons for opposition to SEZs emerge out of displacements and the consequent forced migrations of marginalized sections, with the connivance of the state machinery. This was witnessed in the Communist Party–ruled state of West Bengal. Critics have described these developments as "internal colonialism," "primitive globalization," "governance by corporations," and "unmitigated disaster," and they have pronounced SEZs as neoliberal enclosures in India. Votaries of the SEZ project only the positive potential of these zones for employment generation, poverty reduction, and human development. But there are some important areas of concern as well.

Section 49 of the SEZ Act empowers the central and state governments to modify or withdraw the application of any law (except labor laws) in these zones. Significantly, the act instructs the state governments to declare SEZs as "public utility services" and invests the governance of SEZs to the development commissioner (DC). The application of the former clause nullifies the bargaining power of employees and laborers working in SEZs. Further, only special courts with the key role of the DC can try and settle any civil dispute within an SEZ or any trial of a "notified offense." Significantly SEZs are neither clearly defined by the World Trade Organization (WTO) and General Agreement on Trade and Tariffs, nor are they subject to dispute-settlement proceedings, except in matters of export subsidies and import substitution.

Central laws have not addressed issues like urban management in the wake of rapid urbanization induced through SEZs, environment impact assessment, or protection of tribals. Some civil society organizations have conducted public audits of SEZs in Maharashtra and questioned the SEZ policy of Indian government. In many cases, like in the state of Goa, people have forced the government to scrap the SEZ policy altogether. In another case, 1,500 farmers of Avasari Khurd village in the Pune District of Maharashtra have joined hands to use their barren land to form their own SEZ. Contradictory findings in relation to the employment of women, plight of contract labor (owing to exemption from the Contract Labor [Regulation and Abolition] Act, 1970), cost-benefit analysis of SEZs, claims and counter claims of employment generation, land acquisitions, and issues of rehabilitation and resettlement present a rather complex picture of the state of SEZs in India and will play a crucial role in the social and economic formation of India in the 21st century.

YOGESH SNEHI

See also Economy; Globalization; Outsourcing and Offshoring

Further Reading

Aggarwal, Aradhna. "Impact of Special Economic Zones on Employment, Poverty and Human Development." Working Paper No. 194. New Delhi: Indian Council for Research on International Economic Relations, 2007.

Gopalakrishnan, Shankar. "Signs of an Impending Disaster." *Seminar: A Symposium on Special Economic Zones* 582 (2008): 25–31.

Mukherji, Rahul, and Aparna Shivpuri Singh. "Investing in the Indian Special Economic Zones: A Background Paper." Working Paper 12. Institute of South Asian Studies (ISAS), Singapore, 2006. www.isasnus.org/events/workingpapers/12.pdf.

Palit, Amitendu, and Subhomoy Bhattacharjee. *Special Economic Zones in India: Myths and Realities.* New Delhi: Anthem, 2008.

Samaddar, Ranabir. "Primitive Accumulation and Some Aspects of Work and Life in India." *Economic and Political Weekly* 44(18) (2009): 33–42.

Special Economic Zones in India, Ministry of Commerce and Industry, Department of Commerce. Accessed April 28, 2011. http://www.sezindia.nic.in.

Vaidya, Chetan, and Vijay K. Dhar. "Special Economic Zones (SEZs) and Their Implication on Urban Management and Regional Planning in India." Working Paper 1. National Institute of Urban Affairs, New Delhi, 2008. http://www.niua.org/discussion_papers_2008.asp.

✦ SRI LANKA, RELATIONS WITH

Relations with Sri Lanka have been guided largely by India's concerns about its security and Sri Lanka's fears of its powerful neighbor. A shared Tamil ethnic composition with Sri Lanka has been a tricky issue threatening India's internal as well as external security. The geographical proximity and the comparatively uneven size of India and Sri Lanka have served mostly as negative factors. Although Sri Lanka, after independence, began its relations with India with some trepidation, by the mid-1950s the two nations had come to share regional concerns. In the 1970s, Sri Lanka's prime minister Mrs. Sirimavo Bandaranaike struck close ties with Indian prime minister Mrs. Indira Gandhi. However, from 1977, the divisive policies instituted by Sri Lankan president Junius Richard Jayawardene and his successor, Ranasinghe Premadasa, created a severe strain in bilateral relations. While the post–Cold War era brought both countries relatively close, the prolonged ethnic war on the island between the government of Sri Lanka and the Liberation Tigers of Tamil Elam (LTTE), a Tamil militant organization that was defeated militarily only in May 2009, left India in a difficult predicament.

Sri Lanka, an island only 270 miles from north to south and 141 miles east to west, is separated from India by the narrow 22-mile Palk Strait of the Gulf of Mannar. Of its 21 million people, about 18 percent are Tamils, some of whom have lived in the north and east of the island for many centuries, while others were brought from southern India in the late 19th and early 20th centuries by the British to work the coffee and tea plantations in the central highlands. The first bilateral issue of consequence, one that became sticky for some 40 years, was the issue of citizenship for these Tamil plantation workers. At independence, Sri Lanka refused to recognize them as citizens. Over the years more than 500,000 Tamils were repatriated to India, while the rest managed to get citizenship rights by 2003.

A second, more vexatious, issue between India and Sri Lanka has involved Tamils living in the north and east, and also in the south among the Sinhalese. From the time of the

1958 anti-Tamil riots through the major pogrom of 1983, waves of Tamil refugees to India increased dramatically. Disaffected Tamil youth by this time had formed the LTTE and other militant groups, which began receiving weapons and training from India's Research and Intelligence Wing (RAW) to fight the majority Buddhist Sinhala government for security in their Sri Lankan Tamil homelands of the north and east. Although India, especially under Indira Gandhi, supported the cause of Sri Lankan Tamils, neither Gandhi nor her successors promoted the concept of an autonomous independent Tamil state, as this had the potential to undermine India's own constitutional framework. President Jayawardene's knowledge of India's support for Tamil militancy and his deliberate pro-Western tilt in foreign policy, while India was aligned with the Soviet Union in a 15-year Friendship Treaty, did little to contribute to mutual trust.

In May 1987, when the LTTE gained control of the north of the island, Jayawardene imposed an economic blockade on the Jaffna peninsula, causing thousands of its Tamil civilians to starve. Obliging Tamil Nadu's demand to help the Jaffna Tamils, Indian prime minister Rajiv Gandhi airdropped food and supplies on Jaffna. To prevent a further unauthorized intervention, Jayawardene agreed in July 1987 to the Indo-Lanka Accord, a bilateral agreement aimed at disarming the LTTE and other militant groups, sending the Indian Peace Keeping Force (IPKF) to protect Tamils in the north and east, devolving substantial powers to a newly created northeast province, and forbidding Sri Lanka to allow outside powers to use its ports for military or broadcasting facilities. But when the LTTE refused to lay down its arms, the IPKF was forced to fight the LTTE. This turned into a genuine fiasco, as the LTTE began to receive clandestine support from Prime Minister Premadasa. After he was elected president in 1988, Premadasa asked the beleaguered IPKF to leave the island. In May 1991 the LTTE scored revenge by assassinating Rajiv Gandhi. Ironically, two years later, Premadasa met the same fate at LTTE's hands. By this time, the Indian government had not only banned the LTTE from its soil but had also adopted caution in dealing with Sri Lanka.

The next decade witnessed improving bilateral relations, with agreements forged in trade and defense. India pledged its commitment to Sri Lanka's unitary sovereignty and territorial integrity. In late 1999 and early 2000, when the LTTE gained an upper hand militarily in the north and east, President Chandrika Kumaratunga made a plea to the Indian prime minister Atal Bihari Vajpayee for military assistance. Weighing its past debacle, as well as the sentiments of its Tamil populations, India turned down the plea but agreed to assist in the evacuation of trapped army cadres in the north, provided that a cease-fire could be attained between the army and the LTTE. In consultation with India, Norway brokered a cease-fire in 2002 between Kumaratunga and the LTTE. Because of the LTTE's consistent demand for independent statehood, the sporadic talks that followed over the next four years did not bear fruit. As a result, both sides quietly mobilized their militaries. To prevent Sri Lanka from constantly turning to China and Pakistan, India provided military training and assistance and stepped up its naval patrol to curb LTTE smuggling.

After Mahinda Rajapakse won the Sri Lankan presidency in November 2005, in part the result of an LTTE Tamil boycott, violence began to escalate and then turned into a full-scale war. As a result of secession within LTTE forces, the government was able to secure the Eastern Province. The government began its attack on the LTTE in earnest in early 2007. In preparation for this offensive, China provided aid on a large scale, for which it was given access to Sri Lanka's ports and the seabed off the island's northwest coast to explore for oil. Pakistan also played a very significant role in providing arms and expertise. To counter Chinese and Pakistani influence, the Indian government covertly supported Rajapakse's mission but encouraged him overtly to arrange a cease-fire in order to appease its own Tamil populations. As the military pushed north, eventually confining the LTTE and hundreds of thousands of civilians to a small strip of land, people in Tamil Nadu demanded that the Indian government stop the government offensive. While continuing its plea for a cease-fire, India sent humanitarian aid and doctors to attend to wounded and starving Tamil civilians.

Since Rajapakse decided not to allow nongovernment aid workers access to the Wanni region in the north, where thousands of civilians were trapped during the army's last offensive against the LTTE, the United Nations (UN), backed by the European Union, the United States, and India, called for a cease-fire to save civilian lives. Bolstered by support from China and Russia, Rajapakse continued the offensive, disregarding the gravity of attendant civilian casualties. Undeterred, Sri Lanka's military pushed its offensive to the maximum, destroyed the conventional LTTE force along with its leaders, and declared victory in May 2009.

A few days later, the United Nations Human Rights Council (UNHRC) convened a special session to weigh the possibility of a formal probe into Sri Lanka's and the LTTE's war crimes and into Sri Lanka's treatment of war refugees. The United States, France, and Britain also pressured the International Monetary Fund (IMF) to delay implementation of a $1.9 billion loan. India felt that this Western strategy was detrimental to the cause of the approximately 300,000 Tamil refugees in need of immediate rehabilitation. Sensitive to outside interference in its own internal issues, such as the problems in Kashmir and Assam, India joined China, Russia, Pakistan, and other countries in successfully blocking the UNHRC resolution. To counter Chinese influence, big business concerns in India are pushing its Congress Party–led government to play a more assertive role throughout South Asia. Only time will tell how this strategy translates into Indo–Sri Lankan relations.

SREE PADMA

See also South Asian Association for Regional Cooperation

Further Reading
Bush, Kenneth D. *The Intra-Group Dimensions of Ethnic Conflict in Sri Lanka.* New York: Palgrave Macmillan, 2003.

Krishna, Sankaran. *Postcolonial Insecurities: India, Sri Lanka, and the Question of Nationhood.* Minneapolis: University of Minnesota Press, 1999.

The Lanka Academic. Accessed April 28, 2011. http://theacademic.org.

Stedman, Stephen John, Donald S. Rothchild, and Elizabeth M. Cousens. *Ending Civil Wars: The Implementation of Peace Agreements.* Boulder, CO: Lynne Rienner, 2002.

✦ STOCK EXCHANGE MARKETS

Bombay Stock Exchange Limited is the oldest stock exchange in India as well as in Asia. It was established as "The Native Share and Stock Brokers Association" in 1875. The Bombay Stock Exchange, popularly known as the BSE, is the first stock exchange in the country to obtain permanent recognition in 1956 from the government of India under the Securities Contracts (Regulation) Act, 1956. The BSE has played a vital role in the development of the Indian capital market, with a presence in 417 cities and towns. The BSE provides an efficient and transparent platform for trading in equity, debt instruments, and derivatives. The BSE's Online Trading System (BOLT) is a proprietary system of the exchange. It is BS 7799-2-2002 certified, which establishes it as an internationally recognized security framework providing best practices for information, personnel, network, and physical security. The regulatory authority for the Indian stock market is the Securities and Exchange Board of India (SEBI), which is entitled to protect the investors' interests and to regulate and develop the securities market. The main index of the BSE is called the BSE SENSEX (or simply SENSEX). It is composed of 30 financially sound company stocks, which are reviewed and modified from time to time.

Given its large geographic area and the prevalence of the typical floor-based trading system until 1994, a total of 22 stock exchanges were created to cater to the needs of investors in every part of India. Three basic models were adopted: associations of individuals, limited liability companies (without profit sharing), and

A man checks his mobile phone as he walks past the Bombay Stock Exchange, Dalal Street, Mumbai, Maharashtra, February 2006. India's stock exchanges have become increasingly important in global financial markets. (AP Photo/Rajesh Nirgude)

companies limited by guarantees. Regardless of the form of organization, all were recognized by the tax authorities as nonprofit entities, or entities in which their members had no claim to operating surpluses. Although the surpluses generated were not explicitly distributed, exchanges provided various services to their members invariably below cost, with the subsidy element varying from exchange to exchange.

Exchanges enjoyed subsidies in many forms. The respective state governments allotted land for constructing the buildings for exchange operations and brokers' offices on nominal terms. Until recently, the government of India had adopted the concept of regional stock exchanges (RSEs), defining the operating area of each exchange. A public company was required to list its stock on the RSE nearest its registered office.

A listed company had to pay listing fees, both initial and annual, and such fees were linked to the size of its issued capital. For most RSEs, listing fees were the main source of income. Each exchange enjoyed monopoly rights in securities trading in the city of its location. Investors had no mechanism to protect themselves from collusive behavior by the stock brokers. This monopoly also led to the creation of fragmented markets that were shallow, inefficient, and cost ineffective. Brokers generally dealt with investors through a multilayered chain of intermediaries, increasing the cost of transaction.

Since exchanges prohibited corporate membership, all brokerage entities were either proprietary or partnership concerns. Although the liability of a brokerage firm was unlimited, this did not mean much to investors, as almost all the brokerage firms were poorly capitalized. Brokerage firms distributed most of the profits at the end of each accounting year, transferring them to their family members. Thus, in the event of a firm's insolvency, investors were the main losers.

The capital market reforms process was launched in 1992 in response to the infamous Harshad Mehta Scam, which shook the banking system and the capital markets. Some prominent stockbrokers fraudulently diverted huge sums of money from banks (government-owned and private banks, as well as prominent foreign banks) and manipulated 270 million shares, causing the BSE to shed 570 points in a day. The diversion of bank funds to personal accounts artificially inflated the prices of their favorite stocks. This brought into the forefront severe deficiencies in the existing trading and settlement system. The apparent boom in equity markets caused by such fraudulent practices attracted thousands of gullible investors who hoped to make quick gains. The bubble burst after some investigative journalists exposed the scam. When the banks demanded funds back from the brokers, it triggered a market collapse. The banks lost an estimated $2 billion, and the crisis was a major embarrassment for the Indian government, which had just launched a series of reforms in the securities markets.

The government promptly imposed reform measures in the securities markets, the highlight of which was the birth of the National Stock Exchange (NSE). The new exchange operated in accord with globally accepted best practices, both in trading and settlement systems. The NSE is India's largest securities exchange in terms of daily trade numbers. It offers automated electronic trading of a variety of securities, including equity, corporate debt, central- and state-government securities, commercial paper, CDs, and exchange traded funds. The exchange has more than 1,000 listed members and is owned by more than 20 different financial and insurance institutions. The NSE specializes in three market segments: wholesale debt, capital market (automated screen-based trading system), and derivatives, including futures and options that form the largest segment of the exchange. Within six years of its inception, the NSE's impact on the Indian capital markets was so overwhelming that the rest of the exchanges, except for the BSE, became virtually defunct. As a survival strategy, 10 regional exchanges set up subsidiary companies that became members of NSE and BSE. The systems and procedures introduced by the NSE have been accepted by the SEBI and were made applicable to the other exchanges. The new trading system has encouraged price competition resulting in lower bid-ask spreads. As a result, transaction costs are estimated to have declined by a factor of 8 to 10 after the NSE came to dominate the Indian market.

PARAMITA GUPTA

See also Economy; Financial Institutions, Development; Money and Foreign Exchange Markets; World Trade Organization, Relations with

Figure 4   India market value of publicly traded shares

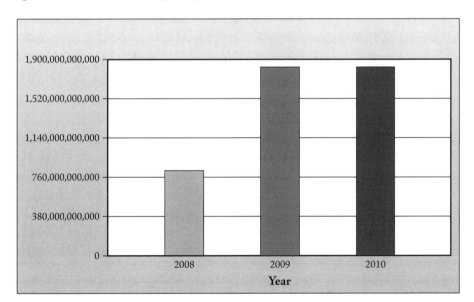

Year	Market Value of Publicly Traded Shares	Rank	Percent Change	Date of Information
2008	818,900,000,000	16		2006
2009	1,819,000,000,000	8	122.13%	December 31, 2007
2010	1,819,000,000,000	8	0.00%	December 31, 2007

Source: "India Market Value of Publicly Traded Shares," Indexmundi, http://www.indexmundi .com/india/market_value_of_publicly_traded_shares.html.

Further Reading

Berg, William, "The Indian Stock Market." December 27, 2005. http://EzineArticles.com
    /?expert=William_Berg.

Bombay Stock Exchange. "Bombay Stock Exchange Limited: The Edge is Efficiency." Accessed April 28,
    2011. http://bseindia.com.

"The Evolution of Indian Stock Market." Accessed March 5, 2010. http://www.articlesbase.com
    /investing-articles/the-evolution-of-indian-stock-market-1942167.html.

✦ SUBRAMANIAM, LAKSHMINARAYANA

Lakshminarayana Subramaniam (b. 1947) is one of India's leading south Indian violinists, a composer and conductor, and an outstandingly versatile musician. His opus fuses
several Indian and Western musical styles without compromise. Famous for his virtuosic performances in the Karnatic tradition and his convincing performances of Hindustani music,
Subramaniam, often known simply as "Mani," has also distinguished himself as a violinist,
composer, and conductor in the Western classical tradition, and as a jazz performer.

Subramaniam has never abandoned his deep roots in Indian music. In his long career, he
has performed and recorded extensively as both a soloist and accompanist for many of the
stars in both the Karnatic and Hindustani musical systems. He has played with such highly
regarded south Indian vocalists as Chembai Vaidyanatha Bhagavatar, K. V. Narayanaswamy,
S. Srinivasa Iyer, M. Balamuralikrishna, and M. D. Ramanathan, as well as the percussionist
Palghat Mani Iyer. His knowledge of the Hindustani system of north India is such that he has
performed and recorded with musicians of the caliber of Ali Akbar Khan, Rais Khan, V. G.
Jog, and Jasraj and Zakir Hussain.

His prodigious discography of more than 200 recordings and numerous concerts around
the world include collaborations with, inter alia, such violin virtuosos such as Yehudi Menuhin, Ruggiero Ricci, Jean-Luc Ponty, and Stéphane Grappelli (their recording together is
called *Conversations*). During his forays into jazz, he has performed with such jazz legends
as Herbie Hancock, Joe Sample, Stanley Clarke, Maynard Ferguson, Ravi Coltrane, Al Jar-
reau, and Larry Coryell. His film scores include three films by Mira Nair—*Salaam Bombay*
(1988), *Mississippi Masala* (1991), and *Kama Sutra: A Tale of Love* (1996), and he provided
contributing music for Bernardo Bertolucci's *Little Buddha* (1993). Subramaniam's orchestral
compositions have been performed by some of the world's leading orchestras, including the
New York Philharmonic Orchestra with Zubin Mehta (*Fantasy on Vedic Chants*), the Swiss
Romande Orchestra (*Turbulence*), the Kirov Ballet (*Shanti Priya*), the Oslo Philharmonic
Orchestra (*Concerto for Two Violins*), and the Berlin Opera (*Global Symphony*), the live concert of which was broadcast simultaneously to 28 nations to celebrate the 50th anniversary of
the United Nations (UN) in 1995.

Trained by his father, V. Lakshminarayana Iyer, Subramaniam began his career at age six,
playing with two of his brothers, L. Shankar and L. Vaidyanathan. When the trio broke up

all of them launched solo careers. A medical degree from Madras Medical College entitles Subramaniam to the honorific "Dr." in his name. He subsequently finished a master's degree in music from the California Institute of the Arts. Among his honors, Subramaniam was awarded both the Padma Shri (1988) and Padma Bhushan (2001) awards from the government of India.

Subramaniam is currently married to Kavita Krishnamurthi, a vocalist. Formerly, he was married to the late Vijayashree (Viji) Subramaniam, who was also a vocalist. He is the father of violinists Seetaa Subramaniam and Ambi Subramaniam, with whom he performs.

J. ANDREW GREIG

See also Khan, Ali Akbar; Khan, Vilayat; Music, Devotional; Shankar, Ravi

Further Reading
Floyd, Leela. *Indian Music.* London: Oxford University Press, 1980.

✦ SURAT

The city of Surat in the state of Gujarat is widely known for diamond polishing and synthetic textiles and is one of the most prominent and rapidly growing cities in India. According to the 2001 Census of India, Surat is the nation's 10th-largest city. It is a city with a glorious past that once dominated both the indigenous and the Indian Ocean trading networks. Geographically located midway between Mumbai and Ahmedabad, the rise and fall of Surat has also been closely linked with these two cities. In 1994 Surat was revisited by a deadly plague, which the city responded to with a clean-up campaign. It has since been declared the second-cleanest city in the country, after Chandigarh, by INTACH (Indian National Trust for Arts and Culture, Bangalore).

The city is popularly believed to have been founded by Malik Gopi or Gopinath, a Brahmin trader-administrator in the early decades of the 16th century. Early Portuguese writers like Duarte Barbosa (d. 1521) mention the port of Surat, but in this period it was clearly overshadowed by its twin, Rander, located on the opposite bank of the Tapi River. Rander was also known by its community of Navayat Muslims, or Malik Momins, who were Shi'as and traced the origin of their group to followers of the Abbasid caliphs living at Kufa around 750 CE. These were famous in the western part of the Indian Ocean as pilots and navigators. Rander ultimately declined, which paved the way for the rise of Surat. By 1540 it emerged as a major center of transshipment and as a staging point between Sumatra and merchants from both Southeast and West Asia.

Surat, during the Mughal period (1526–1858), turned into the emporium of India, exporting cloth and gold. Its major industries were textiles and shipbuilding. The city was famous for *kinkhab* cloth and the weaving of coarse saris, silk cloth, and *kinkhab dupattas* (a long scarf), and production of these items was a major industry. In 1795 there were 15,777 looms, one-third of them operated by Muslims and the rest by Khatris and Kanbis (now known as Patidars). Large ships and boats were also built there, and in 1650 extensive repairs to the English ship *Falcon* (500 tons) were carried out. The shipbuilding yard at Surat was maintained until 1785. Surat's prosperity grew under the Mughals throughout the 17th century. It was also an important pilgrimage center for Indian Muslims as the port of embarkation for the *hajj* (pilgrimage to Mecca). For this reason, Surat was also known as "Babul Macca," the Gateway to Mecca. The city had various *caravansarais* (inns), as well as mosques to cater to both the trading communities and the pilgrims.

For almost 150 years, Surat was truly a multicultural and cosmopolitan city. The first Europeans to confront Surat were Portuguese. After Vasco da Gama (ca. 1460–1524) voyaged around the Cape of Good Hope to Calicut on May 20, 1498, the Portuguese with their naval might rapidly occupied strategic locations in the Indian Ocean. By 1559 they entrenched themselves in Daman, south of Surat. They started controlling the Indian Ocean by sweeping the Arabs from the Arabian sea lanes and imposing their own passport system (*cartez*) on Indian shippers for safe conduct. The arrival of the Dutch and the English, however, spelled the end of Portuguese domination throughout Asia. The Portuguese were routed in 1612 by the English, and in 1640 the Dutch wrested Malacca (in Malaysia) from their control. From 1612 the English had a continuous station in Surat; the Dutch had arrived earlier, in 1602, and founded the United Dutch East India Company. By 1615 the Dutch also had a regular establishment in Surat. The French made an appearance in the city as well, especially French Capuchin missionaries. By the first half of the 18th century, however, Surat began declining with the emergence of the English as the sole power in Indian Ocean trade. This also coincided with the declining authority of the Mughal Empire after the death of Mughal emperor Aurangzeb in 1707 and the concentration of commercial activities in Bombay (Mumbai), which had been acquired by the English.

The reemergence of Surat began in the early 20th century. Surat's prosperity was primarily based on *jari* embroidery (the application of gold and silver thread over fine textiles); handloom weaving, which was later upgraded to power-loom weaving; and diamond polishing. However, unlike the traditional sectors elsewhere in India, the early years of the 20th century in Surat witnessed a revival of traditional industry. In 1909 a survey estimated that there were around 500 dealers and 8,000–10,000 workers in the *jari* industry. Surat's industry continued after independence, and a major expansion occurred in the 1980s when the export market grew rapidly. The industry may be divided into three major segments: *akharedars* (self-employed artisans), traders/manufacturers, and workers or wage earners. The *akharedars* mainly use family labor, and they earn commission based on the volume of work. Traders/manufacturers primarily work as family units and either own small units in which they manufacture goods or outsource work on a contract basis. A large number of workers who do not have choice and control over either the market or the manufacturing process make up the third group. This workforce mainly consists of women. Initially Muslims controlled this industry, but since 1930 it has been almost exclusively controlled by the Rana caste or the Gola caste of Hindus.

Surat is now one of the largest centers in the world for the production of nylon and polyester synthetic fabrics. From the 1950s onward the central as well as the state governments extended a number of fiscal incentives for the growth of small industries. On the recommendation of the Textile Inquiry Committee (1954), a program to encourage the conversion of the ordinary looms into improved (semi-automatic) looms or into decentralized power looms was introduced. In terms of certain excise regimes, concessions were granted on power-loom cloth, promoting it over mill-made textiles.

In the early 1980s, a prolonged textile strike in Mumbai provided further impetus to the power-loom industry in Surat. As production of textile cloth declined in Mumbai, entrepreneurs began to invest in power looms in Surat. The families that were traditionally engaged in weaving, mainly of the Khatri, Kanbi, and Vania upper and middle castes, played a leading role in the textile boom. Over the years, in addition to using power looms, these families diversified into processing art-silk fabrics, filament sizing, twisting and texturing, manufacturing textile machinery, and wrap knitting. Apart from Khatris and Kanbis, who constitute the largest group in the power-loom sector, Vanias (both Jains and Hindus) and Patidars also have major shares in the industry. Other groups with considerable share in power looms are the Muslim Memons and Khojas. These two groups own around 12 to 15 percent of the power looms. Over the years, migrants from the Punjab and Rajasthan who worked as traders and commission agents in the 1960s have also started investing their capital, generated through usury and commodity exchange, in looms and other processes of clothmaking. With the growth of power looms the processing industry also developed.

A large percentage of the looms function as small or family units. These are run by self-employed local weavers who also maintain direct links with large industries for the continuous supply of yarns and other materials. Alongside these genuine entrepreneurs there also exist units that are designed to circumvent the rules of the Factory Act. In such cases, the ownership of looms is divided among the names of existing or imaginary family members, though in all other respects looms are operated and managed by one family under one roof. This fragmentation system is locally known as *bhagala*. Power looms are installed in what are known as *sheds*, which generally house 8, 12, 16, or 20 looms. There are around 25,000 manufacturers or power-loom owners in and around Surat. Smaller units have 12 looms, and the average-size manufacturing unit has 20 looms.

In comparison to textiles, diamond polishing is a recent industry. Local lore informs that a Surat entrepreneur, returning with a boat laden with diamond cutters from East Africa, started the city's polishing industry in 1901. The systematic rise of the diamond-polishing industry also goes back to the 1950s. The rise was a direct outcome of the rapidly growing demand for small diamonds in the industrial market. The growth in demand for diamonds,

Employees examine and evaluate diamonds on the floor of Sanghvi Exports in Surat, Gujarat, February 2005. Surat has historically been an important port for imports and exports. (Santosh Verma/Bloomberg via Getty Images)

coupled with the scarcity of labor in foreign manufacturing centers, provided the most powerful incentive to the development of the industry.

The municipal government in Surat is as old as Bombay and Ahmedabad municipalities and was established in 1852 under a Government of India Act in 1850. The city was later governed under the Bombay Provincial Municipal Corporation Act of 1949, and in 1964, with the rise of the population, the Surat municipality became Surat Municipal Corporation (SMC). The SMC has three wings: the general body, the standing committee, and the municipal commissioner. The general body consists of elected representatives, and it elects the mayor and deputy mayor. The members of the standing committee are elected by the general body from among its members. It is headed by the chairman, who is appointed by the state government and is the executive head of the SMC.

In the second half of the 1950s the De Beers company started an aggressive advertising campaign to persuade every American male to buy diamonds for his sweetheart. This campaign, which was later extended to Europe, proved immensely successful—in fact it is one of the most successful advertising campaigns ever launched. The demand for small, good-quality diamonds skyrocketed. European diamond workshops could not keep up with demand, and European labor was too expensive to get a good profit from the sale of small diamonds.

A turning point came in 1954, when the Import Replenishment Scheme was introduced. Under this scheme diamond traders could import rough diamonds from the

Diamond Trading Company in London and from other sources abroad. Against the exports of cut and polished diamonds to foreign countries, a certain import replenishment entitlement was given under this scheme. This act is regarded as the origin of the "diamond miracle," which was to transform the diamond-cutting sector in India, and Surat in particular, in the coming decades. The act came as a boon when a huge stock of jewelry was unloaded on the Indian market by princes, such as the Nizam of Hyderabad and the maharajas of Darbhanga, Baroda, and Jamnagar. It was against the export of this jewelry that rough diamonds were allowed to be imported. Other reasons for the revival of the Indian diamond industry were a recession in Western Europe and the United States, and the closing of the Suez Canal between 1956 and early 1957.

During the 1960s and early 1970s the international diamond market started booming. The market in the West for small, low-quality diamonds skyrocketed. To promote exports, the government set up the Gems and Jewelry Export Promotion Council in 1966.

The main entrepreneurs of the diamond industry were initially Jain Vanias of north Gujarat. Later Patidars from Saurashtra entered the industry. Since only a small investment is required to buy a lathe machine, or *ghanti*, the scope for upward mobility is quite high. With the growth of the diamond-polishing industry in the 1960s and the early 1970s, Saurastrian Kanbi Patels, who were already in Surat, started inviting families and caste and village relations from Saurastra to come to the city to work in the diamond industry. They came in large numbers—especially after three years of drought and famine in Saurastra from 1972 to 1974. Initially the Patel migrants worked as diamond cutters while the owners were local Surat businessmen and Palanpur Banias. The latter also had a firm control over the local diamond trade. However, in the course of the 1970s, many early Saurastrian pioneers were able to start their own diamond workshops and factories. They rapidly turned into wealthy factory owners and diamond traders. A good part of the industry is still run along caste and kinship lines, and the entire sector is highly unorganized. However, attempts have been made to regulate it.

The Surat diamond industry has a share of 42 percent of the world's total rough diamond cutting and polishing businesses. The industry underwent a severe crisis in 2008 as demand slowed in the wake of the worldwide economic recession. The recession exposed various drawbacks in the system, as workers are paid on the basis of the number of diamonds cut and polished, and units faced an acute shortage of manpower as retrenched workers were skeptical about coming back due to the small amount of money paid them. This forced the units to offer incentives to the workers. With a revival in demand from Western consumers, a section of the industry began its shift to solitaires. The focus on the high-value segment has also increased awareness of the need for skilled workers.

The industry still faces an acute labor shortage, particularly a shortage of skilled labor. In small and cramped units, the working conditions, health issues, and safety standards are invariably found to be extremely poor. The working area is often reported to be cramped, inadequately lit, lacking proper ventilation, unsafe, and unclean.

Though the wages of power-loom and diamond workers have increased in the last two decades, they do not correspond to the rise in prices, and they have not enjoyed any substantial improvement in their standard of living. Labor laws are constantly flouted, and the threat of workers losing their jobs looms large. In addition, only a tiny percentage of workers receive work throughout the month.

In recent decades a good number of large-scale industries have also come up in Surat, in and around Hazira and Kawas. Some of the major industries include KRIBHCO, Reliance, Oil and Natural Gas Corporation Limited, and ESSAR. Because of this industrial growth, the price of land and the costs of construction, transport, and essential services have all risen. These years have also witnessed a tremendous expansion of the city boundary, and a clear contrast can be observed in urban morphology between the old, or the heart of the city, and newly developed localities that encircle the traditional hub. It has also significantly changed the social composition of the city.

The social fabric of the city comprises communities and subcastes like Parsis, Muslims, Jains, Christians, and Hindus, which are further divided into castes and subcastes (*jnatis*) like the Daudi Bohras and Kanbis (artisans), Khatris (weavers), Golas (rice pounders), Ghanchis (oil pressers), and Suthars (carpenters), to name a few. Along with this cluster, there are communities with a relatively recent arrival in the city, including Marathi-speaking migrants from neighboring regions of Maharastra and a migrant working class from Orissa, Andhra Pradesh, Bihar, and Uttar Pradesh. There is also a sizable and visible presence of migrants (known as *hiraghasus*, or diamond cutters) from the Saurashtra region dominating the diamond and textile sectors, and Marwari traders from neighboring Rajasthan.

By one estimate 30 percent of the total population consists of Surtis who have stayed in the city for more than four generations. Brahmans include Anavil, Nagar, Audichya, and other subcastes. Vania and Jains, who are traditionally in trade and business, lived for generations in localities like Vadifalia, Sonifalia, Gopipura, Nanavat, Chowk, and Haripura. Now these groups have dispersed to the outskirts of recently developed areas of Athwa Lines and Piplod in exclusive localities. Khatris dominate the weaving industry. Scheduled castes of Bhangis and Meghwals are still employed in the work of cleaning. Vankars earlier formed a large section of textile workers. However, with the decline of textile production in recent years, they have moved into different sectors of the economy.

Like Hindu society, Muslim society is also not a monolithic community and is divided along kin-based affiliations. The community is divided mainly into local Muslims, immigrant Muslims, or Sunni Muslims, who claim their genealogy in West Asia (Saiyed, Shaikh, Moghul, and Pathan), and those who are converted from indigenous Hindu groups. While the community of Nawabs establishes its direct linkages with the Mughal nobility, Saiyeds and Shaikhs consider themselves to be at the top of the social hierarchy.

The Parsi population in Surat is estimated to be only around 3,500, yet they have a substantial presence in the cultural and philanthropic activities of the city.

Besides people from Gujarat, Surat has also attracted migration from Orissa, Andhra Pradesh, Bihar, Rajasthan, and Maharashtra. Maharastra, because of its proximity, has traditionally provided a good number of migrants. Surat has been the favorite destination for people from the Khandesh belt of Maharashtra (districts of Dhule, Jalgaon, and Nashik). Along with them, people from the districts of Nagpur, Buldana, Bhandara, and Raigadh have historically migrated to Surat. Migrants from these neighborhood regions of Maharashtra have been settled in Surat for more than two to three generations; their marriages take place in Surat itself, and their second and third generations have been born and brought up in the city. This is not the case with migrants from other parts of nation, who continue to maintain strong social and cultural ties with their native regions. A majority of migrant working-class people from Orissa, Andhra Pradesh, Bihar, and Uttar Pradesh normally come to the city as individuals without their families. Nearly the entire population of migrant workers lives in nearly 300 slums and informal settlements, located within as well as outside the city. Migration from Rajasthan is a relatively recent phenomenon and goes back to the early 1990s. A large number of Rajasthani migrants are in the textile and auxiliary sectors and have also entered into diamond polishing, petty sales, and trading.

A special feature of Surat's social fabric is the proximity and economic interdependence of different social groups. This mutual dependence has contributed significantly to the maintenance of communal harmony in the city; yet, the history of the city is not free from communal outbreaks. In 1969, when Ahmedabad and the rest of Gujarat experienced horrifying riots, communal relations remained on an even keel. Apart from a few skirmishes, Surat remained calm in the 1970s and for a major part of the 1980s. In 1990 rioting took place in a number of localities when Lal Krishna Advani (b. 1927), one of the prominent political leaders of the Bharatiya Janata Party (BJP), founded in 1980, was arrested for his campaign to construct a temple dedicated to the Hindu god, Rama, at the site of the old Babri Mosque in Ayodhya, Uttar Pradesh. The communal tension continued, and clashes were reported from predominantly Muslim localities in 1991 and 1992. Following the demolition of Babri Mosque on December 6, 1992, large-scale communal riots engulfed the entire city, claiming more than 200 lives and damage to the tune of more than a million rupees in less than one month of communal strife.

In August 1994 Surat received another shock with the outbreak of plague, which was reported to be the deadly pneumonic plague. In panic, some 300,000 people fled the city in a matter of 48 hours. There were around 1,000 suspected cases, in which 103 were diagnosed as plague patients; around 80 people died within 15 days between September 18 and October 7. Along with this, nearly 4,000 suspected plague patients, including those who fled from the city, were found in several other parts of the country. This took place almost a century after the previous outbreak.

Since the communal violence of 1992 and the plague of 1994, the city has expanded tremendously both in terms of its physical boundaries as well as in terms of the diversification of capital inflow and social fluidity. New areas like Hazira (an industrial locality) and Pandesara (a working-class locality) are no longer outside the city limits. Similarly, new middle-class localities like Adajan, Piplod, and City Lights came into prominence as residential areas for those in the upwardly mobile service industry as well as for the nouveau riche. These localities also redefine new social orders as they do not house people on the basis of the old traditional social categories of caste and subcaste.

SADAN JHA

See also Gujarat

Further Reading

Das, Gupta, Ashin. *Indian Merchants and the Decline of Surat, c.1700–1750*. Wiesbaden: Franz Steiner, 1979.

Desai, Kiran, and Aparajita De. *Hindu Muslim Relations in Gujarat: Caste Studies of Surat and Vadodara*. Surat: Centre for Social Studies, 2003.

Engelshoven, Miranda. "Rural to Urban Migration and the Significance of Caste: The Case of the Saurashtra Patels of Surat." In *Development and Deprivation in Gujarat: In Honour of Jan Breman*, edited by Ghanshyam Shah, Mario Rutten, and Hein Streefkark, 294–313. Delhi: Sage, 2002.

Gokhale, Balkrishna Govind. *Surat in the Seventeenth Century: A Study in Urban History of Pre-Modern India*. London: Curzon, 1979.

Haynes, Douglas. *Rhetoric and Ritual in Colonial India: The Shaping of a Public Culture in Surat City, 1852–1928*. Berkeley: University of California Press, 1991.

Sahu, Gagan Bihari, and Das Biswaroop. *Income Remittances and Urban Labour Markets: Oriya Migrant Workers in Surat City*. Bhubaneswar: Adhikar, 2008.

Shah, Ghanshyam. *Public Health and Urban Development: The Plague in Surat*. New Delhi: Sage, 1997.

Subrahmanyam, Sanjay. "A Note in the Rise of Surat in the First Half of Sixteenth Century." *Journal of the Economic and Social History of the Orient* 43(1) (2000): 23–33.

Surat Municipal Corporation. Accessed April 28, 2011. http://www.suratmunicipal.org/.

✦ SURYA, VASANTHA

Vasantha Surya (b. 1942) is a gifted poet, translator, journalist, and writer in both Tamil and English. Born in New Delhi during the freedom movement, Surya had a patriotic, yet cosmopolitan upbringing. She completed high school in Washington, D.C., where her father was a diplomat at the Indian embassy. After returning to India, she received her B.A. in history from Bombay University. Surya inherited her poetic talent and social consciousness from both her mother and her father. Her fascination for English and American literature was balanced by lessons in Tamil inculcated by her mother. This rich background led Surya to explore the possibilities of other national literatures and to begin writing herself. Her first piece of writing was a descriptive essay in English on Kerala, for which she won the prestigious National Gold Key award for students. Her return to India expanded her knowledge of Indian history, so that she became a keen observer of India's fledgling democracy and its challenges. Turning to journalism, the theme of social justice became central to her articles for *The Hindu*, *The Indian Express*, and *Frontline*. Surya also began composing poetry, which reflected local concerns, in the idiom of Indian-English. After a few years' residence in Germany, she became proficient in German and cultivated an interest in that nation's poetry. She later translated the poetry of Rainer Maria Rilke (1875–1926) into both Tamil and English. She describes translation as her "passion," but she prefers to use the term "transcreation," as she believes the best translations convey the nuances of the original text into the Indian-English idiom. She refers to Indian languages as the "many chambered" mansions of contemporary consciousness.

Surya's two poetry volumes were well received, especially by the acclaimed veteran poets A. K. Ramanujan (1929–1993) and Keki Daruwala (b. 1937). *The Stalk of Time* (1985), in fact, was short-listed for the Commonwealth Poetry Prize. *A Word Between Us* (2003) is a fierce, trenchant, yet exuberant collection of poems on such contemporary themes as religious fanaticism ("Trident"); exploitation ("Servant"); and women ("Pativrata"). She has also translated *The Ballad of Budhni* into English. This was based on a Bundeli Hindi poem about police atrocities in a Madhya Pradesh village. Her translations of 20th-century Tamil fiction portray women as both victims and agents. Such novels include *Yamini* (1996), which was about a young girl; *Contemporary Tamil Short Fiction* (2000); *A Place to Live* (2005), edited by Dilip Kumar; "Muthumeenakshi," about a child widow in 1912, in *A. Madhaviah: A Biography and a Novella* (2004); *Birthright* (*Kadaisee Varai* in Tamil; 2005), on female feticide; and *The Defiant Jungle*, by Sa. Kandasamy (2009), on the destruction of a virgin forest by developers. Among her English works are sections of *Whose News?*, edited by Ammu Joseph and Kalpana Sharma (1993). She has recently emerged as a writer and illustrator of children's fiction in English and Tamil. She evocatively recreates the imaginary world of children in *Mridu in Madras*, which she has translated into Tamil. Episodes of *Thithilee Tales* have been serialized for *The Hindu*, and she has published a children's *Ramayana* in *Chatterbox*. She combines her writing with activism. She and her husband conduct classes for disadvantaged children, teach English classes for nurses at a Chennai hospital, and organize free health care in villages.

SITA ANANTHA RAMAN

See also Literature

Further Reading

Raman, Sita Anantha. *Women in India: A Social and Cultural History.* 2 vols. Santa Barbara, CA: ABC-CLIO, 2009.

Vasantha, Surya. *Mridu in Madras*. New Delhi: Rupa, 2007.

Vasantha, Surya. *The Stalk of Time*. Chennai: CRE-A, 1985.

Vasantha, Surya. *A Word between Us*. Chennai: Sandhya, 2003.

Vasantha, Surya, trans. *Contemporary Tamil Short Fiction*. Edited by Dilip Kumar. Chennai: East-West Publishers, 2000. Reprinted as *A Place to Live* (Mumbai: Penguin, 2005).

Vasantha, Surya, trans. *The Defiant Jungle (Saayavanam in Tamil)*, by Sa. Kandasamy. Chennai: New Horizon Media, 2009.

Vasantha, Surya, trans. *Yamini*, by Chudamani Raghavan, Chennai: Macmillan, 1996.

T

✦ TAMIL NADU

Tamil Nadu, the "country of the Tamils," encompasses over 50,000 square miles on the southeast coast of India. The town of Kanyakumari, where the Indian Ocean meets the Bay of Bengal and the Arabian Sea, is at its most southern point. With a population of nearly 70 million people, Tamil Nadu is the seventh most populous state in India; it also has the highest percentage of people, some 45 percent, living in urban areas. Known as Madras until 1969, it is the heartland for the diasporic Tamil community now found in many parts of the world, most notably Malaysia and Singapore, where Tamil is an official language. Tamil is the official language of Tamil Nadu, but English is widely understood as the city of Chennai produces some half-dozen English-language daily and evening newspapers; small percentages of people speak Telegu, Kannada, and Malayalam—like Tamil, Dravidian languages—and Urdu, the language of Muslims. A dry and hot state with temperatures ranging between 55°F and 109°F, it depends on the two monsoon seasons of the southwest monsoon (June–September) and the northeast monsoon (October–December) for its water. It is divided into 32 districts with Chennai, the capital, being the fourth-largest city in India. The governor heads the state but the administration is led by the chief minister and his cabinet. The unicameral Legislative Assembly seats 235 members. It sends 39 members to the Lok Sabha, the lower house of Parliament in New Delhi. The main political parties in the state are the Dravida Munnetra Kazhagam, the All India Anna Dravid Munnetra Kazhagam, the Congress Party, and the smaller Pattali Makkal Katchi.

Archaeological sites dated to nearly 2000 BCE, where the script Tamil Brahmi was used, attest to the long period of habitation in Tamil Nadu. In 72 CE the apostle Saint Thomas is believed to have been buried in Chennai after a 20-year mission in southern India. His remains were removed to Italy in the 3rd century although his original tomb, one of only three shrines built over the remains of one of Christ's apostles (the other two are Saint Peter's in Rome and Santiago de Compostela in Spain for Saint James), is located in the Basilica of the National Shrine of Saint Thomas in Chennai. The state encompassed such early dynasties as the Pandhyas (6th–10th centuries), with its capital at Madurai, and the Pallavas (ca. 600–ca. 912) before the Cholas, noted in inscriptions as early as the third century BCE, established a powerful dynasty between the 9th and 13th centuries. The Cholas not only dominated all of southern and eastern India as far as Bengal and Sri Lanka but they also spread Indic culture throughout Southeast Asia as they developed trading ties with Srivijaya in modern Indonesia to protect trade with China. More important, Madurai hosted its academy, or *sangam*, from about the 2nd century, and it produced over 2,000 *sangam* poems written by over 500 poets, many of them women. These were collected in nine anthologies and along with the *Tolkappiyam* are not only a grammar of the Tamil language but also a guide to early Tamil life. The *Silappadikaram* (*The Ankle Bracelet*), a 3rd-century romance and the most celebrated piece of writing from the Sangam period, is, likewise, a great treatise on Tamil civilization. These make up the great works of *sangam* literature and are at the heart of classical Tamil learning. By the middle of the 14th century the whole of southern India was ruled by the Vijayanagara Kingdom until the city of Vijyanagar was sacked in 1565 by Muslims. The British arrived as traders at Madras in 1639 and over the next century and a half became the paramount power in India with Madras being one of the three presidencies of British India.

Due to this rich history Tamil Nadu has numerous historical sites and the city of Chennai is the center of a vibrant cultural life based around Tamil culture and language. The Meenakshi or Sundareshvara Temple dedicated to the Hindu god Shiva and located in the city of Madurai is one of the most remarkable Hindu temple complexes in India. Mahabalipuram, the city of the "Seven Pagodas," located 37 miles south of Chennai and a UNESCO World Heritage Site, is a port city founded in the 7th century by a Pallava king, and it is now a craft center and, like Madurai, a popular tourist site. Tanjavur, the capital of the Cholas, is renowned for its Temple of Brahadisvara, the "Temple of the Big God" and it became the heart of Tamil culture renowned even today for its bronze figurines, handicrafts, metallic inlay plates, and musical instrument, the *veenai*. It was also the birthplace of three 19th-century musicians who established the Karnatak music tradition and the home of the Tanjavur quartet who systematized the Bharatanatyam dance tradition of southern India. Tiruchirappalli, also known as Trichy, is located 200 miles south of Chennai in the center of the state and contains the Rock Fort, which hovers over the city, and Thiruvanaikava Temple. Udagamamandalam, or Ootacamund (Ooty), is one of Tamil Nadu's renowned hill stations located in the Nilgiri hills, or the Blue Mountains, made famous by the British who tried to re-create the landscape and architecture of England in the green and pleasant land 7,500 feet high in the hills.

A lake in the courtyard of the Meenakshi temple in Madurai, Tamil Nadu. Dedicated to the Hindu god Shiva, it is one of the largest temple complexes in India. Although mentioned in ancient Tamil texts, the current buildings are dated to 1600. (Sergey Kushnir/Dreamstime.com)

Chennai, situated on a flat coastal plain and fronted by the magnificent Marina Beach, over seven miles long, is the heart of modern Tamil culture and life. The extended metropolitan area has a population approaching 10 million. It is a thriving industrial area with both a traditional automobile industry and also high tech businesses. It is India's second-largest exporter for the IT service industry, hosting such multinational corporations as Dell, Motorola, Samsung, and Sony, and such Internet-based services as Amazon, eBay, and PayPal. Two rivers, the Koovam and the Adyar, wend their lazy way through the city and they are linked by the 2.5-mile Buckingham Canal. The port of Mylapore was built by the Pallavas and the Portuguese port of São Tome was established after their arrival in 1522. The modern city was built around the British Fort Saint George, which they founded in 1640, and it has been expanding ever since. Chennai has an international airport and it is a major railroad terminus. It is an educational center boasting numerous institutes of higher education with a fine reputation: they include the Indian Institute of Technology; the University of Madras, one of the oldest universities in India, having been established in 1857; the Ramakrishna Vivekanada College; and the Madras Christian College. Cricket is the most popular sport in the city and the M. A. Chidambaram Stadium hosted games for the 2011 Cricket World Cup. The Chennai Super Kings play in the Indian Premier League. In addition to Chennai's rich cultural, social, and intellectual life, the Tamil film industry is located in the district of Kadambakkam and plays a special role in Tamil society. Tamil cinema produces the second-largest number of films in the world after

Bollywood in Mumbai and they are not only shown in India but are exported around the world as well. In a remarkable development, a number of people in the Tamil movie industry have gone on to careers in politics, even leading the state as chief ministers. Above all, however, Chennai is renowned for its six-week-long music festival in December–January. It is a showcase of Karnatak music and dance. Over 1,000 *kutcheris* ("concerts") held either in small halls that hold less than 100 people or large auditoriums that hold 300 people are performed by some 600 singers, dancers, actors, and musicians. The rich intellectual, cultural, and business life of Chennai help make Tamil Nadu one of the most vibrant states in the union and one of several areas of India that have a special cultural identity.

ROGER D. LONG

See also Diaspora, Indian; Dravidian Movement; Dravidian Munnetra Kazhagam Parties; Languages and Scripts; Newspapers, Indian-Language; Sri Lanka, Relations with; Surya, Vasantha.

Further Reading

Government of Tamil Nadu. *Tamil Nadu, Human Development Report.* New Delhi: Social Science Press, 2003.

Leonard, A. G. *Tamil Nadu Economy.* New Delhi: Macmillan, 2006.

Kannammal, S. Geetha. *An Introduction to Tourism in Tamil Nadu.* Chennai: University of Madras, 2007.

Palanithurai, G. *A Handbook for Panchayati Raj Administration.* New Delhi: Concept Publishing, 2007.

Planning Commission, India. *Tamil Nadu Development Report.* New Delhi: Academic Foundation, 2005.

Rajayyan, K. *Tamil Nadu: A Real History.* Madurai: Ratna Publications, 2005.

Ramasamy, A., ed. *History of Universities in Tamil Nadu.* Karaikudi: Alagappa University, 2002.

Swaminathan, A. M. *Food Security, Policy Options for Tamil Nadu.* New Delhi: Academic Foundation, 2009.

Tamil Nadu. Accessed April 28, 2011. http://www.tn.gov.in.

Tata Institute of Social Sciences. *The State and Civil Society in Disaster Response: An Analysis of the Tamil Nadu Tsunami Response.* Mumbai: Tata Institute of Social Sciences, 2005.

✦ TEEN MURTI BHAVAN

Teen Murti Bhavan, the Nehru Memorial Museum and Library (NMML), was built in 1930 and designed by Robert Tor Russell (1888–1972), chief architect for the Public Works Department of the government of India and famous for designing Connaught Circle (1928–1934) in the center of New Delhi, was originally named Flagstaff House and was the residence of the commander in chief of the British Indian Army. Following independence in 1947, the house became the official residence of India's first prime minister, Jawaharlal Nehru (1889–1964; prime minister 1947–1964), who lived there for 16 years until his death on

May 27, 1964. After his death, Teen Murti Bhavan was made into a museum and library promoting modern Indian history and containing an invaluable collection of materials devoted to Nehru and his era. The house gets its name from the Teen Murti ("three statues") Memorial built in memory of Indian soldiers who died in World War I (1914–1918) fighting as part of the Indian Army, which stands in front of its extensive grounds. The Nehru Memorial Museum and Library Society was established in 1966 and is an autonomous institution under the Ministry of Culture. It has a large collection of historical research material and attracts scholars from all over India and the world who visit to consult its extensive materials. It has an agreement with the British Library in London with which it exchanges research materials and this, along with its own voluminous materials, makes it a premier research center for South Asian studies. It has four major constituents: the Memorial Museum, a library on modern India, the Centre for Contemporary Studies, and a planetarium. The Nehru Planetarium has an active educational program and offers programs for students and amateur astronomers. On the grounds of the museum, where entrance is free, is a granite rock inscribed with excerpts from Nehru's historic "Tryst with Destiny" speech delivered during the midnight session of the Indian Constituent Assembly on August 14–15, 1947, at the time of India's independence. An annual Jawaharlal Nehru Memorial Foundation lecture delivered by eminent world leaders and academics can cover national and global science or social and economic issues. It is held at the Bhavan annually on April 1. In addition to the annual lecture the library hosts conferences and round tables on the pressing issues of the day; many of the proceedings and findings of the meetings are published by NMML and this activity makes NMML one of the leading intellectual sites in Delhi.

SHEEBA HÄRMÄ

See also Asiatic Society of Bengal; Asiatic Society of Mumbai; New Delhi

Further Reading

James, J. C. *Sir Banister Fletcher's a History of Architecture.* New York: Scribner, 1975.
Nehru Memorial Museum and Library. Accessed April 28, 2011. http://nehrumemorial.com/.
Nehru Memorial Museum and Library. *NMML Manuscripts: An Introduction.* New Delhi: Nehru Memorial Museum and Library, 2003.
Nehru Planetarium: Nehru Memorial Museum and Library, New Delhi. Accessed April 28, 2011. http://nehruplanetarium.org/.

✦ TELANGANA

The term "Telangana" means "region of Telugu" or "land of Telugu" and denotes an ethnonationalist movement by Telugu-speaking people in the south of India to carve out a separate state from territories mostly located in the state of Andhra Pradesh. Telugu is a

Dravidian language and the third most widely used language in India. The term "Telangana," however, is a misnomer since it is applied only to a limited region in Andhra Pradesh, while Telugu is the language of the whole of Andhra Pradesh. In fact, the state of Andhra Pradesh was formed by taking adjacent regions with Telugu-speaking populations from Hyderabad and Tamil Nadu. The term "Telangana" was designated to distinguish the Telugu region from Marathwada (the land of Marathi) as part of the long bygone Hyderabad state. However, this term has come to stay and distinguishes the 10 districts of Andhra Pradesh roughly located in the northwest—Warangal, Adilabad, Khammam, Mahabubnagar, Nalgonda, Rangareddy, Karimnagar, Nizamabad, Medak, and Hyderabad, the present state capital of Andhra Pradesh—that border Madhya Pradesh in the north and Maharashtra in the west. In the new millennium the demand for the creation of Telangana has become a powerful one. Telangana leaders responsible for such separatist agitations have always expressed concern about the lack of regional development when compared with the rest of Andhra Pradesh. Statistical analysis based on the use of resources, industrialization, per capita income, and production have, however, shown such concerns to be baseless, but the arguments persist, especially among adherents of Telangana. On December 9, 2009, the government of India announced that it would begin studying the process of establishing the state of Telangana within the Indian union.

LAVANYA VEMSANI

See also Hyderabad

Further Reading
Ahmad, Syed. *The Telengana Districts.* Hyderabad: Hyderabad Geography Association, 1956.
Bernstorff, Dagmar. *Region and Nation: The Telengana Movement's Dula Identity.* London: School of Oriental and African Studies, 1977.
Kumar, V. Anil. "DISCUSSION: Why Telangana? Why Now?" *Economic and Political Weekly* 42(9) (2007): 790.
Pavier, Barry. *The Telengana Movement, 1944–51.* New Delhi: Vikas, 1981.

Telecommunications. *See* Media and Telecommunications

✦ TELEVISION

After its humble beginnings in 1959 and two decades of unhurried growth, where programming was mainly instructional, television development in India suddenly accelerated in the 1980s, as more and more of the country was brought under the umbrella of national television. In 1976, television was formally separated from All India Radio, which had hitherto overseen its activities, and set up as a discrete entity called Doordarshan (a literal translation into Hindi of the English word "television"). In 1997, the government established Prasar Bharati to oversee the activities of both Doordarshan and All India Radio and to ensure their autonomy.

The next leap forward came in 1991, with the arrival of the cable and satellite revolution through the intermediary of Star TV, beamed from Hong Kong. The growth figures for cable and satellite television are staggering. In 1991 there was, in addition to the 5 state-owned terrestrial channels, 1 satellite channel: Star TV. With the arrival of the Indian-owned Zee TV in 1992, the number of satellite channels had doubled. But within three years there were 48 terrestrial and satellite channels, and by 2003 the Indian public had a mind-boggling 224 channels to choose from. With total revenues of 111 billion rupees ($2.5 billion) in 2002, expected to rise to 139 billion rupees ($22.5 billion) by 2010, television provides over 60 percent of the revenue from the entertainment sector. Today India is the third-largest market for cable subscribers in the world, after the United States and China.

As for the viewers, in 2003 there were 84 million households with access to terrestrial television, of which 41 million households also had access to cable and satellite. Since each household is calculated as consisting of 5.5 individuals, it translates into a potential daily audience of nearly a half-billion viewers for terrestrial television and a quarter of a billion viewers for cable and satellite.

The most impressive feature of Indian television has been its exponential growth. Despite a late start, television is now the fastest-growing area of entertainment in India, and the forecast for Indian television, particularly regional television, is one of continued growth. As penetration of terrestrial, cable, and satellite television into the rural areas increases, the regional sector is expected to grow considerably.

As of 2006 there were a total of 192 million households in India—56 million in urban areas. Of these, 43 million receive terrestrial television, with 27 million households also subscribing to cable and satellite networks. There is room for growth in urban areas, particularly in cable and satellite television connectivity.

There are 136 million rural households, of which only 39 million receive terrestrial television and 13 million have cable and satellite connections. Cable and satellite penetration in regional hinterlands, away from the main commercial capitals, is particularly low, and the scope for growth in the rural areas is tremendous. However, growth in television connectivity in the hinterland will depend on improved infrastructure, particularly the availability of electricity in the rural areas.

The way toward greater organization of the cable networks may come through large operators, known as multi-system operators (MSOs), who act as middlemen by taking signals from the broadcasters and passing them on to the local *cablewallahs*, or cable operators. MSOs such as InCableNet and Siti-Cable are keen to offer households and businesses broadband Internet connections through cable television. They are therefore seeking to improve the communications infrastructure by upgrading the networks, sometimes even the "last mile," which cable operators usually control.

Direct to home (DTH) technology has been discussed as the future for television in India. DTH refers to the distribution of satellite and cable channels using digital technology in Ku Band, which provides signals directly to the subscriber's premises. The biggest advantage of DTH technology is that it renders the role of the cable operator redundant. Digital technology and signal compression also create savings on transponder services while allowing for greater numbers of channels. However, the more expensive addressable system and aerial dish required for DTH result in increased costs for the subscriber, a very important consideration in mass media diffusion in India.

Although the results of surveys published by the Federation of Indian Chambers of Commerce and Industry (FICCI), the *Economic Times*, and other newspapers and magazines, tend to vary, they all agree that the regional channels and general entertainment in Hindi garner over 80 percent of the total viewership and comprise the largest segment of the market. The programs include prime-time soaps, quiz shows, music contests, comedy programs, and talk shows. Star TV's Star Plus channel, which now broadcasts entirely in Hindi, leads the field in entertainment, with 45 of the nation's top 50 programs, followed by Sun TV, Gemini TV, Sony Entertainment, ETV, and Zee TV.

The most watched category of general entertainment is the soap opera. The first Indian "prodevelopment" serial was *Hum Log*, which enjoyed unprecedented success. The serial had 157 episodes and ran for 17 months during 1984 and 1985. It sought its inspiration from Mexico's Televisa. Much of early Indian television serials was prodevelopment programming, consisting of television serials created with the aim of social development. Started in South America, the model, which combines entertainment with education, was considered worth pursuing by public television broadcasters such as Doordarshan.

At any given time, every broadcaster in Hindi and the regional languages has at least one and often more soaps. They are generally about extended families, with the struggle for power among various members of the extended family dominating the action. Central to these conflicts are the vicious power struggles between the mother-in-law (*saas*) and the daughter-in-law (*bahu*). Since most Indians, both in the cities and villages, live in extended families with several generations cohabiting under one roof, these soaps find great resonance with audiences. These *saas-bahu* struggles are epitomized in long-running soaps such as Star TV's Hindi-language *Saas Bhi Kabhi Bahu Thi*. Others include *Kahani Ghar Ghar Ki* (Star), *Des Mein Nikla Hoga Chand*, *Kkoi Dil Mein Hai*, and *Kkusum* (Sony). The leader of the pack is *Kyunki Saas Bhi Kabhi Bahu Thi*, which, in order to keep ahead of the rest, must come up with ever-more innovative and daring ideas. For example, its production company, Balaji Telefilms, was the first to decide to shoot some of its episodes in Australia.

The soaps target female audiences, and most run only on weekdays. Drawing on unrestrained feminine greed and ambition, first introduced to Indian viewers by *The Bold and the Beautiful*, which was screened by Star TV in the early 1990s, Indian soaps are intense family dramas. "Television clearly loves the new nasty [female villain] who seduces husbands, steals boyfriends, exchanges babies and manipulates mothers-in-law," writes critic Kaveree

Bamzai. So popular are negative female characters that when the serial *Des Mein Nikla Hoga Chand* began to slide in the ratings, director Aruna Irani allegedly decided to expand the predatory female's role. The series' subsequent rise to the ranks of the top 15 television shows was proof that nasty women have the best ratings.

The soaps concentrate on affluent, urban, unhappy Indians and unfailingly narrate incidents of rape, divorce, and extramarital relationships. "A good soap asks for the impossible," says television's top writer Manohar Shyam Joshi, who invented the genre with *Hum Log* and *Buniyaad.* "It must be high drama which can masquerade as reality." In the once squeaky clean *Saas Bhi Kabhi Bahu Thi*, Tulsi, the mother-in-law, vows to avenge her pregnant daughter, who was recently raped by her son-in-law and framed her boyfriend for a murder he did not commit; in *Kkoi Dil Mein Hai*, the recently widowed Kajal is forced by the family to marry her brother-in-law, whom she once loved, but he is now married to her best friend; in *Kkusum*, Garv finds that a one-night stand with Kali, whom he once loved, leaves her pregnant, and that now he really loves his wife, Kali's stepsister; and in *Tanav*, everyone lives unhappily ever after—Mrs. Malik has a boy toy, her husband is sleeping with his secretary, her stepdaughter has discovered that her lover is married, and her son, who is gay, has AIDS. Adultery, ambition, AIDS, murder, madness, seduction, betrayal, impotence, rage: these are the subjects that are advanced on a transfixed Indian public. Manohar Shyam Joshi despairs of the contemporary soaps: "Earlier the episode would climax with a stirring dialogue. Now it closes with a slap, a shriek, and a cuss word."

In 2003, as an antidote to the surfeit of *saas-bahu* dramas, Sony introduced a new serial called *Jassi Jaissi Koi Nahin*. Its central character, Jassi, is an earnest but clumsy secretary with braces and thick spectacles. The series was a surprise hit because the ugly duckling role is said to have reassured hundreds of ordinary-looking girls about their self-worth. Secretaries frequently invite Mona Singh, the actress who plays Jassi, as guest of honor to their events. Storywise, it also leaves open the possibility for Jassi to turn into a beautiful swan. To capture the mood of the nation, the Indian postal services have even commemorated a new postal cover and cards in her honor. Imitations of *Jassi Jaissi Koi Nahin*, such as *Yeh Meri Life Hai*, *Saakshi*, and *Dekho Magar Pyar Se*, have not been as successful as the original.

Quizzes and game shows are also extremely popular on Indian television. The most successful was *Kaun Banega Crorepati?*, an Indian version of *Who Wants to Be a Millionaire?* that aired in the late 1990s and was hosted on Star by a mature Amitabh Bachchan, the biggest star of Hindi cinema. The program is said to have revived the fortunes of the faltering channel. Attempts by other channels to replicate the success with other film stars were not effective, pointing to the newness of format and charisma of the superstar for the extraordinary success of the program.

In 2004, Sony and Star TV's music channel, Channel V, both launched Indian versions of *Pop Idol* with a celebrity panel of judges. Ten Indian cities competed to find a winner on Channel V's *Super Singer*, while Sony's *Indian Idol* limited the search to the four major cities. Music contests have been popular on Indian television for over a decade. *Antakshari*, where

Bollywood actor Shahrukh Khan, who succeeded Amitabh Bachchan as game show host, poses at a press conference for television channel Star Plus's game show, *Kaun Banega Crorepati*, the Indian version of *Who Wants To Be A Millionaire*, in New Delhi, December 2006. Television shows have become as popular in India as they are in many other parts of the world. (AP Photo/Mustafa Quraishi)

each contestant has to sing a song beginning with the final syllable of the previous singer's lyrics, first began on Zee TV in 1993 and has maintained a loyal audience ever since. In 1995 the channel started a second musical contest, *Sa Re Ga Ma*.

In addition to programs on the various general entertainment channels, the two major channels dedicated to music are MTV and Channel V. Initially, MTV broadcast only Western music but found that the only way to penetrate the Indian market was to offer Indian (and Indian film-based) music. International music now constitutes just 2 percent of all music on Indian television, with 98 percent devoted to Indian music delivered by young male and female DJs who speak "Hinglish," a Hindi-English patois most popular with the young. The two channels have revolutionized Indian music and created a whole new genre of Indipop, sung in Hindi, English, and Hinglish. They have also fueled a boom in the music videos market.

Other prime-time programs on Indian-language channels include Simi Garewal's interviews with stars and celebrities and Sanjeev Kapoor's cooking program, *Khana Khazana*.

Detective action series, such as *Ak . . . tion Unlimited Josh*, are largely imitations of *Miami Vice* featuring muscular men fighting crime. They are aimed to interest male audiences fatigued by daily doses of *saas-bahu* extended family traumas. In an Indian version of *Crimewatch UK*, the city police departments describe certain crimes that actually have been committed and seek public assistance in solving them. Current comedy programs feature writer, director, and producer Aatish Kapadia, whose work includes *Khichdi* and its sequel *Instant Khichdi*. Kapadia is also behind the program *Sarabhai vs. Sarabhai* and *Main Office Tere Angan Ki*, whose titles are spoofs on Hindi films and plays. Other popular comedy programs include *Office Office* and *LOC*. A new channel entirely devoted to comedy, called Smile TV, came on the air in 2004.

Indian television also offers at least three imitations of *Sex and the City: Dil Kya Chahta Hai* on Star TV, *Kuchh Love Kuchh Masti* on Sahara, and *Kabhi Haan Kabhi Naa* on Zee TV. In general, however, copies of Western shows are not particularly popular. An early imitation of *Friends*, remade on Zee TV as *Hello Friends*, failed to excite the public. Reality shows such as *Big Brother*, however, began as early as 1993 and have become popular, with some shows having an Indian formula and others licensed from abroad.

Major companies that provide the content for general entertainment on television include Balaji Telefilms, Cinevista Communications, Padmalaya Telefilms, Sri Adhikari Brothers, Pritish Nandy Communications, Ronnie Screwvala's UTV, and Crest Communications. Entertainment in English, including films, is largely provided by Zee English, Zee MGM, Star World, Star Movies, HBO, AXN, and Hallmark and constitutes just under 2 percent of the total viewership in India. The National Geographic and Discovery channels usually dub their programs into Hindi.

Hindi films attract around 4 percent of total viewership on Indian television. Doordarshan as well as all cable and satellite channels screen feature films in Hindi and in regional languages. There are also channels dedicated to screening Hindi films, such as B4U, Zee Cinema, and Sony Max. Independent cable operators who are not affiliated with MSOs often offer a film channel with films in Hindi, English, and regional languages as a "goodwill gesture" to their subscribers. These screenings are mostly without authorization and include the screening of pirated videos. Some are even said to offer soft porn films late at night.

The rise of dedicated news and news-based channels is a recent phenomenon on Indian television. After decades of total control by Doordarshan on the dissemination of news throughout the nation, the cable and satellite networks first opened the doors to foreign news channels after Star began broadcasting to India in 1991. But it was not long before the cable and satellite networks began to provide national, regional, and local news in regional languages. Today, news channels in Hindi and the regional languages attract the largest percentage of news viewership.

In 2005, there were 32 dedicated news channels offering news and news-based programs, 10 of them in English and the rest in Hindi and all the major languages of India. Of these, 10 channels have recently come on the air, including channels that offer business news in Hindi, such as Zee Biz, Videocon, CNBC-TV18, and NDTV. An additional 20 Indian channels are preparing to enter the market. The planned new arrivals include one produced by Bennett, Coleman & Co. (owners of the English-language newspaper *Times of India*) and Reuters.

The most successful news channel is the Hindi-language Aaj Tak, owned by Living Media India, which also owns the news magazine *India Today*. The company's success can be attributed to its decision to woo the small businesses that had previously been shunned by advertisers as too insignificant or down-market. In doing so, it broke advertising records and showed that dedicated news channels could be lucrative business. The success of Aaj Tak encouraged other broadcast companies to start news channels in regional languages.

Zee News and Star News are the next most-watched news channels. Star News became a serious contender in the business of news services when it switched its services to Hindi in 2003. Until then its Hindi news service was provided by NDTV, a company that previously provided a weekly roundup of news and events for Doordarshan. NDTV is now an independent 24-hour news channel in Hindi. Aaj Tak and NDTV have both started a new English-language service called Headlines Today and NDTV 24x7, respectively. The increased competition among the news channels has resulted in attractive packaging and high production values. The English-language Headlines Today, for instance, is said to have trained its newscasters with CNN.

Sun TV has dedicated news channels in Tamil and English, Udaya TV in Kannada, and Asianet in Malayalam. It will soon have 2 new channels in Telugu and Malayalam. Sahara Samay, which already has 4 dedicated news channels, is set to roll out another 31 city-centric news channels. English-language transnational news channels available in India are CNN and BBC World. CNBC has also launched an Indian channel, CNBC India.

Doordarshan's national and regional channels also carry news in Hindi, English, and most regional languages. Although Doordarshan is the front-runner in the news channels stakes by virtue of its terrestrial monopoly and access to 51 percent of the nation's households, its presentation is perceived as progovernment and dull. In 2004, Doordarshan inaugurated two new dedicated channels to broadcast live all proceedings in the Lok Sabha and Rajya Sabha, the lower and upper houses of the Indian Parliament. It is hoped that the election in 2004 of several former film stars to Parliament might evoke greater interest in watching the Indian legislators at work.

According to the survey published in the *Economic Times*, the cable and satellite news channels' share of viewership, which was just 2 percent a few years ago, has risen to 6–7 percent. Advertising revenues have accordingly increased too. News channels corner 14 percent of the total television advertising revenue. The reason for this disproportionate share of revenue is the perception that the genre mainly attracts men, who are the decision makers for the purchase of high-value goods in most families. Also, news viewers are often perceived as the opinion formers of the nation. Advertisers therefore consider them a significant emerging market.

Cricket dominates sports in India, and it is the most important game on television. To many, cricket inspires a religious fervor akin to that inspired by only one other staple of Indian culture: cinema. No other sport generates the same nationwide interest and excitement.

The yearlong calendar of cricket matches in India and abroad dominates the intense bidding war for the rights among sponsors for the matches. There are a variety of interregional matches, but more important are the test and one-day international (ODI) matches played among the handful of cricket-playing nations of the world. The most important of all these matches are without doubt the World Cup matches and any match that features India playing Pakistan. They command the highest fees for advertising—about $25,000 for a 10-second spot (as compared with $2 million for the Super Bowl in the United States).

Because of India's abysmal international performance in most sports other than cricket, the national interest in sports channels is not as great as elsewhere in the world. However, field hockey, tennis, and football are growing in popularity. The new Indian sports stars, such as Sania Mirza in tennis and Narain Karthikeyan in Formula One racing, are beginning to emerge on the international stage and may spur more broadcasts of these sports on Indian television.

Star Sports, Zee Sports, Doordarshan's DD Sports, and ESPN are the main sports channels in India.

Religious and mythological soaps have been a perennial feature on Indian television, and all channels have at least one (but usually several) such series on air at any given time. Recently the major religious serials were *Shree Ganesh* and *Shree Krishna* on Sony, *Ma Shakti* on Star Plus, *Jai Ganesh* on Zee TV, *Brahma Vishnu Mahesh* and *Sati Savitri* on SABe, *Draupadi* on Sahara, with Doordarshan's *Ramayan* and *Mahabharat* repeated on Zee and Sony, respectively. In 2004, the toughest fight for audiences was between Sony's *Devi* on the goddess Durga and *Sarrthi* about Lord Krishna from Star Plus.

In addition to the religious and mythological serials, nine channels have emerged over the last five years entirely devoted to spreading the word of God. These are *Aastha, Sanskar, Maharishi, Om Shanti, Maa TV, Sadhna, Jagran* (sponsored by Zee TV), GOD (a Christian channel based in Jerusalem), and Quran TV (for Muslims). The competition among the seven Hindu channels is intense, particularly since many offer similar fare of devotional music, religious discourses, astrology, celebrations of religious festivals, and sometimes fund-raising projects, and programs about the work of nongovernmental organizations. They all cater to an older audience, but the battle for the hearts and minds of younger viewers is always on. Most of the channels depend on a handful of male and female speakers: Sant Morari Bapu, Guru Maa, Sukhbodhanandji, Sudhanshu Maharaj, Asaram Bapu, and the more cosmopolitan Jaya Rao.

An emerging television market is that for children's programs. There are currently six major channels for children: Cartoon Network, Nickelodeon, Splash, Animax, POGO, and Hungama, with the imminent arrival of a seventh, Walt Disney International. Children's programs constitute nearly 10 percent of the broadcasts on Indian television, and nearly 70 percent of these programs feature cartoons.

Sony's Animax, Turner International's POGO, and UTV's Hungama started broadcasting in January 2004. Hungama, an Indian channel launched by UTV with the intention of broadcasting original programs for children as well as interactive game shows made entirely in India, is an entirely new phenomenon and is being watched with great interest by the other media companies. UTV and its owner, Ronnie Screwvala, who produces television programs for Doordarshan, Star TV, Gemini, Vijaya, and Sun TV, are also involved in the production of Hindi films. For Hungama, UTV has created a governing body entirely made up of children who offer advice on programming.

Indian programs on cable and satellite are popular among the 20 million Indian expatriates living in North America, Europe, Africa, and Southeast Asia. The Zee network, along with Sony, has been the prime mover in the international arena. Sony was the first channel from the subcontinent to be launched in the United States, where the Ethnic American Broadcast Company (EABC) distributed it on the DirecTV DTH platform. Zee beams transmissions to Fiji, the United Kingdom, and mainland Europe, as well as South Africa. It also reaches out to immigrant Indians in Asia and Australia. The network has expanded into a 24-hour telecast in the United States, from its previous 2-hour daily broadcast. Former Indian tennis champion Vijay Amritraj owns the downlinking and distribution rights in North America for Doordarshan's international channel, DD India. Recently the Israeli cable network, Hot, launched a free channel called Hot Bombay, dedicated to Bollywood films.

The international broadcasts include Indian programs and sometimes programs specially made for the immigrant population overseas, which constitutes an important revenue and target for advertising. So lucrative is the overseas market that many Indian programs such as the musical quiz-cum-singing contest *Sa Re Ga Ma* are shot in the United States and the United Kingdom with Asian audiences.

The Indian television scene continues to experience phenomenal growth as we enter the second decade of the 21st century. Several publications provide a running commentary on the growth and character of Indian television. For an up-to-date source for statistics and analysis of the Indian television industry, see televisionpoint.com, whose logo tells it all: Indian TV always. All the way.

ASHA KASBEKAR RICHARDS

See also Bollywood; Doordarshan; Soap Operas

Further Reading
Bamzai, Kaveree. "Mean Queens." *India Today*, April 7, 2003.
Bamzai, Kaveree. "The New Face of News." *India Today*, April 28, 2003.
Bamzai, Kaveree. "Reality Check." *India Today*, November 22, 2004.
Chandra, Anupama. "Script Writers: A Flourish of the Pen." *India Today*, January 31, 1996.
ET Intelligence Group. "The ET Television Survey, 2003: It's a Home Theatre, It's a Multiplex, It's a TV." *Economic Times*, September 26, 2003.
Federation of Indian Chambers of Commerce and Industry (FICCI). *The Indian Entertainment Sector: In the Spotlight.* Mumbai: KPMG, 2003.
Government of India. *India 2010: A Reference Annual.* New Delhi: Publications Division, Ministry of Information and Broadcasting, 2010.
Joshi, Namrata. "Satellite Channels: Westward Bound." *India Today*, August 10, 1998.

Temple of Somanatha. *See* Somanatha Temple

✦ TERRITORIES

India is divided politically into 29 states and seven Union Territories (including the National Capital Territory of Delhi). The seven Union Territories are Andaman and Nicobar Islands; Chandigarh; Dadra and Nagar Haveli; Daman and Diu; Lakshadweep; New Delhi; and Puducherry. They are administered by the president of India through his or her representative, the administrator. In the Andaman and Nicobar Islands, Delhi, and Puducherry the administrators are lieutenant governors. In Chandigarh the governor of the state of the Punjab is the administrator. Daman and Diu are administered by the administrator of Dadra and Nagar Haveli. Lakshwadeep has its own administrator. The national capital territory of Delhi has a Legislative Assembly and a council of administrators, as does Puducherry. Accordingly, the governance of these different territories is flexible and varies from territory to territory. In the case of Delhi and Puducherry, certain bills passed by the respective legislatures must have the assent of the president of India.

ROGER D. LONG

See also Andaman and Nicobar Islands; Chandigarh; Dadra and Nagar Haveli; Daman and Diu; Lakshwadeep; New Delhi; Puducherry

Further Reading

Association of Urban Management and Development Authorities. *States/UTs of India: A Profile.* New Delhi: Association of Urban Management and Development Authorities, 2007.

Boland-Crewe, Tara, and David Lea. *Territories and States of India.* London: Europa Publications, 2010.

✦ THACKERAY, BALASAHEB KESHAV

Balasaheb ("Bal") Keshav Thackeray (b. 1923) is the founder and supreme head of the right-wing Hindu nationalist party the Shiv Sena ("Army of Shivaji"), founded on June 19, 1966. The Maratha king Shivaji (1630–1680) was a Hindu king who rebelled against the Muslim rulers of India and is one of Hindu India's most revered figures. He is held in equally high esteem by the Congress Party in Maharashtra. Bal Thackeray is the son of noted writer and social reformer Keshav Sitaram (KC) Thackeray, and he was born in the city of Pune on January 23, 1923. His political philosophy was largely shaped by his father, a leading figure in the Samyukta Maharashtra Movement (SMM), founded in 1956, which advocated the creation of the linguistic state of Maharashtra. It brought together Marathi activists of diverse political persuasions. The senior Thackeray reportedly supported the strategic use of violence but broke from the SMM because of the prominent place of Communists within the movement. The efficacy of violence and a fervent anti-Communist stance would become key elements of Bal Thackeray's beliefs and the Shiv Sena's political platform.

Bal Thackeray began his professional career as a political cartoonist with the English-language daily the *Free Press Journal*. At the *Free Press*, Thackeray wielded the caricature as a political weapon but was forced to temper his biting commentary. In 1960, he left the *Free Press* to start his own political weekly, *Marmik*, where he could exercise complete editorial control. On the pages of *Marmik*, Thackeray openly criticized politicians and voiced his vehement anti-Communism, which grew even stronger during the China-India War of 1962. By this time, *Marmik* had attracted a significant following among Mumbai's lower-middle-class and white-collar Maharashtrians. In the mid-1960s, Thackeray played directly to this audience by publishing lists of corporate executives employed in Mumbai, highlighting how many of them were "outsiders" and South Indians in particular. The implication was that these "outsiders" were taking jobs away from "native" Maharashtrians.

In 1966, Thackeray abandoned his long-standing aversion to party politics and formed the Shiv Sena to advocate more strongly for the place of Maharashtrians in Mumbai's professional and political landscape. His movement gathered momentum after the Shiv Sena's first public meeting was held in October 1966 in Mumbai's Shivaji Park. When larger-than-expected crowds of working- and middle-class Maharashtrians showed up and expressed their support for his pro-Maharashtrian message, Thackeray set about building the Shiv Sena into an organized political movement. Declaring himself the *pramukh* ("chief") of the Shiv Sena, Thackeray employed military metaphors and slogans advocating physical strength to mobilize his followers and to bring in adherents to the party.

In the late 1960s and early 1970s, Thackeray built the party by forming temporary alliances with nearly all of Maharashtra's political parties. In a controversial move, he came out in support of Prime Minister Indira Gandhi (1917–1984; prime minister 1966–1977, 1980–1984) and the Congress Party (founded in 1885) during the emergency between June 25, 1975, and March 21, 1977. Partly reflecting his support for authoritarian politics and partly a pragmatic move to avoid repression, this support also showed Thackeray's deft political maneuvering. The move, however, was met with dissent from both leaders and rank-and-file members of the Shiv Sena, and Thackeray had to work to repair the damage caused by the alliance.

Ever a controversial figure, Thackeray has attracted significant attention to himself and the party by making statements expressing admiration for Hitler, inciting violence against Muslims, expressing support for the Tamil Tigers, and taking strong stances on aspects of popular culture, including a fervent opposition to the celebration of Valentine's Day. Although he handed the official mantle of the party to his son, Udhav (b. 1960), in 2003, Thackeray remains the party's supreme leader and *senapati*. Suffering from numerous health problems, however, he now makes few public appearances, although his image remains prominently displayed on election posters and he continues to publish editorials in the Shiv Sena daily newspaper, *Saamna*.

LIZA WEINSTEIN

See also Maharashtra; Mumbai; Shiv Sena

Further Reading
Hansen, Thomas Blom. *The Saffron Wave: Democracy and Hindu Nationalism in Modern India.* Princeton, NJ: Princeton University Press, 1999.
Hansen, Thomas Blom. *Wages of Violence: Naming and Identity in Postcolonial Bombay.* Princeton, NJ: Princeton University Press, 2001.
Jaffrolet, Christophe. *The Hindu Nationalist Movement in India.* New York: Columbia University Press, 1996.
Mehta, Suketu. *Maximum City: Bombay Lost and Found.* New York, Knopf, 2004.
Patel, Sujata, and Alice Thorner. *Bombay: Metaphor for Modern India.* New Delhi: Oxford University Press, 1995.
Swami, Praveen. "'The General' in His Labyrinth." *Frontline Magazine* 15(18) (August 29–September 11, 1998). www.hindunet.com/fline/fl1518/15180200.htm.

✦ THAPAR, ROMILA

Romila Thapar is an exceptionally gifted Marxist historian and, as of 2010, the most well-known historian in India and someone who enjoys an international reputation as an expert on ancient India. She was one of the pioneers in writing against colonial stereotypes about Indian history and its supposed lack of a sense of time or historical consciousness. Accordingly, she has been in high demand as a speaker and has made numerous broadcasts for the BBC. She was born in India in 1931 in a Punjabi-speaking family and was raised in various parts of India, as her father was in the Indian Army and was transferred from post to post. After completing her undergraduate education at Punjab University she received a PhD from the University of London in 1958. After returning to India she began teaching in the Punjab but ended her long teaching career at Jawaharlal Nehru University, New Delhi, where she is professor emerita. She also continues to teach and lecture abroad and she has spent time at Cornell University, Dartmouth College, the University of Chicago, the University of California at Berkeley, the University of Michigan, the University of Washington, and the University of Pennsylvania, as well as the Collège de France in Paris, amid a long list of universities where she has been invited to teach and lecture. She is also an honorary fellow of Lady Margaret Hall at the University of Oxford.

The recipient of a long list of honorary degrees from universities around the world, in 2003 she was appointed the first Kluge Chair in Countries and Cultures of the South at the John W. Kluge Center at the Library of Congress. The center was set up to bring together "the world's best thinkers." In 2008 she was awarded the John W. Kluge Prize in the Human Sciences, an award given for lifetime achievement "in the study of humanity."

Thapar is the author of more than 20 books, a number of which have become classics and have remained on the required reading list for undergraduate and graduate students for several decades, and dozens of articles.

Some 50 years after it was originally published in 1961 by Oxford University Press at the Clarendon Press, *Ashoka and the Decline of the Mauryas* remains the single most consulted volume on the súbject, has been continually in print, and is considered required reading on the topic. Generations of students have studied and cherished the volume. In 1999 Oxford University Press reissued the study, for which Thapar offered a new afterword, bibliography, and index.

Her original research on ancient India was incorporated into the first volume of the Penguin history of India, *A History of India I* (1966), a general survey of the history of India from the earliest times to the 1300s. Continually in print and distributed worldwide by Penguin Books, it is widely used as a textbook for undergraduate Indian history classes in India and in the West. She revised this book as *The Penguin History of Early India: From the Origins to 1300* (London: Penguin, 2003). For many people it is the standard guide on ancient India.

Her other renowned studies include *Ancient Indian Social History: Some Interpretations* (New Delhi: Orient Longman, 1978); *Interpreting Early India* (New York: Oxford University Press, 1992); *Śakuntalā Texts, Readings, Histories* (New Delhi: Kali for Women, 1999); *Cultural Pasts: Essays in Early Indian History* (New Delhi: Oxford University Press, 2000); *India: Another Millennium?* (New Delhi: Viking, 2000); *Early India: From the Origins to A.D. 1300* (London: Allen Lane, 2002); *Somanatha, the Many Voices of a History* (New Delhi: Viking, 2004); and *The Aryan: Recasting Constructs* (Gurgaon: Three Essays Collective, 2008).

Thapar has performed a long list of services to her profession and was elected president of the Indian History Congress in 1983 and appointed a corresponding fellow of the British Academy in 1999. She became the chancellor of the University of Hyderabad in 1999. She was also a member of the textbook committee of the Indian Council for Historical Research and she has made many contributions to school textbooks.

She has taken a number of controversial stands with regard to a number of issues, such as on the Aryan invasion-migration theory, the sack of Somanath, and the Hindu epics. She declined to accept the Padma Bhushan award given by the government of India in 1992 and then in 2005 on the grounds that she only accepted awards given by academic institutions or by those connected with her professional work. Her decision, however, was not universally well received. She had earlier been criticized for her statements with regard to Babri Masjid, and M. F. Hussain, a controversial painter of India. She also raised controversy in the United States when she joined the California Hindu textbook controversy by signing a petition opposing the revisions proposed by the Indian community of California in 2006.

LAVANYA VEMSANI

See also Secularism

Further Reading

Thapar, Romila, R. Champakalkshmi, and Savepalli Gopal. *Tradition, Dissent and Ideology: Essays in Honour of Romila Thapar*. New Delhi: Oxford University Press, 1996.

✦ THEATER

A high risk of oversimplification underlies any attempt to survey Indian theater, primarily because it exists in so many languages. The Indian Constitution at present names 22 official languages, while the Sahitya Akademi (India's national academy of letters) recognizes 24, which in itself proves the impossibility of differentiating between greater and lesser linguistic traditions. All these languages, each with millions of speakers, as well as many others and the hundreds of dialects, possess distinctive histories of theater, some of them several centuries old. Thus, to discuss "Indian" theater is like discussing the theater of Western Europe, which has about as many languages, and which no self-respecting scholar today would undertake because of the variety of literatures involved. Neither can any Indian critic claim to know all the major Indian languages, so how can he justify writing about them? The Indian situation gets further complicated by low literacy, as a result of which folk theaters often do not even use written texts, so the researcher cannot depend on standard methods of literary analysis.

As in other Indian activities, the ancient, medieval, and modern coexist in theater, too. Interested visitors can experience three broad performance traditions: the classical Sanskrit, albeit rare, dating back at least a millennium; the multifarious folk forms, most of which originated several hundred years ago, in the Middle Ages; and the urban drama, a product of the 19th century when colonial models influenced regional literatures. Understandably, Western viewers are more intrigued by the classical and folk theaters, attracted by their exotic otherness, whereas educated Indians tend to concentrate attention on their modern city drama, associating it with secular and social progress. An objective picture of Indian theater, however, must take all varieties into account, especially given the fact that most Indians still live outside urban culture.

In certain Hindu temples in the southern state of Kerala, two ancient forms of Sanskrit theater survive. Some historians believe that Kutiyattam can boast of an unbroken continuity of 2,000 years; if true, it is possibly the world's oldest extant theatrical tradition. Typically, it performs specific scenes from classical plays, especially those by the oldest known Indian dramatist, Bhasa, in a mix of Sanskrit, Prakrit (the local vernacular when Sanskrit was spoken by the elite), and old Malayalam (Kerala's regional language). Staged in purpose-built heritage playhouses called *kuttampalam* within the temple precincts, it features stylized acting with *mudras* (codified hand and facial signs and gestures), adhering to performance manuals carefully preserved and handed down over the centuries.

Similarly devotional in nature and using written scripts, Krishnattam is an even rarer form now seen only at the Guruvayur Temple in Kerala. It may have evolved out of a predecessor

400 years ago, dedicated to the worship of Krishna. Visible similarities with the elaborate costumes and makeup of Kathakali dance-drama suggest that it could have had a hand in the latter's creation, but it certainly looks more graceful and refined in comparison, without Kathakali's greater physical vigor and sound. Its stories, delivered in Sanskrit, come from Krishna mythology.

In villages across the country, many folk theaters continue to flourish—and some languish—in the local dialects. These examples of the oral tradition normally have connections with religious festivities but sometimes, though notionally presented as an offering to the community deity, they incorporate a more democratic outlook, including topical allusions and even political satire. Increasingly, however, this vast section of Indian performance has lost audiences to commercial cinema and come under threat of eventual extinction on account of television's outreach to all corners of the nation. Probably the most endangered are the various puppeteering and shadow-theater forms, facing unbeatable competition from the technological world of lights and shadows. It would be a sad day, indeed, if in the foreseeable future the beautiful shadow puppetry of the southern coasts, the progenitors of their world-famous Indonesian descendants, should have to extinguish their lamps for good due to financial nonviability.

Nevertheless, every state and language has at least one rural genre that remains hugely popular to this day: Bandi Pethir, the Kashmiri slapstick farce; the Naqqal and Swang female impersonators in Punjabi; the annual Ramlila cycle in Hindi, worshipping Rama; the enchantingly musical Nautanki, in Urdu (or Hindustani); the populist Jatra in Bengali and its namesake in Oriya; the classicist Ankiya Nat in Assamese; the lyrical Ras Lila of Manipuri, dedicated to Krishna; collective Kuchipudi dance-drama in Telugu; the acrobatic Terukkuttu in Tamil; Kathakali in Malayalam, now internationally renowned; the spectacular gods and demons of Yakshagana in Kannada; the raucous Tamasha in Marathi; and the satirical Bhavai in Gujarati. All of them, partly because of their open-air locations, but also because realism was only a recent British import, employ loud and declamatory acting, substantial song and dance, colorful costumes, and negligible sets and properties.

Rejecting what they considered their backward and superstitious folk inheritance, English-educated and sophisticated Indians began to write plays imitating Western precepts in the 19th century. Realistic, reformist, socialistic, and protest drama emerged, trends that developed down to present times, regardless of language. As a result of their head start in colonial cultural relations with the British, the cities of Calcutta (now Kolkata) and Bombay (Mumbai) show the most cosmopolitan theater history, followed by New Delhi, the capital of independent India.

As the preindependence professional companies declined, film having seduced their clientele away and full-time theater no longer commercially tenable, strictly amateur groups committed to "serious" theater took over. The groups' members work in daytime careers or freelance on-screen (though, ironically, television viewing has eaten into theatergoing) and in advertising spots but rehearse in the evenings after office hours. Typically, the director

Arya Babbar, second right, portrays an Indian Army soldier in the play *Operation Cloudburst*
directed by his mother Nadira Babbar, wife of Bollywood actor Raj Babbar in Gauhati, August 5,
2005. The play is based on the conflict in Assam. Indian theater has a long and vibrant tradition.
(AP Photo/Anupam Nath)

heads the troupe, frequently acting the lead, unlike in the West. Although the central and
state governments provide some subsidies nowadays, the limited budgets available mean that
less money gets earmarked for sets, lights, costumes, and sound. Groups usually do not own
auditoriums; they book halls in advance and, if successful, tour on invitation.

A zonal overview of urban theater can begin with Bengal, whose capital, Kolkata, has
around 200 active groups, the largest number in India. They owe intellectual allegiance to
two iconic directors of the 1960s: the poetical Sombhu Mitra, who established the pioneering
contribution of Rabindranath Tagore to modern Indian theater; and the political Utpal Dutt,
author of witty revolutionary drama. The playwright-director Badal Sircar inspired many
across India, as he rejected the proscenium to experiment with flexible studio space, then
street theater and performances in villages, innovating a socially conscious "Third Theater" that
discarded stage technology and ticket revenue—he passes around a cloth for voluntary donations afterward. Left-wing Brechtian influence remains strong, but many seniors (dramatists
Manoj Mitra and Mohit Chattopadhyaya, directors Rudraprasad Sengupta, Bibhash
Chakraborty, Ashok Mukhopadhyay, and Arun Mukherjee) question partisan ideology now,
a movement much more noticeable among younger directors like Suman Mukhopadhyay,
Kaushik Sen, and Bratya Basu. Several women directors focus on gender issues, while children's theater has a growing following.

To the east, Manipuri theater won attention in the 1980s for aesthetically synthesizing folk heritage, tribal ritual, and contemporary stagecraft under Heisnam Kanhailal, Lokendra Arambam, and Ratan Thiyam but is now caught up in the vortex of insurgent violence and debates on the demerits of both politicization and exoticization. Arun Sarma is the main dramatist of neighboring Assam, which boasts a robust traveling "mobile theater" business and increasing interest in neglected folklore, for example of the Bodo and Karbi ethnic groups. In Orissa, commercial "opera" companies still rule the roost, while the foremost author, Manoranjan Das, has moved from concerns of alienation and man's self-destructive nature, regarded as too remote by some critics, to folk roots.

In the southern region, political theater has many different colors. Tamil drama ranges from the Dravidian chauvinism of C. N. Annadurai and M. Karunanidhi to Cho Ramaswamy's unsparing sarcasm and Komal Swaminathan's Marxism. Indira Parthasarathy, the most respected current playwright, is partial to Tamil literary and philosophical history. Among groups, Koothu-p-pattarai formed a pioneering repertory offering traditional physical training, while newer ones promote Dalit (underprivileged castes) and female empowerment. Malayalam theater shifted from the explicitly Communist works of Thoppil Bhasi in the 1950s, to the anti-illusionistic and symbolist drama of C. N. Srikanthan Nair and G. Sankara Pillai, and then to K. N. Panikkar's self-directed plays based on Kerala's innumerable indigenous performing arts.

Telugu theater, in Andhra Pradesh, also saw a phase of realistic protest drama under actor-director Acharya Atreya, while the Praja Natya Mandali combine continues to present rousing leftist folk-based rural and street theater attacking exploitation. Kannada theater, in adjoining Karnataka, shot to fame nationally in the 1970s with the unabashed theatricality of director B. V. Karanth and the complex plays of actor Girish Karnad, folklorist Chandrasekhar Kambar and the angry absurdist P. Lankesh, ably succeeded now by the younger H. S. Shiva Prakash. The rural institute Ninasam and Bangalore's Rangayana run dynamic repertory companies.

Up north, Hindi provides the greatest variety of theater, its linguistic umbrella covering a family of related dialects in half a dozen states, as well as the sister language of Urdu or Hindustani. Habib Tanvir was its chief figurehead, a director, writer, actor, and composer of Brechtian folk parables, at home whether in refined Urdu or rustic Chhattisgarhi. Ebrahim Alkazi, architect of the National School of Drama (NSD) in Delhi, made that city the nucleus of Hindi theater today. But because of Hindi's status as national language, Hindi theater is almost as advanced in such metropolises as Mumbai and Kolkata. Mohan Rakesh trailblazed contemporary Hindi drama in the 1960s, on malfunctioning human communication, but nowadays wide experimentation in form, design, and locale takes place, notably by women directors and scriptwriters such as Amal Allana, Kirti Jain, and Anuradha Kapur, all associated with NSD and its repertory.

Farther north, Punjabi theater has earned attention through the directors Neelam Man Singh Chowdhry, who tours her sensuous productions with Naqqals internationally, and Gursharan Singh, who persevered in taking street theater for social change to peasants in the face of Sikh separatism. Punjabi drama stretches from Balwant Gargi's Marxist-cum-Freudian takes on passion to C. D. Sidhu's more native sources. Kashmiri theater had faded away in the 1980s under threats from militants, who burned down the venerable Tagore Hall in Srinagar, and artists fled. Fortunately, a revival of folk performances has occurred since 2001, and the efforts of director M. K. Raina to reintroduce theater to Srinagar have borne fruit.

Activities in the west center on Mumbai, which has theater in Marathi, Gujarati, Hindi, and English. The reigning trio of Marathi dramatists included the controversial Vijay Tendulkar, with varied political and psychological themes; Mahesh Elkunchwar, a specialist in charged domestic atmospheres; and Satish Alekar, fond of metatheater. Performance gained considerably from the perfectionism of Vijaya Mehta as director and the naturalism of Shreeram Lagoo as actor. A popular mainstream industry thrives, but so do the groups, with Awishkar in the vanguard. Recently, an influx of talent from interior Maharashtra has resulted in great variety, the younger generation too numerous to name here. The much-derided Gujarati commercial theater in Mumbai produced some interesting plays on Mahatma Gandhi, while Gujarat itself hosts most of the amateur groups in that language, among whom Garage Studio in Ahmadabad has made a name in developmental theater. Madhu Rye is respected as an important dramatist.

English theater in Mumbai has achieved a high standard of technical slickness since the 1980s, though its mixed-lingo "Hinglish" sex farces simply play to the gallery. However, Indians based all over the country have written excellent English drama, from Asif Currimbhoy's topical subjects and Girish Karnad's self-translations (initially staged by the Madras Players) to Mahesh Dattani's family relationships (his winning of the Sahitya Akademi Award in 1994 granted official acceptance to Indian-English drama) and Manjula Padmanabhan's provocative activism. Prime Time Theater, jointly operated from Mumbai and Delhi, has built a reputation for serious content in English theater.

A paucity of theater education affects India today—with only a dozen theater departments in its 250 universities and the NSD the single recognized conservatory (which unfortunately requires fluency in Hindi). A few university theaters, like the Thrissur School of Drama (Kerala), Andhra University and Aurangabad University (Maharashtra), have impacted their states positively, demonstrating the need for more such interventions for the future health of the art.

ANANDA LAL

See also Literature

Further Reading

Dharwadker, Aparna. *Theatres of Independence: Drama, Theory, and Urban Performance in India since 1947.* Iowa City: University of Iowa Press, 2005.

Hollander, Julia. *Indian Folk Theatres.* New York: Routledge, 2007.

Kambar, Chandrasekhar, ed. *Modern Indian Plays.* 2 vols. New Delhi: National School of Drama, 2000–2001.

Lal, Ananda, ed. *The Oxford Companion to Indian Theatre*. New Delhi: Oxford University Press, 2004.

Mukherjee, Tutun, ed. *Staging Resistance: Plays by Women in Translation*. New Delhi: Oxford University Press, 2005.

Varadpande, M. L. *Concise Dictionary of Indian Theatre*. New Delhi: Abhinav, 2007.

Yarrow, Ralph. *Indian Theatre: Theatre of Origin, Theatre of Freedom*. Richmond, UK: Curzon, 2001.

✦ THEOSOPHICAL SOCIETY

The Theosophical Society is an organization dedicated to the investigation of spiritual phenomena. It was founded in 1875 in New York by Madame Helena Petrovna Blavatsky (1831–1891) and Henry Steel Olcott (1832–1907). The term "theosophy" means divine wisdom, and its roots can be traced back to neo-Platonist and gnostic traditions in the thought of the fourth-century philosopher Porphyry. Theosophy represents a revival of the *philosophia perennis* ("perennial philosophy"), a belief that everything was derived from an eternal, unitary principle that was essentially spiritual. This principle was manifested most dramatically by individual enlightened beings.

Olcott was an American army colonel who fought in the American Civil War and worked on a commission investigating the assassination of President Abraham Lincoln (1809–1865; president 1861–1865). As a young man, Olcott became interested in spiritualism and investigated psychic phenomena and wrote about his findings. While working as a journalist, he met Blavatsky, a Russian émigré and spiritualist in a farmhouse located in Vermont where he was investigating some supernatural events. He became the first president of the Theosophical Society.

Arriving in America in 1873 after a divorce, Blavatsky published esoteric works: *Isis Unveiled* (1877), a work concerned with the occult, and *The Secret Doctrine* (1888), a work that presented a vision of the universe evolving from its original spiritual form to its present material status. The spiritual evolution included souls that were identical to the universal soul and were reborn depending on their karmic condition. This book rested on three major principles: existence of one absolute reality, the appearance and disappearance of cycles of the universe, and the identity of all souls with the single universal soul. Referring to her work as "Esoteric Buddhism," she also published *The Voice of Silence* (1889) that was alleged to have been originally written in an ancient language which has never been identified. She claimed to have studied with spiritual masters in Tibet and that she could communicate with these masters telepathically during her life.

Olcott and Blavatsky traveled together to India where they established a headquarters in 1879 on the outskirts of the city of Madras, and they also went to Sri Lanka and other Asian countries. While in Sri Lanka, Olcott immersed himself in Buddhism before becoming a promoter of the religion during the era of Western colonialism, and he defended the island's Buddhists from Christian missionaries. Because he was appalled by the Sinhalese ignorance of their own religion, Olcott's efforts on behalf of Buddhism culminated with his creation of a Buddhist catechism consisting of 14 principles, a work that went through many editions, printings, and languages and was used in many Buddhist countries for the purpose of instruction.

Even though Olcott was a strong advocate for Buddhism, the major principles of the society consisted of an attempt to synthesize Buddhist and Hindu notions in a quest for core beliefs that govern all religions. Olcott and Blavatsky accept the doctrine of karma and rebirth, the existence of astral bodies, and other types of spiritual ideas. They also became involved with the Ārya Samāj, a Hindu reform movement founded in 1875, although they never merged into a single entity. The society was also involved with the Indian National Congress, a political party founded in 1885 that played a major role in the drive for independence.

A couple of additional important figures were Annie Besant (1847–1933) and C. W. Leadbetter (1854–1934). Besant led the Adyar theosophists in India, adopted the cause of Indian nationalism, and played an instrumental role in establishing Central Hindu College in 1898, which later, in 1916, became Benaras Hindu University. Leadbetter, an Englishman born in 1854, became a convert to Buddhism and was considered a gifted clairvoyant, but he fell from grace when it was discovered that he was a pedophile. His forced resignation and later readmittance led to a schism in the organization. Leadbetter discovered Jiddu Krishnamurti (1895–1986), a young boy and son of an associate of the movement, and he was proclaimed to be the next World Teacher, which was equivalent to acclaiming him a messiah. This eventually led to the creation of the Order of the Star, an organization created to promote this new messiah. Krishnamurti later, in 1929, dissolved the Order of the Star and resigned from the Theosophical Society and began a long lecturing and writing career based from his adopted home in Ojai, California.

CARL OLSON

See also Hinduism; Religion

Further Reading
Campbell, Bruce F. *Ancient Wisdom Revisited: A History of the Theosophical Movement.* Berkeley: University of California Press, 1980.
The Theosophical Society International Headquarters, Adyar. Accessed April 28, 2011. http://www .ts-adyar.org.

✦ TIBETAN DIASPORA

Tibet, the "Shangrila" of Western imagination, caught the world's attention in 1959, the year etched as the turning point in the history of Tibet: it witnessed the military invasion of Tibet by the People's Republic of China (PRC) and the consequent flight of the 14th

Dalai Lama, Tenzin Gyatso (b. 1935), and approximately 80,000 Tibetans to northern India. According to the exiled Tibetan government's report, the worldwide distribution of the Tibetan diaspora approximates 145,150 people, of which 119,438 reside in India, Nepal, and Bhutan. A small percentage are scattered in Australia, the Far East, Great Britain, Denmark, Norway, and Sweden with the largest concentration being in Switzerland. In the last 14 years, with the support of the U.S. government, more and more Tibetans have been immigrating to the United States.

In India, Tibetans found a great deal of sympathy. Under the leadership of the Dalai Lama, the Tibetan exile administration was first established in the hill station of Mussoorie in Uttarakhand. In 1960, Dharamsala was chosen as the seat of office of the Central Tibetan Administration (CTA). The central task of the CTA was the rehabilitation and restoration of the dignity and freedom of Tibetan refugees. Notwithstanding the lack of legal standing, a legislative body known as the Assembly of Tibetan People's Deputies (ATPD) was established. In 2006, the ATPD was renamed the Tibetan Parliament-in-exile. Of the total 46 members, 43 are elected every five years as representatives of the three provinces of Tibet, the religious sects, and the Tibetans of Europe and North America. The remaining three are nominated by the Dalai Lama. In efforts to further democratize the process, the members of Parliament were empowered to elect members of the Kashag (the Council of Ministers), which is the executive branch of the administration. A constitution, known as the Charter of Tibetans in Exile, and the Tibetan Supreme Justice Commission were also instituted. In 2001, amendments to the charter provided for the direct election of the *kalon tripa* (the highest executive authority) by members of the exile community worldwide. The *kalon tripa* in turn nominates the other *kalons* (cabinet members). Samdhong Rinpoche ("Precious One") Lobsang Tenzin (b. 1939) became the first directly elected *kalon tripa* on September 5, 2001.

The portfolios under the Kashag are the Departments of Religion and Culture, Home, Education, Finance, Security, Information, International Relations, and Health. International offices of the government-in-exile have been set up in New Delhi, Kathmandu, London, Geneva, New York, Moscow, Brussels, Canberra, Tokyo, Pretoria, and Taipei.

From its inception the government-in-exile, with the support of the Indian government, has given the greatest importance to the education of Tibetan refugee children. The Department of Education currently oversees the education of approximately 28,000 students in 83 Tibetan schools in India, Nepal, and Bhutan. The Tibetan Children's Village in Dharamsala and the Tibetan Homes Foundation in Mussoorie are two autonomous bodies under the Department of Education that, with financial aid from foreign organizations, have developed into recognized and reputable schools playing a vital role in the education of Tibetan children.

In the initial years of exile, everything in India was alien for the Tibetan refugees: the people, air, water, heat of the plains, mosquitoes, food, and, of course, the language. Under the aegis of the government of India, the refugees were settled in remote, uninhabited lands. Many were employed in the construction of roads. Many of them died due to the severe heat and hardship. But they persevered. Through trials and tribulations, they learned not only to live but to adapt successfully to their new environment. However, despite their success, the Tibetan refugees in India are essentially stateless people who hold Indian registration certificates.

Critical to the understanding of the Tibetan diaspora is the influence of China on Tibet. To comprehend the nature of the Tibetan diaspora it is important to scrutinize the world of Tibetan society and civilization inside Tibet today. Because Chinese rule continues to transform Tibet in profound ways, Tibetan life, directly and indirectly, influences Tibetans living in India and elsewhere.

At the center of Tibet and Tibetans stands the Dalai Lama. Revered as the "Boddhisattva of Compassion" and the reincarnation of the 13th Dalai Lama, the current 14th Dalai Lama's legitimacy comes from the faith of his people. His unique position allows him to be the religious and temporal authority of his people. He engenders awe and devotion. In exile he also inspires national will and a sense of mission in his people.

Although the Tibetan diaspora is scattered all over the world, the engine of change in Tibetan identity, outside of Tibet, is driven by the Tibetan community living in India. Occupation and exile created a new consciousness. It created opportunities for Tibetans to recognize their true identity. The Dalai Lama's efforts in 1988 to draw international attention to the Tibetan crisis by addressing the European Parliament in Strasbourg, and his Five-Point Peace Plan for Tibet, was rejected by the PRC, which called his efforts a "disguised form of independence." Since then the Dalai Lama has invalidated the Strasbourg Proposal as the basis for finding a peaceful resolution to the Tibetan crisis. Since 1992, he has constantly reiterated his position of "no independence" in return for "genuine autonomy." But, despite this conciliatory position and despite giving up the quest for independence, China's unwillingness to engage in any direct talk with the Dalai Lama has only served to fuel Tibetan frustrations inside Tibet and in the diaspora. From protest figures fighting against an "unjust" rule, Tibetans have more recently been elevated to the role of human rights victims, endowed with political agency, and tenaciously challenging the PRC.

YOSAY WANGDI

See also Dalai Lama, 14th

Further Reading
Central Tibetan Administration. Accessed April 28, 2011. http://tibet.net.
Saklani, Girija. *The Uprooted Tibetans in India: A Sociological Study of Continuity and Change.* New Delhi: Cosmo, 1987.
Shakabpa, W. D. *Tibet: A Political History.* New Haven, CT: Yale University Press, 1967.
Wangdi, Yosay. "Displaced People, Adjusting to New Cultural Vocabulary: Tibetan Immigrants in North America." In *Emerging Voices: The Experiences of the Underrepresented Asian Americans,* edited by Huping Ling, 71–89. New Brunswick, NJ: Rutgers University Press, 2008.
Wangdi, Yosay. "Tibetan Identity: Transformations within the Diaspora." *Global Studies Journal* 1(1) (2008): 91–100.

✦ TIMES OF INDIA, THE

The *Times of India* is the largest circulating English-language daily newspaper in India. It retains the name of its British publisher and printer, Bennett, Coleman & Co., on its masthead, even though the company passed into Indian hands in 1946. It was first owned by the industrialist Ramkrishna Dalmia (1893–1978) and subsequently by the Sahu Jain industrial family, with the current chairman, publisher, and director all members of the Jain family. In 2008, the newspaper claimed a circulation of 3.1 million, making it also the world's largest-selling newspaper in English and placing it in the top 10 largest-selling newspapers in any language in the world. According to the Indian Readership Survey (2008), it has a readership of 13.3 million.

The *Times of India* began life as a biweekly, the *Bombay Times and Journal of Commerce*, in Bombay (Mumbai) in 1838 and was renamed to its present title in 1861. It built up a steady circulation in Britain and Europe as well as in the Indian subcontinent, becoming a daily in 1850. It was an Anglo-Indian newspaper, British owned and edited, and its last British editor, Ivor S. Jehu (1908–1960), resigned only in 1950. It soon developed a reputation as the premier national newspaper in India and was praised

A reader of *The Times of India* outside his home in Hyderabad, Andhra Pradesh, October 2010. *The Times of India*, founded in Mumbai in 1838 as a semi-weekly newspaper, is now, with a daily circulation of over three million, the world's largest English-language newspaper across all formats (broadsheet, tabloid, compact, Berliner and online). It is part of the world's biggest, most thriving, and most dynamic newspaper industry. (Deshakalyan Chowdhury/AFP/Getty Images)

as such by successive British colonial governments. Though conservatively run, it reserved its journalistic right to be critical of official policies and successfully managed to retain its editorial independence. It developed overseas editions and its editors covered the subcontinent on behalf of the *Times* of London. The heyday of the paper began when T. J. Bennett (1852–1925) became sole proprietor in 1894 and along with a master printer, F. M. Coleman, whom he brought from England, he set the paper on the road to commercial and journalistic success. He expanded the premises, introduced modern technology, and imported experienced British journalists to write for the paper. Though he returned to England in the early 20th century and became a Conservative member of Parliament where he represented the Sevenoaks Division of Kent from 1918 until 1923, he continued to write for the paper and was alive to the political and economic problems of India and supported Indian demands for eventual self-government. The *Times of India* was among the first British newspapers to employ Indian subeditors on its staff starting in the early 1920s.

The paper has tried to retain some of the same spirit of independence and today may be said to uphold a centrist political stance. It was a profitable concern under British rule and though after independence it continued to be successful, it faced increasing competition from other newspapers, newsmagazines, and different news media. In response, from the 1990s, an aggressive management strategy was introduced that transformed the look of the newspaper as well as its content and coverage, with it now being marketed as a mass-distributed consumer product. It also initiated newspaper price wars with an ever-decreasing cover price. Overall, such measures have had their intended effect on depressing competition and raising sales, making the *Times of India* arguably the most profitable newspaper in the country. However, there is concern in some quarters at the potential impact of this commercialization on its editorial and journalistic quality. The newspaper is now printed from more than 20 different centers, including Ahmedabad, Bhopal, Chandigarh, Chennai, Delhi, Goa, Hyderabad, Kanpur, Kolkata, Lucknow, Patna, Pune, Ranchi, Mumbai, and Nagpur. In keeping with the trend of daily journalism in India, the newspaper comes with several supplements on specific days of the week; for instance, the *Times Wellness* is issued on Saturdays and *Times Life* on Sundays. In addition, each of the city editions has city specific supplements, for example, there is the *Bombay Times*, *Delhi Times*, *Kanpur Times*, and *Chennai Times*. The newspaper itself is part of a vast media empire owned by the Times Group, which also includes in its stable the *Economic Times* and the *Mumbai Mirror*, as well as the *Navabharat Times* and the *Maharashtra Times*, and daily newspapers in Hindi and Marathi.

CHANDRIKA KAUL

See also Media and Telecommunications

Further Reading

Balakrishnan, K. *The Times of India: 150 Years On.* New Delhi: Times of India, 1988.

Kaul, Chandrika. "Bennett, T. J."; "Montagu, Edwin S."; "Ritchie, Sir Richmond". In *New Dictionary of National Biography.* Oxford: Oxford University Press, 2004.

Kaul, Chandrika. *Reporting the Raj: The British Press and India, c. 1880–1922.* Manchester, UK: Manchester University Press, 2003.

Natarajan, S. *A History of the Press in India.* Bombay: Asia Publishing House, 1962.

✦ TOURISM

Since the end of the Cold War and with the country's increasing focus on development and integration into the global economy, India has come to understand that tourism has the potential to contribute enormously to economic growth and the accumulation of foreign exchange. Traditionally, India has been a destination for culture and heritage; the iconic Taj Mahal represents one of the Seven Wonders of the World. The country's tourism landscape is adorned with palaces, temples, the Himalayan mountain trails, and much, much more in a land of more than 1.1 billion people of different ethnic backgrounds and home to more than 415 different languages.

The government agency concerned with the policy, regulation, and development of tourism is the Ministry of Tourism headed by a union minister. Each state, however, is given considerable autonomy in marketing its heritage either independently or jointly with the Ministry of Tourism. Other key organizations forming national policies and participating privately are the India Tourism Development Corporation Limited, the Indian Institute of Tourism and Travel Management, the Indian Institute of Skiing and Mountaineering, the National Council for Hotel Management and Catering Technology, and the National Institute of Water Sports.

In 2002, the National Tourism Policy was introduced with the primary aim for tourism to be an engine for economic growth and to act as a multiplier effect and deliver employment opportunities and alleviate poverty. One of the benefits of promoting India as a tourist destination is the rapid development of infrastructure projects such as airports, roads, and first-class hotel accommodations. In the five-year plan from 2007 to 2012, India is building more than 4,000 miles of national highways every year with a budget of $78.54 billion and 10 new airports, with an upgrade of 39 existing ports at the cost of $7.7 billion. This infrastructure construction and expansion bodes well for tourism destinations that are rapidly increasing the number of visitors.

The Indian hospitality industry is also greatly improving facilities with both midrange and high-end accommodations springing up in Kolkata, New Delhi, Mumbai, Bangalore, and Chennai. International hotel brands such as the Sheraton, Marriott, Hilton, and Hyatt, to name just a few, have increasingly established themselves in major Indian cities as they see vast potential in the Indian tourism industry. Three major domestic chains, the Taj Hotels, the Oberoi Hotels, and the Leela Hotels, have also expanded their presence over the years within India. The first two have also established a number of fine hotels overseas. People with land and property and in a position to exploit the opportunities in the tourism business have also invested heavily to transform their palaces, farms, and buildings into accommodations and visitor sites. A famous example of this is the renowned former palace, Taj Lake Palace Udaipur, managed by the Taj Hotels group.

Despite being at a nascent stage, Indian medical tourism is expected to grow dramatically, with an expected 1.2 million visitors, and contribute $2.4 billion gross domestic product (GDP) by 2012. The advantages India possesses in this area include low-cost labor and the availability of a wide range of medical treatments, including options to be treated by traditional medical practitioners. One other development in the tourism industry is the development of facilities and the availability of specialists in yoga and ayurvedic medicine. They are promoted in many cities as well as in suburban settings. One of the states at the forefront of ayurvedic spa treatment and tourism promotion is the state of Kerala, which has been on an aggressive drive to promote a range of experiences from ayurveda and Kathakali dance to stays at beach and backwater resorts along one of its famous beaches, canals, lakes, lagoons, or estuaries.

In the promotion of tourism, India's film industry, known as Bollywood, is another key player influencing both outward and inbound markets. More and more films are

Tourists watch domesticated temple elephants that will be used in a procession during the Trichur Pooram Festival in Trichur, about 47 miles from Cochin, Kerala. International visitors and India's growing middle class have created a vast and expanding tourist industry. (AP Photo)

shot with overseas settings and this has in some ways given a stimulus for Indians to explore the world. Indeed, many countries, particularly Singapore, the United States, and European countries have benefited from such productions. Bollywood films are also widely watched in Singapore, Malaysia, Indonesia, and Pakistan (and also in the diasporic market). Such cultural exports also anchor the admiration for all things Indian both in culture and destination. One recent movie, *Slumdog Millionaire*, has increased India's standing as a destination for international visitors, and there is growing evidence of a new type of tourism: slum tourism.

The 2010 promotion of India as a tourist destination was done with an overarching theme titled "Incredible India." This theme promoted the rich and diverse attractions available in the country. In 2008, the top five countries sending tourists to India, contributing almost 50 percent of the tourists, were the United States, Great Britain, Bangladesh, Sri Lanka, and Canada. Popular destinations for visitors are the capital city New Delhi and the states of Maharashtra, Tamil Nadu, Uttar Pradesh, and Rajasthan. The number of tourists has steadily increased over the decades to about 4.3 million travelers. In 2008, the tourism industry brought in $100 billion, and that figure is expected to more than double to $275 billion by 2018.

KAILASAM THIRUMARAN

See also Medical Tourism

Further Reading
Incredible India. Accessed April 28, 2011. http://www.incredibleindia.org.
Ministry of Tourism. Accessed April 28, 2011. http://www.tourisminindia.com.
Nicholson, Louise. *India*. Washington, DC: National Geographic, 2007.

Tourism, Medical. *See* Medical Tourism

Tribes, Scheduled. *See* Scheduled Tribes

Tripura. *See* Northeastern States

U

Union Territories. *See* Territories

✦ UNITED NATIONS, RELATIONS WITH

As a founder member of the United Nations (UN), India has been a firm supporter of the Purposes and Principles of the United Nations. It has made significant contributions to the furtherance and implementation of the aims of the organization and to the evolution and functioning of its various specialized programs. It stood at the forefront during the UN's tumultuous years of struggle against colonialism and apartheid, its struggle toward global disarmament and ending the arms race, and toward the creation of a more equitable international economic order. At the very first session of the UN, India raised its voice against colonialism and apartheid, two issues that have been among the most significant of the UN's successes in the last half century. India exulted in the UN's triumph and saw in the UN's victory a vindication of the policy relentlessly pursued by it from its initial days at the world forum. On October 25, 1946, the head of the Indian delegation to the UN, Vijayalakshmi Pandit (1900–1990), younger sister of the Indian prime minister Jawaharlal Nehru (1889–1964; prime minister 1947–1964) made her maiden speech to the UN in which she pledged the support of the government and people of India of its firm commitment to the principles of peace and justice as enshrined in the UN Charter.

India, in fact, reflecting the interests of Nehru in internationalism, has been a founder member of most international organizations, especially of the UN and its specialized agencies. Consequently, support to and strengthening of the world organization is an important element of India's foreign policy. The principal purpose of India's foreign policy vis-à-vis the UN is to pursue three closely related goals: a significant role in the shaping of international relations in the 21st century, a movement toward a nonviolent and humane international system, and the promotion of conditions for a sustainable and relatively equitable pattern of international development.

Roughly four closely interlinked phases are identifiable in India's association with the UN since World War II. The first phase covers the years up to the late 1940s and includes the last days of the British Raj when India was a participant in the UN Conference on International Organization held in San Francisco between April 25, 1945 and June 26, 1945. The conference resulted in the creation of the United Nations Charter and was readied for signature on the last day of the conference. As a consequence, India was one of the original members of the UN. The second phase of the relationship between India and the UN concerned crisis situations from Korea, such as during and after the Korean War (1950–1953), and the civil war in the Congo when 39 Indians were killed in the peacekeeping and humanitarian mission between 1961 and 1964, and others have been lost since. As part of the third phase and one of India's early concerns in the United Nations was that all states should be represented in the organizations of the UN so that the UN would truly represent a diversity of opinion and serve as a viable instrument for the peaceful settlement of international disputes. In the fourth phase, India plays a consistent and energetic role in the arenas of arms control and disarmament.

India has taken active part in UN peacekeeping operations (PKO) on four continents. Its most significant contribution has been to maintain peace and stability in Africa and Asia. It has demonstrated its capacity to commit large numbers of troops over prolonged periods of time under very challenging circumstances, and India is the second-largest contributor of troops to the UN. India provided a paramedical unit to facilitate the withdrawal of the sick and the wounded in Korea during 1950–1953 and after the cease-fire of 1953, India was appointed the chairman of the Neutral Nations Repatriation Commission. One brigade of the Indian Army participated in the operation in Korea that was authorized by the UN General Assembly through the Uniting for Peace resolution, Resolution 377 (V) of November 3, 1950, by providing guards for the prisoners of war of all the belligerent countries.

India also contributed to maintenance and promotion of peace in the Middle East. The United Nations Emergency Force (UNEF) was created in 1956 following cessation of hostilities between Egypt and Israel. India provided an infantry battalion, which accounted for the bulk of the UN force. From 1956 to 1967, more than 12,000 Indian troops took part in UNEF. In the UN operation in Namibia in 1967, Indian military observers were responsible for the smooth withdrawal of foreign troops, the peaceful holding of general elections in November 1989, and the subsequent handing over of authority to the local government when Namibia became independent on March 21, 1990. When the UN took steps to restore peace after the civil war and to conduct elections in Mozambique in its United Nations Operation in Mozambique (ONUMOZ) between December 1992 and

December 1994, India provided a large contingent of staff officers, military observers, and an independent headquarters company, as well as engineers and a logistics company. One of the biggest UN peacekeeping operations was in war-ravaged Cambodia. In February 1992 the UN Security Council authorized the establishment of an operation, the United Nations Transitional Authority in Cambodia (UNTAC), which would, inter alia, supervise the cease-fire between Cambodia and Vietnam and the withdrawal of foreign troops, control and supervise the administrative structure of the country, and organize and conduct free and fair elections. During the UNTAC operation India provided an infantry battalion, military observers, and a field ambulance unit. India has also regularly sent military observers to various other UN operations including operations in El Salvador in 1991 and in Liberia in 1994. India provided a contingent comprising one infantry battalion and support elements to the UN assistance mission in Rwanda after the UN approved the UN assistance mission to Rwanda on October 5, 1993. It helped to ensure security for refugees and to create conditions for free and fair elections. Also in Africa, the Indian Army has been participating in the successive phases of the UN mission in Angola since 1989. The Indian contingent comprised one infantry battalion group, one engineering unit, staff officers, and military observers. In view of its experience in de-mining, India has, at the urging of the United Nations, made significant contributions to clearing mines in various missions in Rwanda, Mozambique, Somalia, Angola, and Cambodia.

India has been a strong supporter of the UN's Millennium Development Goals (MDGs), which were devised in September 2000 at the UN Millennium Summit held at the UN Headquarters in New York. The MDGs are eight goals targeted to be achieved by 2015 in response to the world's basic development challenges. The MDGs were adopted by 189 nations and signed by 147 heads of state and governments. The eight MDGs break down into 21 quantifiable targets that are measured by 60 indicators.

Goal 1: Eradicate extreme poverty and hunger
Goal 2: Achieve universal primary education
Goal 3: Promote gender equality and empower women
Goal 4: Reduce child mortality
Goal 5: Improve maternal health
Goal 6: Combat HIV/AIDS, malaria, and other diseases
Goal 7: Ensure environmental sustainability
Goal 8: Develop a Global Partnership for Development

The MDGs synthesize, in a single package, many of the most important commitments made separately at various international conferences and summits of the 1990s; recognize explicitly the interdependence between inclusive growth, poverty reduction, and sustainable development; acknowledge that development rests on the solid foundations of democratic governance, the rule of law, respect for human rights, and maintenance of peace and security; are based on time-bound and measurable targets accompanied by specific indicators for monitoring progress; and bring together, in the eighth goal, the responsibilities of developing countries with those of developed countries, founded on a global partnership endorsed at the International Conference on Financing for Development in Monterrey, Mexico, in March 2002 and again at the Johannesburg World Summit on Sustainable Development in August 2002.

In addition to its other UN activities, India is one of the largest contributors to the core resources of the United Nations Fund for Population Activities (UNFPA) and the United Nations Children's Emergency Fund (UNICEF). India is also a major contributor to the core resources of the World Food Program and its contribution to these funds is higher than that of many of the 30 countries belonging to the Organization for Economic Co-operation and Development, which was founded in 1961.

India has contributed $100,000 to the UNCTAD Trust Fund for the least developed countries. It has also been contributing $50,000 per annum to the ITC Global Trust Fund since its inception in 1996. It also makes substantial voluntary contributions to a number of other UN organizations such as UNEP, Habitat, the UN Drug Control Program, UNRWA, UNIFEM, and UN Volunteers.

India took an active part in the drafting of the Universal Declaration on Human Rights of 1948 when Dr. Hansa Mehta (1897–1995), a Gandhian political activist and social worker who led the Indian delegation, made important contributions, especially in highlighting the need for reflecting gender equality. India is fully committed to the rights proclaimed in the declaration and is a signatory to the six core human rights covenants and also the two Optional Protocols of May 2000 to the Convention of the Rights of the Child signed in New York in 1989.

India has been advocating a holistic and integrated approach that gives equal emphasis to all human rights—based on their interdependence, interrelatedness, indivisibility, and universality—and reinforces the interrelationship between democracy, development, human rights, and international cooperation for development.

India has played an active role as member of the Commission on Human Rights (CHR) since its creation in 1947. It was elected in 2006 to be a member of the newly established Human Rights Council (HRC), which replaced the CHR, by securing the highest number of votes among the contested seats. India was reelected in 2007 again by securing the highest number of votes. India attaches great importance to the HRC and is committed to making the council a strong, effective, and efficient body capable of promoting and protecting human rights and fundamental freedoms for all.

India became the seventh country to ratify the UN Convention on the Rights of Persons with Disabilities after it had participated actively in the deliberations of the ad hoc committee of the UN General Assembly on finalization of the convention in 2009. The enactment in India of the Persons with Disabilities Act (Equal Opportunities, Protection of Rights and Full Participation) in 1995 marked a significant step toward providing equal opportunities for people with disabilities and its support of the UN Convention on the Rights of Persons with Disabilities was an extension of its policy.

India, however, feels disrespected and underappreciated in the UN as it believes it should be a permanent member of the UN Security Council. The rationale behind India's claim for permanent membership of the expanded Security Council is threefold. First, India contributes substantially to the total UN budget and it has made tangible contribution to UN PKOs. Apart from its financial contribution, India has dispatched military personnel to various trouble spots around the globe including the Congo, Korea, Angola, and Bosnia.

Second, when the UN was created in 1945 there were only 51 member states, whereas that number has now quadrupled to 191 states. In order for proper governance and transparent democratic procedures, India feels there should be a greater representational balance. In 1945, 1 member in the Security Council represented about 5 countries, whereas in 2005, 1 member of the Security Council represents 13 countries. In addition, India, along with Japan and Germany, has emerged as one of the world's leading economic powers. Similarly, developing countries such as India and Brazil have carved a niche for themselves by being upper-tier economies achieved through their immense reservoir of manpower and skilled labor.

Third, the end of the Cold War has paved the way for new issues such as international terrorism and the spread of weapons of mass destruction to come to the fore. Other causes for concern emanate from nonmilitary threats such as HIV/AIDS, poverty, and environment degradation. The changed geopolitical circumstances demand concerted action in a reformed decision-making body in the form of a widely represented Security Council. India believes an expanded permanent membership would generate vigorous debate ultimately leading to solutions in the spirit of consensus building and ensure what it believes is India's rightful place in the world's most powerful body.

Overall, India has played a very constructive role in the shaping and the evolution of the UN from its inception in 1945 to the present time. It is expected that India will continue to be a significant contributor to UN activities, and India's multifaceted role, as reflected in the UN mission and its objectives, will continue at a high level. In January 2011, for example, India was elected to a two-year term on the Security Council.

MOHAMMED BADRUL ALAM

See also Foreign Policy

Further Reading

Bandyopadhyaya, Jayantanuja. *The Making of India's Foreign Policy: Determinants, Institutions, Processes, and Personalities.* Bombay: Allied Publications, 1980.

Dutt, V. P. *India's Foreign Policy in a Changing World.* New Delhi: Vikas, 1999.

Kumar, Satish, ed. *The United Nations at 50: An Indian View.* Delhi: UBS Publishers, 1995.

Mody, Nawaz B., and B. N. Mehrish, eds. *India's Role in the United Nations.* Bombay: Allied Publishers, 1995.

Patnaik, Saroj K., Jaya Krushna Baral, and Jagdish Sharma. *United Nations, India and the New World Order.* New Delhi: Mittal, 2004.

Rajan, M. S. *India and International Affairs: A Collection of Essays.* New Delhi: Books, 1999.

✦ UNITED STATES, RELATIONS WITH

The United States, the oldest democracy in the world, and India, the largest democracy in the world with 600 million voters, would be expected to have at least friendly relations or be natural allies. However, that was not the case until recently. Relations between India and the United States were ambiguous, fragile, lukewarm, and mutually suspicious during the Cold War. However, the two nations have fostered close diplomatic, economic, and strategic security ties after the Cold War ended in 1991 and especially since September 11, 2001. The image of India as a "basket case" country a generation ago has changed to that of a burgeoning economic giant and a knowledge industry superpower in the making. India is forecasted to emerge among the top five global economies by 2030 and is expected to become one of the most important strategic partners of the United States.

The relations between India and the United States between the 1950s and 1980s were either lukewarm or tense due to Cold War politics. The United States followed the policy of containment—that is, to contain the spread of Communism and the perceived Soviet threat by military, diplomatic, and economic means, especially encircling the Soviet Union with a ring of friendly nations in military alliances such as the North Atlantic Treaty Organization (NATO), the Southeast Asia Treaty Organization (SEATO), and the Central Treaty Organization (CENTO). It perceived India's independent foreign policy of nonalignment— of reserving the right to side with either bloc in an international crisis based on the merits of each case—as tantamount to alignment with the Soviet Union, especially after 1971, and denounced such policy as "immoral" in an ideologically divided world. Pakistan, which considered India as its number one enemy and a threat to its very existence, joined the American-sponsored alliance system in 1954 and became a major factor in Indo-U.S. relations. Although the United States supported India in the 1962 Sino-Indian War and provided generous food aid in 1966, the relations between the two were tense following the 1965 Indo-Pakistan War, in which Pakistan used American arms. The relationship reached an all-time low during and after the Bangladesh crisis of 1971 in which President Richard Nixon (1913–1994; president 1969–1974) adopted the policy of "tilt" toward Pakistan. President Jimmy Carter (b. 1924; president 1977–1981), who took a personal interest in India, visited New Delhi in January 1978, but India's refusal to sign the Non-Proliferation Treaty prevented any significant improvement in the relations between two nations. Bilateral relations became tense again in the early 1980s when America resumed military aid to Pakistan in support of anti-Soviet mujahideens who were fighting from Pakistani territory against the 1979 Soviet invasion and occupation of Afghanistan.

India's effort to develop its nuclear capability was a major source of tension in its relations with the United States for decades after India conducted its first "peaceful nuclear explosion" in May 1974. The United States responded by enacting legislations to thwart India and Pakistan from acquiring nuclear weapons. India resented the U.S. nonproliferation policy and labeled it as "nuclear apartheid." When India conducted five nuclear tests at Pokharan in May 1998, which were followed by Pakistani nuclear tests, the United States imposed economic sanctions on both nations. However, the thaw in Indo-U.S. relations came about a year later when President Bill Clinton (b. 1946; president 1993–2001) demonstrated America's good faith to India by taking a principled stand on the Kargil War between India and Pakistan in 1999. The Pakistani prime minister Nawaz Sharif (b. 1949; prime minister May–July 1993, 1997–1999) had sought America's help in resolving the conflict and met with Clinton in July 1999. In that meeting Clinton exerted pressure on Nawaz and persuaded him to commit to withdraw all Pakistani forces to their side of the line of control, a politically unpopular decision in Pakistan. Clinton also kept India informed about his stand on this conflict. The United States thereby won India's trust, and it ushered in a new era of cooperation and close relations between the two nations. In March 2000 President Clinton visited India and launched a strategic partnership between the United States and India that culminated in the 2008 nuclear agreement under President George W. Bush (b. 1946; president 2001–2009).

The bilateral civilian nuclear agreement, proposed by President Bush in 2005 and ratified by the Senate in 2008 with the support of Democrats, deepened the trust and cooperation between the two governments. The restriction on nuclear commerce, imposed on India in the 1970s, was thus lifted even though India is not a party to the Non-Proliferation Treaty; India is the only nuclear weapons state granted such exception as a result of the intense lobbying by the Bush administration. The Bush administration sought to help India emerge as a great Asian power to counterbalance the growing power and influence of China. The unprecedented level of cooperation between Washington and New Delhi in many areas, including counterterrorism, defense, and intelligence, continued under the Barak Obama (b. 1961; president 2009–) administration, though there were fears on the part of India that the new administration would downgrade U.S. policy toward India. While there are areas of disagreement between India and the United States such as the Obama administration's anti-outsourcing and limiting of H-1B visas stands, the Obama administration approved the largest military weapons' sale worth $2.1 billion to India—the sale of eight P-8 Poseidons, the most sophisticated antisubmarine aircraft—and, in clear departure from its past policies, India's military has conducted exercises with every branch of the U.S. armed services. President Obama emphasized the enduring bond and continued cooperation between the United States and India, rooted in strong democratic values, at the first state dinner of his presidency at which he honored India's prime minister Manmohan Singh (b. 1932; prime minister 2004–) in November 2009. This was followed by Obama's visit to India in November 2010.

India is an emerging economic power. Propelled by its 1991 liberalization policies, the economy has grown at a fast rate in the first decade of the 21st century (9 percent in 2008);

it is predicted to be among the leading economies of the world by 2020 and the fourth-largest economy by 2050. The United States is India's number one trading partner; their bilateral trade increased almost tenfold between 1988 and 2008, from $4.5 billion to more than $43 billion. With the rapid growth of the Indian middle class, estimated to rise to 650 million in 2025 from 200 million, U.S. companies view India as a lucrative market; the United States has emerged as India's largest investment partner ($9 billion in direct investment). The U.S.-India economic, diplomatic, and military relations are, therefore, likely to deepen based on overlapping interests, shared values, and improved political, economic, and trade relations.

SUNIL K. SAHU

See also Foreign Policy

Further Reading

Balachandran, Gopal. "Nuclear Realpolitik: The Prospects for Indo-US Relations." *Australian Journal of Asian Affairs* 61 (2007): 544–553.

Bertsch, Gary, Seema Gahlaut, and Anupam Srivastava, eds. *Engaging India: US Strategic Relations with the World's Largest Democracy*. New York: Routledge, 1999.

Feigenbaum, Evan A. "India's Rise, America's Interest: The Fate of the U.S.-India Partnership." *Foreign Affairs* 89 (2010): 76–91.

Kapur, S. Paul, and Sumit Ganguly. "The Transformation of U.S.-India Relations." *Asian Survey* 47 (2007): 642–656.

Lak, Daniel. *India Express: The Future of the New Superpower*. New York: Palgrave Macmillan, 2008.

Sridharan, Kripa. "Explaining the Phenomenon of Change in Indian Foreign Policy under the National Democratic Alliance Government." *Contemporary South Asia* 15 (2006): 75–91.

Talbott, Strobe. *Engaging India: Diplomacy, Democracy, and the Bomb*. New Delhi: Penguin, 2004.

U.S.-Indo Nuclear Deal. *See* Indo-U.S. Nuclear Deal

✦ UTTARAKHAND

Ancient Hindu scriptures refer to the region of Uttarakhand as *Dev Bhoomi* or the "Abode of Gods." The people of Uttarakhand pride themselves on the sanctity of their homeland's high mountains and rivers where many important Hindu pilgrimages take place. On November 9, 2000, the government of India made the region the 27th state in the union but named it Uttaranchal, much to the dismay of the local population. Finally, seven years later in 2007, the people's wishes were granted and Uttaranchal became Uttarakhand. In many ways this seven-year struggle for a place name reflects the various problems faced by the state today.

Uttarakhand is a Sanskrit word meaning the "northern section" but refers specifically to the mountainous regions of Garhwal and Kumaon that form two divisions of the state of Uttarakhand. It is located in northwestern India with Tibet (China) and Nepal to the north and east, respectively, the Indian states of Himachal Pradesh and Haryana to the west, and Uttar Pradesh to south. Deciduous and coniferous forests and alpine meadows cover the mountains that make up approximately 93 percent of the 31,767 square miles of state territory fringed by a narrow belt of fertile lowlands. Nanda Devi, Badrinath, Kamet, and Trishul are among the highest peaks in the state, and nestled among these are glaciers such as Gangotri and Yamnotri—sources of the Ganges and Yamuna rivers—that provide sustenance to millions of people living in the north Indian plains. For hundreds of years, these mountains and glaciers have attracted pilgrims from all over India. Haridwar, a city located on the banks of the Ganges where it descends into the plains, is one of four places in India that hosts the three-month-long Kumbh Mela festival celebrated every 12 years by millions of people.

The indigenous people of Uttarakhand call themselves Paharis (hill people) and believe they are culturally distinct from the Maidanis (people of the plains). The folklore of Uttarakhand binds Paharis of Garhwal and Kumaon together, even though they speak different languages and share mutual animosity in their struggle to carve out their own state from India's most populous state, Uttar Pradesh, to which they were arbitrarily assigned after the country's independence from Britain in August 1947. Garhwal and Kumaon had comprised 16 percent of the land area of Uttar Pradesh but accounted for less than 5 percent of its population. For the Paharis the state capital of Uttar Pradesh, Lucknow, seemed disconnected not only because of its inaccessibility but also because the government could not empathize with the needs of the hill people since representatives were mostly from the plains. This disconnect led to their economic underdevelopment. Neglect by Uttar Pradesh was evident in the lack of transportation infrastructure, electricity, drinking water, and basic health services, as well as employment opportunities in the hills compared to the plains. Forest and water resources were used mainly to benefit people living in the plains.

The Mandal Commission's recommendations in 1994 whereby the government of India declared a 27 percent reservation (affirmative action) for other backward castes triggered a populist movement toward statehood. Although desire for a separate hill state first surfaced in the 1920s and 1930s, it was not until the 1990s that a group of people, mostly students and government workers of the region, actively demanded a separate state. Upper-caste people of the hills, which make up 95 percent of the population, feared they would lose what little they had in terms of government jobs and opportunities for higher education because backward castes from the plains of Uttar Pradesh would gain advantage in these institutions in the hills where backward castes were only 5 percent of the population. Nevertheless, the separatist movement always claimed economic backwardness in the hills and preservation of the environment as being the main reasons behind their demand for statehood.

The latter justification for demanding statehood was not just spin to put the movement into a more noble light. Uttarakhand is known around the world as the place that gave rise to the famous Chipko Movement of the 1970s. It was a spontaneous, nonviolent, grassroots action led by rural women who literally hugged trees to protect them from being cut down by logging companies. Another important environmental action was the Anti-Tehri Dam

Movement led by the octogenarian Sunderlal Bahuguna (b. 1927) that aimed to halt the construction in the Himalayas of one of the largest hydroelectric projects in the world. Despite decades of protest by the people of Tehri, the dam was completed in 2003 at a cost of $1.2 billion. It is estimated that more than 40,000 people lost their homes to the reservoir. Many of those displaced by the dam have yet to be resettled by the state government. This massive investment has robbed the rural population in Tehri of drinking water and electricity that is diverted during many months of the year to Uttar Pradesh and Delhi.

With the formation of a new state comes a new capital. Ironically, the current "interim" capital of Uttarakhand, Dehradun, which is the most congested and polluted city in the region, is far away from the hills and controlled again by people from the plains. The location of the capital in Dehradun also displeases the people of Kumaon because it is located in Garhwal. Plans for a new capital in a remote part of the state on the border of Garhwal and Kumaon have been discussed for the last 10 years; a foundation stone was even placed with much pomp and circumstance by the leaders of the separatist movement, but to no avail.

Ten years after statehood, not much has changed for the hill people of Uttarakhand. The livelihood of the Paharis still depends on raising livestock, bartering homemade crafts, and the meager variety of crops that grow in the temperate climate and poor soil. Even though 65 percent of the state's population is still involved in agriculture, it accounts for less than a quarter of its gross domestic product (GDP). Jobs for the rural educated youth are still scarce in the hills even though literacy rates in the state are well above the national average. Almost half the men in the region have migrated to the plains or joined the military to support families who earn a living from their fragmented land holdings worked mostly by Garhwal and Kumaon women. The Garhwal Regiment and the Kumaon Regiment, both infantry regiments established by the British government in India, continue to be among the largest employers of men. The tourism sector does, however, employ a large number of people. Many come to enjoy the national parks and wildlife sanctuaries within a state 65 percent covered in forests, a remarkable figure considering that only 15 percent of India's total area is forested. The Corbett National Park, the Rajaji National Park, and the Nanda Devi Biosphere Reserve are Uttarakhand's important conservation areas. Yet, with only 217 miles of railroads operating in the plains, two semifunctional airports in the entire state, and the Delhi-Dehradun highway still not completed, it may take some time before tourism reaches an economy of scale in the region. However, much of the revenue gained from current tourism fills the pockets of Delhi-based developers of high-end hotels and resorts. Today, the annual per capita income in Uttarakhand has stagnated at $700.

Recently the government of India announced a multimillion dollar project to establish an Indian Institute of Management (IIM) in Kashipur, a city on the plains, while there has been no apparent drive to build any infrastructure for the proposed capital in the hills. And the state Legislative Assembly currently is housed in a small building with only one exit.

KEN WHALEN

See also Mandal Commission

Further Reading
Guha, Ramachandra. *The Unquiet Woods: Ecological Change and Resistance in the Himalaya*. Berkeley: University of California Press, 2000.
Joshi, Alok. "Uttaranchal: All in a Name." BBC News, February 13, 2002. http://news.bbc.co.uk/2 /low/south_asia/1816892.stm.
Kumar, Pradeep. "Uttarakhand: One Year After." *Economic and Political Weekly* 36(51) (2001): 4692–4693.
Mawdsley, Emma. "Uttarakhand Agitation and Other Backward Classes." *Economic and Political Weekly* 31(4) (1996): 205–210.
Sharma, D. D. *Cultural History of Uttarakhand*. New Delhi: Indira Gandhi National Centre for the Arts, 2009.
Uttarakhand Public Service Commission (UKPSC), Gurukul Kangri, Haridwar. Accessed April 28, 2011. http://ukpsc.gov.in.

✦ UTTAR PRADESH

Uttar Pradesh (UP), situated in the Gangetic heartland, is the most populous state in India. A region with vast tracts of fertile land and some of India's major rivers, it is noted for its flourishing agriculture. Known as the United Provinces in colonial India, it was renamed Uttar Pradesh in 1950. Literally, "Northern Province," Uttar Pradesh aptly refers to the region's geographical location within the Indian nation. UP is located along India's international border in the north that it shares with Nepal, while in various directions it shares borders with eight other Indian states: Bihar, Chhattisgarh, Jharkhand, Haryana, Himachal Pradesh, Madhya Pradesh, Rajasthan, and Uttarakhand, as well as the national capital, Delhi.

The present-day multicultural and social makeup of the state reflects the rich historical legacy it has inherited, particularly the presence of multiple religious traditions. It has been a center of Hindu religion as it contains Varanasi or Benaras, one of the holiest places in India for Hindu pilgrimage, and Mathura and Ayodhya, considered the birthplaces of the Hindu deities Krishna and Rama, respectively; these cities are also destinations for Hindu pilgrims. For followers of Buddhism, Sarnath is where the Buddha (ca. 566–466 BCE) gave his first sermon and Kushinagara is where he died. The UP was one of the first places in India where Muslims settled. Later, Muslim dynasties ruled from Rampur, Lucknow, and Jaunpur, cities that developed and spread Muslim culture in northern India. For the followers of Jainism, Uttar Pradesh houses several Jain sites of historical significance where shrines at Allahabad, Ayodhya, Mathura, and Benaras offer sources to learn about the lives and activities of Jain *tirthankaras* ("fordmakers"), or religious preachers.

In the UP, the existence of different religious traditions is marked by both harmonious living and religious conflict. The UP has seen the coming together of Hindus, Muslims, and others resulting in the development of a composite and syncretic culture that is clearly visible in the everyday life of its inhabitants. From shared food and clothing and from music to language, this special historical development has created what has been referred to as the "Ganga-Yamuna culture," implying the coexistence of different cultures and faiths for centuries along the banks of the rivers Ganges and Yamuna—the two holiest rivers in northern India. The term "Ganga-Yamuna" is often used to describe India's secular outlook. The strong presence of different cultures, however, has also led to severe conflict, primarily between Hindus and Muslims. Periodically the two communities have clashed over religious symbols. Communal riots on a large scale occurred in 1992 when a 450-year-old mosque, the Babri Mosque at Ayodhya, was razed to the ground by Hindu activists who claimed the site was the birthplace of the Hindu god Rama. This incident was the result of a right-wing nationwide movement and in turn triggered riots across India.

The UP has the second-largest state economy after Maharashtra, which contains the huge and vibrant international city of Mumbai. The main source of livelihood for the people of the UP is agriculture, although the state also contains a number of industries, both heavy industry and light industry. Sugarcane, rice, wheat, pulses, vegetables, and fruits are grown throughout the state. Important industries include textiles, leather goods, paper, machine tools, metal works, and information technology. Cities such as Moradabad and Ferozabad are known for their craftwork in metal and glass. With Kanpur as the traditional financial and industrial hub, Noida, which is an acronym standing for Naveen Okhla Industrial Development Authority, and located on the Yamuna 12 miles from the vast metropolitan area of Delhi, emerged as a major center for information technology and related services owing to its proximity to the capital, New Delhi.

Different cities of Uttar Pradesh represent the spirit of Indian culture and history. Lucknow, the capital city, is known for its courtly manners, its sumptuous cuisine, and its refined language. Also referred to as the "City of Nawabs," it is one of the leading centers of arts and crafts, including Islamic calligraphy, appliqué art, *chikankari* (delicate wispy white embroidery on cotton and muslin), *shahi kaam* (royal work on clothes often involving gold and silver thread), bone craft, needlecraft, and hand stitching. The cities of Agra and Fatehpur Sikri can be found on the itinerary of every global tourist because of the Mughal monuments of the Taj Mahal at Agra and the capital city complex of Fatehpur Sikri of Emperor Akbar (1542–1605; emperor, 1556–1605). Allahabad and Lucknow are fascinating sites for those interested in colonial history. As previously mentioned, UP is also noted for its numerous pilgrimage sites.

The UP also plays an important role in the political life of India. The state has the honor of contributing the largest number of prime ministers to India: Jawaharlal Nehru (1889–1964; prime minister 1947–1964), Lal Bahadur Shastri (1904–1966; prime minister 1964–1966), Indira Gandhi (1917–1984; prime minister 1966–1977, 1980–1984), Rajiv Gandhi (1944–1991; prime minister 1984–1989), Chaudhary Charan Singh (1902–1987; prime minister 1979–1980), Chandra Shekhar Singh (1902–2007; prime minister 1990–1991), Vishwanath

Pratap Singh (1931–2008; prime minister 1989–1990), and Atal Bihari Vajpayee (b. 1924; prime minister 1996, 1998–2004). The successors of the Nehru-Gandhi family, Sonia Gandhi (b. 1946) and her son Rahul Gandhi (b. 1970), widely tipped to be a future prime minister of India, represent UP constituencies in the lower house of the Indian Parliament, the Lok Sabha, and hence the state continues to play a central role in Indianpolitics. In addition, trends within UP politics have influenced and shaped national political issues and debates. In the last few decades the caste and religious-based politics of the UP have swayed the rest of the nation as witnessed by the increasing intensity of caste identity and the bitter rivalry between different caste groups.

The significance of the UP is further enhanced when one considers its contribution in the fields of literature and education. Its contribution to Hindi and Urdu literature is simply matchless. With literary stalwarts such as Amir Khusrau (1253–1325) and Munshi Premchand (1880–1936), the UP has seen numerous Urdu and Hindi literary figures emerge and shine. The long list includes Harivansh Rai Bachchan (1907–2003), Jaishankar Prasad (1889–1937), Mir Anis (1803–1874), Mir Taqi Mir (1723–1810), and Mahadevi Varma (1907–1987). The UP also houses some of India's leading educational institutions including the Indian Institute of Technology, Kanpur; Benaras Hindu University, Varanasi; Aligarh Muslim University, Aligarh; Allahabad University; and the Indian Institute of Management, Lucknow.

As a state rich in tradition, resources, and political influence it also faces a host of problems connected with India's rapid population growth. These problems include poverty, a low literacy rate, casteism, the need for land reforms, and the increasing political hostility between different castes and classes. Nonetheless, the term "UP" has a special resonance among the people of the state, engenders a special pride among its denizens, and carries a special cachet among the people of the rest of India.

M. RAISUR RAHMAN

See also Ayodhya; Kanpur

Further Reading

Lieten, G. K. "On Casteism and Communalism in Uttar Pradesh." *Economic and Political Weekly* 29(14) (1994): 777–781.

Mathur, M. B. *Uttar Pradesh.* New Delhi: National Book Trust, 1981.

Uttar Pradesh. Accessed April 28, 2011. http://upgov.nic.in/.

Varma, Uma, ed. *Uttar Pradesh State Gazetteer.* Lucknow: Government of Uttar Pradesh, 1994.

V

✦ VARANASI

Varanasi (population 1.057 million) is a city in the northern state of Uttar Pradesh. The name is derived from the confluence of two rivers, the Varuna and the Asi. Both flow into the sacred river Ganges, India's holiest river. Varanasi is India's most important pilgrimage city since Hindus believe that to die in Varanasi leads to release (*moksha*) from the endless cycles of reincarnation.

Bathing in the river at dawn and reciting prayers to the setting sun are daily rituals on the river, which flows from west to east, but Varanasi, on the north bank of the river, is located at a spot where the river turns north. Accordingly, it faces east and the view at dawn as the sun rises is spectacular. The banks of the shore of the Ganges at Varanasi are renowned as being the site of dozens of *ghats*, long, wide stairways on which people pray, meditate, wash, and do their laundry. The "burning *ghat*," where cremation of the dead takes place, is of central importance to the city. Many elderly people come to Varanasi to spend their last days near the holy river, as do *sanyasin*, holy men and women who have renounced their wealth and families to devote themselves to prayer and abstinence. Large palaces, once belonging to wealthy landowners and rajas (princes), line the streets above the *ghats*. Most are now *ashrams* ("retreats"), hostels, or hotels where pilgrims and tourists stay.

Situated on the west bank of the Ganges, Varanasi continues its tradition as a trade center famous for muslin and silks, ivory carving, and perfume. The lustrous, complicated silk saris enhanced with gold and silver thread are a major commodity in the city's economy. Varanasi is also an important educational and cultural center, home of four universities but especially the renowned Benaras Hindu University, founded in 1916, and the Sampurnanad Sanskrit

Hindus take an early morning ritual bath in the river Ganges at Varanasi, Uttar Pradesh. Varanasi is considered one of the holiest sites in India and receives more than a million Hindu, Buddhist, and Jain pilgrims and Indian and foreign tourists annually. (Eddy Van Ryckeghem/ Dreamstime.com)

University, established in 1971, which focuses especially on the study and translation of Sanskrit texts. Indian classical music and dance traditions are also taught and performed at schools in the area.

The history of Varanasi dates back at least 3,000 years and is mentioned in ancient texts such as the *Rigveda*, the *Mahabharata*, and in the *Puranas*. The city was once known as Kashi and was perhaps named after a famous legendary king, Kasha. Another interpretation gives its derivation to the Sanskrit word *kash* meaning to look brilliant or beautiful. As the "city of light," Kashi refers to illumination or enlightenment leading to release from reincarnation. Ancient texts speak of the city as the dwelling place of Shiva, the Hindu god of death and destruction, and there are numerous temples dedicated to him. The myth of the marriage of Shiva, the "Auspicious One," to Parvati, daughter of the Himalayas, tells the story of Shiva choosing Varanasi for their home because of its beauty. The city is also associated with Buddhism, as in the early sixth century BCE, around 527 BCE, the Buddha (ca. 563–ca. 483 BCE) came and preached his famous Deer Park Sermon, his first sermon, and outlined the basic tenets of his faith, or set the "wheel of the law" in motion, at Sarnath, only six miles from the city.

Invasions by Mahmud of Ghazni (971–1030) in 1033 followed by Mohammed Ghori (1162–1206) in 1193 led to Muslim rule over the area. Varanasi became the independent

Kingdom of Kashi in the 18th century. Under British rule, it remained a commercial and religious center. During both the Muslim and British periods, the city was known as Banares. After Indian independence in August 1947, Varanasi became the official Sanskrit spelling and became part of the state of Uttar Pradesh.

RUTH K. ROSENWASSER

See also Hinduism; Uttar Pradesh

Further Reading
Eck, Diana. *Banaras: City of Light.* Princeton, NJ: Princeton University Press, 1982.
Eck, Diana. *Darśan: Seeing the Divine Image in India.* New York: Columbia University Press, 1998.
Varanasi: The Holy City. Accessed April 28, 2011. http://varanasi.nic.in.

Vedanta Movement. *See* Ramakrishna Mission

✦ VIETNAM, RELATIONS WITH

India's relations with Vietnam began with the Geneva Conference in 1954 when Indian mediation there substantially helped the conclusion of the Geneva Agreements. The implementation of those agreements became India's responsibility in its capacity as the chairman of the three-nation International Control Commission (ICC); Canada and Poland are the other two members. India supported Vietnam's nationalist movement against French colonialism and later sided with Hanoi in its drive for the unification of the country regardless of the Communist coloration of the conflict and its global significance for the Cold War. There was considerable admiration for Vietnam's bravery and tenacity as it successfully vanquished the forces of both France and the United States. That background of the triumph of nationalism over the West helped India's attitude toward the new Vietnam as it emerged on the world scene as a unified nation in the mid-1970s.

There was a convergence of strategic relations between India and the new Vietnam as the two countries, on the one hand, opposed China's urge to dominate Asia and the U.S.-China nexus on Cambodia. On the other hand, both India and Vietnam continued their close relationship with the Soviet Union, buying arms and generally following its anti-China policies. Both countries also supported the Heng Samrin (b. 1934) regime (1979–1993) in Cambodia.

The China factor has continued to weigh heavily in the minds of strategists in Hanoi and New Delhi. Both Vietnam and India share long land frontiers and have had unresolved border disputes with China. In Vietnam's case, it also has to keep a watch on its maritime borders with its northern neighbor, which has had serious altercations with Vietnam's navy in the Spratly Islands. India, too, has had apprehensions over China's growing interest in the Bay of Bengal and in the Indian Ocean close to India's Andaman and Nicobar Islands. Therefore, in the view of analysts such as Subhash Kapila, India and Vietnam have "a natural strategic congruence" as to how to restrain China from aggressive actions while keeping it engaged diplomatically.

The new Vietnam openly supported India's bid for a permanent seat on the United Nations Security Council and as Vietnam's participation in the Association for Southeast Asian Nations (ASEAN) became pronounced, it emphasized India's inclusion in ASEAN's deliberations, with an important role in trade matters, notably ASEAN's free trade agreement (FTA).

With the end of its war against the United States, Vietnam improved its trade relations with India. The latter granted Vietnam a most favored nation (MFN) status in 1975 and three years later signed a comprehensive bilateral trade agreement. In 1993, the two countries established the Indo-Vietnam Joint Business Council, which proceeded to propose the removal of legal barriers to increased trade and investment. Four years later, the two countries signed the Investment Promotion and Protection Agreement. Several high-level visits of Indian leaders took place around the new millennium.

Thus, Foreign Minister Jaswant Singh (b. 1938) and Defence Minister George Fernandes (b. 1930) visited Vietnam in 2000 followed by the visit of the Indian prime minister, Atal Bihari Vajpayee (b. 1924; prime minister 1996, 1998–2004) in the following year. In November 2000, the Mekong-Ganga Cooperation was launched in Vientiane, Laos, to develop "strategic cooperation" in tourism, culture, education, and communications with several countries of Southeast Asia; Vietnam was an important member of the new organization.

A high point of mutual cooperation was reached when a series of comprehensive agreements were signed to mark the visit of Prime Minister Nguyen Tan Dung (b. 1949; prime minister 2006–) to India in 2007. The more notable areas of mutual cooperation were information technology, education, and space and nuclear development.

Measures were approved for increased cooperation in fighting drug trafficking and terrorism by improvements in the legal architecture, notably service of summons, execution of warrants, and confiscating instruments of crime. The two countries approved procedures for investigation of financial crimes including cyber crimes designed to inhibit money laundering. India agreed to establish for Vietnam a cyber forensic laboratory costing 22 million rupees. Some of these measures had already been agreed on in a memorandum of understanding (MOU) during the visit of India's home minister Shivraj Patil (b. 1935; minister for home affairs 2004–2008) to Vietnam in 2003 and the visit of Vietnam's minister for public security Gen. Le Hong Anh (b. 1949; minister for public security 2002–) to India in 2004. In that year, the two countries also established direct air links with 20 direct flights per month and the two countries identified each other as major tourist destinations. To make such travel possible, both countries relaxed their visa rules for the visitors from each other's country.

The quantum of trade between the two countries improved substantially following the economic liberalization policies in Vietnam and India. This was notably so in the new millennium as trade figures registering an increase of 20 to 30 percent each year after 2001. From a mere $115 million in 2000 they reached $1 billion in 2006. India's imports from Vietnam were mostly in agricultural products, textiles, handicrafts, and electronics while India's exports included heavy machinery and railroad equipment.

DAMODAR R. SARDESAI

See also Foreign Policy

Further Reading
Kapila, Subhash. "India-Vietnam Strategic Partnership: The Convergence of Interests." Paper #177. South Asia Analysis Group. www.southasiaanalysis.org/%5Cpapers2%5Cpaper177.htm.
Reddy, C. Ravindranatha. *India and Vietnam: Era of Friendship and Cooperation, 1947–1991.* Chennai: Emerald Publishers, 2009.
SarDesai, D. R. *Indian Foreign Policy: Cambodia, Laos, and Vietnam, 1947–1964.* Berkeley: University of California Press, 1968.
Sharma, Gitesha. *India-Vietnam Relations: First to Twenty-First Century.* Kolkata: Dialogue Society, 2004.

✦ VILLAGE EDUCATION COMMITTEES

Village Education Committees (VEC) were developed as part of the decentralized management structure under the District Primary Education Programme (DPEP) in 1994. Their role is to establish a link between the school and the community and be the core structure at the grassroots level for planning, implementing, and coordinating the community-based delivery of primary education. Representation in the VEC aims to be broad, involving all members of the community toward school mapping, community-level monitoring of school programs, and evaluating teacher effectiveness. However, VECs seem to be token institutions with neither teachers nor parents expecting much from them as real participation of the community is depressingly low. One reason for this lack of dynamism is that these committees were formed in a top-down manner based on government directives rather than on the actual needs of the community. Within the DPEP, while VECs are intended to have a pivotal community role, there is no mechanism to regularly collect information and monitor their functioning within specific local contexts. As long as this data is lacking, the representation of women and wider VEC effectiveness is difficult to evaluate. Evidence from nongovernmental organizations (NGOs) and field workers reveal that VECs are often biased in favor of higher caste groups, with very little women's representation and little stake in improving school effectiveness and improving enrollment from deprived sections of society. According to a 2003 World Bank report, around 230,000 VECs, 170,000 parent-teacher associations, and 61,000 school management committees have been formed. The *Pratchi Education Report* in 2002, however, notes that while VECs have been formed in many villages, most are yet to become functional.

SHEEBA HÄRMÄ

See also District Primary Education Program; Education, Development

Further Reading
Mohanty, Jagannath. *Primary and Elementary Education*. New Delhi: Deep and Deep, 2002.
Pratichi Trust. *The Pratichi Education Report*. New Delhi: Pratichi Trust, 2002.
Ramachandran, Vimala, ed. *Gender and Social Equity in Primary Education: Hierarchies Access*. Thousand Oaks, CA: Sage, 2004.
World Bank. *A Review of Educational Progress and Reform in the District Primary Education Program (Phases 1 and II)*. New Delhi: Human Development Sector South Asian Region, 2003.

✦ VISHWA HINDU PARISHAD

The Vishwa Hindu Parishad (VHP) was formed in 1964 by Swami Chinmayananda (1916–1993), Shivram Shankar Apte, and Madhav Golwakar (1906–1973) in response to what its founders believed were growing religious and ideological threats to the traditions and values of India (Hindustan). Created at the height of the Cold War, the VHP's initial thrust was to wrest allegiance and power from what they considered to be corrupt forces tearing India apart, including Christianity, Islam, and Communism.

Initially, it was not an all-Hindu movement but sought cooperation and council from the Sikh, Jain, and Buddhist communities, all of whom had representatives present at the foundational meetings. However, in later years, the VHP would take a decidedly more nationalistic position in domestic politics and a more fundamentalist bent in matters of religion, favoring the various religious traditions under the umbrella of Hinduism. This new tone would alienate the leadership and followers of other Bharati (Indian civilization) faiths.

As part of its original mandate the VHP was to serve as a public interest group for advocating the rights of Hindus, both in India and those who were part of the Hindu diaspora. As a result of these activities the movement enjoyed increasing popularity throughout the 1970s and 1980s, and the VHP expanded its outreach to include work among and for the scheduled castes and other oppressed groups within Indian society. Their philanthropic work included building temples for worship, setting up schools for educating the poor, and funding hospital construction to improve health care.

The VHP has not been shy about inviting controversy in matters of political and religious importance to its members. In 1992, the VHP was part of a larger group of Hindu nationalists that destroyed the centuries-old Babri Mosque at Ayodhya in Uttar Pradesh, claiming that the mosque had been built by Muslim invaders on the very site where a Hindu temple once stood. Moreover, many devout Hindus believed the Babri Mosque sat on the birthplace of Lord Rama, one of the human incarnations of the god Vishnu. The destruction of the mosque led to bloodshed of both Muslims and Hindus.

The VHP's more radical activities led to a desire by some in the membership to take an active role in changing the political landscape of India, including challenging the moderate political parties that had controlled Indian politics since independence. Doing this meant that the VHP needed a close ally, and it found one in the right-wing political party known as the Bharatiya Janata Party (BJP), which had been founded in 1980. The BJP shared much in common with the VHP both in terms of ideology and political goals. Working together, they successfully won control of India's government in the 1998 elections. Though later defeated by the more moderate Congress Party, founded in 1885, the BJP-VHP alliance remains a powerful force in Indian politics.

STEVEN B. SHIRLEY

See also Ayodhya; Bharatiya Janata Party

Further Reading
Bhatt, Chetan. *Hindu Nationalism: Origins, Ideologies, and Modern Myths.* New York: Berg, 2001.
Heath, Deanna, and Chandana Mathur. *Communalism and Globalization in South Asia and Its Diaspora.* London: Routledge, 2010.
Katju, Manjari. *Vishva Hindu Parishad and Indian Politics.* Hyderabad: Orient Longman, 2003.

✦ WATER CONFLICT

Water resources in India over the years have been subjected to tremendous pressures of population growth, urbanization, agriculture, industrialization, and growing pollution. The overexploitation of water and improper management practices have set a dangerous trend that imperils the very availability of water resources for future generations. Water riots have occurred in several parts of Indian cities, and water scarcity has forced people to take desperate measures, often leading to the depletion of existing resources. Inequities in water availability and use have been sources of domestic, national, and regional insecurity. Although water wars do not seem plausible in the near future, interstate conflicts and domestic stress and its spillover into neighboring countries of the region are issues of great concern facing policy planners. Rivers flow across borders, and river basins extend beyond territorial limits.

A country of 24 river basins, India has been host to a large number of riparian conflicts whether within or among countries. The Indus water problem began between India and Pakistan, the India-Bangladesh dispute arose over Ganges waters on Farakka, and the Kosi, Gandak, and Mahakali rivers were involved in history of misunderstandings between India and Nepal. Within India, too, disputes within states exist over the Cauvery and Krishna rivers. Conflicts among riparian states seem to arise in the context of water resource development projects undertaken by states to supplement their water needs. Water can be at the root of conflict in multiple ways. Conflict can occur between states when there are issues of access to and availability of water. Under those circumstances when a state threatens to cut off water supplies to another state, tension may result. Conflict can occur when there are big versus small states or between upper riparian and lower riparian states.

The Indus water system has six rivers: the Indus, the Jhelum, the Chenab, the Ravi, the Beas and the Sutlej. The rivers are so interlinked with a series of canals that in case there is a shortage of water in one, a main link canal can draw water from another. The dispute over these waters arose when India desired that the government of Pakistan replace the supplies that it was receiving from eastern rivers by building link canals from the western rivers. Pakistan refused, as it not only needed the water but also considered itself to be in the right as the lower riparian under international law. It was not until September 19, 1960, that an agreement was signed at Rawalpindi between the prime minister of India and the president of Pakistan. The Indus Water Treaty of 1960 is one of the few examples of successful resolution of a major dispute over an international river basin.

The only unresolved water dispute between the two countries is the Tulbul Navigation Project. Pakistan objects to this Project on the grounds that it violates the Indus Water Treaty by creating storage on the main Jhelum River that has been allocated to Pakistan. The dispute is over the proposed construction by India of the Tulbul Navigation Project, which Pakistan calls Wular Barrage and is located on the Jhelum downstream from Lake Wular. India wants to construct this barrage to control the flow of water in the Jhelum in the lean season (October–February). The flow of water in the Jhelum is about 2,000 cubic feet per second, and its depth is about 30 inches. However, year-round navigability requires the flow and depth of water to be almost 4,000 cubic feet per second.

With multifarious demands of agriculture, navigation, industrialization, fisheries, and inland penetration of seawater in rivers, which are at a very low flow during November–March, the availability of water causes serious problems. A major dispute over water sharing that continued for two decades was the dispute over the Ganges waters. The refusal of India to come to an agreement over the issue of water sharing was seen by Bangladesh as unilateral withdrawal by a big and powerful neighbor. The Ganges-Brahmaputra-Meghna river system falls in a number of countries in South Asia and in China. China contributes solely to the flow of the Brahmaputra, and Nepal contributes to the flow of the Ganges. Both China and Nepal are upper riparian. The remaining two countries, India and Bangladesh, depend heavily on this water system. The dwindling of supplies in the dry season has been a contentious issue between India and Bangladesh, as Bangladeshis receive about 80 percent of their annual freshwater supply through transboundary rivers.

The sharing of Ganges waters in its lean season between India and Pakistan (before 1971) and between India and Bangladesh (after its liberation) has led to confrontation and has remained the biggest cause of conflict between India and Bangladesh. The problems arose due to the construction of a barrage by India, the upper riparian, across the Ganges at a place named Farraka in West Bengal about 10.5 miles upstream from the western border of Bangladesh. The barrage was designed to improve the navigability of the port of Kolkata by flushing out the silt during the lean months by supplying water into the Bhagirathi-Hooghly

River. Despite India's repeated assurances that the barrage would not disturb irrigation schemes and flood control, the Indian government could not convince the Pakistani government of its noble intentions. An Indo-Bangladesh treaty, the Treaty on the Sharing of Ganga Waters at Farakka, was finally signed in 1996 that settled the issue and also covered northern and northeastern states such as Bhutan and Nepal.

India and Nepal have shared a cordial and harmonious relationship in comparison to Bangladesh and Pakistan, but conflicts over the utilization of water resources and riparian rights have occurred between these two nations because of the major rivers originating in Nepal and flowing into India. It is more a matter of harnessing water resources by way of hydropower generation, irrigation, flood control measures, and navigation rather than water sharing. The main rivers—the Ghagra, the Gandak (Kali or Mahakali), and the Kosi—after flowing through Nepal join the great Indian river, the Ganges, in India. The Sarada (1920), Kosi (1954), and Gandak (1959) projects were criticized in Nepal for conferring substantially more benefits to India than to Nepal and resulted in an inequitable treatment under these water resource development projects. These were projects essentially conceived to meet the needs of India with some benefits to Nepal and were designed with Nepal's agreement. Projects suffered from bad planning, poor maintenance, and inefficient implementation, and neither country benefited.

The 1990s saw another major controversy over the Mahakali River in December 1991. Both countries signed a memorandum of understanding to construct a barrage at Tanakpur. India agreed to provide some electricity and water to Nepal.

Interbasin transfers and the sharing of basin water are seen as the means for meeting the steadily increasing needs of a state in terms of irrigation, hydroelectric power, municipal and industrial use, navigation, and transport. Problems have arisen in Punjab over supply sharing, and existing controversy prevails between Tamil Nadu and Karnataka and between Andhra Pradesh and Karnataka.

The river Ravi rises in Himachal Pradesh, enters the plains near Madhopur in Punjab, and then moves along the border between India and Pakistan before merging into the river Chenab. The Beas River flows from its headwaters in Mandi (Himachal Pradesh) and, after flowing for about 285.8 miles, merges into the river Sutlej. Under the Indus Water Treaty of 1960, the Ravi, Beas, and Sutlej were given for exclusive use of India except for a transition period of 10 years during which India was to supply water from these rivers to enable Pakistan to develop a canal system in its territory using the three rivers allocated to it. This period ended in March 1970, after which India had exclusive rights to develop and use the waters. In composite Punjab these three rivers—the Ravi, Beas, and Sutlej—provide ample water for its needs. The subsequent partition of the Punjab into Punjab and Haryana under the Punjab Reorganization Act of 1966 sowed the seeds of discord, as sharing of water was now to be bifurcated between the two states.

The act also stated that a provision for the construction of the SYL Canal (Sutlej Yamuna Link Canal) to divert waters of the river Beas should be made for full utilization of Haryana's share. This considerably reduced Punjab's share of water that it considered essential for its rich agriculture and for its generation of electricity to pump water from tube wells. Prolonged negotiations ultimately resulted in the Rajiv-Longowal Accord, followed by the Ravi Beas Water Tribunal Award.

The Cauvery River is one of the most important rivers of southern India. The river rises in the Western Ghats at an elevation of about 4,399 feet in the state of Karnataka and flows for about 497 miles before flowing into the Bay of Bengal. Tamil Nadu, a small part of the basin of Kerala, the state of Karnataka, and a part of the Union Territory of Puducherry form part of the Cauvery delta, thus making it an interstate river. The discharge in this river basin comes from about 33,900 square miles of catchments from Karnataka and Tamil Nadu.

The upper riparian Karnataka came under severe pressure from these states to release water, and beginning in the 1970s talks between Karnataka and Tamil Nadu went on intermittently for more than two decades but to no effect. The government of India interceded, but the problem remained unsolved. The Supreme Court ordered the establishment of the Cauvery Waters Tribunal, which was established on June 2, 1990. Under an interim award in 1991, the tribunal decided that Tamil Nadu should get 205 thousand million cubic feet (Tmcft) of water every year and asked Karnataka to release waters to Mettur Reservoir in a stipulated pattern. Karnataka expressed its inability to release waters, and Tamil Nadu again appealed to the Supreme Court, but the Court chose not to issue any direction and thought it expedient to ask the prime minister to intervene. The prime minister decided that Karnataka should release 6 Tmcft of water for saving the standing crops of Tamil Nadu and also set up a committee to determine the water needs for saving the standing crops in both states.

In addition to major interstate river water disputes, India has faced other minor interstate disputes over water resources. Disputes over the sharing of waters by the riparian states of the Yamuna River, mainly Delhi and Haryana, with Delhi accusing Haryana of not releasing enough water for the drinking water requirement of the capital's population, has occurred time and again. The list can be exhaustive, with states vying for the river waters in Tamil Nadu–Kerala over the river Bhavani or Orissa and Chhattisgarh vying over the river Indravati as the bone of contention, with the latter alleging that the state was not getting the promised share of its riparian rights.

Apart from riparian conflicts, conflicts over water are also related to socioeconomics and equity. Conflicts occur between people living in the upper catchments and those who live downstream; conflicts also occur because of the social cost of the project through displacement of populations, loss of land by submergence, cultural loss, loss of livelihoods, dispersal of integrated communities, and severance of people's links from the natural resource base. Apart from development, distributional inequality and issues of social inequity are also inherent in the caste and class structure of India. There is a question not only of availability but also of ease of access. Such water-related conflicts also impact ethnic, economic, rural, and urban populations within and across waters.

Apart from the socioeconomic- and equity-related conflicts, there are other potential sources of conflict that can result as pressure over water increases. For example, sectoral

Sardar Sarovar Dam on the Narmada River. Rising in eastern Madhya Pradesh and flowing west for over 800 miles through Madhya Pradesh, Maharashtra, and Gujarat, the Narmada River is the traditional boundary between North and South India. The Dam is but one example of the enormous efforts India has made to harness its waters for drinking and especially for irrigation purposes. (AP Photo/Gujarat State Information Department)

demands in irrigation will increase due to the rapidly growing population. There will be a need for more water storage projects for increased food grain production. There is also a predictable rise in urban population by 2025, with more that 40 percent of the population living in urban areas. Depletion and degradation of the resource will affect the livelihood of a large number of people. This will definitely increase the stress on water. Evidence already supports such scenarios, especially in the case of rural versus urban needs. With increasing urbanization and the growing population of metro cities, stress on water has been increasing. Several cities in Rajasthan, Gujarat, Kerala, and Karnataka have witnessed loss of life resulting from protests of the diversion of water from farmlands to metro cities such as Delhi, Bangalore, and Vadodara. Water drives a wedge between urban and rural populations. Water riots are becoming a common occurrence, with people clashing at several places over access to water. Conflicts related to water can be many and varied in other contexts and levels and between uses and areas. Above all, conflict can and does arise between water availability and accessibility in development and sustainability.

Ensuring access to potable and quality drinking water is essential to preventing waterborne diseases, which are prevalent in India. One of the most important causes of mortality and morbidity is poverty, and its various manifestations are seen in communicable diseases caused by the poor quality of drinking water and unhygienic sanitation. Safe drinking water and sanitation directly impact the health of the people, their productivity, and the quality of life. Waterborne diseases are endemic in Indian cities, frequently becoming large-scale epidemics. Villagers use peripheral and often contaminated surface water sources. Due to lower population density in villages, waterborne diseases are endemic but rarely cause large outbreaks. An estimate shows that diseases spread by Ganges pollution alone deprives the country of nearly 40 million workdays because of ill health. The loss in terms of mortality and economic injury is incalculable.

The depletion, degradation, and inequitable distribution of water resources remains a national security concern, especially when the water in question is in short supply while dependence on it is great and is shared with other often-adversarial states.

VANDANA ASTHANA

See also Water Policy; Water Resources

Further Reading

Fischer, William, ed. *Toward Sustainable Development? Struggling over India's Narmada River.* New York: M. E. Sharp, 1995.
Independent Review. *Sardar Sarovar: Report of the Independent Review.* Ottawa: Resources Future International, 2009.
Roy, K. J., et al., eds. *Water Conflicts in India: A Million Revolts in the Making?* New Delhi: Routledge, 2009.
Shantha Mohan, N. Sailen Routray, and N. Sashikumar, eds. *River Water Sharing: Transboundary Conflict and Cooperation in India.* London: Routledge, 2009.

✦ WATER POLICY

After centuries of colonial rule and expropriation of resources, national economic objectives in the era immediately following colonization emphasized nationalization of extractive and core industrial sectors of the Indian economy as a strategy for economic development of the country. The first prime minister, Jawaharlal Nehru (1889–1964; prime minister 1947–1964), opted for a policy based on centralized planning and development. He envisaged a capital-intensive strategy to achieve both growth and social justice in the country. Thus began an era of large dams and capital-intensive irrigation and agriculture. However, India did not have a national water policy until 1987 even though water management and distribution was allocated to the states in India's quasi-federal structure.

India is a union of states, and as such responsibilities are allocated to the states and the central government in the Indian Constitution. Water is a state subject, with the central government having minimal intervention with regard to water policies unless the water policy becomes a matter of public interest. It was only in 1985 that the Ministry of Water Resources was established due to the growing pressures of diverse water issues. The National Water Resource Council was set up under Prime Minister Rajiv Gandhi (1944–1991; prime minister 1984–1989), under whom India adopted its first National Water Policy in 1987.

The Union Ministry of Water Resources is responsible for coordination, development, conservation, and management of water as a natural resource. The ministry looks into the general policy on water resource development and management, technical and external assistance to the states for irrigation, multipurpose projects, groundwater exploration and exploitation, command area development, drainage, flood control, waterlogging, sea erosion problems, dam safety, and hydraulic structures for navigation and hydropower. The Ministry of Environment and Forests oversees water pollution and control issues, while the Ministry of Power manages hydropower. The Ministry of Urban Development handles water supplies and sewage disposal in urban areas. Water supply in rural areas is taken care of by the Ministry of Rural Development.

It is the individual state government, however, that is primarily responsible for the management of water resources. The administrative control and responsibility for managing water rests with the various state departments and corporations. Urban water supply is generally the responsibility of the municipal corporations and water boards constituted under an act of the state legislative assembly. These boards function autonomously. Currently water supplies, from bulk production to distribution, are taken care of by these corporations and boards. The cost of water is highly subsidized by the state agencies, as water is perceived to be a public good. The rural water supplies are taken care of by the Panchayats (a village council that is popularly elected). Urban Local Bodies (ULBs) generally receive funds in the form of loans or grants from the central and state governments. These local institutions, which are primarily responsible for urban water and rural supplies, were recognized as a third tier of the government by a constitutional amendment in 1993. Under the 73rd and 74th Amendments to the Indian Constitution, these municipal corporations and Panchayats are mandated and empowered to chart out the financial and political character of development on issues such as water supplies and management. Focusing as it did on decentralization in the Indian political system, the amendment was of such a magnitude that it had an impact on the functioning of the political machinery associated with water at the state and substate levels. It is within this administrative setup that policies for water resource management in irrigation as well as rural and urban water supplies are produced, enacted, and implemented. India adopted its first National Water Policy (NWP) in 1987 under the leadership of Prime Minister Rajiv Gandhi in an era when ideas for the transition of the Indian state were actually being germinated.

Over the years, as demands regarding water grew, another draft National Water Policy (1998) was adopted on April 1, 2002. The water policy marks a departure from the 1987 policy in several ways. The policy adopted in 2002 places emphasis on socioeconomic aspects in water policy planning and the needs of the states. The addition to the policy of Sections 11, 12, and 13 reflects the reformist intent of the government in a neoliberal framework and the involvement of the private sector in water source projects.

With the National Water Policy in place, the Ministry of Urban Development went ahead in making major changes to allow 100 percent foreign direct investment (FDI) in urban infrastructure projects. This included development of water supply sources, water distribution, billing, sewage reclamation and reuse, management of unaccounted-for water, manufacture of water supply equipment, and privatization of solid-waste management systems. At present, the central government offers special incentives for investments such as exemption from customs and excise duties on imported machinery and exemption from all taxes for the first five years of water and sewerage projects. The government has provided these fiscal incentives to encourage partnership with the private sector and to attract foreign investment in urban water supply and sanitation projects. In addition, the government further amended the municipal acts to enable ULBs to collaborate with the private sector and to improve governance and management. The goal for India is to meet the Millennium Development Goals of the United Nations (UN), and the Johannesburg goals at the World Summit for Sustainable Development in 2002 commit India to achieving 100 percent coverage in urban water supplies. These supplies are hampered by poor quality of transmission and distribution networks, physical losses ranging from 25 percent to 50 percent, low pressures leading to back siphoning that results in contamination, and water availability ranging from two to eight hours a day.

India has 16 percent of the population of the world and shares 4 percent of the world's water resources and 2.45 percent of the world's land area. Distribution of water resources is highly uneven in time and space, and vast populations live in areas of acute scarcity of water. The country has to grapple with severe critical issues of water because of natural or hydrological conditions and exacerbated human activities. There is leakage of water in the pipelines and irrigation systems due to poor maintenance. In urban areas about a third of all water is lost through leaky pipelines, contributing to the scarcity of water.

Based on per capita renewable water availability, India has enough water to meet the demands of its people. However, despite an estimate of 493,738 gallons of water per person per year, large numbers of people suffer severe water shortages, partially because of uneven availability of water. Floods and droughts are common in the entire country. While national aggregates and average assessments of India's situation in terms of water availability are presently not uncomfortable, there are wide variations, both temporal and spatial, in the availability of water in the country due to extreme floods and absolute scarcity in the region. Apart from hydrological factors, scarcity of water has been exacerbated by bad management and maintenance practices as well as by increasing pollution in the rivers and in the groundwater.

The increase in pollution in river waters is a major concern throughout India. Rivers are the lifeline of water and serve as the primary source of drinking, agricultural, and industrial water. The two major rivers of northern India, the Ganges and the Yamuna, have become highly polluted. Similarly, the Krishna, Cauvery, and Godawari and other rivers in the south and the Brahmaputra in the east are increasingly polluted. Domestic and industrial waste is dumped into rivers. Even where there are waste treatment plants, either they are not operational due to energy shortages or for financial reasons waste is directly dumped into the rivers. The industrial effluents contain hazardous organic and inorganic pollutants. In addition, domestic waste and fecal matter are rich in organic pollutants. During the monsoon, agricultural washout containing pesticides, insecticides, and fertilizer residues further increase river pollution. The dumping of animal carcasses adds to the pollution. The cremation of dead bodies at riverbanks and the religious practice of throwing unburned bodies of sages, saints, and infants directly into the river make the water unhealthy. There are other religious rituals of submerging often insoluble metal or stone representations of deities in the rivers that increase water pollution. However, the main source of pollution is still sewage and municipal effluents, which account for 75 percent of the pollution load in rivers; the remaining 25 percent is contributed by industrial effluents and other pollution sources.

The water used by industry that contains chemicals and heavy metals ultimately makes its way back to the water cycle. Industrial chemicals increase the temperature of water bodies, which is detrimental for sustenance of life downstream. The control of pollution has not been able to keep pace with urbanization and industrialization. Millions of cubic feet of industrial waste are constantly dumped into the water bodies every day in large cities.

Groundwater is also another source of drinking water and is not spared from pollution. A sampling of the groundwater quality at 138 sampling stations in 22 industrialized zones in India revealed that water in all the zones was not fit for drinking purposes due to high bacteriological and heavy metal contamination. It is also estimated that 1.5 million preschool children in India die every year due to the spread of cholera, dysentery, and gastroenteritis. This constitutes 60 percent of the total death toll. The situation has not improved, and the bad quality of water remains a public health hazard.

In 1985 Prime Minister Rajiv Gandhi established a plan for the Ganges Basin cleanup, which has been enforced by the Ganga Project Directorate, under the Central Ganga Authority, to oversee pollution control and the consequent cleaning of the Ganges River. The water quality in the middle stretch of the Ganges, which had deteriorated to classes C and D (the worst class is E, the best A), was restored to class B in 1990 after the implementation of the action plan. However, in several stretches the quality of the river water remains in classes C and D. A similar program for the Yamuna River is in the pipeline, and a national river action plan is being drawn up to clean the heavily polluted stretches of the major rivers of the country.

The legal framework for water quality and its protection began with passage of the first comprehensive legislation, known as the Water Prevention and Control of Pollution Act, in 1974 (amended in 1988) supplemented by provisions of the Environmental Protection Act in 1986 and the Water Cess (Prevention and Control of Pollution) Act in 1977. The National Water Policy (1987 and 2002) of India was the result of the realization of the growing scarcity of water.

The Water Pollution Act of 1974 was the first serious attempt at controlling pollution. The act was the culmination of more than a decade of deliberations between the state and the central government. Given that water is a state subject, the states passed a resolution under the constitution permitting the central government to pass this act so that a uniform code and an organizational structure could evolve.

In order to partially meet the requirements for funds of the bureaucratic network of the Central and State Water Pollution Control Boards, the central government passed the Water Cess Act in 1977 under which each industry and local body was to pay a nominal cess fee on water consumption. The act also gave a rebate of 70 percent of the cess for firms that installed pollution treatment plants and met pollution control standards. In 1991 this rebate was reduced to 25 percent in the interest of resource conservation. However, the Water Cess Act has not been adequate in meeting the expenses of the board or as an effective economic incentive for inducing the firms to take pollution abatement measures because of its nominal incidence. Paying the full cess fee is cheaper than installing pollution control plants. The regulatory power of the boards has therefore remained the major instrument of environmental policy.

The Environmental Protection Act of 1986, also known as the Umbrella Act, was created by the Indian Parliament. This act empowers the central government to take all necessary measures to protect and improve the quality of the environment and to prevent, control, and abate environmental pollution. The act identifies the Ministry of Environment and Forests as the apex nodal agency to deal with environmental problems of the country so that an integrated and holistic policy can be implemented with regard to the environment. Unlike the earlier acts, the scope of the Environmental Protection Act covers water, air, and land and the interrelationships that exist among them as well as human beings and other living creatures.

The Policy Statement for Abatement of Pollution (1992) emphasizes integration of environmental considerations into decision making at all levels. The statement aims to achieve this through prevention of pollution at its source, implementing the best practical technical solutions, requiring that the polluter pays for the pollution and control arrangement, focusing protection on heavily polluted areas and river stretches, and involving the public in decision making. Thus, water laws and policy have come a long way in regard to the goal of pollution control.

The implementation of water laws involves a complex variety of actors. There is a basic division of power between the central government and the states, reflecting the federal nature of the Indian Constitution. While the mandate of the Central Pollution Control Board (CPCB), an agency of the central government, is to set environmental standards for all domestic and industrial plants in India, lay down ambient standards, and coordinate the activities of the State Pollution Control Boards (SPCBs), the oversight, implementation, and enforcement of environmental laws is decentralized and is the responsibility of the SPCBs, which are state agencies. The SPCBs have a two-tier administrative structure to carry out their functions under the law.

The Ministry of Environment and Forests does the overall coordination at the national level and also takes direct responsibility for the states that do not have their own ministry or department of environment. The main functions of the ministry relate to coordination of activities of various central and state authorities established under previous acts, determining emission/effluent standards, getting information about industrial processes, and giving directions for closure or regulation of industries violating pollution standards. The ministry authorizes institutions such as the CPCB and SPCBs to act on its behalf, while the ministry maintains overall control. Under the law and pollution control mechanisms, boards have the necessary powers to enforce pollution standards and compel industries to adopt either clean technologies or cleanup technologies, whichever the industries deem necessary. The other actor in the regulatory process is the industries. The government of India has identified 18 categories of industries as highly polluting, some of which are petrochemical plants, tanneries, paper and pulp plants, dye plants, and pesticide manufacturing. Under the regulatory policy framework, extensive guidelines were set for emission discharges from industries, and minimal national standards were evolved for each specific industry. While the number of highly polluting industries is not predominant in the country, such industries predominate as fuel consumers and consumers of capital.

The government has taken large steps in the constitutional, legal, and administrative fields in order to maintain water quality standards in the surface waters of India. Both the central and state governments have made efforts to contain pollution. But the implementation of laws to maintain water quality standards requires a totally different set of policy contexts: a clear-cut law, a strong and willing bureaucracy, and a long-lasting commitment from the government to provide the needed political and financial support. Implementing water policies represents a great challenge for a vast country. The implementation of regulatory policy has been left to the state boards, whose powers are not limited to advising and information collection but also include the inspection of sewage plants for treatment effluents and the setting up of effluent discharge standards.

VANDANA ASTHANA

See also Water Conflict; Water Resources

Further Reading
Asthana, V. *Water Policy Processes in India: Discourses of Power and Resistance.* Oxford, UK: Routledge 2009.
Desai, B. *Water Pollution in India: Law and Enforcement.* New Delhi: South Asia Publishers, 1992.
Iyer, R. *Water and the Laws in India.* New Delhi. Sage, 2009.
Khator, R. *Environment, Development and Politics in India.* Lanham, MD: University Press of America, 1991.
Thakur, K. *Environmental Protection Law and Policy in India.* New Delhi: Deep and Deep, 1997.

✦ WATER RESOURCES

India is dependent on the southwestern and northeastern monsoons. Rainfall shows great variation in amount and seasonal distributions. The pattern of rainfall in India is greatly influenced by mountain formations. The Himalayas constitute the major mountain range in the north, extending to about 1,553 miles in length. The Himalayas are divided into three distinct ranges: the Greater and Middle Himalayas and the lower Sivaliks. The major hills in the Indian Peninsula are in the Eastern Ghats, the Western Ghats, the Aravallis, the Vindhyas, and the Satpura ranges.

In the northeastern parts of India there is a break where the Garo, Khasi, and Jaintia hills form the bend ranges of the Himalayas. The alignment of the hills with respect to prevailing winds and their elevation profoundly influences the distribution of rainfall all over India, making some areas abundant with rainfall, while in other areas rainfall is acutely scarce. The average annual rainfall is 41 inches, which is the largest anywhere in the world for a country of comparable size. However, annual rainfall amounts fluctuate widely. Over the Khasi and Jantia hills, rainfall is 394 inches a year, while in the north in the Brahmaputra Valley rainfall is 450 inches a year and as much as 40.9 inches in a day. On the other hand, in the extreme west in Rajasthan annual rainfall is as low as 4–6 inches. On the west coast of India, heavy rainfall occurs annually along the slopes of the Western Ghats up to an average of 236 inches, but in certain nearby areas annual rainfall is as low as 20–24 inches. On the east coast, rainfall is highest near the coastal areas and decreases inland. Mount Abu in the Aravalli range experiences annual rainfall of 63 inches, while in the surrounding plains annual rainfall is barely 24 inches. The Himalayas in the east have annual rainfall of about 197 inches but only about 110 inches on the western side of the high mountain area. Snowfall is restricted to the Himalayan region.

Storms and depressions also have their impact. During August and September the largest number of storms and depressions occur over the Bay of Bengal, ultimately passing inland into West Bengal and the Orissa coast. Rainfall occurs in the regions exposed to these moving storms and is as high as 4–8 inches a day. These monsoon depressions play a very critical role in the distribution of monsoon rain over northern India and the peninsula. Their absence leads to droughts. These traveling disturbances yield copious rain in the entire area from north coastal Andhra Pradesh, Orissa, Madhya Pradesh, Bihar, West Bengal, eastern Uttar Pradesh, and the Punjab hills, varying from 39 to 78 inches. Cyclones also occur on the east coast during the premonsoon (April–May) and postmonsoon (October–November) periods. Some cyclones are of severe intensity and cause havoc and devastation.

Sixty percent of India's water resources are found in the main river systems of India. The Ganges, Brahmaputra, and Meghna river systems cover 33 percent of the country. The Himalayan rivers—the Indus, the Ganges, and the Brahmaputra—are snow-fed and perennial and get large summer flows, while the peninsular rivers are dependent on the monsoons and are seasonal. Rivers such as the Godavari, the Krishna, the Pennar, and the Cauvery pass through large tracts of low rainfall regions and as such carry much less water with low yields than do rivers passing through areas with good rainfall.

The hydrological conditions of complex mountain winds, the orientation of mountains, and the variability of rainfall, storms, and cyclones lead to excessive low rainfall areas.

An example of this is Rajasthan, where the Bay of Bengal monsoon clouds are unable to cross the Himalayan barrier.

The principal water resources of India therefore comprise surface water (through streams and rivers) and groundwater. The river systems of India can be classified into two groups: the perennial rivers of the Himalayan region and the rivers of peninsular India. They are often uncertain in their behavior due to a meandering flow or drastic changes in river courses caused by landslides and seismic activity. The peninsular rivers originate at much lower altitudes and flow through areas that are geologically more stable. They are more predictable in their behavior. The flow patterns of the two groups of river systems are different. In the peninsula, the flow is characterized by heavy discharge during the monsoons followed by low discharge during the dry months. In the Himalayan river systems the seasonal dry weather leads to annual cycles of ice depletion; rivers are then fed by melting snow and glaciers. Even in the lean period during the winter the flow is never reduced very much.

The main Himalayan river systems are those of the Indus, the Ganges, and the Brahmaputra. The Indus River, one of the great rivers of the world, rises north of Mansarover in Tibet and flows through Kashmir for a distance of 403 miles in a northwesterly direction. The river then moves past Nanga Parbat into Pakistan. In the plains, the main tributaries of the Indus are the Jhelum, Chenab, Ravi, Beas, and Sutlej rivers.

The river Ganges originates at Devprayag, where two rivers—the Alaknanada and Bhagirathi—meet. The Ganges flows in a southwardly direction and later moves southeasterly through the Great Plains of Farakka, forming the apex of the Ganges Delta. In the Ganges's long course of 1,568 miles, numerous tributaries join the river. One of the major tributaries is the Yamuna, which has its source close to the Ganges. The Ghaghara arises in the Himalayas east of the Ganges, and the

Boys playing on the ghats amidst the pollution in the river Ganges at Varanasi, Uttar Pradesh. Water pollution is one of India's biggest environmental problems and the cause of illness. (Steve Allen/Dreamstime.com)

Kosi arises in the mountain of Nepal. The Kosi contributes water to about 37 percent of the population and covers a cultivable land area of 196,909 square miles.

The Brahmaputra arises in Tibet, where it is known as the Tsangpo. When it emerges from the foothills in Arunachal Pradesh, it is known as the Siang and Dihang. The river becomes the Brahmaputra after being joined by the Dibang and Lohit rivers in its flow through the Assam Valley. The Brahmaputra has smaller catchments than either the Ganges or the Indus and enters Bangladesh with the waters of many tributaries. Flowing southward to join the Ganges in its course through the plains, the Brahmaputra divides into many channels and forms numerous braids that enclose various islands.

The peninsular rivers fall into two categories: coastal and inland. The coastal rivers are comparatively smaller streams. There are only a handful of these rivers that drain into the sea on the east coast, but around 600 rivers drain into the sea on the west coast. The west coast rivers are particularly important. Although they drain only 3 percent of the basins, as much as 14 percent of the country's water resources are contained in them. The inland rivers are of great antiquity. They are stable and well defined in their courses. The rivers flowing westward such as the Narmada and Tapi have narrow elongated catchments, while the eastward-flowing rivers—the Mahanadi, Godavari, Krishna, and Cauvery—are less turbulent and more predictable than the Himalayan rivers.

During 1966–1967 the Department of Agriculture initiated a centrally sponsored groundwater survey and investigation program. The Central Ground Water Board became the organization tasked with studying groundwater resources. The board periodically estimates the total groundwater draft for the whole country. Groundwater utilization for different years is estimated based on groundwater draft. Return flows from irrigation use are assumed as 10–20 percent of the water diverted from the reservoir for irrigation. In the case of localized use of groundwater for irrigation, the return flow is assumed to be negligible. The return flows from domestic and industrial uses either from groundwater or surface water sources are assumed to be 70–80 percent. Because of the hydrogeological variations in the country, the groundwater development potential also varies widely in different states and regions. Although rainfall has been the principal source of groundwater recharge, the recharge from canal seepage and return flow of irrigation was found to be significant while estimating groundwater recharge in the states of Andhra Pradesh, Punjab, Haryana, and Jammu and Kashmir. Recharge ranges from 43 percent to 49 percent in these states, while in the states of Tamil Nadu and Uttar Pradesh it ranges from 24 percent to 28 percent.

The marine water resource is of considerable importance for navigation, fisheries, industrial and domestic products, seafood, oil, and gas. The national coastline has a cradle of port cities, including Mumbai, Panaji, Cochin, Thiruanthanhpuram, Chennai, Nellore, Vishakhapatanam, and Kolkota. Smaller ports include Okha and Dwarka. These port cities provide livelihoods to millions of people through fishing. In Kolkota the fish catch and dried supplement foods provide sustenance to millions of people in West Bengal. The port cities have either rocky or sandy shores. While sandy shores support beautiful beach resorts, the rocky shores are known for infinite oceanic wealth in the form of sea products. The marine waters also provide turtle as well as shrimp, lobster, and other arthropods that are packed and sold as edible food. India produces 1.7 million tons of fish, out of which 35 percent is from freshwater.

VANDANA ASTHANA

See also Water Conflict; Water Policy

Further Reading
Briscoe, J., and R. S. P. Malik. *Handbook of Water Resources in India: Development, Management, and Strategies*. New Delhi. Oxford University Press, 2007.
Iyer, Ramaswamy R. *Water: Perspectives, Issues and Concerns*. New Delhi: Sage, 2003.
Jain, S. K., P. K. Agarwal, and V.P. Singh. *Hydrology and Water Resources of India*. New York: Springer, 2007.

Wealth. *See* Poverty and Wealth

✦ WEST BENGAL

West Bengal is an eastern state of India that was born at the time of India's independence from British imperialism in 1947. Independent India was partitioned into Pakistan and India. The province of Bengal, which had a significant Muslim population, was divided into the Hindu-dominated West Bengal, which was included in India, and the Muslim-dominated East Bengal, which was included in Pakistan. In 1971 East Bengal became the nation of Bangladesh.

Although now belonging to two different nations—India and Bangladesh—the two Bengals share the same ethnoracial characteristics. Ruled for the past 3,000 years by kings who were Buddhist (Maurya, Pala), Hindu (Maurya, Gupta, Sena), Muslim (Turkic, Mughal), and Christian (British, Danish, French), Bengal has come to acquire a rich cultural and religious diversity.

History in West Bengal dates back to the Stone Age. Excavations near the ancient town of Sagardighi in the Mushidabad District unearthed evidence of a civilization that could date back 15,000–20,000 years. Closer to recorded history are the findings at Chandraketugarh, near Barasat in the North 24 Parganas District, of relics of several periods, roughly from the 5th century BCE. These discoveries have led to speculation that this could be the city of Gange in the ancient kingdom of Gangahridai (literally meaning the land that has Ganga at its heart) referred to by Ptolemy, Pliny the Elder, Megasthenes, and Virgil.

Peopled by the Austro-Asiatic, Dravidian, and Tibeto-Burman groups, the region of West Bengal was ruled by non-Vedic kings before the coming of the Indo-Aryans. Bengal became part of the Indo-Aryan civilization from around the 7th century BCE, when the

Magadha Empire included western Bengal. Ruled by kings and emperors who were Hindu or Buddhist, Bengal had a social life that was characterized either by an egalitarian Buddhist society or by a hierarchically structured Brahmin-dominated society. Bengal was part of the Nanda, Maurya, and Gupta empires, and the first king who asserted its independence was Shashanka of Gaur in the 7th century CE. The Buddhist Palas who ruled from the 8th century were followers of the Mahayana and Tantric forms of Buddhism. The Hindu Sena kings followed for about a century, to be defeated in 1204 by the Turkish forces led by Bakhtiyar Khilji of the Slave Dynasty. Bengal was the last frontier conquered by the Turko-Mongols in their drive eastward from Central Asia. The Turks ruled for about two centuries until they were defeated in 1576 by the Mughals, whose empire spanned almost the entire Indian subcontinent. This began the reign of the Bengal nawabs who governed Bengal and remained politically subordinate to the Delhi Sultanate but repeatedly challenged the power of the Mughals.

The 13th–18th centuries saw the coming of innumerable Sufi saints to Bengal and mass conversions to Islam along the south and east of Bengal. There was in fact a significant difference between the western and eastern parts of the Bengal province. The degree of urbanization and the population density were far greater in the north and west of Bengal. The agricultural pattern was more settled, and the larger cities encouraged greater social stratification. The continuous immigration of Brahmins from the north of India aligned the west of Bengal with mainland India's Vedic culture to a degree greater than had been possible in the eastern region of Bengal, which was still largely forested and rural. The Gaudiya Vaishnava movement begun by Chaitanya in the 16th century also influenced the society and culture of western Bengal. Chaitanya's message of bhakti (devotion) and prem (love) as the only qualities necessary to reach God played an important role in diminishing the hold of the caste system. In West Bengal today, the population includes Sikhs, Christians, Jains, and Buddhists, and in areas that are remote from the urban center, animistic worship and innumerable syncretic religions and cults flourish.

The west of Bengal for many centuries had a flourishing trade at its river ports and was popular with merchants from all over the world. By the 18th century, the French and the English had established trading bases at Chandannagar and Calcutta, respectively. Tension between these two nations intensified with the Seven Years' War in Europe, and the English began strengthening their fortifications at Calcutta without the permission of the nawab of Bengal. This angered the nawab, leading to the Battle of Plassey between Bengal and the British East India Company in 1757. The English won the battle and replaced Nawab Siraj-ud-daulah with a titular head, thus effectively taking control of Bengal. A few years later with the Battle of Buxar in 1764, the British position was strengthened over a larger part of India, ushering in the 200-year colonization of India by the British Raj.

The colonial rulers made Calcutta the capital of colonial India, and Bengal functioned as the seat of colonial power for the next two centuries. During these years, some areas of West Bengal underwent rapid industrialization and development. The Mission Press was set up at

Serampore, institutes of higher education were set up at Calcutta, and the first railway line in India was established. Many famines, however, also marked this period, two of which were particularly devastating and killed millions; the famine in 1770 wiped out a third of Bengal's population, and the famine in 1943 killed an estimated 3 million people.

Western education was introduced in the early 19th century to create an indigenous group who would act in the European administrative and trade offices, giving rise to the Bengali middle class. This was the time when Bengal witnessed the Bengal Renaissance: an awakening of modern thinking that challenged orthodox concepts. The reform movements against suttee, child marriage, and other evils of Hindu society placed Bengal at the vanguard of India's movement toward modernity and liberalism. The first concerted rebellion against the colonizers in 1857 began from Barrackpore, a suburb of West Bengal, with the soldier Mangal Pandey and spread rapidly across northern India. This event, known variously as India's First War of Independence or as the Sepoy Mutiny, led to the British Crown taking over the administration of British India from the East India Company.

It was in Bengal that the Indian nationalist movement began to concretize in the latter half of the 19th century. Extreme and revolutionary groups such as Jugantar and Anushilan Samiti emerged to fight the British. The first partition of Bengal in 1905 was seen as an attempt to divide and thereby weaken Bengal along religious lines and was strongly resented, giving rise to the Swadeshi Movement. Based on the principle of economic boycott of English goods, the movement aimed at weakening the British economy and was the most successful of the pre-Gandhian movements against colonialism.

In 1947 the declaration of India's partition into India and Pakistan resulted in bloody riots between Hindus and Muslims. As large numbers of Muslims left West Bengal for eastern Pakistan, an equally large influx of Hindus came into West Bengal. Thousands were killed, traumatized, and made destitute, making this one of the darkest chapters in India's history. The governments and people on both sides of the border coped as best they could in providing shelter and relief to the refugees. The influx of refugees into West Bengal has continued over the years.

Apart from the riots during the Partition of 1947, West Bengal has been marked by religious tolerance and amicable coexistence between the many communities that live here. Immigrants from outside the subcontinent who have been in West Bengal for several generations now include Portuguese, Jews, Armenians, Dutch, and Chinese. Years of exposure to religious traditions of Sufi Islam, Gaudiya Vaishnavism, and Ramakrishna's teachings have made religion in West Bengal significantly tolerant. The long political dominance of the Socialist parties has aided this, and class difference is perhaps more keenly felt than religious differences. The state of West Bengal witnessed a violent uprising during the 1960s and 1970s. This group of radicals, the Naxalites, was led by a section of the Far Left group dissatisfied with the socioeconomic structure, which had remained harshly unequal. They led a violent movement that unleashed terror in the state and had to be brutally suppressed by the government. Despite the promise shown by Bengal in the 19th century, the state has been mired in economic problems of trade unionism, lack of industrialization, and power crises. Since the 1990s, however, the state has begun to show signs of development and economic growth. West Bengal's economy is the third largest in India.

West Bengal is rich in ecology and biodiversity. The state has 1 biosphere reserve, 2 tiger reserves, 5 national parks, and 15 wildlife sanctuaries. There are more than 7,000 species of flora, including bacteria, algae, fungi, bryophytes, pteridophytes, and angiosperms, and more than 10,000 species of fauna. West Bengal has a varied geography. Northern Bengal lies in the foothills of the Himalayas. To the south of this region is the Dooars, an area that has been marked for its ecological diversity, unique in its wealth of flora and fauna. In southern Bengal lie the deltaic region and the mangrove forests known as the Sunderbans, which has a wealth of biological diversity in its wetlands and forests, besides being home to the Royal Bengal Tiger. Crisscrossed by innumerable rivers and rivulets, West Bengal is largely dependent on agriculture, with rice and fish being the preferred diet across the state.

SIPRA MUKHERJEE

See also Kolkata

Further Reading
Bandyopadhyay, Sekhar. *From Plassey to Partition: A History of Modern India.* New Delhi: Orient Longman, 2004.
Chatterjee, Joya. *Bengal Divided: Hindu Communalism and Power Politics.* Cambridge: Cambridge University Press, 1994.
Chatterjee, Partha. *Texts of Power: Emerging Disciplines in Colonial Bengal.* Minneapolis: University of Minnesota Press, 1995.
Eaton, Richard M. *The Rise of Islam along the Bengal Frontier, 1204–1760.* New Delhi: Oxford University Press, 1997.
Sen, Amiya P. *Social and Religious Reform: The Hindus of British India.* New Delhi: Oxford University Press, 2003.
Sengupta, Nitish. *History of the Bengali-speaking People.* New Delhi: UBS Publishers, 2008.

✦ WIDOWS

India has a large number of widows. Census data on widows shows that India has 34.3 million widows ages 10 and above in 2001, or 9.1 percent of the corresponding female population of 377.8 million, and a 2010 forecast figure of 42.4 million (total females 467.1 million, ages 10 and above). The 1991 census counted 26.2 million widows. The percentage of 9.1 percent is higher than for all other South Asian countries at around 7 percent (other than Afghanistan at around 27 percent). East Asia, for example, has percentages at around 7–8 percent (ages 15 and above). China has 8.1 percent and is projected to have

43 million widows in 2010, corresponding to a women's population of 532.9 million, ages 15 and above, and countries with war legacies have higher percentages: Japan, 13 percent; the Koreas, 12.3 percent; and Vietnam, 10.4 percent. Child widows exist due to the early age of marriage that is practiced among sizable proportions of Hindus and Muslims. The areas of India that have the highest percentages of widows are in the states of Bihar, Uttar Pradesh, Rajasthan, Jharkhand, Orissa in northern India, and Andhra Pradesh in southern India. UNICEF defines child marriage as marriage before the age of 18 and cites Indian data for 2007 that shows that 47 percent of women ages 20–24 were married before age 18. The marriage of girls around ages 12–13 is still common, while according to one estimate 15 percent of girls in India's five poorest states get married at or below the age of 10. In fact, the age cohort distribution of widows, according to the 2001 census, shows 0 percent (ages 0–9 years), .1 percent (ages 10–14), .2 percent (ages 15–19), .7 percent (ages 20–24), 1.4 percent (ages 25–29), 2.6 percent (ages 30–34), 4.5 percent (ages 35–39), 7.7 percent (ages 40–44), 11.3 percent (ages 45–49), and 37.5 percent (ages 50 and above).

The study of the condition of widows in India and the impact of their large numbers is heavily neglected by the government, by policy analysts, and by nongovernmental agencies (NGOs) and researchers. This is unfortunate given the incentive structure created by key aspects of widowhood and their negative impact on others; the incentive structure arises from widows' economic insecurity, which is often characterized by severe deprivation, the lack of physical security, and social stigma. In all of this, pivotal roles are played by key Indian social norms with respect to marriage and sexual respectability, together with the role of government. Widows are sometimes referred to under research and NGO program headings as "female-headed households" and "single women," where the primary focus is on single women as a category. Internationally, the popular image of widows is their association with the custom of suttee, a Hindu practice whereby the widow commits ritual suicide by throwing herself on her deceased husband's funeral pyre, although suttee is no longer systematically practiced. Widow deprivation in concentrated form is on display to the world in the town of Vrindavan (Brindaban) in Uttar Pradesh, where abandoned Hindu widows spend the rest of their lives in refuges. Some of the widows have been there since early childhood. The image of extreme social conservativism toward widows is also fueled by the many widows from the elite segment of Indian society, typically the Hindu Brahmin caste, for which remarriage is socially unacceptable and ritualized norms severely restrict daily behavior for the remainder of their lives. While Hindu high-caste social norms for widows are still practiced to varying degrees, for the wider society, characterized as nonelite, widows' social situation is more varied. For example, in lower social groups, widows' remarriage is a much more common occurrence and is due to the material rigors of life and the social norms restricting female employment in large parts of the country. Country-level data on remarriage in India is rare; data calculated for the 1971 Indian census estimated that 33.7 percent of widows across India remarried, while 62.5 percent of men whose wives had died remarried. There is little material on Indian Muslim widows, but available sources give a picture of fewer constraints than their Hindu counterparts, while Christian widows tend to be still less encumbered by restrictions.

The impact of widows on society is largely unappreciated, but an understanding of it is required to make practical headway on core social and economic development concerns, especially for women and girls. This negative impact operates through four factors, closely related to the core negative aspects of widowhood: lack of a welfare state, a high degree of discrimination against women's paid employment, a completely ineffective legal system across large parts of India, and social stigma. The outcome that these elements produce is the privileging of the institution of marriage and, in effect, the legitimating of women through men as the only dependable source of female economic support. This fact is supported by the near universality of marriage in Indian society and the commensurate broad social understanding of its importance and unavoidability for women in particular. Using the broadest and most commonly used Indian socioeconomic generalizations, the north-south distinction across a range of human development indicators (HDIs) shows that widows typically have higher standards of living in southern India, which systematically deteriorates across most of northern India. For example, in a comparison of women's life expectancy at birth between the severely impoverished state of Uttar Pradesh and the advanced state of Kerala, the difference is almost 20 years, at 76 years for Kerala and 57 years for Uttar Pradesh. The fate of widows closely follows the implications of these statistics. This is shown by fewer remarried widows in southern India compared to northern India; in southern India it is generally not socially unacceptable for women to take up paid employment, unlike in northern India. Evidence shows that in northern India the chance of becoming a widow is lower, but women, once widowed, have a higher risk of mortality, while the opposite is true in southern India. Crucially, there is greater social acceptance in southern India of women living on their own, although this is not at Western levels. Concern, especially in northern India, with independent single women is based on notions of sexual impropriety wherein a single woman's morals are always perceived to be in doubt. Widows' deprivation and poverty are largely a northern outcome of the general inability of women to take up paid employment, which is socially sanctioned, resulting in their consequent reliance on male family members and land for subsistence. Land, given that roughly 70 percent of the Indian population is rural, takes on crucial importance to widowed women, particularly in northern India.

Deprivation for widows frequently results from northern India's effectively nonexistent legal system, facilitating effective land theft by relatives and neighbors because court processes, for low-income widows in particular, are too expensive, too lengthy, and open to corruption. In the event that land is stolen or a widow is from a landless low-income family, also a common experience, the added lack of a welfare state largely guarantees destitution if support from the family is not available. This brings into focus the negative incentives, and thus the crucial nature, of widows' deprivation for development. Due to the reliance on family as the only realistic prospect of assistance for the majority of women and due to the social norms of inheritance practices that place property such as land in the hands of male relatives, women place a high degree of emphasis on male children to the detriment of female children. This has given rise to the term "son preference," which also applies to some East Asian countries. The son preference effect is where mothers and families do whatever it takes to ensure that sons survive; this is mirrored by an abnormally high degree of mortality among girls under five years of age in India and girls' significantly lower school participation, both of which primarily occur in northern India. The crucial aspects in the creation of these outcomes are males' effectively exclusive access to paid employment and the fact that daughters leave home when they marry. This has resulted in the social norm of sons being responsible for the financial aspects of care for parents, and this is crucial for widows because women generally outlive men. Therefore, until drastic improvements are made in the reform and enforcement of law and a welfare state is instituted with a strong focus on single women, the threat of widows' deprivation will continue to negatively impact not only married women as they try to hedge against the financial and other insecurities of being without a husband in future years, but also girls' very survival.

Other aspects of widowhood are that young widows without children usually find it easy to remarry, while the opposite is true for women with children. One option in rural settings where control of land is a significant issue is to marry a brother of the deceased husband if one is available. Otherwise, widows generally and older widows in particular often have to accept marriage to significantly older men. Where child marriage is practiced, children can and do become widows. This causes significantly greater risks of degrading circumstances arising for the child widow. The mothers of child widows often feel that the best option for their daughters' welfare is to have them remarry even if they are still very young, such as being below the age of 15. Widows with children, however, do not want to remarry and avoid doing so when possible out of fear of the treatment meted out to the widow's existing children by a new husband and often due to the experience of an abusive marriage. Finally, they fear that as previously married women they may not be fully accepted into the new family. Widows can be discriminated against out of the perception of them as sexual predators, and their presence in public contexts brings questions of the integrity of those with whom they are linked, such as in the case of male employers. Alternatively, widows can be sexual victims twice over, first by being attacked by a man for the purposes of sexual gratification and second by being accused of instigating the man's attack. A case exists of a widow who, in a village context, after being attacked on two occasions was accused by the village council of soliciting the sexual attack. She subsequently committed suicide. Widows in India can face very difficult circumstances.

RISTO HÄRMÄ

See also Family; Women, Status of; Women's Reform Movements

Further Reading
Agarwal, Bina. *A Field of One's Own: Gender and Land Rights in South Asia*. Cambridge: Cambridge University Press, 1994.

Ahuja, Mukesh. *Widows: Role Adjustment and Violence*. New Delhi: Wishwas Prakashan, 1996.

Bhattacharya, Malini. *In Radha's Name: Widows and Other Women in Brindaban*. New Delhi: Tulika Books, 2008.

Bose, Ashish, and Mala Kapur Shankardass. *Growing Old in India: Voices Reveal, Statistics Speak*. New Delhi: BR Publishing, 2004.

Chen, Martha Alter. *Perpetual Mourning: Widowhood in Rural India*. New Delhi: Oxford University Press, 2000.

Chen, Martha Alter, ed. *Widows in India: Social Neglect and Public Action*. Thousand Oaks, CA: Sage, 1998.

Croll, Elizabeth. *Endangered Daughters: Discrimination and Development in Asia*. London: Routledge, 2000.

Drèze, Jean, and Amartya Sen. *India: Development and Participation*. New York: Oxford University Press, 2002.

International Institute for Population Sciences, Mumbai. *National Family Health Survey (NFHS-3), 2005–06*. Mumbai: International Institute for Population Sciences, 2007.

Luce, Edward. *In Spite of the God: The Strange Rise of Modern India*. London: Abacus, 2006.

Nussbaum, Martha C. *Women and Human Development: The Capabilities Approach*. Cambridge: Cambridge University Press, 2000.

Reddy, P. Adinarayana, ed. *Problems of Widows in India*. New Delhi: Sarup and Sons, 2004.

Saxena, Shobha. *Child Marriage in South Asia: Brutal Murder of Innocence*. New Delhi: Regal Publications, 2007.

✦ WOMEN, STATUS OF

"You can tell the condition of a nation by looking at the status of its women," said the first prime minister of India, Jawaharlal Nehru (1889–1964; prime minister 1947–1964). Unlike similar developing countries, India produces an elite world-class category of women, epitomized by graduates of the Indian Institute of Technology Science, the Institute of Technology, and the Indian Institute of Management graduates along with health professionals and a range of internationally known academics, writers, athletes, businesswomen, and actors. Among many notable Indian women are Bina Agarwal (b. 1951), Shabana Azmi (b. 1950), Kamala Das (1934–2009), Nandita Das (b. 1969), Kiran Desai (b. 1971), Vandana Shiva (b. 1952), Kiran Mazumdar Shaw (b. 1953), and Sania Mirza (b. 1986). However, while women can also be found in the Indian space program and firms such as Microsoft, the vast majority of Indian women still face high levels of deprivation and severe gender-based discrimination.

At the broadest levels of analysis of female well-being, northern Indian women, with the exception of the two northern pockets of Himachal Pradesh and Mizoram states, do much worse on standard and nonstandard human development indicators (HDIs) than their southern counterparts. In southern India and for the country as a whole, Kerala state represents a model of women's development, although problems exist for women there as well. Northern attitudes and outcomes for women have been characterized by exceptional gender inequality and extreme discrimination, for which variations in poverty provide only part of the explanation. The evidence suggests that women's status is critically determined by social norms based in cultural beliefs, that is, a synthesis of customary and religious ideas. Many gender deprivation accounts do not fully appreciate this. Notably, while particular forms of Islam practiced in some parts of the world have been implicated in problematic social outcomes as measured by HDIs, the current Indian Hindu society has produced and continues to produce highly detrimental incentives toward gender, with severe outcomes for women. Well-documented accounts exist of widespread girl-child neglect resulting in mortality and low levels of education, wide-scale disinheritance of women, dowry murder, widespread rape and violence against women, and widespread sex-selective abortion against female fetuses mainly in the nonstandard HDIs.

On balance, the Hindu and Muslim societies in India hold equal positions on outcomes for women, with both groups significantly behind other religious denominations. Significantly, Hindu society, due to the caste system, creates the additional dimension of religious class-based discrimination, with negative results for women from the lowest castes. For example, among other problems, they are seen as soft targets for sexual abuse, including rape as a weapon of extortion and as caste discipline by higher-caste men. Custodial rape is common by police. Famous case studies include the renowned cases of Phoolan Devi and Bhanwari Devi, and films have been made about both cases. Women of other religious groups, such as Jain, Christian, and Parsi, do significantly better across all or most HDIs.

Standard HDIs show the following macrotrends for women: literacy has risen from 15 percent in 1960–1961 to 54.2 percent in 2001, mortality for children under age five decreased

Women artisans do appliqué work at a handcrafts business in Orissa. (Samrat/Dreamstime.com)

from 282 deaths per 1,000 live births in 1960 to 90 in 2005, in 2005 there were 86 deaths per 1,000 male births compared to 95 per 1,000 female births, malnutrition manifested in anemia rose from 51.8 to 56.2 percent among all women between 1998–1999 and 2005–2006, female (paid) labor force participation for rural women rose from 31.8 to 32.7 percent (virtually no change) and for urban women from 13.4 to 16.6 percent from 1972–1973 to 2004–2005, and the total fertility rate changed from 5.9 in 1960 to 3.11 children per woman in 2005. Thirty percent of infants at birth would qualify for intensive care if they were born in California. Approximately 70 percent of the population of India is rural. The social distribution shows that 82 percent of household heads are Hindu, 13 percent are Muslim, 3 percent are Christian, 2 percent are Sikh, and 1 percent are Buddhist, with all others less than 1 percent; 19 percent are low castes (Scheduled Caste), and 8 percent are Adivasi (Scheduled Tribes).

Four key social norms affect the overall status of women in India. First, sexual respectability or reputation causes a restrictive attitude toward economic and social activity of women outside the home and toward the mobility of girls from the start of puberty. Northern rural Hindu and Muslim women are governed by social norms restricting them to home-based work, typically unpaid, and pubescent girls are pulled from school and married based on the notion equating sexual promiscuity with freedom of unsupervised movement. Some 45 percent of the population lives in states in northern India—Bihar, Jharkhand, Madhya Pradesh, Orissa, Rajasthan, and Uttar Pradesh—where this attitude and related practices exist. The percentages of unmarried women ages 15–49 for 1998–1999 who worked outside the home were 11 percent in Uttar Pradesh, 13 percent in Rajasthan, 17 percent in Bihar, 9 percent in Haryana, 9 percent in Punjab, 23 percent in Orissa, and 31 percent in Madhya Pradesh. In contrast with China, large numbers of Chinese factory workers are unmarried rural teenage girls who have migrated for work purposes.

Second, single women are seen as socially deviant, given the social norm of mandatory marriage, and marriage in India is nearly universal, as marriage and domestic activity are still seen as the main life achievement and role of a woman in all social groups. The failure to marry can cause damage to a family's reputation, thereby inhibiting the marriage of siblings and damaging social capital. This extends in some cases to widows, who in some rural locations are accused of witchcraft and are attacked; evidence for this exists in Bihar, Jharkhand, Rajasthan, and Orissa states.

Third, marriage norms play a significant role in the lives of Indian women in a variety of aspects. Marriage as early as possible is preferred, often just after puberty for rural society, and is common across all social groups. The average age of marriage is 15–16 years of age or on completion of a level of education, while the emphasis on sexual purity means that many rural girls are permanently removed from school, although this mainly occurs in the central and northern states. There is a preference that the education level of the bride be limited. The level of education is based on social class—for example, primary school level for unskilled workers, secondary school level and possibly undergraduate level for urban dwellers, and postgraduate level for elite groups, although generally no higher than a master's degree—and in all cases education level for the wife should be less than that of the husband. Men and women form marriages that are typically arranged with little input from prospective brides and grooms in most social groups. In northern India, the level of contact permitted between the wife and her parents is limited. Remarriage is effectively prohibited for widows by many segments of Hindu Brahmins (highest caste) and some other Hindu castes, while Muslims do not hold views with punitive outcomes for widows. There are widely held attitudes that effectively prohibit interreligious marriage, while Hindu intrareligious marriage between different castes depends on which sex is of the lower caste and how far apart in the caste hierarchy the two castes are. The giving of dowries is widely practiced by all faith groups.

Fourth, with regard to inheritance, while Hindu women especially are widely disinherited by husbands' relatives and by siblings, there was an improvement in inheritance law for Hindu women in 2005. It should be noted that there are specific faith-based laws covering each religious community with regard to the family.

The cumulative impact of these social norms results in widespread economic dependence of women on men. Compounding this is a nonexistent welfare state, with the government's own admission of the collapsed public primary health care system in several regions for reasons other than underfunding, and the fact that women are ignorant of many areas of legislation. Women depend on husbands and in older age on sons. Otherwise, severe poverty is likely in widowhood. This has led to son preference, which causes the neglect of girls in rural society and mass abortion of female fetuses. Widow deprivation has played a significant role in the girl-child deprivation and female fetus abortion phenomena.

RISTO HÄRMÄ

See also Family; Women's Reform Movements

Further Reading

Agarwal, Bina. *A Field of One's Own: Gender and Land Rights in South Asia*. Cambridge: Cambridge University Press, 1994.

Anderson, Siwan. "Why Dowry Payments Declined with Modernization in Europe and Are Rising in India." *Journal of Political Economy* 3(2) (2003): 269–310.

Chaurasia, Alok Ranjan, and S. C. Gulati. *India: The State of Population, 2007*. New Delhi: Oxford University Press, 2008.

Chen, Martha. *Perpetual Mourning: Widowhood in Rural India*. New Delhi: Oxford University Press, 2000.

Dreze, Jean, and Amartya Sen. *India: Development and Participation*. New Delhi: Oxford University Press, 2002.

Dube, Leela. *Anthropological Explorations in Gender: Intersecting Fields*. New Delhi: Sage, 2001.

Gangoli, Geetanjal. *Indian Feminisms: Law, Patriarchies and Violence*. Burlington, VT: Ashgate, 2008.

Hasan, Zoya, and Ritu Menon, ed. *The Diversity of Muslim Women's Lives in India*. New Brunswick, NJ: Rutgers University Press, 2005.

International Institute for Population Sciences and ORC-Macro International. *National Family Health Survey (NFHS-3), 2005–06: India*, vol. 1. Mumbai: International Institute for Population Sciences, 2007.

Jha, Jyotsna, and Dhir Jhingran. *Elementary Education for the Poor and Other Marginalised Groups: The Real Challenge of Universalization*. New Delhi: Manohar, 2005.

Kapadia, Karin, ed. *The Violence of Development: The Politics of Identity, Gender and Social Inequalities in India*. New York: Zed Books, 2002.

Kumar, Ravi, ed. *The Crisis of Elementary Education in India*. New Delhi: Sage, 2006.

National Family Health Survey. 3 vols. Mumbai: International Institute of Population Studies, 1992–2006.

Rai, Shirin M. *The Gender Politics of Development*. London: Zed Books, 2008.

Sagade, Jaya. *Child Marriage in India: Socio-legal and Human Rights Dimensions*. New Delhi: Oxford University Press, 2005.

Sangtin Writers. *Playing with Fire: Feminist Thought and Activism through Seven Lives in India*. Minneapolis: University of Minnesota Press, 2006.

✦ WOMEN'S REFORM MOVEMENTS

During the Vedic period in India (2500–1500 BCE) women held a high position in society with the Hindu texts the *Rigveda* and the *Yajurveda* highlighting women's education and role in family and society. In the post-Vedic period, the Laws of Manu as recorded in the *Manusmirti*, composed around 200 CE, gave women a subordinate status to men. This subordinate status was used to impose regressive rules and regulations on women, advocated male supremacy, and dealt with such issues as barring women from public functions; child marriage; and suttee, the funeral practice whereby a widow would immolate herself on her husband's funeral pyre. The concept of womanhood as delineated in the *Manusmirti* contributed directly to the formation of women's reform movements and galvanized 19th-century social reformers to focus their work on women's issues. Between the 1820s and the 1850s reformers set up organizations such as the Brahmo Samaj (founded in 1828) in eastern India in Calcutta, the Prarthana Samaj (founded in 1867) in western India in Bombay, the Arya Samaj (founded in 1875) in northern India at Rajkot, and the Theosophical Society (founded in 1875) in southern India at Madras. In each of these organizations women's issues were raised and discussed. Prior to the reformers, illiterate women such as Rassundari Devi (b. ca. 1809), taught themselves reading and writing. Devi and others went on to write gender-focused accounts of their lives during this timeframe, and Devi wrote the first autobiography by an Indian woman highlighting women's issues. Raja Ram Mohan Roy (1774–1833) of Bengal was the first to initiate the cause of women and denounce the caste system. The Prarthana Samaj was founded by Brahmins to prove that the Hindu religious tradition was not the source of the legitimacy of women's societal roles. The Arya Samaj emphasized the education of both girls and boys. Pandita Ramabai (1858–1922) was the first Indian woman to publicly advocate female education and women's rights by traveling all around India with her brother arguing for the emancipation of women. In 1881 she gave evidence before the Hunter Commission set up by the British to examine the state of education in India; the commission's report was issued in 1884. Ramabi emphasized the need for the abolition of child marriages and the promotion of women's education. In Bengal in 1905 the Swadeshi Movement, a movement to promote the purchase of indigenous goods and boycott British imported products, gave women a prominent role in nationalist activities on a large scale, but mass mobilization began in 1910 with the Bharat Stri Mahamandal, which opened offices in 11 cities to promote women's issues, especially female education. The Women's Indian Association, founded in 1918 in Andhra Pradesh, was the first organization to unite all women for mutual assistance. Its goal was and is to offer assistance "to distressed women and children." The National Council of Women in India, founded in 1925, strives to remove legal barriers to women. The All India Women's Conference in 1927 became recognized as the most important women's group. Communist and non-Communist groups alike, whatever their political persuasion, also worked to improve women's conditions. The result of all these women's movements in various parts of the country involving women of a number of ideological, class, and social perspectives was that reform movements contributed to significant changes in the law dealing with women's rights, status, and privileges. Among them were acts such as the Hindu Widow Remarriage Act of 1856, the Child Marriage Restraint Act of

Indian activists from the Self Employed Women's Association (SEWA) and other organizations representing workers from the unorganized sector shout slogans during a protest rally in New Delhi, August 2007. The activists were demanding that the Indian government table the bill for "Social Security for Unorganised Workers," which was a promise of the Common Minimum Programme of the United Progressive Alliance government. They were demanding that pension and health insurance be included in the bill. (Manpreet Romana/AFP/Getty Images)

1929, the Hindu Women's Right to Property Act of 1937, the Hindu Marriage Act of 1955, the Hindu Succession Act of 1956, the Suppression of Immoral Traffic in Women and Girls Act of 1956–1957, and the Dowry Prohibition Act of 1961.

These pieces of legislation greatly improved the status of women in India. However, contemporary women's movements in India began in 1972 with the *chipko* movement, an environmental movement in the Himalayan foothills in which women played a prominent part, and people hugged trees to prevent them from being cut down. In 1974 the first feminist women's group, the Progressive Organization of Women, was set up. Inspired by the United Nations (UN) declaration of 1975 as the year of women, many grassroots women's organizations were formed. With the rise of activists such as Medha Patkar (b. 1954), Brinda Karat (b. 1947), and Madhu Kishwar (b. 1959), the contemporary women's movement in India focuses on fighting for educational rights and opportunities for women, gender equality, economic empowerment, the prevention of domestic violence and sexual exploitation, reproductive rights, abortion rights, divorce, and various issues dealing with the cultural stereotyping of women. The Self Employed Women's Association, more commonly known as SEWA and registered in 1972, represents the practical outcome of the reform movement. SEWA is a trade union representing poor self-employed women who earn a living through labor or various sorts, including manual labor, and small businesses.

SHEEBA HÄRMÄ

See also Family; Women, Status of

Further Reading
Duley, Margot I., and Mary I. Edwards. *The Cross-Cultural Study of Women: A Comprehensive Guide.* New York: Feminist Press, 1986.
Gupta, Shakuntla. *Women Development in India: A Comparative Study.* New Delhi: Anmol, 2005.
Olivelle, Patrick. *Manu's Code of Law: A Critical Edition and Translation of the Mānava-Dharmaśāstra.* Oxford: Oxford University Press, 2005.

✦ WORLD BANK, RELATIONS WITH

India's involvement with the World Bank dates back to its inception at Bretton Woods, New Hampshire, after World War II. India was among the 17 countries that met in Atlantic City in June 1944 to prepare the agenda for the Bretton Woods conference and among the 44 countries that signed the final agreement that established the World Bank. In fact, the name "International Bank for Reconstruction and Development" (IBRD) was a suggestion made by India to the drafting committee. The Indian delegation was led by Sir Jeremy Raisman (1892–1978), who served as a finance member of the government of

India during 1939–1945, and included Sir C. D. Deshmukh (1896–1982), governor of the Reserve Bank of India (1943–1950) who later become India's finance minister (1950–1956); Sir Theodore Gregory, the first economic adviser to the government of India; Sir R. K. Shanmukhan Chetty (1892–1953), who later became independent India's first finance minister (1947–1952); A. D. Shroff (1899–1965), one of the architects of the Bombay Plan published in 1944 for the economic development of India after independence; and B. K. Madan (1911–?), later India's executive director in the International Monetary Fund (IMF).

World Bank lending to India started in 1949 when the first loan of $34 million was approved for the Indian railways. In the first decade (1949–1959), the World Bank made about 20 loans to India amounting to a total of $611 million. During 1960–1969, overall loans to India increased to $1.8 billion, about three times the level in the previous decade. The period 1970–1979 was marked by a large increase in the absolute volume of International Development Association (IDA) lending, and the IDA share in total World Bank assistance reached a high of 80 percent. However, in the 1980s India's share in total IDA lending declined to 25 percent and was updated by the more expensive World Bank lending, which increased to $14.7 billion during 1980–1989.

The long-term relationship between the World Bank and India displays certain trends. In the early years, the World Bank closely collaborated with the more active United States Agency for International Development (USAID) to force policy changes. Hence, the World Bank's involvement was not as direct and visible as in the 1980s and 1990s. However, after the 1980s the World Bank, along with the IMF, played a more direct and visible role in India's policymaking.

Despite India's prominence in the World Bank's loan portfolio and the World Bank's importance in India's external borrowings, these were, in aggregate, modest for India's economy. The loans accounted for less than 1 percent of the gross national product and were seldom more than a couple of dollars per capita. However, their relative importance has been greater in certain sectors and time periods. In particular, the World Bank has been one of India's most reliable sources of external financing when the country suffered a balance of payments problems, such as in the 1960s, after the first and second oil shocks, and during 1990–1991.

PARAMITA GUPTA

See also World Economic Forum; World Trade Organization, Relations with

Further Reading
Kirk, Jason A. *India and the World Bank: The Politics of Aid and Influence.* New York: Anthem, 2010.
World Bank. *World Bank Engagement at the State Level: The Cases of Brazil, India, Nigeria, and the Russian Federation.* Washington, DC: World Bank, 2010.

✦ WORLD ECONOMIC FORUM

The World Economic Forum (WEF) is an independent international organization incorporated as a Swiss not-for-profit foundation. The WEF is committed to improving the state of the world by engaging leaders in partnerships to shape global, regional, and industry agendas. Its objective is to achieve a world-class corporate governance system in which values and rules are equally important. The WEF believes that economic progress and social development are endogenous to business sustainability, hence its motto "entrepreneurship in the global public interest."

Members of the WEF include companies that are driving forces in the world economy. The typical member company is a global enterprise with more than $5 billion in turnover (this may vary by industry and region). Additionally, these enterprises possess the following characteristics: (1) They rank among the top companies within their industry and/or country, and (2) they play a leading role in shaping the future of their industry and/or region.

Over the course of its 38-year history, the WEF has achieved a proud record of accomplishments in advancing progress on key issues of global concern. In 1979 the WEF became the first nongovernmental institution to initiate a partnership with China's economic development commissions, spurring economic reform policies in China.

The WEF's annual meeting in 2010 held in Davos, Switzerland, featured the "India Everywhere" project, which is the largest-ever Indian participation at the WEF. The event was attended by senior representatives from the government and by business leaders from different sectors, including the finance minister, the commerce and industry minister, the deputy chairman of the Planning Commission, the minister of tourism, and the chief ministers of Delhi, Rajasthan, and Kerala.

PARAMITA GUPTA

See also World Bank, Relations with; World Trade Organization, Relations with

Further Reading
World Economic Forum. "India Economic Summit 2010." Accessed April 28, 2011. http://www.weforum.org/events/india-economic-summit-2020.

✦ WORLD TRADE ORGANIZATION, RELATIONS WITH

India is a founding member of the General Agreement on Tariffs and Trade (GATT) of 1947 and its successor, the World Trade Organization (WTO), that came into effect in January 1995 after the conclusion of the Uruguay Round of Multilateral Trade Negotiations. The purpose of India's participation in an increasingly rule-based system in the governance of international trade is to ensure more stability and predictability, which ultimately would lead to more trade and prosperity for itself and the 134 other nations that now comprise the WTO. India also automatically avails of most-favored nation status and national treatment for its exports to all WTO members.

India was an active participant in all rounds of GATT negotiations and in the post-WTO era continues to be an important voice in discussions to launch a new round of multilateral trade negotiations. The focal point of such discussions has been to ensure a fair distribution of rights and obligations between developed and developing countries and to address the developmental concerns of poor countries. India's negotiating strategy has evolved vis-à-vis its overall trade and development strategy and policy orientation. The country's earlier strategy was largely defensive, in line with its import substitution policies. But the initiation of economic reforms following the balance of payments crisis of 1991 altered India's views on the opportunities, benefits, and threats of engaging in the multilateral trading system and has led to the adoption of a more forward-looking negotiating strategy.

PARAMITA GUPTA

See also World Bank, Relations with; World Economic Forum

Further Reading

Barua, Alokesh, and Robert Mitchell Stern. *The WTO and India: Issues and Negotiating Strategies.* New Delhi: Orient Black Swan, 2010.

Natchiappan, E. M. Sudarsana. *India and WTO.* Chennai: University of Madras, 2007.

Nigam, R. L. *WTO and India.* New Delhi: Max Ford Books, 2006.

Thakur, Anil Kumar. *WTO and India.* New Delhi: Deep and Deep, 2007.

✦ YADAV, LALU PRASAD

Lalu Prasad Yadav (b. 1948) is the founder and president of Rashtriya Janata Dal (National People's Party), founded in 1997; former union minister of Indian Railways; and a member of the Lok Sabha, the lower house of Parliament. He was born into a poor peasant family in Phulwaria village in Gopalganj in northern Bihar. Due to the generosity of his elder brother, Mukund Rai, Yadav was able to continue his education and earn his law degree from Patna University (founded in 1917). He began his political career early as an active student leader in the 1970s in Patna, organizing protest movements against social injustices meted out to the Dalits (untouchables) and other minorities. He was greatly inspired by the Socialist leader Jayaprakash Nayaran (1902–1979) and participated in all of Narayan's rallies against government policies, especially during the State of Emergency (1975–1977) of Prime Minister Indira Gandhi (1917–1984; prime minister 1966–1977, 1980–1984), for which Yadav was jailed for several months. He contested his first Lok Sabha election in 1977 from the Chapra constituency in Bihar becoming, at 29, one of the youngest members of Parliament. As a result, he became one of the leading figures in Bihari politics. He then became a member of the Bihar Legislative Assembly for two terms and in 1989 became the leader of the opposition at the center by joining the Janata Dal (founded in 1999).

In 1990 Yadav headed the Janata Dal government in Bihar as the chief minister and served in that capacity until 1997. His decision to implement the recommendations of the Mandal Commission (1990) by providing reservations in the state won him accolades from Dalit communities. Yadav also professed close affinities to the plight of the Muslims, and his commitment to communal harmony between the Hindus and the Muslims was tested within a few

The charismatic and controversial Lalu Prasad Yadav, former chief minister of Bihar whose wife, Rabri Devi, followed him as chief minister, enabling him to maintain power and influence behind the scenes. He also served as Indian Railways minister. He was famous for his "caste politics," when he mobilized poor Muslims and Dalits (untouchables) to support his political agenda of favoring the poor and for his remarkable job of making Indian railways more efficient and profitable. (AP Photo/Ajit Kumar)

months of attaining office when he arrested Lal Krishna Advani (b. 1927), the leader of the Bharatiya Janata Party (founded in 1980), as Advani entered the boundary of Bihar on his journey to build the Ram Janmabhoomi Temple in Ayodhya in the United Provinces. Under Yadav's leadership the state of Bihar remained free of communal riots at a time when many other Indian states were dealing with severe interreligious disturbances after the demolition of Babri Masjid in December 1990. Since then Yadav has dominated the politics of Bihar even after resigning from the post of chief minister in 1997 on corruption charges when the state government was charged with the embezzlement of $267 million in the husbandry department. Although Yadav was imprisoned for these charges, he quickly installed his wife as the state's chief minister.

In 1997 Yadav announced the formation of a new political party, the Rashtriya Janata Dal, in order to establish a political party with influence at the center. The Rashtriya Janata Dal lent support to the Indian National Congress Party–led government in 2004 to prevent the Bharatiya Janata Party alliance from obtaining power. Yadav was then appointed the union minister of railways (2004–2009). Indian Railways, Asia's largest rail network, faced severe financial losses and deficits, but Yadav made it a profitable and self-sufficient industry through, among other things, downsizing, outsourcing, introducing innovative products, and increasing freight charges. Subsequently the management of Indian Railways under Yadav has become a case study at the premier Indian Institute of Management. The success of Indian Railways also attracted management students at Harvard University and the Wharton School of the University of Pennsylvania, who visited India and participated in lectures organized at Rail Bhawan, the headquarters of Indian Railways in New Delhi in 2006.

Rashtriya Janata Dal decided not to contest the 15th Lok Sabha elections in 2009 with its present allies, including the Indian National Congress Party, and opted instead for an alliance with Mulayam Singh Yadav (b. 1939) of the Lok Dal (founded in 1974) and Ram Vilas Paswan (b. 1946) of the Lok Janshakti Party (founded in 2000). These parties did poorly in the elections, and Yadav reiterated his unconditional support to the new government headed by Prime Minister Manmohan Singh (b. 1932; prime minister 2004–) after the election defeat.

FATIMA A. IMAM

See also Ayodhya; Bharatiya Janata Party; Bihar; Railroads; Yadav, Mulayam Singh

Further Reading

Jha, Neena, and Shivnath Jha. *Lalu Prasad, India's Miracle.* Ghaziabad: The Beginning Foundation, 2008.

Neelkamal, Neelam. *Laloo Prasad Yadav: A Charismatic Leader.* New Delhi: Har-Anand Publications, 1996.

✦ YADAV, MULAYAM SINGH

Mulayam Singh Yadav (b. 1939) is a leader of the Samajwadi Party, which he founded in 1992, in the Lok Sabha, the lower house of Parliament, from the Mainpuri constituency in Uttar Pradesh. In Uttar Pradesh, Yadav is known for his strong commitment to social justice and secularism. He belongs to the Aheer caste of Etawah and champions the rights of the backward castes or untouchables (Dalits) by advocating reservations (quotas) for them at all levels. As a young man struggling to receive an education in the small village of Sifai in Etawah, Yadav was greatly inspired by Ram Manohar Lohia (1910–1967), a Socialist leader and member of the Indian National Congress (INC), and joined in Lohia's demonstrations against the government. Yadav completed his graduate studies at Jain Inter College, Mainipuri, where he became a lecturer. He started his political career by contesting a Uttar Pradesh state assembly election on a Socialist Party ticket in 1967 and became the youngest member of the assembly. The protest movement against the State of Emergency imposed by Prime Minister Indira Gandhi (1917–1984; prime minister 1966–1977, 1980–1984) established Yadav on the national stage, and he was jailed for his involvement. He served as a Uttar Pradesh state minister during 1977–1980 and then assumed leadership of the Janata Dal (founded in 1977) in 1989.

Although Yadav started his first term (1989–1991) as the chief minister of Uttar Pradesh in 1989 with strong support from the right-wing Bharatiya Janata Party (founded in 1980), he lost the support of the party when he opposed party president Lal Krishna Advani (b. 1927) and his Ram Janmabhoomi Temple movement in Ayodhya and arrested followers of the movement for instigating communal strife. As a result, in 1992 Yadav formed his own party, the Samajwadi Party, and became the chief minister of the United Provinces for the second time (1993–1995) by allying with the Bahujan Samaj Party (founded in 1984). During his second tenure as chief minister, Yadav was involved in a controversy regarding the demand of separate statehood for Uttarkhand (the northern part of Uttar Pradesh that became a separate state in 2000). The supporters of the demand for Uttarkhand alleged that Yadav had ordered its activists shot during peaceful demonstrations. Within two years he lost the support of the Bahujan Samaj Party and had to resign from his post. The Bahujan Samaj Party leader Mayawati (b. 1956) accused Yadav of harassing her when the party withdrew its support for his government in 1995.

In 1996 Yadav contested the 11th Lok Sabha elections from the Mainpuri constituency, joined the central government led by Prime Minister H. P. Deve Gowda (b. 1933; prime minister 1996–1997), and was appointed defense minister. The central government collapsed in 1998, and Lok Sabha elections were held. Yadav was inducted into the Union ministry, again with the defense portfolio, in Inder Kumar Gujral's (b. 1919; prime minister 1997–1998) United Front government, although that government too only lasted a year. After the fall of the government, Yadav continued to serve as the leader of the opposition at the center and did not support the governments led by either the Bharatiya Janata Party (1999–2004) or later by the Congress Party (2004–2009). In Uttar Pradesh, however, Yadav remained a powerful leader and served as the state's chief minister for the third time during 2003–2007. Yadav and his party enjoy the support of the backward castes (Dalits) and the Muslims, receiving most of their support from the rural areas, but Bahujan Samaj Party leader Mayawati continues to challenge Yadav by portraying herself as the real leader of the Dalits in the state.

FATIMA A. IMAM

See also Ayodhya; Bharatiya Janata Party; Uttarakhand; Uttar Pradesh

Further Reading

Shafiuzzaman. *The Samajwadi Party: A Study of Its Social Base, Ideology, and Programme.* New Delhi: APH, 2003.

Sharma, Ashok Kumar. *Mulayam Singh Vichara aur Chintana: Ideas and Philosophy.* New Delhi: Dayamanda Poketa Buksa, 2005.

Singh, Ram, and Anshuman Yadav. *Mulayam Singh Yadav: A Political Biography.* New Delhi: Konark, 1998.

✦ YOGA

The word "yoga" is derived from *yoke*, which means "union," as the goal of yoga is to create union between the body and the mind. There is, however, no agreement on yoga's origin, definition, or classification, which is considered one of the most complicated multidimensional body and mind practices. Yoga used to be a "Made in India" philosophy and belongs mainly to Indian history and religion, but during India's long history, yoga has moved from religion to philosophy to politics and from a local to a global practice.

Yoga's long history goes back, as does India's, more than 5,000 years. As some steatite seals found in archaeological excavations (3000–2700 and 1750 BCE) show, yoga postures

A young instructor, left, teaches yoga as elderly women practice at a park in Kolkata, West Bengal. Yoga, an ancient Indian practice, is seen as a means to both physiological and spiritual well-being. (AP Photo/Bikas Das)

were being practiced in ancient times. Yoga started as a religious practice for Hindus. In fact, the word "yoga" appears often in the "Bhagavad Gita" ("The Lord's Song"), a section within the Hindu epic *Mahabharata* (ca. 500–400 BCE).

Although most of the research on yoga concludes that it originated in India, others argue that a Neolithic settlement named Mehrgahr (now Afghanistan) had many parallels to early yoga.

Yoga's definitions have changed from time to time and from region to region. Patanjali, who is the systematizer of yoga (ca. 150 BCE), defined yoga as "the restraining of the mind-stuff (*chitta*) from taking various forms (*vrittis*)." The more recent definition set by Paramahansa Yogananda (1893–1952) in the 20th century stated that yoga was a method for restraining the natural turbulence of thoughts, which otherwise impartially prevents all men from glimpsing the true nature of the spirit.

Yoga became more widely known in the West in the late 19th century by Swami Vivekananda (1863–1902), who brought Vedanta and yoga to the United States on September 11, 1893, when he gave his first address to the Parliament of Religions held at the Art Institute of Chicago, where yoga was localized and reshaped to make it belong to the whole world. The philosophy of yoga entered politics, as it was essential to the living philosophy of nonviolence of Mohandas Karamchand Gandhi (1869–1948) as he led the Indian National Congress (INC), (founded in 1885), in its fight for independence from Britain.

Despite yoga becoming a part of the cultures of people all around the world, the Indian government still considers yoga to be a part of Indian heritage. The Indian Yoga Association, sponsored by the Ministry of Health and Family Welfare, was accredited in October 2008 by the government of India to, among other things, create global standards in yoga education. As a self-regulatory body of renowned yoga schools in India, the Indian Yoga Association, a nonprofit, nonpolitical, and nonreligious body, aims at maintaining and promoting the different Indian yoga traditions.

Yoga is no longer just a physical practice. Extensive research is being conducted that has resulted in the publication of articles trying to reach beyond the typical physical exercise culture of yoga. In doing so, practitioners of yoga are attempting to address the many other dimensions of the practice of yoga while at the same time examining issues that impact the global yoga community as a whole.

Yoga is also no longer a Hindu religious practice. Yoga classes can be found in many non-Hindu countries, including Muslim countries. Yoga continues to be a tool to manage stress, support good health, and develop an individual's spirituality.

NILLY KAMAL EL-AMIR

See also Diet and Health; Hinduism; Religion

Further Reading

Discover Yoga Online. Accessed April 28, 2011. http://www.Discover-yoga-online.com.

Gandhi, J. *Peace by Peaceful Means: Peace and Conflict, Development and Civilization.* London: Sage, 1996.

Vivekananda, Swami. *Raja Yoga.* New York: Ramakrishna-Vivekananda Center, 1970.

Yoga Journal. Accessed April 28, 2011. http://www.yogajournal.com.

Yogananda, Paramahansa. *Autobiography of a Yogi.* 12th ed. Los Angeles: Self-Realization Fellowship, 1990. The charismatic and controversial Lalu Prasad Yadav, former chief minister of Bihar whose wife, Rabri Devi, followed him as chief minister, enabling him to maintain power and influence behind the scenes. He also served as Indian Railways minister. He was famous for his "caste politics," when he mobilized poor Muslims and Dalits (untouchables) to support his political agenda of favoring the poor and for his remarkable job of making Indian railways more efficient and profitable. (AP Photo/Ajit Kumar)

Selected Bibliography

✦

Abbas, K. A. *Indira Gandhi: Return of the Red Rose*. Mumbai: Popular Prakashan, 1966.

Abdullah, Sheikh. *Flames of the Chinar: An Autobiography*. Translated by Khushwant Singh. New Delhi: Viking, 1993.

Abraham, Itty. *The Making of the Indian Atomic Bomb: Science, Secrecy and the Postcolonial State*. London: Zed Books, 1998.

Acharya, Shankar. *Essays on Macroeconomic Policy and Growth in India*. Delhi: Oxford University Press, 2008.

Afshar, H., ed. *Women, State, and Ideology*. Basingstoke, UK: Macmillan, 1987.

Agarwal, Bina. *A Field of One's Own: Gender and Land Rights in South Asia*. Cambridge: Cambridge University Press, 1994.

Agarwal, Supriya, and Urmil Talwar. *Gender, History and Culture: Inside the Haveli*. Jaipur: Rawat, 2009.

Agnes, Flavia. "Hypocritical Morality." *Manushi* 149 (October 2005): 10–19.

Agnes, Flavia. "Protecting Women against Violence: Review of a Decade of Legislation, 1980–1989." *Economic and Political Weekly* 27(17) (1992): 19–33.

Agnes, Flavia. *State, Gender and the Rhetoric of State Reform, Gender and Law*. Bombay: RCWS, SNDT, 1995.

Agrawal, A. *Chaste Wives and Prostitute Sisters: Patriarchy and Prostitution in the Bedias of India*. Delhi: Routledge, 2008.

Ahluwalia, Isher Judge. *Industrial Growth in India: Stagnation since the Mid-Sixties*. Delhi: Oxford University Press, 1985.

Ahluwalia, Isher Judge, and I. M. D. Little, eds. *India's Economic Reforms and Development: Essays for Manmohan Singh*. New Delhi: Oxford University Press, 1998.

Ahmed, Akbar S. "Bombay Films: The Cinema as Metaphor for Indian Society and Politics." *Modern Asian Studies* 26(2) (1992): 289–320.

Ahmed, Imtiaz. *State and Foreign Policy: India's Rose in South Asia*. New Delhi: Vikas, 1993.

Ahuja, M. L. *Electorial Politics and General Elections in India, 1952–1998*. New Delhi: Mittal, 1998.

Aiyar, M. S. *Rajiv Gandhi's India: Politics, Economics, Foreign Policy and Perspective*. Hyderabad: Sangam Books, 1998.

Akbar, M. J. *India: The Siege Within*. Rev. ed. New Delhi: UBS Publishers, 1999.

Akbar, M. J. *Kargil: Cross Border Terrorism*. New Delhi: Mittal, 1999.

Akbar, M. J. *Kashmir: Behind the Veil*. New Delhi: Rohi, 2002.

Akbar, M. J. *Nehru: The Making of India*. London: Viking, 1988.

Akbar, M. J. *Riot after Riot: Caste and Communal Violence in India*. Harmondsworth: Penguin, 1988.

Alexander, M. K. *Madame Gandhi: A Political Biography*. North Quincy, MA: Christopher Publishing House, 1969.

Alexander, P. C. *My Years with Indira Gandhi*. New Delhi: Vision Books, 1991.

Ali, Aruna Asaf. *Private Face of a Public Personality: A Study of Jawaharlal Nehru*. New Delhi: Radiant, 1989.

Ali, S. Mahmud. *The Fearful State: Power, People, and Internal War in South Asia*. London: Zed Books, 1993.

Ali, Tariq. *An Indian Dynasty: The Story of the Nehru-Gandhi Family*. New York: Putnam, 1985.

Ali, Tariq. *Pakistan: Military Rule or People's Power*. New York: Morrow, 1970.

Allen, Douglas, ed. *Religion and Political Conflict in South Asia, India, Pakistan, and Sri Lanka*. Westport, CT: Greenwood, 1992.

Aloysius, G. *Nationalism without a Nation in India*. 3rd ed. New Delhi: Oxford University Press, 2000.

Alvares, Claude, and Ramesh Billorey. *Damning the Narmada: India's Greatest Planned Environmental Disaster*. Kuala Lampur: Third World Network, 1988.

Amaravati, Mallappa. *China, India and Japan: A Review of their Relations*. Jaipur: ABD Publishers, 2004.

Amnesty International, India. *Human Rights in India: The Updated Amnesty International Report*. New Delhi: Vistaar Publications in Association with Amnesty International Publications, 1993.

Anderson, Michael R., and Sumit Guha. *Changing Concepts of Rights and Justice in South Asia.* New Delhi: Oxford University Press, 2000.

Anderson, R., and S. Damle. *The Brotherhood in Saffron: The RSS and Hindu Revivalism.* Boulder and London: Westview, 1987.

Anderson, R. S., and W. Huber. *The Hour of the Fox: Tropical Forests, the World Bank, and Indigenous People in Central India.* Seattle: University of Washington Press, 1988.

Ansari, Sahibzada Yusef. *Sonia Gandhi: Triumph of Will.* New Dehli: India Research Press, 2006.

Appadurai, Arjun. *Modernity at Large: Cultural Dimensions of Globalization.* Minneapolis: University of Minnesota Press, 1996.

Arnold, David, and Stuart Blackburn. *Telling Lives in India: Biography, Autobiography, and Life History.* Indianapolis: Indiana University Press, 2004.

Arora, A., and S. Athreye. "The Software Industry and India's Economic Development." *Information Economics and Policy* 14 (2002): 253–273.

Arunachalam, Jaya, and U. Kalpagam, eds. *Development and Empowerment: Rural Women in India.* Jaipur: Rawat, 2006.

Ashwini, Chhatre, and Casan Saberwal. *Democratizing Nature: Politics, Conservation, and Development in India.* New Delhi: Oxford University Press, 2006.

Assayag, Jackie, and Chris Fuller. *Globalizing India: Perspectives from Below.* Anthem Studies in Development and Globalization Series. London: Anthem, 2005.

Asthana, Vandana. *Water Policy Processes in India: Discourses of Power and Resistance.* New York: Routledge, 2009.

Augustine, P. A. *Social Equality in Indian Society.* New Delhi: Concept Publishing, 1991.

Austin, Granville. *The Indian Constitution: Cornerstone of a Nation.* Oxford, UK: Clarendon, 1966.

Austin, Granville. *Working a Democratic Constitution: The Indian Experience.* Delhi: Oxford University Press, 2002.

Awasthy, G. C. *Broadcasting in India.* Bombay: Allied, 1965.

Ayer, S. A. *The Lone Sentinel: Glimpses of Morarji Desai.* Bombay: Popular Depot, 1960.

Ayres, Alyssa, and C. Raja Mohan. *Power Realignments in Asia: China, India and the United States.* New Delhi: Sage, 2009.

Azad, Salam. *Contribution of India in the War of Liberation of Bangladesh.* New Delhi: Bookwell Publications, 2006.

Baber, Zaheer. "'Race,' Religion and Riots: The 'Radicalization' of Communal Identity and Conflict in India." *Sociology* 38 (2004): 701–718.

Bacchetta, Paola. *Gender in the Hindu Nation: RSS Women as Ideologues*. New Delhi: Women Unlimited, 2004.

Bacchetta, Paola. "Militant Hindu Nationalist Women Reimagine Themselves: Notes on Mechanisms of Expansion." *Journal of Women's History* 10 (1999): 125–140.

Bagchi, Amiya Kumar. *Capital and Labour Redefined: India and the Third World*. London: Anthem, 2002.

Bagchi, Amiya Kumar. "Public Sector Industry and Quest for Self-reliance in India." *Economic and Political Weekly* 17 (1982): 615–628.

Bagchi, Sanjoy. *The Changing Face of Bureaucracy: Fifty Years of the Indian Administrative Service*. New Delhi: Manohar, 2007.

Bahl, Vinay. *The Making of the Indian Working Class: A Case of the Tata Iron and Steel Company, 1880–1946*. New Delhi: Sage, 1995.

Baird, Robert D. *Religion and Law in Independent India*. New Delhi: Manohar, 2005.

Bajpai, Asha. *Child Rights in India: Law, Policy, and Practice*. New Delhi: Oxford University Press, 2003.

Baker, C. J. *An Indian Rural Economy: The Tamilnad Countryside*. Oxford: Oxford University Press, 1990.

Balachandran, G. *India and the World Economy*. Delhi: Oxford University Press, 2005.

Balasubramanyam, V. N. *The Economy of India*. London: Weidenfeld and Nicolson, 1984.

Balraj, Krishna. *India's Bismarck/Sardar Vallabhbhai Patel*. Mumbai: Indus Source Books, 2008.

Banaji, Shakuntala, ed. *South Asian Media Cultures: Audiences, Representations, Contexts*. London: Anthem, 2010.

Banerjee, Bani P. *Handbook of Energy and Environment in India*. New Delhi: Oxford University Press, 2005.

Banerjee, N., ed. *Indian Women in a Changing Industrial Scenario*. London: Sage, 1991.

Banik, Dan. *Starvation and India's Democracy*. New York: Routledge, 2009.

Bannerjee, S. *India's Simmering Revolution*. London: Zed Books, 1984.

Bannerji, Sumanta. "The Politics of Violence in India." In *Internal Conflict in South Asia*, edited by Kumar Rupesinghe and Khawar Mumtaz, 81–95. London: Sage, 1996.

Bardhan, Pranab. *The Political Economy of the Development of India*. Oxford, UK: Blackwell, 1984.

Bardhan, Pranab, and T. N. Srinivasan, eds. *Rural Poverty in South Asia*. New York: Columbia University Press, 1988.

Barnett, Marguerite Ross. *The Politics of Cultural Nationalism in South India*. Princeton, NJ: Princeton University Press, 1976.

Barrow, Ian J. "India for the Working Classes: The Maps of the Society for the Diffusion of Useful Knowledge." *Modern Asian Studies* 38(3) (2004): 677–702.

Baruah, Arunima, ed. *Women in India*. New Delhi: Anmol, 2003.

Baruah, Sanjib. *Durable Disorder: Understanding the Politics of Northeast India*. Oxford: Oxford University Press, 2007.

Baruah, Sanjib. *India against Itself: Assam and the Politics of Nationality*. New Delhi: Oxford University Press, 2001.

Baruah, Sanjib. *Postfrontier Blues: Toward a New Policy Framework for Northeast India*. Washington, DC: East-West Center Washington, 2007.

Basdeo, Sahadeo. "Enhancing Cooperation between India and Canada in the Era of Globalisation and Deregulation." *British Journal of Canadian Studies* 19(1) (2006): 77–97.

Basrur, Rajesh M. *Challenges to Democracy in India*. New Delhi: Oxford University Press, 2009.

Basu, Amrita. *Two Faces of Protest: Contrasting Modes of Women's Activism in India*. Berkeley: University of California Press, 1992.

Basu, Amrita, and Atul Kohli, eds. *Community Conflicts and the State in India*. New Delhi: Oxford University Press, 1998.

Basu, Aparna, and Bharati Ray. *Women's Struggle: A History of the All India Women's Conference, 1927–2002*. New Delhi: Manohar, 2003.

Basu, B. D. *History of Education in India*. New Delhi: Cosmo, 1999.

Basu, Dilip K., and Richard Sisson, eds. *Social and Economic Development in India: A Reassessment*. New Delhi: Sage, 1986.

Basu, Kaushik. *India's Emerging Economy*. New Delhi: Oxford University Press, 2005.

Basu, Srimati. *She Comes to Take Her Rights: Indian Women, Property and Propriety*. Albany, NY: SUNY Press, 1999.

Basu, T., P. Datta, S. Sarkar, T. Sarkar, and S. Sen. *Khaki Shorts, Saffron Flags*. Hyderabad: Orient Longman, 1993.

Bates, Crispin. *Beyond Representation: Colonial and Postcolonial Constructions of Indian Identity*. Oxford: Oxford University Press, 2006.

Bates, Crispin, and Subho Basu. *Rethinking Indian Political Institutions*. London: Anthem, 2005.

Bathla, Seema. "Trade Policy Reforms and Openness of Indian Agriculture: Analysis at the Commodity Level." *South Asia Economic Journal* 7 (2006): 19–53.

Baud, I. S. A. *Form of Production and Women's Labour: Gender Aspects of Industrialization in India and Mexico*. New Delhi: Sage, 1992.

Baud, I. S. A., and G. A. de Bruijne, eds. *Gender, Small-Scale Industry, and Development Policy.* London: IT Publications, 1993.

Baviskar, Amita. "Between Violence and Desire: Space, Power and Identity in the Making of Metropolitan Delhi." *International Social Science Journal* 55 (2003): 89–98.

Baviskar, Amita. *In the Belly of the River: Tribal Conflicts over Development in the Narmada Valley.* New Delhi: Oxford University Press, 1995.

Baxi, Upendra. *The Future of Human Rights.* 3rd ed. New Delhi: Oxford University Press, 2008.

Baxi, Upendra, and Subho Basu, eds. *Crisis and Change in Contemporary India.* New Delhi: Sage, 1995.

Baxter, Craig. *The Jana Sangh: A Biography of an Indian Political Party.* Philadelphia: University of Pennsylvania Press, 1969.

Bayliss-Smith, T. B., and S. Wanmali, eds. *Understanding Green Revolutions.* Cambridge: Cambridge University Press, 1984.

Bayly, Susan. *Caste, Society and Politics in India from the Eighteenth Century to the Modern Age.* The New Cambridge History of India Series. Cambridge: Cambridge University Press, 2001.

Benei, Veronique. *Schooling Passions: Nation, History, and Language in Contemporary Western India.* Stanford, CA: Stanford University Press, 2008.

Beteille, Andre. *The Backward Classes in Contemporary India.* Delhi: Oxford University Press, 1992.

Beteille, Andre. "Caste in Contemporary India." In *Caste Today,* edited by C. J. Fuller, 150–179. Delhi: Oxford University Press, 1996.

Beteille, Andre. *The Idea of Natural Inequality and Other Essays.* Delhi: Oxford University Press, 2003.

Beteille, Andre. "The Reproduction of Inequality: Occupation, Caste, and Family." *Contributions to Indian Sociology* 25 (1991): 3–28.

Beteille, Andre. *Society and Politics in India: Essays in a Comparative Perspective.* New Delhi: Oxford University Press, 1998.

Bhagwati, Jagdish. *India in Transition: Freeing the Economy.* Oxford, UK: Clarendon, 1993.

Bhagwati, Jagdish, and Padma Desai. *India: Planning for Industrialization: Industrialization and Trade Policies since 1951.* Oxford: Oxford University Press, 1970.

Bhagwati, Jagdish, and T. N. Srinivasan. *Foreign Trade Regimes and Economic Development, India.* New York: National Bureau of Economic Research, 1976.

Bhai, N. *Harijan Women in Independent India.* Delhi: BR Publishing, 1986.

Bharadwaj, A. N. *Problems of Scheduled Castes and Scheduled Tribes in India.* New Delhi: Light and Life, 1979.

Bharadwaj-Badal, Sangeeta. *Gender, Social Structure and Empowerment: Status Report of Women in India.* Jaipur: Rawat, 2009.

Bharat, Shalini. "Attitudes and Sex-Role Perceptions among Working Couples in India." *Journal of Comparative Family Studies* 26(3) (1995): 371–388.

Bhargava, G. S. *Morarji Desai: Prime Minister of India.* Delhi: Indian Book Company, 1977.

Bhargava, Rajeev. *Politics and Ethics of the Indian Constitution.* New Delhi: Oxford University Press, 2008.

Bhargava, Rajeev. *Secularism and Its Critics.* Delhi: Oxford University Press, 1998.

Bhargava, Rajeev, Amiya Kumar Bagchi, and R. Sudarshan. *Multiculturalism, Liberalism, and Democracy.* New York: Oxford University Press, 1999.

Bhargava, Rajeev, and Kalyani Dutta. *Women, Education, and Politics.* New Delhi: Oxford University Press, 2005.

Bharucha, Rustom. *In the Name of the Secular: Contemporary Cultural Activism in India.* Delhi: Oxford University Press, 1998.

Bhasin, K., R. Menon, and N. S. Khan, eds. *Against All Odds: Essays on Women, Religion and Development from India and Pakistan.* Delhi: Isis International and Kali for Women, 1994.

Bhatia, Krishan. *Indira: A Biography of Prime Minister Gandhi.* London: Praeger, 1974.

Bhatia, Nandi. *Modern Indian Cinema.* New Delhi: Oxford University Press, 2009.

Bhatnagar, Rashmi Dube, and Reena Dube. *Female Infanticide in India: A Feminist Cultural History.* Albany, NY: SUNY Press, 2005.

Bhatt, Ela R. *We Are Poor but So Many: The Story of Self-Employed Women in India.* Oxford: Oxford University Press, 2006.

Bhatt, Ela R., ed. *Shramshakti.* New Delhi: Report of the National Commission on Self-Employed Women and Women of the Informal Sector, 1988.

Bhatt, R. K. *History and Development of Libraries in India.* New Delhi: Mittal, 1997.

Bhatt, S. C. *Satellite Invasion of India.* New Delhi: Gyan, 1994.

Bhattacharjee, Arun. *Rajiv Gandhi: Life and Message of India's Second Slain Prime Minister.* New Delhi: Ashish, 1992.

Bhattacharya, Rabindra N. *Environmental Economics: An Indian Perspective.* New Delhi: Oxford University Press, 2002.

Bhattarcharjea, A. *Kashmir: The Wounded Valley.* New Delhi: UBS Publishers, 1994.

Bhushan, K., and G. Katyal. *A. P. J. Abdul Kalam: The Visionary of India.* New Dehli: APH Publishing, 2002.

Bhutani, Sudarshan. *A Clash of Political Cultures: Sino-Indian Relations, 1957–1962.* New Delhi: Roli Books, 2004.

Bidwai, Praful, Harbans Mukhia, and Achin Vanaik, eds. *Religion, Religiosity, and Communalism.* New Delhi: Manohar, 1996.

Bidwai, Praful, and Achin Vanaik. *New Nukes: India, Pakistan and Global Disarmament.* Oxford, UK: Signal Books, 2000.

Biswas, Asit K., Olli Varis, and Celia Tortajada. *Integrated Water Sources in South and South-East Asia.* New Delhi: Oxford University Press, 2004.

Boillot, Jean-Joseph. *Europe after Enlargement: Economic Challenges for EU and India.* New Delhi: Academic Foundation, 2007.

Borooah, R., et al, eds. *Capturing Complexity: An Interdisciplinary Look at Women, Households and Development.* New Delhi: Sage, 1994.

Bose, Pablo S. "Critics and Experts, Activists and Academics: Intellectuals in the Fight for Social and Ecological Justice in Narmada Valley, India." *International Review of Social History* 49 (2004): 133–157.

Bose, Sugata. *Agrarian Bengal Economy, Social Structure and Politics, 1919–1947.* Cambridge: Cambridge University Press, 1986.

Bose, Sugata, ed. *South Asia and World Capitalism.* Delhi: Oxford University Press, 1990.

Bose, Sugata, and Ayesha Jalal. *Modern South Asia: History, Culture and Political Economy.* 2nd ed. New York: Routledge, 2004.

Bose, Sugata, and Ayesha Jalal. *Nationalism, Democracy, and Development: State and Politics in India.* Delhi and New York: Oxford University Press, 1999.

Bose, Sumantra. *Kashmir: Roots of Conflict, Paths to Peace.* Cambridge: Harvard University Press, 2003.

Bose, Tapan, and Rita Machanda, eds. *States, Citizens and Outsiders: The Uprooted Peoples of South Asia.* Katmandu: South Asian Forum for Human Rights, 1997.

Bouton, Marshall M., and Philip Oldenburg. *India Briefing: A Transformative Fifty Years.* Armonk: M. E. Sharpe, 2000.

Brands, H. W. *India and the United States: The Cold Peace.* New York: Twayne, 1990.

Brass, Paul R. "Class, Ethnic Group and Party in Indian Politics." *World Politics* 33 (1981): 449–467.

Brass, Paul R. *Ethnic Groups and the State.* Totowa, NJ: Barnes and Noble, 1985.

Brass, Paul R. *Ethnicity and Nationalism: Theory and Comparison.* New Delhi and London: Sage, 1991.

Brass, Paul R. *Factional Politics in an Indian State: The Congress Party in Uttar Pradesh.* Berkeley: University of California Press, 1965.

Brass, Paul R. *The Politics of India since Independence.* 2nd ed. Cambridge: Cambridge University Press, 1994.

Brass, Paul R. *The Production of Hindu-Muslim Violence in Contemporary India.* Seattle: University of Washington Press, 2003.

Brass, Paul R. "The Punjab Crisis and the Unity of India." In *India's Democracy,* edited by Atul Kohli, 169–213. Cambridge: Cambridge University Press, 1994.

Brass, Tom. *New Farmers' Movements in India.* New YorkY: Routledge, 1995.

Brecher, Michael. *Nehru: A Political Biography.* London: Oxford University Press, 1959.

Brecher, Michael. *The Politics of Succession in India.* Westport, CT: Greenwood, 1976.

Brecher, Michael. *Succession in India: a Study in Decision-making.* Oxford: Oxford University Press, 1966.

Breman, Jan. *Of Peasants, Migrants and Paupers.* New Delhi: Oxford University Press, 1985.

Breman, Jan. *Footloose Labour.* Cambridge: Cambridge University Press, 1996.

Breman, Jan, Isabelle Guerin, and Aseem Prakash. *India's Unfree Workforce: Of Bondage Old and New.* Oxford: Oxford University Press, 2009.

Brines, Russell. *The Indo-Pakistani Conflict.* London: Pall Mall, 1968.

Briscoe, John, and R. P. S. Malik. *Handbook of Water Resources in India.* New Delhi: Oxford University Press, 2007.

Briscoe, John, and R. P. S. Malik. *India's Water Economy.* New Delhi: Oxford University Press, 2006.

Brosius, Christiane. *Empowering Visions: The Politics of Representation in Hindu Nationalism.* London: Anthem, 2004.

Brosius, Christiane. *India Shining: Consuming Pleasures of India's New Middle Classes* New Delhi: South Asia Routledge, 2009.

Brosius, Christiane, and Melissa Butcher, eds. *Image Journeys: Audio-Visual Media and Cultural Change in India.* New Delhi: Sage, 1999.

Brown, Judith M. *Modern India: The Origins of an Asian Democracy (The Short Oxford History of the Modern World).* 2nd ed. Oxford: Oxford University Press, 1994.

Brown, Judith M. *Nehru.* London: Longman, 1999.

Brown, Judith M. *Nehru: A Political Life.* New Haven, CT: Yale University Press, 2005.

Brown, Lester. *Seeds of Change: The Green Revolution and Development in the 1970s.* London: Praeger, 1970.

Brown, Rebecca, and Nicholas Thomas. *Art for a Modern India, 1947–1980 (Objects/Histories).* Durham, NC: Duke University Press, 2009.

Bruckner, Heidrun, et al. *The Power of Performance: Actors, Audiences, and Observers of Cultural Performances in India*. New Delhi: Manohar, 2007.

Buck, Tracy. "The 'Femina' Mystique: Reading Inconsistencies in India's Most Popular Women's Magazine." *SAGAR: A South Asia Graduate Research Journal* 12 (2004): 39–54.

Buechler, Stephanie. "Local Responses to Water Resource Degradation in India: Groundwater Farmer Innovations and the Reversal of Knowledge Flows." *Journal of Environment Development* 14 (2005): 410–438.

Bullion, Alan J. *India, Sri Lanka, and the Tamil Crisis, 1976–1994*. London: Pinter, 1995.

Burger, A. S. *Opposition in a Dominant Party System*. Berkeley: University of California Press, 1969.

Burghart, Richard, C. J. Fuller, and Jonathan Spencer. *The Conditions of Listening: Essays on Religion, History, and Politics in South Asia*. Delhi: Oxford University Press, 2008.

Burman, B. K. Roy. *Beyond Mandal and After: Backward Classes in Perspective*. New Delhi: Mittal, 1992.

Burman, B. K. Roy. "The Problem of the Untouchables." In *Tribe, Caste and Religion in India*, edited by Romesh Thapar, 82–93. Delhi: Macmillian, 1977.

Burman, J. Roy. "Hindu-Muslim Syncretism in India." *Economic and Political Weekly* 31 (1996): 1211–1215.

Butalia, Urvashi. *The Other Side of Silence: Voices from the Partition of India*. Durham, NC: Duke University Press, 2000.

Butalia, Urvashi. "Women and Communal Conflict: New Challenges for the Women's Movement in India." In *Victims, Perpetrators or Actors? Gender Armed Conflict and Political Violence*, edited by Fiona Clark and Caroline Moser, 99–114. London: Zed Books, 2001.

Byres, T. J. "Charan Singh: An Assessment." *Journal of Peasant Studies* 15(2) (1988): 139–189.

Byres, T. J. "The New Technology, Class Formation, and Class Action in the Indian Countryside." *Journal of Peasant Studies* 8(4) (1981): 405–454.

Byres, Terence, ed. *The State and Development Planning in India*. Delhi: Oxford University Press, 1993.

Byres, Terence, and Ben Crow. *The Green Revolution in India*. Milton Keynes, UK: Open University Press, 1983.

Calman, Leslie J. *Protest in Democratic India: Authority's Response to Challenge*. Boulder, CO: Westview, 1985.

Candland, Christ. *Labor, Democratization and Development in India and Pakistan*. New York: Routledge, 2008.

Carras, Mary C. *Indira Gandhi in the Crucible of Leadership.* Boston: Beacon, 1979.

Carter, Anthony. *Elite Politics in Rural India.* Cambridge: Cambridge University Press, 1974.

Cassen, Robert. *India: Population, Economy, Society.* New York: Macmillan, 1978.

Cassen, Robert, and Vijay Joshi. *India: The Future of Economic Reform.* New Delhi: Oxford University Press, 1995.

Centre for the Study of Developing Studies. *State of Democracy in South Asia.* New Delhi: Oxford University Press, 2008.

Chakaravarty, Sumita S. *National Identity in Indian Popular Cinema, 1947–1987.* Austin: University of Texas Press, 1993.

Chakrabarti, Rajesh. *The Financial Sector in India.* New Delhi: Oxford University Press, 2006.

Chakrabarty, Bidyut. *Communal Identity in India: Its Construction and Articulation in the Twentieth Century.* New Delhi: Oxford University Press, 2003.

Chakrabarty, Bidyut, and Rajat Kumar Kujur. *Maoism in India: Reincarnation of Ultra-Left Extremism in the 21st Century.* New York: Routledge, 2009.

Chakrabarty, Bidyut, and Rajendra Kumar Pandey. *Indian Government and Politics.* New Delhi: Sage, 2008.

Chakrabarty, Dipesh. "Culture in Working Class History." Edited transcript of a lecture delivered by the author and the discussion that followed at the V. V. Giri National Labour Institute in Noida, Uttar Pradesh, on November 25, 1998, http://www.indialabourarchives.org/publications/Dipesh%20Chakrabarty.htm.

Chakrabarty, Sukhamoy. *Development Planning: The Indian Experience.* Delhi: Oxford University Press, 1987.

Chakraborty, A. K. *Kargil: Inside Story.* Noida: Trishul Publications, 1999.

Chakraborty, S., ed. *Rural Women's Claim to Priority: A Policy Debate.* Delhi: Centre for Women's Development Studies, 1985.

Chakravarti, Ashok. *Aid, Institutions and Development.* New Delhi: Oxford University Press, 2005.

Chakravarti, Uma, and Nandita Haksar. *The Delhi Riots: Three Days in the Life of a Nation.* New Delhi: Lancer International, 1987.

Chakravarty, A. S. *National Identity in Indian Popular Culture.* New Delhi: Oxford University Press, 1998.

Chakravatty, Paula. "Translating Terror in India." *Television New Media* 3 (2002): 205–212.

Chakraverty, Sukhamoy. *Development Planning: The Indian Experience.* New Delhi: Oxford University Press, 1998.

Chalam, K. S. "Human Resources Development in South India." *Journal of Social and Economic Development* 2 (2002): 291–313.

Chandavarkar, Rajnarayan. *History, Culture and the Indian City.* Cambridge: Cambridge University Press, 2009.

Chandavarkar, Rajnarayan. *Imperial Power and Popular Politics: Class, Resistance and the State in India, 1850–1950.* The Cambridge Studies in Indian History and Society Series. Cambridge: Cambridge University Press, 1998.

Chandhoke, Neera. *Beyond Secularism: The Rights of Religious Minorities.* New Delhi and Oxford: Oxford University Press, 1999.

Chandhoke, Neera. *State and Civil Society: Explanations in Political Theory.* New Delhi and London: Sage, 1995.

Chandra, Bipan. *Essays on Contemporary India.* New Delhi: Har-Anand, 1993.

Chandra, Bipan, Aditya Mukherjee, and Mridula Mukherjee. *India after Independence.* New Delhi: Penguin, 1999.

Chandra, Ramesh, and Neela Gokhale. *First Woman President of India: Pratibha Patil.* New Delhi: Kalpaz, 2008.

Chandra, Satish. *State, Pluralism, and the Indian Historical Tradition.* New Delhi: Oxford University Press, 2008.

Chandra, Shanta Kohli. *Development of Women Entrepreneurship in India: A Study of Public Policies and Programmes.* New Delhi: Mittal, 1991.

Chandra, Shanta Kohli. *Family Planning Programme in India: Its Impact in Rural and Urban Areas, 1970–1980.* New Delhi: Mittal, 1987.

Chaplin, Susan E. "Cities Sewers and Poverty: India's Politics of Sanitation." *Environment and Urbanization* 11 (1999): 145–158.

Chapnick Mukhopadhyay, Carol Chapnick, and Susan Seymour. *Women, Education and Family in India.* Boulder, CO: Westview, 1994.

Charlton, Sue Ellen M. *Comparing Asian Politics: India, China, and Japan.* 3rd ed. Boulder, CO: Westview, 2009.

Chary, M. Srinivas. *The Eagle and the Peacock: U.S. Foreign Policy toward India since Independence.* Westport, CT: Greenwood, 1995.

Chary, Manish Telikicherla. *India, Nation on the Move: An Overview of India's People, Culture, History, Economy, IT Industry, and More.* Bloomington, IN: iUniverse.com, 2009.

Chatterjee, P. C. *Broadcasting in India.* New Delhi: Sage, 1991.

Chatterjee, Partha. *The Nation and Its Fragments: Colonial and Postcolonial Histories.* Princeton, NJ: Princeton University Press, 1993.

Chatterjee, Partha. *The Partha Chatterjee Omnibus.* Oxford: Oxford University Press, 2000.

Chatterjee, Partha. *A Possible India: Essays in Political Criticism.* New Delhi: Oxford University Press, 1999.

Chatterjee, Partha. *State and Politics in India.* New Delhi: Oxford University Press, 2008.

Chatterjee, Partha, ed. *Wages of Freedom: Fifty Years of the Indian Nation-State.* New Delhi: Oxford University Press, 1997.

Chatterjee, Partha, and Pradeep Jeganathan. *Community, Gender and Violence.* New York: Columbia University Press, 2001.

Chatterjee, Rupa. *Sonia Gandhi: The Lady in Shadow.* New Delhi: Butala Publications, 1998.

Chatterji, Angana P. *Violent Gods: Hindu Nationalism in India's Present; Narratives from Orissa.* Gurgaon: Three Essays Collective, 2009.

Chatterji, Ruchira. *The Behaviour of Industrial Prices in India.* Delhi: Oxford University Press, 1989.

Chaudhry, Praveen K., and Marta Vanduzer-Snow. *United States and India: The Formative Years through Declassified Documents.* New Delhi: Sage, 2008.

Chaudhuri, Pramit. *The Indian Economy: Poverty and Development.* London: Crosby Lockwood Staples, 1978.

Chaudhuri, Sudip. *The WTO and India's Pharmaceuticals Industry.* New Delhi: Oxford University Press, 2005.

Chaurasia, Alok Ranjan, and S. C. Gulati. *India: The State of the Population, 2007.* New Delhi: Oxford University Press, 2008.

Chellaney, Brahma. *Asian Juggernaut: The Rise of China, India, and Japan.* New York: HarperCollins, 2010.

Chellaney, Brahma. *Nuclear Proliferation: The U.S.–Indian Conflict.* New Delhi: Orient Longman, 1993.

Chellaney, Brahma, and Vivek Chibber. *State-building and Late Industrialization in India.* Princeton, NJ: Princeton University Press, 2004.

Chhachhi, Amrita. "Forced Identities: The State, Communalism, Fundamentalism and Women in India." In *Women, Islam and the State*, edited by D. Kandiyoti, 218–242. Philadelphia: Temple University Press, 1991.

Chhibber, Pradeep. "Why Are Some Women Politically Active? The Household, Public Space, and Political Participation in India." *International Journal of Comparative Sociology* 43 (2002): 409–429.

Chiriyankandath, James. "'Communities at the Polls': Electoral Politics and the Mobilization of Communal Groups in Travancore." *Modern Asian Studies* 27(3) (1993): 643–665.

Chopra, J. K. *Women in Indian Parliament: A Critical Study of Their Role.* New Delhi: Mittal, 1993.

Chopra, Kanchan Ratna, and Virkam Dayal. *Handbook of Environmental Economics in India.* New Delhi: Oxford University Press, 2009.

Chopra, Rohit. *Technology and Nationalism in India: Cultural Negotiations from Colonialism to Cyberspace.* Amherst, NY: Cambria, 2008.

Choudhury, Golam Wahed. *Pakistan's Relations with India, 1947–1966.* London: Pall Mall, 1968.

Choudhury, R. A., Shama Ghamkar and Aurobindo Ghose. *The Indian Economy and Its Performance since Independence.* Delhi: Oxford University Press, 1990.

Chowdhry, Prem. "'First Our Jobs Then Our Girls': The Dominant Caste Perceptions on the 'Rising Dalits.'" *Modern Asian Studies* 43(2) (2009): 437–479.

Chowdhry, Prem. "Private Lives, State Intervention: Cases of Runaway Marriage in Rural North India." *Modern Asian Studies* 38(1) (2004): 55–84.

Chowdhry, Prem. *The Veiled Women: Shifting Gender Equations in Rural Haryana, 1880–1990.* Delhi: Oxford University Press, 1994.

Citizens Commission on Bonded and Child Labour (India). *Freedom from Bondage.* New Delhi: Indian Social Institute, 1995.

Clark, Alice, ed. *Gender and Political Economy: Explorations of South Asian Systems.* New York: Oxford University Press, 1993.

Clymer, Kenton J. *Quest for Freedom: The United States and India's Independence.* New York: Columbia University Press, 1995.

Cohen, Stephen Philip. *India: Emerging Power.* Washington, DC: Brookings Institution Press, 2002.

Cohen, Stephen Philip. *The Indian Army: Its Contribution to the Development of a Nation.* 2nd ed. New Delhi: Oxford University Press, 2001.

Committee on the Status of Women in India. *Towards Equality: Report of the Committee on the Status of Women in India.* New Delhi: Government of India, Ministry of Education and Social Welfare, Department of Social Welfare, 1975.

Cooper, Darius. *The Cinema of Satyajit Ray: Between Tradition and Modernity.* Cambridge: Cambridge University Press, 2000.

Copland, Ian. *Jawaharlal Nehru of India, 1889–1964.* Leaders of Asia Series. Queensland: University of Queensland Press, 1980.

Copland, Ian. "Lord Mountbatten and the Integration of the Indian States: A Reappraisal." *Journal of Imperial and Commonwealth History* 21(2) (1993): 385–408.

Copland, Ian, and John McGuire. *Hindu Nationalism and Governance.* New Delhi: Oxford University Press, 2007.

Corbridge, Stuart. "The Ideology of Tribal Economy and Society: Politics in the Jharkhand, 1950–1980." *Modern Asian Studies* 22 (1988): 1–42.

Corbridge, Stuart, and John Harriss. *Reinventing India: Liberalization, Hindu Nationalism and Popular Democracy.* Cambridge, UK: Polity, 2000.

Corbridge, Stuart, Glyn Williams, and Manoj Srivastava. *Seeing the State: Governance and Governmentality in India.* Cambridge: Cambridge University Press, 2005.

Cossman, Brenda, and Ratna Kapur. *Secularism's Last Sigh? Hindutva and the (Mis)Rule of Law.* Delhi and Oxford: Oxford University Press, 2001.

Costa, Benedict. *India's Socialist Princes and Garibi Hatao.* Ludhiana: Kalyani Publishers, 1973.

Cousins, Norman. *Talks with Nehru.* London: J. Day, 1951.

Crook, Nigel, ed. *The Transformation of Knowledge in South Asia: Essays on Education, Religion and Politics.* New Delhi: Oxford University Press, 1996.

Cullity, Jocelyn. "The Global Desi: Cultural Nationalism on MTV India." *Journal of Communication Inquiry* 26 (2002): 408–425.

Currie, Bob. *The Politics of Hunger in India: A Study of Democracy, Governance and Kalahandi's Poverty.* Basingstoke, UK: Macmillan, 2000.

Currie, K. "The Indian Stratification Debate: A Discursive Exposition of Problems and Issues in the Analysis of Class, Caste and Gender." *Dialectical Anthropology* 17 (1992): 115–139.

Dahiwale, S. M., ed. *Understanding Indian Society: The Non-Brahmanic Perspective.* Jaipur: Rawat, 2005.

Dahiya, Bharat. "Hard Struggle and Soft Gains: Environmental Management, Civil Society and Governance in Pammal, South India." *Environment and Urbanization* 15 (2003): 91–100.

Daiya, Kavita. *Violent Belongings: Partition, Gender, and Postcolonial Nationalism in India.* Philadelphia: Temple University Press, 2008.

Dalmia, Yashodhara. *The Making of Modern Indian Art: The Progressives.* Oxford: Oxford University Press, 2001.

Dalmia, Yashodhara, ed. *Contemporary Indian Art: Other Realities.* Mumbai: Marg, 2002.

Dalmia, Yashodhara, and Salima Hashmi. *Memory, Metaphor, Mutations: Contemporary Art of India and Pakistan.* Oxford: Oxford University Press, 2007.

Dalvi, J. P. *Himalayan Blunder: The Curtain-Raiser to the Sino-Indian War of 1962.* Dehra Dun: Natraj, 1997.

Damodaran, A. K., and U. S. Bajpai, eds. *Indian Foreign Policy: The Indira Gandhi Years.* London: Sangam, 1990.

Dandekar, V. M. *Indian Economy, 1947–1992,* vol. 1, *Agriculture.* New Delhi: Oxford University Pres, 1994.

Das, Arvind N., and Marcel van der Linden, eds. *Work and Social Change in Asia: Essays in Honour of Jan Breman.* New Delhi: Manohar, 2003.

Das, Dipendra Nath. *Child Labour in India: A Study on Magnitude, Dimension and Determinants.* Delhi: Sage, 1996.

Das, Gurcharan. *India Unbound: The Social and Economic Revolution from Independence to the Global Information Age.* New York: First Anchor Books, 2002.

Das, M. N. *The Political Philosophy of Jawaharlal Nehru.* London: Allen and Unwin, 1961.

Das, Veena. *Critical Events: An Anthropological Perspective on Contemporary India.* New York: Oxford University Press, 1995.

Das, Veena. *Handbook of Indian Sociology.* New Delhi: Oxford University Press, 2004.

Das, Veena. *The Oxford India Companion to Sociology and Social Anthropology.* New Delhi: Oxford University Press, 2003.

Das, Veena, ed. *Mirrors of Violence: Communities, Riots, and Survivors in South Asia.* New Delhi: Oxford University Press, 1992.

Das Gupta, Chidananda. *The Painted Face: Studies in India's Popular Cinema.* New Delhi: Roli Books, 1991.

Datar, Chhaya, ed. *Struggle against Violence.* Calcutta: Bhatkal and Sen, 1995.

Datt, Ruddar. *Lockouts in India.* New Delhi: Manohar, 2003.

Datta, Anindita. "MacDonaldization of Gender in Urban India: A Tentative Exploration." *Gender, Technology and Development* 9 (2005): 125–135.

Davies, Paul. *What's This India Business? Offshoring, Outsourcing, and the Global Services Revolution.* London: Nicholas Brealey, 2008.

D'Costa, Anthony. *The Long March to Capitalism: Embourgeoisment, Internationalisation and Industrial Transformation in India.* New York: Palgrave Macmillan, 2005.

D'Cruz, Premilla, and Shalini Bharat. "Beyond Nuclear: The Indian Family Revisited." *Journal of Comparative Family Studies* 32(2) (2001): 167–195.

De, Shobhaa. *Superstar India: From Incredible to Unstoppable.* New York: Penguin Global, 2009.

Deolalikar, Anil B., and the World Bank. *Attaining the Millennium Development Goals in India.* New Delhi: Oxford University Press, 2005.

Derrett, J. Duncan. *Religion, Law, and the State in India.* London: Faber, 1968.

Desai, A. R. *Caste and Communal Violence in Independent India*. Bombay: C. J. Shah Trust, 1985.

Desai, Ashok. *India's Telecommunications Industry: History, Analysis, Diagnosis*. New Delhi: Sage, 2006.

Desai, I. P. "Anti-Reservation Agitation and Structure in Gujarat Society." *Economic and Political Weekly* 16 (1981): 819, 821–823.

Desai, Jatin. *Kargil and Pakistan Politics*. New Delhi: Commonwealth, 2000.

Desai, Manali. *State Formation and Practices of Democracy in India*. New York: Routledge, 2006.

Desai, Meghnad. *Agrarian Power and Agricultural Productivity in South Asia*. Berkeley: University of California Press, 1985.

Desai, Meghnad. *Development and Nationhood: Essays in the Political Economy of South Asia*. New Delhi and Oxford: Oxford University Press, 2005.

Desai, Meghnad. "India: Emerging Contradictions of a Slow Economic Development." In *Explosion in a Subcontinent*, edited by R. Blackburn, 11–50. Harmondsworth, UK: Penguin in association with New Left Review, 1975.

Desai, Morarji. *The Story of My Life*. 3 vols. New Delhi: Pergamon, 1979.

Desai, Tripta. *India-USA Diplomatic Relations, 1940–2002*. New Delhi: Munshirm Manoharlal, 2006.

Deshpande, Ashwini. *Globalization and Development*. New Delhi: Oxford University Press, 2007.

DeSouza, Peter Ronald, and E. Sridharan. *India's Political Parties*. Readings in Indian Government and Politics Series. New Delhi: Sage, 2006.

Devi, Phoolan. *The Bandit Queen of India: An Indian Woman's Amazing Journey from Peasant to International Legend*. Guilford, CT: Lyons, 2006.

Dey, S. K. *Power to the People? A Chronicle of India, 1947–67*. Bombay: Orient Longman, 1969.

Dhagamwar, Vashudha. *Law, Power and Justice: Protection of Personal Rights under the Indian Penal Code*. New Delhi: Newbury Park, CA: Sage, 1992.

Dhar, A. N. *Indira Gandhi, the "Emergency," and Indian Democracy*. New Delhi: Oxford University Press, 2000.

Dharwadker, Aparna Bhargava. *Theatres of Independence: Drama, Theory, and Urban Performance in India since 1947*. New Delhi: Oxford University Press, 2006.

Dirks, Nicholas B. *Castes of Mind: Colonialism and the Making of Modern India*. Princeton, NJ: Princeton University Press, 2001.

Divan, Shyam, and Armin Rosencranz. *Environmental Law and Policy in India*. Delhi and Oxford: Oxford University Press, 2000.

Dixit, J. N. *India-Pakistan in War and Peace*. New York: Routledge, 2002.

Dixon, R. B. *Rural Women at Work: Strategies for Development in South Asia*. Baltimore: Johns Hopkins University Press, 1978.

DN. "Reservations and Class Structure of Castes." *Economic and Political Weekly*, (1990): 83.

Dorin, Bruno, ed. *The Indian Entrepreneur: A Sociological Profile of Businessmen and Their Practices*. New Delhi: Manohar, 2003.

Dossani, Rafiq. *India Arriving: How This Economic Powerhouse Is Redefining Global Business*. New York: Amacom, 2007.

Douglas, Ian Henderson, Gail Minault, and Christian Troll. *Abul Kalam Azad: An Intellectual and Religious Biography*. Oxford: Oxford University Press, 1993.

Dreze, Jean. *Public Report on Basic Education in India*. Oxford: Oxford University Press, 2000.

Dreze, Jean, et al., eds. *The Dam and the Nation: Rights of Religious Minorities*. New Delhi: Oxford University Press, 1997.

Dreze, Jean, and Amartya Sen. *Hunger and Public Action*. Oxford: Oxford University Press, 1989.

Dreze, Jean, and Amartya Sen. *India: Economic Development and Social Opportunity*. Delhi: Oxford University Press, 1995.

Dua, B. D., et al. *Indian Judiciary and Politics: The Changing Landscape*. New Delhi: Manohar, 2007.

Dube, Saurabh. *Postcolonial Passages: A Reader in Contemporary History-writing on India*. Oxford: Oxford University Press, 2006.

Dubey, Sharada. *First among Equals: Presidents of India, 1950 to Present*. London: Westland, 2009.

Dudrah, Rajinder Kumar. *Bollywood: Sociology Goes to the Movies*. New Delhi: Sage, 2006.

Dunn, D. "Gender Inequality in Education and Employment in the Scheduled Castes and Tribes of India." *Population Research and Policy Review* 12 (1993): 52–70.

Duyker, E. *Tribal Guerillas: The Santals of West Bengal and the Naxalite Movement*. New Delhi: Oxford University Press, 1987.

Dwivedi, K. C. *Right to Freedom and the Supreme Court*. New Delhi: Deep and Deep, 1994.

Dwivedi, Rishi. *Urban Development and Housing in India, 1947 to 2007*. New Delhi: New Century, 2007.

Dwyer, R. *All You Want Is Money, All You Need Is Love: Sex and Romance in Modern India*. London and New York: Cassell, 2000.

Dwyer, Rachel, and Christopher Pinney, eds. *Pleasure and the Nation: The History, Politics and Consumption of Popular Culture in India*. New Delhi: Oxford University Press, 2006.

Dwyer, Rachel, and Divia Patel. *Cinema India: The Visual Culture of Hindi Film.* New Brunswick, NJ: Rutgers University Press, 2002.

Dyson, Tim, et al. *Twenty-First Century India.* New Delhi: Oxford University Press, 2004.

Echeverri-Gent, John. *The State and the Poor: Public Policy and Political Development in India and the United States.* Berkeley: University of California Press, 1993.

Elliott, Carolyn M. *Civil Society and Democracy: A Reader.* New Delhi: Oxford University Press, 2003.

Engineer, A. A. *Communalism and Communal Violence in India: An Analytical Approach to Hindu-Muslim Conflict.* New Delhi: Ajanta, 1989.

Engineer, A. A. *Communal Riots in Post-Independence India.* Hyderabad: Sangram Books, 1984.

Engineer, A. A. *Secular Crown on Fire: The Kashmir Problem.* New Delhi: Ajanta, 1991.

Engineer, A. A. *The Shah Bono Controversy.* Hyderabad: Orient Longman, 1987.

Engineer, A. A., ed. *The Gujurat Carnage.* New Delhi: Sangram Books, 2003.

Engineer, Asghar Ali, and Amarjit S. Narang, eds. *Minorities and Police in India.* New Delhi: Manohar, 2007.

Environmental Services Group. *Dams on the Narmada: The Official View.* New Delhi: Environmental Services Group, 1986.

Erdman, Howard I. *The Swatantra Party and Indian Conservatism.* Cambridge: Cambridge University Press, 1967.

Etienne, Gilbert. *India's Changing Rural Scene, 1963–1979.* Oxford: Oxford University Press, 1983.

Fakhri, S. M. Abdul Khader. *Dravidian Sahibs and Brahmin Maulanas: The Politics of the Muslims of Tamil Nadu, 1930–1967.* New Delhi: Manohar, 2008.

Farouqui, Ather. *Muslims and Media Images.* Oxford: Oxford University Press, 2009.

Farred, Grant. "The Double Temporality of Lagaan: Cultural Struggle and Postcolonialism." *Journal of Sport and Social Issues* 28(2) (2004): 93–114.

Fazila, Vazira, and Yacoobali Zamindar. *The Long Partition and the Making of Modern South Asia: Refugees, Boundaries, Histories.* New York: Columbia University Press, 2010.

Fernandes, Leela. *India's New Middle Class: Democratic Politics in an Era of Economic Reform.* Minneapolis: University of Minnesota Press, 2006.

Fernandes, Leela. "Nationalizing 'the Global': Media Images, Cultural Politics and the Middle Class in India." *Media, Culture and Society* 22 (2000): 612.

Flavia, Agnes. *Law and Gender Inequality: The Politics of Women's Rights in India.* New Delhi: Oxford University Press, 2004.

Flavia, Agnes. "Protecting Women against Violence: Review of a Decade of Legislation, 1980–1989." *Economic and Political Weekly* 27 (1992): 19–33.

Forbes, Geraldine. *Women in Modern India.* Cambridge: Cambridge University Press, 1996.

Forland, Tor Egil. "'Selling Firearms to the Indians': Eisenhower's Export Control Policy, 1953–54." *Diplomatic History* 15(2) (1991): 221–244.

Forum against Oppression of Women. *Working Women in Mumbai Bars: Truths behind Controversy; Results from Survey among 500 Women Dancers across Mumbai.* Juhu, Mumbai: Research Centre for Women's Studies, SNDT Women's University, 2005.

Fox, Richard G., ed. *Urban India: Society, Space and Image.* Monograph and Occasional Papers Series 10. Durham, NC: Duke University Press, 1970.

Frank, Katherine. *Indira: The Life of Indira Nehru Gandhi.* New York: Houghton Mifflin Harcourt, 2002.

Frankel, Francine R. *India's Green Revolution.* Princeton, NJ: Princeton University Press, 1971.

Frankel, Francine R. *India's Political Economy, 1947–2004: The Gradual Revolution.* 2nd ed. New Delhi: Oxford University Press, 2006.

Frankel, Francine R., et al. *Transforming India: Social and Political Dynamics of Democracy.* Delhi: Oxford University Press, 2002.

Frankel, Francine R., and M. S. A. Rao, eds. *Dominance and State Power in Modern India.* Delhi: Oxford University Press, 1989.

Freitag, Sandria. *Collective Action and Community: Public Arenas and the Emergence of Communalism in North India.* Berkeley: University of California Press, 1989.

Froerer, Peggy. *Religious Division and Social Conflict: The Emergence of Hindu Nationalism in Rural India.* New York: Berghahn Books, 2007.

Frykenberg, Robert Eric. *Christianity in India: From Beginnings to the Present.* Oxford: Oxford University Press, 2010.

Fukuda-Parr, Sakiko, and A. K. Shiva Kumar. *Handbook of Human Development.* New Delhi: Oxford University Press, 2009.

Fuller, C. J. *The Camphor Flame: Popular Hinduism and Society in India.* Princeton, NJ: Princeton University Press, 2004.

Gadgil, Madhay, and Ramachandra Guha. *The Use and Abuse of Nature: Incorporating This Fissured Land; An Ecological History of India and Ecology and Equity.* Oxford: Oxford University Press, 2005.

Gadgil, Madhay, and Ramachandra Guha. "Ecological Conflicts and the Environmental Movement in India." *Development and Change* 25 (1994): 101–136.

Gaines, Elliot. "Interpreting India, Identity, and Media from the Field: Exploring the Communicative Nature of the Exotic Other." *Qualitative Inquiry* 11 (2005): 518–534.

Galanter, Marc. *Competing Equalities: Law and the Backward Classes in India*. Berkeley: University of California Press, 1984.

Galanter, Marc. "Pursuing Equality: An Assessment of India's Policy of Compensatory Discrimination for Disadvantaged Groups." In *Social and Economic Development in India*, edited by D. K. Basu and R. Sisson, 129–152. New Delhi: Sage, 1986.

Galanter, Marc. "Pursuing Equality in the Land of Hierarchy." In *Law and Society in Modern India*, edited by M. Galanter, 185–207. New Delhi: Oxford University Press, 1991.

Galbraith, J. Kenneth. *Ambassador's Journal*. Boston: Houghton Mifflin, 1969.

Gandhi, Indira. *India: The Speeches and Reminiscences of Indira Gandhi*. London: Rupa, 1975.

Gandhi, Indira. *My Truth*. Delhi: Grove, 1981.

Gandhi, Nandita. "Impact of Religion on Women's Rights in Asia." *Economic and Political Weekly* 23 (1988): 127–129.

Gandhi, Nandita. *When the Rolling Pins Hit the Streets*. London: Zed Books, 1996.

Gandhi, Rajmohan. *Gandhi: The Man, His People, and the Empire*. Berkeley: University of California Press, 2008.

Gandhi, Sonia, ed. *Freedom's Daughter: Letters between Indira Gandhi and Jawaharlal Nehru, 1922–39*. London: Hodder and Stoughton, 1989.

Gandhi, Sonia, ed. *Two Alone, Two Together: Letters between Indira Gandhi and Jawaharlal Nehru, 1940–64*. London: Hodder and Stoughton, 1992.

Gangar, Amrit. "Films from the City of Dreams." In *Bombay: Mosaic of Modern Culture*, edited by Sujata Patel and Alice Thorner, 210–224. Delhi: Oxford University Press, 1996.

Gangrade, K. D., and J. A. Gathia, eds. *Women and Child Workers in Unorganised Sector: NGOs Perspectives*. New Delhi: Concept Publishing, 1983.

Ganguly, Sumit. *Conflict Unending*. New York: Columbia University Press, 2002.

Ganguly, Sumit. *The Crisis in Kashmir: Portents of War, Hopes of Peace*. Cambridge: Cambridge University Press, 1999.

Ganguly, Sumit. *South Asia*. New York: New York University Press, 2006.

Ganguly, Sumit, and Neil Devotta, eds. *Understanding Contemporary India*. Boulder, CO: Lynne Rienner, 2003.

Ganguly, Sumit, Larry Diamond, and Marc F. Plattner. *The State of India's Democracy*. Baltimore: Johns Hopkins University Press, 2007.

Ganguly, Sumit, and Devin T. Hagerty. *Fearful Symmetry: India-Pakistan Crises in the Shadow of Nuclear Weapons*. Seattle: University of Washington Press, 2006.

Ganguly, Sumit, and Lee H. Hamilton, eds. *The Crisis in Kashmir: Portents of War, Hopes of Peace*. Cambridge: Cambridge University Press, 1999.

Ganguly, Sumit, and S. Paul Kapur. *India, Pakistan, and the Bomb: Debating Nuclear Stability in South Asia.* New York: Columbia University Press, 2010.

George, Abraham. *India Untouched: The Forgotten Face of Rural Poverty.* Chennai: East West Books, 2004.

George, Rosen. *Contrasting Styles of Industrial Reform: China and India in the 1980s.* Chicago: University of Chicago Press, 1992.

George, T. J. S. *Krishna Menon: A Biography.* London: Jaico, 1964.

Ghose, Bhaskar. *Doordarshan Days.* New Delhi: Penguin/Viking, 2005.

Ghose, S. K. *The Crusade and End of Indira Raj.* New Delhi: Intellectual Book Corner, 1977.

Ghosh, Jayati. "Development Strategy in India: A Political-Economic Perspective." In *Nationalism, Democracy and Development,* edited by Sugata Bose and Ayesha Jalal, 165–183. New York: Oxford University Press, 1998.

Ghosh, Partha S. *BJP and the Evolution of Hindu Nationalism: From Periphery to Centre.* New Delhi: Manohar, 1999.

Ghosh, S. C. *The History of Education in Modern India, 1757–1998.* Hyderabad: Orient Longman, 2009.

Gibbons-Trikha, Jacqueline A. "Sanctuary: A Women's Refuge in India." *Journal of Developing Societies* 19 (2003): 47–89.

Glaeser, Bernhard, ed. *The Green Revolution Revisited: Critique and Alternatives.* London: Allen and Unwin, 1987.

Glazer, Sulochana Raghavan, and Nathan Glazer, eds. *Conflicting Images: India and the United States.* Glendale, MD: Riverdale, 1990.

Gokhale, Jayashree. *From Concessions to Confrontation: The Politics of an Indian Untouchable Community.* Bombay: Popular Prakashan, 1993.

Gokulsing, K. Moti, and Wimal Dissanayake. *India Popular Cinema: A Narrative of Cultural Change.* Hyderabad: Orient Longman, 1998.

Gooptu, Nandini. "Caste and Labour: Untouchable Social Movements in Urban Uttar Pradesh in the Early Twentieth Century." In *Dalit Movements and the Meanings of Labour in India,* edited by Peter Robb, 277–298. Delhi: Oxford University Press, 1993.

Gopal, D., ed. *Australia in the Emerging Global Order: Evolving Australia-India Relations.* Delhi: Shipra, 2002.

Gopal, Sarvepalli. *Anatomy of a Confrontation: Ayodhya and the Rise of Communal Politics in India.* London: Zed Books, 1993.

Gopal, Sarvepalli. *Jawaharlal Nehru.* New Delhi: Oxford University Press, 2003.

Gopal, Sarvepalli. *Radhakrishnan: A Biography.* New Delhi: Oxford University Press, 1992.

Gopal, Sarvepalli, ed. *Anatomy of a Confrontation: The Babri Masjid-Ramjanmabhumi Issue.* New Delhi: Penguin, 1991.

Gore, M. S. *The Social Context of an Ideology: Ambedkar's Political and Social Thought.* New Delhi: Sage, 1993.

Gossman, Patricia. *The Human Rights Crisis in Kashmir: A Pattern of Impunity.* New York: Human Rights Watch, 1993.

Gothoskar, Sujata, ed. *Stuggles of Women at Work.* 2nd ed. New Delhi: Vikas, 1997.

Gottlob, Michael. *Historical Thinking in South Asia.* New Delhi: Oxford University Press, 2006.

Gottschalk, Peter. *Beyond Hindu and Muslim: Multiple Identity in Narratives from Village India.* Oxford: Oxford University Press, 2000.

Govinda, R., and the National Institute of Educational Planning and Administration (India). *India Education Report.* New Delhi: Oxford University Press, 2002.

Goyal, Anupam. *The WTO and International Environmental Law.* New Delhi: Oxford University Press, 2006.

Graham, Bruce Desmond. *Hindu Nationalism and Indian Politics: The Origins and Development of the Bharatiya Jana Sangh.* Cambridge: Cambridge University Press, 2007.

Grewal, J. S. *The Khalsa: Sikh and Non-Sikh Perspectives.* New Delhi: Manohar, 2006.

Grewal, J. S., and Indu Banga, eds. *Punjab in Prosperity and Violence: Administration, Politics, and Social Change, 1947–1997.* New Delhi: K. K. Publishers for Institute of Punjab Studies, Chandigarh, 1998.

Guha, Ramachandra. *India after Gandhi: The History of the World's Largest Democracy.* New York: Ecco, 2007.

Guha, Ramachandra. *Social Ecology.* Delhi: Oxford University Press, 1998.

Guha, Ramachandra. *The Unquiet Woods: Ecological Change and Peasant Resistance in the Himalaya.* New Delhi: Oxford University Press, 1989.

Guha, Ramanchandra, and Madhav Gadgil. *Ecology and Equity.* New Delhi: Penguin, 1995.

Guha, Sumit. *Environment and Ethnicity in India, 1200–1991.* Cambridge: Cambridge University Press, 2006.

Guhan, S., and Samuel Paul, eds. *Corruption in India: Agenda for Action.* New Delhi: Vision Books, 1997.

Gulati, Ashok, and Tim Kelley. *Trade Liberalization and Indian Agriculture.* Delhi and Oxford: Oxford University Press, 2001.

Gulati, Leela. *Profiles in Female Poverty: A Study of Five Poor Working Women in Kerala.* Delhi: Hindustan Publications, 1981.

Gupta, Akhil. *Postcolonial Developments: Agriculture in the Making of Modern India.* Durham, NC: Duke University Press, 1998.

Gupta, Akhil, and Kalyanakrishnan Sivaramakrishnan. *The State in India after Liberalization: Interdisciplinary Perspectives.* New York: Routledge, 2010.

Gupta, Bhabani Sen. *Rajiv Gandhi: A Political Study.* New Delhi: Konark, 1989.

Gupta, Dipankar. *Nativism in a Metropolis: The Shiv Sena in Bombay.* New Delhi: Manohar, 1982.

Gupta, Dipankar. *Social Stratification.* 13th ed. Delhi: Oxford University Press, 2007.

Gupta, K. R. *India's International Relations.* 2 vols. New Delhi: Atlantic Publishers and Distributors, 2009.

Gupta, Nilanjana. *Switching Channels: Ideologies of Television in India.* New Delhi: Oxford University Press, 1998.

Gupte, Pranay. *Mother India: A Political Biography of Indira Gandhi.* New York: Scribner, 1992.

Gupte, Pranay. *Vengeance: India after the Assassination of Indira Gandhi.* New York: Norton, 1985.

Gusain, H. K. *Political Views and Thoughts of Nehru.* New Delhi: Cyber Tech Publications, 2009.

Hansen, Thomas Blom. *The Saffron Wave: Democracy and Hindu Nationalism in Modern India.* Princeton, NJ: Princeton University Press, 1999.

Hansen, Thomas Blom. "The Vernacularisation of *Hindutva*: The BJP and Shiv Sena in Rural Maharashta." *Contributions to Indian Sociology* 30 (1996): 177–214.

Hansen, Thomas Blom. *Wages of Violence: Naming and Identity in Postcolonial Bombay.* Princeton, NJ: Princeton University Press, 2001.

Hansen, Thomas Blom, and Christophe Jaffrelot. *The BJP and the Compulsions of Politics in India.* 2nd ed. New Delhi: Oxford University Press, 2001.

Hanson, Albert Henry. *The Process of Planning: A Study of India's Five-Year Plans, 1950–1964.* Oxford: Oxford University Press, 1966.

Hardgrave, Robert L. *The Dravidian Movement.* Delhi: Popular Prakashan, 1965.

Hardgrave, Robert L. *India under Pressure.* Epping: Bowker, 1984.

Hardgrave, Robert L. *The Nadars of Tamilnad.* Berkeley: University of California Press, 1969.

Hardtmann, Eva-Maria. *The Dalit Movement in India: Local Practices, Global Connections.* New Delhi: Oxford University Press, 2009.

Harihar, Bhattacharya. *Communism in Tipura.* New Delhi: Ajanta, 1999.

Harrison, Selig. *India: The Most Dangerous Decades*. Madras: Oxford University Press, 1965.

Harrison, Selig S., Paul H. Kreisberg, and Dennis Kux, eds. *India and Pakistan: The First Fifty Years*. Woodrow Wilson Center Series. Cambridge: Cambridge University Press and Woodrow Wilson Center Press, 1999.

Harrison, Selig S., and K. Subrahmanyam. *Superpower Rivalry in the Indian Ocean: Indian and American Perspectives*. Oxford: Oxford University Press, 1989.

Harriss, John. *Power Matters: Essays on Institutions, Politics, and Society in India*. New Delhi and New York: Oxford University Press, 2009.

Harriss-White, Barbara. *India Working: Essays on Society and Economy*. Cambridge: Cambridge University Press, 2003.

Harriss-White, Barbara, and S. Janakarajan. *Rural India Facing the 21st Century: Essays on Long-Term Village Change and Recent Development Policy*. London: Anthem, 2004.

Harshe, Rajen. "India-Pakistan Conflict over Kashmir: Peace through Development Cooperation." *South Asia Survey* 12 (2005): 47–60.

Hart, Henry C., ed. *Indira Gandhi's India: A Political System Reappraised*. Boulder, CO: Westview, 1976.

Hasan, M., ed. *Knowledge, Power and Politics: Educational Institutions in India*. New Delhi: Roli Books, 1998.

Hasan, Mushirul. *Living with Secularism: The Destiny of India's Muslims*. New Delhi: Manohar, 2007.

Hasan, Mushirul. *Moderate or Militant: Imaging India's Muslims*. Oxford: Oxford University Press, 2008.

Hasan, Mushirul. *Nationalism and Communal Politics in India*. New Delhi: Manohar, 1991.

Hasan, Mushirul. *The Nehrus: Personal Histories*. London: Mercury Books, 2006.

Hasan, Mushirul, ed. *India's Partition: Process, Strategy and Mobilization*. Oxford: Oxford University Press, 1994.

Hasan, Mushirul, ed. *Nehru's India: Select Speeches*. Oxford: Oxford University Press, 2007.

Hasan, Mushirul, and Nariaki Nakazato, eds. *The Unfinished Agenda: Nation-Building in South Asia*. New Delhi: Manohar, 2001.

Hasan, Zoya. *Parties and Party Politics in India*. New Delhi: Oxford University Press, 2002.

Hasan, Zoya. *Politics of Inclusion: Caste, Minority, and Representation in India*. Oxford: Oxford University Press, 2009.

Hasan, Zoya. *Quest for Power: Oppositional Movements and Post-Congress Politics in Uttar Pradesh*. New Delhi: Oxford University Press, 1998.

Hasan, Zoya, and Ritu Menon. *Unequal Citizens: A Study of Muslim Women in India.* New Delhi: Oxford University Press, 2004.

Hasan, Zoya, Eswaran Sridharan, and Ratna M. Sudarshan, eds. *India's Living Constitution.* London: Anthem, 2005.

Hawley, John C. *India in Africa, Africa in India: Indian Ocean Cosmopolitanisms.* Bloomington: Indiana University Press, 2008.

Hayward, Ruth Finney. *Breaking the Earthenware Jar: Lessons from South Asia to End Violence against Women and Girls.* Katmandu: UNICEF, 2000.

Heitzman, James. *Network City: Planning the Information Society in Bangalore.* Oxford: Oxford University Press, 2004.

Heller, Patrick. *The Labor of Development: Workers and the Transformation of Capitalism in Kerala, India.* Ithaca, NY: Cornell University Press, 1999.

Heller, Peter, and Govindra Rao. *Sustainable Fiscal Policy for India.* New Delhi: Oxford University Press, 2006.

Herring, R. J. *"Land to the Tiller": The Political Economy of Agrarian Reform in South Asia.* London: Yale University Press, 1983.

Hewitt, Vernon. *Reclaiming the Past? The Search for Political and Cultural Unity in Contemporary Janmu and Kashmir.* Manchester, UK: Manchester University Press, 1997.

Human Rights Watch Children's Rights Project, Human Rights Watch/Asia. *The Small Hands of Slavery: Bonded Child Labor in India.* New York: Human Rights Watch, 1996.

Humbers, Philippe. *The Rajiv Gandhi Years: Sunshine and Shadows.* New Delhi: Vimot, 1992.

Hurst, Evelin. *Women's Political Representation and Empowerment in India: A Million Indiras Now?* New Delhi: Manohar, 2004.

Ilaiah, Kancha. *Why I Am Not a Hindu: A Sudra Critique of Hindutva, Philosophy, Culture, and Political Economy.* Calcutta: Samya, 1996.

Inden, Ronald. *Imagining India.* Chicago: University of Chicago Press, 1990.

India Kargil Review Committee. *From Surprise to Reckoning: The Kargil Review Committee Report, New Delhi, December 15, 1999.* New Delhi: Sage, 2000.

International Institute for Non-Aligned Studies [IINS]. *35 Years of Non-aligned Movement: Documents, 1961–1996.* New Delhi: IINS, 1997.

Ishil, Hiroshi, et al. *Social Dynamics in Northern South Asia.* New Delhi: Manohar, 2007.

Jabbar, Naheem. *Historiography and Writing Postcolonial India.* New York: Routledge, 2009.

Jacobsohn, Gary J. *The Wheel of Law: India's Secularism in Comparative Constitutional Context.* Princeton, NJ: Princeton University Press, 2005.

Jadhav, K. N. *Dr. Ambedkar and the Significance of His Movement.* New Dehli: Lahooti Fine Press, 1993.

Jaffrelot, Christophe. *Ambedkar: Leader of the Dalits, Architect of the Indian Constitution.* London: Hurst, 2001.

Jaffrelot, Christophe. *The Hindu Nationalist Movement in India.* New York: Columbia University Press, 1998.

Jaffrelot, Christophe. *The Hindu Nationalist Movement in Indian Politics, 1925 to the 1990s: Strategies of Identity-Building, Implantation and Mobilisation (with Special Reference to Central India).* London: Hurst, 1996.

Jaffrelot, Christophe. *India's Silent Revolution: The Rise of the Lower Castes.* London: Hurst, 1999.

Jaffrelot, Christophe. *The Sangh Parivar: A Reader.* Delhi: Oxford University Press, 2005.

Jaffrelot, Christophe. "The Subordinate Caste Revolution." In *India Briefing: Quickening the Pace of Change,* edited by A. Ayres and P. Oldenburgh, 121–158. Armonk, NY: M. E. Sharpe, 2002.

Jain, B. M. *Global Power: India's Foreign Policy, 1947–2006.* Lanham, MD: Lexington Books, 2009.

Jain, C. K., ed. *Women Parliamentarians in India.* New Delhi: Surjeet, 1993.

Jain, P. C., ed. *Indian Economic Crisis: Diagnosis and Treatment.* New Delhi: Concept Publishing, 1992.

Jain, R. K. *The Kashmir Question, Etc.: Soviet South Asian Relations, 1947–1973.* Oxford, UK: Martin Robertson, 1979.

Jaiswal, S. *Caste: Origin, Function and Dimensions of Change.* New Delhi: Manohar, 1998.

Jal, Janak Raj. *Presidents of India, 1950–2000.* New Delhi: Regency Publications, 2002.

Jalal, Ayesha. *Democracy and Authoritarianism in South Asia: A Comparative and Historical Perspective.* Cambridge: Cambridge University Press, 1995.

Jalal, Ayesha. *Partisans of Allah: Jihad in South Asia.* Cambridge: Harvard University Press, 2008.

Jalal, Ayesha. *The Sole Spokesman: Jinnah, the Muslim League and the Demand for Pakistan.* Cambridge: Cambridge University Press, 1994.

Jalan, Bimal. *India's Economic Crisis: The Way Ahead.* Delhi: Oxford University Press, 1991.

Jannuzi, F. Tomasson. *India in Transition: Issues of Political Economy in a Plural Society.* Boulder, CO: Westview, 1989.

Jayakar, P. *Indira Gandhi: A Biography.* New Delhi: Viking, 1992.

Jayal, Niraja Gopal. *Democracy and the State: Welfare, Secularism, and Development in Contemporary India.* 2nd ed. New Delhi: Oxford University Press, 2002.

Jayal, Niraja Gopal. *Democracy in India*. New Delhi: Oxford University Press, 2009.

Jayal, Niraja Gopal, and Sudha Pai, eds. *Democratic Governance in India: Challenges of Poverty, Development and Identity*. New Delhi: Sage, 2001.

Jayal, Niraja Gopal, Amit Prakash, and Pradeep K. Sharma. *Local Governance in India: Decentralization and Beyond*. New Delhi: Oxford University Press, 2006.

Jayawardena, Kumari, and Mulathi de Alwis, eds. *Embodied Violence: Communalizing Women's Sexuality in South Asia*. New Delhi: Kali for Women, 1996.

Jeffery, Craig, Patricia Jeffery, and Roger Jeffery. "Dalit Revolution? New Politicians in Uttar Pradesh, India." *Journal of Asian Studies* 67(4) (2008): 1365–1396.

Jeffery, Patricia, and Amrita Basu, eds. *Appropriating Gender: Women's Activism and Politicized Religion in South Asia*. London: Routledge, 1997.

Jeffery, Patricia, et al. *Labour Pains and Labour Power: Women and Childbearing in India*. London: Zed Books, 1989.

Jeffery, Patricia, and Roger Jeffery. *Don't Marry Me to a Plowman! Women's Everyday Lives in Rural North India*. Boulder, CO: Westview, 1996.

Jeffery, Patricia, Roger Jeffery, and Craig Jeffery. "Islamization, Gentrification and Domestication: 'A Girls' Islamic Course' and Rural Muslims in Western Uttar Pradesh." *Modern Asian Studies* 38(1) (2004): 1–54.

Jeffery, Roger. *The Politics of Health in India*. Berkeley: University of California Press, 1988.

Jeffery, Roger. *What's Happening to India? Punjab, Ethnic Conflict, Mrs. Gandhi's Death and the Test for Federalism*. Basingstoke, UK: Macmillan, 1986.

Jeffery, Roger, and Patricia Jeffery. *Confronting Saffron Demography: Religion, Fertility, and Women's Status in India*. New Delhi: Three Essays Collective, 2006.

Jeffery, Roger, and Patricia Jeffery. *Population, Gender and Politics: Demographic Change in Rural North India*. Cambridge: Cambridge University Press, 1997.

Jeffery, Roger, and Jens Lerche, eds. *Social and Political Change in Uttar Pradesh: European Perspectives*. New Delhi: Manohar, 2004.

Jeffery, Roger, and Nandini Sundar. *A New Moral Economy for India's Forests?* New Delhi and Thousand Oaks, CA: Sage, 1999.

Jeffrey, Robin. *India's Newspaper Revolution: Capitalism, Technology and the Indian Language Press, 1977–1999*. New York: Palgrave Macmillan, 2000.

Jeffrey, Robin. "The Mahatma Didn't Like Movies and Why It Matters: India's Broadcasting Policy, 1920s-90s." *Global Media and Communication* 2 (2006): 204–224.

Jeffrey, Robin. "Testing Concepts about Print, Newspapers, and Politics: Kerala, India, 1800–2009." *Journal of Asian Studies* 68(2) (2009): 465–489.

Jenkins, Rob. *Democratic Politics and Economic Reform in India*. Cambridge: Cambridge University Press, 1999.

Jenks, Andrew L. *Perils of Progress: Environmental Disasters in the Twentieth Century*. Upper Saddle River, NJ: Prentice Hall, 2010.

Jiwani, Yasmin. "The Exotic, the Erotic and the Dangerous: South Asian Women in Popular Film." *Canadian Woman Studies* 13(1) (1992): 42–46.

Johnson, B. L. C. *Development in South Asia*. Harmondsworth, UK: Penguin, 1983.

Joshi, Anuradha, and Mick Moore. "Enabling Environments: Do Anti-poverty Programmes Mobilize the Poor?" *Journal of Development Studies* 37 (2000): 25–26.

Joshi, B. R., ed. *Untouchable! Voices of the Dalit Liberation Movement*. London: Zed and MRG, 1986.

Joshi, Barbara R. *Democracy in Search of Equality: Untouchable Politics and Indian Social Change*. Delhi: Hindustan Publishing, 1982.

Joshi, Chand. *Bhindranwale: Myth and Reality*. New Delhi: Vikas, 1984.

Joshi, Chitra. *Lost Worlds: Indian Labour and Its Forgotten Histories*. London: Anthem, 2005.

Joshi, S. R., and Trivedi, B. *Mass Media and Cross-Cultural Communication: A Study of Television in India*. Report No. SRG-94-041. Ahmedabad: Development and Educational Communication Unit, Indian Space Research and Organisation, May 1994.

Joshi, Sarat C. *Gandhian Social Work*. New Delhi: Akansha Publishing House, 2009.

Joshi, Varsha, and Surjit Singh. *Culture, Polity and Economy*. Jaipur: Rawat, 2009.

Juergensmeyer, Mark. *Religious Nationalism Confronts the Secular State*. New Delhi: Oxford University Press, 1994.

Jumani, U. *Dealing with Poverty: Self-Employment for Poor, Rural Women*. London: Sage, 1991.

Kabir, Nasreen. *Talking Films: Conversations on Hindi Cinema with Javed Akhtar*. Oxford: Oxford University Press, 2002.

Kakar, Sudhir. *The Colours of Violence*. New Delhi: Viking, 1995.

Kalia, Ravi. *Gandhinagar: Building National Identity in Postcolonial India*. Columbia: University of South Carolina Press, 2004.

Kalpagam, U. *Labor and Gender: Survival in Urban India*. New Delhi: Sage, 1994.

Kamal, Nath. *India's Century: The Age of Entrepreneurship in the World's Biggest Democracy*. New York: McGraw-Hill, 2007.

Kamath, H. V. *Last Days of Jawaharlal Nehru*. Calcutta: Jayasree Prakashan, 1977.

Kamath, P. M. *India's Policy of No First Use of Nuclear Weapons: Relevance to Peace and Security in South Asia*. New Delhi: Anamika Publishers, 2009.

Kanna, V. Venkat. *Law and Child Labour in India.* New Delhi: Anmol, 2002.

Kannabiran, K., and V. Kannabiran. "Caste and Gender: Understanding Dynamics of Power and Violence." *Economic and Political Weekly* 26 (1991): 2130–2133.

Kannabiran, Kalpana, and Ranbir Singh. *Challenging the Rules of Law: Colonialism, Criminology and Human Rights.* New Delhi: Sage, 2008.

Kapur, Ashok. *Pokhran and Beyond: India's Nuclear Behaviour.* 2nd ed. New Delhi: Oxford University Press, 2003.

Kapur, Devesh, and Pratap Bhanu Mehta. *Public Institutions in India: Performance and Design.* New Delhi: Oxford University Press, 2005.

Kapur, Rajiv. *Sikh Separatism: The Politics of Faith.* New Delhi: Vikas, 1987.

Karlekar, Hiranmay. *In the Mirror of Mandal: Social Justice, Caste, Class and the Individual.* New Delhi: Ajanta, 1992.

Karnad, Bharat. *India's Nuclear Policy.* Westport, CT: Praeger, 2008.

Kasbekar, A. "Hidden Pleasures: Negotiating the Myth of the Female Ideal in Popular Hindi Cinema." In *Pleasure and the Nation: The History, Politics, and Consumption of Public Culture in India,* edited by Rachel Dwyer and Christopher Pinney, 268–308. New Delhi: Oxford University Press, 2000.

Katju, Manjari. *Vishva Hindu Parishad and Indian Politics.* New Delhi: Orient Longman, 2003.

Katzenstein, Mary F. *Ethnicity and Equality: The Shiv Sena Party and Preferential Politics in Bombay.* Ithaca, NY: Cornell University Press, 1979.

Kaul, Venita, and the World Bank. *Reaching Out to the Child.* New Delhi: Oxford University Press, 2004.

Kaur, Raminder. *Performative Politics and the Cultures of Hinduism: Public Uses of Religion in Western India.* London: Anthem, 2005.

Kaur, Raminder, and Ajay J. Sinha. *Bollywood: Popular Indian Cinema through a Transnational Lens.* New Delhi: Sage, 2005.

Kavoori, Anandam P., and Aswin Punathambekar. *Global Bollywood.* New Delhi: Oxford University Press, 2009.

Kazmi, Fareed. *The Politics of India's Conventional Cinema: Imagining a Universe, Subverting a Mutiverse.* New Delhi: Sage, 1999.

Keay, John. *Democracy and Discontent: India's Growing Crisis of Governability.* Cambridge: Cambridge University Press, 1992.

Keer, Dhananjay. *Dr. Ambedkar.* Bombay: Popular Prakashan, 1954.

Kerr, Ian J. *Engines of Change: The Railroads That Made India.* New York: Praeger, 2006.

Kerr, Ian J. *Railways in Modern India.* New Delhi: Oxford University Press, 2001.

Kessinger, Tom G. *Vilyatpur, 1848–1968: Social and Economic Change in a North Indian Village*. Berkeley: University of California Press, 1974.

Khan, S. "Systems of Medicine and Nationalist Discourse in India: Towards 'New Horizons' in Medical Anthropology and History." *Social Science and Medicine* 62(11) (2006): 278–297.

Khan, Saira. *Nuclear Weapons and Conflict Transformation: The Case of India-Pakistan (Asian Security Studies)*. New York: Routledge, 2008.

Khan, Yasmin. *The Great Partition: The Making of India and Pakistan*. New Haven, CT: Yale University Press, 2008.

Khan, Yasmin. "India Divided: State and Society in the Aftermath of Partition: The Case of Uttar Pradesh 1946–52." DPhil dissertation, Oxford University, 2005.

Khare, R. S. *Caste, Hierarchy, and Individualism*. New Delhi: Oxford University Press, 2006.

Khilnani, Niranjan M. *Iron Lady of Indian Politics: Indira Gandhi in the Balanced Perspective*. Delhi: H. K. Publishers, 1989.

Khilnani, Sunil. *The Idea of India*. London: Penguin, 2003.

King, Robert D. *Nehru and the Language Politics of India*. New Delhi: Oxford University Press, 1997.

Kirk, Jason A. *India and the World Bank: The Politics of Aid and Influence*. London: Anthem, 2010.

Kirpal, Dhillon. *Identity and Survival: Sikh Militancy in India, 1978–1993*. New Delhi: Penguin India, 2006.

Kishwar, Madhu. *Deepening Democracy: Challenges and Governance and Globalization in India*. New Delhi and Oxford: Oxford University Press, 2006.

Kishwar, Madhu, and Ruth Vanita. "The Burning of Roop Kanwar." *Race and Class* 30 (1988): 59–67.

Kishwar, Madhu, and Ruth Vanita. *In Search of Answers: Indian Women's Voices from Manushi*. New Delhi: Manohar, 1996.

Kitchlu, T. N. *Windows in India*. New Delhi: Ashish, 1993.

Klingensmith, Daniel. *One Valley and a Thousand: Dams, Nationalism, and Development*. Oxford: Oxford University Press, 2007.

Kochanek, Stanley A. *The Congress Party of India*. Princeton, NJ: Princeton University Press, 1968.

Kochanek, Stanley A. "Liberalisation and Business Lobbying in India." *Journal of Commonwealth and Comparative Politics* 34 (1996): 155–173.

Kochanek, Stanley A. "The Politics of Regulation: Rajiv's New Mantra." *Journal of Commonwealth and Comparative Politics* 23 (November 1985): 189–211.

Kochanek, Stanley A. "Regulation and Liberalization Theology in India." *Asian Survey* 26 (1986): 1284–1308.

Kochanek, Stanley A. "The Transformation of Interest Politics in India." *Pacific Affairs* 68 (1996): 529–550.

Kochanek, Stanley A., and Robert L. Hardgrave. *India: Government and Politics in a Developing Nation*. 7th ed. Boston: Thomson-Wadsworth, 2008.

Koenraad, Elst. *Ram Jammabhoomi vs. Babri Masjid: A Case Study in Hindu-Muslim Conflict*. New Delhi: Voice of India, 1990.

Kohli, Atul. "Centralization and Powerlessness: India's Democracy in a Comparative Perspective." In *State Power and Social Forces: Domination and Transformation in the Third World*, edited by Joel S. Migdal, Atul Kohil, and Vivienne Shue, 89–107. Cambridge: Cambridge University Press, 1994.

Kohli, Atul. *Democracy and Development in India: From Socialism to Pro-Business*. New Delhi: Oxford University Press, 2009.

Kohli, Atul. *Democracy and Discontent: India's Growing Crisis of Governability*. Cambridge: Cambridge University Press, 1990.

Kohli, Atul. *India's Democracy*. Princeton, NJ: Princeton University Press, 1988.

Kohli, Atul. "Politics of Economic Liberalisation in India." *World Development* 3 (1989): 305–328.

Kohli, Atul. *The State and Poverty in India: The Politics of Reform*. Cambridge: Cambridge University Press, 1989.

Kohli, Atul. *The Success of India's Democracy*. Cambridge: Cambridge University Press, 2001.

Kohli, Atul, ed. *India's Democracy: An Analysis of Changing State-Social Relations*. Princeton, NJ: Princeton University Press, 1988.

Kohli, Atul, and Amrita Basu. "Community Conflicts and the State in India." *Journal of Asian Studies* 56 (1997): 391–397.

Kohli, Vanita. *The Indian Media Business*. New Delhi: Response, 2003.

Kolenda, Pauline. "Caste in India since Independence." In *Social and Economic Development in India: A Reassessment*, edited by D. K. Basu and R. Sisson, 106–128. New Delhi: Sage, 1986.

Kothari, Rajni. *Caste in Indian Politics*. New Delhi: Orient Longman, 1970.

Kothari, Rajni. *Politics and the People: In Search of the Humane India*. New York: New Horizons, 1989.

Kothari, Rajni. *State against Democracy: In Search of Humane Government*. New Delhi: Konark, 1988.

Kothari, Smitu, and Harsh Sethi, eds. *Rethinking Human Rights: Challenges for Theory and Action*. Delhi: Lokayan, 1991.

Kothari, Smitu, and Harsh Sethi, eds. *Voices from a Scarred City: The Delhi Carnage in Perspective*. New Delhi: Lokayan, 1985.

Krishna, Ashok, and P. R. Chari, eds. *Kargil: The Tables Turned*. New Delhi: Manohar, 2001.

Krishna, Sankaran. *Postcolonial Insecurities: India, Sri Lanka and the Question of Nationhood*. Minneapolis: University of Minnesota Press, 1999.

Krishnamurthy, Mathangi. "Outsourced Identities: The Fragmentation of the Cross-Border Economy." *SAGAR: A South Asia Graduate Research Journal* 14 (2005): 23–38.

Krishnaswamy, Sudhir. *Democracy and Constitutionalism in India*. New Delhi: Oxford University Press, 2009.

Krueger, Anne O. *Economic Policy Reforms and the Indian Economy*. New Delhi: Oxford University Press, 2002.

Kudaisya, Gyanesh. *"Heartland": Uttar Pradesh in India's Body Politic*. New Delhi: Sage, 2006.

Kulke, Hermann, and Dietmar Rothermund. *A History of India*. 5th ed. London: Routledge, 2010.

Kumar, Amrita, and Prashun Bhaumik, eds. *Lest We Forget: Gujrat, 2002*. New Delhi: World Report/Rupa, 2002.

Kumar, C. Raj, K. Chockalingam, and V. R. Krishna Iyer. *Human Rights, Justice, and Constitutional Empowerment*. New Delhi: Oxford University Press, 2007.

Kumar, Deepak, ed. *Science and Empire: Essays in Indian Context, 1700–1947*. Delhi: Anamika Prakashan, 1991.

Kumar, Dharma. "The Affirmative Action Debate in India." *Asian Survey* 32 (1992): 290–302.

Kumar, Dharma, and Meghnad Desai, eds. *The Cambridge Economic History of India*, vol. 2, *c.1751–c.1970*. Cambridge: Cambridge University Press, 1983.

Kumar, Neelam. *Women and Science in India*. New Delhi: Oxford University Press, 2009.

Kumar, Nita. *The Artisans of Banaras: Popular Culture and Identity, 1880–1986*. Princeton, NJ: Princeton University Press, 1988.

Kumar, Nita. *The Politics of Gender, Community, and Modernity*. New Delhi: Oxford University Press, 2007.

Kumar, Radha. *The History of Doing: An Illustrated Account of Movements for Women's Rights and Feminism in India, 1800–1990*. New Delhi: Kali for Women, 1993.

Kumar, Ravindra. *The Social History of Modern India*. New Delhi: Oxford University Press, 1983.

Kumari, Ved. *The Juvenile Justice System in India: From Welfare to Rights*. New Delhi: Oxford University Press, 2004.

Kumar Singh, Ujimal. *Political Prisoners in India*. New Delhi: Oxford University Press, 1998.

Kundu, Amitabh, et al. *India Social Development Report*. New Delhi: Oxford University Press, 2006.

Kux, Dennis, and Daniel P. Moynihan. *India and the United States: Estranged Democracies, 1941–1991*. Honolulu: University Press of the Pacific, 2002.

Lak, Daniel. *India Express: The Future of the New Superpower*. New York: Palgrave Macmillan, 2009.

Lal, Ananda. *The Oxford Companion to Indian Theatre*. New Delhi: Oxford University Press, 2004.

Lal, Ananda. *Theatres of India: A Concise Companion*. New Delhi: Oxford University Press, 2009.

Lal, Deepak. *The Hindu Equilibrium: Cultural Stability and Economic Stagnation*. New York: Oxford University Press, 1988.

Lal, Sheo Kumar, and Umed Raj Nahar. *Extent of Untouchability and Pattern of Discrimination*. New Delhi: Mittal, 1990.

Lal, Vinay. *The History of History: Politics and Scholarship in Modern India*. New Delhi: Oxford University Press, 2003.

Lal, Vinay. *Political Hinduism: The Religious Imagination in Public Spheres*. New Delhi: Oxford University Press, 2009.

Lal, Vinay, and Ashis Nandy, eds. *Fingerprinting Popular Culture: The Mythic and the Iconic in Indian Cinema*. New Delhi: Oxford University Press, 2006.

Lamb, A. *Kashmir: A Disputed Legacy, 1846–1990*. Hertingfordbury, UK: Roxford Books, 1991.

Lamb, Sarah. *White Saris and Sweet Mangoes: Aging, Gender, and Body in North India*. Berkeley: University of California Press, 2000.

Landy, Marc, and Jaya Arunachalam. *Structuring a Movement and Spreading It On: History and Growth of the Working Women's Forum in India, 1978–2003*. Frankfurt: IKO-Verlag fur Interkulturelle Kommunikation, 2003.

Lapierre, Dominique, and Javier Moro. *It Was Five Past Midnight in Bhopal: The Epic Story of the World's Deadliest Industrial Disaster*. New York: Grand Central Publishing, 2002.

Larson, Gerald James. *Religion and Personal Law in Secular India: A Call to Judgment*. Bloomington: Indiana University Press, 2002.

Lateef, Shahida. *Muslim Women in India*. London: Zed Books, 1990.

Lewis, John P. *India's Political Economy: Governance and Reform.* Delhi: Oxford University Press, 1995.

Liddle, Joanna, and Rama Joshi. *Daughters of Independence: Gender, Caste and Class in India.* London: Zed Books, 1986.

Lieten, G. K. *Power, Politics and Rural Development: Essays on India.* New Delhi: Manohar, 2003.

Linnemann, H., and C. H. Hanumantha Rao, eds. *Economic Reforms and Poverty Alleviation in India.* New Delhi: Sage, 1996.

Little, John T. "Video Vacana: Swadhyaya and Sacred Tapes." In *Media and the Transformation of Religion in South Asia,* edited by Lawrence Baff and Susan S. Wadley, 254–283. Philadelphia: University of Pennsylvania Press, 1995.

Llewellyn, J. F. *Legacy of Women's Uplift in India.* New Delhi and Thousand Oaks, CA: Sage, 1998.

Low, D. A. "Pakistan and India: Political Legacies from the Colonial Past." *South Asia* 25(2) (2002): 257–272.

Lucas, Robert E. B., and Gustav F. Papanek, eds. *The Indian Economy: Recent Development and Future Prospects.* Westview Special Studies on South and Southeast Asia. Boulder, CO: Westview, 1988.

Luce, Edward. *In Spite of the Gods: The Rise of Modern India.* New York: Anchor Books, 2008.

Ludden, David. *An Agrarian History of South Asia.* Cambridge: Cambridge University Press, 1999.

Ludden, David. "India's Development Regime." In *Colonialism and Culture,* edited by Nicholas Dirks, 247–287. Ann Arbor: University of Michigan Press, 1992.

Ludden, David. *The New Cambridge History of India,* vol. 4, pt. 4, *An Agrarian History of South Asia.* Cambridge: Cambridge University Press, 1999.

Ludden, David. *Peasant History in South India.* Princeton, NJ: Princeton University Press, 1985.

Ludden, David, ed. *Contesting the Nation: Religion, Community, and the Politics of Democracy in India.* Philadelphia: University of Pennsylvania Press, 1996.

Ludden, David, ed. *Making India Hindu.* Delhi: Oxford University Press, 1996.

Ludden, David, ed. *Reading Subaltern Studies: Critical History, Contested Meaning and the Globalization of South India.* London: Anthem, 2002.

Madan, T. N. *Modern Myths, Locked Minds.* New Delhi: Oxford University Press, 1997.

Madan, T. N. *Religion in India.* Delhi: Oxford University Press, 1997.

Madan, T. N. "Secularism in Its Place." In *Secularism and Its Critics,* edited by R. Bhargava, 747–759. New Delhi: Oxford University Press, 1998.

Madan, T. N., ed. *Muslim Communities of South Asia: Culture, Society, and Power.* New Delhi: Manohar, 1995.

Madan, Vandana. *The Village in India.* New Delhi: Oxford University Press, 2004.

Mahar, J. Michael, ed. *The Untouchables in Contemporary India.* Tucson: University of Arizona Press, 1972.

Maharatna, Arup. *Demographic Perspectives on India's Tribes.* New Delhi: Oxford University Press, 2005.

Maheshwari, Shriram. *Public Administration in India: The Higher Civil Service.* New Delhi and New York: Oxford University Press, 2005.

Mahmood, Cynthia Keppley. *Fighting for Faith and Nation: Dialogues with Sikh Militants.* Philadelphia: University of Pennsylvania Press, 1997.

Maini, Tridivesh Singh. *Humanity amidst Insanity: Hope during and after the Indo-Pak Partition.* New Delhi: UBS Publishers, 2009.

Majid, Abdul. *Legal Protection to Unorganized Labour.* New Delhi: Deep and Deep, 2000.

Majumdar, Boria. "When North-South Fight, the Nation Is Out of Sight: The Politics of Olympic Sport in Post Colonial India." *International Journal of the History of Sport* 23(7) (2006): 1217–1231.

Majumdar, Boria, and Nalin Mehta. *India and the Olympics.* New York: Routledge, 2009.

Malhotra, Anshu. *Gender, Caste, and Religious Identities.* New Delhi: Oxford University Press, 2002.

Malik, Hafeez. *Moslem Nationalism in India and Pakistan.* Washington, DC: Public Affairs, 1963.

Malik, Iftikhar. *The History of Pakistan.* Westport, CT: Greenwood, 2008.

Malik, Yogendra K. "The Akali Party and Sikh Militancy: Move for Greater Autonomy or Secessionism in Punjab?" *Asian Survey* 26 (1986): 345–362.

Malik, Yogendra K., and V. B. Singh. *Hindu Nationalists in India: The Rise of the Bharatiya Janata Party.* Boulder, CO: Westview, 1994.

Malik, Yogendra K., and Dhirendra K. Vajpeyi. *India: The Years of Indira Gandhi.* Leiden: Brill Academic, 1988.

Mallick, Indrajit, and Sugata Marjit. *Financial Intermediation in a Less Developed Economy: The History of the United Bank of India.* New Delhi: Sage, 2008.

Mallick, Ross. *Development, Ethnicity and Human Rights in South Asia.* New Delhi: Sage, 1999.

Mallick, Ross. *Development of a Communist Government: West Bengal since 1947.* Cambridge: Cambridge University Press, 2007.

Mallick, Ross. *Indian Communism: Opposition, Collaboration, and Institutionalization.* New Delhi: Oxford University Press, 1994.

Mani, V. S. *Handbook of International Humanitarian Law in South Asia.* New Delhi: Oxford University Press, 2007.

Mankekar, D. R., and Kamala Mankekar. *Decline and Fall of Indira Gandhi.* New Delhi: Vision Books, 1977.

Mankekar, Purnima. *Screening Culture, Viewing Politics: An Ethnography of Television, Womanhood, and Nation in Postcolonial India.* Durham, NC: Duke University Press, 1999.

Mann, T. K. *Administration of Justice in India: A Case Study of Punjab.* New Delhi: Concept Publishing, 1979.

Manor, James. "How and Why Liberal and Representative Politics Emerged in India." *Political Studies* 20 (1990): 20–38.

Manor, James. "The Political Sustainability of Economic Liberalization in India." In *India: The Future of Economic Reforms,* edited by Robert Cassen and Vijay Joshi, 339–364. New Delhi: Oxford University Press, 1995.

Manor, James. *Power, Poverty and Poison: Disaster and Response in an Indian City.* New Delhi: Sage, 1993.

Manor, James. "Tried, Then Abandoned: Economic Liberalisation in India." *Institute of Development Studies Bulletin* 18 (1985): 39–44.

Manuel, Peter. *Cassette Culture: Popular Music and Technology in North India.* Chicago: University of Chicago Press, 1993.

Markovits, Claude. *History of Modern India, 1480–1950.* London: Anthem, 2004.

Markovits, Claude. *UnGandhian Gandhi: The Life and Afterlife of the Mahatma.* London: Anthem, 2004.

Marston, Daniel P., and Chandar S. Sundaram. *A Military History of India and South Asia: From the East India Company to the Nuclear Era.* Bloomington: Indiana University Press, 2008.

Marwah, Ved. *Uncivil Wars: Pathology of Terrorism in India.* New Delhi: Indus, 1995.

Masani, Minocheher Rustom. *The Communist Party of India: A Short History.* Mumbai: Bharatiya Vidhya Bhavan, 1967.

Massey, J. *Dalits in India: Religion as a Source of Bondage or Liberation.* New Delhi: Manohar, 1995.

Mather, Hari Mohan. *India: Social Development Report 2008.* Delhi: Oxford University Press, 2008.

Mathur, Kuldeep. "Does Performance Matter? Policy Struggles in Education." Unpublished manuscript, 2001.

Mathur, Kuldeep, and Niraya G. Jayal. *Drought, Policy and Politics in India: The Need for a Long Term Perspective.* New Delhi: Sage, 1993.

Maxwell, Neville. *India's China War.* London: Cape, 1970.

May, Daiane Kroeger. "Pharmaceutical Crisis in India: Transcending Profits with Human Rights." *Wisconsin International Law Journal* 10 (1991): 40–77.

Mayer, Adrian C. *Caste and Kinship in Central India: A Village and Its Region.* Berkeley: University of California Press, 1960.

Mazari, Shireen M. *The Kargil Conflict: Separating Fact from Fiction.* Islamabad: Center for Strategic Studies, 1999.

Mazumdar, Indrani. "Unorganized Workers of Delhi and the Seven Day Strike of 1988." http://www.indialabourarchives.org/publications/Indrani%20Mazumdar.htm.

Mazumdar, Ranjani. *Bombay Cinema: An Archive of the City.* Minneapolis: University of Minnesota Press, 2007.

Mazzarella, William. *Shoveling Smoke: Advertising and Global Contemporary India.* Delhi: Oxford University Press, 2003.

McHodgkins, Angelique Melitta. "Indian Filmakers and the Nineteenth-Century Novel: Rewriting the English Canon through Film." MA thesis, Miami University, 2005.

McLain, Karline. *India's Immortal Comic Books: Gods, Kings, and Other Heroes.* Bloomington: Indiana University Press, 2009.

McMillan, Alistar. *Standing at the Margins.* New Delhi: Oxford University Press, 2005.

Mediratta, S. K. *Handbook of Law, Women, and Employment.* New Delhi: Oxford University Press, 2009.

Meera, Kosambi. *Crossing Thresholds: Feminist Essays in Social History India.* Ranikhet: Permanent Black, 2007.

Mehra, Parshotam. *Essays in Frontier History: India, China, and the Disputed Border.* New Delhi: Oxford University Press, 2007.

Mehra, Parshotam. "India's Border Dispute with China: Revisiting Nehru's Approach." *International Studies* 42 (2005): 357–365.

Mehrota, Santosh K. *India and the Soviet Union: Trade and Technology Transfer.* Cambridge: Cambridge University Press, 1991.

Mehrotra, Santosh, et al. *Universalizing Elementary Education in India.* New Delhi: Oxford University Press, 2005.

Mehta, Bhattacharya Rini, ed. *Bollywood and Globalization: Indian Popular Cinema, Nation, and Diaspora.* London: Anthem, 2010.

Mehta, Jagat S. *Negotiating for India: Resolving Problems through Diplomacy: Seven Case Studies, 1958–1978.* New Delhi: Manohar, 2006.

Mehta, Nalin. *India on Television: How Satellite TV Has Changed the Way We Think and Act.* New Delhi: HarperCollins, 2008.

Mehta, Nalin, ed. *Television in India: Politics, Culture, and Globalization.* London: Routledge, 2008.

Mehta, Nalin, and Mona Mehta. *Politics, Conflict and Society in Gujarat: Fifty Years of a Modern Indian State (1960–2010).* New York: Routledge, 2010.

Mehta, Ved. *Rajiv Gandhi and Rama's Kingdom.* New Haven, CT: Yale University Press, 1994.

Mendelson, Oliver, and Marika Vicziany. *The Untouchables: Subordination, Poverty and the State in Modern India.* Cambridge: Cambridge University Press, 1998.

Menon, Dilip. *Cultural History of Modern India.* New Delhi: Social Science Press, 2006.

Menon, Nivedita. *Gender and Politics in India.* New Delhi: Oxford University Press, 2002.

Menon, Raja. *Weapons of Mass Destruction: Options for India.* New Delhi: Sage, 2005.

Menon, Ritu. *Borders and Boundaries: How Women Experienced the Partition of India.* New Brunswick, NJ: Rutgers University Press, 1998.

Menon, V. P. *The Story of the Integration of the Indian States.* Delhi: Orient Longman, 1956.

Menon, V. P. *The Transfer of Power in India.* Rev. ed. Hyderabad: Sangam Books, 1999.

Metcalf, Barbara D., and Thomas R. Metcalf. *A Concise History of Modern India.* 2nd ed. Cambridge: Cambridge University Press, 2006.

Michael, S. M., ed. *Dalits in Modern India: Vision and Values.* New Delhi: Vistaar, 1999.

Mies, Maria. *Indian Women and Patriarchy: Conflicts and Dilemmas of Students and Working Women.* New Delhi: Concept Publishing, 1980.

Mines, Mattison. *Public Faces, Private Lives: Community and Individuality in South India.* Berkeley: University of California Press, 1994.

Ministry of Finance, Government of India. *Economic Survey, 2008–2009.* New Delhi: Oxford University Press, 2009.

Ministry of Housing and Urban Poverty Alleviation and United Nations Development Programme. *India Urban Poverty Report, 2009.* New Delhi: Oxford University Press, 2009.

Mishra, Girish. *Economic History of Modern India.* Delhi: Pragati Publications, 2002.

Mishra, J. *Equality vs Justice. The Problem of Reservations for Backward Classes.* New Delhi: Deep and Deep, 1996.

Mishra, Pankaj. *Temptations of the West: How to Be Modern in India, Pakistan, Tibet, and Beyond.* New York: Picador, 2007.

Mishra, Vijay. *Bollywood Cinema: Temples of Desire.* London: Routledge, 2002.

Misra, B. B. *Government and Democracy in India.* Delhi: Oxford University Press, 1986.

Misra, B. B. *The Indian Middle Classes.* Oxford: Oxford University Press, 1961.

Mistry, Dinshaw. "India's Emerging Space Program." *Pacific Affairs* 71 (1998): 151–174.

Mitchell, Lisa. *Language, Emotion, and Politics in South India: The Making of a Mother Tongue.* Bloomington: Indiana University Press, 2009.

Mitra, A. "Voices of the Marginalized on the Internet: Examples from a Website for Women of South Asia." *Journal of Communication* 54 (2004): 492–510.

Mitra, Asok. *Calcutta Diary.* London: Cassell, 1977.

Mitra, Asok. *The New India, 1948–1955: Memoirs of an Indian Civil Servant.* Bombay: Popular Prakashan, 1991.

Mitra, Sharmila. "The Movement of Women's Emancipation within the Bengali Muslim Community in India." *Women's History Review* 15(3) (2006): 413–422.

Mitra, Subrata. *Power, Protest and Participation: Local Elites and the Politics of Development in India.* London: Routledge, 1992.

Mitra, Subrata. *The Puzzle of India's Governance: Culture, Context and Comparative Theory.* London: Routledge, 2006.

Mitra, Sumit, and Anita Kaul. "Doordarshan: The Tedium Is the Message." *India Today,* May 31, 1982.

Mittal, Mukta. *Educated Unemployed Women in India.* New Delhi: Anmol, 1994.

Mohan, P. V. S. Jogan, and Samir Chopra. *The India-Pakistan Air War of 1965.* New Delhi: Manohar, 2005.

Mohan, Rakesh. *Facets of the Indian Economy.* New Delhi: Oxford University Press, 2002.

Mohanty, Manoranjan, et al. *Grass-roots Democracy in India and China.* New Delhi: Sage, 2007.

Momen, Mehnaaz. "Can Secular Liberal Politics be Reincarnated in India?" *Journal of Asian and African Studies* 40 (2005): 243–260.

Moog, Robery S. "Elite-Court Relations in India: An Unsatisfactory Arrangement." *Asian Survey* 38 (1998): 410–423.

Mooij, Jos. "Food Policy in India: The Importance of Electoral Politics in Policy Implementation." *Journal of International Development* 11 (1999): 625–636.

Mookerjea-Leonard, Debali. "Divided Homelands, Hostile Homes: Partition, Women and Homelessness." *Journal of Commonwealth Literature* 40 (2005): 141–154.

Mookherjee, Dilip. *The Crisis in Government Accountability*. Oxford: Oxford University Press, 2004.

Moon, Vasant. *Growing Up Untouchable in India: A Dalit Autobiography*. Lanham, MD: Rowman and Littlefield, 2001.

Moraes, Dom. *Indira Gandhi*. Boston: Little, Brown, 1980.

Moraes, Dom. *Mrs. Gandhi*. London: Cape, 1980.

Morey, Peter, and Alex Tickell, eds. *Alternative Indias: Writing, Nation and Communalism*. Amsterdam: Editions Rodopi BV, 2005.

Morris-Jones, W. H. *The Government and Politics of India*. Fayetteville, AR: Hutchinson, 1971.

Mujeeb, Muhammad. *Dr Zakir Husain*. New Delhi: National Book Trust, 1972.

Mukarji, Nirmal, and Balveer Arora, eds. *Federalism in India: Origins and Development*. New Delhi: Vikas, 1992.

Mukherjee, J. R. *An Insider's Experience of Insurgency in India's North-East*. London: Anthem, 2007.

Mukherjee, Rila, and M. N. Rajesh, eds. *Locality, History, Memory: The Making of the Citizen in South Asia*. Cambridge, UK: Cambridge Scholars Publishing, 2009.

Mukherji, Rahul. *India's Economic Transition*. New Delhi: Oxford University Press, 2007.

Mukherji, Rahul. "Interests, Wireless Technology and Institutional Change: From Government Monopoly to Regulated Competition in Indian Telecommunications." *Journal of Asian Studies* 68(2) (2009): 491–517.

Mukhopadhyay, Nilanjan. *The Demolition: India at the Crossroads*. New Delhi: Indus, 1994.

Mukhopadhyay, Swapna, ed. *Women's Health, Public Policy, and Community Action*. New Delhi: Manohar, 1998.

Mukhopadhyay, Swapna, and R. Savithri. *Poverty, Gender and Reproductive Choice: An Analysis of Linkages*. New Delhi: Manohar, 1998.

Mukta, Parita. "Gender, Community, Nation: The Myth of Innocence." In *States of Conflict: Gender, Violence and Resistance*, edited by Susie Jacobs et al., 163–178. New York: Zed Books, 2000.

Mullatti, Leela. "Families in India: Beliefs and Realities." *Journal of Comparative Family Studies* 26(1) (1995): 11–26.

Muraleedharan, T. "Imperial Migrations: Reading the Raj Cinema of the 1980s." In *British Historical Cinema: The History, Heritage and Costume Film*, edited by Claire Monk and Amy Sargeant, 144–162. London: Routledge, 2002.

Murthy, Padmaja. *Managing Suspicions: Understanding India's Relations with Bangladesh, Bhutan, Nepal, Sri Lanka*. New Delhi: Institute for Defence Studies and Analysis, 2008.

Nag, Chitta Ranjan. *Post-colonial Mizo Politics, 1947–1998*. New Delhi: Vikas, 1999.

Naipaul, V. S. *India: A Wounded Civilization*. Toronto: Vintage, 2003.

Naipaul, V. S. *A Million Mutinies Now*. New York: Viking Penguin, 1991.

Nair, Janaki. *The Promise of the Metropolis: Bangalore's Twentieth Century*. New Delhi: Oxford University Press, 2005.

Naito, Masao, et al. *Marga: Ways of Liberation, Empowerment, and Social Change in Maharashtra*. New Delhi: Manohar, 2008.

Nambissam, G. B. "Equity in Education: Schooling Dalit Children in India." *Economic and Political Weekly* 31 (1996): 1011–1024.

Nanda, B. R. *Jawaharlal Nehru: Rebel and Statesman*. New Delhi: Oxford University Press, 1995.

Nanda, B. R., ed. *Indian Foreign Policy: The Nehru Years*. New Delhi: Vikas, 1976.

Nandimath, O. V. *Handbook of Environmental Decision Making in India*. New Delhi: Oxford University Press, 2009.

Nandy, Ashis. "The Changing Popular Culture of Indian Food: Preliminary Notes." *South Asia Research* 24 (2004): 9–19.

Nandy, Ashis. "Indian Popular Cinema as a Slum's Eye View of Politics." In *The Secret Politics of Our Desires: Innocence, Culpability and Indian Popular Cinema*, edited by A. Nandy, 1–18. London: Zed Books, 1988.

Nandy, Ashis. *The Romance of the State and the Fate of Dissent in the Tropics*. New York: Oxford University Press, 2003.

Nandy, Ashis. *Time Warps: Silent and Evasive Pasts in Indian Politics and Religion*. New Brunswick, NJ: Rutgers University Press, 2002.

Nandy, Ashis, ed. *The Secret Politics of Our Desires: Innocence, Culpability and Indian Popular Cinema*. Delhi: Oxford University Press, 1996.

Nandy, Ashis, et al. *Creating a Nationality: The Ramjanmabhumi Movement and Fear of the Self*. New Delhi: Oxford University Press, 1995.

Nandy, Ashis, and Ramin Jahanbegloo. *Talking India*. New Delhi: Oxford University Press, 2006.

Nandy, Pritish. "The Rediff Business-Interview with Shashi Gopal." 1999. http://rediff.com/business/1999/sep/08nandy.htm.

Narain, Vrinda. "Negotiating the Boundaries: Gender and Community in India." LLM thesis, McGill University, 1997.

Narayan, Jayaprakesh. *Prison Diary, 1975*. Edited by A. B. Shah. Bombay: Popular Prakashan, 1977.

Narayan, Jayaprakesh. *Swaraj for the People.* Varanasi: Sarva Sangh Prakash, 1963.

Nargolkar, Vasant. *JP's Crusade for Revolution.* New Delhi: S. Chand, 1975.

National Resource Centre on Child Labor. *Child Labour in India: An Overview.* Noida: National Resource Centre on Child Labor, V. V. Giri National Labour Institute, 2001.

Nauriya, A. "Dalit-Intermediate Caste Alliance: Call to Greatness." *Economic and Political Weekly* 29(27) (1994): 1640–1643.

Nayar, Baldev Raj. *American Geopolitics and India.* Columbia, MO: South Asia Books, 1976.

Nayar, Baldev Raj. *Globalization and Politics in India.* 2nd ed. New Delhi: Oxford University Press 2008.

Nayar, Baldev Raj. *The Modernization Imperative and Indian Planning.* Delhi: Vikas, 1972.

Nayar, Baldev Raj, and T. V. Paul. *India in the World Order: Searching for Major-Power Status.* Cambridge: Cambridge University Press, 2003.

Nayar, Kuldip. *The Judgement: Inside Story of the Emergency in India.* New Delhi: Vikas, 1977.

Nayar, Kuldip, and Kushwant Singh. *Tragedy of Punjab: Operation Bluestar and After.* New Delhi: Vision Books, 1984.

Nayyar, Deepak. *Liberalizaion and Development.* New Delhi and Oxford: Oxford University Press, 2008.

Nayyar, Deepak. *Trade and Globalization.* New Delhi and Oxford: Oxford University Press, 2008.

Needham, Anuradha Dingwaney, et al. *The Crisis of Secularism in India.* Durham, NC: Duke University Press, 2007.

Nehru, Jawaharlal. *The Discovery of India.* New Delhi: Penguin, 2004.

Nehru, Jawaharlal. *Jawaharlal Nehru's Speeches, 1946–64.* 5 vols. Delhi: Publications Division, Ministry of Information and Broadcasting, Government of India, 1949–1968.

Nehru, Jawaharlal. *Nehru, the First Sixty Years: Presenting in His Own Words the Development of the Political Thought of Jawaharlal Nehru and the Background against Which It Evolved.* Edited by Dorothy Norman. New York: John Day, 1965.

Nehru, Jawaharlal. *The Oxford India Nehru.* Oxford: Oxford University Press, 2007.

Nehru, Jawaharlal. *Toward Freedom.* New York: Day, 1942.

Nilekani, Nandan. *Imagining India: The Idea of a Renewed Nation.* New York: Penguin, 2010.

Ninan, Sevanti. *Through the Magic Window: Television and Change in India.* New Delhi: Penguin, 1995.

Niranjana, Tejaswini. "Nationalism Reconfigured: Contemporary South Indian Cinema and the Subject of Feminism." *Subaltern Studies* 11 (2001): 138–166.

Nirmal, C. J. *Human Rights in India*. New Delhi: Oxford University Press, 2002.

Nissam, Urlah B. *India: Economic, Political and Social Issues*. Hauppauge: Nova Science Publishers, 2008.

Nizamani, Haider. *The Roots of Rhetoric: Politics of Nuclear Weapons in India and Pakistan*. Westport, CT: Praeger, 2000.

Noorani, A. G. *Constitutional Questions and Citizens' Rights*. New Delhi: Oxford University Press, 2006.

Noorani, A. G. *Constitutional Questions in India: The President, Parliament, and the States*. New Delhi: Oxford University Press, 2000.

Nossitar, Tom. *Communism in Kerala*. London: Hurst, 1982.

Nossitar, Tom. *Marxist State Governments in India*. London: Pinter, 1988.

Nugent, N. *Rajiv Gandhi: Son of a Dynasty*. London: BBC Books, 1990.

Nussbaum, Martha. *The Clash Within: Democracy, Religious Violence, and India's Future*. New Delhi: Permanent Black, 2007.

Oldenburg, Veena Talwar. *Dowry Murden: The Imperial Origins of a Cultural Crime*. Oxford: Oxford University Press, 2002.

Ollapally, Deepa M. *The Politics of Extremism in South Asia*. Cambridge: Cambridge University Press, 2008.

Omvedt, G. "The Anti-Caste Movement and the Discourse of Power." *Race and Class* 33 (1991): 15–27.

Omvedt, G. *Dalits and the Democratic Revolution: Dr. Ambedkar and the Dalit Movement in Colonial India*. New Delhi: Sage, 1994.

Omvedt, G. *Dalit Visions*. New Delhi: Orient Longman, 1995.

Omvedt, Gail, J. O'Neil, T. Orchard, R. C. Swarankar, J. F. Blanchard, K. Gurav, and F. Moses. "Dhanda, Dharma, and Disease: Traditional Sex Work and HIV/AIDS in Rural India." *Social Science and Medicine* 59 (1999): 851–860.

Oommen, T. K. "Rural-Urban Continuum Reexamined in Indian Context." *Sociologia Ruralis* 7 (1967): 30–48.

Oza, B. M. *Bofors, the Ambassador's Evidence*. New Delhi: Konark, 1997.

Oza, Rupal. *The Making of Neoliberal India: Nationalism, Gender, and the Paradoxes of Globalization*. New York: Routledge, 2006.

Padhy, K. S., and P. K. Panigrahy. *Socialist Movement in India*. Columbia, MO: South Asia Books, 1992.

Page, David, and William Crawley. *Satellites over South Asia: Broadcasting, Culture and the Public Interest*. New Delhi: Sage, 2001.

Pai, Sudha. *Dalit Assertion and the Unfinished Democratic Revolution.* New Delhi: Sage, 2002.

Panagariya, Arvind. *India: The Emerging Giant.* Oxford: Oxford University Press, 2008.

Pandey, Gyanandra. *Remembering Partition: Violence, Nationalism and History in India.* Cambridge: Cambridge University Press, 2001.

Pandey, Gyanandra. *Routine Violence: Nations, Fragments Histories.* Stanford, CA: Stanford University Press, 2006.

Pandey, Gyanandra, ed. *Hindus and Others: The Question of Identity in India Today.* New Delhi: Viking, 1993.

Pandey, Nishchal N. *India's North-Eastern Region: Insurgency, Economic Development, and Linkages with South-East Asia.* New Delhi: Manohar, 2008.

Pandey, Ram Darshan. *Fundamental Rights and Constitutional Amendments.* Delhi: Capital Publishing House, 1985.

Pandit, Vijaya Lakshmi. *The Scope of Happiness.* New York: Crown, 1979.

Panikkar, P. N., ed. *The Concerned Indian's Guide to Communalism.* New Delhi: Penguin, 1999.

Pankaj, Ashok. "Review Article: India's Political Economy, 1947–2004: The Gradual Revolution." *South Asia Research* 26 (2006): 201–206.

Pant, Harsh V. *Contemporary Debates in Indian Foreign and Security Policy: India Negotiates Its Rise in the International System.* New York: Palgrave Macmillan, 2008.

Parikh, Kirit S., and R. Radhakrishna. *India Development Report, 2004–2005.* New Delhi: Oxford University Press, 2004.

Parikh, Narahari. *Sardar Vallabhbhai Patel.* Ahmedahad: Navajian, 1971.

Parikh, Sunita. *The Politics of Preference: Democratic Institutions and Affirmative Action in the US and India.* Ann Arbor: University of Michigan Press, 1997.

Parish, Steven M. *Hierarchy and Its Discontents: Culture and the Politics of Consciousness in Caste Society.* Philadelphia: University of Pennyvania Press, 1996.

Patel, I. G. *Glimpses of Indian Economic Policy.* Delhi: Oxford University Press, 2004.

Patel, Sujata, and Kushal Deb, eds. *Urban Studies.* New Delhi: Oxford University Press, 2006.

Patel, Sujata, and Jim Masselos. *Bombay and Mumbai: The City in Transition.* Oxford: Oxford University Press, 2005.

Patel, Tulsi. *Fertility Behaviour.* 2nd ed. New Delhi: Oxford University Press, 2006.

Pathak, Zoya, and R. S. Raja. "Shahbano." *Signs* 14 (1989): 558–582.

Patibandla, M., and B. Petersen. "The Role of Transnational Corporations in the Evolution of a High-Tech Industry: The Case of India's Software Industry." *World Development* 30 (2002): 1561–1577.

Pattanaik, Prasanta K. *Essays on Individual Decision-making and Social Welfare.* New Delhi and New York: Oxford University Press, 2009.

Patwari, A. B. M. *Mafizul Islam: Fundamental Rights and Personal Liberty in India, Pakistan, and Bangladesh.* New Delhi: Deep and Deep, 1988.

Paul, T. V., ed. *The India-Pakistan Conflict: An Enduring Rivalry.* Cambridge: Cambridge University Press, 2005.

Pavarala, Vinod, and Kanchan K. Malik. *Other Voices: The Struggle for Community Radio in India.* New Delhi: Sage, 2007.

Perkovich, George. *India's Nuclear Bomb: The Impact on Global Proliferation.* Berkeley: University of California Press, 2001.

Pettigrew, Joyce. *The Sikhs of the Punjab: Unheard Voices of State and Guerilla Violence.* London: Zed Books, 1995.

Pinney, Christopher. *The Coming of Photography in India.* New Delhi: Oxford University Press, 2008.

Pinney, Christopher. "Introduction: Public, Popular, and Other Cultures." In *Pleasure and the Nation: The History, Politics and Consumption of Public Culture in India,* edited by Rachel Dwyer and Christopher Pinney, 1–34. Oxford: Oxford University Press, 2001.

Pinney, Christopher. *Photos of the Gods: The Printed Image and Political Struggle in India.* London: Reaktion Books, 2004.

Post, J. "Professional Women in Indian Music: The Death of the Courtesan Tradition." In *Women and Music in Cross-Cultural Perspective,* edited by Ellen Koskoff, 97–109. New York: Greenwood, 1987.

Pothen, S. *Divorce: Its Causes and Consequences in Hindu Society.* Columbia, MO: South Asia Books, 1996.

Potter, David. *India's Political Administrators: From ICS to IAS.* New Delhi: Oxford University Press, 1996.

Powers, Janet M. *Kites over the Mango Tree: Restoring Harmony between Hindus and Muslims in Gujarat.* Westport, CT: Praeger, 2008.

Prakash, Ved. *New Towns in India.* Durham, NC: Duke University, Program in Comparative Studies on Southern Asia, 1969.

Pranab, Bardham. *The Political Economy of Development in India.* New Delhi: Oxford University Press, 1998.

Prasad, A. *Reservation Policy and Practice in India: A Means to an End.* New Delhi: Deep and Deep, 1991.

Prasad, Madhava. "Cinema and the Desire for Modernity." *Journal of Arts and Ideas* 25 (1993): 71–76.

Prasad, Madhava. *Ideology of the Hindi Film: A Historical Construction.* Delhi: Oxford University Press, 1990.

Prasad, Rajendra. *Autobiography.* Bombay: Asia Publishing House, 1957.

Presler, Franklin A. *Religion under Bureaucracy: Policy and Administration for Hindu Temple in South Asia.* Cambridge: Cambridge University Press, 2008.

Price, Monroe E., and Verhulst, Stefan G., eds. *Broadcasting Reform in India: Media Law from a Global Perspective.* New Delhi: Oxford University Press, 1998.

PricewaterhouseCoopers and FICCI. *The Indian Entertainment Industry: An Unfolding Opportunity.* New Delhi: FICCI, March 2005.

Pritchett, Frances W. "The World of Amar Chitra Katha." In *Media and the Transformation of Religion in South Asia,* edited by Lawrence Babb and Susan Wadley, 76–106. Philadelphia: University of Pennsylvania Press, 1995.

Projected and Actual Population of India, States and Union Territories, 1991. New Delhi: Office of the Registrar General, April 4, 2001.

Puniyani, R. *Contemporary India: Overcoming Sectarianism and Terrorism.* Gurganon: Hope India, 2008.

Puniyani, R. *Fundamentalism: Threat to Democracy.* Maithri: Tiruananthurana, 2007.

Purandare, Vaibhav. *The Sena Story.* Mumbai: Business Publications, 1999.

Puri, Balraj. *Kashmir towards Insurgency.* Bombay: Orient Longman, 1993.

Puri, G. *Hindutva Politics in India.* Delhi: UBSP, 2005.

Puri, Jyoti. *Woman, Body, Desire in Post-Colonial India: Narratives of Gender and Sexuality.* New York: Routledge, 1999.

Purushothaman, Sangeetha. *The Empowerment of Women in India: Grassroots Women's Networks and the State.* New Delhi: Sage, 1998.

Quanyu, Shang. "Sino-Indian Friendship in the Nehru Era: A Chinese Perspective." *China Report* 41 (2005): 237–252.

Quigley, D. *The Interpretation of Caste.* Oxford: Oxford University Press, 1993.

Racine, Josianne, and Jean-Luc Racine, eds. *Viramma: Life of an Untouchable.* London: Verso, 1999.

Radhakrishna, R., and Indira Ghandi Institute of Development Research (Bombay, India). *India Development Report, 2008.* New Delhi: Oxford University Press, 2008.

Radhakrishna, Rokkam. *Handbook of Poverty in India*. 3rd ed. New Delhi: Oxford University Press, 2006.

Rahman, Anika. "Religious Rights Versus Women's Rights in India: A Test Case for International Human Rights Law." *Columbia Journal of Transnational Law* 28 (1990): 473–498.

Rai, Ajai K. *The Kargil Conflict and the Role of the Indian Media*. New Delhi: Centre for Defence Studies and Analyses, 2001.

Raj, Christopher Sam, and Abdul Nafey, eds. *Canada's Global Engagements and Relations with India*. Delhi: Manak Publications, 2007.

Raj, K. N., ed. *Essays on the Commercialization of Indian Agriculture*. Ithaca, NY: Cornell University Press, 1985.

Raja, Saraswati, M. *Satish Kumar, and Stuart Corbridge: Colonial and Post-Colonial Geographies of India*. New Delhi: Sage, 2006.

Rajadhyaksha, Ashish. "The Epic Melodrama: Themes of Nationality in Indian Cinema." *Journal of Arts and Ideas* 25 (1993): 55–70.

Rajadhyaksha, Ashish. "Neo-Traditionalism: Film as Popular Art in India." *Framework* 32 (1986): 20–67.

Rajadhyaksha, Ashish, and Paul Willemen. *Encyclopedia of Indian Cinema*. New Delhi: Oxford University Press, 2002.

Rajagopal, Arvind. *The Indian Public Sphere: Readings in Media History*. New Delhi: Oxford University Press, 2009.

Rajagopal, Arvind. *Politics after Television: Hindu Nationalism and the Reshaping of the Public in India*. Cambridge: Cambridge University Press, 2001.

Rajan, Sunder Rajeswari. "Rethinking Law and Violence: The Domestic Violence (Prevention) Bill in India, 2002." *Gender and History* 16(3) (2004): 769–793.

Rajimwale, Anil, Krishna Jha, and Bobby Poulose. "Oral History Documentation of Indian Labour Movement." http://www.indialabourarchives.org/publications/anilrajimwale.htm.

Rajshekar, V. T., and Y. N. Kly. *Dalit: The Black Untouchables of India*. Atlanta: Clarity, 2009.

Raju, A. Subramanyam. *Democracies at Loggerheads: Security Aspects of U.S.-India Relations*. New Delhi: South Asian Publishers, 2001.

Raka, Ray, and Mary Fainsod Katzenstein. *Social Movements in India*. New Delhi: Oxford University Press, 2005.

Rakshit, Mihir. *Macroeconomics of Post-reform India*. Delhi and Oxford: Oxford University Press, 2009.

Rakshit, Mihir. *Money and Finance in the Indian Economy*. New Delhi: Oxford University Press, 2009.

Ram, Nandu. *Beyond Ambedkar: Essays on Dalits in India*. New Delhi: Har-Anand, 1995.

Ram, Ronki. "Ravidass Deras and Social Protest: Making Sense of Dalit Consciousness in Punjab (India)." *Journal of Asian Studies* 67(4) (2008): 1341–1364.

Ramaiah, A. "Identifying Other Backward Classes." *Economic and Political Weekly* 27 (1992): 1203–1207.

Raman, Sita. *Women in India: A Social and Cultural History*. New York: Praeger, 2009.

Ramanujam, G. *Indian Labour Movement*. New Delhi: Sterling Publishers, 1990.

Ramappa, T. *Competition Law in India*. New Delhi: Oxford University Press, 2006.

Ramaswamy, Sumathi. "Body Language: The Somatics of Nationalism in Tamil India." *Gender and History* 10(1) (1998): 78–109.

Ramaswamy, Sumathi. *Passions for the Tongue: Language Devotion in Tamil India*. Berkeley: University of California Press, 1997.

Ramaswamy, Vijaya, ed. *Re-Searching Indian Women*. New Delhi: Manohar, 2003.

Ranganathan, Maya. "Television in Tamil Nadu Politics." *Economic and Political Weekly* 41(48) (2006): 4947–4951.

Rani, N. Indra. "Child Care by Poor Single Mothers: Study of Mother-Headed Families in India." *Journal of Comparative Family Studies* 37(1) (2006): 75–95.

Rao, Badrinath Krishna. "Religious Minorities under Hindu Hegemony: The Political Economy of Secularism in India." PhD dissertation, University of Alberta, 1999.

Rao, C. H. Hanumantha. *Agriculture, Food Security, Poverty, and Environment: Essays on Post-reform India*. New Delhi: Oxford University Press, 2005.

Rao, M. Govinda. *Development, Poverty, and Fiscal Policy*. Delhi: Oxford University Press, 2004.

Rao, S. L. *The Partial Memoirs of V. K. R. V. Rao*. New Delhi: Oxford University Press, 2002.

Rao, V. K. R. V. *India's National Economy, 1950–1980: An Analysis of Economic Growth and Change*. New Delhi: Sage, 1983.

Rawat, Ramnarayan S. "Making Claims for Power: A New Agenda in Dalit Politics for Uttar Pradesh, 1946–48." *Modern Asian Studies* 37(3) (2003): 585–612.

Ray, Nisith Ranjan. *Dimensions of National Integration: The Experiences and Lessons of Indian History*. Calcutta: Punthi-Pustak, 1993.

Ray, R. *The Naxalites and Their Ideology*. New Delhi: Oxford University Press, 1988.

Ray, Raka, and Seemin Qayum. *Cultures of Servitude: Modernity, Domesticity, and Class in India*. Stanford, CA: Stanford University Press, 2009.

Ray, Shovan. *Handbook of Agriculture in India*. New Delhi: Oxford University Press, 2007.

Raychaudhuri, Tapan. *Perceptions, Emotions, and Sensibilities: Essays on India's Colonial and Post-colonial Experiences.* New Delhi: Oxford University Press, 2005.

Reddy, D. Narasimha, and Srijit Mishra. *Agrarian Crisis in India.* Oxford: Oxford University Press, 2009.

Reddy, O. Chinnappa. *The Court and the Constitution of India.* New Delhi: Oxford University Press, 2008.

Reddy, Y. V. *Lectures on Economic and Financial Sector Reforms in India.* Delhi: Oxford University Press, 2005.

Reed, Thomas C., and Danny B. Stillman. *The Nuclear Express: A Political History of the Bomb and Its Proliferation.* Osceola: Zenith, 2009.

Richardson, John M., Jr., and S. W. R. de. A. Samarasinghe. *Democratisation in South Asia: The First Fifty Years.* Kandy: International Centre for Ethnic Studies, 1998.

Riemenschneider, Dieter. *The Indian Novel in English: Its Critical Discourse, 1934–2004.* Jaipur: Rawat, 2005.

Robb, Peter. *A History of India.* New York: Palgrave Macmillan, 2004.

Robinson, Andrew. *Satyajit Ray, the Inner Eye: The Biography of a Master Film-Maker.* New York: I. B. Tauris, 2004.

Robinson, E. A. G., and Micheal Kidron, eds. *Economic Development in South Asia: Conference: Papers and Discussions.* London: Macmillan, 1970.

Robinson, Francis. "The Congress and the Muslims." In *Indian National Congress and Indian Society, 1885–1985,* edited by Paul R. Brass and Francis Robinson, 162–183. New Delhi: Chanakya, 1987.

Robinson, Francis, ed. *The Cambridge Encyclopedia of India, Pakistan, Bangladesh, Sri Lanka, Nepal, Bhutan, and the Maldives.* Cambridge: Cambridge University Press, 1989.

Rodrigues, Valerian. *The Essential Writings of B. R. Ambedkar.* Delhi: Oxford University Press, 2005.

Role of Chitra Katha in School Education. Bombay: India Book House Educational Trust, 1987.

Rose, Kalima. *Where Women Are Leaders: The SEWA Movement in India.* London: Zed Books, 1992.

Rose, Leo O., and Richard Sisson. *War and Secession: Pakistan, India and the Creation of Bangladesh.* Berkeley: University of California Press, 1990.

Rothermund, Dietmar. *An Economic History of India: From Pre-Colonial Times to 1991.* New York: Routledge, 1993.

Rothermund, Dietmar, ed. *Liberalising India: Progress and Problems.* New Delhi: Manohar, 1996.

Rotter, Andrew Jon. *Comrades at Odds: The United States and India, 1947–1964*. Ithaca, NY: Cornell University Press, 2000.

Roy, Arundhati. *The Algebra of Infinite Justice*. New Delhi: Penguin, 2002.

Roy, Arundhati. *The Cost of Living*. New York: Modern Library, 1999.

Roy, Beth. *Some Trouble with Cows: Making Sense of Social Conflict*. Berkeley: University of California Press, 1994.

Roy, Srirupa, and Julia Adams. *Beyond Belief: India and the Politics of Postcolonial Nationalism*. Durham, NC: Duke University Press, 2007.

Roy, Tirthankar. *Outline of a History of Labour in Traditional Industry in India*. Noida: V. V. Giri National Labour Institute, 2001.

Roy, Tirthankar. *Rethinking Economic Change in India: Labour and Livelihood*. New York: Routledge, 2007.

Rubin, R. Barnett. "Economic Liberalization and the Indian State." *Third World Quarterly* 7 (1985): 942–957.

Rudolph, Lloyd I., and Susanne Hoeber Rudolph. *In Pursuit of Lakshmi: The Political Economy of the Indian State*. Chicago: University of Chicago Press, 1987.

Runckle, Susan. "Bollywood Beauty and the Construction of 'International Standards' in Post-Liberalisation Bombay." *SAGAR: A South Asia Graduate Research Journal* 11 (2004): 37–57.

Russell, Ralph. "Indian Nationalism—Before and after Independence." *Socialist History* 13 (1998): 23–36.

Rutten, M. "A Historical and Comparative View on the Study of Indian Entrepreneurship." *Economic Sociology: European Economic Newsletter* 3(2) (2000): 3–16.

Saberwal, S. *India: The Roots of Crisis*. New Delhi: Oxford University Press, 1986.

Sachdeva, Pardeep. *Dynamics of Municipal Government and Politics in India*. Allahabad: Kitab Mahal, 1991.

Saez, Lawrence. *Federalism without a Centre: The Impact of Political and Economic Reform on India's Federal System*. New Delhi and London: Sage, 2002.

Sagade, Jaya. *Child Marriage in India*. New Delhi: Oxford University Press, 2005.

Sahasranaman, P. B. *Handbook of Environmental Law*. New Delhi: Oxford University Press, 2009.

Sahay, Uday. *Making News: Handbook of Media in Contemporary India*. New Delhi: Oxford University Press, 2006.

Sahgal, Nayantara. *Indira Gandhi: Her Road to Power*. New York: F. Unger, 1982.

Sahgal, Nayantara. *Indira Gandhi's Emergence and Style*. Durham, NC: Carolina Academic Press, 1979.

Sahu, Naba Krishna. *Electoral Politics in Federal India*. New Delhi: Gyan, 2006.

Saladin, Matthias. "Applications of Geographic Information Systems for Municipal Planning and Management in India." *Journal of Environment Development* 11 (2002): 430–440.

Salwi, Dilip. *Homi J. Bhabha: Architect of Nuclear India*. New Delhi: Rupa, 2004.

Samanta, Amiya K. *Gorkhaland: A Study in Ethnic Separatism*. New Delhi: Khama, 1996.

Sandhu, Ranvinder, ed. *Urbanization in India*. New Delhi: Sage, 2003.

Sangwan, O. P., ed. *Social System and the Dalit Identity*. New Delhi: Commonwealth, 1995.

Sanjay, Srivastava. *Constructing Post-colonial India: National Character and the Doon School*. New York: Routledge, 1998.

Sarangi, Asha. *Language and Politics in India*. New Delhi: Oxford University Press, 2009.

SarDesai, D. R. *India: The Definitive History*. Boulder, CO: Westview, 2008.

SarDesai, D. R. *Indian Foreign Policy in Cambodia, Laos, and Vietnam, 1947–1964*. Berkeley: University of California Press, 1968.

SarDesai, D. R., and Anand Mohan, eds. *The Legacy of Nehru: A Centennial Assessment*. New Delhi: Promilla, 1992.

SarDesai, D. R., and Raju C. G. Thomas, eds. *Nuclear India in the Twenty-first Century*. New York: Palgrave, 2002.

Sarhadi, Ajit Singh. *Punjabi Suba: The Story of the Struggle*. Delhi: U. C. Kapur, 1970.

Sarila, Narendra Singh. *The Shadow of the Great Game: The Untold Story of India's Partition*. New York: Carroll and Graf, 2006.

Sarkar, Sumit. *Beyond Nationalist Frames: Postmodernism, Hindu Fundamentalism, History*. Ranikhet: Permanent Black, 2002.

Sarkar, Sumit, and Tanika Sarkar. *Women and Social Reform in Modern India: A Reader*. Bloomington: Indiana University Press, 2008.

Sarkar, Tanika. *Hindu Wife, Hindu Nation: Community, Religion and Cultural Nationalism*. Bloomington: Indiana University Press, 2010.

Sarma, N., and B. Banerjee. *Nuclear Power in India: A Critical History*. New Delhi: Rupa, 2008.

Sasikumar, S. K. "International Labour Migration from Independent India." http://www.indialabourarchives.org/publications/sksasikumar.htm.

Sathe, S. P. *Judicial Activism in India*. 2nd ed. Delhi: Oxford University Press, 2003.

Sathyamurthy, T. V. *India since Independence: Studies in the Development of the Power of the State; Centre-State Relations: The Case of Kerala.* Columbia, MO: South Asia Books, 1985.

Sathyamurthy, T. V. *Social Change and Political Discourse in India: Structures of Power, Movements of Resistance,* vol. 3, *Region, Religion, Caste and Gender in Contemporary India.* New Delhi: Oxford University Press, 1996.

Scaria, Arul George. *Ambush Marketing.* New Delhi: Oxford University Press, 2008.

Schenk, Hans, ed. *Living in India's Slums: A Case Study of Bangalore.* New Delhi: Manohar, 2001.

Schofield, Victoria. *Kashmir in Conflict: India, Pakistan and the Unending War.* 2nd rev. ed. London: I. B. Tauris, 2002.

Schwartzberg, Joseph E., ed. *A Historical Atlas of South Asia.* 2nd ed. New York: Oxford University Press, 1992.

Seabrook, J. *Love in a Different Climate: Men Who Have Sex with Men in India.* London: Verso, 1999.

Seghal, R. "Kiss and Sell? Don't Try It in India." *Multinational News International* 7(3) (May 2001): 8–9.

Selbourne, D. *An Eye to India: The Unmasking of a Tyranny.* Harmondsworth, UK: Penguin, 1977.

Selliah, S. *The Self-Employed Women's Association, Ahmedabad.* Geneva: International Labor Office, 1989.

Sen, Amartya. *The Argumentative Indian: Writings on Indian History, Culture and Identity.* New York: Picador, 2006.

Sen, Amartya. *Development as Freedom.* Oxford: Oxford University Press, 2001.

Sen, Amartya. "Indian Development: Lessons and Non-Lessons." *Daedalus* 118 (1989): 369–382.

Sen, Amartya, and Jean Drèze. *India.* New Delhi: Oxford University Press, 2005.

Sen, Amartya, and Jean Drèze, eds. *Indian Development: Selected Regional Perspectives.* New Delhi: Oxford University Press, 1997.

Sen, Amartya, and Pranab Bardhan. *The Political Economy of Development in India.* New Delhi: Oxford University Press, 1985.

Sen, E. *Indira Gandhi: A Biography.* London: Owen, 1973.

Sen, Mala. *Death by Fire: Sati, Dowry Death and Female Infanticide in Modern India.* London: Weidenfeld and Nicholson, 2001.

Sen, Mala. *India's Bandit Queen: The True Story of Phoolan Devi.* London and San Francisco: Pandora, 1991.

Sen, Ronojoy. *Articles of Faith: Religion, Secularism, and the Indian Supreme Court.* New Delhi: Oxford University Press, 2010.

Sen, Samita. "Gender and Class: Women in Indian Industry, 1890–1990." *Modern Asian Studies* 42(1) (2008): 75–116.

Sen, Sarbani. *The Constitution of India: Popular Sovereignty and Democratic Transformations.* New Delhi: Oxford University Press, 2007.

Sen, Sukomal. *Working Class of India: History of Emergence and Movement, 1830–1990.* Calcutta: K. P. Bagchi, 1997.

Sengupta, Ramprasad. *Ecology and Economics: An Approach to Sustainable Development.* Oxford: Oxford University Press, 2004.

Seshan, N. K. *With Three Prime Ministers: Nehru, Indira, and Rajiv.* New Delhi: Wiley-Eastern, 1993.

Sethi, Geeta, and the World Bank. *Fiscal Decentralization to Rural Governments.* New Delhi: Oxford University Press, 2004.

Shah, A. M. "Rural-Urban Networks in India." In *Country Town Nexus,* edited by K. L. Sharma and Dipankar Gupta, 11–42. Jaipur: Rawat, 1991.

Shah, Amrita. *Hype, Hypocrisy, and Television in Urban India.* New Delhi: Vikas, 1997.

Shah, Ghanshyam. *Caste and Democratic Politics in India.* London: Anthem, 2004.

Shah, Ghanshyam. *Social Movements in India: A Review of Literature.* New Delhi: Sage, 1990.

Shah, Kirit K. *History and Gender Some Explorations, India.* New Delhi: Rawat, 2005.

Shani, Giorgio. *Sikh Nationalism and Identity in a Global Age.* New York: Taylor and Francis, 2007.

Shani, Ornit. *Communalism, Caste and Hindu Nationalism.* Cambridge: Cambridge University Press, 2007.

Shani, Ornit. "The Rise of Hindu Nationalism in India: The Case Study of Ahmedabad in the 1980s." *Modern Asian Studies* 39(4) (2005): 861–896.

Shankar, Shylashri. *Scaling Justice: India's Supreme Court, Anti-Terror Law, and Social Rights.* New Delhi: Oxford University Press, 2009.

Sharma, Archana. "Fusion over the Airwaves: South Asians and Radio Pedagogy." *SAGAR: A South Asia Graduate Research Journal* 10 (2003): 50–77.

Sharma, Arvind. *Hinduism and Human Rights: A Conceptual Approach.* 2nd ed. New Delhi: Oxford University Press, 2005.

Sharma, K. L. "Caste and Class in India: Some Conceptual Problems." *Sociological Bulletin* 33 (1981): 1–27.

Sharma, Kusum. *Ambedkar and the Indian Constituion.* New Delhi: Ashish, 1992.

Sharma, R. *Breaking Silence*. Delhi: Anhad, 2006.

Sharma, Satish. *Modernism and Planned Social Change: A Study of Two Villages in India*. Hong Kong: Asian Research Service, 1982.

Sharma, Shelendra D. *China and India in the Age of Globalization*. Cambridge: Cambridge University Press, 2009.

Sharma, Shyam Sunder. *Legal Aid to the Poor: The Law and Indian Legal System*. New Delhi: Deep and Deep, 1993.

Sharman, Rita, and Thomas Polemon. *The New Economics of India's Green Revolution*. Ithaca, NY: Cornell University Press, 1993.

Shastri, Vanita. "The Politics of Economic Liberalization in India." *Contemporary South Asia* 6 (1997): 27–56.

Sheel, Ranjana. *The Political Economy of Dowry: Institutionalization and Expansion in North India*. New Delhi: Manohar, 1999.

Shenoy, Sudha R. *India: Progress or Poverty? A Review of the Outcome of Central Planning in India, 1951–1969*. London: Institute of Economic Affairs, 1971.

Shiva, Vandana. *The Violence of the Green Revolution: Ecological Degradation and Political Conflict in Punjab*. Dehra Dun: Research Institute for Science and Ecology, 1989.

Shrestha, Ava, et al. *The Impact of Armed Conflicts on Women in South Asia*. New Delhi: Manohar, 2007.

Shukul, H. C. *India's Foreign Policy: The Stategy of Nonalignment*. New Delhi: Chanakya, 1994.

Silva, Mangalika de. "Nationalism and Sexuality: The Intersection of Gender and Power in South Asia." *Nivedini-A Sri Lankan Feminist Journal* 8 (2000): 61–89.

Simeon, Dilip. "The Politics of the Labour Movement: An Essay on Differential Aspirations." http://www.indialabourarchives.org/publications/dilip_simeon.htm.

Sims, Holly. *Political Regimes, Public Policy, and Economic Development: Agricultural Performance and Rural Change in the Two Punjabs*. New Delhi: Sage, 1988.

Singer, Wendy. *'A Constituency Suitable for Ladies': And Other Social Histories of Indian Elections*. New Delhi: Oxford University Press, 2007.

Singh, Anita Inder. "Keeping India in the Commonwealth: British Political and Military Aims, 1947–49." *Journal of Contemporary History* 20(3) (1985): 469–481.

Singh, Anita Inder. "Imperial Defence and the Transfer of Power in India, 1946–1947." *International History Review* 4(4) (1982): 191–209.

Singh, Bhupinder. *Autonomy Movements and Federal India*. Jaipur: Rawat, 2002.

Singh, Har Mohinder. *History and Development of Dalit Leadership in India*. Raleigh, NC: Ivy Publishing House, 2009.

Singh, K. S., ed. *Tribal Movements in India*. 2 vols. New Delhi: Manohar, 1982.

Singh, Patwant, and Harji Malik. *Punjab: The Fatal Miscalculation*. New Delhi: Patwant Singh, 1985.

Singh, R. G. *The Depressed Classes of India: Problems and Prospects*. New Delhi: Stosius/ Advent Books Division, 1986.

Singh, Raja. "Purity and Pollution: The Dalit Women within India's Religious Colonialism." *SAGAR: A South Asia Graduate Research Journal* 12 (2004): 79–103.

Singh, Ujjwal. "Political Prisoners in India Pre- and Post-Independence." PhD dissertation, University of London, 1996.

Singh, Yogendra. *Social Stratification and Change in India*. New Delhi: Manohar, 1977.

Singha Roy, Debal K. *Women, New Technology and Development: Changing Nature of Gender Relations in Rural India*. New Delhi: Manohar, 1995.

Sinha, S. P. *Lost Opportunities: 50 Years of Insurgency in the North-East and India's Response*. New Delhi: Lancer Publishers, 2008.

Sisson, Richard, and Leo E. Rose. *War and Secession: Pakistan, India, and the Creation of Bangladesh*. Berkeley: University of California Press, 1991.

Sivaramakrishnan, K., and Arun Agrawal. *Regional Modernities: The Cultural Politics of Development in India*. Stanford, CA: Stanford University Press, 2003.

Sivaramakrishnan, K. C., Amitabh Kundu, and B. N. Singh. *Handbook of Urbanization in India: An Analysis of Trends and Processes*. New Delhi: Oxford University Press, 2005.

Sivaramayya, B. *Matrimonial Property Law in India*. New Delhi: Oxford University Press, 2002.

Smita, G. "Modern Messages Told the Traditional Indian Way." *Media Asia*, (December 12, 2002): 2.

Smith, Donald E. *India as a Secular State*. Princeton, NJ: Princeton University Press, 1963.

Sobhan, Rehman, ed. *Bangladesh-India Relations: Perspectives from Civil Society Dialogues*. Dhaka: University Press, 2002.

Solomon, Rakesh H. *Globalization, History, Historiography: The Making of a Modern Indian Theatre*. London: Anthem, 2010.

Sonalkar, Wandana. "An Agenda for Gender Politics." *Economic and Political Weekly* 34 (1999): 24–29.

Sonwalker, Prasun. "India: Makings of Little Cultural/Media Imperialism?" *International Communication Gazette* 63 (2001): 505–519.

Sooryamoorthy, R., and K. D. Gangrade. *NGOs in India: A Cross-Sectional Study*. Westport: Greenwood, 2001.

South Asia Human Rights Documentation Centre. *Handbook of Human Rights and Criminal Justice in India.* 2nd ed. New Delhi: Oxford University Press, 2007.

South Asia Human Rights Documentation Centre. *Handbook of Human Rights and Humanitarian Law.* New Delhi: Oxford University Press, 2007.

Srampickal, J. *Voice to the Voiceless: The Power of People's Theatre in India.* London: Hurst, 1994.

Srikandath, Sivaram. "Cultural Values Depicted in Indian Television Advertising." *International Journal of Mass Communication Studies* 48 (1991): 165–176.

Srinivas, M. N. "The Caste System in India." In *Social Inequality,* edited by A. Beteille, 265–272. Harmondsworth, UK: Penguin, 1997.

Srinivas, M. N. *Collected Essays.* Oxford: Oxford University Press, 2004.

Srinivas, M. N. *Indian Society through Personal Writings.* Oxford: Oxford University Press, 1998.

Srinivasan, Shobha. "Breaking Rural Bonds through Migration: The Failure of Development for Women in India." *Journal of Comparative Family Studies* 28(1) (1997): 89–92.

Srinivasan, T. N., and Suresh D. Tendulkar. *Reintegrating India with the World Economy.* Washington, DC: Peterson Institute, 2003.

Srivastava, C. P. *Lal Bahadur Shastri, Prime Minister of India, 1964–1966: A Life of Truth in Politics.* Oxford: Oxford University Press, 2006.

Srivastava, Dayawanti. *Selected Speeches of Lal Bahadur Shastri, June 11, 1964 to January 10, 1996.* New Delhi: Publications Division, 2007.

Statesman, Calcutta. *Bofors: The Unfinished Story.* Calcutta: Statesman, 1989.

Stern, Robert W. *Changing India: Bourgeois Revolution on the Subcontinent.* 2nd ed. Cambridge: Cambridge University Press, 2003.

Streeten, Paul, and Michael Lipton, eds. *The Crisis of Indian Planning: Economic Policy in the 1960s.* Oxford: Oxford University Press, 1968.

Stone, Elaine Murray. *Mother Teresa.* Mahwah, NJ: Paulist Press, 1999.

Subedi, Surya P. *Dynamics of Foreign Policy and Law.* New Delhi: Oxford University Press, 2005.

Subramaniam, Chitra. *Bofors: The Story behind the News.* New Delhi: Viking, 1993.

Subramanian, K. S. *Political Violence and the Police in India.* New Delhi: Allied Publishers, 2002.

Subramanian, S. *Rights, Deprivation, and Disparity.* New Delhi: Oxford University Press, 2006.

Subramanyam Raju, A., et al. *Maritime Cooperation between India and Sri Lanka.* New Delhi: Manohar, 2006.

Sundar, Nandini, Roger Jeffery, and Neil Thin. *Branching Out: Joint Forest Management in India*. Oxford: Oxford University Press, 2002.

Sundar, Ram. *Rajiv Gandhi: Visionary of Modern India*. New Delhi: Kanishka Publishing House, 2008.

Sury, M. M. *Fiscal Policy Developments in India, 1947 to 2007*. New Delhi: New Century, 2007.

Swami, Praveen. *India, Pakistan and the Secret Jihad: The Covert War in Kashmir, 1947–2004*. New York: Routledge, 2007.

Taeube, F. "Culture, Innovation, and Economic Development: The Case of South Indian ICT Clusters." In *Innovation, Learning, and Technological Dynamism of Developing Countries*, edited by S. Mani and H. Romjin, 202–228. New York: United Nations Press, 2004.

Talbot, Ian. *Divided Cities: Partition and Its Aftermath in Lahore and Amritsar, 1947–1957*. Oxford: Oxford University Press, 2006.

Talbot, Ian. *The Partition of India*. Cambridge: Cambridge University Press, 2009.

Talbot, Ian, and Darshan Singh Tatla. *Amritsar: Voices from between India and Pakistan*. Basingstoke, UK: Palgrave Macmillan, 2007.

Talbot, Ian, and Darshan Singh Tatla. *The Partition of India*. New Approaches to Asian History Series. Cambridge: Cambridge University Press, 2009.

Talbot, Ian, and Shinder Thandi, eds. *People on the Move: Punjabi Colonial and Post-Colonial Migration*. Oxford: Oxford University Press, 2004.

Talbott, Strobe. *Engaging India: Diplomacy, Democracy, and the Bomb*. Washington, DC: Brookings Institution Press, 2006.

Tandon, B. B., V. K. Agnihotri, and H. Ramachandran. "Globalization and Decentralization: Emerging Issues from the Indian Experience." *International Review of Administrative Sciences* 67 (2001): 505–523.

Tarlo, Emma. *Clothing Matters: Dress and Identity in India*. Chicago: University of Chicago Press, 1996.

Tarlo, Emma. *Unsettling Memories: Narratives of the "Emergency" in Delhi*. Berkeley: University of California Press, 2001.

Taylor, Jay. *The Dragon and the Wild Goose: China and India, with New Epilogue*. New York: Praeger, 1991.

Tellis, Ashley J. *India's Emerging Nuclear Posture: Between Recessed Deterrent and Ready Arsenal*. Santa Monica, CA: RAND Corporation, 2001.

Thakur, Janardan. *Indira Gandhi and Her Power Game*. Delhi: Vikas, 1979.

Thakur, Sankarshan. *The Making of Laloo Yadav: The Unmaking of Bihar*. New Delhi: HarperCollins, 2000.

Thapan, Meenakshi. "Embodiment and Identity in Contemporary Society: Femina and the 'New' Indian Woman." *Contributions to Indian Sociology* 38 (2004): 411–444.

Tharoor, Shashi. *India: From Midnight to the Millennium and Beyond*. New York: Arcade Publishing, 2006.

Tharoor, Shashi. *Nehru: The Invention of India*. New York: Arcade Publishing, 2004.

Thieme, John, and Ira Raja. *The Table Is Laid: The Oxford Anthology of South Asian Food Writing*. Oxford: Oxford University Press, 2009.

Thomas, Raju G. C. *Democracy, Security, and Development in India*. New York: Palgrave Macmillan, 1996.

Thomas, Raju G. C. *Perspective on Kashmir: The Roots of Conflict in South Asia*. Boulder, CO: Westview, 1992.

Thompson, T. "Revealed: Bollywood Craze That Is Fuelling London's Vice Rackets." *Observer*, July 27, 2003. http://www.guardian.co.uk/crime/article/0,,1006717,00.html.

Thorat, Sukhadeo. *Dalits in India: Search for Common Identity*. New Delhi: Sage, 2008.

Thoraval, Y. *The Cinemas of India*. Chennai: Macmillan India, 2001.

3iNetwork. *India Infrastructure Report, 2006*. New Delhi: Oxford University Press, 2006.

3iNetwork. *India Infrastructure Report, 2007*. New Delhi: Oxford University Press, 2007.

3iNetwork. *India Infrastructure Report, 2008*. New Delhi: Oxford University Press, 2008.

3iNetwork. *India Infrastructure Report, 2009*. New Delhi: Oxford University Press, 2009.

Throgmorton, J. A. "The Rhetorics of Policy Analysis." *Policy Sciences* 24 (1991): 153–179.

Tilak, Shrinivas. *Religion and Aging in the Indian Tradition*. Albany, NY: SUNY Press, 1989.

Tinker, I., ed. *Persistent Inequalities: Women and World Development*. New York: Oxford University Press, 1990.

Tomlinson, B. R. *The Economy of Modern India, 1860–1970*. The New Cambridge History of India Series. Cambridge: Cambridge University Press, 2008.

Topalova, Petia. "Three Emperical Essays on Trade and Development in India." DPhil dissertation, Massachusetts Institute of Technology, 2005.

Toye, John. *Public Expenditure and Indian Development Policy, 1960–1970*. Cambridge: Cambridge University Press, 1981.

Trehan, Jyoti. *Crime and Money Laundering: The Indian Perspective*. New Delhi: Oxford University Press, 2004.

Tripathi, Dwijendra. *Alliance for Change: A Slum Upgrading Experiment in Ahmedabad*. New Delhi: TATA McGraw-Hill, 1998.

Tripathi, Dwijendra. *Business Communities of India.* New Delhi: Manohar, 1984.

Tripathi, Dwijendra. *Business Houses in Western India: A Study in Entreprenurial Response, 1850–1956.* New Delhi: Manohar, 1990.

Tripathi, Dwijendra. *Business and Politics in India: A Historical Perspective.* New Delhi: Manohar, 1991.

Tripathi, Dwijendra. *The Oxford History of Indian Business.* New Delhi: Oxford University Press, 2004.

Trivedi, H. R. *Scheduled Castes' Quest for Land and Social Equality.* New Delhi: Concept Publishing, 1995.

Tully, Mark. *India: Forty Years of Independence.* New York: Braziller, 1988.

Tully, Mark, and Z. Masani. *From Raj to Rajiv.* London: British Broadcasting Corporation, 1988.

Tully, Mark, and Jacob Satish. *Amritsar: Mrs. Gandhi's Last Battle.* Calcutta: Rupa, 1985.

Uberjoi, J. P. S. *Religion, Civil Society and the State: A Study of Sikhism.* Delhi: Oxford University Press, 1996.

United Nations Development Programme. *Human Development Report 2004.* New York: Oxford University Press, 2004.

United Nations Development Programme. *Human Development Report 2005.* New York: Oxford University Press, 2005.

Upadhyay, Archana. *India's Fragile Borderlands: The Dynamics of Terrorism in North East India.* New York: I. B. Tauris, 2009.

Upadhyaya, Prakesh Chandra. "The Politics of Indian Secularism." *Modern Asian Studies* 26(4) (1992): 81–53.

Vaidyanathan, A. *Agricultural Growth in India: Role of Technology, Incentives, and Institutions.* New Delhi: Oxford University Press, 2009.

Vaidyanathan, A. *Indian Economy: Crisis, Response and Prospects.* New Delhi: Orient Longman, 1995.

Vaidyanathan, A. *India's Water Resources: Contemporary Issues on Irrigation.* New Delhi and New York: Oxford University Press, 2008.

Vanaik, Achin. *The Furies of Indian Communalism: Religion, Modernity, and Secularization.* London: Verso, 1997.

Vanaik, Achin. *The Painful Transition: Bourgeois Democracy in India.* London: Zed Books, 1990.

Vanaik, Achin. "Rajiv's Congress in Search of Stability." *New Left Review* 154 (1985): 55–82.

Vanderbok, William G. "Critical Elections, Contained Volatility and the Indian Electorate." *Modern Asian Studies* 24(1) (1990): 173–190.

Van Der Veer, Peter. "'God Must Be Liberated!' A Hindu Liberation Movement in Ayodhya." *Modern Asian Studies* 21 (1987): 283–301.

Van Der Veer, Peter. *Religious Nationalism: Hindus and Muslims in India*. Berkeley: University of California Press, 1994.

Van Dyke, Virginia. "The Anti-Sikh Riots of 1984 in Delhi: Politicians, Criminals and the Discourse of Communalism." In *Riots and Pogroms*, edited by Paul Brass, 201–220. Basingstoke, UK: Macmillan, 1996.

Vanita, Ruth. *Love's Rite: Same-Sex Marriage in India and the West*. New York: Palgrave Macmillan, 2005.

Vanita, Ruth. *Queering India: Same-Sex Love and Eroticism in Indian Culture and Society*. New York: Routledge, 2002.

Van Schendel, Willem. *A History of Bangladesh*. Cambridge: Cambridge University Press, 2009.

Varadarajan, Siddharth. *Gujarat: The Making of a Tragedy*. New Delhi: Penguin, 2002.

Varma, Ajay Prakash, Poonam S. Shauhan, and M. M. Rehman, eds. *Indian Labour: A Select Statistical Profile*. New Delhi: Manak Publications, 1997.

Varma, Pavan. *The Great Indian Middle Class*. Delhi: Penguin, 1989.

Varshney, Ashutosh. *Ethnic Conflict and Civic Life: Hindus and Muslims in India*. New Haven, CT: Yale University Press, 2002.

Varshney, Ashutosh. *Democracy, Development, and the Countryside: Urban-Rural Struggles in India*. Cambridge: Cambridge University Press, 1995.

Vasudev, Uma. *Two Faces of Indira Gandhi*. Delhi: Vikas, 1977.

Vasudevan, Ravi. *Making Meaning in Indian Cinema*. New Delhi: Oxford University Press, 2002.

Vicziany, Marika, and Jayant Bapat. "Mumbadevi and Other Goddesses in Mumbai." *Modern Asian Studies* 43(2) (2009): 511–541.

Vindhya, U. "'Dowry Deaths' in Andhra Pradesh, India: Response of the Criminal Justice System." *Violence Against Women* 6 (2000): 1085–1108.

Virdi, Jyotika. *The Cinematic ImagiNation: Indian Popular Films as Social History*. New Brunswick, NJ: Rutgers University Press, 2003.

Vohra, N. N. *India and Australia: History, Culture and Society*. Delhi: Shipra, 2009.

Vora, Rajendra, et al. *Region, Culture, and Politics in India*. New Delhi: Manohar, 2006.

Vyas, A., and S. Singh. *Women's Studies in India: Information Sources, Services, and Programmes.* New Delhi: Sage, 1993.

Wade, Robert. *Village Republics: Economic Conditions for Collective Action in South Asia.* Cambridge: Cambridge University Press, 2007.

Walker, David. "General Cariappa Encounters 'White Australia': Australia, India and the Commonwealth in the 1950s." *Journal of Imperial and Commonwealth History* 34(3) (2006): 389–406.

Wallace, Paul. "Sikh Minority Attitudes in India's Federal System." In *Sikh History and Religion in the Twentieth Century,* edited by J. T. O'Connell, 256–273. Toronto: University of Toronto Center for South Asian Studies, 1988.

Wallace, Paul. "The Sikhs as a 'Minority' in a Sikh Majority State in India." *Asian Survey* 3 (1986): 363–377.

Wallace, Paul, and Surendra Chopra, eds. *Political Dynamics and Crisis in Punjab.* Amritsar: Guru Nanak Dev University, 1988.

Wallace, Paul, and Ramashray Roy. *India's 1999 Elections and 20th Century Politics.* New Delhi: Sage, 2003.

Watal, Jayashree. *Intellectual Property Rights in the WTO and Developing Countries.* New Delhi: Oxford University Press, 2003.

Wardhaugh, Julia. "The Jungle and the Village: Discourses on Crime and Deviance in Rural North India." *South Asia Research* 25 (2005): 129–140.

Webber, David J. "The Distribution and Use of Policy Knowledge in the Policy Process." *Knowledge and Policy* 4 (1991): 6–35.

Webster, John C. B. *A History of the Dalit Christians in India.* San Francisco: Mellen University Press, 1992.

Webster, John C. B. *Religion and Dalit Liberation: An Examination of Perspectives.* New Delhi: Manohar, 1999.

Webster, John C. B. "Who Is a Dalit?" In *Dalits in Modern India: Vision and Values,* edited by S. M. Michael, 68–79. New Delhi: Vistaar, 1999.

Weiner, Myron. *The Child and the State in India: Child Labor and Education Policy in Comparative Perspective.* Princeton, NJ: Princeton University Press, 1991.

Weiner, Myron. *The Indian Paradox: Essays in Indian Politics.* New Delhi: Sage, 1989.

Weiner, Myron. "The Regionalization of Indian Politics and Its Implications for Economic Reform." In *India in the Era of Economic Reforms,* edited by Jeffrey Sachs et al., 337–367. New Delhi: Oxford University Press, 1999.

Weiner, Myron, and M. F. Katzenstein. *India's Preferential Policies.* Chicago: University of Chicago Press, 1981.

Widmalm, Sten. *Kashmir in Comparative Perspective: Democracy and Violent Separatism in India.* Oxford: Oxford University Press, 2006.

Wijk-Sijbesma, Christine van, et al. *Water and Sanitation: Institutional Challenges in India.* New Delhi: Manohar, 2006.

Wilkinson, Steven I. *Religious Politics and Communal Violence.* New Delhi: Oxford University Press, 2007.

Wilkinson, Steven I. *Votes and Violence: Electoral Competition and Ethnic Riots in India.* Cambridge: Cambridge University Press, 2004.

Williams, Rina Verna. *Postcolonial Politics and Personal Laws.* New Delhi: Oxford University Press, 2006.

Wirsing, Robert G. *India, Pakistan and the Kashmir Dispute: On Regional Conflict and Its Resolution.* New York: St. Martin's, 1998.

Wolpert, Stanley. *India and Pakistan: Continued Conflict or Cooperation?* Berkeley: University of California Press, 2010.

Wolpert, Stanley. *Gandhi's Passion: The Life and Legacy of Mahatma Gandhi.* New York: Oxford University Press, 2001.

Wolpert, Stanley. *India.* 4th ed. Berkeley: University of California Press, 2009.

Wolpert, Stanley. *Jinnah of Pakistan.* New York: Oxford University Press, 1984.

Wolpert, Stanley. *Nehru: A Tryst with Destiny.* New York: Oxford University Press, 1996.

Wolpert, Stanley. *A New History of India.* 8th ed. Oxford: Oxford University Press, 2008.

Wolpert, Stanley, ed. *Encyclopaedia of India.* 4 vols. New York: Scribner, 2006.

Wood, John R. *The Politics of Water Resource Development in India: The Case of Narmada.* London: Sage, 2007.

Wood, Michael. *India.* New York: Basic Books, 2007.

World Bank. *Enhancing Women's Participation in Economic Development.* Washington, DC: World Bank, 1994.

World Bank. *From Competing at Home to Competing Abroad.* New Delhi: Oxford University Press, 2007.

World Bank. *India: Re-Energizing the Agricultural Sector to Sustain Growth and Reduce Poverty.* New Delhi: Oxford University Press, 2005.

World Bank. *India: Unlocking Opportunities for Forest-Dependent People.* New Delhi: Oxford University Press, 2006.

World Bank. *India Land Policies for Growth and Poverty Reduction.* New Delhi: Oxford University Press, 2007.

World Bank. *India Rural Governments and Service Delivery*. New Delhi: Oxford University Press, 2008.

World Bank. *Wasting Away: The Crisis of Malnutrition in India*. Washington, DC: World Bank, 1999.

Wyatt, Andrew. *Decentering the Indian Nation*. New York: Routledge, 2003.

Zachariah, Benjamin. *Developing India*. New Delhi: Oxford University Press, 2005.

Zachariah, K. C., et al. *Return Emigrants in Kerala: Welfare, Rehabilitation, and Development*. New Delhi: Manohar, 2006.

Zakaria, Rafiq. *The Widening Divide: An Insight into Hindu-Muslim Relations*. New Delhi: Viking, 1995.

Zavos, John. *The Emergence of Hindu Nationalism in India*. New Delhi: Oxford University Press, 2003.

Zavos, John, Andrew Wyatt, and Vernon Hewitt. *The Politics of Cultural Mobilization in India*. Oxford: Oxford University Press, 2004.

Zelliot, E. *From Untouchable to Dalit: Essays on Ambedkar Movement*. 3rd ed. Columbia, MO: South Asia Books, 2005.

Zutshi, Chitralekha. *Languages of Belonging: Islam, Regional Identity and the Making of Kashmir*. New Delhi: Permanent Black, 2003.

About the Editors and Contributors

✦

EDITORS

Arnold P. Kaminsky
Professor of History, California State University, Long Beach

Roger D. Long
Professor of History, Eastern Michigan University

EDITORIAL ADVISER

Damodar R. SarDesai
Navin and Pratima Doshi Chair in Indian History (Emeritus) and Professor Emeritus,
History, University of California, Los Angeles

CONTRIBUTORS

Zahid Shahab Ahmed
School of Humanities, University of New England (Australia)

Mohammed Badrul Alam
Professor of Political Science, Jamia Millia University (India)

Rashmi Umesh Arora
Postdoctoral Research Fellow, Department of Accounting, Finance and Economics, Griffith
University (Australia)

Vandana Asthana
Assistant Professor of Government, Eastern Washington University

Jesudas M. Athyal

Associate Editor, *Dictionary of South Asian Religions*

Melia Belli

Assistant Professor of Asian Art History, University of Texas at Arlington

Shereen Bhalla

Bilingual and Bicultural Studies, University of Texas, San Antonio

Stuti Bhatnagar

PhD Candidate, School of International Studies, Jawaharlal Nehru University (India)

Nilanjana Bhattacharya

Lecturer in Comparative Literature, Department of English and Other Modern European Languages, Visva-Bharati University, India

Jeffrey C. Blutinger

Barbara and Ray Alpert Endowed Chair in Jewish Studies and Associate Professor of History, California State University, Long Beach

Christiane Brosius

Chair of Visual and Media Anthropology, Karl Jasper Centre of Transcultural Studies, Asia and Europe in a Global Context Cluster, University of Heidelberg (Germany)

Joseph P. Byrne

Professor of Honors Humanities, Belmont University

E. L. Cerroni-Long

Professor of Anthropology, Eastern Michigan University

Elizabeth Chatterjee

Senior Research Fellow, History, All Souls College, Oxford (UK)

Upendra Choudhury

Professor of Political Science, Aligarh Muslim University (India)

Gareth Davey

Professor of Psychology, University of Chester (UK)

David Efurd

Visiting Assistant Professor of Art History, Skidmore College

Nilly Kamal El-Amir

Faculty of Economics and Political Science, University of Cairo (Egypt)

Nicholas Farrelly

Associate Investigator, College of Asia and the Pacific, Australian National University (Australia)

Juli Gittinger
PhD Candidate, Religious Studies, McGill University (Montreal, Canada)

Gloria G. Gonzales
Adjunct Professor, Asian Studies and Multicultural Studies, Palomar College

J. Andrew Greig
U.S. Diplomatic Service, Retired

Paramita Gupta
Assistant Professor of Finance, California State University, Long Beach

Risto Härmä
Project Manager, Faith Regen Foundation (UK)

Sheeba Härmä
UK South Asian Manager/Project Head, Oxfam GB

James M. Hastings
Assistant Professor of Asian and World History, Wingate University

Phyllis K. Herman
Associate Professor of Religious Studies, California State University, Northridge

Amy Holmes-Tagchungdarpa
Assistant Professor of Tibetan, Chinese, and Himalayan History, University of Alabama

Fatima A. Imam
Assistant Professor of History, Lake Forest College

B. M. Jain
Former Professor and Senior Research Scientist in Political Science, South Asia Studies Centre, University of Rajasthan (Jaipur, India)

Andrew L. Jenks
Associate Professor of History, California State University, Long Beach

Sadan Jha
Assistant Professor, Centre for Social Studies, Veer Narmad, South Gujarat University (Surat, India)

Sushmita Kashyap
Freelance Reporter and Mediaperson; Consultant, Asian Centre for Human Rights (Assam) for CORDAD (Netherlands)

Chandrika Kaul
Lecturer in Modern History, School of History, University of St. Andrews (Scotland)

Medha Kudaisya
Department of History, Faculty of Arts and Sciences, National University of Singapore (Singapore)

Ananda Lal
Professor and Head, Department of English, Jadavpur University (Kolkata)

Brendan P. LaRocque
Assistant Professor of History, Saint Benedict and Saint Johns University

Peter Lyon
Reader Emeritus in International Relations and Research Fellow, Institute of Commonwealth Studies, University of London

Surjit Mansingh
Adjunct Professor at the School of International Service, American University, Washington D.C.; formerly Professor of International Politics at Jawaharlal Nehru University, New Delhi (India)

Sharmina Mawani
Lecturer, Institute of Ismaili Studies, and Vice President, Gujarat Studies Association (UK)

Andrew McGarrity
Lecturer in South Asian and Indo-Tibetan Studies, Department of Indian Subcontinental Studies, University of Sydney (Australia)

Deepak K. Mishra
Associate Professor, Centre for the Study of Regional Development, School of Social Sciences, Jawaharlal Nehru University (New Delhi)

Anjoom Mukadam
Lecturer, Institute of Ismaili Studies, and President, Gujarat Studies Association (UK)

Prabhati Mukherjee
Professor Emeritus, Indian Institute of Advanced Studies, Simla, India

Sipra Mukherjee
Associate Professor of English, West Bengal State University (India)

Shoma Munshi
Professor of Anthropology and Head of the Social Science Division, American University of Kuwait (Kuwait)

Taberez Ahmed Neyazi
South Asia Programme, National University of Singapore

Bala Raju Nikku
Head of the Department of Social Work, Kadambari Memorial College of Science and Management (Kathmandu, Nepal)

Carl Olson
Professor, Department of Philosophy and Religious Studies, Alleghany College

Tom Owen-Smith
PhD Candidate, Department of Linguistics, School of Oriental and African Studies (UK)

Sree Padma
Executive Director, ISLE Program, and Lecturer, Asian Studies, Bowdoin College

M. Raisur Rahman
Assistant Professor of History, Wake Forest University

Sita Anantha Raman
Associate Professor Emerita of History, Santa Clara University

Nalini Rao
Associate Professor of World Art, Soka University of America

Sanaa Riaz
PhD Candidate in Anthropology, University of Arkansas

Asha Kasbekar Richards
Freelance Journalist specializing in popular culture; former teacher at the taught Indian Cinema, University of London

Emily Rook-Koepsel
PhD Candidate, History, University of Minnesota

Ruth K. Rosenwasser
Curatorial Consultant, South Asian Art, Lowe Art Museum, University of Miami

Sunil K. Sahu
Frank L. Hall Professor of Political Science and Professor of Political Science, DePauw University

Anup Saikia
Reader in Geography, Gauhati University (India)

Amal Sanyal
Associate Professor of Economics, Lincoln University (Canterbury, New Zealand)

Colleen Taylor Sen
Food Historian and Journalist, specializing in food of the Indian subcontinent

Raman N. Seylon
Assistant Professor of History, Bridgewater State University

Steven B. Shirley
Assistant Professor, Keimyung University (Korea); Distinguished Fellow, Central American Institute of Asia Pacific Studies (Taipei, Taiwan)

Brian Shoesmith
Honorary Professor of Communications and Contemporary Arts, Edith Cowan University (Western Australia)

Caleb Simmons
PhD Candidate, Department of Religion, University of Florida

Yogesh Snehi
Assistant Professor of History, DAV College, Amritsar (India)

Tulasi Srinivas
Assistant Professor, Sociology and Anthropology, Department of Communication Studies, Emerson College

Eric Strahorn
Assistant Professor of History, Florida Gulf Coast University

Ramesh Thakur
Distinguished Fellow, Centre for International Governance and Innovation, Professor of Political Science, and Director of the Bailsillie School of International Affairs, University of Waterloo (Canada)

Kailasam Thirumaran
Lecturer in Tourism and Hospitality Management, James Cook University (Australia), Singapore Campus

Anil Varughese
Assistant Professor, School of Public Policy and Administration, Carleton University (Ottawa, Canada)

Lavanya Vemsani
Associate Professor of History, Department of Social Sciences, Shawnee State University

Antonella Viola
Department of History and Civilization, European University Institute (Florence, Italy)

Steve Wall
Instructor, English, Philosophy, and Humanities, Hillsborough Community College, Plant City Campus

Yosay Wangdi
Associate Professor of History, Grand Valley State University

Jay Weinstein
Professor of Sociology, Eastern Michigan University

Liza Weinstein
Assistant Professor of Sociology, Department of Sociology and Anthropology,
Northeastern University

Ken Whalen
Assistant Professor of Geography, American University of Afghanistan (Kabul, Afghanistan)

Eleanor Zelliott
Laird Bell Professor of South Asian History, Emerita, Carleton College

Index

✦